The Role of Women in Librarianship 1876-1976:

The Entry, Advancement, and Struggle for Equalization in One Profession

By Kathleen Weibel and Kathleen M. Heim
with assistance from Dianne J. Ellsworth

A Neal-Schuman Professional Book

ORYX PRESS
1979

Operation Oryx, started more than 15 years ago at the Phoenix Zoo to save the rare white antelope—believed to have inspired the unicorn of mythology—has apparently succeeded. The operation was launched in 1962 when it became evident that the animals were facing extinction in their native habitat of the Arabian peninsula.

An original herd of nine, put together through *Operation Oryx* by five world organizations now number 47 in Phoenix with another 38 at the San Diego Wild Game Farm, and four others which have recently been sent to live in their natural habitat in Jordan.

Also, in what has come to be known as "The Second Law of Return," rare biblical animals are being collected from many countries to roam freely at the Hai Bar Biblical Wildlife Nature Reserve in the Negev, in Israel, the most recent addition being a breeding herd of eight Arabian Oryx. With the addition of these Oryx, their collection of rare biblical animals is complete.

Copyright © 1979 by Kathleen Weibel, Kathleen M. Heim, and Dianne J. Ellsworth

Published by The Oryx Press
3930 E. Camelback Road
Phoenix, AZ 85018

Published simultaneously in Canada

Printed and Bound in the United States of America

Distributed outside North America by
Mansell Publishing
3 Bloomsbury Place
London WC1A 2QA, England
ISBN 0-7201-0819-5

Library of Congress Cataloging in Publication Data

Main entry under title:

The Role of women in librarianship, 1876—1976.

(A Neal-Schuman professional book)
Bibliography: p.
Includes indexes.
1. Women librarians—United States—Addresses, essays, lectures. I. Weibel, Kathleen. II. Heim, Kathleen M. III. Ellsworth, Dianne J.
Z682.2.U5R64   331.4'81'02   78-27302
ISBN 0-912700-01-7

This work is dedicated to all those library workers who share a vision of equality for women, particularly Anita R. Schiller and Margaret Myers, scholars, role models, activists, and friends.

Contents

American Librarianship

Preface

Librarianship is a profession initially dominated by men in numbers and later, because of their relative ease of access to the profession, by women. Yet librarianship manifests a dual career structure for men and women which tends to be based on socially acceptable male and female roles. This structure changes only as perceptions of appropriate roles alter. Administration, scholarship, and technology are the province of men in librarianship. Guidance, nurturance, routinization, and popular culture are the province of women.

In the final quarter of the nineteenth century, when women entered the library work force in any number, librarianship was a male sphere considered acceptable work for women because of their role as culture keepers. Within librarianship some definite female spheres were established, e.g. children's librarianship, and women could and did advance within them. Although as early as the turn of the century librarianship was perceived as a woman's profession, transfer to the profession's male spheres, particularly the administration of large prestigious libraries, continues, even today, to be as difficult as entrance into a male dominated workforce.

The Role of Women in Librarianship 1876-1976: The Entry, Advancement and Struggle for Equalization in One Profession is a sourcebook compiled to provide a history of the first hundred years of a profession traditionally classed as a "women's profession" and to document the continuing struggle of women within that profession to achieve full opportunity and recognition.

Two major sections comprise the book: an anthology of forty-four selections from the library literature of Great Britain and the United States and an annotated bibliography, international in scope, of over one thousand items, with author, title, and subject index. One index provides access to the introduction and anthology sections.

The anthology selections were chosen to include a broad spectrum of thought and data on the role of women in British and American librarianship from a variety of sources and in a variety of styles. The selections are demonstrative rather than representative although the number of documents appearing in each section is a proportional sample of the literature that appeared in the period covered. Criteria for inclusion included: discussion of major issues; illustration of the role of women in the development of librarianship; interpretation as well as presentation of data; and extent of influence upon the library profession. No biographies were included unless the material was incorporated into a document treating women on a broader scale. Biographical notes on contributors follow the Introduction. Some selections have been edited or excerpted from longer documents; this is noted in each case. Selections are arranged chronologically.

The annotated bibliography is designed to be read as a chronology of issues, themes, data, and opinions on the role of women in librarianship as well as a guide to literature not reprinted in the anthology. While the focus of the bibliography is on English speaking nations, documents from other countries were also cited and annotated when located. The bibliography is based on an extensive search of library literature, the specifics of which are described in the bibliography's introduction. The introduction also explains the construction of the bibliography and offers suggestions for its use. All the documents cited, with the exception of those which were not annotated, were read by the editors.

The Role of Women in Librarianship 1876-1976 is the result of a series of collaborative efforts. In the process of preparing this work the editors discovered that a related project was being undertaken by Dianne J. Ellsworth and Mary Cross. Believing that there was a need and market for both books and that as feminists our responsibility was to cooperate to produce better coverage of the field, communication between the two projects was begun. The publishers of the Ellsworth/Cross book, however, chose not to pursue the project. In keeping with our feminist philosophies we chose to collaborate with Dianne J. Ellsworth and merge the Ellsworth/Cross book with ours to produce *The Role of Women in Librarianship 1876-1976*. The process of combining two similar but unique projects has at times been difficult but we believe that both the book and our personal growth have benefited and for this we are grateful. We would particularly like to acknowledge our thanks to the American Library Association Social Reponsibilities Round Table Task Force on Women for preliminary bibliographic efforts upon which this book builds and expands; Maxine K. Rochester and Margaret Myers who identified many obscure items; Suzanne LeBarron, Howard Harris, and Diane G. Kadanoff who helped untangle citations; Grethe Jacobsen and Willa Schmidt who translated German, Dutch, and Scandinavian language materials; Priscilla Neal and Judith Tuohy of the University of Wisconsin-Madison Memorial Library Interlibrary Loan Department; Andrey Orr and Jean Rideout of the University of Wisconsin-Madison Library School Library; Philip Gary Heim who typed and helped ready the bibliographic portion of this work for publication; Carol Royce, Tamara Winston, and Alice Hergenraden who typed various portions of the book; Rhonda Gandel who assisted in organizing the anthology; and Pamela R. Broadley who helped proofread portions of the anthology, compiled the Title Index, and compiled the major portion of the Biographical Notes on Contributors.

The institutional support provided by the University of Wisconsin-Madison Library School; University of Wisconsin-Extension; and the University of Illinois Graduate School of Library Science over the two years we have worked on this project has been of considerable assistance.

Special thanks is due to Julie Ann Chase for the subject index to the bibliography and to Susan Ruth Stein for the index to the work as a whole.

Dianne J. Ellsworth's contributions to the book are so intertwined with our own that it is difficult to distinguish them. Her assistance in all aspects of the book was fundamental to its completion. Without the encouragement and support of Patricia Glass Schuman, our editor and friend, we would neither have begun this project nor completed it. We also appreciate the patience and support of the staff of The Oryx Press: Phyllis Steckler, Joan Crawford, and especially Kaye Reed, who turned the manuscript into a book, even though we didn't meet the deadlines. Also we are grateful to the authors and publishers who have granted us permission to reprint their material. Finally to the many friends and workers in libraries who have encouraged us, thank you.

Kathleen Weibel
Albany, New York

Kathleen M. Heim
Urbana, Illinois

December 15, 1978

Introduction

Librarianship is one of a few professions with a history of hospitality to women. This is particularly true in westernized nations. In the United States, for example, 82% of citizens reporting their 1973 occupation in the librarian, archivist, curator category were women.[1]

This hospitality has not meant equality for women within the profession. Women's status in librarianship, as in nursing, social work, and teaching, reflects the societal pattern of women's place in the work force. All four professions have been termed semi-professions and are accorded less status, remuneration, and control than more prestigious male-dominated professions, such as law and medicine. All four share, albeit to varying degrees, dominance of the professional work force by women, and control of the professional institutions by men.[2]

Women are the majority of practitioners in librarianship, but they are vastly underrepresented in management roles. The larger, the more scholarly, the better financed the library or library-related institution, the more likely it is that the administrator will be male while librarians who work with children in public libraries or elementary schools are usually female. Although women outnumber men in academic libraries, the ratio is much lower than in any other type of library. More library educators are male than female and more males than females have earned the PhD in librarianship. The major commercial library periodicals are edited by men, with the exception of one devoted to work with children and youth. Even when both sexes hold equal positions in terms of responsibility, men tend to earn higher salaries.[3]

Women have been encouraged to enter the profession and have been offered opportunities for advancement, but many of the forces which limit them in society have also frustrated their achievement of equality in librarianship. Of course, there are individual women whose careers belie this, but they are the exception rather than the norm.

The functional role of librarian has been performed ever since there was a need to organize, preserve, and provide access to the records of society, but librarianship did not emerge as an organized profession until the latter half of the nineteenth century. In the United States this is dated from 1876 when the American Library Association and the *Library Journal* were founded, and the U.S. Bureau of Education issued its report on librarianship (1876-02*). In Great Britain the date 1877, the year the Library Association was established, serves a similar purpose.

Women entered librarianship in both countries during an expansion of the tax-supported public library movement and an increase in the number of academic libraries resulting from the growth of higher education. The rapid

*Refers to citation in the annotated bibliography beginning on page 295.

development of libraries, which were labor intensive organizations, created a need for a large, preferably educated, work force. Concomitant with this was the increasing number of women who had taken advantage of educational opportunities lately opened to them, many of whom were eager to enter the labor market.

Traditionally associated with the male sphere, paid employment has been open to women only under conditions appropriate to the prevailing perception of woman's role. Librarianship, particularly public librarianship, met these conditions because it involved service, transmittal of societal values and culture, focus on the individual, and attention to detail. It was a genteel calling seen as a logical extension of woman's traditional roles in the home and family. As long as librarianship was perceived primarily as an extension of the scholarly life, and access to the centers of scholarship were denied to women, the role of librarian had been primarily male.

During the medieval period in Europe, when convents as well as monasteries served as intellectual centers, both nuns and monks functioned as librarians; at least one convent produced a major encyclopedia. Yet, in the eleventh and twelfth centuries, when the centers of learning were transferred to cathedral schools and ultimately universities, both of which systematically excluded women, there is no evidence that women carried out librarian functions. During the Renaissance, and later in Tudor England, several women did develop book collections, but they were not the administrators or organizers of their collections. Women participated more actively in Europe's intellectual life during the seventeenth and eighteenth centuries, but with few notable exceptions they were primarily patrons rather than producers or organizers of knowledge. With compulsory education and the development of colleges for women in the nineteenth century, women moved into the intellectual world in numbers significant enough to impact their roles in the labor force.[4]

Women were recruited for librarianship only when it became economically necessary and socially acceptable. Library literature of the late 19th century emphasizes that although women earned lower salaries, they often performed the same functions as men and may even have performed them better (†1878-01 and p. 5; †1880-01 and p. 7; 1899-11, among others). The library movement expanded more rapidly than did its base of philanthropic and public support. Hiring women was originally a means of maintaining and even extending service without increasing costs. Working in libraries was socially acceptable for women because the field was seen as a fitting extension of women's traditional behavior pattern. Dee Garrison points out that librarianship "quickly adjusted to fit the narrowly circumscribed sphere of women's work, for it appeared similar to the work of the home, functioned as cultural activity, was philanthropic in nature, required no great skill or physical strengths, and brought little contact with the rougher parts of society," (1976-06).

Librarianship has fairly consistently, if self-consciously, dealt in its journal literature with the role and status of women and the impact of their numerical dominance. Despite this emphasis, the profession's predominance by women has until recently been largely ignored in the monographic and journal literature dealing with the development of librarianship, libraries, and library associations. The sex composition of the profession has also been ignored in study after study of the characteristics of library workers, including salary and employment status. This situation continues even with today's heightened awareness of women's roles. Largely overlooked as an area of study by other disciplines such as labor market analysis and sociology of occupations, librarianship's knowledge of itself and its relation to the rest of the work force, particularly women, is also limited. The reemergence of the women's movement, its impact on librarianship, and the development of an interdisciplinary approach to the study of women have resulted in increasing attention to the analysis of the role and status of women in American librarianship. Yet, this attention is not reflected in recent general historical studies of the profession in either the United States or Great Britain.[5] Women in librarianship have been mainly treated by women scholars such as Garrison (1976-06) or Grotzinger,[6] and as anthologized pieces or conference papers. Rarely have women been integrated into a history of the profession. This pattern parallels the development of women's studies in other disciplines; it reflects the fact that women's significance and contributions to society were largely ignored until documented by women themselves. Male library historians deal gingerly with the subject of women if they deal with it at all. Edward Holley, a noted library historian, prefaces his recent discussion of American women librarians with the comment: ". . . a mere male certainly has his gall in talking about the 'gentle ladies' in our profession. . . ."[7]

While the subject has been dealt with primarily in the more plentiful literature of Great Britain and the United States, the role of women in librarianship has also been of concern in many other countries, including New Zealand (1969-09), Japan (1976-13), Germany (1939-02), and South Africa (1940-05). Since the 1970s, Canadian literature on women in librarianship has been more substantial than that of Great Britain, in part due to the existence of *Emergency Librarian,* a feminist library journal. The Australians have also devoted considerable time in their literature to women in librarianship, including an analysis of women's entry and current status in the profession (1972-03). The American literature of the seventies, however, provides the beginning of an analytical framework for the examination of the role of women in librarianship. This literature is typified by Schiller (1974-09 and p. 222) and Garrison (1972-73 and p. 201).

The literature on librarianship relating to women can be classified into seven broad categories. These are:

—opinion pieces both condemning and supporting women's role in the profession (Chennell: 1902-03 and p. 41; Pierce: 1902-06 and p. 45)*;

—exhortations to women (Ahern: 1899-03 and p. 22);

—descriptions of women's status in librarianship (Freedman: 1970-16 and p. 189);

—statistical studies including data on women (Bryan: 1952-01 and p. 128);

—similar reports of studies which focused solely on women (Ward: 1966-02 and p. 159);

—news of action or activities related to women which appear regularly ("Up in Arms": 1918-01-02-03 and p. 76);

—historical or sociological analysis of the role of women in librarianship (Corwin: 1974-31 and p. 259).

---

*The documents cited as representative of the literature categories are reprinted in the anthology section of this volume as well as included in the annotated bibliography. Entry numbers, e.g. 1902-03, refer to the bibliographic citation. Page numbers refer to the location in the anthology.

The extensively annotated bibliography (pp. 295-441) reviews the literature of women in librarianship. Its detail is designed to enhance the reader's use and understanding of the articles and excerpts from American and British library literature included in the anthology.

Together, the anthology and the bibliography document women's entry, advancement, and struggle for equalization in the library profession. These two parts should be used jointly. The bibliography provides an overview; the anthology illustrates major issues, themes, voices and styles from American and British literature.

Materials were included in the bibliography if they contributed to an understanding of the role of women in librarianship. Biographical items were not included unless they were collective biographies discussing women in a context larger than their own careers. Materials on such issues as the image of librarians, or on groups of library workers, such as library assistants who are primarily women, were included only if they specifically addressed their topic as a woman-related issue.

Criteria for inclusion in the anthology are the same as those for the bibliography, with three additional constraints. First, the literature must consider or illustrate issues significant to the role of women in librarianship. Second, documents must not only represent data or biographical information, but must also include analysis and interpretation. Third, they must have been published in Great Britain or the United States and focus on the status of women in librarianship in those countries. Literature discussing the international status of women in librarianship was also used only when the article was published in the United States or Great Britain.

The literature reprinted in the anthology is discussed in this introduction in chronological order, with each section preceded by a brief synopsis of each time period. These sections reflect the major periods in the history of women and of librarianship.

EMERGENCE OF AN ORGANIZED PROFESSION 1876-1900

Entry into the profession is the major theme of the early literature of women in librarianship. During the mid-nineteenth to early twentieth centuries, the composition of the library work force in the United States and Great Britain moved from predominantly male to female. So pronounced was this alteration that society's perception of the librarian stereotype changed from fussy old man with scholarly demeanor to that of mousy disapproving spinster.

The first selection, excerpts from "Historical Sketches of the Ladies' Library Associations of the State of Michigan," is an example of women's role in establishing libraries. The women of the Ladies' Library Associations, although not librarians themselves, were instrumental in founding libraries throughout the state of Michigan. They were precursors of the Women's Clubs which actively promoted libraries later in the twentieth century. (For an analysis of the work of the Ladies' Library Associations see 1954-01.)

The excerpt from "Transactions and Proceedings of the Conference of Librarians Held in London," provides evidence of women's progress within the library profession. Among the American attendees at this founding conference of the Library Association of the United Kingdom were Justin Win-

sor, William F. Poole, and Lloyd Smith. Their comments indicate that women
were commonly employed in American libraries, as assistants, as catalogers,
and in some instances as heads of libraries. Yet as Smith observes ". . . in England a lady-librarian was scarcely ever heard of. . . ."

The entry of women into the public library field in Great Britain is described by Alderman Thomas Baker in "The Employment of Young Women
as Assistants in Public Free Libraries." He notes that a growing interest in
women's rights, as well as the economy of hiring women, led to the experiment in women's employment—an experiment he regards as successful.

In "Women in Libraries: How They are Handicapped," Melvil Dewey
delineates the desirability of library work for women with college backgrounds and summarizes his opinion as to why women of equal ability were
not receiving pay equal to men: women's health is poorer; they lack business
and executive training and permanence in their plans; they leave employment
to marry or tend to families; and they are unable to do heavy work in addition
to their duties, while men can. Dewey does observe that if women were given
training, and if they planned a career rather than viewed work as a stopover
prior to marriage, they probably would do as well as men. However, he concludes: "There are many uses for which a stout corduroy is really worth more
than the finest silk."

Disparity in pay between men and women was also discussed at the 1892
meeting of the American Library Association. "Proceedings of the Fourteenth
American Library Association Conference: The Women's Meeting," which
offered a generally optimistic view of women's opportunity in the library field,
are reprinted in full. While the meeting concluded with a motion that a
women's section be formed within ALA, no further mention of the section is
found in the literature. Quite possibly the protest against the formation of
such a section, made by Tessa Kelso (1892-02 letter), prevailed. She stated,
"There is but one standard of management for a live business and sex has
nothing to do with it."

The effect of formal training for librarianship, or the lack of it, provides
the theme for several of the articles that follow. Miss Richardson,* in "Librarianship as a Profession for Women," compares the status of women in American and British librarianship. Among her conclusions is that the lack of formal
library training in Great Britain hinders women's entry and advancement in
the profession. She also points out that while women sometimes held positions
in British public libraries they were generally not employed by the large
reference or academic libraries. The American situation was similar, but not
with the absoluteness found in the more tradition-bound British society.

Mary Eileen Ahern, an active and influential American librarian, discusses "The Business Side of a Woman's Career as a Librarian," suggesting
many practical methods by which women may attain the business-like
qualities needed for success. Ahern notes the paradox that a woman entering
the business world, of which libraries are a part, must "forget she is a woman
and at the same time keep it ever before her that she is a woman."

Discussions similar to Miss Richardson's and those of the American Library Association Women's Meeting, but international in scope, took place at
the 1899 International Congress of Women. The theme was "Women in the
Professions." Excerpts from the conference proceedings, entitled "Women Li-

*No first name is available for Miss Richardson.

brarians," are reprinted here. Mary Wright Plummer outlines the training of women as librarians and the development of library education in the United States. M. S. R. James describes the need for education for librarians and surveys the international status of women in librarianship. Toulmin Smith and B. L. Dyer detail the history and status of women in British libraries. Smith suggests that more women librarians are active in Great Britain "than is commonly supposed." Reports of the speeches and discussion at the Congress caused considerable controversy in the British library press over whether the status of women in librarianship was accurately portrayed (see, for example, The Bibliography reference number 1899-14).

THE MOVE TOWARDS SUFFRAGE: 1901-1921

With entry achieved, attention turned to the status of women within the profession. The First World War both expanded and exposed the limits of opportunities for women in librarianship. Although the majority of librarians were not militant, in their expression of concern about equal opportunity and equal pay, the tone of the literature became more strident during the move toward suffrage. Accompanying this assertiveness was an emerging backlash against the growing number of women in the profession.

In a series of articles appearing in the British *Library World,* a lively debate on the qualifications and role of women in librarianship ensued between Frank Chennell and Kate Pierce. The debate lasted the better part of 1902 (1902-03-06-07-08-10) and inspired a survey on women in British libraries, the results of which were also printed in *Library World* (1902-09). Only the first two sallies are reprinted here. In "Lady Assistants and Public Libraries," Chennell argues ". . . that this heavy incursion of the lady assistant into the ranks of our profession should be received with some gravity." Pierce, described in *Library World* as an outspoken "champion" of women's rights, responds in "Women in Public Libraries," that Chennell has overlooked major points in the matter of women's employment. "If Mr. Chennell once admits that a good girl is better than a bad boy, then the whole of his case against women falls to the ground." Ultimately Chennell subsided "somewhat gracefully" and Pierce goes on to do similar battle several years later (1907-05).

Salome Cutler Fairchild's "Women in American Libraries," is a full scale survey of women in American librarianship. She undertook the task at the request of Herbert Putnam, Librarian of Congress and President of the American Library Association. Fairchild concludes that women "do not hold the positions offering the highest salaries, and broadly speaking do not receive equal remuneration for the same grade of work." The explanations offered for this situation are essentially the same as the criticisms of women made by Dewey in "Women in Libraries: How They Are Handicapped." Among these are lack of mobility, delicate physique, emotionalism, willingness to work for less pay, and conservatism. Fairchild notes that these comments come from women as well as men. She concludes: "To the ambitious every form of handicap acts as a spur. In the long run, however, women may prefer to work mainly in those lines where they can if they will equal men—in the various forms of scholarly effort; and in those where they naturally excel him—in positions where the human element predominates."

In "The Prospect: An Address Before a Graduating Class of Women," Herbert Putnam expands on the view of male and female natures alluded to by Fairchild. Putnam is an articulate believer in the positive value of traits he attributes as natural to women and looks to women's franchise as a means of bringing morality into the political arena. Yet, if women are to move into the professional world they must take on such male traits as a sense of proportion and initiative. Putnam discusses these and the complementary female traits, offering advice on "the question for woman, looking to her own advancement . . . how, without diminution of [the female traits], she may gain the balancing virtues which thus far, distinctively, she lacks."

Mizpah Gilbert surveys the status of women in European as well as American and British libraries in "The Position of Women in Public Libraries." She believes that by women's "own work she stands or falls in the future. If in Great Britain, by indolence or by adopting the policy of *laissez faire,* she remains chiefly the hewer of wood and drawer of water then she will have none to blame but herself." The work of the Library Assistants' Association Committee on Women, which functioned from 1913 until the First World War, is described.

An article and letters in response, reprinted under the title "Women Assistants and the War," reveal the opportunities opened to women in British librarianship during the First World War and the conflict engendered by a realistic appraisal of these opportunities.

In "Up in Arms," an editorial and letters reprinted from *Public Libraries,* an American library journal edited by Mary Eileen Ahern, the limits imposed on women librarians' service in the libraries of the army camps are described. The editor concludes: "If one were justified at any time in saying that library work is 'a man's job' it would occur in regard to a library that was in a community of 35,000 men, but there is room even then for women to assist."

BETWEEN THE WARS: 1922-1940

The backlash in the literature intensified between World Wars I and II, as did the examination of women's place and impact on the profession. Although women continued to comment on their situations, they were defensive rather than offensive, as they had been during previous periods. Slowly, discourses on women's unique qualifications closed, replaced by discussions concerning the need to recruit men.

In her "Sex Disqualification," Marjorie Peacock, an outspoken apologist for women in British librarianship wrote, ". . . We have reached the critical and dangerous point for women when, openly, sex is no disqualification, yet in secret it is a most powerful handicap." An overt example of the discrimination outlined by Peacock is described in the editorial "Men Versus Women Librarians."

The background and current status of women in British librarianship is reviewed by Miss W. M. Thorne in a "Librarianship As A Career for Women," speech given to the Junior Section of the Library Assistants' Association. For women "slowly but surely a new vista [has] opened up" primarily because of the opportunities available to women during the First World War. Women's predominance in the field of children's librarianship—". . . the natural place for women"—is emphasized.

An area of librarianship in which women do not readily participate, academic librarianship, is discussed by J. I. Wyer in "Women in College Librarianship." ". . . While women are holding their own in the American women's colleges, in colleges for men or coeducational institutions they are represented, with very few exceptions, only in small, relatively unimportant institutions."

The effect of the number of women in librarianship is faced head on in a 1933 "Problems" column of the *Wilson Bulletin for Librarians* when the question is asked: "Should the preponderance of women in the American library profession be considered an evil?" The letter from an English library worker raising the issue and four of the replies are reprinted. For additional responses, see 1933-02. Generally the answers are "no," although many are qualified by comments on the suitability of women for only certain types of library work and the need to recruit qualified men to balance the profession.

Stewart Smith directly confronts the issue of women's commitment to their careers in "Librarianship—Stop-Gap or Profession?" He concludes that encouraging men to enter library work is the primary way to achieve the "career librarians" the profession must have if it is to advance.

In a 1938 editorial, "The Weaker Sex?," *Library Journal* noted that although an apparent scarcity of candidates for administrative positions in public and college libraries existed, women were not being considered for these posts. Comments were invited. Eleven letters were published (1938-06 letters) of which five are reprinted. Opinions and tone vary, but it is generally agreed that women must take responsibility for improving their status despite the prevalence of men on library boards and hiring committees which presents a formidable obstacle—men tend to hire men.

The impression created by "The Weaker Sex?" "if allowed to pass unquestioned might have an unfortunate effect on the attitude and ambition of young women in, or about to enter, the profession" according to Robert S. Alvarez. In "Women's Place in Librarianship," he presents data from his dissertation (1939-01) to demonstrate that women hold the leading positions in American public libraries and library associations. In a letter following the publication of the article (1938-11 letter), W. H. Kaiser points out that if the data discussed by Alvarez in his narrative were placed in columns for easy comparison, none of the statistics presented would show that women have a share of administrative positions proportionate to their number in the profession.

Katharine Stokes responds to the issues raised by Stewart Smith and to the lack of any comment other than her own (1936-01 letter) engendered by his article "Warning—Soft Shoulders." Stokes sees marriage as a positive, rather than a negative factor in a man's career. Women should also be able to combine career and family if they choose, but they can not expect special treatment if they wish to "work shoulder to shoulder with men."

In the benchmark *American Librarianship from a European Angle*, Wilhelm Munthe, a Norwegian university librarian prominent in international librarianship, surveys the development of librarianship in the United States. His chapter, "Librarianship a Feminine Vocation?", is reprinted in its entirety. The number of women in librarianship is seen as both a cause and effect of low salaries. The predominance of women is not a victory for women's rights. "The sad part of this is that the feminization of any organization is always a sure sign of an underpaid profession." The contributions of women to American librarianship are acknowledged and the negative aspects of their participation in the profession, such as the gossipy tone of library literature, catalogued. Munthe concludes his observations with the recommendation that more men must be recruited to American librarianship.

Rena Cowper reviews the recent flurry of literature on women in American libraries in "Not in Our Stars" and asks: "America protesteth: What of Britain?" Her conclusion is that despite suffrage and improved legal status, there is still blatant discrimination. Mindful of the threat to democracy in the European political situation, she calls on British women in librarianship to stabilize themselves not only to secure their own interests but also their larger freedoms.

WORLD WAR II AND AFTER: 1941-1965

From World War II until the mid-sixties, library literature moves from relative silence on the role of women to discussions of whether sex discrimination exists within the profession. Although concern about the "over-feminization" of librarianship continues, by the close of this period even married women were considered for their potential in the library labor market.

"Shall the Misses Be Masters?" asks A. G. S. Enser in the title of an article raising the alarm that the British library profession will become over-feminized. Enser's concern is documented with statistics gathered from membership lists of the *Library Association Yearbooks*. It generates much heated discussion in the letters column of the *Library Association Record* (1948-01 letters) in which personal experience, further analysis of statistics, and historical documentation are mixed with accusations and recriminations. The conclusion? More women may be entering the profession but they are not obtaining the more prestigious credentials or positions in any greater number.

Ralph Munn's response to the calls for recruiting more men into American librarianship also generated considerable comment (1949-03 letters; 1950-03 and letter). In his article "It's a Mistake to Recruit Men," Munn warns against the profession accepting men of mediocre calibre just because they are men and looking for a "secure and not too difficult job."

A dual career structure for men and women was found in the study of public library personnel undertaken by psychologist Dr. Alice Bryan as part of the Public Library Inquiry—a multi-disciplinary examination of the American public library as a social institution. Excerpted for reprint from *The Public Librarian* are data and analysis supporting this conclusion, as well as Dr. Bryan's other findings on women in public librarianship: women predominate at all levels of library work except in the administration of large libraries; male librarians consistently have higher academic qualifications than women whose qualifications tend to be based either on experience or on the older library training programs; tensions exist between men and women, particularly expressed by middle management women. Dr. Bryan's study marks a significant departure in the literature of women in librarianship because her investigation of women was fully integrated into carefully designed research in the public library segment of the profession.

"Women in Librarianship," by Marion Wilden-Hart, demonstrates that in 1956 matters were still far from satisfactory for women librarians in Great Britain. She discusses the causes of the situation including women themselves, the attitudes of their male colleagues, and the need to differentiate between professional and nonprofessional library functions.

Sylva Simsova addresses an issue of much concern to British women librarians in "Married Women In Libraries." A married woman herself, she does not believe that marriage is necessarily a critical factor in a woman's career, although the birth of the first child is. She reviews the status of maternity leave, child care and problems in reentering the labor force after child raising. Women are urged to complete their qualifications as insurance of their ability to re-enter the profession. In the letters which follow the article (1961-06 letters), the merits of working mothers, the availability of part-time work, and the capability of women to carry out both adequate careers and family lives are debated.

Discrimination in librarianship is explored by Miriam Holden, book collector and long time advocate of women's rights in "The Status of Women Librarians," a speech given at the 1965 convention of the National Women's Party. The National Women's Party had been founded by Alice Paul and other American suffrage leaders who believed that the women's movement should not have been satisfied with the Nineteenth Amendment, but should have immediately begun full scale efforts to obtain the Equal Rights Amendment. Holden's speech is a feminist analysis of the status of women in librarianship whose "plight . . . is an example and a warning to us all." She concludes that "the challenge to American women of the sixties is to support an effective campaign to erase sex bias in job recruitment for top positions. Only through such action can we prevent our male-dominated hiring practices from forcing women workers to remain second-class citizens in an economy of abundance."

Responding to Holden's charges in an editorial entitled "Tokenism at the Top?" Eric Moon, Editor of *Library Journal*, challenges Holden's statistics but comments "we are not brave — or foolish — enough to take sides on *this* issue." In the only letter on the editorial (1965-09 letter), Robert Jordon supplements Moon's statistics and concurs with Holden.

THE SECOND FEMINIST MOVEMENT: 1966-1976

Action on issues affecting women in librarianship along with scholarly examination of the role of women marks the literature of the mid-sixties to 1976 — the reemergence of the feminist movement. Women in librarianship joined with other women in a liberation movement based on a conscious articulation of conditions, principles, and ideology. The status of women in librarianship continued to be documented and analyzed as it had since 1876, but now with the realization that the condition of women in librarianship is as much the result of the societal condition of women as of the forces within the profession or the characteristics of individual librarians.

The availability of a pool of married women librarians able to meet the staffing needs of British libraries is the subject of Patricia Layzell Ward's "Women in Librarianship." Excerpts from this study, commissioned and published by the Library Association, are reprinted here. Ward concludes that qualified married women were available, but that assistance in the form of child care, part-time positions, and refresher courses would facilitate their re-entry into the profession. "Women in Librarianship" was well reviewed (1966-02 Reviews) and reported in the literature (1966-05). It served as a model for a similar study in New Zealand (1969-09).

Arnold Sable deals with the stereotype of the librarian in "The Sexuality of the Library Profession," providing a brief history of the stereotype, its change from male to female, its basis in reality, and its implications for the profession. Sable accepts the theory of innate male and female characteristics.

(For a discussion of the stereotype which does not agree with this view, see 1976-19).

"The Liberated Librarian? A Look at the 'Second Sex' in the Library Profession" acknowledges that "male ascendancy" has improved the salaries of American librarians, but argues for an end to male dominance of the profession. Author Janet Freedman offers a number of practical means for bringing women more fully into the policy-making positions in librarianship, including shared jobs. Her article engendered both pro and con comment and reports of part-time work experiences (1970-16 letters).

In an article which won him the male chauvinism award of the American Library Association's Social Responsibilities Round Table Task Force on Women (1971-25), John Carey takes issue with the assumption that the status of women in librarianship results from discrimination due to prejudice. Refuting Anita Schiller's analysis, while agreeing with her data (1970-11), Carey asks ". . . how can such a large majority be held down by such a small minority?" "Overdue: Taking Issue with the Issues" raised strong comment in the *Wilson Library Bulletin* letters column (1971-11 letters).

Helen Lowenthal's article "A Healthy Anger," which appeared in the September 1, 1971 issue of *Library Journal* devoted to women in librarianship, (1971-27) reflects the growing influence of the women's movement. Lowenthal provides a sex role based analysis of the library profession and suggests that women examine why they choose librarianship as a career. She calls on women to direct their anger at the situations which perpetuate inequality and sex role definition. The one letter written in response to Lowenthal states "all you liberationists: stop trying to make me unhappy!" (1971-27D letter).

In a benchmark article on women in librarianship, historian Dee Garrison argues that the feminization of librarianship lead to the evolution of the public library as a marginal institution. Feminization, as used in "The Tender Technicians," refers both to the profession assuming the aspects and norms of women's role as culture keepers and nurturers, and to the influx of women into the field. Garrison's article represents both a bridge to the interdisciplinary area of women's studies and a significant contribution to the history of the development of the library profession.

Garrison's article is followed by the equally significant "Women in Librarianship." Librarian Anita Schiller's analysis and review of the status of women in American librarianship covers a broader span than Garrison who focuses on the emergence of the profession. Her review of the literature demonstrates a consistent pattern of salary and position differentials between men and women in all types of libraries. Schiller also reviews the changes in sex composition of various areas of librarianship such as library education, questions the assumptions of the traditional research framework used to analyze women's professions, and discusses such specific variables as mobility, education and personal characteristics. Current activism within the professional associations is also covered.

Building on the analysis done by Sharon Wells in her 1967 Master's thesis (1967-03), Margaret Corwin adds considerable documentation to the understanding of women's role in American librarianship in "An Investigation of Female Leadership in Regional, State, and Local Library Associations, 1876-1923." Corwin found that although women were extremely active in state and local associations, they were not well represented at the national level. She concludes that ". . . when the inferior legal status of women and the traditional social role of women are taken into account, female librarians were probably more active in leadership positions in the library field than might initially have been expected." Her article is of importance not only for its value as a research report, but because it is the only article on women in librarianship published to date in the prestigious *Library Quarterly.*

Patricia Ward updates her 1966 study "Women in Librarianship" in a 1975 *Library Association Record* article. She finds that the proportion of qualified British women working in the profession continues at a high level and that pay parity is more of a reality. The proportion of women in senior posts in Great Britain is still not high and British women ". . . have not organized themselves within the profession as have women librarians in the United States."

A review of the literature from 1970-1975, "American Librarianship" by Anne Brugh and Benjamin Breed, appeared in the second issue of the scholarly *Signs: Journal of Women in Culture and Society.* The authors emphasize the socioeconomic and historical bases for sex segregation in the structuring and development of the profession. Research areas are suggested to ". . . help define goals and to collect the data needed, if women in librarianship are to make the profession more than a dead-end for the majority of practitioners."

A speculative look at the future of librarianship is provided in the final selection, "Toward a Feminist Profession" by Kathleen Weibel. It was written for the centennial issue of the *Library Journal* and discusses and analyzes librarianship from the perspective of its numerical dominance by women, its female attributed characteristics, and its potential for actualizing the tenets of feminism.

FOOTNOTES

1. *1975 Handbook on Women Workers* (Washington, DC: U.S. Department of Labor, Employment Standards Administration, Women's Bureau, 1975).

2. Amitai Etzioni. *The Semi Professions and Their Organizations* (Glencoe, IL: The Free Press, 1969).
Study Commission on Undergraduate Education of Teachers. *Teacher Education in the United States: The Responsibility Gap* (Lincoln, NE: University of Nebraska Press, 1976).
Pat Diangson, Diane F. Kravetz, and Judy Lipton. "Sex-Role Stereotyping and Social Work Education," *Journal of Education for Social Work* 11 (Fall, 1975) 44-49.
Sandy Mannino. "The Professional Man Nurse: Why He Chose Nursing and Other Characteristics of Men in Nursing," *Nursing Research* 12 (Summer, 1963):185-186.

3. For a review of current research findings the articles, "Status of Women in Librarianship," in the *ALA Yearbook.* (Chicago, IL: American Library Association). 1976: Anita Schiller (1976-09); 1977 and 1978: Kathleen Weibel; 1979 (in press) Kathleen Heim.

4. There is much work currently being done on the history of women in European intellectual life. For an overview and sampling of current research see: Reneta Bridenthal and Claudia Koonz, eds. *Becoming Visable: Women in European History.* (Boston, MA: Houghton Mifflin, 1977).

5. In the United States:
Sidney C. Jackson. *Brief History of Libraries and Librarianship in the West* (New York: McGraw-Hill, 1974).
Elmer D. Johnson and Michael H. Harris. *History of Libraries in the Western World* 3rd Edition. (Metuchen, NJ: Scarecrow Press, 1976).
Dennis Thomison. *History of the American Library Association 1876-1972* (Chicago, IL: American Library Association, 1978).
In Great Britain:
W. A. Mumford. *A History of the Library Association 1877-1977* (London: The Library Association, 1977).
Michael J. Ramsden. *A History of the Association of Assistant Librarians: 1895-1945* (Falkirk: Association of Assistant Librarians, 1973).

6. Laurel Grotzinger. "Dewey's 'Splendid Women' and Their Impact on Library Education," in Harold Goldsteen, ed. *Milestones to the Present: Papers from Library History Seminar University* (Syracuse, NY: Gaylord Professional Publications, 1978), pp. 125-152.

7. Edward Holley. "Scholars, Gentle Ladies, and Entrepreneurs: American Library Leaders, 1876-1976," in *Milestones to the Present*, pp. 80-108.

Biographical Notes on Contributors

Compiled by Pamela R. Broadley, Kathleen M. Heim, and Dianne J. Ellsworth

INTRODUCTION

Because women's contributions to librarianship have been obscured by time and custom, it was often difficult to find biographical information about early women librarians. Those women still living were contacted personally. Numerous current biographical directories and reference books were also used. In the case of American women, two sources were helpful: *Dictionary of American Library Biography*, edited by Bohdan S. Wynar; and Cynthia Cumming's *A Biographical-Bibliographical Directory of Women Librarians*. Biographical information on early British women librarians was even more difficult to find. Michael J. Ramsden's *A History of the Association of Assistant Librarians: 1895-1945*, provided some information, but in many cases only the post held by the contributor at the time she wrote the article included was available. Male librarians have had considerably better biographical coverage, and their biographical histories were verified in standard biographical tools. Whenever possible biographical information was verified through personal contact with the contributor.

CONTRIBUTORS

Ahern, Mary Eileen (1860-1938)

Mary Eileen Ahern graduated from the Library School of Armour Institute of Technology in Chicago in 1896. After working as a school teacher, she became assistant state librarian of Indiana, a position she held from 1889 to 1893, at which time she became the state librarian. In 1895, she became editor of *Public Libraries*, continuing in that position until 1931. During this time, she also spent seven months (January-July 1919) as a publicity agent in France for the American Library Association, organized the Indiana Library Association and, in 1896, helped establish the library department of the National Education Association.

Alvarez, Robert Smyth (1912-   )
   With a Ph.D. in Library Science from the University of Chicago, Robert Alvarez has held a succession of library directorships since 1941. Starting his career in the Brockton, Massachusetts public library, where he served for two years, he moved on to the Nashville public library from 1946-1959 before continuing his career in California. From 1959-61, he was director of the Berkeley Public Library and since 1966, Dr. Alvarez has served in that capacity at the South San Francisco Public Library. Besides these library responsibilities, Dr. Alvarez has gained considerable experience in the fields of editing and publishing and is currently accountable for three publications: *Administrator's Digest, Business Information* and *Superintendent's Digest.*

Baker, Thomas
   At the time the article, "The Employment of Young Women as Assistants in Free Public Libraries," was published, Alderman Baker was vice president and chairman of the Manchester Public Free Libraries Committee.

Barker, Tommie Dora (1888-   )
   Tommie Dora Barker received her degree from Emory University Library School in 1909 and began her career in the Alabama Department of Archives and History in Montgomery, Alabama. In 1911, she became an instructor at the Atlanta Library School where she became director in 1915. In 1930, she left this position to become regional field agent in the south for the American Library Association. She held this post until 1936 when she became dean of Emory University Library School. Upon retirement, in 1954, she held the position of director. Ms. Barker was a member of ALA (on council 1923-28, 1937-42; director of library education division 1950-53; chairperson membership committee 1946-51).

Beede, Benjamin R. (1939-   )
   Benjamin Beede holds an M.L.S. from Rutgers University Graduate School of Library Science.
   Aside from a year-long position as supervisor of reference services in the Linden, New Jersey public library, Mr. Beede's career has been based at the Rutgers University School of Law Library where he supervised technical services from 1969-71 while pursuing a political science doctorate degree at the University. Since 1971, he has served as a public services supervisor in the Rutgers Law Library and is currently ranked as associate professor. Among Mr. Beede's other professional achievements are his contributions to library literature, several political science publications and offices held in professional organizations including president, Greater Philadelphia Law Library Association (1974-75) and Editorial Advisory Board for *New Jersey Libraries,* published by the New Jersey Library Association, 1976-77.

Bixby, A. F.
   At the time her article was published, Mrs. A. F. Bixby was a member of the Ladies' Library Association in Union City, Michigan.

Borden, Arnold K.
   At the time he wrote his response, Arnold Borden was at the University of Pennsylvania.

Brugh, Anne E.
   Anne Brugh received an M.A.L.S. from the University of Michigan in 1951 and was also awarded an M.A. in history from Rutgers University in 1976.

She has held several posts at the Douglass College Library at Rutgers serving in the circulation department from 1955-68 and working in her present capacity as reference librarian since 1969. Besides many job related activities such as implementing a bibliographic instruction program at Douglass College Library, Ms. Brugh has been involved in several Rutgers University AAUP chapters and has also held numerous offices in the New Jersey Library Association, among them secretary-treasurer of the College and University Section, 1966-68; 1971-72.

Bryan, Alice I. (1902-   )

Alice Bryan received a Ph.D. from Columbia in 1934 and was appointed head of the psychology department at the Pratt Institute School of Fine and Applied Arts shortly thereafter. While employed at Pratt, Dr. Bryan also served as a consulting psychologist to Columbia's School of Library Service. Eventually, in 1939, she became a full professor at that school where she remained until retirement. Dr. Bryan is the author of *The Public Librarian* published in 1953, and she has held membership in several professional organizations.

Carey, John T. (1939-   )

After obtaining a master's degree from Simmons College in 1968, John Carey became assistant regional administrator for the Western Regional Public Library System (1968-69); director of the public library in Groton, Connecticut (1969-71); media services librarian at St. Mary's College of Maryland (1971-72); and is currently Supervisor of the cataloging section of the National Audiovisual Center, Washington, D.C. His primary professional interests are in cataloging and audiovisual materials. He was president of the Eastern Connecticut Film Circuit.

Chennel, Frank

At the time of his controversial debate with Kate Pierce, Frank Chennel was librarian at Willisden Green Library in England.

Clarke, Olive E.

In 1912, Olive Clarke attended the inaugural meeting of the South Coast Branch of the Library Assistant's Association, an organization that was founded in 1895 and changed its name to the Association of Assistant Librarians in 1922. She was employed at the Islington Public Library when she was elected honorary member of the L.A.A. in 1914. She held the title for a year until she married W. C. Berwick Sayers, one of the pioneers of the Association, and then moved to Wallasey where her new husband had recently been appointed chief librarian.

Corwin, Margaret Ann (1949-   )

Holding two master's degrees from the University of Chicago, one in library science and one in humanities as well as a master's in urban studies from Loyola University, Margaret Ann Corwin's major professional emphasis is in the field of information services for various planning and research agencies. From 1973-1975, she started an information center for the planning division of a major shopping center and new community developer. She also functioned as a research analyst for the company. Ms. Corwin is currently the director of information services for the American Society of Planning Officials, assuming such responsibilities as writing technical reports, publishing a newsletter and managing a research service for agency members of the Association. In addition to job-related publications, Margaret Corwin's articles on professional women have appeared in the *Library Quarterly* and *Chicago History*. She is an associate member of the American Institute of Planners.

Cowper, Alexandrina Stewart (1916-   )

The professional life of Alexandrina Cowper, F.L.A., has been centered in Edinburgh, Scotland where she has served in the public library (1935-45), taught English and history at the Leith Academy, (1946-49), and worked as librarian at Trinity Academy (1950-67). In 1967, Ms. Cowper was appointed senior tutor librarian at the Edinburgh College of Commerce where she is currently employed. She has published a number of papers on Scottish history and has contributed articles to *Library World* and *Library Assistant.*

Curtis, Florence R.

At the time she wrote her letter, Florence Curtis was director of the Hampton Institute Library School.

Cutler, Mary S.

See Fairchild, Mary Salome Cutler.

Daniels, Marietta

See Shepard, Marietta Daniels.

Dewey, Melvil (1851-1931)

The active professional life of Melvil Dewey, which spans the years 1872-1905, defies capsulization since throughout this period Dewey was involved in shaping so many of the major elements of the profession. During 1876 alone, the year that he came into prominence, Dewey published the classification system which is named for him, was instrumental in initiating the *American Library Journal* and was appointed its managing editor, and helped found the American Library Association. With his zealous organizational instinct, visionary idealism and leadership talent, Dewey assumed command of many top posts and offices for the duration of his career. Some of his accomplishments that had outstanding impact on the field were his founding of formal library training programs at Columbia and Albany, his establishment of the New York Library Association which set the precedent for the founding of other state organizations, and his pervasive efforts to transform the State Library into what he called a "people's college" to be used in "educating the masses."

Dyer, Bertram L. (1869-1909)

Bertram Dyer was educated at King's College in London and became one of the early influential members of the A.A.L. He held two posts in England, namely junior assistant in the Kensington Public Library in 1882 and sub-librarian in charge of the Brompton Branch Library. From here, Mr. Dyer emigrated to South Africa where he assumed a leading role in the development of libraries, organizing the first library conference in the colony. The meeting became, under Dyer's influence, a permanent feature of the Annual Conference of the South African Association for the Advancement of Science. Until his death, Mr. Dyer maintained his affiliation with A.A.L. and also contributed to the organization's publication, *Library Assistant,* of which he had been the original editor.

Enser, A. G. S. (1915-   )

A. G. S. Enser, F.L.A., F.R.S.A., has been employed in a series of public libraries after completing his education at Nottingham University College. He has held posts at Nottingham, Swansea, and Tottenham Public Libraries before assuming his present position of borough librarian of Eastbourne in 1958. Among his publications are an index of *Filmed Books and Plays* and articles contributed to *Library Association Record, Library World,* and the *Encyclopaedia of Librarianship.*

Fairchild, Mary (Salome) Cutler (1853-1921)

After graduating from Mount Holyoke Seminary in 1875 and working as a cataloger in a small rural library, Salome Fairchild was hired by Melvil Dewey as a cataloger in his library at Columbia College. When Dewey opened his library school at the College, he appointed her instructor of cataloging, and when the school moved to Albany in 1890, Dewey made her vice-director. She served there as a talented administrator and inspiring teacher until 1908. During this time, she was in charge of the New York State Library for the Blind. She also wrote extensively, publishing at least seventeen articles on such subjects as library service to children and women in librarianship. Salome Fairchild was active in the ALA serving twice as vice president and also as chairperson of the ALA exhibit at the 1893 World's Columbian Exposition in Chicago. Until her death, she toured the country lecturing on such topics as American library history and book selection.

Freedman, Janet

Janet Freedman received a master's degree from Simmons College, Graduate School of Library Science in 1962 and since then has held a number of library posts in the greater Boston area, serving first in a suburban public library, later as director of a junior college library, and more recently has worked in various capacities at the Salem State College Library in Salem, Massachusetts. Among other achievements at that institution, Ms. Freedman has administered the graduate program for school library certification, and as director of public services, she has developed a complete instructional program in the use of information resources reaching students at every level. She has also taught an undergraduate course at Salem State entitled, "Women in Today's World" and published articles on topics ranging from women librarians to school library/media centers. A member of many professional organizations, Ms. Freedman has organized programs and workshops at several professional conferences. She is currently director of the Library Communication Center, Southeastern Massachusetts University.

Garnett, Richard (1835-1906)

Aside from his literary endeavors, which produced numerous original and scholarly works, Richard Garnett's major outlet for his love of books existed in his professional activities at the British Museum. In 1851, he became an assistant in the library there under the direction of Anthony Panizzi. Until his retirement in 1899, Dr. Garnett's major responsibilities included cataloging, supervising the printing of the general catalog and keeper of printed books. He served as president of the Library Association from 1892-3 and was a frequent contributor to *Transactions,* the Association's periodical. Dr. Garnett also edited a series of library manuals before his retirement from the British museum.

Garrison, Dee (1934-   )

Dee Garrison is a member of the history department at Livingston College, Rutgers University. She completed her education at the University of California with a degree in intellectual and social history. She is the author of *Apostles of Culture: The Public Librarian and American Society, 1876-1920* (New York: Macmillan, Inc., 1979). Her area of specialization within women's history is the study of professional and radical women. She is presently completing a study of women psychoanalysts and is beginning a biography of Elizabeth Gurley Flynn. Her two articles on women in librarianship are cited in the bibliography: 1972-73; 1976-06.

Gilbert, Mizpah

Mizpah Gilbert was at the Fulham Public Library. In 1916, Miss Gilbert resigned her membership on the A.A.L. Council when she was appointed borough librarian of Newark-upon-Trent. She had been an active member of the A.A.L. for a decade.

Hewins, Caroline Maria (1846-1926)

Caroline Hewins received her library training at the Boston Athenaeum under William Frederick Poole from 1866-67, and her library career commenced when she became librarian of the Hartford, Connecticut Public Library in 1875, a post she held for fifty years. Through her lectures at library schools and educational workshops, her writings and her capable administration of the Hartford library, Ms. Hewins became a major supporter of the public library movement and is particularly recognized for her contribution in the area of children's services. Her professional activities include founding the Connecticut Library Association and persuading the state legislature to create the Public Library Committee, a model for future state library commissions. Vice president of ALA in 1891, she was later responsible for establishing the Children's Section of the organization in 1900.

Holden, Miriam Young (1893-   )

Book collector and consultant on women in history, Miriam Holden founded a library collection in her own name containing books and records of women's role in civilization; her political, legal, and economic status; and her progress in education, science and religion. Miriam Holden has also lectured widely on the status of women in history, co-authored a book, *The American Woman in Colonial and Revolutionary Times, 1565-1800,* and lent her expertise and support to numerous organizations, among them the N.Y. Urban League, the Columbus Hill Birth Control Clinic, Participation of Women in Postwar Planning, Council Friends of Columbia University Libraries, The World's Center for Woman's Archives, and the National Women's Party.

Howell, A. Mrs.

At the time the article was published, Mrs. Howell was a member of the Ladies' Library Association in Union City, Michigan.

Hyatt, Ruth (1916-   )

With a certificate in library science from the Pratt Institute, Ruth Hyatt held positions in several public libraries including those in Somerville, Belmont and Fitchburg, Massachusetts; Hartford and Greenwich, Connecticut; and New York City. Her career culminated in 1916 with the post of head librarian of the public library in Farmington, Connecticut. While head librarian at Fitchburg, Ms. Hyatt also coordinated the Clark University evening college program in library techniques. Among other professional activities, she was a member of the advisory board for *The New Standard Encyclopedia* and a member of the Connecticut Advisory Council on Regional Library Service.

James, M. S. R.

M. S. R. James began her career in England where she was librarian of People's Palace in London from 1887 to 1894 and was elected Honorary Fellow of the A.A.L. in 1895.

In 1899 when her speech, "Women and Their Future in Library Work" was delivered, she was employed by the Library Bureau in Boston, Massachusetts.

Lightfoot, Robert Mitchell Jr. (1910-   )

Robert Lightfoot holds an M.S. in sociology from the University of Virginia and was granted a B.S. in library science by Syracuse University in 1940. After two academic posts, Mr. Lightfoot entered the field of librarianship in 1936 when he became librarian of Keystone Junior College. Since then he has worked in libraries at North Carolina State College, Louisiana Polytech Institute, Missouri Valley College and the Air War College. In 1955, Mr. Lightfoot assumed the directorship of Bradley University Library where he remained until retirement in 1975. He has also edited two professional periodicals, *the Missouri Librarian Association Quarterly* (1951-1952) and *Alabama Librarian* (1953-55).

Lowenthal, Helen

Helen Lowenthal was awarded the M.S.L.S. from Simmons College in 1970. She has worked in several New England libraries including the Boston Public and the Massachusetts Institute of Technology Humanities Library while studying at Simmons. After graduating, Ms. Lowenthal served as reference librarian at the Brookline, Massachusetts public library before becoming director of the town library in Springfield, Vermont. At present, she directs the Goodnow Library in Sudbury, Massachusetts. Throughout her career, she has held membership in state library associations and has been devoted to women-related issues in the profession as evinced by her participation in an MLA Ad Hoc Committee on Professional Rights and Responsibilities and the Boston Task Force on Women's Issues in Librarianship.

Mann, Margaret (1873-1960)

Margaret Mann studied for two years at the Armour Institute in Chicago, and during her lifetime gained widespread recognition for remarkable cataloging and teaching abilities. Among the challenging cataloging operations undertaken by Ms. Mann were the standardization of cataloging practices at the University of Illinois and supervision of its entire cataloging process; the publication of the classified catalog at the Carnegie Library of Pittsburgh; and organizing the Engineering Societies Library catalog in New York City. Besides serving as vice president and member of the executive board of ALA, she was also chosen by the organization to write a textbook on cataloging as part of their curriculum study series. In 1938, she retired from her position of associate professor of cataloging at the University of Michigan.

Moon, Eric (1923-   )

British-born Eric Moon, F.L.A., received his library education in 1949 at Loughborough College in London, and after nineteen years of library posts in England, worked as director of public library services in St. Johns, Newfoundland (1958-59). Since he became editor of *Library Journal* in 1956, Mr. Moon's career has leaned towards publishing. He was with R. R. Bowker Company, first serving as general director and later director of education development until he became president of Scarecrow Press. A staunch defender of civil rights and intellectual freedom, Mr. Moon's professional interests also include book selection, public relations, bibliography and library education. He has contributed widely to professional publications and held offices in numerous professional organizations; most notably, Mr. Moon was elected president of the ALA in 1976.

Munn, Ralph (1894-1975)

After receiving his library degree from the New York State Library School at Albany in 1921, Ralph Munn held posts in the Seattle, Washington and Flint, Michigan public libraries before becoming director of the Carnegie Library of Pittsburgh in 1928. Mr. Munn served in that capacity until his retirement in 1964. At the same time, he was dean of the Carnegie Institute of Technology until 1962 and was elected to the ALA presidency in 1939. During his career, Mr. Munn was an advocate of library cooperation and public library development, principles that he advanced while serving on the Pennsylvania Governor's Commission on Public Library Development (1930-31), as a delegate to the U.N. Conference on Libraries in 1950, and through his foreign consulting activities in Australia, New Zealand, Central and South America.

Munthe, Wilhelm (1883-1966)

Born in Oslo in 1883, Wilhelm Munthe was educated at the universities of Berlin, Copenhagen and Upsala. His entire professional career took place at the University Library of Oslo where he was first appointed an assistant in 1908 and was eventually promoted to the top position of "Overbibliotekar" in 1922. However, Dr. Munthe's professional activities were both national and world-wide in scope. In 1920, he founded the Norwegian Public Libraries Association. Throughout his career, he visited libraries in many countries and wrote many works, including the well-known publication, *American Libraries from a European Angle*, the result of a Carnegie Corporation invitation to prepare a report on American library practices. Dr. Munthe was elected president of the International Federation of Library Associations and honorary vice president of the British Library Association in 1951.

Peacock, Marjorie

At the time her article was published, Miss Peacock was employed at the Wallasey Public Library in England.

Petherbridge, Miss

Miss Petherbridge was an active member of the A.A.L. in its early years, having presented a paper entitled "American Library Schools" at the 1895 general meeting. That same year, she was elected Honorary Fellow of the Association, but was obliged to resign the position in 1899 after the remarks she made at the International Congress of Women regarding women in librarianship created considerable discord in the Association.

Pierce, Kate E. (1873-1966)

Kate Pierce served as librarian of Kettering Public Library from 1896-1939. She holds the distinction of being the first woman councillor of the Library Association.

Plummer, Mary Wright (1856-1916)

Mary Plummer studied librarianship in Melvil Dewey's first class at the School of Library Economy at Columbia College from 1887-1888. After working as a cataloger for two years at the St. Louis Public Library, she was employed by the Pratt Institute Free Library where in 1895, she became both head of the library school and director of the library. Miss Plummer left Pratt in 1911 to organize and administer the first library school of the New York Public Library where she served until her death. Her activities at the latter two institutions gained her the reputation of a pioneer in the field of library education and children's librarianship. At Pratt, Miss Plummer instituted a children's room in the library and separate, specialized training programs for scholarly and children's librarians. She wrote numerous articles appearing in *Library Journal* and *ALA Bulletin* as well as the section on training for librarianship published in the ALA *Manual of Library Economy*. Miss Plummer also held several important offices in library organizations, including second woman president of ALA.

Poole, William Frederick (1821-1894)

William Poole who created, as one of his first professional endeavors, the *Index to Periodical Literature* that bears his name, made many remarkable contributions to the library world during his forty-seven year career. Gaining initial experience at the Mercantile Library Association of Boston and the Boston Athenaeum, he inaugurated such innovations as the dictionary catalog. He did an outstanding job of developing staff, collections and services, particularly at the Boston Athenaeum. In 1868, Mr. Poole left the Athenaeum and became a consultant for nine different libraries prior to embarking on some of his most significant contributions. For the next sixteen years, Poole devoted his energies to transforming the Cincinnati Public Library and the Chicago Public Library into two major, successful institutions. His final accomplishment came with the opportunity to create, in 1887, the recently-endowed Newberry Library. It should also be noted that Mr. Poole participated in the founding meeting of the ALA and served first as vice president and later as president for two years.

Putnam, George Herbert (1861-1955)

Herbert Putnam held a succession of library directorships commencing with his posts at the Minneapolis Athenaeum (1884-1887), the Minneapolis Public Library (1887-1891) and the Boston Public Library (1895-1899). While at the Boston Public, Putnam testified before the Joint Committee of the Library concerning his vision of the Library of Congress' national role, a philosophy that he was able to put into action when he assumed his forty-year position as head of that Library in 1899. Under Putnam's guidance, the Library became a great national institution, an agency that promoted the standardization of library methods and library cooperation. In the course of broadening the Library's national role, Mr. Putnam succeeded in gaining generous financial support from Congress and establishing a pattern of service to government, scholars and professional librarians. Through the initiation of policies and programs during his administration, the collection expanded to over six million volumes; the Legislative Reference Service was established; the Library of Congress Classification scheme was inaugurated; access to the Library was extended; and the equivalent of a union catalog was started.

Richardson, Miss

At the time her article was published, Miss Richardson was an assistant in the St. Helen's Library, England.

Sable, Arnold T. (1930-   )

Mr. Sable's previous posts include director of the Kingston City Library, New York and director of the Adriance Memorial Library in Poughkeepsie, New York (until 1970). He presently is a member of Kibutz Kapri in Israel.

Sanders, Minerva (1837-1912)

Receiving little formal education, Minerva Sanders became librarian of Pawtucket (R.I.) Public Library in 1876. She is noted for such innovations as allowing children to use the library and adopting the open shelf policy, a principle which she singlehandedly defended at the 1889 ALA convention in St. Louis. Locally, Ms. Sanders was instrumental in building up school libraries, and she also held office in the Rhode Island Library Association. She was elected councillor at the 1904 meeting of ALA.

Sanders, S. H.

Mr. Sanders was a library worker from Harrow-on-the-Hill, England at the time his controversial letter, which provoked the Wilson Bulletin Contest, was written.

Sargent, M. E.

M. E. Sargent was a spokeswoman at the Women's Meeting at the 14th American Library Association Conference in 1892. No other biographical information was available.

Savord, Ruth

At the time she wrote her letter, Ruth Savord was librarian for the Council on Foreign Relations, Inc., New York, N.Y.

Schiller, Anita R.

Anita R. Schiller is reference librarian/bibliographer at the University of California, San Diego. Her research on the status of women began with her study, "Characteristics of Professional Personnel in College and University Libraries," funded by the USOE in 1967-68, and performed at the University of Illinois Library Research Center, where she was a research associate until 1970. She has served as editor of the "Aware" column in *American Libraries,* on the editorial board of *College and Research Libraries,* on the ALA Council, and has been a member of the ALA SRRT Task Force on Women since its formation. She received a Council of Library Resources Fellowship in 1976, and in 1978-79 was appointed Ralph R. Shaw Visiting Scholar at Rutgers Graduate School of Library and Information Studies.

Shepard, Marietta Daniels (1913-   )

Marietta Daniels Shepard has a wide educational background which has led to a varied professional life.

She graduated from the University of Kansas in 1934 with an A.B. in Spanish; she received an M.A. in Romance languages from Washington University in St. Louis in 1945 while concurrently attending Columbia University in New York, receiving her B.S.L.S. in 1943. She is fluent in Spanish, French and Portuguese.

Ms. Shepard began her career as an order assistant at the Kansas City (Mo.) Public Library, moved on to become chief of circulation at Washington University Library, and later was a special assistant to the Librarian of the Library of Congress. She was associate librarian of the Pan-American Union for 20 years.

She has held many positions in Central and South America including director of libraries and professor of library science at the Normal School Santiago in Panama; consul for the reorganization of libraries in Havana, Cuba; held concurrent professorships of library science in Ecuador and Panama.

Ms. Shepard has also been a member of ALA since 1934 and was on its executive board. In addition, she was a member of the UNESCO panel, and Pan American liaison for the Committee of Women's Organizations.

Shera, Jesse Hauk (1903-   )

Awarded a Ph.D. in library science from the University of Chicago in 1944, Jesse Shera has had a distinguished career in librarianship with his major posts including assistant director of the University of Chicago Library, associate professor in the Graduate Library School at the University of Chicago, dean and professor of library science at Case Western Reserve University and director of the Center for Documentation and Communication Research. Dr. Shera's major professional interests, reflected in his profuse publication of monographs and journal articles, center on education for librarianship, library history and the theory of classified documentation. Dr. Shera's career is marked by professional awards, diverse professional activity and association membership. Offices held in these associations include ALA Council (1965-69); chairman of the ACRL publications committee (1957-59); CNLA executive board (1964-); president of AALS (1964-65); and president of the Ohio Library Association (1963-64). Dr. Shera retired from active duty as dean of the Case Western Reserve Library School in 1970 and currently holds the title of professor and dean emeritus.

Simsova, Sylva (1931-   )

Educated in Prague, Czechoslovakia, Sylva Simsova, F.L.A., has worked in a number of British public libraries since 1951 including the Islington, Hackney, Stoke-Newington, and Finchley public libraries. In 1964, Ms. Simsova assumed a teaching position at the School of Librarianship, Polytechnic of North London where she currently holds the rank of senior lecturer. Since 1961, Ms. Simsova has contributed to an array of professional publications including Volume Two of *The Encyclopaedia of Library and Information Science, Research in Librarianship, Library Association Record,* and *Libri.*

Smith, Lloyd Pearsall (1822-1866)

Lloyd P. Smith was a man of learning and a descendant of James Logan, the Philadelphia benefactor whose will gave preference for appointing his heirs to positions in the Philadelphia Library Company. Appointed as a "hereditary librarian" in 1848 and succeeding his father as director in 1851, Mr. Smith remained at this post until his death. He was a rather conservative librarian who believed that locked cases for all books would facilitate service, since the librarian would have better control over the collection. He did, however, take advantage of ideas learned at professional meetings to improve his own library, and in fact, was a founder of the ALA. Active in the Association, he served as vice president, executive board member and councillor.

Smith, Stewart Worland (1905-   )

Mr. Smith has worked in several libraries throughout the country beginning with Milwaukee Public Library in 1929. He left his position as chief of the historical department in 1940, accepting a post in the Fitchburg (Mass.) Public Library. In 1944, he began a two-year directorship of the Lincoln, (Neb.) City Libraries after which he was director of the St. Louis County Library until 1968. Presently, Mr. Smith is a consultant. He is credited with the invention of several circulation innovations including the audio charge system. From 1949-50, he was president of the Missouri Library Association.

Smith, Toulmin
   At the time the conference proceedings were published, Miss Smith was librarian at Manchester College, Oxford.

Stokes, Katharine Martin (1906-   )
   Katharine Martin Stokes studied at the University of Michigan for her master's degree in English and her master's degree and Ph.D. in library science. The first twelve years of her library career were spent in Pennsylvania where she held, among other jobs, the position of assistant librarian at the Pennsylvania State College Library. After three years as circulation librarian at the University of Illinois (1945-48), she was librarian at Western Michigan University from 1948-67. While at Illinois, Dr. Stokes edited *Illinois Libraries* and from 1949-50 edited *Michigan Librarian.* Until her retirement in 1972, Dr. Stokes was employed as the College and University Library Specialist, Division of Library Services, U.S. Office of Education. She has remained active, planning the D.C. meeting of the International Federation of Library Associations in 1974 as the Conference Secretary. Since 1975, she has been a volunteer docent in the Folger Shakespeare Library, Washington, D.C.

Thorne, Miss W. M.
   At the time the article was published, Miss Thorne was at St. Bride Institute Library in England.

Tyler, Alice Sarah (1859-1944)
   Alice Tyler graduated from the University of Illinois Library School in 1894 and became an assistant at the Decatur Public Library before moving on to the Cleveland Public Library in 1896. There she began her teaching career while serving as catalog librarian and lecturer in the library's summer school. Between 1900-1912, Ms. Tyler was director of the summer library school at the State University in Iowa and was also secretary of the Iowa State Library Commission, editing the bulletin of the Commission for one year. The remainder of her professional life was spent at the Case Western University Library School where she held the administrative and academic posts of director (1913-1925) and dean and professor of library science (1925-1929). Ms. Tyler's participation in professional associations during this time is also impressive: she was president of the Ohio Library Association (1916-17), president of the Association of American Library Schools (1918-19), and president of ALA (1920-21).

Ward, Patricia Layzell
   Patricia Layzell Ward, M.A., Ph.D., F.L.A., was previously on the research staff at the Polytechnic of North London School of Librarianship. Currently, she holds the position of principal lecturer, research and liaison and is engaged in preparing up-dated reports on the question of women in librarianship for government and professional committees concerned with manpower planning for the profession in the U.K.

Weibel, Kathleen
   Kathleen Weibel received her M.L.S. from Columbia School of Library Service and worked at the New York and Chicago public libraries prior to pursuing a doctorate in library science at the University of Wisconsin. While studying for that degree, Ms. Weibel taught at the University of Wisconsin Library School and also coordinated the COLEPAC continuing education project for the University of Wisconsin Extension Service. She is currently Continuing Education Consultant with the New York State Library.

Wilden-Hart, Marion

Marion Wilden-Hart has held a wide range of library positions including lecturer at the Department of Librarianship, Birmingham University; coordinator of acquisitions at Syracuse University; and library advisor in Malaysia. At present she is a member of the faculty of art and design in charge of learning resources at Brighton, Polytechnic.

Winsor, Justin (1831-1897)

A member of the Boston aristocracy and noted historian, Justin Winsor first became involved in the library profession when he was appointed director of the Boston Public Library in 1868 after serving on the Board of Trustees for two years. The results of his emerging administrative creativity soon drew him recognition from the library world. His innovations included promotion of popular fiction, branch libraries and Sunday opening. In 1877, Winsor accepted the directorship of the Harvard College Library and again introduced new services and policies such as student stack privileges, bibliographic instruction and interlibrary loans. Mr. Winsor also took an active role in the formation and development of the ALA, serving as the organization's first president from 1876-1885. He was elected president again in 1897 and shortly before his death, he lead the American delegation to the Second International Library Conference.

Wyer, James Ingersoll (1869-1955)

After receiving his degree at the New York State Library School at Albany in 1898, James Wyer spent seven years as librarian at the University of Nebraska where he clearly established his reputation in the profession and cultivated his interest in education for librarianship. His most significant achievements took place when he succeeded Melvil Dewey as director of the New York State Library and Library School in 1908 and assumed the staggering task of rebuilding the great library after it was demolished in the tragic Capitol fire of 1911. Wyer successfully reconstructed the institution to conform to his vision of the ideal state library; the policies and programs he instituted as director reflected his conviction that the library should provide statewide service and function as the coordinating agency for library activities throughout the state. Recognition for Wyer's achievements as an educator came in 1915 when he was elected president of the Association of American Library Schools. A prolific writer, James Wyer contributed regularly to *Library Journal* and *Library Quarterly* and wrote an influential textbook on the subject of reference work. He held several major organizational posts, among them, ALA president.

The Role of Women in Librarianship 1876-1976:

The Entry, Advancement, and Struggle for Equalization in One Profession

PART

I

1876-1900
EMERGENCE OF AN
ORGANIZED PROFESSION

Historical Sketches of the Ladies' Library Associations of the State of Michigan

Compiled and Arranged by Mrs. A.F. Bixby and Mrs. A. Howell

UNION CITY LIBRARY ASSOCIATION

During the winter of 1872, a few enterprising women, who not being allowed to vote, yet felt the need of some sphere in which to exert their powers of usefulness, formed a Christian Association, thinking to benefit some one by denying themselves the privilege of playing whist or drinking milk punch. They were energetic, courageous, ferocious, if need be, in the cause. They talked in public and prayed in private over the wickedness which abounded, and some went so far as to enter the billiard halls and drinking saloons to convince men that they were on the highway to ruin. But they were women, and what could poor, weak women do who were not allowed the right of suffrage? They could only speak and weep and supplicate over the depravity of the age. After a few months of toil and wailing, with no visible improvement as to the amount of liquor drank, cards shuffled, dances abandoned, or souls saved, the conclusion was reached that a Christian Association would not work, but perhaps something else would. What should that something else be? After much argumentation, it was decided that nothing could be more beneficial to a rising generation than cultivation of the mind, and how better to promote this intellectual growth than by select reading?

All agreeing in this, with some addition as to numbers, a start was made by the remodeling of themselves into dramatists. In this role they were eminently more successful, coming out ahead at the end of two evenings on the stage, with something over seventy dollars as a nest-egg.

The young men of the place, seeing the undertaking well under way, and having in their possession moneys also gained in the laudable but unsuccessful formation of a Young Men's Christian Association, now came gallantly to the front, and presented the ladies with the hard-earned assets, amounting to thirteen and one-half dollars. But with the cash came this condition: "We

Excerpt reprinted from *Historical Sketches of the Ladies' Library Association of the State of Michigan*. Adrian, Michigan, Times and Expositor Steam Print, 1876:133-135.

must select our own books." The baby institution was only too glad to accept this milk of human kindness, even though it did come with an insinuating proviso. Therefore, with the understanding that no dime novels were to be purchased, the capital on hand was increased to $83.80. Then, for fear so large an amount might tempt thieves to break through and steal, 'twas thought best not to wait for further contributions, but to immediately turn greenbacks into books, to satisfy the mental cravings of the populace.

Sixty-three volumes were purchased, a shelf selected, librarian chosen, tickets issued, and the Union City Public Library was fairly on its feet. The prodigy grew slowly, and in passing through the various diseases incident to childhood, was several times on the point of dissolution, but the assiduous care of the most earnest brought it alive, but most feeble, to the fall of 1875, when it was decided to adopt a more vigorous treatment; in other words, they would be legally incorporated. A reorganization was the result of the council.

Under the renovated constitution the officers, consisting of President, Vice President, Clerk, Treasurer, Collector and Librarian, with five directors, constitute the board, who shall have entire supervision of the business affairs of the Association. A new name seemed advisable under the circumstances, therefore the Union City Public Library merged into the Ladies' Library Association.

With the new government and re-christening, came a stroke of good fortune, by way of a gift most generous. Messrs. Corbin and Tucker presented the Association with a large, pleasant room in their new brick building, on Broadway. Then the cry went out, "come and help us," that we may make a presentable appearance in our new home.

The Light Guards, of Coldwater, heard the appeal, and like true knights of old, hurried bravely to the rescue of the fair ones. Generously devoting the entire proceeds of one of their entertainments to the cause they had espoused, the ladies were thereby enabled to purchase furniture for the new apartment, and make an addition of sixty volumes to the library.

Being now in good moving order, they went "up in the world," in more senses than one, for the change was most favorable, and a rapid improvement has been the result. To prove it—

At the time of our reorganization (October, 1875), our worldly possessions consisted of a bottle of mucilage, a small stained wood case, and less than two hundred books, with only fifty ticket holders. No apparent interest, except on the part of the two librarians, who alone kept alive the vital spark on which its existence depended. And more, at the mercy of the benevolent for a shelter. How now? At the present date (May 15th, 1876), we own a beautiful room *nicely furnished*, with the exception of a carpet, a fine black walnut case, eight feet in length, neatly finished with sliding doors, drawers, etc., a model for the others we are to have *some day*. In the old one a small (as yet) museum is being collected. A choice selection of 388 volumes, among which is Appleton's new American Encyclopedia. Our ticket holders increased to 120, with, best of all, a general waking up of the people to the needs of the village in this direction, seems to verify the old adage, "merit does much but fortune more."

Transactions and Proceedings of the Conference of Librarians Held in London

October, 1877

Mr. Lloyd P. Smith, V.P., was surprised that in England a lady-librarian was scarcely ever heard of, while in America the great majority of librarians were women. Very good librarians they were, and he was sorry to say that they were too often underpaid. A lady-librarian had told him that she found that one of a librarian's proper qualifications was to be able to live on two meals a day, and pay for one out of his or her own pocket.

Professor Justin Winsor, V.P., said:—In the Boston Public Library two-thirds of the librarians are women. In American libraries we set a high value on women's work. They soften our atmosphere, they lighten our labour, they are equal to our work, and for the money they cost—if we must gauge such labour by such rules—they are infinitely better than equivalent salaries will produce of the other sex. For from £100 to £160 a year we can command our pick of the educated young women whom our Colleges for Women are launching forth upon our country—women with a fair knowledge of Latin and Greek, a good knowledge of French and German, a deducible knowledge of Italian and Spanish, and who do not stagger at the acquisition of even Russian, if the requirements of the catalogue-service make that demand. It is to these Colleges for Women, like Vassar and Wellesley, that the American library-system looks confidently for the future. I think, if I may say it, that it will be a happy day for England when the number of your governesses is so diminished as to be more equal to the demand, by a portion of them substituting the wider sphere of library-work for the enervating care of the idealess young. I am glad to offer to you as one of our American deputation the late librarian of Wellesley College, who is with us. That institution, a few miles from Boston, with all the surroundings of park and lake that can make a spot alluring, will show you a lady for its president, others of her sex for her supporters in the professional chairs, and three or four hundred students in gowns that become them because they are women. It is to such institutions that America looks, in the face of the great educational problem whose right solution is to determine her destiny. The solution of that problem is an ennobling work, and libraries and women are to play no mean part in it.

Excerpt reprinted from *Transactions and Proceedings of the Conference of Librarians Held in London, October, 1877.* London, Chiswick Press, 1878:177.

Mr. W.F. Poole, V.P., said:— Women are largely employed as assistants in our American libraries, and in many instances they have charge of libraries. Some of our most accomplished cataloguers are ladies, and they find constant employment in this special work, at compensation quite as large as the librarians of some of the principal libraries in the English provinces receive. My chief office-assistant and cataloguer is a lady, and a more competent person for the position I do not desire. There is a feeling in America that positions in libraries belong to ladies, and they are employed and paid the same pay as would be received by men who could do the work as well and perhaps better.

The Employment of Young Women as Assistants in Public Free Libraries

by Alderman Thomas Baker

The employment of young women as assistants in public free libraries in this country is a recent experiment which I believe was first tried in Manchester, and was the result of circumstances which I will endeavour to detail. For nineteen years after the formation of the Manchester Public Free Libraries boys and young men only were employed as assistants. Good wages were paid them, and their work was of a lighter and pleasanter kind than that of many other employments. No dissatisfaction was ever expressed with the work, but the younger boys considered it a grievance to have to remain after ordinary office hours, when other boys were playing; and the elder ones learnt, as they advanced in years, that they were becoming qualified for better paid situations: for it happens in Manchester, and it may be the same in other commercial centres, that intelligent youths of seventeen or eighteen years of age are found competent to do work often assigned to men, for which they get better paid as youths than they would be if of men's estate. The consequence of this has been that the older and better class of youths, whose intelligence and general bearing have been developed by two or three years' training in the libraries, have been able to obtain other situations with a greater increase of wages than their years warranted. This occurred so often as to give the chairman of the committee an impression that situations were held, and perhaps sought for, only as stepping-stones to something better. Neither the chances of promotion to better positions in the reference library, nor to appointments as branch librarians combined with a reasonable increase of wages, were sufficient to keep the young men in the service of the committee, while the frequent vacancies which occurred caused much trouble and inconvenience in the maintenance of that order and efficiency which are essential to the carrying out successfully of the work of the libraries. At this time the subject of woman, her rights, duties, and employment—particularly her exclusion from certain trades and professions—was engaging the attention of thoughtful people. Their chairman suggested to the committee that young women should be tried as assistants in the libraries. To this they assented; and, though it was

Reprinted from *Transactions and Proceedings of the Second Annual Meeting of the Library Association of the United Kingdom Held at Manchester, September 23, 24, and 25, 1879*. London, Chiswick Press, 1880:32-33.

known that the number of women was greater in proportion to that of the other sex, it did not occur to them that the situations they had to offer would be so much sought after, and by so superior a class of applicants as made their appearance. As it was customary to advertise for youths as vacancies occurred, a similar proceeding was adopted now that it was decided to try the other sex; and an advertisement in the following words was inserted in the *Manchester Guardian* of September 5, 1871:—"Manchester Public Free Libraries.— Wanted, a respectable, intelligent young woman as assistant in the Free Libraries. Apply to the Chief Librarian, Campfield." This advertisement, which, if it had been for a boy, would have elicited a response from only a few applicants, brought up a host of young women candidates. After inquiring into the qualifications of about twenty, and taking their names and addresses, the remaining applicants were informed that more had already appeared than were required. Three of the young women who had applied were engaged at the merely trial wages of six shillings per week. One of them was assigned to the Campfield Lending Library, one to the Ancoats branch, and one to the Chorlton branch; and after a short trial, when they were found to be efficient, their wages were adequately increased. The branch librarians would have preferred continuing on the old system, but they did not allow this feeling to interfere with the carrying out of the wishes of the committee; and now, I believe, there is not one of them who is not in favour of the change. The experiment answered in every way, and it was one of the first inquiries of the committee, as they met month after month, how the young women assistants did their work? It has been to the committee a subject of great gratification that they have been the means of introducing young women to a new class of labour, and that they have been able to employ so many of them. They have at this time thirty-one in their service—four in the reference library, and twenty-seven in the branches—at wages varying according to length of service and ability, from ten to eighteen shillings per week. They are regular in their attendance, attentive to their duties, uniformly courteous to borrowers, and contented with their employment and position, evincing no disposition to leave. Few of them have left, except from such causes as bad health or being about to marry. The relief to the chairman of the committee is, I can assure you, very great; for there are now few changes, and if a vacancy does occur, there are many applicants for it. The committee have never had occasion to repeat their advertisement. In November last year, when the boys' room in connexion with the Chorlton Branch Library was first opened, it was so filled with boys that the number of assistants had to be increased without delay. The first three young women whose names were in the book of applicants were communicated with and engaged there and then. They took their places the next night, and began library work as half-timers, from five o'clock P.M. to nine every evening, at the wages of ten shillings per week, with the prospect of appointment as full assistants as vacancies occurred; and one of these young women has now a full engagement at the library at fourteen shillings per week. As the wages list is revised, which is once a year, this assistant, if she continues to give satisfaction, will have her remuneration raised till she ultimately has eighteen shillings per week, which is the maximum sum the committee at present give to the women assistants. There are qualities in which the female assistants are scarcely equal to male ones, and the librarians like to have one youth at their command: he is better for any rough work there may be, such as opening and shutting windows, going errands, also in reaching books from the higher shelves, and perhaps in case of disorder in the reading-rooms, though this is of very infrequent occurrence; but for attendance on readers and applicants for books, they prefer the girls.

Women in Libraries: How They Are Handicapped

by Melvil Dewey

There is a large field of work for college-bred women in promoting the founding of new libraries, infusing new life into old ones, or serving on committees
or boards of trustees where their education and training will tell powerfully
for the common good. Active interest of this kind may fairly be expected of
every college graduate.

In the more direct work for which salaries are paid, there is an unusually
promising field for college girls and in few lines of work have women so nearly
an equal chance with men. There is almost nothing in the higher branches
which she cannot do quite as well as a man of equal training and experience;
and in much of library work women's quick mind and deft fingers do many
things with a neatness and despatch seldom equaled by her brothers.

My experience is that an increasing number of libraries are willing to pay
for given work the same price, whether done by men or women. Yet why are
the salaries of women lower? In all my business and professional life I have
tried to give women more than a fair chance at all work which I had to offer.
Experience has taught me why the fairest employers, in simple justice, usually
pay men more for what seems at first sight the same work. Perhaps these
reasons may help you to avoid some of the difficulties.

1. Women have usually poorer health and as a result lose more time from
illness and are more crippled by physical weakness when on duty. The difficulty is most common to women, as are bright ribbons and thin shoes and long
hair, but it is a question of health, not of sex. A strong, healthy woman is
worth more than a feeble man for the same reason that a strong man gets more
than a weak woman.

2. Usually women lack business and executive training. Her brothers
have been about the shops and stores and in the streets or on the farm hearing
business matters discussed and seeing business transacted from earliest childhood. The boys have been trading jack knives and developing the business
bumps while the girls were absorbed with their dolls. It would be a miracle at
present if girls were not greatly inferior in this respect and it is this fact which
accounts for so few prominent chief librarianships being held by women. But
this is the fault of circumstances, not necessarily of sex, and women who have
somehow got the business ideas and training and have executive force are get-

Address given March 13, 1886 before the Association of Collegiate Alumnae.
Excerpts reprinted from *Library Notes* 1 (October 1886):89-92.

ting the salaries that such work commands. When girls have as good a chance to learn these things, I doubt not that they will quite equal their brothers and will keep cash and bank accounts and double entry books for their private affairs. A man brought up girl-fashion, as not a few are, proves just as helpless on trial and as a result gets only a "woman's salary."

3. Lack of permanence in her plans is one of the gravest difficulties with women. A young man who enters library work and later thinks of a home of his own, is stimulated to fresh endeavors to make his services more valuable. Many a young man's success in life dates from the new earnestness which took possession of him on his engagement. But with women the probability or even the possibility that her position is only temporary and that she will soon leave it for home life does more than anything else to keep her value down. Neither man or woman can do the best work except when it is felt to be the life work. This lack of permanence in the plans of women is more serious than you are apt to realize. If woman wishes to be as valuable as man she must contrive to feel that she has chosen a profession for life and work accordingly. Then she will do the best that is in her to do as long as she is in the service and if at any time it seems best to change her state, the work already done has not been crippled by this "temporary" evil.

4. With equal health, business training and permanence of plans, women will still usually have to accept something less than men because of the consideration which she exacts and deserves on account of her sex. If a man can do all the other work just as well as the woman and in addition can, in an emergency, lift a heavy case, or climb a ladder to the roof or in case of accident or disorder can act as fireman or do police duty, he adds something to his direct value; just as a saddle horse that is safe in harness and not afraid of the cars, will bring more in nine markets out of ten, than the equally good horse that can be used only in the saddle. So in justice to those who wish to be fair to women, remember that she almost always receives, whether she exacts it or not, much more waiting on and minor assistance than a man in the same place and therefore, with sentiment aside, hard business judgment cannot award her quite as much salary. There are many uses for which a stout corduroy is really worth more than the finest silk. . . .

We greatly prefer college-bred women in selecting new librarians: 1. Because they are a picked class selected from the best material throughout the country. 2. Because the college training has given them a wider culture and broader view with a considerable fund of information all of which will be valuable working material in a library as almost nowhere else. 3. Because a four years' course successfully completed is the strongest voucher for persistent purpose and mental and physical capacity for protracted intellectual work. 4. Chiefly because we find that the training of the course enables the mind to work with a quick precision and steady application rarely found in one who has not had this thorough college drill. Therefore we find it pays to give higher salaries for college women. . . .

The salary to women for the first year is seldom more than $500 and at present few have grown to over $1,000, though here and there $1,200 to $1,500 are paid to women of experience. But there is no reason why a woman cannot do the same work for which our leading librarians receive $3,000 to $5,000 and I have no doubt that as women of education, with thorough technical training and experience come forward, the salaries will rapidly increase. For this highest grade work the demand exceeds the supply and will grow steadily with the new development of the library system. If one finds many more well paid positions for teachers, there are vastly more competitors for each of these places than for that of the trained librarian. After careful study it seems to me that to an earnest woman of superior ability the library field already offers in its present period of rapid growth as good an opening financially as teaching.

Proceedings of the Fourteenth American Library Association Conference: The Woman's Meeting

The Woman's Meeting was called to order May 19 at 2:30 P.M. by Miss Mary S. Cutler, who briefly explained that the call for the meeting had come from the Secretary of the Association, and called on the members to nominate a chairman. Miss E.M. Coe, of the New York Free Circulating Libraries, was elected chairman, and Mrs. Melvil Dewey, Secretary. Miss Cutler presented by title a paper on

WHAT A WOMAN LIBRARIAN EARNS

The work of the modern librarian is so little understood that an outline of what it covers may not only prove interesting reading, but also throw light on the question of what should be a fair financial return for this service to the reading public.

The librarian must be both a good business woman and an educator in the highest sense of the word. First, she must build up the library. Her problem is as follows: Given a multitude of books and a limited fund, to select those best suited to the needs and tastes of her particular readers. She must buy the books and keep exact business records. She must take an inventory of stock once a year. She must present to the trustees both a monthly and annual report on work and finances. She must be familiar with recent thought in library architecture, as she is often called on to suggest plans for a new building or for the enlargement of an old one.

She must make the resources of the library available by a wise classification of books; by a catalog which indicates clearly to the reader if the book he seeks is in the library, also what books on a subject are most valuable for his purpose; by individual help, being ready at any moment to drop other work and spend an hour or two if need be in hunting up answers to questions from all sorts and conditions of readers. She must also devise and carry on a system of charging books which shall secure their safety, at a minimum of work and waiting for both borrowers and attendants.

Reprinted with permission from the "Proceedings of the Fourteenth American Library Association Conference, Lakewood." *Library Journal* 17 (August 1892):89-94.

She must inspire her assistants, even those of the lowest grade, with her own ideals, so that the spirit of courtesy and of helpfulness shall pervade the place like an atmosphere.

She is not content to satisfy the demands made on the library; she creates a demand.

She establishes a close connection between the library and the public schools, gaining the cooperation of the teachers in bringing up a generation of readers with pure tastes and a genuine love of good reading. She grants special privileges to reading and art clubs, buying with reference to their needs. The librarian is one of the most efficient promoters of university extension, as the library is its natural centre. She prints lists of books and articles on topics of current interest, buys books for the mechanic and the foreigner, talks with the foreigner in his own language, cooperates with the church and press in local forms. The librarian must be in touch with the latest and best thought of the time and with the growth of her own community, making the library an active, aggressive, educational force.

All this and more is being done by the modern librarians, both men and women.

How much money does the woman-librarian receive, and how much is received by women who fill subordinate library positions?

An official statement has been secured of salaries paid to all the women employed in 25 of the most prominent libraries in the country, prominent from their size, wise administration, and efficiency. They represent 15 States, two Eastern, three Middle, eight Western, and two Southern, and several types of libraries, free public, subscription, state, and college. Other statistics which follow are also official.

Three hundred and ninety-six women are employed in 25 prominent libraries, receiving from $240 to $1,500, an average salary of $570. This includes work of all grades, and the average is greatly reduced by the large number required to do mechanical work in comparison with the few needed for supervisory and independent work.

Fifteen women of recognized ability, trained as apprentices in large libraries or in the school of experience, receive from $550 to $2,000, an average salary of $1,150; 38 women, trained in the Library School which was opened in 1887, receive from $600 to $1,500, an average salary of $900. The 15 highest salaries paid to library school women average $1,090. Seven women as librarians of State libraries receive from $625 to $1,200, an average salary of $1,000. The 24 men filling similar positions receive an average salary of $1,450.

From all of the preceding lists have been selected 37 women who have made a decided success of the work. Their salaries, tabulated as follows, are effected by local conditions, and are in many cases not in proportion to the value of services rendered:

One at $2,000; one at $1,800; one at $1,740; four at $1,500; one at $1,320; one at $1,300; six at $1,200; one at $1,100; two at $1,080; six at $1,000; five at $900; four at $800; three at $700; one at $550.

From these figures and a general estimate based on a large acquaintance with librarians, I conclude that a woman occupying a subordinate position in a library, where faithfulness, accuracy, and a fair knowledge of books are the only essentials, can expect from $300 to $500. A good cataloger, or a librarian with average ability and training, can expect to receive from $600 to $900. A

woman with good natural ability and fitness for the work, with a liberal education and special training, can expect $1,000 at the head of a library, or of a de-
partment in a large library, with a possible increase to $1,500 or $2,000.
Women rarely receive the same pay for the same work as men.

Salaries are lowered: (1) By political influence in certain libraries supported by the city and state, which discourages good work by making the
tenure of office uncertain. (2) By the fact that working among books is considered an attractive and "genteel" employment, without the severe strain of
teaching. (3) Because many library trustees have not the modern conception
of a library and are content with inferior work. (4) Because many other library
trustees take advantage of a woman's willingness to work for less than she
earns when she knows her work is useful. The women in one well-known library accept, year after year, for high-grade service the pitiful dole of twenty
cents an hour.

Salaries tend to increase and are increasing steadily because there are so
few men or women able to meet the growing demand for trained librarians.

A woman's fitness for library work is proved. She has already a recognized place in the profession. She has contributed somewhat to the literature
of the subject and holds offices of honor in the American Library Association.
This is due largely to the liberal spirit of the leaders in the library movement
of the last twenty years.

In England she has no such place. At the last conference of the Library
Association of the United Kingdom the President apologized to me for what
he called the dullness of the sessions, saying that of course there could be
nothing in the discussions of a library association to interest ladies.

In America her position in the future will be what she has power to make
it. She has a fair chance, and if she fails it will be her own fault. A genius for
organization, executive ability, and business habits, a wide knowledge and
love of books amounting to a book-instinct, and the gift of moving and inspiring other minds are absolutely essential to the highest success. The palm of
honor and of opportunity waits for her who shall join a genius for organization to the power of a broad, rich, catholic, and sympathetic womanhood. The
work is worth the best energies of the strongest minds, and in the long run will
win appreciation and proper financial support.

Mrs. M.R. Sanders spoke on

READING-ROOMS; WHAT A WOMAN MAY DO IN THEM

The opportunities for influencing readers, specially boys; the firmness
and tact often required to preserve order and discipline; what a woman may
accomplish in cases where a man's physical strength is usually thought necessary.

Miss Middleton, Miss Green, and Miss James each gave bits of personal
experience.

The chairman asked Miss Green to say something from her own experience as to "exactness in cataloging" and of women "as bookkeepers." She had
found young women, on the whole, more exact, more willing to take pains.
The balance, in her experience, was a little in favor of the girls. As to book-
keeping, she mentioned one case in a prominent public library, where a
woman, without any assistant, had been bookkeeper for twenty years, and in
all that time had never been known to make a mistake that could be criticised.

Time being limited, Miss M.E. Sargent read by title her paper on

WOMAN'S POSITION IN LIBRARY SERVICE

In lieu of any opinions of my own I present for your consideration and for discussion what I have been able to gather as to a woman's possibilities and also her limitations in such service. I quote first from a librarian's views: "Some doubt has been expressed of the capacity of a woman to manage a city library. The objectors, I think, must be unacquainted with the recent library history of Massachusetts. Many of our large libraries are administered by women, and I have never heard that they did not give as much satisfaction to trustees and the public as men." The writer then speaks of the excellent work of Miss James of Wilkes-Barre, of Miss Thurston at Newton, of Miss Hayward at Cambridge, Miss Chandler of Lancaster, and some others. "Besides these there are 97 other women who are librarians of public libraries in this State and 51 who are librarians of libraries not public. That is to say, out of 427 libraries 156 are in charge of women. . . . A woman may be imbued with all the modern ideas of librarianship—of assisting the public, of teaching the public, elevating the public." Referring to libraries outside of Massachusetts he cites the splendid work of Miss Coe, the head of the New York Free Circulating Library.

In quite an opposite strain are the following words from a trustee's standpoint: "My reason for preferring a man for the head of a library in a large city is not based on what may be called library *per se*. It is connected with the business side of the librarian's position. Unfortunately women are hedged about with rules of decorum and courtesy which somewhat interfere with their usefulness in many relations in a municipal or a business community; with the trustees, for instance, who may change from time to time—may include conflicting elements—may comprise men of rough or at least of downright and positive character. A man's relations with such a board are freer and more likely to be influential than a woman's, because he can talk right *at* them and *with* them, without offense on either side. He is usually accustomed to hasty and unfair criticism and knows how to meet it effectively. With the city government—especially the council who make appropriations—a man can work far more efficiently than a woman can. He can go out among them at their offices and stores, or in the City Hall corridor; can learn what influences are brought to bear on them, and so benefit the library in a score of ways closed to a woman. With the rougher class of the community, with laborers and artisans, a man, for obvious reasons, can do more effective work. Women, more rarely, have the disciplinary power over a mixed force of men and women under them than men do; but that is rather a personal matter, to be tested in experience. Some women have it in a marked degree; many men are lacking in this direction. Now I am not bigoted; perhaps these views are wrong, but they are founded on a wide business experience, and an observation of many libraries and librarians all over this country. My theory seems to be generally accepted in practice, at any rate; for men are at the head of most if not all the libraries in large cities."

For myself, with Miss Willard, I feel that "we should study the largeness of life and not its limitations." We should be divine optimists, "who, rowing hard against the stream, see distant lights of Eden gleam, and know the dream is not a dream."

"We are hedged about with rules of decorum and courtesy." Max O'Rell has said that unsexing in America has been a blessed thing for us.

"The freedom enjoyed by American women has enabled them to mould themselves in their own fashion. They do not copy any other women; they are original. I can recognize an American woman without hearing her speak. You have only to see her enter a room or a car and you know her for Jonathan's daughter. Married or unmarried, her air is full of assurance, of a self-possession that never fails her, and when she looks at you or talks to you her eyes express the same calm consciousness of her worth. They say in France that Paris is the Paradise of women. If so, there is a more blissful place than Paradise; there is another word to invent to give an idea of the social position enjoyed by American ladies. If I had to be born again and I might choose my sex and my birthplace I would shout at the top of my voice, "Oh, make me an American woman."

And then again, in dealing with the rougher elements above alluded to, force does not always mean "bayonets and cannon balls." The silent and unseen are still the strongest powers of all. A scientific age is proving what faith has always taught, that "thought and will and love are the only forces that endure."

"Time is the great alembic in which all are tested." The work of Miss Mitchell in science, of Miss Edwards in Egyptology, may be cited as examples of what can be accomplished by women.

With the true love for the work, with a similar devotion and the needed inspiration and aspiration, why cannot a like result be accomplished in *our* service, and why may we not be able to prove that our possibilities outweigh our limitations. We can at least console ourselves with the thought expressed by Thoreau, "It is the business of mankind to polish the world, and every one who works is scrubbing some part."

"Where your heart is interested, let your life take part; where your life takes part, let your heart glow."

"Some evils must be trampled down
  Beneath our feet, if we would gain,
In the bright fields of fair renown,
  The right of eminent domain.

"Standing on what too long we bore
  With shoulders bent and downcast eyes,
We may discern—unseen before—
  A path to higher destinies."

In closing the chairman spoke of the interest, freedom of discussion, and special value to the young librarians of such meetings as this. Voted: That a committee be appointed to organize a Woman's Section of the A.L.A., to report at the next conference in Chicago. The Chair appointed Miss H.P. James, Mrs. Melvil Dewey, and Miss H.E. Green, with power to add to the committee. Adjourned.

Annie Dewey, *Secretary pro tem.*

Librarianship as a Profession for Women

by Miss Richardson

Now that women are entering as competitors in almost every field of labour formerly looked upon as belonging exclusively to the sterner sex, it may not be uninteresting to hear a little about library work as a profession for women.

In the first place, let us look for a moment at the mere routine work which goes on in every free library, and which is done for the most part by the assistants, — I refer to the labelling, repairing and issuing of books. The first two will in all probability be done more quickly and neatly by a girl than a boy; and as regards the issuing of books, there is an advantage in having at least one female assistant, as many of the lady borrowers prefer to be attended to by one of their own sex. In those libraries which have separate reading-rooms for ladies, it is also essential that a female assistant should look after the room and attend to the renewal of the papers and periodicals placed there.

But to proceed to the real work of a librarian, that which is done for the most part behind the scenes, such as choosing new books, classifying and cataloguing them, attending to correspondence, and the numerous other duties which are comprised in a librarian's work. Here, too, a woman will be as much at home as a man, and will make the institution under her charge a success.

In America, women are taking their places in this ever-widening sphere of labour, and proving that they can do work of this kind quite as well as their brothers. There they have more opportunities of getting a fair trial than we in England possess, for library committees are convinced that librarianship is a profession eminently suited to earnest women of education and refinement, and give them every encouragement accordingly.

The Library School at Albany seems to be doing a good work in training and sending out women ready to labour for the uplifting of those in the towns where their lot is cast, and that good may be done amongst the readers, especially young readers, cannot be denied.

Now that so much more education is considered necessary for every station in life, libraries will soon be found in every town in the kingdom, and this will open up a vast field of labour for both men and women. It is only lately that librarianship has been included amongst the professions at all, and it depends mainly on librarians themselves whether their work is recognised by the outside public or not.

Reprinted with permission from *The Library* 6 (1894):137-142.

A paper was read at the second annual meeting of the Library Association, held in Manchester in 1879, by the late Alderman Thomas Baker, who was then chairman of the libraries' committee, on "The Employment of Young Women as Assistants in Free Public Libraries." [See page 7.] Mr. Baker said he believed the plan was first tried in the Manchester libraries, and had proved a success. At that time they were only employed as assistants; but since then ladies have held the position of librarians in the branches of the Manchester library, who have, doubtless, in the first place, served in the capacity of assistant in one of the libraries under the corporation.

A girl who enters a library as assistant, and intends to make the work her life-work, if we may so call it, neglects no opportunity of learning as much as possible of the technical part of librarianship, and at the same time tries to improve herself in general knowledge. There is not much time for very deep study of any subject, for the hours in a library are usually very long; but a librarian, male or female, who is always on the alert to find out the books which will be most useful to borrowers and persons who come to seek information of various kinds, will make the institution under his or her charge more popular and flourishing than one who is very learned in any one subject, and, perhaps, oblivious of the fact that the visitors to a library do not all incline to the same study as himself, but expect a little attention to their needs and wants from the librarian. At the same time one can never know enough, and must be ever ready for fresh ideas, and prepared to learn as much as possible.

Women are employed in many of the great American libraries, and even hold the post of chief librarian in some of them. There, however, they are specially trained at the Library School, and are put on an equality with men, and so obtain the same advantages. Some go in for cataloguing as a speciality; this is suited to the quiet, shy women, who, though fully qualified for the work, prefer to do that part of it which may be accomplished away from public view. Others, who do not shine in cataloguing, are well fitted to meet and aid those who come to consult the books under their charge. Some combine both qualities, and are fitted to take control of a library. In England women are not yet admitted into the old and large reference libraries which are scattered over the country, nor into the libraries connected with our colleges, but they are gradually making their way as librarians in the public libraries which are springing up in many of our provincial towns. In this position they must have an all-round knowledge of library work, and be able to help the readers and borrowers in their search for works on special subjects, or even to direct the reading of those who are unable to make a wise choice for themselves.

Here I may just mention that women have acquired rather a bad reputation for being slow in coming to a decision, and when asked to give an opinion on a disputed point or to recommend the best book on a certain subject, they hesitate, are not quite sure, and so on. This is a fault to which many women are prone, and one which must be cured if they are to work on the same level as men. If a woman means to get on in library work, she must learn to be self-reliant, and to make up her mind at once when a decision is to be made. It must be owned, however, that this reproach is not so much deserved as it was some years ago. Girls are now taught on the same principles as boys in many cases, and instead of being made *fine ladies* are taught business habits from childhood, and left to use their own judgment in various matters. This sort of education is bearing fruit already, and the girls who have had this advantage are readier to compete for the same work as their brothers than those who have been brought up in the old-fashioned way. A woman may have as solid an education as a man, and use it as a means of earning a livelihood, and still be a womanly woman.

The wider the education possessed by a librarian the more successful the work is likely to prove, and now that librarianship is being found to be as well suited to the capacity of woman as man, there will be keen rivalry between the sexes, for our colleges. Girton and Newnham amongst the number, are sending out year by year women who are well taught, self-reliant, and ready to work to the best of their ability in whatever calling they have chosen. That of librarianship will be, I think, one which will commend itself to many as a means of helping others in the search after knowledge, and will also be found an agreeable employment. Miss Black, who was one of the first two librarians at the People's Palace, London, formerly of Newnham College, Cambridge, passed the graduation examinations, and would have obtained the degree had she been a man. Miss James, the late librarian, had three ladies as assistants, two of whom studied at Newnham College, and the other at Lady Margaret Hall, Oxford. All these ladies have found the work most attractive, and, to quote their own expressed opinions, they think there is at present no occupation more suited to women who are fairly well educated, and possess a real love of books. It ought not to be taken up as a mere pastime however, for nothing can be done in this work without earnestness, interest and thoroughness, also devotion to books. At Blackpool, Bridgwater, Darlaston, Darwen, Glossop, Nantwich, Poole, Fleetwood, Middleton, Northwich, Sittingbourne, Willenhall, Carnarvon, Galashiels, Hawick, Selkirk, and Widnes, ladies fill the office of librarian. At Peel Park Library and Regent Road, Salford, and at two or three of the branch libraries at Manchester, ladies are employed as librarians. In addition to the above named towns, the following libraries employ female assistants, viz.:—Battersea, Clerkenwell, Westminster and Chelsea, London; Aberdeen, Derby, Doncaster, Edinburgh, Oldham, Nottingham, Paisley, Sheffield, Glasgow (Stirling's Library, Baillie Institution), Bradford, Bristol, Manchester, Liverpool, and St. Helens, and the three lady librarians at Blackpool, Salford, and Widnes have female assistants.

But to be a successful librarian, a woman must have a practical training in all the work connected with a library; and to get this it is necessary that she should become, in the first place, an assistant to some librarian, who will teach her the technicalities of his craft.

England has not as yet found it necessary to establish a special college for the training of librarians, such as is in successful operation in the United States, but still something has been done, and the L.A.U.K. examinations of library assistants is a step in the right direction; and, doubtless, before long, all applicants for the post of librarian will have to produce certificates from this body. As women prove their capability for this kind of work, better appointments than those they now fill will be thrown open to them; and they will be engaged in the higher positions in our great libraries, and will so work and use their talents that their influence will be felt by many in towns other than those in which their work lies. But that time has not yet come; they must, at present, be content to wield their sway over the libraries which are so quickly springing up around us, and let their work, by its quality and usefulness, prove them fit for still better things.

Another hindrance to the employment of women in libraries is, that many enter the field, not with the view of making it a life-work, but merely as a means to an end. They think it a pleasant sort of work, but do not intend to remain at it. Now, the best work cannot be done, unless it is felt to be the work on which one's life is to be spent, and few or no women will remain in a library after marriage, for instance. But if their work is to be a real work, this must not be an obstacle. Let the work be done during the time they are engaged in it — be it long or short, — in such a manner, that when they leave it, it has not to be done over again by the next comer, but is as perfect as it is possible to make it.

At present, the employment of women as librarians is in its infancy, but is sure to prove a success; for girls who make up their minds to embrace the library profession as their life-work will work patiently and well, and will lose no opportunity of learning all that will aid them in their duties, and will show that, given the same opportunities as boys, they will do equally as well in this as in many other professions, and may, perhaps, excel some of them.

In conclusion, I would just remark that we do not wish to supplant our male friends in this work, but only ask that fair opportunities may be given to those of our sex who are anxious and willing to become labourers in this field of public work.

The Business Side of a Woman's Career as a Librarian

by Mary Eileen Ahern

In this day and age we hear *ad infinitum* and almost *ad nauseam* much discussion of woman's work and place in the economy of nature and in the material world. Without going into any of the reasons, or combating any of the arguments for or against the present status of women in any place, we must recognize the fact that there is a vast army of women who are in the labor market today, involuntarily or otherwise. Of these we need only consider such as come within the scope of our own profession, or in the many relations it bears to other movements of the day.

Women in library work as professionals is distinctly an American idea. There are but very few women in library work in England, and none of them in responsible positions. One of the incidents that excited most comment at the International Conference in 1897 was the presence of so many women librarians in the American party. There is, therefore, a special duty laid upon those women who are in the work, as well as those just taking it up, to prove their fitness for coming before the public in the capacity of serving in any position in the library profession.

There is a type of an individual that has always been recognized, and everywhere honored, when it reaches the development described as womanly. The library profession, be it said in the beginning, offers a pleasant and profitable field of action for womanly women. There is no room for any other kind in this work, just as there is not in any other serious field.

No woman can hope to reach any standing or field for effective work in the library profession, any more than in any other, who does not bring to it that love which suffereth long and is kind, is not puffed up, does not behave itself unseemly, vaunteth not itself, thinketh no evil, is fervent in spirit, and diligent in business. That there are many such, the rolls of those in high places amply testify. That there are some who have not caught the meaning of their work one's daily experience and observation make clear.

There is still some discrimination against the sex in the minds of library boards, it is true, but on the women in the world to which most library trustees belong must fall in a large measure the blame, though the women librarians are not wholly to be excused.

Reprinted with permission from *Library Journal* 24 (July 1899):60-62.

One of the first and most important lessons which a woman who enters the business world needs to learn is the seeming paradox to forget she is a woman, and at the same time keep ever before her that she is a woman. She should lose all sight of preliminary bounds which are perfectly proper in the relations of the social world, but which do not exist in the business world. That there would exist a more ideal condition of affairs if the business world were more polite, and recognized that certain forms and ceremonies make people happier, may be true, but that it does not write its code under these lines is beyond dispute.

In meeting the obligations which are assumed on entering this field of labor, as in all others, no consideration should be demanded in the fulfillment of the duties connected therewith, on any grounds that would not be justifiable were a man in the place. It may work extra hardship on a woman who has duties to perform outside the library, if she obeys the rule to be at her desk at 9 o'clock every morning, but that is not considered sufficient excuse for her tardy arrival. If arrangement is made by the library, which will relieve the pressure on her, a favor has been granted, not a right conceded.

On the business side of library work all ideas of sex, color, or previous conditions are properly eliminated. A woman is engaged to do certain things because as an individual she is supposed to be able to perform them, and no question of privilege other than as an individual should be looked for. The sooner the women who are in the busy working world comprehend this point and act accordingly, the sooner the problem of women's wages, positions, and promotions will be settled.

As for the second part of the paradox, every woman who, by force of circumstances, is compelled to be a part of the machinery of public affairs, owes it not only as a duty to herself, but to every other woman so situated, to try to live up to the finest ideals of womanhood. No woman striving ever so hard to play the part of a man has ever succeeded in doing more than to give just cause for a blush to the rest of her kind.

The dignified woman never has any complaint to make of those with whom she comes in contact in a business life. She need not be so frigid in her demeanor as to be repellent, but she can be possessed of a winning sweetness which comes from a sympathetic attitude towards others, and which will only be emphasized by the quiet calm that is the outward evidence of mental equipoise. The flippant answer or banter is nowhere more out of place than in serving in a public library. It detracts from the proper feeling that a library is a source of help and light and sweetness, which it is the duty of every one engaged in the work to keep before the eyes of the public. If nature has not endowed the woman who desires to enter the library profession with this dignity of manner, this commendable characteristic, it is well to set about its cultivation at once, for it is a well-known fact that it is quite as easy to train a set of manners as a set of morals, and as the attribute of dignity can be classified under both headings, it can be easily seen what rare advantages belong to the woman who can claim it as her own.

Then there is another attribute which has no place in the equipment of a woman librarian, and that is that almost indefinable something called "feelings." It is sometimes called a form of egotism, though not generally recognized as such by its possessor, but which nevertheless is as self-centered as the conceit which springs from vanity, and while it may not be so arrogant, is hardly less provoking.

As a matter of fact, it seems to me, after a long service of years for the public, that in this work-a-day practical world the less one thinks about one's self and one's feelings the better, and the best chance of happiness lies in forgetting our own individuality altogether and living for others.

In library work, as in other work, the personality of the woman which comes nearest the ideal woman as she is found anywhere else is the important equipment upon which a large share of her success or failure depends.

In contemplating library work as a livelihood, the first thing to consider is the fact that the outside of the books will require attention as well as the inside, and the fact that a girl likes to read is not necessarily *prima facie* evidence that she will make a good librarian, or certainly is not a prime requisite for a technical librarian who is somewhat hampered in her cataloging or classifying, unless a liking of that kind is constantly held in check.

The chief requisite of a librarian, I should say, and the one in which observation would lead me to say there is greatest lack among women in general, is executive ability and a knowledge of business methods. I do not mean to be understood as belittling general culture and technical knowledge: they, of course, are essential; but more librarians possess the latter than may be found exercising the former, and, as the head of an institution, the first qualifications are most necessary. The detail of arrangement may be left to another; but the librarian herself must meet the most exacting public—the public which gets something for nothing—and with tact, judgment, and skill win its approval of her plans for meeting the needs of the community. She must have skill in managing others, and setting them to do her bidding without a loss of that sympathetic relation between librarian and staff so necessary for success in managing the institution. The woman librarian, more than the man, has to be on her guard against personalities entering into her administration. I have been told over and over of the trial it was to hold themselves at the proper point where they could be the friend of those about them and at the same time maintain the place of an officer on duty. Only executive ability will carry one safely through these things, and serious thought should be given to its cultivation, for it can be acquired.

To this executive ability must be added a sense of business principles and what may be termed appreciation of the situation.

While learning the forms and processes necessary to the easy running of a library, it should be borne in mind that there is also the other side. While a librarian should know how to meet her reading public, she should also know how to meet her board. While she should know how to charge and discharge the books which the public takes, she should also be capable of auditing accounts and buying intelligently, and by that I do not mean *what* she buys so much as how she buys. A librarian, in order to be a success, must be acquainted, and thoroughly so, with the business world, its methods and rules, its requirements and privileges. A librarian may be in close touch with her readers, she may have an elaborate system of cataloging and classification, but if her reports come up to the library board in a slipshod, confused state, bearing signs of a lack of what is termed business sense, her standing with them is imperilled, and where a librarian has lost the admiration of her board her influence in that field is at an end.

When a business house receives an order for goods, well prepared, clear as to what is wanted, definite as to price and carriage, it takes a real pleasure in filling it, and, because of its clearness, time is saved to both the buyer and the seller, which to the latter, at least, is always money.

One of the weak places in the woman librarian's equipment is a lack of generous charity for what she considers the professional failings of others in the work. If one weak place in the armor of a fellow-worker is discovered, like a knight of old, she fastens her attention on that alone, despite the fact that there may be 50 strong points beside it, and even the weakness under the direction of its possessor may not be so glaring a fault as it appears in the eyes of the faultfinder. Think only of the good points, look for them, and do not let any one else know that you see where the shortcomings lie, and after a while you will not be quite sure that you saw them yourself. There is room for good workers always, and water will find its level. Hunt for the good things in other people's libraries, and it will not be long until the often expressed opinion of men, that women in business are jealous of each other's success, will die out for want of material to support it.

If there is a particular part of library work that you find more congenial than another, work toward reaching it, and if you are properly fitted for it the chances of its coming to you are decidedly increased. But, if you undertake to do something else, the fact of its not being your choice has no bearing on the performance of it in the very best way possible, and here comes in the question of salary. Women in business are accused, and not without cause, of slighting their work because the salary is not commensurate with the duties which they are called on to perform. Have a distinct understanding before beginning work as to what you are to receive for your work, and then do it the very best you are able. If you find that you have sufficient reason for being dissatisfied with the remuneration speak to the proper persons about it, and then abide honorably by the decision. One has no right by shirking his legitimate work to cast reproach on the whole body of workers. If you are at the head of affairs make it a point to tell definitely, and in good season, what those about you may depend upon both as to positions and salaries. It is said that women managers are too apt to consider such things as personal matters, and are weak in dealing with them. It is just as much the right of an assistant to know definitely about these things as it is for the President of the United States to know of his term and salary.

In the correspondence which brings requests for employment I have seen a disposition to do certain things which form the reasons of labor unions. I refer to the practice of cutting under the salary received by the majority for certain work. Librarians as a class are paid less than school teachers, while their work is about on the same basis. This is, in a large measure, the fault of librarians themselves. They do not work on this problem in harmony, and there is still too much "influence" back of giving places. I have my doubts about sending for a position the name of a girl who is willing to work for nearly nothing, for I cannot help thinking that her talents are not in demand in the market, or else she does not intend to carry out her contract, and her work will amount to about the same as the salary she asks.

Librarianship is a delightful and helpful field for work to those who will rise to its possibilities, but there is no room for thoughtless, indifferent posing here, as there is nowhere else. An army of noble women have done heroic work in opening the doors of the business world to their sisters; it is an obligation resting on every woman who enters these doors to add something to the credit of the army, and it is little less than criminal to detract from the reputation so hardly earned of being faithful conscientious workers.

Women Librarians

Excerpts from the International Congress of Women of 1899 . . .

INTRODUCTION

Dr. Richard Garnett strongly urged women not to accept too low remuneration for library work, pointing out that not only was this unjust to themselves, but would be likely to produce opposition to their employment in libraries on the part of librarians in general, whose salaries were very inadequate as it was, and who would naturally object to their scale of wages being lowered still further by competition. He eulogised the general fitness of women for employment in libraries, and particularly mentioned the pleasure he had always received from the frequent visits of American lady librarians to the British Museum.

THE TRAINING OF WOMEN AS LIBRARIANS

By Miss Mary W. Plummer

There is no training for women librarians which might not with equal propriety be called training for men librarians; and indeed, the four Schools of Library Training in the United States admit men to their classes, though the majority of their students are women. The reasons for the latter fact are not far to seek. The library-student must be well-educated and well-read, and women who are so equipped gravitate toward the professions and the arts rather than toward business-life. Librarianship is regarded by them not only as a profession but as an agreeable one, and they elect it while still in college, or renounce in its favour the more wearing occupation of teaching. It appeals to those to whom social standing is a matter of importance, the librarian of the town or village being considered, as a rule, the social equal of the best among the townspeople. To those women who are fond of books, the prospect of a life passed among them, even if the situation be somewhat comparable to that of Tantalus, offers a strong attraction. The salaries of head-librarians are on about the same scale as those of professors in colleges and teachers of high school and grammar grades, varying according to the size and importance of the library to be administered. Women are willing to accept more modest sal-

Excerpts reprinted from *The International Congress of Women of 1899: Women in the Professions.* Volume II, Edited by the Countess I. Aberdeen. London, T. Fisher Unwin, 1900:211-232.

aries than men, if the wage seems a just one for the work. They do not ask to be paid for being women. Fewer men enter the library schools, partly because the attention of young men of scholarly tastes is not sufficiently called to the field, partly because the energies of most American men seem to tend naturally toward commercial life, and partly because young men as a rule are not willing to accept the salaries offered to beginners. The result is that the men of the profession are largely librarians by experience rather than by training, and that they hold nearly all the best-paying positions, while the trained women occupy positions under them or take the headship of libraries of somewhat smaller size and importance. The relations of the men and women of the profession are in nowise inharmonious, and the leading spirits among the men are most active in the effort to advance the salaries of women. When boards of library directors shall be more generally composed of both men and women, the opportunities of women librarians to show what they can do in positions of the first rank will perhaps be more frequent.

The idea of a school for the training of library assistants was in the air for some time before it was finally embodied in the School of Library Economy at Columbia College, New York. This school opened its doors in January, 1887, to a class of nineteen or twenty, chiefly young women, and continued its sessions until June, 1889, when it was transferred to the New York State Library, at Albany, the chief librarian of Columbia College, Mr. Melvil Dewey, who was head of the school, having been appointed to the State librarianship and required to take up his residence at the capital city.

From this parent school three other schools, under the charge of three of the earlier graduates have arisen—that of Pratt Institute, in Brooklyn, New York, in 1890; that of Drexel Institute, in Philadelphia, in 1892; and that at Armour Institute, in Chicago, in 1894, this last being now transferred to Illinois State University.

The schools have developed differences of practice as they have advanced, though the theoretical part of the training is the same. The parent school, connected as it is with the large reference-library of the State and with the Board of Regents of the State University, has at its service the machinery of these institutions, a large collection of illustrative material, and a large staff of instructors whose time is wholly given to the work of the school. It conducts a summer school for six weeks, in the early summer, for librarians or library-assistants, who can take that length of time to improve themselves in the knowledge of their work and then return to their libraries. It offers to conduct correspondence courses also. It gives the preference among applicants to college graduates, and accepts the college diploma in lieu of an examination. It has a one-year course, at the end of which students who have done especially creditable work are admitted to special courses in the second year, if they desire.

The Pratt Institute School is connected with an almost unique professional school, and at the same time does the work of a free circulating and free reference library for the city of Brooklyn, thus offering its students the opportunity of practice in all departments of the work before going out to take positions. It does not accept the college diploma in place of an examination; regarding general information, culture, and personal qualifications as the gifts most necessary for the librarian and believing that the college diploma does not guarantee these. Its entrance examinations and personal interviews are designed to test the applicant in these particulars, and the college diploma is regarded only as an added qualification. The student of its first-year course goes out equipped with an all-round knowledge of and practice in library technique, and it offers at present a choice of two special courses in the second year, one for the training of children's librarians, and one, as yet not given in the other schools, called the historical course, including the cataloguing of early printed books, and the study of manuscripts, etc.

The Library School at Drexel Institute is also connected with a professional school, and is at the same time free to the citizens of Philadelphia. It has a one-year course, similar to that of the first year at Pratt Institute.

The school at the University at Illinois has been made one of the regular schools of the university, which students, after a two years' course, may elect to study in, though encouraged to take the full four years' course of the university.

As the comprehensive character of public library work in the United States brings to light the needs of various classes of the public and the lack of means to meet these needs, the library schools, fully abreast of the situation, present new fields of training for the student who would be a specialist; for instance, the opening of separate departments for children in a few libraries, and the announcement of the problems peculiar to these departments, set the schools at work at once selecting those students most likely to succeed in the work with children and preparing courses of study and training for them.

The success of the schools in meeting a need of the profession is undoubted. Even where local prejudice is so strong that a library dares not employ a trained outsider on its staff, the fact that other libraries have trained assistants has been the means of introducing competitive examinations for filling library positions, and procuring a higher level of intelligence in the local staff. And frequently, when the establishment of a town library is in prospect, the local candidates for positions who are far-seeing go to a library school for instruction, and are able thus to present themselves as applicants for the library positions with the weight of both training and local candidacy to aid them. Had no library schools been founded, the increasing needs of students and the growing tendency of women's clubs toward study would have necessitated a higher grade of library assistant than the average one of the past, appointed to and perhaps kept in his position by political influence, and the schools would have been forced into being. With the introduction of school training, salaries have advanced, vacations have lengthened, hours have shortened, and all the consideration due to brain workers is gradually being conceded.

A feature of the training of the schools is its resemblance to seed sowing. There is a vitality in it that keeps alive and growing in the graduate at work the enthusiasm and interest of the student. The practical problems that meet her at the outset prove that everything has not been learned in the school, that there are emergencies the school did not and could not provide for, and she realises that she is still in school and still learning; and the sheer interest of the daily work carries her on even after the impetus of the school training may have lost its force.

In the early days there was some doubt as to the consequences for the actual library assistant of an influx of trained workers into the ranks each year. But so far the number from the four schools is limited to about a hundred graduates per year—a number soon absorbed among the many libraries of the country, without any disastrous effect upon the assistants already in service. For those who cannot leave their positions to take the year of training there are local library clubs, the library periodicals, staff meetings, and other agencies of self education, and the wise assistant or librarian avails herself of them, recognising the signs of the times and trying to adapt herself to the new occasions which require new duties.

No demand upon the schools is more constant than that from the town or village library, organised and carried on by hit-or-miss methods, for trained help to come and reorganise the library, set it going in the proper way, and incidentally train those in charge of it to continue the work. So much of this training and organising has been done that it has seemed at times as if students might specialise in normal methods and devote themselves to this branch of work.

If anything, it is the small or medium-sized library that realises most keenly its deficiencies, and is most likely to want assistants from the schools; but so practical have been the teachings of the schools and so adaptable the graduates, that even the prejudice of the older and more conservative libraries has given away. The college and reference-libraries have been among the last to admit the new influence. One graduate introduced into a doubting library and successful in her work means more conviction of the value of the schools than anything that their advocates can say.

This is more than a technical question.

The special adaptation of well-educated, refined young men and women to a particular educational work, such as we now recognise the work of libraries to be, means raising the level of a whole calling, making it really what it has only pretended to be—a profession. It means putting at the service of the scholar, of the student, of the lettered and unlettered, of the young people and children, an army of cultured persons whose delight it is to serve and to make themselves ever more fit for serving.

WOMEN AND THEIR FUTURE IN LIBRARY WORK

By Miss M.S.R. James, Librarian of the Library Bureau, Boston (United States)

It has frequently been urged against the inhabitants of Great Britain that they are not quick at the uptake, and it is stated that in the matter of education Great Britain is still lamentably behind other countries, and particularly so in the matter of technical training of all kinds, though recent years have developed a marked tendency in all directions to lessen the reproach. Technical or secondary education has come to be regarded as an essential continuation of the training in elementary schools and is a potent factor in causing the realisation of the imperative necessity for providing students with books which, owing to obvious reasons, they are unable to purchase for themselves. Hence the increasing establishment of libraries in manufacturing districts, towns, and communities, all over the world. That the best of tuition if required both for elementary and secondary education, and that the standard expected is high, is not to be wondered at, but that such service should be in a majority of instances inadequately remunerated, partly from lack of funds, partly from the inability of governing bodies to appreciate the far-reaching effects of such service, is greatly to be deplored. The public library and librarian of any community or educational institute, should be regarded as part, and a very important part, of the machinery of technical, secondary, and higher education. Carlyle says, "Libraries are the universities of the people," and this being so, the library committee, librarian, and staff cannot be too carefully selected. If the best professors and instructors are not too good for a university, the best educated, most widely-read, and highly-cultured persons cannot be too good for library work, which in its requirements is kaleidoscopic, and in its demands on the literary resources and the brains of its librarian, variable and sudden. It is, unfortunately, impossible for most library boards, of public libraries under the Acts, to command the services of highly-educated librarians or assistants, owing to the small incomes produced by the rate, and until recently it has not been generally considered necessary for a librarian or an assistant to have any particular qualification for the work. The librarians of these libraries have themselves to a great extent been instrumental in raising their status to its present position, which is not yet sufficiently high, it being obvious that if specialised knowledge is required of teachers before they can embark in the perilous venture of tuition, it is equally necessary to require at least some show of educational fitness from librarians, who are rightly expected to be well up in all works in modern science, industries, economics, and all branches of literature; to be able to recommend the best and latest editions of any subject; to suggest lists of books for purchase, and after approval to buy them, with some regard for business economy, and to classify and catalogue them so that they shall be promptly available; who, in addition to these requirements, must possess unfailing patience, tact, courtesy, executive ability, secretarial instincts, knowledge of accounting, an appreciation of humour, the keen perceptions of a good indexer, and unobtrusive ability to penetrate the minds of inquirers for the elucidation of their somewhat involved demands, together with the up-to-date, on-the-spot alertness of the man of business. It is, of course, possible to be a born librarian—there have been many instances, but even so, a practical working knowledge of library administration is simply an addition, and no detraction to its possessor. It is, however, not exceptions, but the general average for whom rules have to be made. The above-stated requirements simply tend to show that, from their possession of them, educated women are peculiarly fitted for such work, and it is a source of great wonderment to every one who has considered the subject that so few women have been employed in British libraries in really responsible positions. For some reason or another their employment seems only to have been contemplated as possible in connection with public libraries under the Acts (except the brilliant exceptions of Miss Toulmin Smith, librarian of Manchester College, Oxford, and Miss Guiness, of Holloway College), where, from the nature of things, as already explained, their services are limited and scope confined. Not that it is impossible for women employed in public libraries under the Acts to better their condition, but in the majority of cases very little can be expected from the class of women employed, executive ability last of all; and salaries, though almost at the sweating limit, owing to financial economics, are in a good many instances quite as much as the work is worth. Mr. McFarlane, in his "Library Administration," says of women assistants that "there seem to be no objections to them other than those commonly alleged against women's work," and writes that they are "specially useful in a juvenile department"; at the same time speaking of the cheapness of their labour, he adds, "that there is as yet no serious question of employing women in the more scholarly libraries," though he goes on to tell of a lady who assisted in the arrangement and cataloguing of the Tapling collection of postage stamps in the British Museum.

Women are, I believe, employed in catalogue and index work at the Royal Society; one of them to my knowledge was a graduate of Newnham College. At Dr. Williams's library in Gordon Square, W.C., women are employed; a Miss Abbott was for a long time librarian at Hampstead subscription library. A Miss Stamp was head of the Notting Hill library before it came under the Acts, and she is registered as one of the few women members of the L.A.U.K. who attended meetings of that association in its early days. For some time women have been employed in libraries in London and elsewhere, though in what capacity it is difficult to discover, and there must doubtless have been others in country towns and districts. Indeed, at the present day a woman of the old school is employed as librarian of a country library presented to the little town of Woodbridge, Suffolk, by one Thomas Seckford, of old time charitable inclination; and a woman is employed at the subscription library in the "Ancient House," Buttermarket, Ipswich, Suffolk; in addition to one employed by Mr. W. Palmer in his library at Reading, to which post she was appointed in 1879, I believe. An American woman, Miss Hattie Johnson, was employed for a year or more as cataloguer in the National Library of Dublin, Ireland; she has given her experiences before the New Hampshire Library Club. (See *Library Journal,* February, 1899, page 69.) Women generally manage their college libraries, though it does not appear to be done with any great degree of system, or technical or practical knowledge. Women are also to be found in subscription and society libraries. I can, however, find only nineteen English libraries employing women as chief librarians, and their salaries appear to average £45 to £80 per annum. What is expected for this, or what other compensation there may be, if any, I am unable to state. With a view to saving the time of any one sufficiently interested to go into the matter, I have at the end of this paper appended a list of references to various English and American periodicals and papers. Manchester Public Library began to employ women as assistants in 1871, and found them "specially good in dealing with boys." The applicants, who were numerous, were recruited from among the daughters of tradesmen and shopkeepers, and received at first from 10s. per week to £80 a year, according to experience and ability. Manchester employs women as heads of branch libraries as well. Battersea, Chelsea, Clerkenwell, Derby, Oldham, St. Helens, Salford, Blackpool, Paisley, Liverpool, Bristol, and many other libraries have followed suit, and now require an elementary entrance examination before appointment, which is a step in the right direction. Aberdeen employs women who have a university certificate, but the value of this statement is considerably lessened when we learn that their remuneration was only 10s. per week at commencing, a sum, even taking into consideration the cheapness of provincial life, utterly insufficient for a well-educated, refined, self-respecting woman, no matter how economical. The status of the librarian is all the time being raised, more is expected, and rightly, for it is a position of great responsibility and one of unlimited possibilities and far-reaching influence on future generations, an exaggerated statement, you think, perhaps—but run it down and it will be seen to be emphatically true. Unfortunately, up to the present in Great Britain it does not appear to have been realised that the labourer is worthy of his hire if he or she proves this by the quality of their work. In foreign countries we find the employment of women not much more extensive. In Italy Signorina Sacconi (now Signora Sacconi-Ricci) of the Marucellian Library, Florence, distinguished herself by her work, inventions, and report on libraries, and though no longer actively employed she still takes a great interest in all matters pertaining to library work. In Norway we find Fröken Valborg Platou, who has been employed as chief librarian at Bergen for over fifteen years. She receives about £124 a year, and employs a woman assistant, whose hours are five and a half per day, who receives £22 per year; there is also a woman caretaker, whose hours are six per day and remuneration £28 per year — a significant statement! In Sweden, women have been employed as assistants for some years. In Austria, at Vienna, they are employed as assistants, and in the Ottendorfer Library at Zwittau, Germany, the librarian is a woman. In Switzerland, at the Fribourg Cantonal Museum, a woman is director. In France there appears to be no record of the employment of women, but every one knows of the finished work of Mlle. Pellichet, of 30, Rue Blanche, Paris, as a cataloguer of the incunabula in the National Library of France. She is now travelling all over France obtaining data for a catalogue of further collections. In Honolulu, Sandwich Islands, a Miss Mary Burbank presides over the library. In Canada women are extensively employed, though I have not found many as chiefs. In Australia, where, I am told, there are openings, a few women are employed as assistants, and there are a few in South Africa: one from Cape Town attended the International Conference of 1897.

In the United States we find, as in other occupations, the elysium of women: it is almost the exception not to find women in libraries, where they have proved themselves indispensable as organisers, administrators, cataloguers, and indexers, and also in the management of the children's department — an increasingly important position. Their work as educators is respected and recognised, and their position is assured both as regards the public and the library board, excepting in cases, happily on the decrease, where politics are allowed to debase the value of public library administration and development.

Newspapers are coming to find that indexes are of great value to them; periodicals and magazines, etc., all ought to have indexes, and I feel sure that English publishers will begin to see with the eyes of their American competitors, that it pays to have some one who *knows* in this department of their work, and that educated, scientific, thorough work is essential to their businesses. Moreover, where there are village libraries to be organised, selected, classified, and catalogued, who so well fitted for this work as a woman? Then there are prison libraries, lighthouse libraries, school libraries, workhouse libraries, and ships' libraries. The average Atlantic liner's library catalogue would disgrace a child, despite its fine cover. In America women go out organising new, and reorganising old libraries with great success; they go to the library desiring to be put in thorough up-to-date order, spend a month or more as is required straightening things out, and then turn the reins of perfected government over to the local appointed librarian. There is no reason against, and every reason for, the same kind of work being done by Englishwomen, and many little libraries are sorely in need of revision on modern lines.

There are travelling libraries. I think Mr. Stead employs women in his venture, and in addition private libraries and museum libraries, so we see that if the present prospects are not exactly glowing, there are possibilities, and though we have seen that public libraries under the Acts do not afford such scope or opportunity as yet, there are others.

There is also bibliographical work, and I have an inkling that there is a good deal to be done in palaeography, and if all this fails, there is, as a *pièce de résistance* the catalogueless library of St. Petersburg, Russia, which is sorely in need of the services of a new cataloguer.

DISCUSSION

Miss Toulmin Smith, Librarian, Manchester College, Oxford, said: In considering what are the prospects for women in the profession of librarian we will cast a glance backwards for a moment, to get a true perspective of our subject.

Libraries we have had for centuries, hoards of treasured learning in manuscript and print, in cathedrals, inns of court, colleges and universities, and not least in some of the historic private mansions of old and wealthy families. Later on, academies, learned societies, and government offices, including the Houses of Parliament, made their collections, each having its own *raison d'etre.* The irony of time and fate has brought about that the term of "minor libraries" is applied by some to these important adjuncts to scholarship, the pioneers of modern reading. They do not, as a rule, appeal to the "man in the street," but it is obvious that they led the way for the wider spread of book education and the consequent desire for libraries that should satisfy general wants. Then came the period of institutes, clubs, Athenaeums, and circulating libraries maintained by shareholders and subscribers, many of which still have a vigorous existence. But with all these there was no *profession,* and no woman librarian (acknowledged) among them. That splendid institution, the library of the British Museum we must pass by; no woman can yet pass its portals, though a whisper of such a possibility was once heard. The public free library is, as all know, a creation of our own day; I well remember the great interest taken by my father in the opening of the Birmingham Free Library, one of the earliest of these, forty years ago. The great strides made, especially in primary education, and in the mental training of women, the changed aspects of civilisation, increased powers of locomotion and restlessness of social life, have made the public library in countries like England and America a necessity; a place where current knowledge of men and things may quickly be attained, where literature and history in their noblest and best forms may be easily reached by the mass of the people.

In the United Kingdom the number of public libraries under the Acts since 1845, together with about 40 other free and public libraries, is 397, according to the Library Association Yearbook for 1899. The full extent of the public libraries is not yet reached, their numbers will increase with local wants and powers. The 1899 Yearbook gives the number of other miscellaneous libraries at about 813, while Mr. Greenwood's Yearbook of 1897 puts the number of libraries not under the Acts at about 1,100. It is difficult to reach the exact figure, but we may take it that there are in all quite 1,450 libraries in these islands, excluding private collections. Our colonial brethren too are not behind, the number of their libraries, in Africa, Canada and West Indies, Australasia, and Asia, including India, in 1897 showed a total of 426, most of them being public.

As regards the professional position of women as librarians, we may remember that as a "profession" for men, librarianship is but of recent date. The older libraries, save in exceptional cases, such as the British Museum, the Bodleian at Oxford, or the Advocates' Library at Edinburgh, did not call for a staff of assistants; with a moderate staff of books and a limited number of readers the post of librarian could be filled by a man of literary or antiquarian tastes with careful habits, who would learn his business as he went along, helped by a certain tradition. The formation of the Librarians' Association in 1878 showed the growing sense of responsibility among those in charge of the new public libraries, and it was but in 1882, not nineteen years ago, that Mr. Tedder, of the Athenaeum Club, read a paper at the Cambridge meeting on "Librarianship as a Profession," sketching in the leading qualifications and duties necessary for those who would seriously take up this walk in life. It was considerably later that the preliminary training courses were established, and that the Association obtained its charter, which gave this occupation a recognised and honourable status. The growth of the free libraries movement has given birth to the profession, the training and culture for which must affect, in their turn, the keepers of all kinds of libraries who would march with the times. If men therefore have so recently entered into their inheritance, women may bide their time in patience, confident of success before long.

Libraries may be divided into two classes, the first comprising the public free library, where any one of the neighbourhood may not only read but may borrow books for home reading; the second various, including college and special libraries of all kinds not open to the general public, but each meant for a certain circle of readers; many gathered to illustrate special lines of study, some of them ancient rather than modern. For women the first class has at present offered the most opportunities in this country; the work is regular and well-ordered, some of it is mechanical or departmental, much demands the resource and intelligent interest of the worker. In the second class but few women have yet found admittance, though some of these have been good appointments, and for competent women there seems no reason why a considerable opening should not gradually arise in various institutions.

The capacity of women for library work, and their particular aptness for it, have not now to be proved. Mr. Tedder, who from the beginning has warmly encouraged their employment, spoke of their success as a "recognised fact" years ago, pointing, of course, to the American as well as to the English experience; and Bodley's present librarian told me the other day that "women's work is absolutely as good as that of men." But while the latter gentleman dissuades women from becoming librarians because, as he says, there is no opening and they are so poorly paid, Mr. Tedder thinks otherwise. "I have always been of the opinion," he writes me, "that there is a fair prospect for women in library work, but they must make themselves competent. They should procure experience and professional training, especially in the difficult art of cataloguing. Good catalogues are scarce. . . . There is fair prospect for them, provided they are not afraid of work and possess a good preliminary education." I find a point greatly in their favour is the influence which they possess for quiet and order. Alderman H. Rawson, of Manchester, speaking at the International Library Conference of 1897, said, "Their services in the reading-rooms set apart for boys are especially valuable, exercising a restraining influence over the lads, and conducing to quietness, order, and decorum." And the effect of replacing men by women in St. Phillip's Library at Bristol, formerly subject to nightly disturbances, has been quite remarkable (W.S. Selby in the *Librarian's Assistant* for June, 1899).

It is perhaps hardly fair, with differing circumstances, to compare the position of the English to the American women in libraries, but more has been done in England than is commonly supposed. In Bristol since about 1875 or 1876, in Manchester since about 1879, "young women have been selected for the public library service"; at both places they are required to pass an elementary examination; the ages on appointment vary, in Bristol from 15 to 18, in Manchester from 16 to 23. At present the salaries at Bristol range from £26 to £60 a year; the branch librarians at Manchester receive £60 to £90 a year, the assistants 10s. to 21s. a week. At Bristol 35 women are employed, in the four grades of junior and senior assistants, branch sub-librarian, and branch librarian; and their duties embrace the entire work of a public library, including binding. At Manchester there are 85 women, of whom five are heads of branch libraries, each with a senior assistant, but otherwise not classified. I asked my kind informants, Mr. E. Norris Mathews and Mr. Chas. W. Sutton, the chief librarians of Bristol and Manchester, whether any women trained by them had been sent to other libraries; both replied in the negative, thus indicating that the demand for qualified women has not yet been large (a recent advertisement for a lady assistant with experience in public library work shows, however, that it is beginning). Women join the Library Assistants' Association, as well as participate in the examinations instituted by the Librarians' Association.

In an excellent paper printed in the *Library* (journal) for 1894, Miss Richardson, of St. Helens Public Library, rightly says, "As women prove their capability for this kind of work better appointments than those they now fill will be thrown open to them." [See page 18.] She gives a list of places in the United Kingdom where women were then employed; at 14 libraries in England and four in Scotland women were assistants; at 18 libraries in different towns, besides two or three branch libraries in Manchester, women were the librarians, in several cases with a female assistant. These did not include the two ladies at the People's Palace (London), Miss Black, succeeded by Miss James, the latter of whom had three assistants, all college women (from Newnham and Lady Margaret's). The most recent statistics on the subject, gathered and printed in the *Library Assistant* (June, 1899) by the editor, Mr. B.L. Dyer (to whose courtesy I am indebted for the advance sheet) are fairly encouraging. He gives the following figures (with details which I omit):—

Of rate-supported libraries, 28 have women librarians; 16 branch librarians in four places are women; 48 employ women assistants, to the number of 255 altogether.

Mr. Dyer omits eight libraries in Miss Richardson's lists, but altogether 81 public libraries (branches included) now employ women, against 37 in 1894.

Of nonrate-supported libraries little published information is available; Mr. Dyer notes 11 with women librarians and 13 with assistants; 24 in all. Besides these I may mention Dr. Williams' Library, London, where are two women assistants; a highly capable woman is librarian to the Education Department; the Newcastle College has a woman librarian, and another has been librarian at the Yorkshire College, Leeds, for fourteen years, discharging the ample duties for seven hundred students and their professors with the help of a woman assistant. Recently, too, librarians are being or have been appointed to some of the women's colleges, as Holloway, Somerville, and Newnham, and doubtless other women's colleges will follow the example.

Competence on the part of women, and the power of library authorities to offer fair salaries seem to be what are needed to develop further openings.

Mr. B.L. Dyer (Editor of *The Library Assistant*, and hon. sec. of the Library Assistants' Association) regretted to find the women working as librarians and assistants in British rate-supported libraries unrepresented at the meeting. Library assistants had been described as deplorably ignorant and ill-educated, and as being mainly drawn from the uneducated classes. Cultured college women had been invited to an easy victory over them, and to thrust them from their uneducated leisure by a six months' voluntary service. He would assure them that assistants came mainly from the same class as the elementary teachers and the civil servants of the second division, and that the education of the men and women was not below that level. Reference had been made to the success of two ladies, who had never worked in a library, at a bibliography examination conducted last year by the Library Association, but he would ask women not to expect too easy a victory over these so-called board-school boys, because only just recently two assistants had scored 100 percent, and two others 90 percent in a similar examination. He deplored an attack on a class of public servants who were doing a useful work, and he had to ask why this triumph over early difficulties by means of the educational means of the day was not mentioned. When the educational ladder was complete, he helped to see girls from the board schools attain as high places as boys had done at Oxford and Cambridge, and he would ask if it were a matter of shame to that Kensington board-school lad who just recently obtained a senior wranglership that the rudiments of his education were obtained in a board school? In a profession, as in a university, it mattered not where the raw material came from, but what it was developed into. A very optimistic view had been taken of librarianship as a profession; hundreds of persons sought to enter public libraries under the impression that posts in them were highly-paid sinecures for literary leisure. Those who thought that pursued an *ignis fatuus*. The work was hard, the hours long, and the pay miserably poor. High attainments were expected of a librarian, as well as administrative capacity; but the average salary paid to him was not £90 a year for some sixty hours per week. The average salary paid to an assistant for rather less hours was not £40. He knew librarians, and women librarians, who were practically on duty for seventy-eight hours a week for £50 a year; and he knew assistants who worked seven days a week, and had but a single evening off duty per week from year's end to year's end. The busiest hours of a library were the evening hours, and he would ask women to think twice before they lightly undertook the labour of standing four hours at a time continuously issuing and receiving books like a clerk at a railway ticket office. Even in London and other large towns evenings off were rare luxuries, and he could mention one town where a youth of twenty-six, in receipt of 15s. a week, had not had a night's holiday, except Sunday, for three years. Where was room for the influence of cultured college ladies here? Those who sought positions in the apparently genteel, but hard-worked and ill-paid profession should think twice if these desired a living wage or a leisured ease, owing to the very limited incomes of the great majority of libraries, and the long hours they were open. The commencing salary offered in London to library assistants was only seven or eight shillings a week, for forty-eight hours' work, and he could assure any woman voluntarily undertaking the duties of an assistant for six months without pay, as had been suggested, that after a much more prolonged period of drudgery in the routine of a library they would know very little of the literary side of the work. Optimistic theories of halcyon days of literary leisure were very pretty, but a few questions asked at the nearest library would reveal facts in strong opposition to these fancies, and would discourage all but those who had a real love for the work, and were willing to give laborious days for very little emolument.

Miss Margaret Windeyer (New South Wales) said: In speaking of librarianship as a profession for women, and in considering the different courses of technical training which afford an opportunity of acquiring a knowledge of the minutiae of library economy, it must not be forgotten that a librarian who shall be successful in the highest sense must have a personal fitness and inherent qualifications for library work. The value of an accurate knowledge within the sphere of library economy will be greatly enhanced if a librarian is equipped with tact, patience, discrimination, and executive ability; and to these attributes there must be added, not necessarily the scholarship that an earlier generation demanded of its librarians, but an even and persistent attention in the direction of newly published books, an alertness in acquiring knowledge of recent discoveries in science and the arts, and an insight into human character which will express itself in sympathy and goodwill. In a public library it depends largely upon the librarian whether the books read are those that will give a stimulus to a man's best energies, rest to a tired woman, a vision of fairyland to a lonely child.

A sympathy developed by contact with the world will help librarians in their daily work, as demonstrators in the laboratories of intellect, as libraries have been termed; an enthusiasm for their work will add interest to the details of shelf-listing, cataloguing, and of the lending department work; and executive ability will in many ways increase the usefulness of the library in their neighbourhood. Among the fundamental principles of successful management of free public libraries is the complete recognition of the relation of the library to the public as a centre for their educational development; and as a basis of literary organisation there should be the idea that a librarian is a public servant whose service is of the highest order. Women who recognise that librarianship is a profession adapted to the capacity and attainments of highly educated women will do all in their power to raise library professional standards among women to the heights of dignity and usefulness which have been reached by some women librarians.

Among the interesting developments in library school work in the United States has been specialisation in different departments by students, in order to fit themselves for those positions which require certain distinct qualifications. The student with a knowlege of philanthropic questions can become fitted to be the librarian in a college settlement lending library; the woman of wide attainments prepares for a position as reference librarian in a college library; and as librarians in the children's room, which is such an important part of a large public library, there is unlimited scope for the usefulness of those who are fitted by temperament and inclination for their work, which will be of even greater value after special study; and the woman of enthusiasm will enjoy her work in any organisation which sends travelling libraries, boxes of carefully selected books, to sparsely settled districts, to a far greater degree if she has studied the history of library extension and development, and understands the scope and usefulness of such work.

When one considers the value and importance of public libraries in the community, and in view of the absorbing interest that library work has for those engaged in it, we must hope that many more people will become interested in librarianship as a profession for women.

PART

1901-1921
THE MOVE TOWARDS
SUFFRAGE

Lady Assistants in Public Libraries

by Frank Chennell

The librarian of a large suburban library is reported to have recently stated that any vacancy occurring among the senior assistants in the institution he controls, will, in future be filled by promotion from the junior staff, the places of the latter to be filled by the appointment of *girl assistants.*

I trust that it will be generally and readily admitted that this heavy incursion of the lady assistant into the ranks of our profession should be considered with some gravity.

It is not my intention to approach the matter from any selfish standpoint of competition.

Whether the increase in the number of lady workers in our libraries be fair or the reverse to coming librarians should not greatly concern us. The ubiquitous female now competes in every profession, and, in many, it cannot be gainsaid, most worthily.

Two simple and obvious remedies should suggest themselves to the would-be librarian. Either to outstrip his lady competitor in efficiency, or — to marry her.

It would be presumption, and outside the scope of this article, to even suggest which of these two alternatives is to be preferred.

Nor do I propose to discuss the matter from the standpoint of the library. The Committee, or the librarian, is responsible for these innovations in the appointment of staffs, and they alone are best able to decide whether the institution they conduct has, or has not, benefited either pecuniarily, or in the ability with which it is governed.

What, I think, is of greater importance, and should concern us all, is the probable effect this increasing substitution of girl labour for that of lads, may have upon our profession generally.

There is no need to submit an elaborate table of statistics to show the rising tendency of committees, and perhaps of librarians to add to the number of lady-workers in public libraries. I have roughly glanced through some eighty reports, received during the year, and embracing public libraries throughout the country. Twenty-eight of these show upon their staff page the names of female assistants. Fifteen from the provinces, and thirteen from London.

Reprinted with permission from *Library World* 4 (March 1902):245-248.

Without soliciting information from each of our libraries it would be difficult to obtain complete and reliable figures upon this question. Many librarians being quite content to let their own name suffice for staff information.
The only point, however, that I am desirous of emphasising in connection
with these figures is this. A reference to the reports of these self-same libraries
of six and seven years ago discloses no mention, in exactly one half the number, of lady assistants.

The view I am forced to take of this question is that if many libraries
follow the example of the one I have cited the number of training schools for
future male librarians must perforce slowly decrease. The number of coming
men will be considerably thinned, and competition for senior positions will be
less keen because fewer qualified candidates will be available. A fall in competition invariably entails a corresponding diminution of efficiency. We need
a far higher standard in this respect than at present obtains, and to this end
our various associations are striving.

Assistants in libraries throughout the country, have, with commendable
enterprise formed themselves into an union, not, let it be said, for protection,
but that by mutual aid they may so qualify themselves to make even better librarians than their predecessors.

Librarians of public libraries in London have, for some years past, combined for the sole purpose of holding amicable gatherings at which new ideas
may be ventilated and reforms discussed.

The parent association, when not torn and racked by petty dissension
over this or that proposed innovation, strives to the one common end—the
raising of the status of the librarian.

These endeavours can only become thoroughly effective by strenuous
efforts on the part of librarians to secure, and to train as assistants only those
who intend to pursue the calling. This continuity is rarely, if ever, obtained
where female labour is employed. In library work the girl rarely rises beyond
the assistant stage, at which point she too frequently bars the progression of
the other hands.

In this article it would be as unwise and ungallant to introduce any
reference to the relative general mental development of the lady and lad assistant as it would be to express any opinion, one way or the other, concerning
Schopenhauer's dictum that "When Nature made two divisions of the human
race she did not draw the line exactly through the middle." I trust it will also
be unnecessary for me to interpolate reasons why, though the number of
women-workers as helps in the library may increase, there is but slight probability that many will obtain chief control of an institution.

I cannot, however, refrain from giving an apropos quotation from a
recent article on "The Postion of Women in Politics." "Women," the writer
says, "are deficient in public spirit. Their judgment is more apt to be vitiated
by narrow or personal considerations than is the judgment of men, and their
opinions on questions of public morality are more faddy than robust."

The following extract from "The Academy" of December last is a
peculiarly satisfactory confirmation of the veracity of the last statement:—

"The literary world was amused by the reports of the lengths to which a
committee of lady censors had gone in the exclusion of modern novels from
the Boston Public Library on faddist grounds. Such stories as Mr. Henry
James' 'The Two Magics'; Miss Mary E. Wilkins' 'The People of Our
Neighbourhood'; and Sir Walter Besant's 'The Changeling,' were rejected for

frivolous or irrelevant reasons. Mrs. Humphry Ward's 'Eleanor' had been ruled out because 'girls of today would cast about for Manistys, as girls of a bygone day did for Rochesters.'

That women do *not* succeed to chief control is emphasised by a lady writer (Miss Petherbridge) in the current issue of "The Englishwomen's Year Book."

In referring to the retirement of Miss James, late Librarian to the Peoples' Palace Library, she states "Since she gave up the position no woman has come prominently forward in the library world."

She further says "There are two main reasons for this (a) the very poor remuneration, and the *very limited outlook* that awaits the librarian at the end of her training"; (b) "The difficulty of getting trained."

The last obstacle (b) I have endeavoured to show is less difficult now, apparently, than the writer imagined.

The (a) hindrance, *i.e.* that of insufficient remuneration, Miss Petherbridge in her next paragraph solves in a peculiar way by offering the aspiring lady assistant the following advice. "The first step towards becoming an efficient librarian is to enter some good library as *voluntary worker.*" (I am of course responsible for the italics).

One thing is, at present, obvious, though committees of impecunious libraries welcome the girl whose labour can be obtained at two-thirds the cost of that of a lad, these same committees apparently refrain from promoting the lady to any but subordinate positions.

Is it then a *reductio ad absurdam* to infer that if our lady friends absorb a great number of these junior positions there will ensue a decided dearth of assistants, for the higher posts, who have any pretensions to knowledge of library management and routine?

The best assistant, and indeed the most capable librarian, is he who through successive stages has climbed the ladder of his profession from the first step of the raw recruit to the topmost rung.

At the present moment, in institutions throughout the country there are young men qualifying upon meagre salaries, step by step, with tardy promotion, to obtain these better positions. The majority of these students have but one aim — to become fully efficient, but one goal — the librarian's chair. They have adopted the calling as a life one, and have chosen it from a deep-rooted love of books, and an earnest interest in literature. They are students, and must read hard, and perforce late, to pass the examinations wisely instituted by the Library Association. Into each of these masculine footprints it is, then, proposed to place the dainty extremity of a transitory girl assistant, leaving, perchance, the position of sub-librarian and senior assistant open to the stronger persuasion.

Can we justly anticipate that many of these lady helps will continue long in the work? It is indubitably proved that they do not.

A few years, and a newer and better profession opens out to the girl, one in which she knows she is secure. In which she can be neither assailed nor excelled, and in which no male competition can enter. The erstwhile lady assistant in the library, then becomes, perhaps, in a truer sense a librarian's assistant.

But the continuity of the work is broken, and a new girl recruit has to be enlisted and trained, only, in turn, to become efficient in what perhaps later proves of no earthly use to her, and woefully *de*ficient in what is probably essentially necessary.

And now what have these libraries with their ranks of girl assistants gained? The library has possibly been spared a few pounds in salaries. Their work perchance has been equal to that which would have been extracted from male assistants. The girls' advocate will say, and we may perhaps admit, that the *library* has not suffered.

Need we take account of any opinion on the part of the librarian? Basking amorously in their sunny smiles, *he* has thought the arrangement not such a *bad* one! But what of the profession generally?

Though we may exonerate this incursion of the girl assistant from doing any serious hurt to either library or librarian, I maintain, for the reasons I have endeavoured to put lucidly, and for the one thousand and one reasons it would be unwise to submit to print, that the *calling* of the public librarian can but suffer grievous harm by the innovation.

Women in Public Libraries

by Kate E. Pierce

An article in the March number of the *Library World*, on "Lady Assistants in Public Libraries," by Mr. Chennell, of Willesden Green, [See page 41.] dismisses the claims of women to positions as municipal workers in such a tone of absolute confidence, that I am tempted to challenge some of his conclusions. It is with some hesitation that I come forward to raise objections to some of his statements, being but a "lady help" who has incurred the reprobation of the late learned Arthur Schopenhauer and the displeasure of the gallant Mr. F.E. Chennell, who seems to be somewhat afflicted by the jealous thought that he, too, is not "basking amorously" in the "sunny smiles" of "girl recruits," who are anxious to occupy the "footprints" of vastly superior male assistants!

The main point of Mr. Chennell's indictment, stripped of its garnishing of mere conjecture and verbal prolixity, is that women are threatening to oust men and boys from positions in public libraries to which, he assumes, they have earned a proscriptive or traditional right. He does not tell us how men acquired such a valuable freehold as this exclusive right to manage public libraries, nor does he state what his views would have been had libraries from the very first been staffed by women, like the public schools. He simply contents himself with the somewhat gratuitous assumption that women are unfitted for library work, because Schopenhauer, a bilious old German, thought so, and because Mr. Frank Chennell, with a thousand and one reasons up his sleeve, possibly as imaginary as the Arabian Nights, maintains that the profession of librarian will suffer grievous harm by what he is pleased to call an "innovation." Mr. Chennell gives two remedies for getting rid of the "ubiquitous female." The first, to substitute uneducated youths for educated girls, and so assert the divine right of the male animal to boss the show. The mystery is how girls ever obtained a footing in *any* of the many occupations in which they now compete successfully, and on equal terms, with the vastly superior male! The second remedy is, I fear, less simple, as, even in this free country, oriental methods are frowned upon, and a librarian cannot keep on marrying all his girl assistants much as they would appreciate the honour, and this remedy must, therefore, wait till Mormonism or Islamism become recognised institutions!

Mr. Chennell has missed some of the most important points in connection with this matter, and I shall set forth a few which occurred to me when I read his article.

Reprinted with permission from *Library World* 4(May 1902):286-288.

1.—He is very strong all through his paper, on the alleged inferiority of women to men in mental and physical attributes, and thinks that the coming of the lady assistant will mean a great deterioration in the work, pay, and calling of librarians. No proof is given for this extraordinary statement, and Mr. Chennell is careful to conceal the fact that a very large proportion of the boy assistants now employed in public libraries are considered incompetent by their masters; as may be gathered from the constant cry for more classes, more education, and better-class youths altogether, I learn, further, from various sources, that some of the public libraries which have been managed by men from their foundation, are not, by any means, on lines which even Mr. Chennell would approve, and that the proportion of male duffers in the library profession is excessive, considering the total number of librarians.

2.—The great difficulty of obtaining boys, especially in large towns, and in those which cannot afford progressive advances, is entirely overlooked by Mr. Chennell. It is this, more than anything else, which has led to the recent increase in the number of women assistants which has alarmed Mr. Chennell, and it will continue to prove a stumbling-block in many places.

3.—I have been assured by librarians who employ women, that they are much more reliable, honest, and steady than boys; that they remain on one place much longer on the average; and that the number who fall victims to matrimony cause fewer changes than will be found in a staff composed exclusively of boys.

4.—I cannot find any trace of the introduction of women assistants having led to reductions in salaries. On the other hand, I know that the women assistants at Bristol, Battersea, Clerkenwell, Bradford, Manchester and elsewhere are paid better than the corresponding grades of male assistants in other places. This can easily be verified by reference to Greenwood's last "Library Year Book."

5.—Apparently Mr. Chennell has not taken to heart the revelations of the last census. With a considerable majority of women, is it to be supposed that they must not seek every possible means of obtaining a livelihood which can be legitimately found?

6.—Whatever their political or physical shortcomings may be, women have proved themselves enthusiastic, capable, and trustworthy librarians, both in England and America, and not a few of the best ideas in modern American library management have emanated from them. Perhaps Mr. Chennell will point out the living English male librarians who have done as much for library science generally as Mrs. Fairchild (Miss Cutler), Miss Hewins, Miss Plummer, Miss Sharp and the other American ladies, or Signora Sacconi-Ricci, lately a librarian in Florence? There is no need to speak of the Englishwomen who have distinguished themselves as bibliographers, cataloguers, and indexers, because Mr. Chennell says there are none!

7.—Mr. Chennell has not proved, or attempted to prove, that women *deserve* to be superseded in library work. He has only given utterance to certain fears, based more on prejudice or imagination than on actual experience. Perhaps he will favour us with instances in which the employment of women has proved prejudicial to the public interest. On this point I may add that I have not yet heard of any woman librarian being implicated in proceedings which, at the very least, suggest to the unprejudiced bystander, carelessness in the handling of public money.

These are a few points which others may add to or expound, and they establish, I think, the possibility of the existence of another side to the question Mr. Chennell has raised. In a matter affecting the public interest so closely as free libraries, the question of the sex, nationality, creed, or politics of those who are responsible for their good management, is one which need only be raised when there is a huge public outcry against one or the other, or when committees find that their staffs are inefficient, and dismiss them accordingly, irrespective of sex or any other circumstance. If Mr. Chennell once admits that a good girl is better than a bad boy, then the whole of his case against women, such as it is, falls to the ground.

Women in American Libraries

by Salome Cutler Fairchild

A striking illustration of the change of sentiment and practice with reference to the prominence of women in American libraries is afforded by a comparison of three conferences of the American Library Association. At the first meeting of the Association in Philadelphia, 1876, only 12 of the 103 members present were women; at the Chicago meeting in 1893, 166 of the 305 members present were women; at Magnolia in 1902, the largest conference yet held, 736 out of 1018 members present were women. The change as shown by attendance is thus from about eleven percent in 1876 to nearly 72 percent in 1902.

The *Library Journal*, commenting editorially (November, 1876) on the first meeting, says: "They (the women) were the best of listeners and occasionally would modestly take advantage of gallant voices like Mr. Smith's, to ask a question or offer a suggestion."

Miss Caroline M. Hewins, librarian of the Hartford (Ct.) Public Library, has the distinction of being the first woman to lift her voice in a meeting of the American Library Association. In 1877 at the second meeting, in New York, she asked whether in any other state besides Massachusetts the income from the dog tax was used to support the public library.

Miss Mary A. Bean, at that time librarian of the Brookline Public Library, was the first woman to appear on a library program. She read a paper on "The evil of unlimited freedom in the use of juvenile fiction" at the Boston meeting in 1879.

In 1893, of the 28 papers making up the so-called "World's Fair papers," six were written by women. In 1902, of the 21 formal papers printed in the Proceedings, three were by women. In the same year two of the seven section meetings were presided over by women; one was the Children's Section, the other was a large general evening session in which prominent men like Dr. Canfield and Dr. Dewey gave addresses. The names of 36 men and 16 women, excluding foreign delegates, appear on the present program. From the role of modest listener in 1876 to a representation of nearly one-third on the program of an international conference is a long step. The proportion of participation in the work of the conference is still small in relation to the proportion of attendance.

Reprinted with permission from *Library Journal* 29 (December 1904):157-162.

It would appear to me, therefore, evident that there is practically no discrimination with regard to sex in the American Library Association. For many years women have been constantly represented on the Council and Executive Board. Any woman who has anything to say may be sure of a fair chance and no undue favor in saying it. What she may write or say or do in the work of the Association is usually rated at its real worth. I may not be a fair judge, but it would seem to me that the work of women in the Association shows a pleasing lack of self-consciousness. There is very little posing or apparent effort to be conspicuous. The broad-minded attitude of the men who have been leaders in the library movement from 1876 to the present day accounts for the place of women in the American Library Association.

Quite another question, however, is her place in the library field itself. What proportion of women are holding responsible positions? Are those positions varied or confined within narrow lines? Are her services considered valuable as tested by a money standard? I have undertaken to gather some statistics which may throw light on the relative service of men and women in American libraries, both as regards the character of that service and its remuneration. The inquiry does not particularly interest or attract me, but I am glad to undertake it because of my confidence in the judgment of our president who thinks that such a statistical statement, with a slight analysis of the statistics, will be of value.

I have used as a basis for inquiry 100 libraries originally chosen as representative for a course of lectures on American libraries given by me in the New York State Library School. A tentative list was secured as follows: Mr. W.S. Biscoe, of the New York State Library, and the writer of this paper, read through with some care the list of libraries contained in "Public, society and school libraries," published by the Bureau of Education in 1901, checking those that seemed in any way worthy to be considered. The tentative list thus formed was submitted to about 43 librarians, as follows: all the members of the Council and Executive Board of the A. L. A. 1902-3, the directors of library schools, and persons specially familiar with the libraries of certain states. The list of representative libraries thus formed includes all large general libraries in the country and a selection of smaller libraries of different types in different parts of the country. Special collections like the Surgeon-General's Office at Washington have been excluded. The following is the list of 100 representative libraries thus selected:

REPRESENTATIVE LIBRARIES

PUBLIC

Free, circulating, endowed or tax-supported

Boston P. L.	Washington, P. L. of D. C.
Chicago P. L.	Newark F. P. L.
Philadelphia F. L.	Northampton, Forbes L.
Cincinnati P. L.	Peoria (Ill.) P. L.
Baltimore, Enoch Pratt F. L.	*Brooklyn, Pratt Instiute F. L.
New York P. L.	*Hartford P. L.
Cleveland P. L.	*Newton (Mass.) F. L.
Detroit P. L.	*Brookline (Mass.) P. L.

*Have a woman as librarian.

Buffalo P. L.
St. Louis P. L.
Brooklyn P. L.
Worcester F. P. L.
San Francisco F. P. L.
Milwaukee P. L.
Springfield (Mass.) City L. Ass'n.
*Minneapolis P. L.
Pittsburgh, Carnegie L.
*Indianapolis P. L.
Providence P. L.
Denver P. L.
Scranton P. L.
*Utica P. L.
*Wilkes-Barre, Osterhout F. L.
*Philadelphia, Drexel Institute L.
*Dover (N. H.) P. L.
*Evanston (Ill.) F. P. L.
*Medford (Mass.) P. L.
Gloversville (N. Y.) F. L.

*Los Angeles P.L.
*Omaha P.L.
Syracuse Central L.
New Haven F. P. L.
*Dayton (O.) P. L.
*Kansas City (Mo.) P. L.
Somerville (Mass.) P. L.
New Orleans, Fisk F. and P. L.
Salem (Mass.) P. L.
*Burlington (Vt.) Fletcher F. L.
Wilmington (Del.) Inst. F. L.
*Atlanta, Carnegie L.
*Dubuque (Ia.) Carnegie-Stout P. L.
*North Adams (Mass.) P. L.
*Jamestown (N.Y.)
  James Prendergast F. L.
*Oak Park (Ill.) Scoville Inst. L.
*Eau Claire (Wis.) P. L.
Galveston (Tex.) Rosenberg
  Library.

FREE REFERENCE

Newberry L., Chicago.
Peabody Institute L., Baltimore
John Crerar L., Chicago

Grosvenor L., Buffalo.
Watkinson L., Hartford.
Howard Memorial L., New Orleans.

GOVERNMENT

Library of Congress, Washington.
New York State L., Albany

Massachusetts State L.,
  Boston.

UNIVERSITY OR COLLEGE

Harvard University.
*Chicago, University of.
Columbia University.
Yale University.
Cornell University.
Pennsylvania, University of.
Michigan, University of.
Princeton University.
Brown University.
Johns Hopkins University
Dartmouth College.
California, University of.

Amherst College.
Bowdoin College.
Wisconsin, University of.
*Vermont, University of.
Wesleyan University.
Mass. Inst. of Technology
Oberlin College.
Nebraska, University of.
*Northwestern University.
*Illinois, University of.
Adelbert College.
Leland Stanford Jr. University

WOMEN'S COLLEGES

*Wellesley College.
*Vassar College.

*Bryn Mawr College.
*Mount Holyoke College.

PROPRIETARY

Phila., Library Company of.

Boston Athenaeum L.

New York Society L.

Providence Athenaeum L.

Redwood L., Newport

SUBSCRIPTION

N. Y., Mercantile L. Assn of.

Phila., Mercantile L. Co. of

St. Louis Mercantile L. Assn.

San Francisco, Mechanics' Inst. L.

The following blank was sent to the 100 representative libraries:

I have been asked by the President of the American Library Association to prepare for the printed Proceedings of the St. Louis Conference a statistical statement on "Women in American Libraries." Will you cooperate to that end by filling the following blank for the library which you represent:

1. Total number of staff members.
2. Total number of women.
   1 and 2 should include all full-time employees, excluding janitors.
3. State relative salaries of men and women for:
   1. Positions involving administrative responsibility.
   2. Responsible positions, technical and otherwise, not administrative.
   3. Others.

in the following form:

Administrative Responsibility.		Other Responsible Positions.		Others.	
Men	Women	Men	Women	Men	Women
1 at $5000	1 at $2100	1 at $2400	1 at $1500	2 at $720	7 at $900
2 at 2400	3 at 1800	3 at 2100	3 at 1200	2 at 600	5 at 720
		3 at 1500	4 at 900	3 at 480	21 at 600
		3 at 1200		4 at 360	14 at 480
					3 at 360

State frankly (so far as you are willing) the policy of the library board and your individual opinion as to the employment of women on a library staff. Mention all the advantages and limitations which occur to you. Indicate positions or lines of work for which you may think women specially fitted, or unfitted, with reasons. Every statement regarding individual libraries shall be held as entirely confidential.

Will you kindly give the matter immediate attention.

Very truly yours,

Salome Cutler Fairchild.

Replies have been received from 94 of the 100 libraries. A few declined to answer the questions regarding salaries.

Dividing the 54 public libraries investigated into two groups by size, and including in the larger group the first 21, the Newark library being the last of the first group, the following is true: In 19 out of 21 libraries in the large library group the librarians are men, the Minneapolis and Indianapolis libraries being the two in the charge of women. In 21 out of 33 libraries in the small library group the librarians are women. Men are in charge of each of the six reference and of the three government libraries. Of the 24 college or university libraries (excluding those exclusively for women), 20 have men as librarians, four have women, namely, Chicago, Vermont, Northwestern and Illinois. Women are in charge of the four women's college libraries. Men are in charge of the five proprietary and of the four subscription libraries. Thirty-one of the 100 representative libraries are in charge of women.

In the first group, including 21 large public libraries, all reported, but only 18 reported fully. Of these, 46 administrative positions are held by men, 73 by women. In the second group, of 33 smaller public libraries, 29 reported fully. Of these, 11 administrative positions are held by men, 29 by women. In the free reference libraries reporting, all administrative positions are held by men. In the government libraries, 24 are held by men, five by women. Of the 19 college libraries reporting fully (excluding those for women only), 47 administrative positions are held by men, 14 by women. All the administrative positions in the four women's college libraries are held by women. No women hold administrative positions in the five proprietary or four subscription libraries. In all statements made above regarding administrative positions, the head positions are included.

The following is a summary of facts with reference to responsible positions not administrative. Of 18 reporting fully in the large library group, 69 are held by men, 205 by women. Of 29 reporting fully in the small library group, eight are filled by men, 77 by women. In the free reference libraries reporting one such position is filled by a man, seven by women. In the government libraries, 102 by men, 84 by women. Of the 19 college libraries reporting fully (excluding those for women only), 20 are held by men, 44 by women. All such positions in the women's college libraries are held by women. In the five proprietary and four subscription libraries reporting, six are held by men, seven by women.

Of the 94 libraries of various types reporting, 514 subordinate positions are filled by men and boys, 1211 by women and girls.

2958 is the total number of persons employed by all the 94 libraries reporting; 2024 is the total number of women. One library employs only men, 21 employ only women, 10 employ less than one-half women, 36 from one-half to three-quarters women, and 25 more than three-quarters women.

In tabulating salary returns only public libraries have been considered. The number of libraries of the other types is small, the number reporting is smaller than for public libraries and fewer women are employed. The comparison of salaries would therefore be of little value.

In the large library group the highest salary reported for men is $7000, the lowest $3000; the highest salary paid to a woman is $2100.* The average highest salary paid to men holding responsible positions not administrative is $1208, to women $946. The average mean salary paid to men and boys in subordinate positions is $532, to women and girls $530. It will be remembered that the statistics include pages but not janitors or part-time employees.

The highest salary paid to a man as librarian in the small library group is $3000, the lowest $1500, the average $2118. The highest salary paid to a woman as librarian in this group is $2000, the lowest $800, the average $1429.

The figures prove that women greatly outnumber men in the libraries selected. It is a safe conclusion that they outnumber them by a larger proportion in the libraries of the country. They hold a creditable proportion of adminis-

*Not the highest salary paid to a woman in American libraries.

trative positions but seldom one involving large administrative responsibility. They outnumber men in responsible positions other than administrative, but they seldom hold the most responsible of such positions in the largest libraries or in those which might be called distinctly libraries for scholars. They vastly outnumber men in other positions. Broadly speaking, they hold a large number of important positions, seldom the most important.

They do not hold the positions offering the highest salaries, and broadly speaking, apparently they do not receive equal remuneration for the same grade of work.

The utmost kindness and courtesy have been invariably shown by librarians in stating the peculiar advantages and limitations of women, and most replies have been full, frank and discriminating. They throw considerable light on conditions as shown by statistics.

Economic reasons go far to explain the situation.

"Women will accept much smaller salaries than men of equal ability and preparation. There is an abundant supply of women who will work for less than men require and generally can afford to do so. Therefore, women drive men out of the library profession as they do out of the teaching profession."

"Women do not cost as much as men. This you may say is a mean advantage, but with little money and many books needed it is a very potent one."

Library trustees in filling a position can usually choose from a larger number of women than of men who are fitted by natural ability, education, training and experience to do the work. A woman thus chosen will usually accept a lower salary and remain satisfied with the salary longer than a man would. If she has others dependent on her support the burden is more likely to decrease than to increase, and her social obligations are less in a pecuniary way. She is more likely than a man to prefer a comfortable position at a moderate salary among her friends to strenuous responsibility at a high salary in a distant city. Women in the future may have more people dependent on their support. They will never have so many as men. A growing desire in the single woman for independence, for personal comfort and for travel may make her more ambitious.

Women are quite generally acknowledged to work under a handicap because of a more delicate physique. This shows itself in less ability to carry calmly the heavy burdens of administrative responsibility, to endure continued mental strain in technical work or to stand for a long period. It also doubtless accounts for the "nerves and tears" mentioned by one librarian (a woman) and the "tears" mentioned with profuse apologies by a man. It is quite probable that the physical handicap of women will be reduced as greater emphasis is placed on the importance of athletics and of out-of-door life and sports for girls. I do not see how it can be eliminated. Whether women will ever hold the highest administrative positions in libraries may remain perhaps an open question. That such positions are not now held by women is a fact. It is evidently believed by men holding such positions and probably by trustees holding the appointing power, that women are not in the present stage of civilization fitted to hold such positions. The following reasons are given:

1. She has not the temperamental fitness for the exercise of large authoritative control over a mixed staff.
2. She is not in touch with the world of affairs.
3. She is distinctly unbusinesslike.
4. She shuns rather than courts responsibility.

5. She is conservative and afraid of legitimate experiments.

6. She lacks originality.

7. She lacks a sense of proportion and the power of taking a large, impersonal view of things.

Some of the criticisms just cited have come from women. In many cases men stating certain disadvantages of women as a class have recognized that exceptional women are not only free from them but positively excel in the opposite direction. It is quite possible that with larger experience they may as a class rise above all disadvantages and ultimately hold the highest positions. There could be no agreement on such a point and individual opinion is of slight value. It is doubtless true that since women fill satisfactorily administrative positions of considerable importance, they might easily hold some others now held by men. A certain degree of conservatism and prejudice in the appointing power should not be left out of account. It may also be said on the other side that in the medium-sized libraries, of which so many women have charge, some one or more of the trustees may in reality deal with city officials and make business decisions which would fall to the librarian if a man. How far such is the case it would be impossible to discover. But I know that trustees frequently elect a man instead of a woman because as they say they have not time to devote to the business interests of the library. They assume that a woman would not have business capacity. Such sentiments on the part of trustees account for what I believe to be a fact that a woman is seldom appointed from the outside to a head position in even the medium sized libraries. She is promoted from a responsible position in the same library or she was made librarian when the institution was small.

It is quite generally conceded that in positions which do not involve the highest degree of executive or business ability but which require a certain "gracious hospitality," women as a class far surpass men. Such positions are: the head of a small or medium sized library, first assistant and branch librarian in a large public library, the more important positions in the loan department and all work with children, both in the children's room and in cooperation with schools. Here it is said her "broad sympathies, her quick wits, her intuitions and her delight in self sacrifice" give her an undoubted advantage.

One librarian writes:

"The enthusiasm a woman usually puts into her work is a great leaven and tends to lift the most monotonous task out of the commonplace."

And again:

"There should be at least one woman in a responsible position on every large staff where women are employed. There is always a certain amount of housekeeping and of matronizing (he might have said mothering) which is essential for the health and comfort of all concerned."

There are a few exceptions, but it is the consensus of opinion that, granted equal educational advantages, women are as well fitted as men for technical work, even the higher grades of cataloging. They are preferred by most libraries reporting for all ordinary cataloging positions because of "greater conscientiousness, patience and accuracy in details."

Women and girls are generally preferred to men or boys in the routine work of a library. They are thought to be more faithful and on the whole more adaptable. The lack of permanence because of marriage is largely balanced by the fact that boys who take clerical positions in a library generally do so as a stepping stone to other work. Women lose more time on account of illness and their health must be more carefully watched. They are more subject to petty jealousies, more easily upset and demoralized in their work by little things. Although in the main more conscientious than boys, girls show a curious lack of reliability in the matter of punctuality. Women in charge of libraries have not infrequently told me that the hardest thing they had to do was to make the girls on the staff realize that it is dishonest to be habitually five or ten minutes late in the morning.

One librarian of large experience sums up his highly appreciative estimate of the work of women by comparing them to a familiar character—

"There was a little girl,
And she had a little curl
  Right in the middle of her forehead.
When she was good
She was very, very good,
  And when she was bad she was horrid."

It is interesting to observe the proportion of men on the staffs of libraries in charge of women. Of such libraries reporting, by far the greater proportion of them have a staff made up entirely of women. In most others (there are exceptions) the masculine element is represented by pages, or by men who do evening work, or who fill comparatively unimportant positions. It seems to me that the library serving a constituency of men and women can render better service through a staff on which the important positions are divided between the two sexes. Men and women represent different elements, they look at things from a different point of view. If they work together side by side in an individual library as they do in the home, in social life, in the church, and as they already do in the library association, each contributing his or her best, the result is broader, richer and more vital than if men alone or women alone take part.

The economic reasons already dwelt upon operate in many libraries to prevent such an arrangement. One reporting library attempts as even as possible a division of positions between the sexes. In many other libraries I suspect such a division is recognized as an ideal.

Reviewing all the facts it seems clear that women in American libraries have accomplished much creditable work which has won generous recognition. Still more avenues of opportunity are open. At the same time, on account of natural sex limitations, and also actual weakness in the work of many women as well as because of conservatism and prejudice, many gates are at present closed to women.

To the ambitious every form of handicap acts as a spur. In the long run, however, women may prefer to work mainly in those lines where they can if they will equal men—in the various forms of scholarly effort; and in those where they naturally excel him—in positions where the human element predominates.

The Prospect:
An Address Before a
Graduating Class of Women

by Herbert Putnam

The privilege which you accord me is an agreeable one, and I should wish to take full profit of it. I am not, therefore, willing to use it in the exposition of some general theme, unrelated to the occasion, even though convention might sanction such a choice. Instead, I shall venture some reflections inevitable to the occasion itself—what it means, what it portends.

And the first is as to the phenomenon itself—a group of young women specifically trained for vocation not merely domestic, and about to proceed into it. A recent phenomenon, the like of which was not seen in the world until the nineteenth century, and late in that. Its bearing and its interest in its relation to the problem of the sexes, and the relations of woman, as a sex, to the community, are obvious. But its significance as part of a world movement is of a concern far greater. It is an expression at once of a tendency in social evolution and of a conviction in democracy. The tendency is that towards individualism; the conviction, that of the responsibility of the individual as such. They are both phases or incidents of that evolution which, in other phases, the lawyer describes as a change from status to contract; the historian as a change from feudalism to democracy; and the sociologist as a change from homogeneity to heterogeneity. For each implies a development of the individual as the unit. Granting him the unit—and, under democracy, free—diversity follows; for there is nothing in nature so diverse as the individual, and responsibility follows, for democracy looks directly to him, and he cannot escape by a reference merely to his caste or sect or social order, or any convention. He cannot, even by a reference to his sex. Still less can he by a reference to his status; for as a limitation or exemption this no longer exists. He has indeed ceased to be static; he has become dynamic. And the power within him for which he is responsible, which he is called upon to exercise, is the power to work.

Work. We talk much—and healthily—of "service." That, however, is a term of different import. It may imply a larger range and a broader social relation, but the relation is not a new one. It has existed since the beginning of society, and it has manifested itself at different times in various forms—many

Address given June 12, 1912 before the graduating class of Simmons College.
Reprinted with permission *Library Journal* 37 (December 1912):651-658.

worthy, some heroic. But the idea of work as in itself a dignity, a privilege and an obligation, is, I think, a new one. It also issues from the social conscience; it implies a resultant benefit to society; but in expressing it, society seems to declare that this most important benefit is to come from energizing each one of its units. The development of self, the application of one's own individual powers to some useful activity, is to precede service to others.

> To *believe* thoroughly in one's own self, so that one's own self be thorough —
> were to *do* great things, my lord.

That belief, on such a basis, may thus be the condition of useful service to others. At all events, it is itself the healthiest basis of a progressive community life.

And the second phenomenon which I cannot overlook, because it interests me extremely, is the fact that you who have recognized and accepted this obligation are women, not men. How is that fact to affect you, how is it to affect the business and society upon which you are to enter?

Now, the time has passed when the phenomenon would have caused either business or society to look upon you askance. Woman in vocation — a multitude of women in diverse vocations — are now accepted facts; and while discussion is still rife over her relation to industry or office — and apprehension over the effect of this upon the calling to which ancient tradition dedicated her — and there is still protest accordingly, this protest has become sporadic. And it seems now admitted that so long as the state fails to provide a home and a husband (if she would accept him) for every woman, a large percentage of women *must* engage in industry or take office; that it is creditable that they should do so; and that, having become thus independent units in society, they are entitled to the privileges — or should be subject to the duties — of that participation in the conduct of the affairs of the community — that is to say, the ballot and what it implies — accorded to the other independent units, with not merely personal, but property rights to be safeguarded.

You will, therefore, be accepted without demur. You will be welcomed. And there will be nothing in the general attitude of business or society to impair the high hope with which you leave here.

But when you have entered upon the actual relations of business or office you will encounter certain difficulties. You will find certain limitations which seem to curtail that "fair chance" which you were led to expect. It remains a "fair chance" within your own sex, but it appears to be but a partial chance as against the other sex. It seems limited by some prejudice in favor of that other sex. If this exists, it can only be due to convictions based on observation and experience. Upon what superior traits of men, in business or office, is it based?

You may well consider.

The first is *manliness*. Now, this isn't any quality or aptitude within the individual himself. It is rather a certain bearing or relation between him and his "job," him and his superior, him and the occasion or the exigency of the moment. Its existence in the man assures that he will bear a large good or a large ill with equal steadiness; that he will accept the small ills as merely incidental — what the golfers call "rubs o' the green"; and that, behind any act which affects him or his authority, he will recognize that there may be, there probably are, considerations larger than himself, larger, perhaps, than his superior who makes the decision, and imperative upon the latter. That same manliness enables him not merely to accept a decision, but to abide by it; and similarly to abide uncomplainingly by an understanding in which he has acquiesced, even though he prove the loser by it.

The absence of this, habitual, attitude in woman is not evident in her attitude towards the larger ills; for she bears keener ills more patiently and with greater fortitude than man. It is not serious in her attitude toward the larger good, should it come. But it causes her to be peevish toward the smaller ills and to distort them; it causes her to ascribe personal, and, therefore, sinister, motives to official action which affects her unfavorably, and causes her often to repudiate, after the event, understandings which have resulted to her disadvantage. She may have "overlooked" something, or she may merely have been too sanguine, and she wishes to "go back upon" the bargain. A man, in like case, may wish it equally. But he will not betray the wish. With him "a bargain is a bargain"; an understanding, no matter how expressed, is a contract. And through the experience of centuries he has come to abide by his contracts as final. His manliness is bound up in them. To evade the consequences of them, to ask indulgence is, he would say, to "squawk."

But this isn't because he is a man. It is only because this attitude has been developed in him by experience. There is no reason why it should not be equally developed in woman after a similar experience. Meantime, I mention it as one of those distinctions between the sexes, considered characteristically, which you will find operative in the minds and the decisions of administrators, whose organization includes both men and women.

The second characteristic distinction *is* a trait—it is *sense of proportion.* But this, also, and especially, is the result of ages of experience in affairs. In certain fields it is the result of mere culture—"the ability to see large things large, and small things small"; but in affairs it can come only through experience. And a sex which till recently has, as a sex, devoted itself to the particular and the personal, inevitably carries into any new field of activity the same concentration and allegiances. To it all is still detail; all the relations and motives are still personal. There *is* no wood, for the trees. And the trees themselves signify, chiefly as they affect or are affected by certain human relations.

Now, there is profit in this, of which I shall speak presently. The loss in it is that it sets the detail above the general result, the part above the whole. It prevents the particular individual from recognizing the relation between his part and the whole; it causes him to exaggerate the fact of the moment, or the method that is habitual; and it renders him *inflexible.* As compared with men, women in business represent the inflexible; so much so that any administrator will tell you of his despair in persuading them to change a process or method, and very likely, of his final recourse to an appeal purely personal—which succeeds, not because it conquers their convictions, but because, being women, it wins their sympathy.

In so far as a defect, this inflexibility accounts, I suppose, for the failure of woman as a sex to develop, except within narrow areas, the inventive faculty; or in music and the arts, the creative faculty; or in administrative work, to show what is called "initiative."

The characteristic of modern industry is organization. This means differentiation, which, in turn, means for any individual worker specialization in some detail which is subordinate to the whole, and yet contributory to it. Now, in the handling of this detail as such, in the mastery of it, in consistent devotion to it, woman is superior to man. But in the sense of its larger relation, not as a fact in itself, but as part of a whole, she is still his inferior. She does not, as he must and does, so clearly realize that in such an organization the whole is not merely made up of its parts, but the effectiveness of the whole is conditioned by the efficiency of each of its parts; and, therefore, that an enlargement or perfection of the whole requires, from time to time, a modification of each part, a readjustment of its relation with the other parts. The efficiency of an employee includes his ability to recognize this; his opportunity lies in the recognition of it. It does not suffice that he should apply himself devotedly to the detail assigned him, as such; he is also to view this detail in its larger relations, is to consider it in its contributory relations as it may affect the general results, increase or improve the output, reduce the cost.

Now, this involves both insight and the power of generalization. And in neither, applied to affairs, is woman as yet the equal of man. She immerses, enmeshes herself in the particular. Her treatment of this may be complete. But at any one moment she is bounded by it. A man may handle it less perfectly, and yet reveal in his handling of it a conception of its larger relations which will indicate his ability to handle a larger task. The woman may have the ability for the larger task, but it will not develop until the task is assigned. It awaits the need, and the proof of it awaits the call.

That is why the call, to her, less often comes. For that indication of an ability beyond the job in hand is what is called "initiative." No one can define more exactly what this is. But it is what every administrator is looking for in his subordinates, and it is the basis and the condition of promotion. An employee lacking it is not conscious of the lack; he is as little conscious of it as of his lack of sense at a particular color. Nor can it be proved to him by argument. He can rarely be satisfied of it by illustration. Meantime, he doesn't "get on." He complains and asks, "Why?" He has done, done faithfully, everything assigned him, but still the same things continue to be assigned him—at the same salary; while A and B, his one-time associates, have been advanced from one thing to another—larger responsibilities, larger pay. But they showed "initiative"! How *could* he show initiative when his work was so routine?

Yet any administrator will tell you that there is not a position in his establishment, down to the humblest, not a work the most elementary and routine, where initiative cannot be shown.

The head of a western corporation, having occasion to sign several thousand bonds in a New York banking house, called for a boy to blot his signatures. He was assigned six in succession, and only one satisfied him, so various may be the methods of so simple a process as applying a blotter to a slip of paper. How did the successful boy differ from the others? He could not say in particular, only there was a "something" in his way of "handling the job" that was distinctly different. That boy seemed to "gauge" him, to discern whatever was peculiar in *his* manner and method, and to put himself into sympathy with these. The relation instituted became immediately *harmonious,* and the result in proportion. Such was his explanation. Insight!—and yet in how seemingly trivial an affair. But trivial as it was, it satisfied this man of large experience that that lad would reach far, a judgment confirmed when he learned that he was a student of a western college, applying his vacation to earning his tuition fees for the ensuing year.

The employee who doesn't "get on," and is told that the reason is because he lacks initiative, meets this explanation in different ways. The manly one returns to his task determined to throw himself into it with the same zeal, but also to project himself out of it; to study opportunities of it in relation to that whole to which I referred, and to study his associates and their ways, who seem to be advancing more rapidly than he. He may succeed in imitating them; he may fail. It may not be "in him." But at least he has met the issue in a manly fashion. In doing so he has gained the respect and the interest of his superior.

The other way of meeting it, which is the despair of an administrator, is for the employee to detect in the explanation of "lack of initiative" a mere subterfuge, and to see behind it as the real obstacles those sinister personal influences of which I have spoken. This disposition is, unfortunately, the more natural if he be a woman. Together with that inflexibility, that lack of elasticity, it accounts for the inferior ability of women in business or office to readjust themselves to their work, to vary and develop their relation to it, so as to offer evidence of qualities suited to a higher one; and it accounts, also, for the reluctance of their chiefs to assign them to a higher position, because, while a man might be so assigned as an experiment by which, having agreed, he will abide, a woman is apt, in spite of the agreement, to dispute the later judgment of her failure as also due to some indisposition to grant her "a fair chance."

In general, this difference between men and women in their business or official relations may be summarized or explained as a difference in equilibrium. The equilibrium of the man is dynamic, and therefore progressive. It is the result of constantly adjusting himself to new conditions and new relations, of seeking to avail himself of new forces. The equilibrium of woman is still static—the survival of ages of passivity in relations which were fixed, among conditions which were imposed. Neither is a final characteristic of sex. If the former has come from experience, the latter may yield to a similar experience.

But having thus far noted certain of the obstacles which you are to encounter in the competitions of business or office, let me turn, gratefully, to the offsetting assurances which you will carry with you. And especially those of sex.

The largest success in business and office being conditioned upon qualities predominantly associated thus far with men, there is a common assumption that when a woman engages in industry or takes office she must take on certain traits distinctively masculine, and make place for these by laying off certain others distinctively feminine. Disbelieve it. And, understand, I am not referring to what are called "the graces of womanhood." I am not proposing to sentimentalize about those. No woman consciously or deliberately lays them off. Folly if she did. They are an asset in business and office as they are anywhere else, and the loss of them is a complete loss; there is no substitute for them in anything that can be imitated from the other sex.

The traits actually in question are rather such as I have attempted to describe as the product of the distinctive cumulated experience of man in affairs. They are, in part, qualities within himself, but they are due also to a way of looking at things, an attitude, a relation, which from habit have become instincts. But they are not for that, essentially or in a congenital sense, masculine—not even the one of them which I have entitled "manliness"; for manliness in the sense in which I meant it isn't masculinity, nor need men have any monopoly of it. So, certain of the other virtues which I have enumerated belong merely to the ethics of a business or official relation. And if there is a characteristic relative lack of them in woman as a sex, this is but a present defect.

But if woman has a defect of these virtues, she has also the correlative virtues of certain of these defects. The relative inability to generalize is due to an absorption in the particular, which means a devotion which is in itself a virtue; the lack of sense of proportion which causes her to exaggerate the significance of the trivial, is due to a similar absorption and devotion; her occasional peevishness is the result of an absorption, a devotion, which has become excessive, so that it has worn upon her nerves and upset her balance; the dread of change in any fact or method is due to loyalty to the thing which is, and to which she has dedicated herself; the instinctive reference to a personal standard or motive is due to a similar loyalty otherwise directed.

All these virtues, distinctively feminine, are assets. They are of great import in business; and so far from laying them off, you should confidently hold fast to them. They have a substantial market value; and they have also a tremendous social value. If they do not make for progress, they assure stability. If in business or office they do not lead to promotion, they at least assure preference in the positions which are subordinate. They are, of course, static, rather than dynamic: they hold to that which is, the relation established against a new one proposed. But in business and in institutions, this side also must be represented; in society and in politics it is essential. It is the conservative, as distinguished not merely from the progressive, but from the radical and the willful. And as it is distinctively a feminine trait, it may be not merely a distinctive superiority of yours in the competitions of business, but your distinctive contribution to the welfare of society and the state.

For the welfare of society and the state requires that what might be called the masculine and the feminine natures shall be equally operative, the former urging, the latter restraining; that to the dynamic shall be opposed the static; to the progressive, the conservative; to the incessant disposition towards mere expediency, the constant reminder of principle; to mere vigor, refinement; to the disposition to give things the preference over persons, that kind of loyalty which gives persons the preference over things; and, I may add, to the tendency to regard the personal and domestic virtues as of subordinate concern in affairs of state—insistence upon the home and family as the essential unit, and therefore the personal and domestic virtues as of the utmost concern. With the participation of women in the franchise, this latter insistence is to have a marked influence; and one cannot doubt that in the western states where the recall of magistrates is operative it will be exercised at the instance of women for the rebuke of defections in the incumbent, rather moral than political.

To say that such qualities or instincts distinctively feminine are to oppose those distinctively masculine is not to say that they are to defeat them. They are to contend with them, but also to cooperate. They are complementary. And this contention, in ultimate cooperation, is but an enlargement in society of the contention in cooperation of identical qualities or instincts which goes on within the man himself; for any given man is one-half woman, as any given woman is one-half man. The difference is that in the latter case, the contest being subjective, the issue is apt to become confused; in the former, being objective, it stands clear.

I am therefore deeply serious when I say that the perpetuation, the confident assertion, of these feminine traits is of the utmost importance to society. And they are of notable value to business and office. Every administrator will tell you that, and of his frequent occasion for gratitude to them.

The question for woman, looking to her own advancement, is, how, without diminution of them, she may gain the balancing virtues which thus far, distinctively, she lacks.

Now, as concerns the ethics, the need is merely to develop and apply in a special field, new to her, an ethical sense which heretofore she has exercised only in other directions. This is merely a matter of experience, developed by noting the consequences of a failure to exercise it. The experience itself develops a sort of instinct, which, once established, operates without the need of definition or argument. It calls into play what among men stands for "honor." An illustration: a public official was once waited on by a delegation of women with a suffrage petition. He was asked to sign it. Without expressing opinion upon its merits, he remarked that it would obviously be improper for a public official to sign petitions to the legislature in matters not affecting his office. The justice of this view was at once accepted, and the delegation withdrew, apologetic. On the eve of the presentation of the petition, a letter from the proponents was published, setting forth that "the following gentlemen in favor of the petition" had to withhold their signatures because of official propriety; and his name and office were listed with the others.

Now, this was done in the most innocent good faith, the proponents being women. It would scarcely have been possible for them, being men.

As to loyalty also. The mischief is not in the lack of it, but rather in the overintensification and misdirection of it. Loyalty is loyalty, and always, from an ethical standpoint, admirable. But there are four kinds, or directions, of it: there is loyalty to the person, there is loyalty to the corporation or the state, there is loyalty to the fact—that particular fact, the thing which is—and there is loyalty to the idea or ideal. Now, with two of these—to person and to fact— highly active, woman has as yet but imperfectly developed the other two. Here patriotism in crises may be passionate and capable of extreme sacrifice; but it is apt to be induced by attachments purely local or personal. And in business or office it is not the larger whole which she keeps in view, an ideal of which she is conscious, but some objective detail.

The ability to generalize is a condition of the largest success in business, but it is also a condition of efficiency in the smallest relations. It includes the ability to project one's self beyond one's self and the particular. It requires, therefore, imagination. And imagination is a characteristic of all the great captains of industry. But it is also the distinguishing trait of those in subordinate offices who adjust themselves in a harmonious and, therefore, progressive relation with their work and office.

With some people it is undoubtedly born. But this is not to say that it may not be cultivated. And the means of cultivating it are especially two: contact with people, and contact with books; people as diverse as may be accessible, stimulating to new and varying sympathies; books as stimulating as possible, stirring sympathy as such, as well as diversifying the objects of it. And of these two, while the opportunities for the former must vary much with any particular woman, the opportunity for the latter is now equally open to all.

So I come finally—as, perhaps, a librarian should and must—to books as the indispensable aid to your future. And as these books are not the textbooks of a mere craft—not the books training for a definite vocation, but those making for culture—I am free here, as elsewhere, to exalt them, to declare them also the indispensable. Free also to rejoice in the more general studies which you have pursued here, as, even with the end of a livelihood, also vocational studies. For, after all, technique—that is, mere expertness in the handling of method or mechanism—is the least of accomplishments, intelligence the greatest. Technique, merely as such, approximates the individual to the perfection of a machine, but it cannot do more. Intelligence lifts him from the mechanical to the spiritual, from the particular to the general, from mere fact to relations.

And it also shows the fruit in him both of education and of culture; education which enables him not merely (as does a machine) to do well the thing that he has been in the habit of doing, but also "to do well the thing that he has never done before"; and culture which, as I have quoted, enables him "to see large things large and little things small." It is the latter which in business, as in matters of taste, feeling and social conduct, assures him that sense of proportion which means sanity. And flexibility also. "Be supple, David, about things immaterial," enjoins the dominie upon David Balfour. Be supple about things immaterial, is the lesson that woman in business and office needs most of all to learn.

In this view there is *no* study rightly pursued which is *not* vocational; and for the larger vocations and the more progressive relation in any vocation, the more general studies may prove even more effective than those specifically vocational, just as a mind that is buoyant, elastic and capable of independent thinking is of more consequence in affairs than a mere memory stored with facts; and a character that is disciplined to initiative more practical than one equipped merely with ethical precepts.

I trust, therefore, that of all the courses you have pursued here your gratitude will be not least to those which have not in themselves represented any immediate utility; the more because, while the technique furnished by the others might be acquired through actual experience, the peculiar service rendered by the general studies cannot. And you will not suppose or admit that this service is dubious merely because the particular subjects which they treat, or the particular facts which they convey seem to have no direct application to business or affairs. No college graduate should need to be told that the process of mental, as of physical, digestion is not mechanical, but chemical—that it *converts,* and that, therefore, the effect produced may bear no likeness to that which has produced it. The humblest of illustrations satisfies as to this—an ox in a meadow. The very type of muscular strength. But how produced?—by diet of ox? No; by diet of grass.

There is predestination, perhaps. But in the case of studies, and the mind instead of the body, we have for our guidance decisions resting upon observation and experience; and the experience which has observed that the tendency of certain studies—history, science, mathematics, literature, languages— irrespective of any exact knowledge conveyed, is to enlarge the understanding, develop the critical faculty, quicken the sensibilities, refine the taste, and in general to *free* the spirit to an independent exercise of itself, so that they may fitly be termed "liberal" studies (for this is their claim to that title); this experience still, happily, has weight against the superficial assumption that only that preparation for affairs is "practical" which consists in doing precisely the thing which is later to be done for profit.

This latter is not the conviction of men of affairs engaged in the largest operations. I have before me an address by such a one delivered to the graduating class of a school of technology—the words of an engineer addressing prospective engineers. Let me read a passage from it:

"You will soon find that many kinds of knowledge which you have perhaps considered useless are important and essential in your professional work. It is a mistake made by most students, and I have no doubt many of you have made it, to think that the faculty of the school have introduced too many general studies into the course instead of giving all, or nearly all, of the time to purely technical studies and practical work closely related to engineering. To those of you who have had this feeling, I would only say that your views will change as you go on, and in ten years from now you will think more of the judgment of the faculty in these matters than you do at present. There is no doubt that your instructors *could* map out a course which would turn out graduates who would be able to start in practical work with much more ease and readiness than you can; in fact, any boy who had spent the four years you have spent here, in the field or the draughting room, learning practical engineering, would, other things being equal, be able to do routine work in an engineering office much better than you could do it; but, on the other hand, in a very few years you should be far ahead of him. In other words, your instructors have been wise to give you a broad and liberal training and to forego teaching you some of those things which would come nearest to making of you engineers at the time you finish your course in order to give you more of the broad and fundamental principles, the mastery of which will enable you in a reasonable time to become much abler and more valuable engineers than if your training here had aimed to teach you the maximum amount of that kind of technical information which is supposed to be most immediately useful to the young graduate. It is much better for you to have a broad, liberal education and a little engineering knowledge when you leave here than to have a much greater amount of practical and technical knowledge without a liberal education."

A notable declaration that, from a "practical" source; and as it was issued on an occasion such as this, at an institution also preparing for vocation, I trust that I do no treason to your faculty in quoting it here.

Of course, I am not condemning vocational studies. I am merely distinguishing them, and rejoicing that even here I am not called upon to sound a paean in praise of them. You remember the old lady who was so glad that she didn't like beans, for if she did she would undoubtedly eat them; and as she detested them, that would be very unpleasant! I am not quite in similar case, but I suppose we are both reactionaries, and open to all the opprobrium (not political) which that term implies.

I can't quite believe, however, that with respect to studies there is even yet a really thick-and-thin progressive. When it comes to the last analysis, you will find him making distinctions which, consistently applied, would leave all the margin that the "older school" requires. The only really consistent vocationalist is, in fact, the Fiji Islander, who eats the hearts of his enemies in the hope of absorbing their spirit. He, at least, connects directly the results with the cause in its apparent manifestations.

And if these general studies have such an utility in their direct result, how signal their utility in the indirect! I mean in the interests which they excite, the associations which they engender, the resources which they provide. For among other service it is their possible one to give precisely that larger, wider, saner view which is to offset the exaggerations of detail; to cultivate perspective, the sense of proportion; and to promote humor, which, if not a condition, is apt to be an incident of it. The foundation laid here for the impulsive recourse to books—for an appreciation of them as such, for certainty in the choice of them, and for facility in their use—is, I still think, the most signal service and the most enduring which your college has rendered you; that and the community life, with the privilege of slowly maturing in the helpful and stimulating personal contacts which are the privilege of four years in any academic institution.

And I do not overlook the fact that certain of you are directing yourselves to careers in science, rather than to business or affairs. It is no disparagement to science to say that it is "narrow"; for what is narrow may be also deep. And we have been reminded that "the sword of righteousness is also narrow, but it cuts exceeding keen."

But in proportion as the ways of science are narrow, its field more and more specialized, its professional gaze absorbed, there is the greater need of an interest by the man of science in what is outside and beyond, and an initiative in seeking contact with it. Indeed, his largest results depend upon it; for they require in him an imagination which can be cultivated in no more effective way.

To books, however, easily within your reach, there must be added another aid in the lack of which as a sex you are handicapped. This is health. For the intensity of women in office or industry, which may become hysteria, is apt to be the result of a stress which they are physically unable to bear, and which, accordingly, their conscience transfers to their nerves. Their nerves were not meant to bear it, and inevitably give way under it. The remedies for this are too obvious to capitulate. Let me only emphasize that of all those you seek, against such obstacles as you may encounter, none are more important to the final result.

And so you go out to a world full of interest, containing many perplexities, but also many rewards. To those of you who enter the profession to which I belong, I have already, in all that I have said, indicated some of the perplexities. I would gladly expatiate upon the rewards, if that would not seem too partial. They are the rewards incident to an altruistic service, which is none the less a public service in that it does not always carry what is called a public office.

But, indeed, opportunity for public service is by no means limited to those in office. It is open to every one of you who enter upon affairs of any sort which involve relations with your fellows. And the reward, if not apparently direct, may prove sufficient in the mere zest of the service itself.

You go out from here with certain expressions — "ideals," etc. — conventional to such occasions. And your experience with them will seem singular. At first, in your early contacts with life, they will be rudely shocked, perhaps ridiculed. And as, though seemingly true, they are not yet *real* to you, you will begin to doubt them. Later in life they revive and reassemble, and what are now to you mere formulae become then fact. They have always been, and it is only the realization of them that has been deferred. The grateful realization of them later is one of the rewards. There are analogies in nature:

"Mysterious Night! — when our first parent knew
Thee, from report divine, and heard thy name,
Did he not tremble for this lovely frame,
This glorious canopy of light and blue? —
Yes, 'neath a curtain of translucent dew,
Bathed in the rays of the great setting flame,
Hesperus, with the high host of heaven came,
And lo! Creation widened in man's view.
Who could have dreamed such darkness lay concealed
Within thy beams, O Sun? — or who could find,
While fruit and leaf and insect stood revealed,
That to such countless orbs thou mad'st us blind?"

If some illusions must go, there are discoveries which take their place and compensate. These also are surprises.

You recall the experience of Mrs. Mallet in "Roderick Hudson."

> Her marriage had been an immitigable error, which she had spent her life in trying to look straight in the face. . . . But at last, as her child emerged from babyhood, she began to feel a certain charm in patience, to discover the uses of ingenuity, and to learn that, somehow or other, *one can always arrange one's life.*

One can always arrange one's life. Particularly if one be a woman; for deftness in that art, and patience in the practice of it, is the distinction of your sex.

Kant found three questions which every human being puts to himself. "What can I know? What can I do? What may I hope for?" Of these, you have answered the first. You have material for answering the second; you go now to face the third. Face it with confidence. The future contains the answer. And if its answer at first disappoint, or even seem wholly unresponsive, do not despond; for the answer that will finally come may prove, though different, even better than your hope. And if it thwart some apparently just ambition on your individual part, it may, nevertheless, make for the welfare of society, and in doing so will assure you the satisfaction of having contributed your necessary finite part to the infinite design.

The Position of Women in Public Libraries

by Mizpah Gilbert

Resembling the modern novel, this article has a purpose. The reader may remember the story of the man who having a fierce dog put up a notice in very large letters warning trespassers. A friend on seeing the placard said, "I suppose you have made that notice very large so that he who runs may read?" "No," replied the owner, "Not that he who runs may read, but that he who reads may *run!*" Certain facts are here given which cannot be gainsaid; certain opinions offered, which, on the contrary, may be combated. Firstly, I intend briefly to summarise the position of women in public libraries today; secondly, to show, given women's own efforts and desires, what it might be in the future.

Women were first employed as public library assistants in England at Manchester in 1871. The salaries given were £26 to £80 per year, according to the ability of the assistant; £80 was the salary paid to women branch librarians. Many libraries followed the procedure of the Manchester Public Libraries; Clerkenwell was the first London Library to employ women as assistants, but Notting Hill was the first public library to be in charge of a woman. Since these early beginnings controversies, regarding the suitability and aptitude of women for library work have been more or less frequent. A controversy which took place in the pages of the *Library World* in 1904-5 was well summed up by the Editor, who said: "The practical unanimity of the librarians who employ women as to the general excellence of their service is so marked that it is impossible to resist the conclusion that women have completely vindicated their right to rank as first-class librarians."

Now, what are the advantages at present; given that the woman's work is as good as the man's? I will take Great Britain and Ireland first. In the *Englishwomen's Year Book* the average salaries are given as follows:—In London junior assistants receive from £29 to £52 per year. In the provinces £17 10s. to £41 10s. In London senior assistants receive from £58 to £95; in the provinces £52 to £78. No woman is employed as the chief librarian of a municipal library system in London, though one or two are in charge of branch libraries, the salaries ranging from £80 to £120 per year. In the provinces there are women chiefs, though few in number; the average salary being about £110. As far as can be ascertained there are 3,500 library assistants in Great Britain and Ireland, of these 1,500 are women. These figures are approximate. The number of women employed in public libraries has risen considerably during the last few years, and bids fair to become almost equal to that of the men. When asking oneself why so few women assistants become chiefs it is

Reprinted with permission from *Library World* 18 (October 1915):100-105.

only fair, in addition to the other facts, to remember that the average age of the women is much lower than that of the men. The women marry and leave; the men marry and stay. Such, baldly put, is the position as regards women in public libraries in Great Britain today.

I will just touch on the facilities which are granted to women even as to men for qualification as fully trained librarians. First and foremost there are the classes established by the Library Association in library routine; library history, foundation and equipment; classification; cataloguing; bibliography and literature. Aid is thus given to a knowledge of the various branches of library work. The cost of each course of instruction is twelve shillings and sixpence. These classes are conducted orally for London assistants and by correspondence for provincial assistants. Classes are also held under the auspices of the Association in Birmingham and Liverpool. Thus it may be seen that taking railway fares or postage into consideration an assistant may become qualified in the various branches of librarianship for under £5. To obtain the Diploma of the Library Association the six certificates must be obtained; a thesis has to be written on some original subject connected with librarianship, and a knowledge of Latin and one European language other than English is expected. An entrance fee of two guineas is demanded. Three years' practical work in a library is also asked. This briefly sums up the methods by which the qualified municipal librarian of the immediate present and the future will be made. When the cost of becoming a diplomate of the Association is compared with the expense of qualifications in other professions, it is rather ludicrous to think of the comments on the initial expenditure made usually by short-sighted librarians and assistants.

In connection with the question of qualification, it is interesting to note that out of 566 certificated assistants—some of whom are now chief librarians—448 are men; 118 are women. Thus, out of two thousand men in the profession nearly one-quarter or twenty-five percent are sensible of the necessity for qualification; in the case of the women, roughly speaking, eight percent are qualified. These figures are based on the numbers given in the Library Association syllabus of 1913-14.

Now, I will take the United States. I have been fortunate in obtaining at first hand the opinions of several of the foremost librarians of America today. I will give a brief summary of what they say. There are about 14,000 people engaged in library work in the United States at the present time. About 10,000 are women. Some of the largest city libraries are administered by women, *e.g.,* those of Omaha, Portland, Minneapolis, Hartford, Jersey City, and others. Portland and Minneapolis are very large library systems with many branches, the staff numbering over one hundred members in each. The salaries range from $2,000 to $4,000 (£400-£800). Large numbers of secondary cities have their libraries in the charge of women, particularly so in the Middle West and along the Pacific Coast. When it comes to the small sized libraries, 10,000 volumes and under, they are almost without exception in the charge of women. The large majority of subordinate positions in city libraries are held by women with salaries ranging from $450-$2,000 (£90-£400). The past ten years has seen a very decided growth of high school and normal school libraries, chiefly administered by women with salaries ranging from $1,200 to $2,000 (£240-£400). When writing to me on this subject a well-known American librarian said, "Where you find a difference between the salaries paid to men and the salaries paid to women, you will find that the librarian is not of the latest pattern, and accepts without protest what is offered, lest any questioning of the matter might bring about conditions not to her liking." Thus we see in America the women receive from £90 to £800, according to the position. Of course, it must be remembered that the cost of living in the U.S. is higher than it is in England, and also that much must be spent to get any return.

I will just mention briefly the average cost of obtaining qualification in the U.S. There are twelve library schools in various states. Examinations are held for admission for which in states other than New York an entrance fee of £1 is required. Candidates must be over 20 and under 40 years of age. I will take the New York State school as an example. The regular college course is two years, junior and senior. The cost of tuition including lectures and fees is $150 (£30). The circular of information issued by the school says, "The necessary school expenses are seldom less than $425-475" (£80-95). The courses of study are entitled:—1. Administrative; 2. Bibliographic; 3. Practice work; 4. Technical. At the end of the course a certificate is awarded to each student who completes the work satisfactorily and passes the examination at the close. The degree of Bachelor of Library Science (B.L.S.) is conferred upon all graduates of registered colleges; the degrees of Master and Doctor of Library Science are similarly obtained as those of Master and Doctor of Arts in England.

It has been said that the success obtained by the American women in this particular branch of the world's work is due to the fact that on entering the profession they recognise it as their life work, and throw all their powers of mind and body into the occupation they have chosen. "There is no half-heartedness, no taking it up as a stop-gap, and the result is that they have won for themselves and for those who come after them an honoured position in an honourable profession." Mr. Melvil Dewey once said that when he looked to the future he was inclined to think that most of the *men* who would achieve greatness as the ideal librarian would be *women.*

In Germany women are becoming increasingly employed in public libraries, and also in the scientific and college libraries. Near Berlin a library school has been established, in which girls who have passed their 16th year are instructed in all branches of theoretical and practical library work, including shorthand and typewriting. The course which lasts one or two years costs 1,000 marks (about £50). Examinations are held, and diplomas awarded. Assistants with diplomas receive on an average from 2,440 to 2,880 marks (£122-£144), while untrained workers receive 1,200-2,600 marks. The majority of librarians are in favour of employing women assistants, and those who are qualified are much in demand.

In Sweden, Austria, and Belgium women are employed as assistants. I have not been able to glean any information regarding the libraries of France, but the name of Mademoiselle Pellechet, who was the cataloguer of the Incunabula of the National Library of France, will ever be remembered as that of a great librarian.

Holland possesses several women librarians. Indeed, I think it is fair to say that the future of municipal libraries in Holland lies in the hands of women. Dordrecht is a library which is run on quite modern lines; an excellent example of much made out of little, by enthusiasm and energy combined with a love of beauty. Of Hilversum Library the same must be said. The salaries paid are very small; usually the assistants are voluntary workers, and generally the work is a labour of love. Miss Gebhard, of Amsterdam, Miss Mühlenfeld, of Hilversum, and Miss Snouck-Hürgronje, of Dordrecht, are brilliant examples of what women have done for the public libraries of Holland. And others are following in their footsteps. I would recommend any one who cares to read up the progress of library work in Holland to study Miss Snouck-Hürgronje's article on the Dordrecht Public Library, published in the *Library Association Record.* To read it makes a fellow woman librarian proud of her sex.

In 1913 the Council of the Library Assistants' Association, believing that it was necessary to bring the present position of women in library work directly before the notice of the women assistants of the profession, formed a committee. This committee consisted of some of the foremost and enthusiastic women in the profession. It drew up a circular letter embodying the objects of the committee, and endeavouring to show to women assistants the necessity for qualification. The circular pointed out that the women must qualify if the higher positions of the profession in Great Britain were to be open to them. The sole object of the committee was to rouse women to the knowledge that the future of their sex in the profession, was whatever they chose to make it. Over 600 circulars were sent out to the assistants of the United Kingdom, to all those unqualified whose names could be obtained. The circular was well received, and very gratifying were many of the replies. It is known that the committee has accomplished a good work. Curiosity has been aroused, enthusiasm stimulated, and the necessity for qualification in the various branches of library work has been brought before those previously quite ignorant that qualification was necessary or even possible to obtain. Even in large library centres assistants have revealed that they knew nothing of the educational facilities at their disposal; extraordinary as this may appear to the better informed assistant. The activities of the committee have been stopped owing to the war, but although its work was brief much good has resulted.

In an article entitled "Women as Brainworkers," in the *Nineteenth Century* there is a remark on women as librarians. Commenting on the fact that the woman worker to be on a level with the man must do more than he does, the author says that the woman librarian must have a wider range of reading than the man librarian has. That is, to be where he is she must improve on him. If the reason is asked it is simply that the man has attained; the woman has yet to attain. By this I do not mean that the woman librarian must compete against the man librarian. Not at all. That is not the way to achieve success. Men and women are colleagues, not rivals. A woman librarian must regard her male colleague as a fellow-worker, and act accordingly. To aim at the highest, and to get it if she can. The best candidate to secure the best position, irrespective of sex.

There are usually three reasons urged as causes for the lack of enthusiasm of the women assistants for qualification in their work as compared with the men. The apologists urge:—1. Lack of time and facilities for study; 2. Need of money for classes, examination fees, &c.; 3. The probability of marriage, which makes qualification unnecessary. The first two reasons, it is obvious, are equally applicable to men; the third is peculiar to women. These reasons have all the usual grain of truth which all excuses have, but they are, after all, only excuses for something which ought to be done. Much, often too much, is expected at home of women who earn their living outside; too much time taken from leisure moments given to household duties instead of study. The question of the lack of money, too, is highly important. How can a girl, it is argued, earning only a few shillings a week afford the money necessary for the classes, &c.? To this I would reply that the sacrifice of a luxury which seems almost a necessity may be called for, but if qualification is worth having it is worth a little self-sacrifice. It is noticeable, too, that the person who talks loudest about having no money to spend in self-improvement, usually has it, more or less, to waste on self-amusement. As has been remarked, the L.A. certificates are the hall-mark of the qualified assistant. That the librarian of the future must possess them goes without saying. Three excuses: Time, Money, Marriage, these three; but the greatest of these is Marriage. What, it is asked, is the advantage of endeavouring to become qualified if by marriage all time, labour and money spent on it are lost? That is a statement I challenge. No study is ever lost. The woman who has endeavoured to grasp the possibilities of a position in all its fullness cannot by marriage lose the mental grasp and power obtained by such study. Whether she ultimately reaps the full pecuniary benefit or not, she must, it is inevitable, reap the advantage which will accrue to her character by using her mental powers to their utmost.

I believe I have fairly stated the position of women in library work today, and I think the unbiased reader will agree that her status will be decided by herself. By her own work she stands or falls in the future. If in Great Britain by indolence or by adopting the policy of *laissez faire* she remains chiefly the hewer of wood and drawer of water then she will have none to blame but herself. If, on the contrary, she determines to make her way and be ruler as well as subject then she has that also within her grasp. "In nature there are neither rewards nor punishments; there are only consequences." The wise woman will endeavour to qualify herself for a high place. She will work hard. She will protest against the undercutting of man. Such an advertisement as that issued by the Winchester authorities a few months ago is an insult to a qualified woman. If a corporation desires an experienced librarian why should it offer £120 to £150 if a woman is given the position, but £150 to £180 if it is secured by a man? Surely men can see the danger of such an advertisement. Why should not an experienced woman librarian try to obtain the position if she so desires, and yet by no fault of her own, but rather by her virtues, she lowers the financial value of librarianship. As Mr. MacAlister once remarked when discussing this subject, "It is to be hoped that the stale argument in justification of this injustice will not be brought forward that the man may have a family to support as this may just as easily apply to the woman."

Here then is the position of woman in public libraries, present and future. If she takes her position seriously, qualifies for better things, has ambition for higher, who will say that the girl junior assistant of today may not be the woman chief librarian of tomorrow? Not the public, not the men, only herself.

Women Assistants and the War

One result of the present disastrous war is the fact that certain doors in various professions and trades are being opened to women—doors which would otherwise have long remained closed to our sex.

Although we must all regret the cause of the opening of these doors, women cannot regret the effect—the fact that certain advantages must accrue, and in our direction.

In France we hear of women successfully filling positions which have been rendered vacant by the men who have left their work and answered the call of their country—positions which have hitherto been held only by men. As yet, in England, the services of women have not to any great extent been called for but we cannot say what may happen in the near future if some form of compulsory military training calls out still more of our men.

There is unlimited scope today for the capable woman with originality, grit and initiative, for already one sees advertisements for women workers in all branches of work to fill the place of the men who have gone; vacancies for lectureships in colleges where a year or so ago the merits of a woman professor would not have been discussed; vacancies in offices where men only have been employed; vacancies in public libraries, the staffs of which have previously been composed entirely of men.

The women who mean to win through must make up their minds they will be a success by putting their very best into their work; the exercise of tact and understanding, and the necessity for keeping cheerful are some of the means we can employ towards this end, and we must remember that it is the woman with initiative, the woman who does something no one has done before, who gets promotion and who earns the pleasing verdict—"most efficient."

The problem that we are now called upon to face is, that we as women workers are to be put on our trial, and the result of that trial depends on the individual and her work.

For years past women library assistants have been steadily qualifying themselves, only to find in many instances after they have reached a certain point, that the path is blocked to them, and there is no chance of further advance.

One of the chief causes of complaint in our profession has been that the senior positions have invariably fallen to men; the justice or injustice, the truth or untruth, of this statement does not, at the present time, concern us.

Article and letters reprinted with permission *Library World* 17 (January 1915): 197-200.

The most unimaginative of us now admit that when the war is over a great many changes will have taken place, not only nationally and politically, but socially and individually.

It is too early as yet to determine where in the general reorganisation of national life our profession will be; the optimist may foresee brighter days ahead—the pessimist, the end of libraries and librarians for all time.

Who shall say which will prove to be the correct prophet?

But with regard to woman's work there is one thing we can prophesy, and that is, that when the war is over and things are once again straightened out, the library committees who have experienced the services of capable women assistants who have been engaged "for the period of the war" will, as a result of the quality of the work rendered, be unanimous in their desire to retain such services permanently.

There are many ways in which girls can help. A circular letter has been sent by the Secretaries of the Women's Committee to the women members of the Library Assistants' Association asking them by their presence at the meetings of the Association, both in town and the provinces, to fill up the absent places caused by the large number of men of the profession who have answered the call of the flag. If the girls will respond to this appeal and fill up the ranks at the meetings during the coming sessions, when our men return they will find at least one profession in as flourishing a condition as it has ever been, possibly more so. Who can tell?

Another of the many ways in which they can help is by making the library in which they work as cheerful and bright a place as possible to the many harassed and anxious people who may turn to it for relaxation during this time of stress and worry. They may be assured that they will be doing as patriotic a duty as the war poet who is so rampant, or as the women who carry irritating odds and ends of knitting about with them wherever they go. Those who know the reception these poems and discomforts receive will have the added satisfaction of knowing that their work is of use!

There are chances today for the "one talent" assistant.

A small library which the writer know has furnished a good instance of this; a practically unknown member of the staff who has failed to obtain any certificates of the Library Association, has, during the last few months proved to be of great value, entirely owing to the fact that she speaks French fluently.

It will be argued that French is a most ordinary accomplishment, all educated assistants speak French, and so on; but how many of our assistants have been able to converse with ease with the many Belgians who have used our libraries recently?

We are constantly coming across the "Business as usual" phrase—it is a good motto for a public library, and if women will only remember that if they do their best it will be largely through their efforts that the flag of our profession can be kept flying as proudly as ever.

It must be remembered that this is not a time when we must look for material advantages merely, the girl who is out wholly with that idea today will probably find herself as badly off when the war is over, as the man who, for the sake of what he terms his "professional prospects" is hesitating to fulfill his share of the duty he owes to his country.

But remembering the salaries paid to the Mid-Victorian working women and those paid today, we may well be cautious in guessing what are the limits which the future will establish and it is well therefore to stimulate ambition and hopefulness in the junior assistants. They should be reminded that their goal is not such "a long, long way" off as it was even a year ago, that "these are the days of the side car and the one will drive who can best do it"—so learn to drive and teach your juniors.

We have claimed that we are as competent as men and that our work in the library world is as good as that of our male confrères, our claims are now to be tested, it is up to every girl and woman in our profession to show "of what stuff she is made!"

Napoleon's exclamation, "How rare are men!" is still unfortunately true, but the dreary significance of this statement need not hinder library work.

M.F.

LETTERS TO THE EDITOR OF *THE LIBRARY WORLD.*

Sir,—As a woman librarian I should like to express my sympathy, up to a certain point, with M.F.'s article. There is much in it to stimulate us to do our best work and there is good advice in it for those who are in senior positions. Nor can it be anything but right and sensible for us to make the most of our opportunities and to strain every effort to fit ourselves for such duties as we may be called upon to perform. But, whatever happens, we must not lose sight of the services rendered by the men at the front, in almost every case at great personal sacrifice.

When they return to fill the places kept open for them, as we truly hope they may, we want them to feel that women are better able to work side by side with them, each doing whatever is best suited to his or her respective qualifications. Conditions which can bring about a kindly understanding between the men and women who by force of circumstances have to earn a living, must be welcome and to their mutual advantage, and to such conditions we all look forward in the future; if possible at the close of this terrible war.

I am Sir, &c., *A Woman Librarian.*

February, 1915.

Dear Sir,—In the tumult of feeling which the outbreak of war caused throughout the Empire, hundreds of thousands of men, without thought of the check it might mean to their worldly advancement and prosperity, left their work and their offices, and took the oath which would in all probability lead them into terrible danger—perchance to some ghastly death on the field of battle. Let it be granted that the change from the routine and monotony of everyday life and work was pleasant; that the call to arms thrilled the adventure spirit; that some of the men are having the time of their lives; and that, after all, they are only doing their duty. Those who know of something other than the surface gaiety and glory as portrayed in the newspapers, or by the men who are ever-anxious to save their woman folk from a true appreciation of the hardships they undergo, know that doing what is "only their duty" is making men face a strain and horrors which have turned tried and seasoned soldiers into gibbering idiots! Having regard to these things, it is inconceivable that anyone should be found capable of suggesting that the present is a time in which women should strain every nerve to oust and supplant their men competitors in any department of life. It is, I suppose, inevitable that those who are left at home—men as well as women—should meet with professional opportunities which would not have come their way had not the war claimed the other workers; but coldly and deliberately to attempt to occupy permanently places left open by them is to break every rule of fair play. To say that women workers have had to suffer from men's unfairness does not mitigate the offence in the very least. I have sufficient faith in the eternal rightness of things to believe that, should the women of our libraries adopt this attitude of fighting a man when he is down—and that is what it amounts to—their cause would suffer irretrievably, and the day would never dawn when their work would be judged as work and not as the product of a very much cheaper machine than man!

Let them give of their best to their work; let them cheerfully accept more work and longer hours, so that the work of their men colleagues may not be allowed to come to a standstill; let them offer themselves as *voluntary* workers in districts which are too heavily handicapped by the absence of men; let them attend meetings of professional associations, read papers, and take part in debates, so that there shall still be living organizations for the men to come back to. That is the right thing for women as workers to do during the course of the war; that is the thing which the women of France have been doing; that is the thing which the leaders and members of the various woman suffrage and feminist societies have shown that they consider the right thing—the only thing. They have stopped all acts of militancy, all propaganda work, all diatribes against men and their doings.

Let us not be led astray by a chimera!

Olive E. Clarke

Sir,—Napoleon's exclamation, "How rare are men!" is evidently much more true than I thought when I first quoted it. It was the men who first asked me to write the notes for *The Library World;* it is now the men who write or inspire the criticism of my efforts to please them. I commenced by stating that "we must all regret the cause of the opening of these doors." I then wrote the truth. Yet some of your correspondents apparently deny that I was then sincere. Heaven forbid that I should lead any member of the Library Association, or of any other Association, astray—but I am gratified to be referred to as "a fabled fire-breathing monster of Greek mythology, with a lion's head, a goat's body, and a serpent's tail. A horrible and fear-inspiring phantasm, a bogey." This I find is a chimera! Miss Clarke has evidently unintentionally flattered me. A real "Woman Librarian," seems to have correctly interpreted the spirit of my notes. My point is that in most libraries the men have seen to it that the women have not had an opportunity of showing their ability, and I may add in some cases the women have not grasped the opportunity. The opportunity has now arisen, and I was urging women to be sufficiently manlike in their methods to take it. As to dear old Eratosthenes—his ancestor was a grammarian and a philosopher. "How are the mighty fallen!" His descendants have deteriorated—this one cannot make even an inapt quotation from Shakespeare correctly. However, it is apparent that my notes have been of sufficient interest to be read and criticised, and I therefore presume I shall be receiving some acknowledgment for my efforts if only in order to enable me to cover up my "lion's head," or to assist in clothing my "goat's body."

Yours, &c., *M.F.*

Up in Arms

[Here are] two letters unsigned but from two women prominent in library service. Both have made distinct contributions to the up-building of library work in America and have earned the right to express their opinion publicly on the matter of which they speak or any other matter. Moreover, *Public Libraries* thinks their point well taken. If one were justified at any time in saying that library work is "a man's job" it would occur in regard to a library that was in a community of 35,000 men, but there is room even then for women to assist.

The Camp Libraries

The reports from the various quarters where books are being served to the soldiers give much satisfaction to those who have helped make it possible. The situation in all respects is not ideal, but is any situation? As long as poor human nature is of the present grade there will be obstacles to the fulfillment of all our hopes. But in the main, the libraries are taking their place as sources of help and comfort to "our boys" and there is satisfaction in the thought.

The letters from the librarians given in this number show a fine spirit. Others will be given from time to time so that those who are interested will know how the work goes on. It is a great inspiration to be part of so great a movement.

WHY NOT A WOMAN'S AUXILIARY?

Having had considerable experience in "being a woman" and several years' experience in "being a librarian" I am moved to write you regarding the eloquent silence of the Camp Libraries Committee regarding the services to be rendered by women librarians.

After making due allowance for the difficult task the ALA War Service Committee has had in perfecting an organization and the more difficult task of raising the million dollar fund, there would still seem to have been a long enough period elapsed for plans to be formulated and *announced* regarding the most prompt and efficient method of handling the book side of the camp library work. Accepting the fact that the War Department has ruled that women cannot serve within the library buildings in the camps and cantonments, there is still the very large and very important task of selecting, purchasing, and assembling books and preparing the very simple (but necessary) records before the books are really ready for camp use. I believe it is safe to say that in the majority of public libraries in this country such work is done chiefly by women. Why does not the War Service Committee call to its aid representative trained women librarians who are experienced in handling records connected with branches and other methods of distribution in many large public libraries and state traveling library systems? If there has been an

Editorial and letters reprinted from *Public Libraries* 23 (January 1918):22-24.

effort in this direction and there were not sufficient responses, publicity should be given it.

It happens that among my personal acquaintances are three women, who were trained librarians, before their marriages, who have expressed a desire to render patriotic service (without pay) in connection with camp library work; also a number of women now holding important library positions have hoped that opportunity might be offered for them to contribute a period of time in helping in some phase of this vast undertaking, where their skilled library service would be of value.

No one questions the earnest and eager desire of both men and women in the library profession to be of service to their country at this time; and the inclusion of two well-known and competent women librarians on the War Service Committee was logical and accepted as a matter of course. It was, however, equally logical, after the organization was under way, to utilize this majority group of ALA members for definite service in bringing the books to the soldiers. Surely, no one who had part in the campaign for funds but knows how persistently, wholeheartedly and successfully the women librarians labored in season and out of season to reach the quota assigned to each territory.

Possibly there may be some plan on foot for utilizing this available group of skilled workers, in view of the fact that there is a shortage of men librarians, for service. Why should the camp librarians be expected to prepare the books for circulation, when that could be done as well or better at centers elsewhere and the books sent to them ready for use in *real* camp library service with their men. Does the situation indicate that the present plan has been effective? If an auxiliary committee of women librarians would be acceptable to the committee, to work "back of the line" for the camp libraries in these technical capacities, there are scores and, I believe, hundreds of women ready to serve. Why not try it?

"One of the Women."

WOMEN IN LIBRARY WAR SERVICE

From nearly all the camp libraries comes the cry for more help for the actual doing of work and from many of the camps comes the appeal for suggestions and ideas of just what to do, by men who have gone out to take charge.

The ruling of the War Department forbids that women shall work on the inside of the libraries. There are many more effective women library workers than there are men, and if the library boards over the country would treat them in the same way as they have the men, that is allow their salary, and if the government would provide their subsistence, making arrangements for them to live outside the camps if needs be, one would see an impulse and vigor given to the library work in the camps which it must be acknowledged is lacking at the present time.

Would it be unwarranted for the women themselves to organize to carry on where they see things to be done and that are not being done by the men? Miss Addams' story of Betsy Ross and the flag could find a counterpart in the present situation and in camp library service.

A Woman

[The correspondence on this subject must now cease. — Editor.]

PART

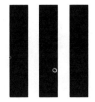

1922-1940
BETWEEN THE WARS

Sex Disqualification

by Marjorie Peacock

The passing of the recent Library Act brings with it the possibility of much development in library work. In addition to the familiar forms of service and extension work which now receive an impetus, certain clauses will result in the establishment of new library areas. It is reasonable to expect, therefore, that there will be a consequent new demand for librarians. This is commonplace and topical speculation. But, apropos, what are the prospects of women workers?

In the history of library labour, we have reached the critical and dangerous point for women when, openly, sex is no disqualification, yet in secret reality it is a most powerful handicap. Perhaps I should be wrong in asserting the general truth of this statement, but I know it to be an absolute fact, in certain quarters, that, when positions fall vacant, a woman's candidature is not considered. Following are the circumstances governing (a) a recent library appointment, and (b) a recent staff regrading.

In case (a) an advertisement was inserted in a paper which is a usual medium for such appointments, notifying a vacancy for an assistant librarian, at so much per annum, and requiring such and such qualifications. My informant intended becoming a candidate for this appointment, but was wisely advised to ascertain first if women candidates were eligible, in order to save a wasted application. She accordingly made the enquiry. This was the reply:— "There is no qualification as to sex. . . . The staff of the department, however, is entirely of men and lads, and I hardly think that the Committee would place a woman in command in present circumstances."

I add no comment, except to emphasise my previous remark as to the danger to women of a situation which neither openly excludes them nor in reality admits them. I would suggest that secret boycott is worse than open boycott; because, whilst identical with the latter in effect, its secrecy disarms criticism. A nice problem arises as to what would be a satisfactory safeguard against secret boycott. Anonymous candidature, on the same principle as that on which the Library Association examinations are conducted, is unsatisfactory. Open candidature permits an appointing body to be influenced by outside knowledge of a candidate's ability—knowledge which has reached it through other channels than the candidate's application. Also, the veil of disguise would be very thin and penetrable in many cases. For example, if candidates were to support their applications by reference to their own published works. Moreover, it is likely that attempts to minimise the chances of disclosure of identity would take the form of an increasing tendency to recognise only examinational certificates as evidence of professional ability.

Reprinted with permission from *Library World* 22 (February 1920):344-346.

Another phase of the sex disqualification problem is shown in case (b). The circumstances are as follows:—Consequent upon the new Library Act, a new staff grading has been put into operation. Within one class there are two employees—one a man, the other a woman. The man has about 18 months seniority of service on the staff, having commenced as a junior assistant under the old grading. He has given three years' voluntary military service. He is a capable and conscientious counter assistant; knows nothing of technical work (i.e., as regards special training or experience); and has hardly done a day's study before, during or since the period of his military service (he has been demobbed about seven months). He holds no L.A. certificates. The woman, on the other hand, was appointed to the library as a senior assistant while he was still on the junior staff. She holds several Library Association certificates. For two years during the war, staff emergencies threw to her lot much of the technical work, unsupervised, including all the classification and cataloguing. Under the new scheme both are graded as technical workers. Very begrudgingly, the woman has been placed on the same financial footing, because of the certificates she holds; but the man attains his financial standing simply because he is a man, and without one call upon his professional credentials. Moreover, he is given seniority of position because of his military service. Trench warfare as a training for librarianship! The whole position bristles with anomalies.

Now, I am a sordid person who works for money rather than love (unlike so many librarians); and if I were in that girl's position I should feel distinctly annoyed. In fact I am annoyed as it is.

The situation is dominated by the old reluctance to agree to equal pay for equal work. It is qualifications *versus* sex; and sex seems to have a good chance of winning. Please understand that I am not claiming respect for the L.A. certificates as such. But what is required of one worker should be required of the other. If the woman has to have certificates, they should be required of the man. If the man's brain and commonsense are sufficient qualification, similar ability in the woman should suffice.

The plea that a man should receive more remuneration for equal work is an old one, and appears to be urged mainly because of his alleged larger expenses in connection with wife, home, etc. Whilst opposing this reason, on principle, I also pause to ask how many bachelors are retained on the financial basis of female employees, because they do not choose to marry? Or how many women with dependents are put on to a male standing because of home expenses?

Unfortunately, the present position is aggravated by the prevailing sentiment in favour of exservice men irrespective of other qualifications. I say "unfortunately." A question of professional status should be decided only by reference to professional ability. The practice of allowing consideration of military service *as such* to influence appointments is professionally unsound and economically unfair.

No. The soldier's satisfactory re-instatement into civil life should be the affair of the authority which wrested him from it. And although private firms may, of course, do as they choose (or as their employees choose) in the matter, public appointments should be made strictly on a professional-capacity basis. By all means, let state, municipal or other funds be earmarked for the purpose of adequately remunerating those who are suffering financial loss owing to the period in which they were involved in the state machine; but let equal work be accorded equal pay, status, and opportunity, irrespective of irrelevant qualifications or sex.

Men versus Women Librarians

It is evident that the ancient city of Winchester does not attach *very* much importance to its public library or to the holder of the office of librarian, or it would not presume to advertise for one who is expected to be "experienced," at the paltry salary of £250 per annum. As if this in itself were not bad enough, the advertisement declares that if the person appointed be a woman, it will be £200 only. If the Winchester City Council really cannot—or will not—pay its librarian more than £250, we hope that it will at least have the self-respect to withdraw the objectionable clause with regard to women, and , if one should be appointed, pay her the extra £50. May we express the further hope that if one of our women members is offered the appointment, she will only accept it on this condition? It will be remembered that a similar course was pursued by the Winchester authorities in 1914, when the salaries offered were £150 and £120 respectively.

In this connection, we are sure that we shall not be misunderstood if we venture to take exception to an Editorial in the October issue of *The Library World*, in which it is suggested that "the library service appeals very strongly to women, and, on the contrary, very little to men of the more able sort. As in America, the best men are not entering the library profession." May we suggest to the editor that the reason lies not so much in the fact that librarianship does not appeal to men as that it is utterly impossible for them to venture or to continue in a profession which offers to a large proportion of its followers, after many years' service, nothing better than some such salary as that to which we have just referred. It is an excellent thing to talk about the ideals of librarianship and about working for the mere love of being associated with fine literature, but these things will not go far towards helping a man to fulfill his duties as a good citizen. If the alleged state of things *is* true, it is no small wonder.

In conclusion, some of us are not made more contented with our lot by this little inference that we are not amongst "the best men" or those "of the more able sort."

Reprinted with permission from *Library Assistant* 15 (November 1921):206-207.

Librarianship as a Career for Women

by Miss W.M. Thorne

Librarianship is not the only career, which, in its infant stages provided employment solely for men. As a matter of fact it seems to be one of the peculiarities of the learned professions in their early years. Architecture, the Law, and the Medical Profession, to name a few that come to my mind, consisted of men only until quite recent days, and when women did begin to creep in, there was, and still is, much prejudice against them. There are very few people who think a woman doctor is as clever as a man, but time will eliminate these opinions, and people will, we hope, have as much confidence in the judgment of the one as the other.

But why *did* the men monopolise the professions? It was through ignorance, in the first instance on the part of our forefathers. They sent their sons to school, but to them it did not seem to matter whether their daughters could read or write, so long as they could do beautiful embroidery and cook a good meal, which arts they learnt presumably, from their mothers.

When the Education Act of 1870 came into force, however, this state of affairs was speedily improved, and from thence-forward, the positions held by women have gradually become more and more important, until *now*, we are well on the way to being recognised as the equals of men in brain power, if not in physical strength. It was the Great War that gave women their opportunity, and I think no one, however unwilling he was to admit the capabilities of women, would say that they did not play their part and prove their worth. It opened up new spheres of employment, and some battles against prejudice having been won, we will take care not to have the fruits of their victories snatched away.

In the Library profession, girls started as junior assistants only. The position was taken with the sole idea of "getting a job," not with the thought of training as a Librarian.

Gradually, however, more responsible posts were given to the extra intelligent, and the number of women employed in Public Libraries increased. Slowly but surely a new vista opened up. The idea of women borough librarians gradually percolated into the minds of existing chiefs, and assistants

Read before Junior Section at Rotherhithe, Dec. 10th, 1924.

Reprinted with permission from *Library Assistant* 18 (January 1925):21-22. Continued (February 1925):33-35.

began to look forward to the time when women should occupy as many of the seats of the mighty as men.

Now, however, very few women enter the profession without the idea of taking it up as a career. A matriculation certificate or its equivalent is essential, and a University Degree is desirable for many reasons, although the years spent in obtaining it are those which are most profitable for getting a practical experience of library routine. The University Course in Librarianship has much the same disadvantages as a degree course—the practical experience is lacking, though in the latter case, of course, there is a good theoretical knowledge. The course for part-time students does not seem to be working out as well as might be hoped, but the University Authorities have asked for information regarding the most convenient time for assistants, with a view, I believe, of trying to make the times of the lectures more suitable.

In one department of the Libraries, women already hold sway. They are installed in nearly every system which has a Children's Section of any pretentions. It is the natural place for women Librarians, although some are much more fitted for the position than others. The mother of a child almost always understands its mind better than the father, and something of the same intuition is present in every woman to a greater or smaller degree. A woman who takes up a position as Children's Librarian must be in love with her job. She must go round and help the little ones choose their books, and recommend to them the better authors. She must be friendly enough to invite their confidence, but must never lose her dignity, or the Library would soon be turned into a beer garden. Yes, a Children's Librarian must be able to do all these things—or else fail to achieve success in her calling.

I would next ask you to consider the question, "Will librarianship ever become a profession for women only?"

Personally I do not think this is at all likely to come about, nor do I think it necessary for making Librarianship wholly satisfactory as a career for women. There are library systems in England run entirely by women, but they are in a very small minority and I see no reason why the percentage should be increased. But I do think that the number of libraries employing men only, should be decreased, and decreased considerably, in fact eliminated altogether. Any library system which employed girls during the war and is now replacing them as they leave, by boys, is I think, taking a distinctly backward step. Thus there does not seem to be any tendency in the direction of making Librarianship a career solely for women, as nursing, nor do I think it necessary, as I said before, in order that it should become a good profession for women to enter.

At present librarianship is not so lucrative as some other professions, although the position now is much better than it was before the removal of the penny rate. As librarians become better educated, the rate of remuneration should increase in a similar proportion, although public opinion will play a large part in that desired improvement. When we ourselves have educated the masses up to realizing that librarianship is as much a skilled profession as doctoring, then we shall have achieved something, and our salaries are sure to increase.

Now having said something about the prospects before us, I will turn, with your permission, to the kind of women most suitable for the career. I have dealt with the special qualities desirable for a Children's Librarian, but they were, for the most part extra to those ordinarily required.

She should be studious, or interest in books and their classification and cataloguing would soon flag. She should be patient, to explain the methods of procedure, and catalogues to simple people. She should be understanding, to be able to gather from a few broken sentences the needs of the person, and sympathetic, to help them in difficulties. A good memory saves much time in "looking up" information while common sense is absolutely invaluable. The faculty for doing neat, tidy and accurate work is one well worth developing as it makes the work of others easier in many respects. A librarian is not encouraged to put all his energies into his work by the thought that if the issues go up his salary will be increased. In a library are housed the Ideals of hundreds of men and women. It is our place to help people to read and understand these matters. We must lend a hand willingly, out of the goodness of our hearts. The libraries are for the benefit of the people, and the librarian must willingly and cheerfully help people to find any information that is wanted.

We have before us a better outlook than any of our predecessors. The scope of librarianship is broadening wonderfully. Most large firms, and all the newspapers of any consequence, have special libraries, and the number is constantly increasing. These libraries must all have a librarian of some sort, and as time goes on, it is to be hoped that properly trained persons will be appointed.

The number of county library schemes too, is rapidly increasing, and women are as suitable for the post of county librarian as men. These schemes, once begun, will never end, but will most assuredly extend in all directions so that assistant county librarians will be needed.

It is up to us to take hold of every slight opportunity that presents itself, not only to improve our own positions, but those of our successors. We have benefitted by the pioneer work done by those who went before, let those who are yet to come, benefit by our work.

Women in College Libraries

by J.I. Wyer

There are in my mail to-day letters from three able, experienced women occupying subordinate but responsible positions in three medium-sized college libraries. All are college graduates. All have received the best library training the country affords. The three hold seven academic degrees. Their ages are thirty, thirty-six and forty-five. All have been continuously engaged in library work since graduating from library school. Two of them are assistant librarians; of these one has never had an active professional chief and has been practically the sole administrator for years. The third is the head of an important department. Each is happy in her present environment, and to my personal knowledge the work of all three is satisfactory to their librarians and college authorities.

In one case the college policy discriminates against women in the matter of salary. In another (where the nominal professor-librarianship is vacant) it seems that no woman will ever be made librarian, and the present assistant, having been practically librarian for years, very properly feels reluctant to continue in her present position under a new man who may or may not be a trained librarian. In the third case the writer knows that she is equal to an independent post, and seeks facts as to her chances for getting it, among college libraries.

These letters raise slightly different aspects of what is at bottom one large question. The writers seek facts and perspective as to the general outlook, rather than advice on individual situations. Undeniably for a generation men have been displacing women as librarians of college libraries, and this has been so noticeable within the last five years as fully to warrant misgiving and uncertainty among women who are ambitious and competent to fill such posts.

The following are some of the facts. Within my own experience, men have replaced women as librarians at Northwestern, Chicago, Kansas, Nebraska, Illinois, Iowa, New Hampshire, and within the past two years at Syracuse, Ohio, Delaware, Pomona. This list might easily be enlarged. I can recall instantly four college libraries where women under professorial librarians have carried the technical and internal administration of the library with such competence as to suggest their ability to run it outright but have been denied this opportunity in favor of men. A review of the most important college libraries now run by women shows that while women are holding their own in the

Reprinted with permission from *School and Society* 29 (February 16, 1929):227-228.

women's colleges, in colleges for men or coeducational institutions they are represented, with very few exceptions, only in small, relatively unimportant institutions.

For years in library placement work I urged both public and college library authorities to take women who could be strongly recommended, instead of men, and on the ground that appeals most to trustees and presidents, that they would get more for their money. But beyond this argument, true as it is, there is the broader one of essential justice in rendering equal pay for equal work. Success in persuading library authorities that the best women are equal to important independent positions was not very encouraging. Those doing most library placement work in this country can cite numbers of cases where men not only of limited library experience but of no library experience or training have been chosen before women of unquestioned ability, professional training and pertinent experience. In the face of these facts, the writers of my three letters can scarcely be encouraged actively to seek new positions or to resign subordinate places with confidence that their experience and abilities will commend them to the independent posts they desire.

The main purpose of this letter is to draw the attention of appointing officers of colleges and universities to a neglected yet thoroughly competent and reasonably plentiful source of library personnel. I am also a bit curious as to the reasons for such consistent male preference. I have never heard one given. Refuge is always taken in the downright statement, "We must have a man," uttered as though that somehow settled the matter. It has always seemed surprising that the library should so long continue to be the sole academic exception to the educational policy of choosing for the head of specialized departments those with special training for and experience in the work they are called to do.

Problems: A Monthly Department of Discussion

Should the Preponderance of Women in the American Library Profession Be Considered an Evil?

A provocative letter, from an English library worker, raises an issue that should provide the stimulus for an interesting (and fervent) discussion. Bluntly stated, the issue is: Should the preponderance of women in the American library profession be considered an evil? What do *you* think? (We hope that some of our male librarians will participate in this discussison.) The letter from England reads:

Dear Sir:

As an outlook differing from most of your readers may possibly be acceptable, I should like to remark on one point concerning American librarianship — gleaned, I must admit, chiefly from the pages of your admirable monthly.

I do think it is regrettable that the profession in America is so largely in the hands of the "gentler sex." To my mind this is incorrigible.

Most of the world's literature has been made by men, and I feel it is in many ways better interpreted by men. The number of women holding senior posts in libraries in this country is negligible, tho for the purely routine work young women are largely employed. But it would seem that, unless the men are not so vocal as the women in the pages of your *Bulletin*, most of the ordinary libraries in the United States are run by the female sex.

Now in this country an inquirer would certainly have much less confidence in a woman, because — thru prejudice or otherwise — it is generally felt the feminine acquaintance with literature of all types is not so comprehensive. As a rule, over here at any rate, a man is generally wider read. Natural curiosity, not mere necessity causes this. Therefore an assistant who has to rely upon a reference book for opinion and information regarding the contents of the world's great books, technical and otherwise, i.e., Darwin or Dickens, cannot converse or instill the same confidence as one who has personal knowledge of the book or books concerned. Again the difference in outlook is most marked — and necessarily so. Can a woman appraise or understand the library requirements of men? Is the preponderance of American borrowers male or female? Yet I should assume in the pres-

Excerpts reprinted by permission from the December 1933 (230-231) and March 1934 (403-407; 409) issues of the *Wilson Bulletin for Librarians.* Copyright © 1933 and 1934 by the H.W. Wilson Company.

ent state of affairs men's library requirements are administered thru the channel of the feminine librarian!

And the fact that the profession has largely become a feminine one has had an adverse effect upon its rightful status—because indisputably the status must be judged by men, who adopt a masculine outlook as a criterion.

Why has the profession become a feminine one in the States? It is certainly not so in this country. Are American men only interested in and attracted towards salesmanship and advertising? Or have libraries grown up piece-meal without adequate financial support sufficient to provide remuneration consistent with the needs and demands of America's most enterprising young men?

I hasten here to add I have no wish to disparage or depreciate the work performed by the large numbers of competent women librarians, or such people as the Editors of the I.A.I., *so far as purely routine jobs are concerned*, but it is in the question of contact where I feel the value of a male librarian is made manifest. Indeed, many of the questions on the more technical topics propounded in libraries in this country would never be gone into by an inquirer confronted by a woman.

Perhaps, however, the service rendered in this country is vastly different from that in the States. Circulation statistics—in fact any statistics—are not held in very high esteem by those over here who look upon library service as something more than the dispensing of fiction to the greatest number.

Until America becomes conscious that her feminized Library Service is not good enough—that is, it is now only scratching on the surface of the world of books—I fear the present short-sighted attitude of ruthless economy will continue. Men must meet and deal with men in questions of appropriations.

S.H. Sanders
Harrow-on-the-Hill

There you have it! We repeat the issue raised by our overseas correspondent: Should the preponderance of women in the American library profession be considered an evil?

RESULTS

Three of the four prize-winning letters this month are written by mere males. (A tie for third place accounts for the extra prize.) Perhaps the ladies were embarrassed by being put on the defensive. At any rate, whatever the merits of this controversy may be, the men demonstrated their wish and right to be heard by writing letters of superior grace, acuteness, and conviction. Do the answers prove anything? Probably not: except the personal reactions of the authors. Nevertheless, one detects in a good many of the letters an undercurrent of feeling that perhaps the entrance of more men into the American library profession would be a welcome phenomenon . . . even to the women! As one of our correspondents emphatically exclaims, "Who's stopping them?" In these times of general low wages and no-wages, it can hardly be contended that the modest salaries of librarians explain the reluctance of young men to study librarianship.

First Prize
Arnold K. Borden
University of Pennsylvania

There is something dangerously explosive about this subject. And when one is led on by fellow staff members to taking the anti-feminine side, can he be banned for trying at the last minute to pull the dynamite out of the fire and beat a hasty, even if traitorous, retreat? For after all, that women librarians need no justification or apology will have incontestable proof in the over-whelming preponderance of briefs that will be received in their support in this controversy.

In fact, it is the occasion of no little surprise that this question should even be raised in our year of grace. Who is it that for so long has carried the light of learning into the tea parlor to maintain our social prestige and bring back topics of throbbing contemporary interest? Who is it that smiles indulgently on the timid college boy when he inadvertently makes for the door with the *World Almanac* under his arm? Who is it that master-minds the catalog and gets the works of Sax Rohmer correctly entered under A.S. Ward? And who is it finally that brushes aside little routines from time to time for the public good yet always contrives to keep our pins separate from our paper-clips, to keep incoming interlibrary loan books listed on blue cards, outgoing on yellow?

It is not to be supposed, however, in giving answer to these rhetorical questions that the genius of women librarians is confined to mere detail. The only suggestion that women do not shine as executives is apt to come from women themselves and one can readily detect the gallantry of their *noblesse oblige* attitude. There is no denying the great strides forward that have been taken under feminine organizing direction in such matters as the proper arrangement of pamphlet collections, the great development of clipping systems, and the application of the vacuum cleaning principle to the hygiene of book-stacks. Altho men can boast a Melvil Dewey only now and then, the genius of the Eternal Feminine is always with us hard at work bringing public understanding into line with the newest cataloging techniques, or devising new explanations for the long sojourn at the bindery of all the periodicals we happen to want.

The most serious problem confronting the library profession today is the large annual loss thru matrimony of so much feminine talent. If any weakness must be admitted in women librarians, it is the possession of qualities which make them such an easy prey to masculine blandishment and sophistry. For the library has special need of the emotional equilibrium which is so characteristic of feminine library staffs until men stride thru the door. And one might pause here in tribute to the mighty efforts made by women to build up library morale. How eloquently and touchingly many of them have written on the subject of *esprit de corps!* Finally, but not least, one should consider the roguish nature of men with whom they have to contend. If proof is needed, it may as well be admitted that even the writer is accused by his twelve-year old nephew of being a "rascal."

And so the circle moves full round as we who set forth to battle the Amazons remain to applaud our victors, suspecting that our only weapon in the finale will be a Cupid's bow.

Second Prize
J.H. Shera
Miami University
Oxford, Ohio

Should the preponderance of women in the American library profession be considered an evil? You may expect me to say "No." — I say "Yes." Such a blunt affirmation, far from being the product of a misogynic spirit, is neither the outgrowth of any conviction concerning the innate superiority of the male—for such dogma the writer holds no brief. But the overt truth of the psychological differences between man and woman cannot be denied; emotionally, temperamentally, spiritually they differ as night from day—yet both are equally essential to complete social unity.

It is indeed banal to prate of the feminization of American culture, tho the too frequent iteration of this vapid truism in no way belies the fact. It ramifies thruout our entire educational system; from the cradle to college the average child's entire cultural contacts are predominately feminine—small wonder that in after years, as a prosperous business man, he inevitably associates women with books and is content to leave the pursuits of literature to his wife. In all this the library profession is but one aspect of our entire social pattern so that reform, if it be forthcoming, must include public education in its entirety.

Inevitable product of woman's newfound economic freedom, the young girl seeking independence has turned to the library and the classroom for the simple reason that there was no place else to go. Even so sanely conservative a writer as Arthur E. Bostwick laments this state of affairs and admits that it is a "pity that the masculine point of view has not oftener been available in this kind of selection" (the selection of children's books). The remedy for all this— open the doors of other careers, business, commerce, finance to the women, and both these and the educational professions would profit thereby. Or, if one be a confirmed Hitlerite or is worried about the falling birth rate, a bachelor tax might be efficacious.

But at best all this is without the pale of the librarian's influence. What can the profession do itself to remedy this state of affairs within its own ranks? The relief is as simple as it is direct: raise the standards of librarianship—to force out the mediocre women?—no—to attract the better men. Require that librarians be true bibliographers; distinguish sharply between true librarians and book-handlers and thus raise salaries, for if librarians would make themselves worth more money they would get more pay. Take the women out of the libraries and put them in responsible political positions and doubtless they will raise library tax appropriations thru their legislative influences.

Mr. Sanders, viewing the English situation from the rarefied heights of Harrow-on-the-Hill, blandly asserts that the English have less confidence in the literary judgments and abilities of women—this from the land of George Eliot and Virginia Woolf, not to mention Fanny Burney and "the immortal Jane." It may well be that the British have erred as far on the side of masculinity as we have gone to the other extreme.

Culture is the complete and harmonious development of *all* the faculties that go to make up the beauty and the strength of human life. It is not to be administered by either sex to the exclusion of the other. The sooner the library profession realizes the need for the injection of more male blood and reorganizes its structure accordingly the sooner will be realized the cultural ideals of Matthew Arnold.

Third Prizes (tie)
"Reuben" from Ohio

Mr. Sanders shrewdly guesses that the higher places in American (presumably public) libraries are over-Rachaelized. Space is lacking to discuss the causes of this condition beyond saying that they are primarily economic, aggravated by Rachael's inclination to perpetuate her own regime.

Rachael often makes good as an executive—exceedingly good—perhaps at an excessive cost. But she succeeds not chiefly thru her femininity, but thru general qualities like breadth, courage, idealism, and managerial capacity which occur at least equally—some of them oftener—in men of corresponding character and education. Distinctively feminine traits handicap perhaps as often as they help her, for example:

Rachael (as Rachael) is notoriously personal and short on objectiveness. Hence, she tends to take criticism hard, inclining either to resent or to over-accept it. She will sometimes indulge in animosities with her sisters which are amusing—or exasperating—but which complicate life on a staff. Her emotionalism can be a great nuisance. She is rather prone to accept authority uncritically, as of book reviewers, and to be carried away by fads.

Rachael likes concrete situations better than general ideas, which is well enough until she needs the light of such an idea in handling a situation. Ideas themselves she adopts rather than originates. She prefers expedients to principles. She is less interested in management than disturbed by the results of poor management. Blue prints and mechanical contriving are out of her line.

Rachael rarely comprehends the interests and standpoint of men readers. She may accept them on faith and do her valiant best to meet them. As head of a large library, she may have a man or two on her staff to run a technical or business section. But even in the large library, the male public suffers; and in the small, it may be forgotten.

Rachael's scholarship—or interest in it—is apt to be sketchy. By "scholarship" I mean not simply a college education and the reading habit, but wide, solid, reasoned information and desirably a living interest in some branch of knowledge for its own sake. The pleasant general reading including much fiction, which Rachael favors, makes her an agreeable conversationalist but no pundit.

At the risk of injustice, I have emphasized the disabilities of Rachael as executive. I have ignored her intelligence, adaptability, conscientiousness, and the special qualities which fit her so admirably for children's and school library work. By such means, a case could be made against men as librarians, and pointed with embarrassing examples.

After all, the problem of man or woman for a given post is largely a matter of individuals, only *all* the requirements and probable emergencies of the position must be considered. It is of serious public and professional concern that a calling which offers so many opportunities for the diverse and complementary gifts of both men and women and which must serve the peculiar needs of each, should be nearly monopolized by either.

Ruth Hyatt
Hartford, Connecticut

It is quite possible that I do not agree with Mr. Sanders that the preponderance of women in American libraries is an evil, because I am a woman. It is also possible that I may have good reasons for disagreement.

It is admitted that women are employed for the purely clerical and routine work in libraries in both England and America. As it is not necessary to discuss them, we will be concerned only with persons in responsible and important positions who care for the needs of the public users of libraries.

I wonder if it is not the attitude of the Englishman toward women which may account for Mr. Sanders' dilemma? For a much longer time women have been accepted on an equal basis with men in America. In business, in politics, in community life, in education, American women have grown into an acknowledged place. In America it is the women who have cultivated the taste for literature, for intellectual achievement, and kept alive and vital the borrowed culture of a European background. For three hundred or more years the men in this country have been too much concerned with the spread of industry, establishment of new business, development of natural resources, the stock market, and chain stores to be bothered overmuch with the satisfying of intellectual curiosity.

After the pioneering and population problem seemed to be holding its own, the women of this country turned their stimulated energy toward the education of the new members of a new country and have persistently fostered the culture that came as a heritage with our English forefathers. With the increasing number of educated women wishing to earn a living it seems quite natural that many should enter the library profession which, as a profession, is certainly cultural.

Mr. Sanders practically accuses us of having libraries inferior to those in England. I cannot argue from first-hand information, but I strongly suspect that the basis for his opinion is laid on his apparent contempt for woman's intelligence and what he reads in the papers. I doubt very much that an inquirer would, in this country, have less confidence in a woman than a man librarian. "Can a woman appraise or understand the library requirements of men?" asks our English skeptic. I believe that the answer is an emphatic, "Yes." Women are more naturally sympathetic and patient interpreters of individual tastes and therefore are better able to be of service to both men and women. Women have long had the confidence of both men *and* women in many fields beside the home. Particularly have they contributed to the maintenance of a national culture and the fostering of intellectual thought.

Women have made our libraries. While men are not negligible in the history of the growth of American libraries, women also have had the educational advantages and intellectual development capable of maintaining a high standard. I cannot compare the standards with those of England, for I do not know its libraries, but I assume that the demand on its service may be somewhat different or Mr. Sanders would not be in such error. We in America may not have the *scholarly* institutions but we keep a high level for the kind of need which the library fills in the cities and communities of this country; a need for recreational reading, practical reference work, and student research. Women have shown themselves intelligent and understanding in their cultural background and sympathetic interpretation, and competent to cope with the executive problems which are a considerable consequence. That the men, whom Mr. Sanders wishes to see in our libraries, are satisfied with the work of women as librarians, as heads of reference work, technical and business departments, and as readers' advisors, is certainly an indication of confidence. One must not be confused by the "lady librarian" of not so many years past, to whom a library position was a solace for a broken heart or thwarted desires. That evil has vanished and women are now educated to the positions of capable librarians who give satisfactory and thoroughly scholarly competence to their work. If women have accomplished all this; have helped to raise and strengthen the basic working standards of libraries; to give wise and intelligent thought to needful inquirers, courteous and sympathetic service to the public, and capable direction to the functions of public libraries; they cannot be considered an evil in the American library profession.

Librarianship—
Stop-Gap or Profession?

by Stewart W. Smith

There is much talk these days among governmental administrators and students of political economy of the necessity for "career" government service. It is being recognized that if there is to be an efficient personnel administering the public business that personnel must be recruited not only from the ranks of those who are adequately prepared but also from among people who intend to make a *life* work of the job in question. As a result, numerous books and articles have appeared stressing this need and the last few years have witnessed the growth of a school of thought which even goes so far as to advocate the creation, in our universities, of departments whose avowed purpose it would be to train people specifically for the government service.

Certainly, if there is truth contained in these arguments, that truth is applicable to the library as well as to other branches of the public service. Insignificant as we are numerically in comparison with other groups of public employees it is, nevertheless, important that we should fall in line and improve our service and personnel thru the adoption of this ideal.

A STEPPING STONE TO MATRIMONY?

As a matter of fact, a close scrutiny of many of our professional ills leads inevitably to the conclusion that they have their roots in a too prevalent tendency among librarians to use their work as a stop-gap rather than as a career. At the risk of inviting the wrath of most women librarians it must be said that they are the most flagrant examples of this tendency to use library work as a stepping stone—usually to a career of matrimony.

Unfortunately the library profession is dominated numerically by women—young women whose intention it is to marry and who at best expect to remain librarians for only a few years. Theirs is, in the majority of cases, a stop-gap philosophy which says in essence, "My salary is low, it is true. I could wish it were more adequate, but after all it is sufficient for the present and soon I shall be married and then it will make no difference. What do I care about improving economic conditions or advancing the profession generally? I am here because I must be doing something, because I don't like school teaching and because I do like books."

Writers of books on vocational guidance and librarians themselves in tones of humility point out that ours is the world's most poorly paid profession. The ALA compiles devastating statistics comparing librarians' salaries with those of teachers and adds further conviction, if any is necessary, of our shameful economic state.

There are numerous reasons why such a condition continues to exist. There is the lack of public appreciation of the librarian's value to the community and there is our failure to promote this appreciation thru adequate publicity. There is the traditional attitude which proclaims the librarian as an exalted idealist with a "calling" into whose scheme of life no preoccupation with things mundane can be permitted entrance. There is the ever present shortage of library funds which has made necessary economies almost resulting in penury and a tendency to devote as much of the available cash as possible to the purchase of reading matter in an effort to promote the library rather than the financial well-being of its employees.

All these factors are involved in the librarian's failure to receive adequate recognition. But there is another condition, embracing to some extent these others and far more potent than they, which explains our general inability to progress as we should. This condition is our collective disinclination to try to remedy the situation. There are exceptions, of course, but the vast majority of librarians are seemingly unwilling to take any active part in a program tending to advance their status in any way.

The above is not in any sense intended as a blanket denunciation of either women librarians or the marriage institution. Any intelligent person will readily admit that women librarians have in the past and still are doing excellent work and making important contributions to the library profession. However, the fact remains that so long as people enter library work with the idea that within a few years they will be out of it, the profession on the whole will suffer and fail to make the progress it should. Obviously, if one does not intend to be employed in a given position for more than a short time, he is not apt to be much concerned with what the status of that position will be in the future.

RECRUIT MORE MEN!

What is the answer? Being a man I hesitate to express my convictions for fear of being accused of masculine jealousy or of being anti-feminist generally. Nevertheless, it seems true, if the foregoing premises are sound, that before librarianship can assume a rank in any way comparable to that of the other learned professions, there must be, first of all, a recruiting of more men to the ranks. This because, in most instances, men will be more apt to stay in library work thruout their lives, and hence will be intensely interested in seeing both the economic and professional status of library work advanced.

How such a result is to be brought about, it is difficult to say. In fact, upon examination the whole problem assumes the aspect of the vicious circle. There are few men in the library profession because salaries are too small to offer inducements to them to enter it, and salaries are small because there are few men in the library profession. The situation may be compared with the teaching profession, which in past centuries was largely the province of men but which was deserted and used as a stop-gap by them because of greater financial inducements in other lines of endeavor and because of the lack of prestige enjoyed by teachers. The result was that teaching, especially in the United States, became more and more the work of women because they were able and satisfied to work for less financial return than were men. Later as our school system expanded, and as men again became active in the teaching profession and the teachers became strongly organized and maintained powerful lobbies, their conditions improved and more and more men have been induced to make teaching their life work.

The history of librarianship is essentially the same. In early times before women generally were afforded the educational opportunities they have today librarians were always men. Then, because of the increased learning made possible thru feminine emancipation, and the development of the public library movement in this country, women became increasingly active in the library profession, both because it was a type of work admirably suited to their abilities and tastes and because they could be employed more cheaply than men.

Such is the present status of the library profession. What the future holds it is, of course, impossible to say. Certain tendencies, however, are apparent. Due to the depression and its accompanying shortage of opportunity and because prospective male librarians have been assured that library work held possibilities for them, there has been a gradual increase in the number of men engaged in library work. Whether or not these men will stay in the profession and others enter it if, and when, the depression lifts, and opportunities in other lines of work offer themselves, depends largely on whether library salaries can be sufficiently advanced to make it possible for men to live decently and to provide for families on their earnings.

"CAREER" LIBRARIANS NEEDED

The question is not whether men will *want* to stay but whether they will be able to do so. As long as a social system prevails in which men occupy the role of providers and women that of home-makers, any talk of equal pay for men and women doing the same work is ridiculous. It is obviously impossible for men to support themselves and their families on the same amount of money that it would cost a single woman without dependents to live. The only just way to solve the problem of comparative salaries of men and women is on the basis of their relative needs.

In addition to the encouraging of men to enter library work, there must be the inculcation among both men and women in the profession of a consciousness of their duty not only to themselves, but to the profession and to those who will be library workers in future years. Even those who use library work merely as a stop-gap must be willing, for the sake of their fellow workers, to make some effort toward the advancement of librarianship if that profession is to flourish and progress.

We *must* have "career" librarians. Library administrators, if they have the best interests of their profession at heart, must adopt long-time plans having as their objective the building up of staffs of workers who intend to be librarians, not for one year or for three, but for their entire lifetimes. Only thus, with librarians aware of their collective needs, striving consciously to satisfy them and making united effort toward professional improvement can our work assume its rightful significance in the eyes of the world and we obtain our merited due of economic adequacy and professional prestige.

The Weaker Sex?

Our attention has been called recently to a problem presented by the Secretary of the American Library Association to the Executive Board and the Board of Education for Librarianship in regard to the scarcity of qualified candidates for administrative positions in public and college libraries. Among the proposed solutions for this problem, several of our readers feel that there has been an undue emphasis placed on recruiting young men for these positions.

In recent years there has been a good deal of unfavorable comment (off the record) on the fact that whenever a position which pays over $3,600 presents itself young men, perhaps of unproved ability, are invariably recommended and pushed, when there may be far more capable women available. In view of the fact that good business opportunities for women in other fields are becoming increasingly available, it seems that the library profession is going backward when it practically closes the doors of its best positions to women. If this trend is allowed to continue, it will become increasingly difficult to attract (and retain) capable young women to the profession, and it will by no means follow that young men of equal or less ability will come in to take their places. As probably 80 to 90 percent of the members of this profession in America are composed of women, hasn't the time come to do something about it, at least, to discuss it openly among ourselves?

Is the library profession to follow that of the teaching profession and have practically all administrative positions filled by men? Are young, ambitious, and intelligent women going to enter into a profession in which the highest they can aspire to is head of a department in a large system or librarian of a small public library? The following figures may, perhaps, be worthy of your deliberation: (1) The 1937-38 Executive Board of the American Library Association consists of thirteen members, four of whom are women; (2) The Council has nineteen women representatives out of a membership of sixty-three; and (3) According to the appointments of current year accredited library school graduates, listed in the November 15, 1937 issue of *The Library Journal,* eighty-six men entered the field as compared to seven hundred and eighty-three women. Is this proportion comparable?

Perhaps you are one of the many who has puzzled over or discussed this problem with other members of the profession over a luncheon, a dinner, or en route to or from a meeting place. If you are, we invite you to continue your discussion in the "Readers' Open Forum" of this magazine which has always taken the lead in encouraging discussion of professional questions in its pages. Opinions pro and con on all subjects, particularly this one, are welcome.

Editorial and selected letters reprinted from *Library Journal* 63 (March 15, 1938):239; (April 15, 1938):294-296; (May 1, 1938):342-343; (June 1, 1938):438; (August 1938):569. Published by R.R. Bowker Co., a Xerox company. Copyright © 1938, by Xerox Corporation.

IN REPLY TO "THE WEAKER SEX?"

It is with considerable reluctance that I comment on the editorial in the issue for March 15, 1938 entitled "The Weaker Sex?", as it seems unfortunate that librarians should have come to be considered on any other basis than their professional competence. But since the question has been raised and since the implication of the editorial seems to be that the A.L.A. is officially considering the question of supply and demand of librarians on the basis of whether they are men or women, rather than basing it entirely on professional competence, then the discussion seems decidedly to be in order.

The question is particularly important to those connected with library schools, for if the policy is accepted and the trend continues for administrative positions to be filled by men, then library schools will be put in a very difficult position; for if they are perfectly honest with prospective women students they will have to tell them the limitations of employment with the result that many of the most desirable recruits will pause before they enter a profession that accepts such discriminations.

The editorial suggests comment on several points and provokes questions on others. First, on the evidence of the record, it seems a fair statement to observe that women have given a very good account of themselves as administrators. Why then has this sudden doubt developed as to the administrative ability of women? Reference is made to the "scarcity of qualified candidates for administrative positions in public and college libraries." This makes one wonder whether women have become responsibility shy or whether they have not been given the opportunity to be considered for these positions or whether our methods for discovering and making known good administrative material are deficient. There must be a considerable number of young women who have been maturing in administrative positions as assistant librarians or heads of departments or even as librarians of smaller colleges and public libraries who are ready for the larger responsibilities suggested.

One wonders also if the employer always specifies that he is seeking a man for these administrative positions, and again one wonders whether, even if he does specify a man, he has his attention called to the fact that very competent women librarians are available — some even who may have qualifications superior to those of the men available. It is on record that in at least one case where a college president wrote to a library school asking for a man librarian, the head of the school sent recommendations of available young men and, at the same time, sent the recommendation of a young woman with the statement that she was better qualified than any of the men suggested. The result was that the woman was appointed and has made a brilliant administrator. It should be recorded also in this connection that some of the leading men in the profession have expressed dissatisfaction with the tendency for only the younger men in the profession to be considered for the better administrative positions.

As to the composition of the Executive Board and the Council of the American Library Association, a further analysis of the membership brings out some interesting facts regarding nominations, elections, etc., and suggests many questions.

An analysis of the membership of the present Executive Board shows that, while four of the members are women, there was opportunity for choice between a man and a woman for five of the other places and a man was elected. For the other four places there was no opportunity given for choice between men and women, only men being put in nomination. Thus, women had the opportunity to have nine places out of thirteen on the present Executive Board where they now have four.

Similarly, as regards the twenty-five elected members of the Council, there are now fourteen men and eleven women composing this group. An analysis of the nominations shows that of the fourteen places filled by men, women had an opportunity to be elected to twelve of them. Thus, women have had the opportunity to be elected to twenty-three of the twenty-five elective places on the Council, where they have been elected to eleven places.

If women feel that their representation on the Executive Board and in the Council is not in proportion to their membership in the A.L.A., they might do well to ponder these figures.

An analysis of the membership of the Nominating Committee and of the nominations and elections over the last ten year period gives further food for thought.

With one exception, the chairman of the Nominating Committee for the past ten years has been a man. The membership has been evenly divided, that is, the men have been in the majority five years and the women five years. However, the women seem to have had better breaks when the women were in the majority. A woman was elected president two of the years when the women had a majority and a woman was elected president the one year when a woman was chairman, though the women were not in the majority as to members. Altogether, for the five years when women were in the majority, the names of forty-three women were put in nomination, while for the five years when men were in the majority, the names of thirty-three women were put in nomination.

Women do not seem to have come off very well in opportunities for the higher offices for the ten year period. Only three women have been permitted to be president in the decade. The word "permitted" is used advisedly for on one occasion when a suggestion of a very distinguished woman librarian for president was sent to the chairman of the Nominating Committee, he replied that sufficient time had not elapsed since the last woman was president for another to be considered, that it would be at least another year before a woman could again be considered for president!

In the case of the first vice-president there have been seven men and three women in the period. When the men were elected, there was no choice as between men and women in five cases, while in the two cases where there was a choice, the man was elected. In the three cases where women were elected, the choice was between women candidates.

As second vice-president, there have been five men and five women. In the two cases where there was a choice between men and women, a man was elected once and a woman once.

A check on the chairmen of boards and committees for the ten-year period shows that approximately 400 chairmen have been men as against approximately 200 women chairmen.

To summarize for the ten years, the names of 118 men have been put in nomination for elective positions and sixty-eight have been elected, while the names of seventy-six women have been put in nomination and forty-three have been elected.

From this analysis of the record, it appears that it is reasonable to feel that more women should be nominated for the elective offices, particularly for the office of first vice-president, which now carries with it the nomination for the presidency. They may not be elected, for it is evident that on whatever basis the women members make their choices among candidates it is not on the basis of sex—nor would anyone advocate that it should be—but at least the opportunity for election should be given, and let them be elected or not according to the will of the membership.

—Tommie Dora Barker,
*Dean, Library School of
Emory University*

My opinion on the editorial in the March 15 issue of *The Library Journal* is that I dislike to have a woman chosen for a position because she is a woman, except where that fact means that she can render more efficient service than a man. The examples are obvious, that of a children's librarian is a case in point.

On the other hand, I believe that there are many positions in which a man can render this more efficient service, for example, in some college or public library. A man can go to men's organizations as a member, not just a speaker. He is welcome to join discussions in hotel or dormitory rooms, at a smoker, or a men's "get-together." Matters of policy are often settled before the matter comes to formal action in a committee. Since a woman has ability and training equal to a man, the conventions and traditions may be the factors which weight the scales in his favor.

I do not believe that an outstanding woman should not have a chance for a good library position unless a man would fit in better and be more useful there. This does not mean that all administrative positions should be filled by men.

—Florence R. Curtis,
Director, Hampton Institute Library School

Now that the feminine constituency of our profession has been invited to discuss openly the present policy of favoring the appointment of young men to administrative positions in public and college libraries, leaving perhaps as the highest attainment for women the position of department head, it is well that we do attempt a prompt consideration of the situation. The future of the young assistant who aspires to high places, who possesses the ability and the training for it, is indeed an uncertain one. It is not plausible to consider that young women of ability who can succeed in other fields will be attracted to such a situation.

The problem as I see it must be approached from three angles: that of the trustees, that of the committees and boards dealing with grants-in-aid to librarians, and that of the librarians already in the profession. Viewing the nation as a whole, we find that library boards and trustees are predominantly men, particularly those of the large library systems. They prefer to search the country over for a man, excellent or mediocre, old or young, to whom to give the librarianship of their particular system, in preference to considering a woman who perhaps has even better qualifications than the man of their choice, and who has given years of service in that system toward learning its problems and needs. She must take a back seat because she is a woman. Will we ever be able to suppose that such a board may choose a woman rather than a man of even equal qualifications?

When one considers the small percentage of women graduates who continue their professional training beyond the accepted B.S. degree, one wonders why there are so few. Is it that most women are satisfied with the preliminary degree and make no attempt to secure higher degrees, or is it that preference and encouragement is given to men in the matter of granting fellowships for advanced study and research. Perhaps a concentrated search should be launched for ability among the young women.

The last hope lies in the librarians themselves. Is it not true that women more than men are willing to assume a subservient role? Many, though they may be few, look forward to the blissful prospect of matrimony and are not particularly interested in advancing their positions. But that does not mean that there are none who seek professional administrative positions and who are well qualified and possessed of positive administrative ability. The woman often possesses much keener insight into the psychology of those with whom she works than the man who loses himself entirely in his work.

We like to think that the emancipation of womankind has been accomplished, but have we completely freed ourselves from the subconscious idea that the men are the lords and masters of the universe? Somehow it is a rather impossible task to try to set ourselves apart from the rest of our sex and try to convince ourselves that as librarians, we are different. Today when a member of the fairer sex speaks before a group of her profession she must be immaculately groomed from her head to her feet to prevent being labelled a freak, especially if her remarks indicate superior intelligence. Otherwise we may spend our time wondering how she can be induced to bob her hair and try a personality coiffure, or wear a more becoming dress, while we make a rather futile attempt to listen to what she is saying. When a man arises to speak immediately afterwards we settle back into our chairs with a mental sigh of relief. There are not so many details to be considered, for no matter how handsome or homely, no matter how intelligent or dull, "he's a man for a' that!"

Yet there are women in the profession capable of commanding the attention of the entire profession by force of their personalities, their abilities and their intelligence. We do need most seriously at this time in our development a Lady Pankhurst who will champion the cause of women in the library profession.

—Marietta Daniels,
Kansas City, Mo., Public Library

MEN VS. WOMEN

I want to congratulate *The Library Journal* for opening its pages to a discussion of a problem—and it is a real problem—which has been concerning the women of the library profession for a long time—the apparent discrimination against their advancement. As is said, there has been a great deal of unfavorable comment but it has all taken place in corners, as it were, and consequently has only served to stir up resentment without giving any opportunity to obtain action.

We are all so busy with our own affairs that we are apt to put aside consideration of such discriminations until they are brought home to us personally although we can all get quite wrought up over events in the Far East, in

Spain and in Germany. Why? Probably it is the power of the press. So if *The Library Journal* puts its power for equal publicity behind this problem, maybe we can get stirred up enough to take some action.

By no stretch of the imagination do I think that anyone will accuse me of belonging to that detestable species known as "feminist" or accuse me of harboring any ideas that women should be given any special consideration because they are women. I have always held that qualifications for any position, in any profession, should be definitely stated and the position should then be filled by the person best qualified, regardless of sex. Personally, it seems to me that the only library positions in this country which, in themselves, demand that the occupant shall be male are those in men's colleges and universities.

Let us look the facts in the face. If I am not mistaken, the procedure in most cases is something like this. When a really responsible position is open, the trustees, directors, or other responsible officials quite rightly consult our professional organization as the logical source where centralized records of professional achievement are on file. What next? Are these requests put through the regular channels of our placement service? Results would lead one to suspect not but rather that placement is made on personal recommendation of officers, most of whom are men and therefore have a natural bias.

In the library profession, as in most other walks of life, one expects to reach the higher administrative positions carrying with them the higher salaries sometime between the ages of thirty-five and forty-five. I think the leaders of the profession have tended to overlook the fact that there were few men entering the profession during the war years and consequently there are few of them in that age group, but we do have a large "war generation" of women who have been acquiring experience over a period of almost twenty years. Granted a good background and training, doesn't this experience make them better qualified than the young man of twenty-five and thirty-five who has only recently emerged from library school, oftentimes having tried and possibly failed in some other field? A generation of capable women are being passed over in favor of young men who have yet to serve their normal period of apprenticeship.

I have had two personal experiences lately—one successful; one unsuccessful. It happened that I was approached by the directors of an important library and asked to make suggestions of men who might direct their library. I did, but at the same time planted the idea that there were several women who, in my opinion, were better qualified than any available man. A woman got the job and the directors have individually thanked me for the suggestion.

The unsuccessful one still rankles. A college president asked me the same question saying he had no specific requirements for either a man or a woman. However, he also consulted some of our men leaders who proceeded to convince him that only a man could successfully administer his library.

We women are not wholly free from blame for this situation. For all too long we have been satisfied to be the "power behind the throne" as assistants to the man in charge; to take our pleasure in doing the job well without any ballyhoo and without seeking or wanting any particular recognition. In most cases, the men have been willing to accept this situation.

Then, too, when one of our women librarians has achieved the seats of the mighty, she has forgotten—or been too busy—to train a successor, for it is a well-known fact in all professions, that when a woman takes over an executive job, at least twice as much is expected of her than of any man in a similar situation. Consequently, when she retires or passes out of the picture, there is no one on hand capable of taking over and the position goes into the open market, so to speak, only it hasn't been much of an "open" market.

Census figures show that there are 30,000 librarians in this country of whom 9/10 are women. If we consider only the libraries serving a population of over 200,000, I wonder if a proper proportion of them are presided over by women. I do not have the figures at hand, but I think we would find the number of men holding positions as chiefs of these libraries out of all proportion to their total number.

Isn't this a problem which our newly formed Trustees Section might well study for they are responsible for giving their communities the best possible administrator. Let there be open discussion pro and con and some better method worked out for suggesting candidates—be they male or female. One suggestion I would make to the Trustees Section is that in a profession that has so few men proportionately the leaders naturally stand out while the truly capable woman is lost in the crowd. Could a plan be worked out to give more publicity to our women leaders so that a list of real eligibles would be public property both when positions are open and also when our nominating committees are looking for officers?

Only when we can assure our college graduates that there is no discrimination can we pick and choose among the candidates proposing to enter the field. Pick and choose we must, for while there are many unemployed librarians, there is a scarcity of those qualified to hold the most responsible positions.

—Ruth Savord
Librarian, Council on Foreign
Relations, Inc., New York, N.Y.

FURTHER DISCUSSION

I have found the reactions to your editorial suggestion that women should be given more of the better library positions quite interesting. It has surprised me, though, that all of the answers have represented the feminine point of view, thus making what is to my mind a highly controversial issue singularly uncontroversial.

As a mere minority male, I should like to present a few points that seem to have been overlooked by your correspondents.

In the first place, I cheerfully admit the truth of the charge that the number of males in better positions is out of proportion to the number of males in the profession. But have the critics of this condition hit on the true reasons for it? Some of it, they intimate, is due to prejudice. I agree. But I do not think that is a major reason. Some, they imply, is due to politics. Again I agree, and do it regretfully.

In the main, however, I think there are much better reasons than these. To begin with, there is a certain prejudice on the part of a large segment of the males of our species toward members of their sex who become librarians. There is a tendency to think (erroneously, of course) of those who enter such a woman-ridden profession as being perhaps a little bit "sissy." The fear of having such an odious adjective applied to him is enough to keep the average male out—with the result that, generally speaking, only men with a genuine love for library work, which is certainly a prerequisite for success in it, are willing to brave the charge or suspicion of being queer and enter the profession. The fact that this prejudice does not exist among women, on the other hand, means that large numbers of girls, on the lookout for what they consider an easy job, study library science. My own experience and observation, both in library school and in libraries, bear out this unkind assumption. Does it not follow, then, that the minority sex should have a disproportionately high representation in the upper brackets of the profession?

Another angle of the situation which has been ignored is the fact that men get higher wages in practically all professions, merely because they are men. This situation is not perhaps, justifiable — but it exists, nevertheless. But why, the critics will say, should we let this be true of librarianship, which is a low-pay profession, anyway? The answer again is pretty clear. It is simply that if male librarians are not good enough to get into the better positions, it is comparatively easy for them to get into other lines of work where they will earn more, while the women, knowing that their pay will probably remain low if they change jobs, are more content to hold their poor ones. Thus we see that at the very start, through greater reluctance to enter the work and greater ease in getting out of it, the poorly equipped men are more easily and more rapidly weeded out than the poorly equipped women.

What I have said implies a certain amount of agreement with the contentions of the ladies who have expressed their views. Yet, at the risk of seeming to contradict myself, I should like to raise a question: Are the men in responsible positions in our profession any more out of proportion to their numbers than they are in allied professions? If we think of the educational field as including all teachers from first grade through graduate school, we will undoubtedly find a preponderance of women — yet how many women are college presidents, school superintendents, or members of boards of trustees? The *World Almanac* for 1938 lists 645 senior colleges and universities in the United States. Of this number only fifty-three have women as heads (134 are colleges for women only), and most of these fifty-three are Catholic colleges for women only, which have a long convent tradition behind them. The number of public school superintendents who are women is also quite low. I know of only one, though I daresay there are some others. The number of women on school boards is fairly high — but such positions, being usually unpaid and involving more worry than anything else, are shunned by most men.

I have just examined the catalogs of thirty men's and co-educational colleges selected at random from our catalog collection, and find that sixteen of them have women as head librarians. Not such a bad proportion for the women, is it, when we consider that all of them have far more men than women on their faculties, and that several have no women with the exception of the librarian? Further, I have just looked over a copy of *The Library Journal* for January 1, 1937, which lists all of the accredited library schools of U.S. and Canada. Of the twenty-six mentioned, twelve seem to be headed by women. That, it seems to me, is a pretty large number, particularly when we recall that in all probability nearly all of the other divisions of the colleges having library schools are headed by men.

Please don't misunderstand me. I do not wish to seem lacking in chivalry, nor do I think all of the good jobs should go to men, or even that most of them should. But I do beg that the ladies of the profession judge us by our merits, and not work up a crusade to put the good positions on a proportional representation basis. To do so would drive out most of the men, and make librarianship even more nearly an all-feminine profession. And that, it seems to me, would keep out more of the best minds than the present system does.

—R.M. Lightfoot, Jr.,
Librarian, Scranton-Keystone Junior College,
La Plume, Pa.

Women's Place in Librarianship

by Robert S. Alvarez

According to a recent editorial in the *Library Journal*,[1] many librarians have the impression that men are always favored for the higher positions and that women are being discriminated against. Such an impression, if allowed to pass unquestioned, might have an unfortunate effect on the attitude and ambition of young women in, or about to enter, the profession. Hence it would seem about time that we had some actual facts and figures to show whether or not such discrimination really exists.

WOMEN IN ADMINISTRATIVE POSITIONS

I doubt if the average librarian realizes how many of our large libraries of all types are headed by women. By "large library" is meant one of over 100,000 volumes. There are 317 libraries of this size in the country and 128, or 40 percent, have a woman as chief librarian. Twenty-five of these women are in charge of libraries having over 200,000 volumes. They are to be found even in such large cities as Newark and Los Angeles.

In libraries of around 160,000 volumes we find about an equal number of men and women as head librarians; in libraries smaller than this the proportion of women to men steadily increases. Women run a good majority of the libraries with between 100,000 and 150,000 volumes, and in the smaller libraries they outnumber the men by four to one. Seven hundred and seventy-one, or 80 percent, of the 968 libraries having between 20,000 and 100,000 volumes are headed by women.

The above figures include chief librarians of all kinds of libraries.[2] Further analysis by type of library shows clearly that the dominant position of the women is not limited to any one type. For instance, in the public library field, women head 64 percent of all institutions with over 50,000 volumes and 91 percent of the institutions with from 20,000 to 100,000 volumes. Taking now the 34 county libraries which have over 50,000 volumes, one finds 82 percent headed by women. Of the 14 county libraries having over 100,000 volumes, 79 percent are headed by women. Even in the college and university field, one finds women in charge of 55 percent of the libraries containing over 20,000 volumes.

Reprinted by permission from the November 1938 (175-178) issue of the *Wilson Bulletin for Librarians*. Copyright © 1938 by The H.W. Wilson Company.

So far we have considered only the position of chief librarian. Below this rank the preponderance of women is so great and so apparent that it requires little discussion here. The assistant librarian of a large library is usually a woman, and 90 percent of the department heads are also women. Taking a few examples from the public library field: one finds that in Philadelphia seventeen of the eighteen department heads are women, in Buffalo nine out of ten are women, and in Los Angeles fifteen out of sixteen are women.

WOMEN IN THE A.L.A.

One finds a similar predominance of women in leading positions in our professional associations. The complaint is often made that men are getting more than their share of the offices in the American Library Association, but the women who complain about this apparently forget that most of these men were *elected*, not appointed; elected, as a matter of fact, by the women themselves since the A.L.A. is largely an organization of women.

If women are in the minority as chairmen of A.L.A. Boards and Committees and as members of the Council and Executive Board, they make up for this by taking the chairmanships of three-fifths of the Round Table groups and two-thirds of the A.L.A. Sections. The many state and regional library associations are completely dominated by women. Three-fourths of the state library associations have women as presidents, and as for their other officers, 93 percent are women. Furthermore, in four cases out of five the president of a library club is a woman.

The position of state library organizer or director of the extension division of a state library is becoming more and more important, and in 80 percent of these positions one now finds a woman. Similarly, eight of the ten state school library supervisors are women.

RECENT APPOINTMENTS

The next question is whether there is now a trend toward the appointment of men to administrative positions. Many believe there is such a trend, but no one has, as yet, presented facts to show it. They may have gained this impression from the following circumstances: In the first place, the appointments which have gone to men have been more widely publicized and discussed than those which have gone to women. In the second place—and this is undoubtedly the more significant explanation—there is a greater turnover of positions held by men. Men tend to move about more than do women, thus adding to the number of male appointments and creating thereby the illusion of a trend toward the appointment of men. A move at the top of the ladder inevitably leads to other adjustments all the way down the line. For instance, the recent appointment of a new Librarian at Harvard University necessitated the appointment, in turn, of a new Head of the Reference Department at the New York Public Library and new chief librarians at New York University, the University of North Carolina, and Fisk University. This series of five appointments, all of men, may have appeared to some librarians as evidence of a trend toward the appointment of men when really it was no such thing. Each man replaced a man, so that the ratio of men to women in administrative positions remained unchanged.

Actually, have there been many instances of late in which women in administrative positions have been replaced by men? So far as I can find there have been very few. Two or three women have recently been replaced by men, but on the other hand, the three women who were last year at the head of large-city libraries—Los Angeles, Cleveland, and Newark—replaced men at the time of their appointments. The recent succession of a man to the Cleveland post merely restores an antecedent condition.

GLANCING AT THE RECORD

During a recent study of trends in the appointment of chief librarians in 142 public libraries situated in cities with over 10,000 population in the seven North-Central states, I noted the sex of each head librarian as compared with that of the predecessor. I found that in cities with from 10,000 to 30,000 population, there were two men and seventy-nine women head librarians. One of the men had been replaced by a woman, and one woman had been replaced by a man. In the remaining instances, men replaced men and women replaced women. In the forty-one cities of from 35,000 to 100,000 inhabitants, there are now only four men administrators whereas twelve of the predecessors were men. In the ten cities with from 100,000 to 200,000 inhabitants, the number of men librarians has increased from four to seven. In the ten cities having over 200,000 population, the ratio of men to women has remained unchanged, one man having been replaced by a woman, and one woman by a man.

The totals for all cities of over 35,000 population show that there are now 19 men and 42 women as chief librarians, whereas in the group of previous appointees there were 24 men and 37 women. In other words, only 31 percent of the present appointees are men while 40 percent of the predecessors were men. Obviously the trend, at least in the North-Central states, is definitely in the direction of more women as chief librarians, rather than the other way around, as generally believed.

Recent appointments in the college field have been more numerous, and admittedly have gone more often to young men. There are, however, several reasons why men have been chosen for these positions. In the first place, their predecessors have been men. Then again, the masculine character of a college faculty seems to call for a male librarian. But more important than these reasons is the fact that the college presidents were looking for persons with a Ph.D. degree, and more men than women have this degree.

CONCLUSION

The surprisingly large number of administrative positions now filled by women should certainly be enough to convince a prospective recruit that there are real opportunities for women in library work. They should also be reassuring to young women already in the field who seem to feel that there is no chance of their ever reaching such heights. Incidentally, any one of these many positions is the equal of anything open to women in, say, the teaching profession. As a matter of fact, there are a good many men who would consider themselves fortunate to get such a position.

The above figures would seem to be conclusive proof of the fact that women really do hold a majority of our administrative positions and, what is more, are maintaining their predominant position in this field despite heavy competition from the ambitious male element. This evidence should convince even the most discouraged feminist that women still rule the library world and that, in all probability, they will continue to do so for some time to come. Our women librarians may rest assured that the path ahead of them is clear, and that they have as good a chance of reaching the top as do their male colleagues. There is no "For Men Only" sign on important administrative positions. There is room at the top for both men and women and librarians can be confident that whatever ability they show will be rewarded, regardless of sex.

REFERENCES

1. . . . "The Weaker Sex?" *Library Journal* 63 (March 15, 1938):232.
2. All such figures were compiled from *Patterson's American Educational Directory.*

Warning—Soft Shoulders

by Katharine M. Stokes

In March 1936, in the pages of this same periodical, I read Stewart W. Smith's article, "Librarianship—Stop-Gap or Profession?" (See page 95.) and my blood promptly boiled. I wrote to the editor at once, feeling certain that he must be expecting a flood of letters from the women of the library profession who read the article. In fact, I thought my indignation would be lost among the letters of many women of more importance, but it relieved my feelings to hit back at such a condescending male attitude in the only way I could.

I looked forward eagerly to the next number of the *Wilson Bulletin* where I expected to read with pride the brilliant retorts of the women in whose professional footsteps I have been attempting to follow. To my amazement, *my own letter* was the only word on the subject! I could scarcely believe we had so little pride in our work. If such apathy were representative of us, then we deserved all Mr. Smith had said.

When I asked my fellow staff members what they thought of such a reaction, the only explanation that arose was the old one, "What's the use? It's a man's world." And no wonder, I thought, if the women show no evidence of wanting their share!

I am not criticizing my seniors for being too much occupied with their accumulated duties or too disillusioned after years of observation to be interested in a situation which they must long since have accepted as inevitable. But my contemporaries should be alert enough with youthful zeal for reform to speak out against any suggestion that they allow themselves to be considered on a different basis from their masculine colleagues.

Traditionally, "Woman's place is in the home," and perhaps the majority of women will always prefer to retain that place. But, there is a large group of American women that finds its fullest expression in following careers which have required special training and abilities. This does not mean that such women would be happy to sacrifice marriage to a career; but rather, it means that the woman who has worked for even a few years in a profession that holds for her much mental satisfaction will feel as unsettled and empty of purpose if she suddenly gives up her position to confine herself to housekeeping and social life, as the business man whose retirement causes people to wonder "what he will do with himself." If she marries a man whose income is such that it will be possible for her to give up her own salary, she may think it wise to continue her professional interests in another way, such as taking an active part in the Friends of the Library group in her community or becoming a member of the Board of Trustees of her own library. (But with the present economic setup, it is more likely that she will need to continue to be gainfully employed if she is to marry at all, for most men of the professional group into which she is likely to marry do not make enough to support a wife comfortably until they are nearing forty.)

MARRIAGE

The young librarian who informs her employer that she is planning to be married is often surprised to find that he reacts in an entirely different way from that which his former confidence in her would have led her to expect. He is likely to explain, very kindly of course, that he will not be able to keep her in his organization after her marriage or that he will be unable to promote her if she remains on his staff. His reason is that her interest will no longer be centered in her work and that her personal life will claim too much of her time and energy to allow her to be of the fullest usefulness to her profession. Naturally, no one told *him* that when he married; in fact, everyone felt that marriage and a family would round out his development and increase his concentration on his work. But he is a *man*, who will not have to be concerned with the running of a household! Yet when his wife has her first baby, he will feel that he cannot leave home to attend a professional meeting which he would ordinarily consider important. Everyone would agree that his personal life should make this claim upon him, but why, then, should a woman be criticized for staying home from her work for a few days to take care of a sick husband?

Many married women who continue their careers prefer not to have children for personal or financial reasons. For those who do want them, satisfactory arrangements should be worked out. In the smaller library, arrangements may be more difficult because of the limited size of the staff which does not permit much flexibility of schedule. But the woman who has a truly professional viewpoint will consider the situation impersonally and resign her position if a leave of absence is impossible. She will usually be able to give her employer ample notice of her plans, and in case she finds it necessary to be away from the library earlier than she expected, the head librarian should be no more upset than if an automobile accident suddenly incapacitates a staff member for months.

It is, of course, the lack of professional viewpoint that has been displayed by some married women which has made many head librarians unwilling to employ them as a class. Very often it is convenient and tactful for an executive to settle individual cases by applying a general rule, but unless exceptions are readily granted a rule may fall heavily upon persons who merit unusual treatment.

I have never happened to know of a professionally trained married woman who did not fulfill the obligations of her position creditably, but I have had enough experience with single women to know that training and ethical behavior do not invariably go together. In a few situations in which I have been involved with untrained married librarians in minor positions, the unpleasantness arising has been enough to make any executive wary. One woman continued to work so far into her period of pregnancy that her appearance caused comment. She should, of course, have made satisfactory arrangements much earlier and saved her employer the embarrassment of approaching her. Another was intermittently unable to come to work for some weeks and finally had her husband take up the matter with the head librarian. Unquestionably, she should have been responsible for her own affairs, not allowing herself the luxury of basking in masculine protection.

BE LIBRARIANS FIRST

A department head was annoyed several times during one winter when she received early morning calls from the husband of a woman working under her: "Mary has a little cold and I think she'd better stay in bed." She was forced to rush to fill the emergencies herself, because she preferred not to inconvenience another employee on such short notice. If the husband had not been so anxious to take care of his wife, she herself would scarcely have had the audacity to tell her chief that she was failing her for such a slight cause.

If we want to work shoulder to shoulder with men, to compete on an equal basis, then we must take care that our shoulder shall not be soft and yielding in a crucial moment. A little of our feminine charm will have to be sacrificed during working hours for the aggressiveness which a career presupposes. And let's not be wistful about it—aren't we flexible enough to bring out our charm all nice and fresh from its daily rest to wear in the evening for the men with whom we do not work?

Librarianship a Feminine Vocation?

by Wilhelm Munthe

This is a touchy point. But we cannot avoid saying something about the over-whelming preponderance of women in the library profession. It is a situation that has obtained ever since Dewey started his first class in 1887, with 19 women and 3 men. Dewey himself foresaw that women were going to be forced out into the vocational and professional world, and it was his idea that they had a better chance in libraries than perhaps anywhere else. Women liked to work with books and literature. It was a quiet sort of business, in which even a timid soul could do good work, without having to come in contact with the coarser side of life. Nor was library work as nerve-racking as teaching.

Library Schools Attract Girls With and Without Initiative. Further-more, Dewey's elementary and didactic method of instruction was rather well suited to women, who found it easy to accept and subordinate themselves to his dynamic personality. And later it developed that for those who had personal initiative and independence there was a broad field of action in the library world.

On the other hand, it is true that right from the start but few men were interested. In those glorious days of "progress" there were so many more attractive pursuits open to them. So it was for the most part only those with strong leanings toward literary studies and activity that sought admission to library schools. From an economic standpoint a library career was not so bad for a single woman, but it had little to offer a man intending to start a family.

Influence On Salaries. Economically, then, there developed a vicious circle: Women took over the library positions because the low salaries did not attract men, and the salaries were low because the positions were held by women. Equal pay for both sexes was at that time unheard of, and even in our day its existence is largely on paper. Whenever one of the higher administrative posts is to be filled, those authorized to make the appointment usually prefer a man and are often willing to increase the salary in order to get him, while the tendency is rather to cut it down if considerations of fairness or lack of male competition necessitates its being given to a woman. The history of American libraries is full of examples of this, right up to recent years.

Dewey himself may well have prophesied that "the librarian of the future will be a woman," yet it is quite likely that he believed the *leading* positions would nearly always be reserved for men. But he did not realize in time that in that event he ought to provide a course of training better adapted to these men. They were not going to come to his elementary library school. So in the course of time there arose a crying need for men in the profession, with the result that outsiders were taken in in great numbers to fill administrative positions. But experiments of this sort did not always turn out so well, and the authorities gradually reconciled themselves to the idea of advancing competent women within the profession to the top positions. And let me say right here, and say it so emphatically that it cannot be misunderstood: many of these women have filled the positions admirably. It has been my good fortune on my three trips to the United States to meet with unquestioned proof of this fact, in Cleveland, Minneapolis, Los Angeles, on the Executive Board and the staff of the A.L.A., and in many other places. I have discussed this question with several of these women and they all agreed that it was a misfortune for the profession that there was so little male competition. But neither did they try to conceal that it really is a "man-sized" job, and that several of their colleagues had broken down prematurely under the nervous strain. In particular, it is difficult for a woman head to command the respect of the city fathers for the needs of the library. But—and I repeat—I have met many women library administrators who radiated vitality and a passion for work. And every one of them recognized the need of more capable men in the library. As the situation is, it often happens that a sizable library staff does not include even one man.

Feminization Symptomatic of Underpaid Professions. At the same time, we find individuals so short-sighted as to interpret this feminine control of the library profession as a victory for women's rights. But the sad part about this is that the feminization of any organization is always a sure sign of an underpaid profession. And there can hardly be any doubt that librarianship is one of the poorest paid professions, considering the preparation required. And one other point: most of the positions with tolerable salaries turn out to be administrative posts held by men. When a profession consists of 87 percent women, whose average salary is approximately $2000 below that of their male colleagues, it indicates an unhealthy condition. I agree with those women who consequently feel that the hope for better standards of pay lies in getting more men to enter the service—but at the bottom.

However, we must take into account that the 5000 public libraries in towns of less than 10,000 inhabitants will probably never be able to offer salaries that will attract able and ambitious men. This will also be true for most of the smaller special libraries. So there will always be a great preponderance of women. But salaries need to be raised, just the same. Besides, there are now other more promising careers open to women with ability, intelligence and initiative.

The need of men librarians is particularly noticeable in libraries with specialized service. The same holds for cataloging and classification in special subjects. Here there has been a dangerous tendency to be satisfied with cheap help. The work being organized as a mechanical routine for the mass-production of catalog cards, no opportunity has been afforded for delving deeper into the literature of the special fields. Add to this consideration the low rate of pay and we have sufficient explanation of the fact that we seldom see men catalogers.

It is quite possible that the beginning salary is attractive enough as pin-money for girls living at home with their parents, but it is distressingly meager when the time comes that they have to take care of themselves, with perhaps the added burden of providing for an aged mother or other relative. Women are themselves the losers by over-feminization. On the other hand, however, it must by no means be forgotten that the library profession offers unusual possibilities for women of extraordinary ability.

Feminine Influences.   This over-feminization cannot of course help putting its mark on the American library system. Among the assets of women as librarians, we must first set down work with children, which, as we know, occupies a larger place in America's library service than in that of any other country. Here women, by virtue of their peculiar qualifications, have the field to themselves. In school libraries they have not yet entirely routed the men. At least, I know for a fact that once at a meeting of school librarians a man turned up among 150 women! Then we will probably also have to put down—as assets and liabilities, respectively—women's strongly developed interest in fiction, especially novels, and their corresponding weakly developed interest in social, technical and natural sciences. We might mention that in local library propaganda women librarians have a tendency to appeal rather to the enthusiasm of the emotions than to the diffidence of reason. Similarly, a veritable tropical luxuriance of sentimental Sunday-school stories continues to flourish in the professional literature. In missionary spirit they are not much behind the Salvation Army. There is too much wishful thinking and ignoring of problems, instead of meeting and solving them. A characteristic illustration of this occurred at the Chicago Conference in 1933, when a male librarian, having stated the need for an investigation of the efficiency of libraries, was answered by a female colleague, who undoubtedly gave utterance to a heart-felt conviction when she said: "Why should we try to measure results? Bread cast on the waters will in some way return to us in manifold measure."

Little Interest in Graduate Study.   Neither can we pass by in silence the fact that the girls who graduate from library school show far less inclination toward advanced study than do their less numerous male classmates. In 1936 men made up 10 percent of the first-year library school enrollment, but 40 percent of the second. A similar situation prevails in other university fields. Williamson's report of 1923 showed that men also picked the best library schools with the highest standards—the lower a school's rating, the lower its percentage of men, both students and teachers.

Finally, we shall probably also have to hold the women responsible for the gossipy tone that prevails in many American library periodicals. To go from a European library journal to one of these is like going from a lecture to a tea-party.

Having ventured these indictments, I hasten to enter as feminine assets that charming spirit of helpfulness, patience, and courtesy, and that sympathetic understanding for even the inarticulate wishes of the public, which are the keynote of the entire service, and have made American libraries unrivaled throughout the world.

And so I leave this ticklish subject with a reference to Professor J.C.M. Hanson's[1] treatment of it elsewhere, in somewhat lighter vein. However, when this champion of the ladies hints that the female electorate of the A.L.A. at times chooses its president more for his handsome outward appearance than for his real qualifications—then I must confess that I cannot imagine whom he has in mind!

But to return to the public and the staff. Something over sixty percent of the library public are women, and consequently a staff of women has special qualifications for understanding and meeting their wishes. But, gradually, as the public library becomes more "man-conscious," and in particular strives to be of use to professional men—in banking, business, trade, industry—it must also provide adequate service for them. They cannot be content with assistants who have only a superficial bibliographical acquaintance with their fields—they need people with basic subject knowledge. For this sort of thing men are naturally better qualified—if they are to be had. And the cry for men is constantly getting louder—even from women leaders in the profession. To cite a single example: In 1931 the Carnegie Corporation appointed a committee to establish the grounds for fellowships in advanced studies. This committee included the president of the Corporation and two outstanding women, Sarah C.N. Bogle of A.L.A. headquarters and Linda A. Eastman of the Cleveland Public Library. Its first reason was short and to the point: "To bring men into the profession."

It is regrettable that in order to hold men of high training library boards have sometimes had to advance young men faster than they deserved. They have jumped past women who in years of service and experience were far ahead of them. In certain of the largest libraries it now looks as though it were difficult for a woman to attain a position of leadership of the third rank. I have heard several bitter expressions of sentiment regarding this situation. For, while we may venture to affirm that women as a rule work best with a man as head, still he must be a man whose professional ability they respect.

Men Administrators or Scholars?　Formerly, it was more the administrative side of the work that interested the few men who chose library careers. And it was undoubtedly here that there was the greatest need for them. This often tended to draw them away from books and from things like cataloging. Knowledge of foreign languages and literature was not infrequently their weakest point. This is now being changed. Today the need is for university men with scholarly tastes and a knowledge of letters and the sciences. To what extent libraries will succeed in keeping those they have, now that the depression is over, depends in large measure on salaries.

Better salaries for men will, I hope, also benefit their women colleagues. For that reason I trust I shall not be taken for a misogynist when I express the hope that the library staff may not become totally emasculated, but may attain, let us say, 30 percent virility.

There is work for both sexes in a library that is to serve all the interests of society.

---

[1]Amerikansk og europeisk bibliotekvesen (in the *Festschrift: Overbibliotekar W. Munthe pa 50 arsdagen.*) Oslo, 1933.

Not in Our Stars

by Rena S. Cowper

In March, 1938, the *Library Journal* editorial entitled "The Weaker Sex" called upon American women librarians to consider their present professional status in the light of the fact that tradition and convention were still awarding the highest administrative posts to men.

Several women replied emphasizing that the necessary qualifications for efficient librarianship—intelligence, personality, wide book knowledge, business aptitude, leadership—were not characteristics peculiar to men. Instances were cited where women had been appointed heads of large public libraries and had administered these very successfully; thus breaking down the old idea that a public institution without a man at the top cannot retain its prestige in the world of affairs. Librarians are to be judged only by one criterion, namely, professional competence.

Robert S. Alvarez took up the challenge in the pages of the *Wilson Bulletin* in an article, "Women's place in librarianship." He gave a statistical survey from which he concluded that it was not just to allege that men are favoured for higher posts. In January last year, again through the medium of the *Wilson Bulletin*, the basis upon which Mr. Alvarez had framed his statistics was queried. A further statistical analysis of the position was made strongly deprecating Mr. Alvarez's assertion that women "have as good a chance of reaching the top as their male colleagues."

The battle was now to the strong. Miss Stokes, circulation librarian, Pennsylvania State College, followed in March with a contrast of the status of the sexes under the caption, "Warning—soft shoulders." Miss Stokes laid her finger on the disease spot which, in an age when women are supposed to be emancipated makes sex democracy in librarianship something yet to be accomplished. And that spot is apathy. Elder women, it would appear, have, with the passage of time, lost that philosophy which welcomes "each rebuff that bids nor sit nor stand but go." Concerning the younger women Miss Stokes writes with point and vigour, declaring they "should have enthusiasm to speak out against any suggestion that they be considered on a different basis from their masculine colleagues."

America protesteth: What of Britain?

H.A. Sharp in *The Approach to Librarianship* says of urban and county libraries, "the more senior posts are often filled by men. . . . Many of the higher posts will doubtless be filled by men for many years to come." The latest edition of the Ministry of Labour pamphlet on librarianship reads, "hitherto appointments as chief librarian have been held almost exclusively by men. . . . Changes are however taking place in some instances. . . ." Not too attractive a prospect for an educated intelligent young woman contemplating a career in library work!

In the 1931 Report on hours, salaries, etc., in British municipal libraries it was acknowledged that "there is little difference between good work whether performed by a male assistant or a female assistant." Why then this continued illogical exclusion of women from higher posts with its concomitant factor of lower salaries? A recent publication, *Unemployment in the Learned Professions,* comments on the irony of such a state of affairs: "This exclusion from the best positions and the fact that women are paid less than men even where they hold identical jobs reflects the determination of man to preserve a monopoly which in most parts of the world he has held for centuries. Professional women more than any other group suffer from this situation, for which there is no excuse."

It is interesting and encouraging to observe that within the profession itself there are men who regard anomalies in salaries between the sexes as unjust, and condemn local authorities for considering female labour as cheap labour. The 1931 Report strongly recommends equality in pay, while B.M. Headicar in his *Manual* advises women to insist on adequate remuneration for the work they are doing. L.R. McColvin, too, has deplored the exploitation of women's work.

The time is more than ripe for women in librarianship to demand the same treatment as their brothers in the questions of appointment to higher administrative posts, equal pay for equal work, and the removal of the marriage bar. But such demands require action, enthusiasm, importunity. Are British women librarians, as Miss Stokes found so many of her American co-workers, indifferent?

Yet how can we women shut our eyes to the unpleasant truth that despite the vote, improved legal status and actually having demonstrated our worth in professions, there still remains against us a barrier of sex discrimination clearly indicating that the freedom of women is far from being as complete as many imagine it to be. And, what is more important, do we ever pause to consider this in its longer perspective of modern politics?

After all, it was the political situation of Europe developing into a world war that, more than any other cause broke down the severest of the opposition to the emancipation of women. That was yesterday and to our advantage. Today the issue lies between democracy and totalitarianism. In *Women Must Choose* Hilary Newitt reviews what has overtaken women under totalitarian rule where, debarred from the professions, they are subtly being drafted into service for the ends of a state in which there is no possible room for women to work out their lives on equal terms with men.

None of us can be too sure of the morrow even in this present stronghold of democracy, this England. I would therefore urge the women of our profession to set their house in order. If we stabilize ourselves within even the specialized limits of our profession we will not only have secured our immediate interests but we will have made a definite contribution towards the greater freedom of our sex in the wider circle of public life in which we are concentrically concerned. Moreover, if the day ever came when professional women were threatened with reactionary forces they would then be able to present a strong united front against which the detrimental subtleties of political creeds could not prevail.

"Not in our stars, but in ourselves": these are the words of the wise. Truly may they be as goads.

PART

IV

1941-1965
WORLD WAR II
AND AFTER

Shall the Misses be Masters?

by A.G.S. Enser

Recently, it has been stated that the American public library system has become grossly over-feminized and that the preponderance of female over male within the profession is having a detrimental effect upon the importance and prestige of public librarianship in the United States of America.

Mr. Charles Nowell spoke on this danger to British librarianship at the Brighton Conference, and Mr. L.R. McColvin, at the Conference of Welsh Library Authorities, held in Aberystwyth recently, also spoke about this subject.

Such warnings by eminent librarians cannot be allowed to pass unheeded, and it can be assumed that due forethought was given to the effect that such words could produce within our profession, before they were uttered in public. The saying, "Hell hath no fury like a woman scorned" must be evident to any mere male librarian who is brave or rash enough to investigate the possible over-feminization of our public librarianship, especially in these days of all-pervading feminine pursuits.

But what are the facts in this country? Is a mountain being made out of a molehill? It is well known that figures can be made to prove any contention and that statistics are usually left to the mathematically minded. However, perhaps rushing in where angels fear to tread, I offer the following comparisons covering a period of ten years, and believe that the figures shown, firstly, will surprise most members of the Library Association, secondly, that they are more than a little disturbing, thirdly, that the warnings of Messrs. Nowell and McColvin are more than justified, and finally, that to be fore-warned is to be fore-armed.

The comparative figures shown opposite are taken in every case, from an examination of the registers of members in the 1937 and 1947 Library Association *Year Books.*

From Table 1 we see that during the past ten years, for every new male member, *six* female members have joined.

From Table 2, for every male member qualifying as an Associate, approximately *two* female members qualified as such.

From Table 3, for every male member qualifying as a Fellow, approximately *two* female members qualified as such.

From Table 4, despite the disparity of comparative male and female membership increase in ten years (213 males to 1,293 females), the percentage of female A.L.A.'s has increased.

TABLE 1

	Total no. of members.	No. of males.	%	No. of females.	%
1937	4,346	2,141	49	2,205	51
1947	5,852	2,354	40	3,498	60
Increase	1,506	213	−9	1,293	+9

Percentage of female increase of total increase = 86%.

TABLE 2

	No. of A.L.A.s.	No. of male A.L.A.s.	No. of female A.L.A.s.
1937	634	376	258
1947	1,428	666	762
Increase	794	290	504

Percentage of female A.L.A.s increase of total A.L.A. increase = 63.5%.

TABLE 3

	No. of F.L.A.s.	No. of male F.L.A.s.	No. of female F.L.A.s.
1937	760	486	274
1947	969	559	410
Increase	209	73	136

Percentage of female F.L.A.s increase of total F.L.A. increase = 65%.

TABLE 4

	No. of A.L.A.s.	% of total membership.	% of male A.L.A.s of total members.	% of female A.L.A.s of total members.	% of male A.L.A.s of total A.L.A.s.	% of female A.L.A.s of total A.L.A.s.
1937	634	14	8.5	6	60	40
1947	1,428	24	11.0	13	47	53

TABLE 5

	No. of F.L.A.s.	% of total membership.	% of male F.L.A.s of total members.	% of female F.L.A.s of total members.	% of male F.L.A.s of total F.L.A.s.	% of female F.L.A.s of total F.L.A.s.
1937	760	17.5	11	6	64	36
1947	969	16.0	10	7	58	42

TABLE 6

Members qualifying during the years 1940-1947.									
	1940	1941	1942	1943	1944	1945	1946	1947	Totals.
Male F.L.A.	22	3	5	5	13	8	45	9	110
Female F.L.A.	13	16	14	21	16	12	31	1	124
Male A.L.A.	14	18	8	9	17	28	71	45	210
Female A.L.A.	22	41	47	59	78	77	140	91	555

From Table 5, as fully qualified members, percentages of females have *increased* and that of males decreased.

Of course, I am aware that conditions during the war years 1939-1945, materially and statistically affected these figures, yet it must be remembered that whilst many male members were on war service, a considerable number of female members were also serving, but I believe that the figures in Table 6 are astonishing to say the least!

Thus, in eight years, 210 males became Chartered Librarians, but so did 555 females. In the same period, 124 female members became fully qualified librarians by examination, at least, to be considered for the highest professional posts.

Considering the number of female members holding qualifications, an examination of the posts they occupy is justified, and herein lies the only crumb of comfort to male members *(but for how long?).*

It is found that no very large municipal library is headed by a female, but women are chiefs at Wolverhampton, Dublin, Preston, Ipswich, Sale and Oldham, whilst deputies of the fair sex reign at Luton, Norwich, Howe, Leamington and Cheltenham, to mention a few. I believe that the writing is on the wall for all to see and considering that females may now become H.M. Ambassadors and Ministers Plenipotentiaries, the chiefships of such "plums" as Manchester, Sheffield, Birmingham, Bristol, Liverpool and even Westminster itself, may one day be occupied by women.

The position in county libraries is worthy of note, since 31 county librarians and 12 deputy county librarians are women. Surely, these figures substantiate my remarks in the preceding paragraph.

I am not rash enough to question the efficiency of women as librarians, and I trust that nothing in this article can be construed as an attack upon the *gentler sex,* but if the figures given prove anything, they surely prove that the British library system is not only in danger of becoming over-feminized, it is so already. Whether this danger can affect the prestige of public librarianship is another question entirely. If the female percentage of representation on local government councils and in Parliament increases in like ratio to the increase in female membership of the Library Association, perhaps we shall then see the complete domination of the profession by women. In 1937, there were 182 males and 21 females occupying seats or offices on the Library Association Council and Branches; in 1947, the figures were 177 males and 46 females, *an increase of 53 percent in female representation.*

However, the post-war years may see the present balance of membership of the Library Association more equalized, even with the handicap of conscription still to be borne by males, but probably the real answer to the problem lies in equality of pay between the sexes, since this would obviate that so prevalent practice of obtaining *quantity* without *quality* in public library staffing by the employment of cheap rate female labour.

If an intake ratio of six females to one male is not over-feminization, then statistics prove nothing, and what has happened in America *cannot* happen here.

It Is a Mistake to Recruit Men

by Ralph Munn

The time has come when the profession should re-examine the traditional belief that librarianship needs more and more men within its ranks. We do need more men, just as we need more women, who possess high qualities of vision, leadership and statesmancraft. But to recruit more and more of the average run-of-mine simply to get men is a mistake. It will operate against the profession, both by filling it with men of mediocre calibre and by discouraging the entrance of superior women.

Librarianship is still, of course, predominantly a woman's calling. The Public Library Inquiry finds, however, that the proportion of men in the accredited library schools has risen from 6 percent in 1920 to 14 percent in 1936, and to 22 percent in 1948. A further increase is forecast for 1949-50.

Library school directors report a stream of male applicants whose qualities are reflected in the following composite: no special interest in libraries or public service, but has read or been told by a vocational adviser that there is a shortage of librarians; is far less interested in salary and advancement than in security — he must have a depression-proof job; no cultural background and would never have gone to college had not the G.I. Bill made that the easiest path to take; college grades satisfactory, but no idea of continued scholarship or development; in short, he is simply looking for a secure and not too difficult job.

FEW $5000 JOBS

We can only hope that not many of the men who comprise this composite got beyond the library school directors. There is danger to the profession, though, in a great increase of men even when they are of average quality. The success of any profession depends upon the well-being of its members. We can draw many of our satisfactions from non-monetary rewards, but a decent standard of living is essential to all of us.

A compilation [see *LJ*, Sept. 1, p. 1185] by Alexander Galt, librarian of the Buffalo Public Library, in May 1949, shows that 20 of our largest public libraries offer only 113 positions with salaries of $5,000 or more; only 326 additional positions carry salaries of $4,000 to $5,000. Other studies have shown

Article reprinted from *Library Journal* 74 (November 1, 1949):1693-1640. Published by R.R. Bowker, a Xerox company. Copyright © 1949, by Xerox Corporation.

that when other types of libraries are added, the number of positions paying $4,000 or more is severely limited. To a single woman without dependents, an annual expenditure of $4,000 will bring the necessities and a few of the frills of living. To a professional man with a family, $4,000 is barely enough to clear the poverty line.

There are several countries in which librarianship reflects the dangers of filling a low-salaried profession with men who are trying to raise and educate families. Those in the lower positions are so much concerned with Junior's need of a winter coat that they can bring no enthusiasm or creative thought to their jobs. Harassed by home responsibilities and expenses, they become hopelessly discouraged and frustrated.

The optimist will insist that all library salaries be raised until they offer adequate support to men with families. That would be a welcome solution, but it is wholly unrealistic at present.

HARMS WOMEN'S POSITION

The Public Library Inquiry confirms what we have all known, that "no one opposes the library, but few are willing to pay much for it." The recent conspicuous advances in library salaries are not due primarily to A.L.A. standards or to our own efforts. They have come naturally from the inflationary factors which have raised the country's entire salary and price structure, and from the old law of supply and demand. There is evidence that inflation has been halted, and that the shortage of librarians is on the way out. Certainly, we must struggle to bring all salaries up to appropriate levels, but we shall no longer have these natural economic forces working for us.

The further limitation of positions which are available to women is perhaps the most dangerous factor in the influx of men.

Women have had to become reconciled to the preference of library boards for men as top administrators. According to my own calculation, and I don't guarantee it, men now direct the public libraries in 71 of the country's 92 cities of more than 100,000 inhabitants. Men are now appearing in much larger numbers as administrators in smaller cities. The universities and major colleges display a strong preference for men, not only as chief librarians but as department heads.

This trend will be extended if the supply of men is greatly enlarged. Men will secure more and more of the attractive positions, not because they are abler than women but simply because governing authorities prefer them. Finally, superior women will no longer enter a profession in which too many of the rewards are reserved for men.

Economic conditions and the status of libraries in American life make it certain that librarianship will offer proportionately few salaries which are adequate for the proper support of a family. Throughout the predictable future it is sure to be mainly a woman's occupation. It should, therefore, be kept attractive to the ablest of women.

We must have men for many positions, to be sure. But let us make certain that they are men who give every promise of raising the standard and prestige of the profession as a whole, and not those who are merely seeking a shabby security in positions to which able women should advance.

The Public Librarian

by Alice I. Bryan

[Editors note: The following material has been excerpted from Dr. Bryan's Chapter Three, "Personal Characteristics," and Chapter Seventeen, "Summary and Conclusions."]

[The following data, collected in the Public Library Inquiry provide some of the] factual base for generalizations about the characteristics, organization, supervision, and education of public library personnel in the United States. From the self-portrait of 2,395 of the men and women now in public library positions, from the description of the personnel practices in the fifty-eight libraries where these librarians work, and from the picture of the thirty-four library schools where many of them were trained, it is possible to identify the primary problems of public library personnel and to make informed judgments as to the most likely solutions for the problems.

In formulating judgments, however, the reader must be mindful of the limitations of the data upon which the findings are based. Their validity and reliability depend upon many factors. Chief among them are the necessary limitations of the samples of librarians, libraries, and library schools that were studied; the methods by which the data were gathered; the percentages of replies received and their distribution within the samples; and the methods by which the data were analyzed. The Inquiry sample as a whole, checked with comparable data from other recent national samplings of the librarian population, appears to provide a reliable basis for conclusions regarding contemporary public library personnel.

But there are differences in the percentage of returns of some of the questionnaires which call for caution in arriving at conclusions from the data. To most of the questionnaires there were adequate responses: a 100 percent return of the questionnaire to library school heads and nearly the same percentage for the questionnaire to library school faculty members; return of requested data from eight of the nine large universities that have library and other professional schools; completed blanks from the heads of fifty-eight of the sixty sample libraries; return of the Inquiry personnel questionnaire from 84 percent of the librarians in the complete sample. But, although the over-all return of the general personnel questionnaire to the librarians was satisfac-

Reprinted from A.I. Bryan: *The Public Librarian*, New York: Columbia University Press, 1952, by permission of the publisher.

tory, only 69 percent of the men in the sample as compared with 85 percent of the women replied. Approximately the same percentages of returns from the Guilford-Martin personality inventory (Factors GAMIN) were received from the men and women librarians. Although 85 percent of the women completed and returned the Strong Vocational Interest Blank, only 33 percent of the men did so. In assessing the significance of the reported differences between men and women, therefore, particularly as to their vocational interests, caution must be used. Despite the limitations indicated, the data on public library personnel reported in the previous pages are probably more representative, more reliable, and touch more aspects of the field than any findings hitherto available.

PERSONAL CHARACTERISTICS

Sex Distribution

Despite the fact that enrollment of male students in the accredited library schools has risen steadily during the past thirty years, public libraries in this country are staffed predominantly by women. Of the 2,395 librarians in the basic sample, 92 percent were women; among these women were found 91 percent of the professional group and 93 percent of the subprofessional group.[1]

Although women far outnumber men on the staffs of the Inquiry libraries, a considerably higher proportion of men hold the higher level positions, as is shown in Table 3.

The greatest concentration of professional employees of both sexes is, of course, in the ranks of the professional assistants; this category (junior and senior grades) includes 87 percent of the women and 65 percent of the men. At the upper end of the distribution, only 4 percent of the women as compared with 15 percent of the men hold positions as head librarians or first-line assistants to the chief. In all the libraries in the basic sample that serve populations of 250,000 or more, all the top administrators are men. Among the subprofessional employees, a few women hold top jobs, but only in very small libraries. These persons, as will be shown in a later chapter, are improperly classified.

Preference of governing authorities for men as top administrators is found not only in the library field but also in almost all occupations in which women are engaged. Attitudes of both men and women librarians toward this situation in their own profession are described in Chapter 5.

Age Distribution

Professional employees in the Inquiry libraries average about twelve years older than those in the subprofessional group. The median age of the professionals, as shown in Table 4, is 42.3 years; of the subprofessionals 30

---

[1]Stigler (cited in footnote 6, Chapter 2), p. 11, reports that women constituted 84.5 percent of all teachers in the United States in 1920, 81.8 percent in 1930, and only 75.3 percent in 1940. He attributes the increase of male teachers partly to the growth of secondary schools, where men are relatively more numerous, and partly, perhaps, to the difficulty experienced by men in obtaining employment in private industry during the thirties.

TABLE 3

TITLE OF LIBRARY POSITION BY SEX

	PROFESSIONAL STAFF			SUBPROFESSIONAL STAFF		
TITLE	*Men* (163) %	*Women* (1,674) %	*Total* (1,837) %	*Men* (33) %	*Women* (428) %	*Total* (461) %
Librarian	6	2	2	..	1	a
Administrative assistant	9	2	3	..	..	..
Division head	11	2	3	..	..	..
Department head	6	5	5	..	a	a
Branch head	..	1	1	..	a	a
Supervisor	3	1	1	..	..	..
Professional assistant-senior	62	81	79	..	2	1
Professional assistant-junior	3	6	6	..	1	1
Subprofessional assistant	..	..	..	100	97	97

[a]Less than one half of 1 percent.

years. The professional men are about three years younger as a group than the professional women; among the subprofessionals the men average about a year younger than the women.[2]

The most significant feature of the age distribution is the "middle-age bulge" in the ranks of the professional women, the group containing almost three fourths of all the employees represented in the table. Only 22 percent of the professional women librarians are under thirty-four years of age as compared with the 52 percent who are between thirty-four and forty-nine. Moreover, in the age brackets below thirty-four we find a steady decline in the percentage of women employees at successively younger levels. With the inevitable further thinning of the ranks of the professional women in the twenties and early thirties through marriage, we can expect an increasing shortage of women librarians to develop during the next ten to fifteen years if present recruiting trends continue. During the same period there also will be an increasing percentage of women approaching the retirement age as the groups now between forty and fifty-five move up the age ladder.

---

[2]According to Stigler's Data (*ibid.*, p.11-12) the median ages of male and female schoolteachers in 1940 were 34.3 and 34 years, respectively. The median age of the women teachers was 1.7 years greater than that of all women in the labor force.

TABLE 4

AGE OF LIBRARIANS BY SEX

	PROFESSIONAL STAFF			SUBPROFESSIONAL STAFF		
AGE	*Men* (163)	*Women* (1,674)	*Total* (1,837)	*Men* (33)	*Women* (428)	*Total* (461)
	%	%	%	%	%	%
Past 63	8	3	4	3	2	2
59-63	4	5	5	..	2	2
54-58	8	8	8	3	2	2
49-53	2	10	10	..	4	4
44-48	10	18	17	3	9	9
39-43	18	21	20	12	11	12
34-38	20	13	13	12	11	11
29-33	23	10	11	16	13	13
24-28	6	9	10	45	25	24
23 or less	..	3	3	6	22	21
Median age	39.3	42.6	42.3	28.8	30.1	30

The present age distribution indicates that a serious recruiting problem now exists in the public library field. At a time when severe shortages already are being felt, it seems evident that an increasingly smaller percentage of professionally trained women are choosing public librarianship as their vocation. The steady increase in the percentage of men who are entering the profession is as yet far too small, numerically, to offset the growing deficiency in woman power.

An analysis of age groups by size of population served shows a steady increase in median age as libraries decrease in size. The median for the professional women in the smallest libraries is 46.5 years; for the subprofessional women, 56.5 years. The age distributions for employees in the various population-size groups follow the overall pattern, but the decline in the percentages of younger women is sharper in the smaller libraries.

Administrative employees, as would be expected, are older on the average than professional assistants. But the top administrators, as a group, are younger than those holding less responsible administrative posts. The age distribution for these three groups of professional employees is shown in Table 5. The top administration group is composed of head librarians and their first assistants; the middle administration group is made up of division heads, department heads, branch heads, and supervisors; the professional assistants include those of both senior and junior grades.

It is significant not only that there is a much larger proportion of men than of women in the administrative groups, but also that the male top administrators are on the average five years younger than the women in this category. This means that men not only have a better chance than do women of reaching the top, but that they get there faster. Among the professional assistants a similar age differential was found; this difference reflects the decreasing number of women who have been entering public library employment during the past ten years.

TABLE 5

AGE OF PROFESSIONAL LIBRARIANS
BY TYPE OF POSITION HELD

	TOP ADMINISTRATOR		*MIDDLE ADMINISTRATOR*		*PROFESSIONAL ASSISTANT*	
AGE	*Men* (23)	*Women* (62)	*Men* (29)	*Women* (149)	*Men* (97)	*Women* (1,375)
	%	%	%	%	%	%
Past 63	18	5	15	10	2	2
59-63	4	9	17	10	..	5
54-58	..	10	17	18	6	7
49-53	4	7	..	13	2	10
44-48	..	23	14	17	12	17
39-43	26	23	24	17	16	20
34-38	30	9	7	10	21	13
29-33	18	8	3	2	31	11
24-28	..	5	3	3	10	11
23 or less	..	1	..	..	..	4
Median age	39.4	44.7	48.4	49.6	36.1	41.6

Parental Background

A majority of the librarians in the basic sample were reared by parents born in the United States. Among the professional group, 64 percent of the men and 74 percent of the women had native-born mothers; 60 percent of the men and 70 percent of the women had native-born fathers. About the same percentage of native-born parents was found for both men and women in the subprofessional group: 70 percent of the men and 71 percent of the women had native-born mothers, 67 percent of the men and 66 percent of the women had native-born fathers.

The educational achievement of the parents of these librarians was superior, on the whole, to that of the general population. The parents of the professional librarians were more highly educated than those of the subprofessionals. Graduation from senior high school was achieved by 60 percent of both the mothers and the fathers of the professional group, by 50 percent of the mothers and 52 percent of the fathers of the subprofessional group. Bachelor's degrees were earned by 9 percent of the mothers and 22 percent of the fathers of the professional librarians, by 7 percent of the mothers and 16 percent of the fathers of the subprofessionals. It is especially noteworthy that one or more graduate degrees were held by 1 percent of the mothers and 13 percent of the fathers of the professional group and by 2 percent of the mothers and 9 percent of the fathers of the subprofessional group. The general pattern of parental education was remarkably similar for men and women librarians.

The parents of these librarians also achieved a higher-than-average occupational level. The fathers of 21 percent of the professional group and 15 percent of the subprofessional were engaged in professional work at the time that our respondents were finishing high school. Another 20 percent of the fathers of both groups were self-employed; an additional 14 percent held managerial positions. A large majority of the mothers, 83 percent of the professionals and 77 percent of the subprofessionals, were not employed outside the home. Only 1 percent of the fathers and approximately 1 percent of the mothers were employed as librarians, but this, of course, is a much larger percentage than in the population at large.

The parents of a majority of both the professional and the subprofessional groups approved their children's choice of librarianship as a career. A larger percentage of the mothers than of the fathers liked the idea. The parents of the professional group were on the whole more enthusiastic than were those of the subprofessionals, a larger percentage of the latter expressing no opinion. Less than 10 percent of the librarians reported that their parents expressed doubt as to the wisdom of choosing librarianship as a life work or definitely disapproved this choice. These findings were consistent for both men and women librarians.

Marriage

The percentage of women librarians in any age group who marry and give up their professional careers is unknown. The proportion of professional women in our sample who are presently combining marriage with a library career is one in four; for the subprofessional women, one in three. Almost two thirds of the professional men and one third of the subprofessional men report that they are married. The divorce rate is higher among the women in both groups than among the men, but considerably lower for these librarians than for the population at large.[3]

Among those who marry, the subprofessional librarians do so on the average about three years earlier than the professionals. The women in both groups tend to marry about a year or so earlier than the men. The median age at the time of the first marriage was 28 years for the professional men and 24.5 years for the subprofessional men; for the professional women it was 26.6 years; and for the subprofessional women 23.9 years. After the age of thirty-five, chances that the single woman librarian will marry and continue her career seem very slim; only 4 percent of the professional and 2 percent of the subprofessional women in our sample were married after having reached that age. But 10 percent of the professional men and 6 percent of the subprofessional men waited until they were thirty-five years old or older to be married.

Librarians as a group select for their mates persons of much higher-than-average educational achievement. The spouses of 52 percent of the married professional men and 41 percent of the married professional women hold college degrees; about half of these spouses hold one or more graduate degrees. Among the subprofessional group the spouses of 18 percent of the married men and 35 percent of the married women are college graduates and about half of them hold one or more graduate degrees. Only 10 percent of the wives of the professional men and 11 percent of the husbands of the professional women had not graduated from senior high school. All the wives of subprofes-

---

[3]Stigler (*ibid.*, p. 11) reports that 24.5 percent of all women teachers in 1940 were married. He gives no marital data for male teachers and no data on incidence of divorce among teachers.

sional men are high school graduates; all but 13 percent of the husbands of subprofessional women had also graduated from high school.

A relatively high proportion of the spouses of these librarians were engaged in professional occupations during their first year of marriage. Included in this group were 36 percent of the wives of the professional men, 37 percent of the husbands of the professional women, and 27 percent and 20 percent, respectively, of the spouses of the subprofessional men and women. The professional men seem partial to librarians as spouses to a much greater extent than are the professional women; the same is true of the subprofessionals, although they are less likely to marry other librarians than are the professionals. Propinquity plus the larger proportion of women than of men on library staffs may explain this phenomenon. Only 36 percent of the wives of the professional men and 9 percent of the wives of the subprofessional men were occupied solely as housewives during their first year of marriage.

The majority of married librarians are fortunate in having spouses who are interested in their work and who give them assistance in pursuing their professional careers. As a group, the professional men receive more help from their mates than do the professional women. Only a very small percentage of the spouses of the professional librarians disapprove of their work and want them to change their careers. The subprofessionals are somewhat less fortunate in the amount of approval and assistance they receive from their mates.

Marriage appears to be far more of an asset in the careers of the professional men than it is for the other groups. Fifty-five percent of the married professional men say their marriages have been either a definite asset or an indispensable factor in their professional achievement, but only 23 percent of the professional women and 20 percent of the subprofessional men and women place marriage on the credit side of the ledger so far as their work is concerned. For 28 percent of the married professional women and 21 percent of the subprofessional women marriage has either made pursuit of their library careers more difficult or has been the chief factor in temporary abandonment of their careers.

The low marriage rate among women librarians seems due more to lack of opportunity than to disinclination to wed. Sixty-four percent of the unmarried professional women and 79 percent of the single subprofessional women say that they would like to marry. Moreover, 39 percent of both these groups of women would like not only to marry, but to give up their library work and devote themselves to homemaking; an additional 3 percent of the professional and 10 percent of the subprofessional women would like to marry and go into some other field of work. Only one third of the professional and one fifth of the subprofessional women who are unmarried profess to be indifferent or disinclined to wed, as compared with 54 percent of the unmarried professional men and 19 percent of the single subprofessional men. . . .

Personality

As compared with the average male university student, the typical male librarian is rather submissive in social situations and less likely to show qualities of leadership. He is within the normal range of masculinity in his attitudes and interests, but he tends to lack confidence in himself and to feel somewhat inferior. His feelings of inferiority, however, seem not to worry him excessively, for he experiences less than average nervous tension and irritability. He shows no great drive for overt activity, but is normally sedentary for his age. On the whole, he seems to have made a reasonably good adjustment to life, and one might guess that stomach ulcers would not be his occupational disease.

The typical female librarian has a personality profile that is remarkably similar to that of her male colleague. As compared with the average woman university student, she is submissive in social situations, lacks self-confidence, feels inferior, has an average amount of drive for overt activity, and feels a normal degree of nervous tension and irritability. She is normally feminine in her attitudes and interests. Like the typical male librarian, she seems reasonably well adjusted.

Within the general personality profile, some rather interesting differences were found between married and single librarians. The married men as a group, compared with the unmarried men, include a larger percentage who score low on general pressure for overt activity, a larger percentage who score high on masculinity of attitudes and interests and on self-confidence, and a larger percentage who show a lack of nervous tension and irritability. There is no difference in percentages of those who score low and high on social ascendancy. Among the married women, as compared with the unmarried, a larger percentage score high on overt activity level, social ascendancy, self-confidence, and femininity. But a larger percentage of the married women than of the single women experience high nervous tension and irritability. Whether these personality traits were present before marriage or developed as a result of marriage cannot be determined from our data. No significant deviations from the typical personality pattern were found for librarians of either sex who are separated, divorced, or widowed. . . .

CONCLUSIONS

The Present Public Library Personnel

The first general conclusion from our study of public librarians is that they are not a clearly defined professional group. No difficulty is encountered in distinguishing two nonprofessional categories among all the people now working in public libraries: the clerical and the maintenance personnel. Their skills are not solely or peculiarly applicable to library operations; for them a job in a public library is primarily a typist's, bookkeeper's, janitor's, or truck driver's job, only secondarily a library job. In some libraries there are also a number of administrative, supervisory, and highly specialized positions requiring full professional training, as defined by librarians, that are clearly recognizable as professional. But there are two other groups of employees, one sometimes called subprofessional and the other a group of highly trained experts in subject matter fields, who at times have an anomalous status.

The so-called subprofessionals, our inquiry revealed, differ significantly from those properly called professionals in almost every major respect. Not only do they lack professional training, but only a third of the subprofessionals, compared to nearly two thirds of the professionals, are college graduates. The median age of the subprofessionals is twelve years younger, and their average length of service ten years less than the professionals. Whereas the professional librarians say that they were strongly motivated in accepting their present library positions by the library's reputation for giving good service and by the opportunities it offered for professional advancement, the subprofessionals as a group are more interested in positions offering good work schedules and pleasant coworkers. Less than one fifth of the subprofessionals, as compared with more than half of the professionals, say that their library work contributes more to their satisfaction in life than does any other interest. Although membership in professional associations is open to the subprofessional group, a much smaller percentage of them than of the professionals actually join the associations and go to their meetings.

Some overlapping was found in the types of work performed by the two groups, but it seems clear that in public libraries subprofessionals have the training, skills, and attitudes which place them in a clerical-technical rather than in a professional category. The use of the word "professional" as part of the term denoting both groups, therefore, implies a false relationship between them.

The lack of clear definition is further evidenced by the tendency in some of the newer library school programs to make the technical training for subprofessional tasks a prerequisite for professional library school education. This continuum implies that subprofessional training is really preprofessional training and that subprofessionals are younger, partly trained members of a homogeneous occupational group, rather than fully-trained members of a nonprofessional group.

The practical reasons for the inclusion of instruction in elementary library techniques as a preliminary step in professional training are clear. They are to be found partly in the fact that the very large number of independent, small public library units call for a single person to perform both professional and technical-clerical tasks, but cannot offer salaries large enough to secure or to justify full professional training of the incumbent. Subprofessionals, then, actually are educated for hybrid professional-clerical positions defined by the institutional necessities of many public libraries as now organized. The subprofessional title was found to be used also in larger libraries. Sometimes it is to provide an internship, that is, a preprofessional temporary post for young people without professional library school training, more often as a legal designation for persons without formal professional education or degrees who are performing a mixture of technical-clerical and professional tasks. In both cases the title adds confusion rather than clarity to the definition of professional librarianship.

Lack of clarity was seen, also, in the various academic time requirements for full professional training recognized until recently by the official system of library school accreditation. Under this system identical professional status was given to graduates from schools in which the professional curriculum was covered in a fifth, or graduate, year and those from schools that included professional training in the four undergraduate years. Again, the justification for such a dual standard for professional training was the existence of many positions to be filled in schools and small public libraries with salary levels and a mixture of duties such that no one with anything but a minimum of academic preparation could be recruited for them.

Finally, it was discovered in our study that persons with graduate academic education but without formal professional library training, holding highly specialized positions within public libraries, were usually classified also as subprofessionals.

Thus, librarianship as a profession with uniform standards of formal training and a common definition of duties does not exist.

The second general conclusion from the Inquiry study is that both the general level and the career pattern of salaries for professional personnel in public libraries are inadequate and tend to be inequitable. The salary median for public librarians was found to be low compared with salaries in other occupations calling for a similar degree of skill and formal education. Unlike some other professions on relatively low salary levels, such as teaching, moreover, no widespread provision exists for insurance covering accidents, illness, or retirement for librarians, and the public library schedules for working hours and vacation do not have any unusually favorable features. The median salary for public librarians designating themselves as professional in the year of our survey (1947-48) was an estimated $300 less than the $2,800 set in that year by the American Library Association as a minimum standard for the beginner's salary on the professional level.

As we have just seen, however, the lack of clear definition of the professional group in public libraries means that the general salary median is a central point in a large range of positions, including those in "one-man" libraries where the librarian performs both clerical and professional duties — often without adequate training for either — and those held by city librarians fully trained and fully occupied in professional work.

A more important defect in the present library salary pattern revealed by our studies was the frequent lack of salary scales equitably and scientifically related to graded positions so as to establish a job and salary career for all entrants from the bottom to the top of a defined profession. Most professional librarians in the Inquiry sample had received salary increases averaging little more than $100 a year, with only two or three promotions in rank over a sixteen-year period. Except for a very small group of city library directors with salaries in the $7,000 to $10,000 plus bracket, the librarian's salary progress typically was from less than $2,000 to less than $4,000.

More particularly, a discrepancy was often found between the classification of jobs on the basis of the employee's accumulation of experience and the difficulty of the work required and the corresponding classification of salaries. The jobs progressed in an orderly fashion from the junior positions to the top position of library director. But the salaries increased only in small amounts from the junior to the middle administrative positions (division, department, or branch heads, and top specialists) that an entering librarian might expect eventually to reach. From these positions there was a large salary jump to the one, two, or three top administrative posts. Thus, most department heads and experienced, highly skilled specialists have salary rewards quite inequitably related to their contribution to the library as an operating institution. Unless they can advance or transfer to one of the few top positions — and in accordance with statistical probability only a few will do so — they end their careers in jobs that are significant professionally, but are substandard financially for persons of their ability.

This unfortunate distortion in the librarian's salary scale is unlike most professional career systems in the public services. There, progress up the salary ladder is generally commensurate with the difficulty and importance of the work performed. This is notably true, for instance, in the Federal civil service, where until recently, at least, the middle positions pushed close to the upper rung of the ladder occupied by the top directive posts. It was found to be true, also, for the salary and promotion systems in the library schools, where there was some lagging behind desirable norms with regard to promotion of faculty members from grade to grade, but where the salary scale was equitably related to the academic grades from the bottom to the top.

The gap in the library salary ladder was found to be complicated—in some degree, perhaps, caused—by the differences in the career opportunities of men and women in the library profession. In a practical sense, the two sexes form separate economic and promotional patterns. Thus, in the Inquiry libraries the men's and the women's salaries start at about the same point, but the men's salaries rise more rapidly than those of the women. Most significant is the larger average range of salary between the beginning and the top positions held by men as compared with those held by women. The women hold proportionately more of the top positions in the smaller libraries, where salaries are smaller, fewer in the larger libraries, where salaries are larger. This situation is reflected in a difference of $300 in median salary in favor of the men. A similar difference was also found between the average salaries of men and those of women faculty members in the library schools.

The percentage of men now holding positions as professional librarians is small—less than 10 percent—but the percentage of men entering the profession is on the increase. The ratio of men to women in the library schools has been growing in recent years, so that the percentage of male students now in the library schools is greater than that of the male professional personnel in public libraries. Our data show, moreover, that the percentage of male librarians in the Inquiry libraries holding academic and professional degrees is considerably higher than the percentage of women degree holders. And the percentage of male students is highest in those library schools providing the most advanced professional training. If these trends continue, women librarians as a group are likely to find themselves still further disadvantaged economically.

The disparity in salaries between the sexes with respect to the library field is not surprising. In practically all the professions it is still a man's world as far as promotion and top economic rewards are concerned. But librarianship is not an occupation that women have recently entered. On the contrary, it was one of the first occupations requiring formal higher education and technical skill in which women could rise unhampered to the top executive posts. Historically, the high quality of library service in relation to very modest salary rewards may be due in large part to the real opportunities for advancement and administrative leadership that librarianship offered women as compared with other occupations open to them.

The progressive removal in the last decades of barriers to significant careers for women in many other occupations and the increasing limitation of opportunities for promotion to the top library positions plus the inequity of salary rewards in the middle positions have created a problem both of morale and of recruiting. Our studies showed that the poorest morale among the present public library personnel is centered in the middle administrative positions, where the quite unnecessary distortion of the salary ladder aggravates the more inevitable tensions involved in the gradual shift from a woman's occupation to a "coeducational" profession. We were not able to make any studies, however, to test the hypothesis that the broadening of occupational opportunities for women of ability, ambition, and spirit and the limitation of opportunities in the library field may be having a subtle but important effect on the quality as well as the number of women attracted to librarianship as a profession.

A third general conclusion from our study is that a large proportion of the personnel now occupying public library positions that call for collegiate and professional education do not have that education and that among the library schools now providing professional education there are great differences in instructional resources. Less than three-fifths of the professional librarians in the Inquiry sample held a bachelor's degree from an undergraduate college. Such a degree is the basic minimum required for regular status in any of the organized learned professions. Only two-fifths of the professional librarians in the sample had met the minimum standard of training set by the librarians themselves for appointment of the lowest professional positions: that is, one year of professional library school education in addition to the academic bachelor's degree. The proportions of those holding the bachelor's and the professional degrees in the sample increased, however, in the younger age groups, so that if present trends continue, these formal inadequacies of academic and professional education are likely to be greatly reduced.

As to the present facilities for professional training, we have already noted the coexistence of four- and five-year library school programs, both conferring full professional status on those who complete them. A major finding of our study was that in other respects the existing "accredited" library schools vary greatly in size, in academic status, and in instructional resources. Nearly a third of the schools in the current year (1950-51) have enrollments of less than forty, a study body scarcely larger than would fill a single classroom. For these small units there is sometimes no more than one faculty member on full time, and the part-time instructors combined contribute no more than the equivalent of one additional full-time faculty member. Such instructional resources could scarcely be thought adequate for a professional curriculum that includes at least five different major subject matters, each with a different background of specialized knowledge. In these smaller units, often existing as parts of undergraduate colleges or even of noncollegiate technical institutes, the library resources are meager, the funds for faculty research and publication—necessary attributes of a graduate-professional instructional center— are nonexistent.

On the other hand, nearly a quarter of the schools in 1950-51 have enrollments of more than a hundred each. A number of these schools and some of the schools with enrollments of less than a hundred, usually existing as organic parts of public or endowed universities, have a faculty personnel, funds, and other facilities for graduate-professional instruction comparable to the newer professional schools in these universities. For the library school faculties, as a whole, the salaries and proportions of members in the higher academic ranks averaged about 10 percent below the best academic norms. But if the small, weak library schools are omitted from consideration, the comparative showing in these matters is not unfavorable. The same is true with regard to teaching load and faculty provisions for permanence of tenure, financial provisions for travel, sabbatical leave, and retirement. Only in funds available for research do the library schools as a whole make a clearly unfavorable showing.

Looked at historically, the trend in library school instructional resources, faculty status, and standards is distinctly favorable. The improvement, it is safe to assume, results from the inclusion of many of the schools as parts of universities where the faculty and the staff have been influenced by the intellectual standards and have shared the intellectual resources as well as the material benefits of salary scales and other provisions applied generally to all parts of the parent institution.

The present inadequacies of the library schools as a group, therefore, are primarily the result of great disparities in resources among these schools themselves. As in the case of the public libraries, improvement does not lie in attempts to improve the teaching resources and standards of all the schools, to set up standards that some of the small and weak institutions cannot hope to meet. The way of improvement, rather, is in the consolidation of facilities in the substantial number of strong library schools existing as parts of universities with generally adequate financial and intellectual resources for teaching and research on a graduate-professional level.

A fourth general conclusion from our study is that the personnel in public libraries is inadequately organized and supervised in terms of modern, scientific personnel management. The lag may be related to the fact that many public libraries are small, independent units where job supervision is necessarily informal and personal. Even here our study indicated that more rather than less systematic procedures would be desirable in such essential matters as definition and allocation of duties, supervision of work, arrangements for vacations and retirement.

But our findings also showed less systematized, planned personnel administration than might be expected in many of the larger public libraries employing hundreds of people. In some of the large city institutions no separate personnel offices with full-time staffs have yet been established. In few of them were the personnel offices in the hands of people with specialized training or experience for their tasks. In a number of instances the library executives seemed unaware of the significance of modern personnel practices or of the value of a personnel office under especially trained leadership.

With this lag in adequate top office organization, it was not surprising to find that in the Inquiry sample scarcely more than half the libraries (only two-thirds of those in the three largest population-size groups) had adopted personnel classification schemes or salary scales; that of the libraries having classification schemes only three-fifths had based them upon job analyses and that fewer still had used job analyses to determine the "relative worth" of each library position in establishing the salary scale; that in setting up personnel classification schemes a number of libraries had classified their employees in terms of training and experience rather than defined positions in terms of particular duties and responsibilities, a reversal of the proper procedure; that in several cases library directors who had a classification scheme and salary scale on paper did not follow its provisions in making appointments and promotions; and that in no more than half the libraries that had classification schemes and related salary scales were these subjected to periodic review and revision.

Nor for the same reason was it surprising to find that in the libraries of the sample there was evidence in many cases of lack of modern personnel procedures for recruiting, selection, and assignment of employees, for in-service training, vacation schedules, payment for overtime, and other provisions for good working conditions; that less than half the libraries have systematic methods of evaluation for promotion and for salary increases; that less than half have developed modern systems for keeping complete records of the essential transactions involved in personnel management; and that a very small proportion carry on anything approaching a systematic evaluation of their personnel procedures and instruments.

The Inquiry sought information on the functioning in the sample libraries of staff associations, trade unions, periodic conferences, house organs, and other devices for maintaining regular two-way communication between the top office, supervisors, and the other workers on all levels, to provide for the regular channeling of suggestions, requests, or grievances and for the presentation of new or revised proposals for programs and policies. There were questions, also, to discover how sensitive public library management has become to the composition and leadership of its small working groups so as to establish maximum loyalties and productivity arising from congenial group relations. The findings here were even more negative than for the more orthodox procedures of personnel management reviewed in the preceding paragraphs. Few librarians, evidently, are yet aware of these newer canons of personnel management, and fewer still have put them into full practice in their libraries.

Here, as in other procedures, public libraries are inadequately equipped with the personnel and have not developed the patterns for the execution of modern personnel policy. In modern, scientific personnel management, as much as in raising salary levels, there is opportunity for improvement of staff morale and the resulting quality of library service.

The fifth general conclusion from the Inquiry study is that the present public librarians are, on the average, oriented by temperament, interest, and training more toward the atmosphere and the working pattern of the traditional public library than toward the purposes and activities of the institution envisaged by the current official public library leaders. The questionnaires, inventories, and interviews administered by the Inquiry have provided a sketch of what the professional workers in the sample libraries are like. These data correct the stock caricatures of librarians based on chance impressions of striking deviants in the profession; they give assurance that librarians as a group do not exhibit markedly eccentric personal characteristics. Indeed, they reveal public librarians as falling within the broad range of personal traits, family backgrounds, civic and political interests characteristic generally of persons in modestly paid intellectual occupations, working on a salary basis rather than in a highly competitive profit-seeking milieu.

On the other hand, the personality inventories returned by the librarians in the sample showed their median scores to be somewhat below the established norms for persons with comparable education in qualities of self-confidence and aggressive leadership. And the returns from the vocational interest blank showed their occupational interests to be more similar to those of artists, writers, and (in the case of men) musicians than to any other cluster of occupations. Other questionnaires returned by the group revealed that with few exceptions these interests have not resulted in creative expression, even as an avocation, so that we may assume their expression to be rather in the form of aesthetic appreciation and critical appraisal.

The reasons given by the librarians for entering the library career, their choices of recreational interests, and their subject-matter backgrounds, as reported in the questionnaires, indicate further that they are as a group predominantly identified with the genteel, bookish, aesthetic tradition and that their preferences and their special knowledge are in the fields of literature, languages, history, arts, and the humanities generally rather than in the scientific-technological and politico-economic specialties and concerns of our time. With these interests, backgrounds, and temperamental preferences, librarians have found a large measure of personal satisfaction and congeniality in the atmosphere and work of the public library as traditionally conceived and organized.

It should be noted that we are here describing only norms, medians, central tendencies among the present public library personnel. In all the traits, interests, and backgrounds mentioned above, the librarians in the Inquiry sample were spread out along a continuum, so that we should find represented among both men and women in the group many gradations of physical energy, aggressiveness, self-confidence, nervous stability, masculinity and femininity of interests and attitudes, as well as the whole range of subject-matter interests and backgrounds. But if there is to be any major shift in public library objectives or activities, the present special orientation of the professional public library personnel needs fully to be taken into account. Group orientations imbedded in professional practices are slow to change, as slow as the processes of raising salary levels, realizing higher educational standards, and introducing new machinery of management and supervision.

Women in Librarianship

by Marion Wilden-Hart

In some professions the place of women is still undetermined and very often underrated. We have yet to elect a woman President of the Library Association, and even for the Councils of the L.A. and A.A.L., the number of women who seek election is shamefully low. This can be attributed to many causes — some of woman's own making, and some inherited from the past.

TRADITIONALISM

L.R. McColvin writing in *Library Staffs*, says "If women are admitted, their presence must not be prejudicial to the interests of men. Equally, however, we must protect the interests of those women who genuinely make librarianship their career." This was his view some years back and it is an opinion that is very often expressed or insinuated today. Mr. McColvin does go on to say "What we seek, therefore, is equality of opportunity and awards." And there is the crux of the problem. On the face of it women today in librarianship have the same opportunity and awards, but closer examination shows this to be not so. How many females have been denied leave of absence to attend a library school in favour of an application from a male? Why is it supposed by a local authority that it costs a man more to keep himself at a school than it does a woman, thus awarding a grant of up to £ 100 less to a woman than to a man? It has been said that it would be a good thing if librarianship were to become a profession for men and an occupation for women and whilst I am in agreement that it is a poor "occupation" for men and quite adequate for women, the professional side has much to offer to women, and what is more important, women have much to offer to the profession. Even in America, where in 1951 92 percent of registered librarians were women, Bryan in *The Public Librarian* admits that a larger proportion of men than women in the administrative groups reach the top and they get there faster. (See page 128.) This last is relevant to much criticism of an administrative female librarian. Many of our deputy women librarians and some chiefs in the past have gained their positions through hard slogging and good luck in the one system in which they have worked. And very often the reputation of all women administrators arises from experience of years and not from effort or achievement which should have won these women a senior position. We have had and still have some first-rate women librarians up at the top, but they have had to fight to get there against greater odds than many male chiefs, and their most for-

Reprinted with permission from the *Assistant Librarian* 49 (May 1956):78-70.

midable obstacle has been the traditional view that women cannot hold office as well as men.

It is true that many men are preferred for senior positions by committees because their status (married or single) will in no way interfere with their work; in fact, it is often assumed that a married man will settle and that a wife is an asset to a man of position. It is also assumed in too many cases that any female employed in the library is suitable for work with children.

RECRUITMENT

Many women entrants to the profession are not interested in librarianship as such, but regard it as a job which seems to hold much promise, opening for them a new world of people and books. Moreover, library work is attractive to a girl with some general education behind her as being a source of culture and a centre of wide general interests. She is unconcerned that a little knowledge is a dangerous thing—and supplying an author or a title when required without knowing anything about the contents of a book, affords satisfaction and a sense of purpose in the work. Indeed, this is perhaps the worst danger into which any recruit can fall; that of regarding routine as an end and of answering enquiries as a means of enhancing her own prestige. She may become library conscious—not for the contents of the books, or the little use made of the library facilities by the public, but conscious of whether the books are perfectly straight on the shelves, whether the borrower's register is up to date, or enough stationery is stamped in the cupboard ready for use. She will in fact become a housekeeper to the library and should she ever rise to being appointed Branch Librarian through her years of service in the one system, she will take as much pride in the appearance of the library as she would of her home. Some of this domesticity is an excellent thing for the profession and many of our library buildings, and the comfort of our staff rooms have been improved by a female hand. S.C. Fairchild in *The Library and its Workers* writes "There should be at least one woman in a responsible position in every large staff where women are employed. There is always a certain amount of housekeeping which is essential for the health and comfort of all."

Generally speaking, women are preferred for clerical work on account of their "greater conscientiousness, patience and accuracy in details." They have a desire to serve and they need (far more than men) personal relationships. Women lose more time on account of sickness and ill-health, and it has been said they are more often late than men, and waste time powdering their noses. They are subject to petty jealousies, more easily upset, and easily demoralized by little things. They need praise more often than men and are easily hurt when they make a mistake. They are more impulsive and emotional than men, but usually possess intuitive sympathy, unselfishness in personal service, and a keen sense of duty. A library is made up of special departments calling for special training, qualifications and abilities, and the public library staff should include persons of many and varied talents. We do not need all qualified people on our staffs. We have room for and need unqualified reliable assistants, and because there is little prospect of promotion in such grades it is unwise and unfair to employ male staff who are of the right calibre for such posts. On the other hand, there are many young girls who take on library work as a stop-gap to marriage, who need work as an outlet, who are willing to work hard and to hold certain responsibilities for a low salary because it suits them and does not demand too much of them in their free time. We need assistants like this, and they are so very much better than a second rate male who has failed at some other job and who seeks librarianship as a last resort. The lack of permanence of young girls in libraries is offset by the number of boys leaving the profession after National Service, and a girl living locally is more likely to stay at one library, since to leave home for a girl often means parental opposition as well as being against her own inclination.

PROSPECTS

A girl on leaving school decides (probably unconsciously) whether to establish economic independence (career girl) or whether to concentrate on her prospects of marriage. Most ambitious young women are aware that men still tend to dislike intellect in women except as a social ornament and that fulfillment in a career may mean unfulfillment in the emotional sphere of marriage. A man generally likes a woman who makes him feel at home, superior and satisfied with himself. Women must be liberated from the belief that the usefulness of their lives depends mainly on whether they find favour with someone else. Few girls go out into the world expecting not to marry and, while this is as it should be, it should not colour a woman's life until the time she is betrothed.

Women often think themselves interesting mainly so far as they are of interest to men. They feel they are valued more as a sex than as a person, and being valued as a type they are likely to behave like a type and are afraid of originality. Being unsure of their own emotions and purpose, they lack confidence and drive. A woman has to exert her influence to be given control and has to show she has initiative before responsibility is given. From a man this is assumed. He is expected to take office, to bear responsibilities, to work things out for himself. Proving her worth is woman's constant battle and aim. Even when she is qualified there is still prejudice and belief that emotion will influence her reason. One is reminded of the man who said, "I don't mind a lady dentist doing the filling, but I must have a man to pull the tooth"! Mr. L.R. McColvin in *Library Staffs*, writes: "If librarianship is to take its just place as a profession, if the librarian is to claim equality of status with other officers, and if he is to represent the needs of the service to committees and councils which are predominantly male, the senior executive and administrative library posts should be held by men." Success of women in the past has been judged by the few who have held administrative senior positions and unfortunately many of these have got there by chance, rather than worth. We have some fine women librarians today and they do take an active part in the profession. Yet it is still unusual for a woman to be asked to give a paper at a meeting and seldom is the fairer sex heard at all in the discussion afterwards. This reluctance to take part until asked is an inherent quality in women and should not be misunderstood. With time for reflection and encouragement, a woman can show her originality and worth and her feminine mind and logic can be an excellent complement to that of her male colleague. The ability to hold high offices depends very much on the individual woman. As a sex, few women seem to be able to ride the storms safely and well without damaging their health. The fact that a woman needs encouragement and help even as a chief does not mean that she will not make a success of the job. After all, many of the greatest men in the world have owed much to their wives who gave them comfort in difficulties, and to their secretaries who kept their work in order.

The success of professional women is dependent not only on the attitude of the public whom they serve, but also on the attitude of their male colleagues. Their status, and the status of the profession as a whole will be improved when the division of staff into professional and non-professional categories is accepted and when posts are filled by specialists to suit the work and not by qualified persons to fill the Grade.

Married Women in Libraries

by Mrs. S. Simsova

The number of women in the profession is increasing rapidly and yet little attention is paid to their problems. While with regard to the teaching profession the 'Come Back' advertisements can be seen on all sides the problem of women in librarianship remains almost unnoticed even in our own press. Occasionally there appears a letter complaining of the major difficulties waiting for women librarians in their jobs. In a recent letter of this kind (*Assistant Librarian*, May, 1961), Mrs. Glass draws the conclusion, in the light of her own experiences, that few women will find it worthwhile to qualify.

It is a waste both from the viewpoint of national economy and the individuals concerned to prevent qualified people from doing jobs for which they have been trained and to discourage new entrants from taking their examination through the fear that they will not be able to use their qualifications if they happen to be women. In this article I would like to examine the position from the viewpoint of a woman who does not let herself be discouraged. What are her chances?

If she decides to stay single her position is not too bad. With the present shortage of men in the profession she is bound to find some promotion although her progress is probably going to be slower than that of her male colleagues. In her professional life she will have nearly equal chances with men; in her personal life, however, she will be denied full development. Very likely she will choose to marry as most of her male colleagues do. After their marriage many women nowadays carry on with their work. No librarian can lose her job through marriage; what she loses are her prospects of promotion. By being married she is expected to be less seriously interested in her profession. This becomes apparent to her when she applies for her first new job. Quite possibly she is going to be interviewed about her domestic life rather than her professional experience and ability. Few authorities will deny her a job if she proves her intentions to be really serious, especially if there are no male candidates and if the grade is not too high. I think that in this respect Mrs. Glass must have been especially unlucky. Having changed my job several times in the last ten years I can say that I have been treated fairly in competition with men in most interviews, in spite of being married. It seems that the conditions are improving all the time; there are many more married women in responsible positions than there used to be.

The second critical period will come with the arrival of her first child. I expect that very few married men among librarians would deny that they

Reprinted with permission from the *Assistant Librarian* 54 (July 1961):130-132.

have improved their qualifications as human beings through being fathers. This is bound to be reflected in their work and therefore both men and women librarians should be encouraged not only to qualify professionally, but also to develop their personal life fully. Probably most women, given the choice, would stay with their children until they grow up and then come back to their profession. They would come back with more experience and with a capacity for detached judgment to gain which the academic staff of universities are sent for long periods of Sabbatical leave. Unfortunately it does not seem to be possible to do this; at least very few women succeed in it. In most cases a woman's career does not finish with marriage, as Mrs. Glass suggests, it finishes when she leaves her job to have children. All her qualifications are wasted for the rest of her life including the many years when her children will no longer depend on her.

The present superannuation regulations, relating to public libraries, make a return to local government after a period of absence difficult. In addition to the usual prejudices against women, married women, women with children—there is the handicap with regard to superannuation of costing the employing authority more than those with an uninterrupted record of service. The chances are that on her return a woman will get only a temporary non-professional job. There are a few lucky ones who have managed to come back to more responsible positions, but most women fail through lack of understanding on the part of the employing authorities.

Thus it seems that if a woman does not want to waste the many years spent on her study and give up all prospects of being able to earn later in life the money she is entitled to by her qualifications she has to carry on with her employment while bringing up her family. This is a very difficult task. What provisions are there for the few who either have to or want to do it?

Maternity leave in local government seems fairly generous. According to the Charter a woman is entitled to eleven weeks before and seven weeks after the birth of the child. The first month is on full pay, the rest on half pay plus Maternity Allowance. Further leave without pay is left to the discretion of the employing authority. This takes good care of the welfare of the expectant mother as most women can work longer than eleven weeks before the baby is due. The seven weeks after the expected date of birth of the child are much too short even if the baby arrives on time which is not always the case. Some babies are several weeks late which shortens the period even more. The mother may be certified as physically fit at the end of six weeks, but it takes much longer to recover full strength again. According to the Charter it is possible to get a further extension of leave without pay. I doubt that any authority would be sympathetic to this kind of request, seeing that some of them are even unwilling to grant leave for study purposes. Later on, as the baby outgrows its first clothes and the mother regains her former fitness, it is not so difficult for her, but it would be easier if mothers with small children could have part-time work. More authorities should follow the example of the L.C.C. who offer part-time professional work in their school libraries.

To sum up: women in the profession should be encouraged to qualify. They should not be asked to sacrifice their personal life to the profession. Marriage and family should be an accepted part of their life, because it is through them that their personalities can be fully developed. The most satisfactory solution for a woman is to retire for a few years when she is expecting her first child and she should have no fears about the future—about not being able to come back. More part-time qualified jobs should be provided to make it possible for her to return sooner. Finally, for those who do not wish to interrupt their service, there should be better understanding of their problems, longer maternity leave and more moral support from their colleagues. Not all children whose mothers go out to work are neglected or grow up to become juvenile delinquents, and working mothers do not love their children less.

As a word of encouragement to those women who wonder whether to qualify because their career would come anyway to an end, I would like to add that there are enlightened authorities who do not discriminate against women as can be seen from the fact that I was given a well-graded job when my baby was six months old.

The Status of Women Librarians

by Miriam Y. Holden

Discrimination against women librarians is a difficult problem to explore for two unusual reasons having to do with the employment of women. First, it is a field in which women have been in the vast majority since 1900. Second, it is a field which is so badly in need of trained personnel that graduates from top library schools currently have a choice of from 10 to 20 jobs from which to select. It therefore cannot be denied that women are offered employment and in large numbers, in this profession.

WHERE and HOW they are employed are the keys to the job discrimination that actually does exist in the field. For while the *education and professional requirements are the SAME* for men and women entering upon a career in library service the REWARDS, once the lower levels of employment have been passed, ARE NOT EQUAL.

Until the middle of this century, service in library work was so badly underpaid that it was left chiefly to women workers. As of 1950, however, shortages of skilled workers in library work became apparent. At that time, salaries started to go up. It was hardly an accident that at the same time men began to choose librarianship for a career in significant numbers. All during the 1950's the salary range rose steadily, and the number of attractive status jobs increased with the establishment of huge federal appropriations for nation-wide library improvement.

The financial and technological revolution developing in the library field is, nevertheless, causing job discrimination against women workers to increase rather than decrease. Although women now represent upwards of 90 percent of the profession of librarian, they are represented in the extreme minority at the top in the few rare jobs that carry highest pay and status. As more attractive salaries and career opportunities open in the future, more men will enter the field to take over even those middle-level jobs now filled by women librarians.

Thus, fully qualified women in library work now face the plain prospect of being relegated to the lowest and middle-range of salaries and status in a profession which they actually dominate by numbers. The objective evidence indicates that for women librarians there is now only TOKENISM AT THE TOP. This trend toward job discrimination will filter down to the middle-level of titled positions during the coming 20-year period unless steps are soon taken to correct the situation.

Reprinted from the August 23, 1965 issue of *Antiquarian Bookman* (AB Bookman's Weekly).

TRENDS IN LIBRARIAN EMPLOYMENT

As examples of the trend, I offer evidence from a study published in the *Library Journal* in 1950. This study revealed that, of ten of the largest library systems in the country, *only 6 percent of the professional librarians on their staffs were men. Yet this 6 percent held roughly 50 percent of the jobs at the main library,* where there are the best chances for advancement as well as professional recognition from beyond the library system itself.

The second example comes from another *Library Journal* study of 1950, which disclosed that *84 percent of the head librarians of the largest college libraries in the country were men.* In a profession where 90 percent of its practitioners are women, only 14 percent of the head librarians are women in the large college libraries. The excuse cannot be offered that women are johnny-come-latelies to university library work, for as early as 1900, there were eleven women members of the University Library staff at Princeton.

New York State set the first official standards for certification of public school librarians in 1930. In the following years, every state has adopted standards for certification of librarians. While the educational requirements, however, are exactly the same for men and women, men are rapidly taking over the best career jobs in this profession.

What is the reason for the apparent willingness of women to step aside and allow men to take over at the top of a profession which women dominate by numbers? In an interview last week with the dean of one of the foremost library schools in the country, I received some very interesting indications. There are no statistics on this, as he was frank to say, but he gave me the following as his informal opinion: The failure of women to advance in any reasonable numbers beyond the middle level of library management probably rests on two bases:

FIRST: ECONOMICS. Women find it difficult to pay for the more advanced degrees, and our culture does not encourage the subsidizing the education of female members of the family much beyond the average level, as it does for males. Therefore, comparatively few women obtain the advanced degrees to qualify for the top jobs.

SECOND: The environment of the job operation itself. As the dean said, "Right or wrong," where men are presidents and board members of colleges and library systems, they usually select men for the management operations positions, because they find men to be more in harmony with their way of thinking. We know there are exceptions to this, but the ratio of women to men in top library executive posts is in favor of MEN. Moreover, this will increase as the pattern of operation of a library or library system becomes more involved and enmeshed in a complex environment of decision making. For such management situations make it all too easy to decide in favor of a man to do the job.

MEN VS WOMEN AS EXECUTIVES

As automation and complex management operations develop in the library field, it is apparent that *men, who control the destiny of these institutions,* automatically look to *men* to manage a field which, in point of NUMBERS, is OPERATED BY WOMEN. It is notorious that the professions and employment fields where women workers predominate are always those which offer the poorest financial rewards. *Librarians as a profession rank below bus drivers in income.* It therefore seems beyond belief that women librarians would be ruled out of attaining the few top rewarding jobs that do exist in their profession.

We know women can function as effectively as men in every profession they have entered. While only 5 percent of American doctors are women, over 70 percent of Russian doctors are women, whose medical skills are recognized as being high level. In Greece, it is said that 80 percent of the coming generation of architectural engineers will be women, because the girls passed college entrance examinations qualifying them for 80 percent of the admissions. This is at a time when women architectural-engineering students in the United States are in a pitiful minority.

We know that in the United States women are the sole support of one out of every ten families. Therefore, each young girl today faces a 10 percent chance of being forced to support her family in an economy which will allow her only a *one-half of one per cent chance of earning more than $10,000 a year to support that family.*

There is no conscious program to exclude women from middle and top management in the library profession. It is, in fact, something much more dangerous for the future of women workers, for *it is being taken for granted,* a cultural compulsive, to write women out of the American economic picture except on the lower levels of financial reward.

LOW COMPENSATION FOR WOMEN

According to Mary Keyserling, director of the Labor Department's Women's Bureau,—a 1963 comparison of the two sexes showed that women received an average of only 59 percent of what men were paid on a full-time basis. Moreover, this is part of a 16-year trend in which women have become increasingly, rather than less, concentrated in the lower-paid, less-skilled jobs. This unfavorable gap is *not* narrowing, it is widening.

A good example of the exclusion of women from consideration for executive training can be found in a recent *Wall Street Journal* article pointing out the need to find ways of recruiting young college graduates for business careers. They report that whereas 40 percent of Harvard graduates of the 1950's wanted to go into business, today only 4 percent have this preference. Recruiting young executive trainees is therefore a serious problem, but no suggestion is made that the solution lies in recruiting brilliant young women college graduates. Here again, women are not even considered for executive trainee programs that may lead on to outstanding careers either in business or in librarianship, which they already dominate numerically.

Automation and the scientific revolution are now transforming our economy. Unless there can be a conscious reversal of the discriminatory attitude toward professional advancement for women, there is going to be a heartbreaking and ever-increasing gap in the wage differential of men and women workers in the United States. The National Woman's Party, always alert to this danger, has never given up its vigilant effort to bring to victory the half-won battle for equality of the sexes.

Our present challenge is to support a program of encouraging young professional women in their struggle for fair employment practices. For example, we must actively challenge, at every opportunity, the accepted discriminatory personnel practices of big business management which hires only men for corporate activities that are actually owned by the majority women stockholders.

We must actively challenge the appointment of men only to top college presidencies of even co-educational institutions, and to the appointment only of men to the managing boards of these colleges. For from these men emanates the continuing practice of eliminating women, no matter how highly qualified, from participating in the rewards of top pay and top jobs which their education and career performance entitle them to have.

The plight of the women librarians is an example and a warning to us all. The challenge to American women of the sixties is to support an effective campaign to erase sex bias in job recruitment for top positions. Only through such action can we prevent our male-dominated hiring practices from forcing women workers to remain second-class citizens in an economy of abundance.

Tokenism at the Top?

by Eric Moon

The library profession is under fire—again. The charge, again, discrimination. The victims this time, scarcely to be called a minority group, are women.

The charge was made by Miriam Y. Holden in May at the Washington Convention of the National's Women's Party. Mrs. Holden's address was titled "Discriminatory Practices in the Recruiting of Women for Leading Positions in the Profession of Librarian." It has been published in the August 23 issue of the *Antiquarian Bookman.*

Says Mrs. Holden: "Although women now represent upwards of 90 percent of the profession of librarian, they are represented *in the extreme minority* (our italics) at the top in the few rare jobs that carry highest pay and status."

She also forecasts that "As more attractive salaries and career opportunities open in the future, more men will enter the field to take over those middle-level jobs now filled by women librarians. Thus, fully qualified women in library work now face the plain prospect of being relegated to the lowest and middle-range of salaries and status in a profession which they actually dominate by numbers." There is, charges Mrs. Holden, "only tokenism at the top."

To support her case, Mrs. Holden quotes some rather old statistics from a 1950 *Library Journal* study which revealed: 1) that in ten of the largest library systems in the country, only six percent of the professional librarians were men, yet this six percent held roughly 50 percent of the jobs at the main library "where there are the best chances for advancement as well as professional recognition from beyond the library system itself"; and 2) that 84 percent of the head librarians of the largest college libraries in the country were men.

On the face of it, Mrs. Holden seems to have a strong case. For example, among the 46 large public libraries for which the Enoch Pratt Free Library issues annual salary statistics, there are only seven which are directed by women.

But then we started looking at some of the other seats of power and prestige in the library profession, and the picture began to look less black and white (male and female). The presidents-elect of both the American and British Library Associations, for example, are women. The president of Special Libraries Association is a woman.

With the surge of federal funds for library services and construction, it seems to us that among those who wield immense and growing power and influence are the state librarians and state library extension heads, and the state school library supervisors.

So what is the picture at the state level? More than 60 percent of the state librarians or heads of state extension departments are women. Among the state school library supervisors, there are only six men.

The library schools, we are sometimes told, are in a position to shape the profession of the future. Of the deans of the accredited library schools, nearly one third are women.

ALA itself is surely one of the most potent forces in librarianship today. There, Mrs. Holden could surely find small cause for complaint. The Deputy Executive Director is a woman. The executive secretaries of no less than eight of the divisions are from the distaff side. The Publishing Department, the *Booklist,* the Office for Recruiting, and the immensely influential Washington Office are all headed by women. Four of the eight members elected to the Executive Board by and from the ALA Council are women. Of the new members elected to the ALA Council this year, 15 of 24 are women. A majority of the members of the highly important Legislative Committee are women.

And finally, among the national library periodicals — which are thought by some to have some influence upon professional opinion — no less than seven have women as chief editors: the *Wilson Library Bulletin, School Library Journal, Special Libraries, Top of the News, Catholic Library World, Library Resources and Technical Services,* and the *LC Information Bulletin.*

We are not brave — or foolish — enough to take sides on *this* issue. But we do feel that Mrs. Holden might make a more convincing case if she brought her statistical ammunition up to date. We present these statistical fragments of our own only to show that her case is not so selectively simple.

PART

V

1966-1976
THE SECOND FEMINIST MOVEMENT

Women and Librarianship

An Investigation into Certain Problems of Library Staffing

by Patricia Layzell Ward

NATURE OF THE PROJECT

There is concern today regarding the social wastage of women, particularly those who are graduates and those who hold a professional qualification.

During the winter of 1962 a series of lectures was arranged by the Association of Assistant Librarians, concerning management problems in libraries. Several speakers discussed staffing problems and the position of qualified married women in librarianship. At this time eight out of every ten new recruits to librarianship were women. Following their comments it appeared that a systematic investigation of women and librarianship was justified and that the following points needed investigation:

1. The shortage of staff in libraries.
2. Whether there was a "reservoir" of qualified married women wishing to re-enter librarianship.
3. Whether there were any steps that could be taken to assist and encourage their return.

METHODOLOGY

Certain limits were placed on the investigation at the outset—it was to be confined to qualified women librarians, permanently resident in the British Isles.

The following points were investigated:

1. *Membership of the Library Association*

The ratio of men to women and the numbers of women qualifying as chartered librarians.

A number of questionnaires were distributed to various categories of librarians as described below. Copies of the questionnaires used are given in the appendix.

Excerpts reprinted from *Women and Librarianship; an Investigation of Certain Problems of Library Staffing.* London, Library Association, 1966. Reproduced by permission of the author and publishers.

2. *Attitude and behaviour of qualified women*

2(a) *Attitude and behaviour of women who studied at certain library schools during selected years*

For this purpose a questionnaire was sent to all women thought to be permanently resident in the British Isles who studied librarianship as full-time students at Manchester College of Commerce, Newcastle College of Commerce, North-Western Polytechnic and University College, London.

The schools were selected for the following reasons:

(a) Manchester for being a large school in the North-West.

(b) Newcastle for being a small school in the North-East.

(c) North-Western Polytechnic for being a large school in the South-East.

(d) University College, London, for being the only post-graduate school at the time that the investigation was carried out.

The investigation was further limited to students who studied at these schools in selected years, namely, 1952/3, 1957/8, 1961/2. It was not possible to study any year before 1952/3 because, prior to this year, some schools had not been established and one school had moved its location and not all of its records were intact. A further reason for selecting 1952/3 as a starting point was that by this time fluctuation in behaviour caused by the Second World War would have diminished. Since the time span is limited, the results must be treated with caution.

14 replies were eliminated from the analysis, 8 were returned only partially completed and 6 were returned by women now resident overseas.

2(b) *Attitudes of qualified women who resigned, or who allowed their membership of the Library Association to lapse in a given year.*

The year selected was 1962 as being the most recent complete year before the start of the investigation; 86 qualified women came into this category, 33 were unmarried, and of these women a number would have resigned on marriage—they were not contacted due to the problems of not having a current address for them.

Thirty-seven of the 53 married women were traced to a recent address and questionnaires were sent to them, 26 (70 percent) of them replied; this represented 53 percent of the total qualified married women who had allowed their membership to lapse during 1962.

Thanks are due to the many chief librarians who helped in tracing former members of their staff.

2(c) *Attitudes of women who were reinstated to membership of the Library Association during a given year*

The year selected was again 1962. The coverage included qualified and non-qualified, married and unmarried women. 65 women were reinstated and questionnaires were sent to them, 44 (68 percent) replying.

2(d) *Attitudes of women who may have been reinstated to membership of the Library Association*

It had been observed that the Appointments column of the *Library Association Record* listed, from time to time, married women who were shown as not having occupied a previous post. It was thought that this might include women returning to the profession. Ten questionnaires were sent out to

TABLE I
RESPONSE RATE BY COLLEGE AND YEAR OF STUDY

School and year		Total number of female students	Number of questionnaires returned	Percentage returned
Manchester	1952/3	18	11	61%
"	1957/8	18	11	61%
"	1961/2	21	16	76%
"	Total	57	38	67%
Newcastle	1952/3	8	5	63%
"	1957/8	12	10	83%
"	1961/2	23	18	78%
"	Total	43	33	77%
North-Western	1952/3	47	27	57%
"	1957/8	30	20	66%
"	1961/2	31	23	74%
"	Total	108	70	69%
University College	1952/3	16	8	50%
"	1957/8	19	16	84%
"	1962/1	14	11	79%
"	Total	49	35	71%
Total		257	176	68%

women listed in 1963, and all were returned; five of them from women who were returning to librarianship after a gap in their careers.

3. *Attitudes of library authorities and chief librarians to the employment of qualified married women*

As no sampling frame has been constructed covering the various types of libraries in different locations in the British Isles, questionnaires were sent to all affiliated (corporate) members of the Library Association listed in the *Library Association Year Book* for 1963. This list covered public, county, university, college, hospital and special libraries. 831 questionnaires were sent out and 665 (80 percent) were returned.

4. *Separate investigations were made into specific points raised by several of the respondents.*

PRESENT SITUATION

Much attention has been placed recently on the changing position of women in society. There are two main factors which must be taken into consideration, in all professions, when planning future recruitment and education.

Women in Higher Education

Firstly, there is the increase in the proportion of students receiving full-time higher education in Great Britain. During the present century the proportion of students in the population has risen from 0.06 percent in 1900/1, to 0.31 percent in 1963. The percentage of women receiving full-time higher education has grown to 7.3 percent, as opposed to 9.8 percent in the case of men, in their age group. However, nearly as many girls as boys pass their G.C.E. at "O" level but fewer, at the present time, stay on into the Sixth Form to take their "A" levels. Of those girls who do pass their "A" levels, the proportion of women entering higher education is the same as that for men.

The type of full-time education that women enter differs, at the present time, from that of men. In 1962/3 a quarter of the students in British universities were women—in the training colleges in England and Wales, two-thirds of the students were women. The proportion of men and women students in schools of librarianship is approximately the same as that for training colleges.

TABLE 2
THE NUMBERS OF MEN AND WOMEN STUDYING FOR THE REGISTRATION EXAMINATION AT MANCHESTER, NEWCASTLE AND NORTH-WESTERN POLYTECHNIC LIBRARY SCHOOLS, IN 1952/3, 1957/8 AND 1961/2

Year	Men		Women		Total
	Number	*Percentage*	*Number*	*Percentage*	
1952/3	46	39%	70	61%	116
1957/8	23	30%	53	70%	76
1961/2	32	31%	74	69%	106
Total	101	33%	197	66%	298

A radical change has taken place in education for librarianship recently. The 1950 syllabus laid down an Entrance Examination which was taken after a year's part-time study; the Registration Examination consisted of four groups comprising seven papers which could be taken one group at a time by part-time study or after taking a year's full-time course at library school. Having passed the Registration Examination, attained the age of 23 years and having completed a period of approved service, a student could apply to be placed on the Register of Chartered Librarians. The Final Examination was arranged in four parts which, as with the Registration Examination, could be taken part by part after part-time study or after a year's full-time course at library school.

In 1964 a new syllabus was introduced. Students with two "A" levels were exempted from an Entrance Examination; students, at the present time, can still take the Entrance Examination* but are being encouraged to take two "A" levels to broaden their education. Students now attend library school for a full-time two-year course—very few part-time courses are now available. The student takes four papers of the Part I (or Intermediate) examination which must be passed at one sitting (deferment is possible in one paper). In their second session at library school, students take six papers from a wide choice to comprise study for the Part II (or Final) examination. These do not have to be passed at one sitting. Having completed a period of approved ser-

---

*The Entrance Examination is to be abandoned from the Winter of 1967, and from that time admission to the Library Association examinations will be limited to those holding either two "A" level passes or a degree.

vice and reached 23 years, the student may ask to be placed on the Register of Chartered Librarians as an Associate. One is now admitted as a Fellow on submission of an approved thesis.

With the reorganization of education in librarianship will come the inevitable increase in the number of full-time students at library schools. Already the number of students taking a full-time course for the Registration Examination has risen from a total of 296 in 1952/3 to 600 in 1962/3. At the North-Western Polytechnic, the intake on a course has risen from 59 for the session September 1961 to June 1962, to 120 for the session which commenced in January 1964.

Students are also being encouraged to enter library school from the Sixth Form and the percentage of school leavers to students who have worked in libraries is likely to increase as the standards for entry to library school are raised. Certain schools of librarianship have already raised their own minimum requirements for entry to two "A" level passes.

WOMEN AND MARRIAGE

The second factor which must be taken into consideration is the increase in the number of women marrying and that women are marrying at an earlier age. C. M. Stewart[1] has estimated that if the marriage rates prevailing in 1957 remained constant, only 5 percent of today's young women will remain single as compared with 15 percent fifty years ago.

Of the sample of students who studied in 1952/3, 48 percent of the respondents expect to be married by 1965, and of those who were students in 1957/8, 74 percent expect to be married by 1965.

TABLE 3
NUMBERS OF WOMEN STUDENTS MARRIED OR ENGAGED TO BE MARRIED AT DECEMBER 1963

Marital State	1952/3		1957/8		1961/2	
	Number	*Percentage*	*Number*	*Percentage*	*Number*	*Percentage*
Students married by 1965	22	48%	38	74%	15	24%
Students who may not be married by 1965	24	52%	16	26%	48	76%
Total	46		54		63	

It has been further estimated that 47 percent of women in the age group 20-24 were married in 1951 as opposed to 56 percent in 1958 and an estimated 60 percent in 1973.

More useful information on the trends in the marriage age of women librarians would have been obtained if the sample of women had been larger and if the investigation had been able to spread over a longer period of time.

The median age for women students on the Registration course was 22 years, and the most frequent age of marriage was 26 years, the majority of married students being married within five years of the end of their course.

With the current changes in the pattern of education for librarianship, the age at which women librarians marry may well be lower in the future as they will possibly complete their full-time education by the age of 21.

The above factors are contributing towards a change in the place of woman in society. She now has a greater opportunity to receive full-time higher education and is not now condemned to a life of celibacy as were women who followed their chosen careers in the earlier part of this century. Houses that are easier to manage with labour-saving devices, coupled with a raising of the surtax level on earned income, have encouraged married women to continue or return to their careers. It is a social waste for women not to have this opportunity.

As the gap between the end of secondary education and marriage narrows, young women will increasingly want their career not only to appeal to them, but will want reassurance that they will have the opportunity to continue their career and to be able to return to it, should they desire a break in their career. If librarianship is to compete with other professions in the recruitment of young women, it is important that an image be presented of a forward-looking profession.

RECOMMENDATIONS

1. That employing authorities should consider the employment of qualified married women on a part-time basis.

2. That librarians should encourage the interest of married women librarians in their area, by inviting them to participate in any professional activities arranged at their libraries, e.g., staff guild meetings.

3. That the Library Association should consider, as a matter of urgency, the publication of a pamphlet encouraging women to return to librarianship.

4. That a central register of part-time posts, particularly suitable for married women not wishing to take up permanent full-time posts, should be maintained at the Library Association. During the period of this investigation a number of persons have written to the author offering part-time or temporary posts for married women.*

5. That the schools of librarianship should organize some short refresher courses for married women.†

6. That women should complete their qualification before considering a break in their careers, and that they should not allow their membership of the Library Association to lapse.

7. That married women not gainfully employed should maintain professional contact by attending professional meetings and weekend courses whenever possible.

● ● ●

*During 1964 the Library Association established an employment register for married women—prospective employers or married women wishing to return to librarianship should contact the Membership Department of the Library Association.

†At the time of going to press it is planned that a refresher course for married women will be held at the School of Librarianship, North-Western Polytechnic, during the session 1965-66.

QUALIFIED FEMALE LABOUR FORCE IN LIBRARIANSHIP

The Proportion of Men and Women in Librarianship

In 1937 the proportion of men and women members of the Library Association was about equal—however, since 1945 the proportion has remained almost constant at 40 percent men to 60 percent women.

TABLE 5
PERSONAL MEMBERSHIP OF THE LIBRARY ASSOCIATION
SHOWING THE PERCENTAGE OF MEN AND WOMEN

Year	Total personal membership	Men		Women	
		Total	Percentage	Total	Percentage
*1937	4,346	2,141	49%	2,205	51%
*1948	6,766	2,719	39%	6,766	61%
1953	10,042	3,935	39%	6,107	61%
1958	10,801	4,434	41%	6,367	59%
1963	12,934	5,153	40%	7,781	60%

Source: *Library Association Year Book* 1937-63.
*Figures quoted by kind permission of A.G.S. Enser.

Although during 1962 the proportion of new members of the association was 80 percent women to 20 percent men, the proportion of members remained constant due to the high proportion of those who resign from membership within a short period of their election, a high proportion of whom must be women.

Qualified Women Librarians

There has been a considerable increase in the number of married women who have been elected as Associates of the Library Association. (See Table 7.) However, . . . this has not been matched by a growth in the number of married women elected as Fellows of the Library Association. . . .

Resignation from the Library Association

The 1963 Establishment and Grading Census of the Library Association asked chief librarians to give figures for persons who retired or resigned from their posts during 1962. It is possible that the figures given in Table 8 will include a number of women who will have resigned on marriage or who have temporarily retired in order to have a family, but who may intend to continue their careers at a later date.

From Table 9 it would appear that fewer married women who are Fellows are removed from the Register, whilst in the case of Associates, there is little significant difference between married women and others.

TABLE 7
PERSONS ELECTED AS ASSOCIATES AND FELLOWS—SHOWN BY SEX

Year	Fellows							Associates						
	Total	Mr. No.	Mr. Percentage	Miss No.	Miss Percentage	Mrs. No.	Mrs. Percentage	Total	Mr. No.	Mr. Percentage	Miss No.	Miss Percentage	Mrs. No.	Mrs. Percentage
1937	93	43	46%	49	53%	1	1%	164	83	51%	81	49%	1	—
1947	40	33	83%	7	18%	—	—	230	103	45%	117	51%	10	4%
1948	71	52	74%	19	25%	—	—	341	150	44%	190	56%	1	—
1949	62	49	79%	13	21%	—	—	242	119	47%	128	53%	1	—
1950	77	60	78%	17	22%	—	—	226	109	48%	116	51%	1	—
1951	70	59	84%	21	16%	1	—	244	105	43%	132	54%	7	3%
1952	59	37	63%	21	36%	1	2%	262	112	43%	149	57%	1	—
1953	51	32	63%	17	33%	2	4%	270	106	39%	150	56%	14	5%
1954	53	34	64%	17	32%	2	4%	316	140	44%	157	50%	19	6%
1955	57	38	67%	17	30%	2	4%	350	158	45%	167	48%	25	7%
1956	51	45	88%	5	10%	1	2%	355	125	35%	198	56%	32	9%
1957	58	43	74%	12	21%	3	5%	307	114	37%	156	51%	37	12%
1958	54	40	74%	13	26%	1	2%	338	137	40%	176	52%	25	7%
1959	49	36	73%	12	25%	1	2%	346	134	39%	163	47%	49	11%
1960	61	46	75%	9	15%	6	10%	320	103	32%	176	55%	41	13%
1961	57	39	68%	13	23%	5	9%	407	143	35%	221	54%	43	11%
1962	50	37	74%	12	24%	1	2%	419	147	35%	214	51%	58	14%
1963	71	40	56%	27	38%	4	6%	576	182	32%	308	53%	86	15%

Source: *Library Association Record* 1937-63.

TABLE 8
PERSONS WHO RESIGNED OR RETIRED DURING 1962 AND WHO LEFT THE PROFESSION ENTIRELY*

	Urban libraries	County libraries	Total
Chartered librarians	71	43	114
Part or unqualified librarians	1,230	506	1,736
Total	1,301	549	1,850

Source: Establishment & Grading Census 1963.
*The Library Association asked how many members of the staff left *because they were leaving librarianship.*

Questionnaires were sent to married women who were chartered librarians and who allowed their membership to lapse or who resigned from membership during 1962. Five out of the twenty-six respondents had been reinstated to membership during 1963. Of those who were not in current membership at the time of the investigation, four were working in libraries and sixteen were not gainfully employed. Sixteen of the twenty-one women not in current membership had attended a full-time course at library school and only five had prepared for the Registration Examination by part-time study. The main reason given for their resignation was for financial reasons (8), others thought that they were unlikely to work outside their homes again (6), two expressed a lack of interest in librarianship. Single reasons given were a lack of interest in the Library Association, one woman was married to a librarian and another preferred to be a member of the Association of University Teachers.

It had been anticipated that a number of married women might resign for financial reasons—hence the inclusion of a question regarding membership fees. Eight respondents said that the fees were reasonable, fourteen would have retained membership at a lower fee, three would not have retained membership even at a lower figure. Married women who are not gainfully employed pay a reduced annual subscription of £1 os. od.—a very reasonable fee when she retains all her membership rights—her qualification, use of the Library Association library, and receives the *Library Association Record* each

TABLE 9
CHARTERED LIBRARIANS REMOVED FROM THE REGISTER 1957-62, EXCLUDING THOSE REMOVED ON DECEASE

Year	Fellows				Associates			
	Total	Mr.	Miss	Mrs.	Total	Mr.	Miss	Mrs.
1957	39	21	11	7	232	69	77	86
1958	24	13	8	3	117	32	42	43
1959	25	13	8	4	125	38	40	47
1960	19	14	5	—	89	32	26	31
1961	17	13	2	2	95	41	23	31
1962	25	12	9	4	116	38	38	40

Source: *Library Association Record* 1957-62.

month, plus any section or branch publication she has opted for. In answer to a question regarding interest in the *Library Association Record,* ten found it of interest, five sometimes found it interesting, one enjoyed parts of it and six never found it interesting at all.

Reinstatement To Membership

It is seen from the above section that a number of chartered librarians who allow their membership to lapse, seek re-election at a later date.

At one time chartered librarians wishing to be reinstated to membership were required to pay the subscription dues in arrears, plus the Registration fee. With a long-lapsed membership it would be expensive to seek re-election. This rule has been amended so that only the Registration fee is payable in addition to the current year's subscription.

TABLE 10
LIBRARIANS RE-INSTATED TO THE REGISTER OF CHARTERED LIBRARIANS 1959-63

Year	Fellows				Associates			
	Total	Mr.	Miss	Mrs.	Total	Mr.	Miss	Mrs.
1959	12	2	5	5	59	30	8	21
1960	4	2	—	2	20	6	5	9
1961	8	8	—	—	21	11	3	7
1962	15	2	6	7	64	29	9	26
1963	—	—	—	—	13	4	1	8

Source: *Library Association Record* 1959-63.

A questionnaire was sent to married women, both qualified and unqualified, who were reinstated to membership during 1962. The majority of unqualified women had only been elected to membership during the period 1951-60. A significant number of qualified women had been elected members between 1930-34.

TABLE 11
TIME OF ORIGINAL ELECTION TO MEMBERSHIP OF MARRIED WOMEN RE-ELECTED IN 1962

	Period of original election							
	1925 -29	1930 -34	1935 -39	1940 -44	1945 -50	1951 -55	1956 -60	1961 -62
Qualified	2	7	4	2	2	3	2	—
Unqualified	1	6	2	3	4	16	15	—
Total	3	13	6	5	6	19	17	—

TABLE 12
QUALIFIED WOMEN LIBRARIANS GAINFULLY EMPLOYED IN 1953, 1958 AND 1963

Year	Unmarried					Married					Percentage working women who married	Total Qualified women working
	Graduate FLA	FLA	Graduate ALA	ALA	Total Qualified unmarried	Graduate FLA	FLA	Graduate ALA	ALA	Total Qualified married		
1953	125	229	120	726	1,200	5	34	16	127	182	13%	1,382
1958	139	246	216	962	1,563	9	53	24	223	309	17%	1,872
1963	136	227	304	1,148	1,815	12	61	48	370	491	21%	2,306

Seven women had forgotten to pay their subscription (17 percent). A high number, 18 (43 percent), had sought re-instatement as they wished to return to librarianship and a further 7 (17 percent) wished to continue with examinations (this was the year immediately preceding the introduction of the new syllabus), and 3 (8 percent) wanted to keep in touch with librarianship. Two women had let their membership lapse on taking up posts in special libraries. Other single reasons put forward were that the regulation regarding payment of subscription arrears had been revised, that the Library Association had now allowed a science subject in place of a language qualification for Associateship, one had spent money on studying, and another had allowed her membership to lapse whilst resident abroad.

Of those who had been reinstated to membership of the Library Association, 25 were married, 4 were divorcees and 2 were widows.

Qualified Women Gainfully Employed at the Time of the Investigation

An analysis was prepared of the qualified women who were members of the Library Association in 1953, 1958 and 1963. The number of qualified women who are married has increased from 182 in 1953 to 491 in 1963, and the percentage of women gainfully employed who are married from 13 percent in 1953 to 21 percent in 1963.

Women graduates.   There has not been an appreciable increase during the last ten years in the percentage of women graduates amongst the total female membership of the Library Association.

TABLE 13
WOMEN GRADUATES EXPRESSED AS A PERCENTAGE OF TOTAL FEMALE MEMBERSHIP

Year	Total women graduates	Percentage of total female membership who are graduates
1953	665	11%
1958	815	13%
1963	952	12%

However, there has been a rise in the number of graduates taking the Registration and Final Examination of the Library Association. In Table 12 it will be seen that the increase in the number of graduate ALAs has more than doubled.

The graduates in the sample of library school students were asked to give the subject of their degree. English and history degrees predominated, and only one student had a higher degree—a Diploma in Education.

TABLE 14
DEGREES HELD BY GRADUATES IN A SAMPLE OF LIBRARY SCHOOL STUDENTS SHOWN BY SUBJECT

Subject	Number
English	15
History	13
French	6
Classics	4
Geography	3
German	2
Philosophy	1
Physics	1
Music	1
Unspecified	1

Ex-students of library schools now working. From the replies to the questionnaires sent to library school ex-students, it was found that 64 percent of the respondents studying in 1952/3 were working in libraries at the present time, 69 percent of the students from 1957/8 and 84 percent from 1961/2.

TABLE 15
LIBRARY SCHOOL EX-STUDENTS WORKING AT THE PRESENT TIME

Year at school	Total number respondents	Total gainfully employed in libraries	Percentage gainfully employed in libraries
1952/3	47	30	64%
1957/8	53	37	69%
1961/2	70	59	84%

Intention to work after marriage. The majority of women today wish to continue their careers after marriage. Of the ex-students, 80 of the respondents were engaged to be married, 59 wished to work for a short period after marriage, 21 hoped to work indefinitely, and only 10 had no intention of working after marriage. It was noted that those women who did not wish to continue with their careers had not, in the majority of cases, completed the Registration Examination.

Type of post held by married women. A.G.S. Enser prepared an analysis of the entries for married women in the *Library Association Year Book* for 1950. He discovered that there were 359 married women listed, of whom 199 were shown as occupying posts in libraries (this includes both qualified and unqualified women). Of those in senior positions—8 were chief librarians, 7 were deputy librarians, 4 county librarians, 3 chief assistants, 5 were children's librarians and 2 were reference librarians. A comparison of the *Year Book* for 1963 reveals that 13 were chief librarians, 7 were deputies, 2 were county librarians, 9 were chief or first assistants, 34 were children's librarians and 10 were reference librarians. A more detailed breakdown is given below for posts and types of library.

Effect of Marriage Upon a Career

The majority of the married respondents to the questionnaires felt that their careers had been affected by marriage. Amongst the group of women who had returned to librarianship, those without children were equally divided as to whether their career had been affected by their marriage.

The principal reason given by married women as affecting their career was the mobility of their husband and the location of his work. Other reasons given were that their careers had been temporarily interrupted by having children or that they would have been more ambitious. A lack of nursery schools and working late in the evening were each cited by only one respondent.

TABLE 16
SENIOR POSTS HELD BY MARRIED WOMEN 1963

Post	Type of library						Total
	Public	County	University National	College	Special	Hospital	
Librarian	13	2	1	38	49	10	113
Deputy librarian	7	1	1	7	5	—	21
Regional librarian ...	1	11	—	—	—	—	12
Deputy regional librarian	—	4	—	—	—	—	4
District librarian	1	3	—	—	—	—	4
Deputy district librarian	1	—	—	—	—	—	1
Chief and first assistants	9	1	—	—	1	—	11
Branch librarian	49	41	—	—	—	—	90
Deputy branch librarian	—	1	—	—	—	—	1
Mobile librarian	2	13	—	—	—	—	15
Reference librarian ..	10	—	—	—	—	—	10
Lending librarian ...	7	3	—	—	—	—	10
Music librarian	3	—	—	—	—	—	3
Law librarian	2	—	—	—	—	—	2
Commercial librarian	1	—	—	—	—	—	1
Technical librarian ..	1	—	—	—	—	—	1
Departmental librarian	—	—	1	—	—	—	1
Reg. children's librarian	—	3	—	—	—	—	3
Church or School librarian	34	8	—	—	21	—	63
Chief cataloguer	3	—	—	—	—	—	3
Cataloguer	7	3	2	—	2	—	14
Senior assistant	73	20	5	2	5	—	105
Lecturer	—	—	—	—	—	—	1

N.B. Note that there is a difference in terminology between different types of libraries.

Husband's reaction to his wife working.   The majority of women who were working reported that their husbands had encouraged them either to continue to work after marriage or to return to their careers. However, the husbands of women who had been students in 1952/3 were equally divided between "encouragement" and "not minding". Of the husbands of women who had been reinstated to membership and had returned to their careers — 18 had encouraged their wives, 8 approved, 3 did not mind and 4 mildly disapproved.

Qualified Women in Retirement

From the table below it will be seen that, notwithstanding the fact that a higher number of qualified married women are working, there is an increasing percentage of married qualified women who are not gainfully employed.

TABLE 17
QUALIFIED MARRIED WOMEN NOT GAINFULLY EMPLOYED IN 1953, 1958 AND 1963

Year	Graduate FLA	FLA	Graduate ALA	ALA	Total qualified married women not working	Percentage qualified women not working
1953	8	36	18	114	176	13%
1958	12	39	42	239	332	16%
1963	18	52	71	473	610	26%

Source: Library Association Year Books, 1953, 1958, 1963.

Reasons for leaving last post.   The majority of married women amongst the students who were not gainfully employed left their last post because they were pregnant. Other reasons, mainly domestic, are shown below.

TABLE 18
REASON FOR LEAVING LAST POST

Reason	Year of study			Total
	1952/3	*1957/8*	*1961/2*	
Pregnancy	10	9	2	21
To look after home—husband	6	2	1	9
Work and household duties too much of a burden	5	—	—	5
Change of location	1	1	—	2
Further study outside librarianship	1	—	—	1
Contract finished	—	—	1	1

The above table shows that only two women left their last post due to a change in the location of their husband's employment, although married women had given this reason as the principal one for their marriage affecting their career.

Returning to Librarianship

Amongst the sample of the library school students who were married and not working, 29 out of 34 hoped to return to librarianship, 4 did not wish to return and one was undecided.

Ninety-six unmarried students replied to a question asking about a possible return to librarianship if they had a break in their careers — 57 thought that they would like to return, 33 replied "No," and 6 thought they might possibly want to return. The proportion of students wishing to continue their careers or to return to librarianship increased with students who had studied in more recent years. They may have been influenced by current reports in the national press regarding the position of women in society today.

Reasons for returning to their careers.   Women amongst the sample of ex-library school students who wished to return to their careers did so, primarily, out of an interest in librarianship; secondly, they felt it was a waste of a qualification not to work; thirdly, they wished to continue their careers; and, fourthly, for financial reasons. Their response to a question asking for the most pressing reasons was, firstly, an interest in librarianship; secondly, to continue with their careers; thirdly, financial reasons; and, fourthly, a dread of suburban motherhood.

Interest in librarianship was the most frequent reason given by women who had already returned to librarianship. Their second reason was financial, thirdly, a desire to continue with their careers, fourthly, because they were bored at home. Last on their list was the feeling that it was a waste of a qualification not to work. Their most pressing reasons were again an interest in librarianship followed by financial reasons.

Length of time away from librarianship.   The number of years spent in retirement by women who had already returned varied between 8 and 15 years. Their age on return is shown below.

TABLE 19
AGE ON RETURN OF WOMEN WHO HAVE RETURNED TO LIBRARIANSHIP

Age group			
20-29	30-39	40-49	50-59
6	8	7	2

Of the students who studied in 1952/3 and who would like to return, half (14) would like to return as soon as possible.

TABLE 20
PERIOD OF TIME THAT MAY ELAPSE BEFORE STUDENTS RETURN TO THEIR CAREERS

Year at library school	*As soon as possible*	*Within 2 years*	*Within 5 years*	*Within 10 years*	*Within 15 years*
1952/3	14	2	2	8	2
1957/8	1	—	5	5	2
1961/2	—	—	—	—	2

If the 1952/3 group of students left their last post on marriage, it appears that they will wait until their children have completed their primary education before returning to their careers.

Children. Very few of the sample of ex-library school students who had continued in or returned to their careers had children. Five respondents had children — 2 had one child and 3 had three children — 2 of the 5 respondents had been widowed. All of their children were at nursery or day school, or were cared for by a close relative.

Amongst the group of women who had been reinstated to membership and had returned to librarianship, 17 had children: three had one child, 11 had two children and 3 had three children. However, only 3 respondents had children under the age of 11 when they returned, 8 had children between 11 and 16, and 6 had children over 17 years of age.

All of the women who were contacted by means of an entry in the Appointments columns of the *Library Association Record* had children — one had one child, 2 had two children, 1 had three children and another had four children. The age range of the children was 6-17 years. One mother had one child at work and another at boarding school. The remaining children attended day school.

Posts on return to librarianship. Of the women who had been reinstated to membership and had returned to librarianship, one-half (12) had returned to work with their previous employer. One had returned to another public library in the locality where she was now resident. Four had moved from public to county libraries. Other single moves from one type of library to another were from a university to a college, special to hospital, public to university, public to special, and, lastly, from a county to a post as library adviser with a bookseller.

Of those women who had been contacted by means of the *Library Association Record* and had returned to librarianship, 3 had worked in public libraries, 2 in county libraries and 1 in a university library. On their return, 3 had moved to college or school libraries, 1 to a county library and another to a public library.

Certain of the sample of ex-students showed a preference for returning to a different type of post in a public library; 9 out of 29 would prefer to work with young people or in a reference library.

Status on return. None of the women who had returned to their careers appeared to have lost seniority — the majority had retired as assistants and had been promoted to senior assistant on their return.

State of professional qualification. As only a few women had completed the Final Examination (1950 syllabus), it might be supposed that some of them might have studied for further examination, or started work upon their thesis whilst they were at home. This was not so, only one respondent amongst the ex-students had studied whilst she was at home. She was an ex-student of University College and had studied for part of the Final Examination.

Of the women who had returned to their careers, two with Registration Examination intended to start work upon a thesis, another, having one part of the Final Examination (1950 syllabus), may start work upon a thesis—their ages are 30, 48 and 52.

CONDITIONS NECESSARY TO ENSURE FULL USE OF THE FEMALE LABOUR FORCE IN LIBRARIANSHIP

Factors Preventing Married Women From Returning to Librarianship

The main factor stated by respondents as preventing their return was the awkward hours worked in various types of libraries, coupled with a lack of part-time posts. The next important reason was a lack of community care for children, and next a lack of domestic help. Other factors put forward in order of importance were—a prejudice against the employment of married women, superannuation problems, a lack of refresher courses and a lack of encouragement to return. One respondent felt that the pay was poor, and another deplored the lack of status of librarianship.

Factors Concerned With Librarianship

Possible discrimination against married women.   Although a number of married women thought that there was a prejudice against the employment of married women, the majority of women who had wanted to return to librarianship had not encountered any difficulty on these grounds (32 had not experienced any difficulty as opposed to 8 who had). One married graduate had searched unsuccessfully for a post as librarian, and had entered the teaching profession.

The attitudes of authorities and librarians to the employment of married women were investigated. Only 8 percent of the authorities responding to the questionnaire preferred not to employ married women. County library authorities showed the highest percentage of discrimination (9 percent).

TABLE 21
AUTHORITIES PREFERRING NOT TO ADMIT MARRIED WOMEN TO THEIR SERVICE—SHOWN BY TYPE OF LIBRARY

Type of library	Total number respondents	Number preferring not to admit married women	Percentage preferring not to admit married women
Public	367	33	9%
County	99	14	14%
University	57	2	4%
College	92	—	—
Special	46	—	—
Hospital	4	1	—
Total	665	50	8%

With regard to geographical location—Eire and Scotland had the highest percentage of discrimination against married women.

TABLE 22
AUTHORITIES PREFERRING NOT TO ADMIT MARRIED WOMEN
TO THEIR SERVICE—SHOWN BY GEOGRAPHICAL LOCATION

Country	*Total number respondents*	*Number preferring not to admit married women*	*Percentage preferring not to admit married women*
England and the Isle of Man ...	497	14	3%
Scotland	45	15	33%
Wales	107	12	11%
Northern Ireland .	8	2	25%
Eire	8	7	88%
Total	665	50	8%

The majority of authorities who preferred not to admit married women to their service gave as a reason economic pressures caused by a high rate of unemployment in their area.

Some comment by respondents on the regional problem is given below:

". . . an old fashioned pre-war idea that two incomes should not go into one home. . . ."

(Welsh public library)

". . . The bias in Ireland (for economic reasons, there is a shortage of jobs) is against the employment of married women. If you have sent . . . to municipal and civil service libraries, you will find them debarred from employing married women. Women must resign on marriage . . . this is a valid serious point in Ireland, because 93 percent of the population is Roman Catholic—it would have been because young married women do not postpone having families, and therefore married women from the point of view of continuity in employment, represent a risk. We find, however, that we can benefit greatly from taking on married women, experienced and well-trained, who have had to resign from Civil Service libraries on account of their marriage and we make the most of this opportunity when it comes our way."

(Irish University librarian)

Librarians' personal attitude.   Chief librarians' personal attitudes to married women on their staff were investigated, as it was felt that some might have a personal bias against married women. Seventeen percent of the librarians preferred not to employ married women, including 21 percent of the public librarians.

As with the authorities' attitudes, chief librarians in Ireland and Scotland showed the highest percentage of personal prejudice against the employment of women.

The most frequent reason for their discrimination was that they felt that a woman's first duty was to her home and family (22 respondents) and a further 15 said they had divided loyalty. Twenty-one respondents said they had a high rate of absence, 8 replied time-table difficulties; however, only one librarian objected to them on the grounds that they wanted part-time work. Other reasons put forward were—that they earned more (by reason of age) than junior staff (7); they leave to have a baby (6); put their home interests first and

TABLE 23
CHIEF LIBRARIANS' PERSONAL ATTITUDE TO THE
EMPLOYMENT OF MARRIED WOMEN

Type of library	Prefers not to employ married women		Only as part-time non-prof.		Prefers unmarried women or men		Total number preferring not to employ married women	
	No.	Percentage	No.	Percentage	No.	Percentage	No.	Percentage
Public	58	16%	3	0.8%	27	7%	88	21%
County	11	11%	—	—	3	3%	14	14%
University . .	4	7%	—	—	2	4%	6	15%
College	3	3%	1	1%	2	2%	5	6%
Special	1	2%	—	—	—	—	1	2%
Hospital	1	25%	—	—	—	—	1	25%
Total	78	10%	4	0.6%	34	5%	116	17%

their job suffers (6); their leave periods are tied to their husbands (5); they have a high rate of resignation (5); they should not be in competition with single persons (3); mobility of their husbands (3); superannuation liabilities (2); they ask for maternity leave (2); they work only for the money (2); they take time off without notice (1); their values of marriage are distorted (1); they cause inconvenience to other members of the staff (1); uncertainty of time they will stay (1).

A selection of comments made by chief librarians which reflect their own attitude to the problem is given below:

". . . no married women in my experience has worked because she wanted to, but because she wanted the money. Naturally her husband and her home were her first concern and work was a secondary. They are invariably unpunctual, try to crowd shopping into tea and lunch breaks, resent evening and Saturday duty and return a high sickness rate . . . other staff resent this and goodwill and discipline tend to suffer."

(Public librarian, male)

". . . I am myself married and have always found that married women who are interested in their work are often better workers than single girls. . . . In this department I have never found that a married woman expects any special privileges or that home affairs interfere with their work; in fact, if anything, they seem to have less emotional upsets than those that are single."

(Public librarian, female)

Hours of work and part-time posts.   These may be considered together. The majority of libraries must always be open for long hours necessitating shift work by staff. Since staff will already be organized for shift work, then it should be comparatively easy to employ women on a part-time basis.

There was an overwhelming preference (30 of 31 respondents) for part-time posts, by the students wishing to return. Those women who had returned would have preferred a part-time post but had, in the majority of cases, to take a full-time post. Those who had returned to a part-time post (4) were working in college, public or county libraries.

Evidence is given below that librarians and authorities are prepared to employ qualified women in a part-time capacity.

Employers' attitude to the employment of married women on a part-time basis.   In the questionnaires sent to employing authorities, a question was asked regarding the total number of women employed, and of these the number who were qualified, and whether they were working on a full- or part-time basis.

TABLE 24
MARRIED WOMEN WORKING IN LIBRARIES 1963

Total staff	Married women employed in professional posts				Married women employed in non-professional posts			
	Part-time		Full-time		Part-time		Full-time	
	No.	*Percentage of total staff*	*No.*	*Percentage of total staff*	*No.*	*Percentage of total staff*	*No.*	*Percentage of total staff*
13,660	178	1%	1,114	9%	2,076	15%	1,138	8%

Whereas 9 percent of the total staff employed were married women employed in professional posts in a full-size capacity, only 1 percent were employed on a part-time basis. It was noticeable that more county libraries had married women employed in a part-time capacity in professional posts.

Authorities were asked whether they were prepared to employ part-time staff or whether they preferred to employ full-time staff only. Eighty-seven percent of the public libraries, 99 percent of the county libraries, 93 percent of the university, 88 percent of the college and 89 percent of the special libraries were prepared to employ staff on a part-time basis.

One of the ex-students made the following comment on this point.

". . . Compared with other professions, except nursing, it is very difficult for a woman to return to librarianship after marriage because of the hours, e.g., four evenings a week until 7 p.m. I think, therefore, that more authorities should employ married qualified women librarians as *part-time* senior assistants, e.g. two could work in a rota so that a reader's advisers desk would be constantly manned by a qualified assistant."

(Unmarried respondent, aged 23)

Arrangement of part-time work.   Questions were put, both to the women in various samples and to the authorities, concerning the arrangement of part-time work, to see whether there was a preference for women to work either for a certain number of hours per day, or a certain number of days per week.

Neither the majority of women or authorities had any particular preference. Where the authorities did have a preference, public, university and college librarians all preferred a number of hours per day.

A selection of comments made by women and chief librarians is given below.

". . . personally I would prefer to work for five days continuously every fortnight, so as to have the week-end free rather than a day off mid-week. Alternatively by rota system work half days on Wednesday and Saturday."

(Married, 43, 4 children)

"A plea for libraries to consider taking part-time cataloguers. I have several married friends who would work mornings or afternoons and cataloguing is eminently suited to this sort of arrangement."

(Married, 33)

"My present job of school librarian is ideal for a married woman as I work a five-day week with regular hours and have four weeks annual leave and Bank Holidays and two extra days at Easter, Whitsun and Christmas. I am in fact doing two part-time jobs and could easily drop one of them and only work 2½ days a week. . . ."

(Married, 27)

". . . at one time we advertised for married women who are qualified librarians who might wish to work on a part-time basis on graded posts. The response was very disappointing and we had only one or two replies. One was from a librarian who wished to work during the school terms only and unfortunately we could not fit her in. We would be happy to employ qualified married women for a few hours each day, or for a few days each week, provided that we can get someone to fill in the rest of the 38 hours doing either professional or non-professional work according to the needs of the service."

(County librarian, female)

"Technical college librarians tend to be a special case. It is in fact an advantage here to have a married woman as my assistant. During the long summer vacation the college is virtually uninhabited and she is pleased to have an extended holiday in the form of annual leave due, time owing for working late during the term and some weeks without pay. . . ."

(College librarian, male)

". . . I have been prepared to arrange for two qualified women to divide up an APT post between them and put out a general advertisement on these lines. Up to date, however, I have never found two qualified women in the same part of the county at the same time so have been unable to experiment on these lines. . . ."

(County librarian, female)

". . . We frequently find that it is often more convenient to employ two married women than one full-time married woman, totalling the same number of working hours."

(County librarian, male)

". . . the married women we have employed as part-time assistants have all been outstanding, extremely reliable and efficient."

(Public librarian, male)

Superannuation Problems

The Local Government Superannuation Act has been a barrier to married women returning to their careers in public and county libraries. At the present time if a woman wishes to return to a post subject to the above Act, she is required to have her contribution paid for the years when she has not been employed either by herself or her employer. In the majority of superannuation schemes this problem does not arise as a woman will withdraw her contribution on retirement and then re-join the scheme on her return—the pension dating from the date of her re-entry and being a reduced pension. This has not been possible in local government; however, a working party of NALGO has had the matter under examination and legislation to amend this section of the Act is expected in the near future.

Refresher Courses

Of those women who had returned to librarianship, 24 would have preferred to have attended a refresher course before their return. Only 6 women did not think it necessary, of whom 3 had been away for less than two years, 2 had worked during their break from librarianship, and 1 had been away for twenty-two years. Of the ex-students who wished to return to their careers, 34 would prefer to attend a refresher course—only 6 did not think it was necessary—3 of whom had attended the course at University College.

One special librarian, returning to work after a gap of six years, attended a two-week course at Aslib and found it very useful. One respondent would have liked to attend a refresher course on moving back to public library work after a short period in a special library.

One unmarried respondent made the following comment on this point: ". . . I consider that refresher courses for married women returning to work will become more and more a necessity of our economic life. As a relatively recent attender of a full-time course (1961-2) I consider that the greatest need will be for a course aimed at showing the progress of librarianship and the present state of co-operation, sources, bibliography and retrieval methods as a whole, rather than a course trying to teach such topics as new issue methods, building design, methods of documentary reproduction—topics which can be picked up during practical experience."

Organization of the course. It was suggested in the questionnaire circulated that the course might be organized as a two-week full-time course, or that attendance should be on one day a week for two months or for two days a week for one month. There was an overwhelming preference for a two-week full-time course.

Professional Contact

Although women might wish to attend a refresher course before returning to their careers, the majority of the respondents who had had a break in their careers had also maintained some form of professional contact during that period.

Professional press. All women who retain their membership of the Library Association (at a reduced fee of £1) continue to receive the *Library Association Record.* In addition to articles on current professional practice, there is also a news supplement. They may also continue to receive publications of sections or groups of the Library Association to which they may belong.

Professional meetings. Of the ex-students who were now married, 36 percent attended professional meetings when these were of particular interest (this percentage includes those working and those not gainfully employed), as opposed to 50 percent of the unmarried women. One-third of the women who were still in retirement, but had been reinstated to membership, attended professional meetings.

Personal contact. Eleven percent of the women who had been students at library school had either husbands or relatives who were librarians. Many

women not gainfully employed at the present time were also in contact with
ex-colleagues or women with whom they had studied at library school. Other
women had made contact at their local library, and some had been invited to
meetings of the staff guild. These were said to be especially valuable, providing professional contact on their doorstep. This contact, if encouraged by the
local chief, may be of value both to the library and the women in retirement as
some women had by reason of this close contact been able to give assistance
during staffing crises. A comment on this point was made by an unmarried respondent.

". . . Can the L.A. think up some sort of 'on call' system in the large
urban areas, such as those running in the nursing and secretarial professions?"

Lack of Encouragement to Return

Several respondents commented that little was being done at the present
time to encourage qualified women to return to librarianship. The Department of Education and Science has produced a leaflet encouraging married
women teachers to return to their careers. The situation is not quite so simple
for librarianship as it is for teaching—for the Library Association is a professional body, not an employing authority. However, some chief librarians are
encouraging married women to return, by placing advertisements in the press
aimed at married women. This is particularly so of the London County Council's* Education Library Service, where half-time posts are offered to married
women with the possibility of working fewer hours in the vacation.

In the paragraphs dealing with the arrangement of part-time work, it can
be seen that several county librarians had tried to recruit married women to
their staffs. The comment below is made by a chief librarian who is herself a
married woman with a family.

"In this day and age it is a fallacy to consider that marriage makes a
woman less competent to continue her interest in librarianship than it does a
man. The incidence of child-rearing can present some personal problems, but
given the will to overcome them and reliable domestic help, a normal happy
home life can make librarianship as satisfying and rewarding for a married
woman as for a married man.

"Our wartime and post-war marriages of female staff produce the following facts: of the 23 marriages, 11 have returned to librarianship after raising a
family; 8 have remained at home with young families so far; 2 have had
families and have taken up teaching; 2 have married and remained in librarianship without having families so far. In our experience the wastage, we consider, will not be great, as of those who have not returned, 10 express a wish to
do so when their families are older, even if only for part-time employment
initially.

Barriers Outside Librarianship

Community care for children.   It is very difficult for a mother to take up a post
before her child reaches the age for entry to primary school. Although many
professions are encouraging married women to return to their careers, very

*Now the Inner London Education Authority.

little is being done to provide more state nursery schools. Such nursery schools have long waiting lists, and unless one is a teacher (for whom special arrangements may be made), or widowed or divorced, it can be difficult to obtain a place for a child at nursery school. It is rare today for a woman to have full-time help in running her home, and few women have a relative to care for their children. In certain localities, groups of professional women have taken action and organized nursery schools for their children.

Domestic help. Very many of the women who have both a job and a home to run would like to have some domestic help to relieve them of some or all of their domestic chores. Today, domestic help is increasingly difficult to find. Refrigerators that enable women to shop at their convenience, washing and washing-up machines, electric mixers, polishers and cleaners have helped to make the running of a home easier.

CONCLUSIONS

1. There is undoubtedly a shortage of staff in libraries today; evidence has been given in Chapter 4 that in 1963 there were 639 graded posts vacant in municipal and county libraries. This does not include new posts which may be created through the expansion of the public library services following the Public Libraries Act, 1964, nor the expansion of other types of libraries.

2. The number of qualified married women who are not gainfully employed, but who have retained membership of the Library Association, has risen from 176 in 1953 to 614 in 1963. Evidence has been given that a number of qualified married women may allow their membership of the Library Association to lapse when they are not working in a library. If encouragement were to be given to these women to return to librarianship, some positive relief would be given to the shortage of staff.

3. Assistance could be given to these women to return by the creation of more part-time posts in libraries and by the provision of refresher courses. Although the Library Association, unlike the Department of Education and Science, is not an employing authority, the publication of a suitable pamphlet, such as that produced for teachers, would encourage married women to return to librarianship.

4. The above point (3) will become increasingly important in the future. It has been shown that an increasing proportion of women librarians may marry, and coupled with this is the probability that they may marry at an earlier age, due to changing social conditions. The change in the pattern of education for librarianship may accelerate this. Under the 1950 syllabus, the most frequent age of marriage for women who had been full-time students at library school was 26 years, the majority marrying within five years of the end of their course. The most frequent age of the women at the birth of their first child was 28, and the majority of women not gainfully employed left their last post because of pregnancy. Hence it was possible that the pattern of their employment was as follows—if they entered librarianship at 18, went to library school at 21, married at 26 and retired at 28, they worked for three to four years before qualifying and for five years after attending library school. (It is admitted that this tendency is drawn from a small sample of women librarians.) The majority of full-time students at the schools of librarianship may in future enter library school directly from the Sixth Form, and they will not

have worked as paid members of a library staff before they sit their Final Examination at a possible age of 20-21 years. They may marry at an earlier age and hence may work for a shorter period before a break in their careers. It is possible that qualified women may have their families in their mid-twenties and to return to their careers in their early thirties. Having raised their families, they may then resume a career which could last until 55-60. It is important that consideration should be given now to the problems of re-training and encouragement for women to return to librarianship

REFERENCE

1. C.M. Stewart, "Future Trends in the Employment of Married Women," *British Journal of Sociology*, December 1961, I-II.

The Sexuality of the Library Profession: The Male and Female Librarian

by Arnold Sable

Everyone is familiar with the stereotype of the librarian: she's a *she*, wears a long, unfashionable dress down to her calves, sits at a desk in view of all library users with a crabbed, tightly pursed look upon her face. Bespectacled, hair pulled back behind her ears, she is unfailingly and eternally middle-aged, unmarried, and most uncommunicative. She exists to put a damper on all spontaneity, silencing the exuberance of the young with a harsh look or a hiss of air. Her only tasks seem to be the checking out of books and the collecting of fines. Books to her are best left upon the library shelves where they do not become dirtied or worn.

This stereotype, although mainly the butt of cartoonists, has been drawn so often that even flesh-and-blood librarians have fallen victim to believing in its reality. She is someone you would not want your son to marry, an ultimately pitiable figure with no "outside interests." She got her job by knowing the mayor, or someone on the board of trustees. There at the desk she will stay, stamping out her books, until her retirement. She will be publicly thanked by these pillars of society at the end of her career for her service to the community.

Today's librarians fight hard to combat the stereotype. They remind cartoonists—and television producers—that, whatever the librarian *might* have been in the past, today she (and he) is an involved, sprightly, up-to-date, smiling individual with enough get-up-and-go to tackle almost anything, even bewildered teenagers, the helpless disadvantaged, and the physically maimed. Their libraries are aware, involved, full of excitement, as pertinent as the headlines. In their efforts to destroy the stereotype, librarians tend to prove how the spinsterish lady could not possibly exist in the noisy, outreaching library of today.

What is important is that librarians, in their efforts to change "the image," have in effect accepted the stereotype. They are acknowledging the possibility of its truth when they expend their energies to show that the real librarian is exactly the opposite. The real librarian is like everyone else, only more so, more attuned to the now. She is interested in the latest in fashion

Reprinted by permission from the April 1969 issue (748-751) of the *Wilson Library Bulletin.* Copyright © 1969 by the H. W. Wilson Company.

clothing and otherwise. The real librarian participates in discussions on important issues even when they might become controversies. Moreover, the real librarian might even be a man with a wife and family, no less, with outside worries, like the rising cost of living and getting the children into a good college.

How did this stereotype develop? The librarian was not always considered an emotionless woman. In the nineteenth century, running a library was considered a man's job. For example, from its establishment in 1841, all the head librarians of Poughkeepsie's public library were men. It was not until 1920 that the library had as the tenth head librarian its first female. Books and men *did* go together in the nineteenth century. Men always predominated when it was a question of who was to be in charge of books. At the first convention of the American Library Association in 1876, of the 104 attendees only 13 were women. When it came to libraries, men were everywhere.

The male dominance of the library profession continued into the twentieth century. But the librarian stereotype was changing into the one we know today. The nineteenth and eighteenth centuries caricatured the librarian as the bibliophile, a pale, undernourished man who lived only for his books. What was it that changed the popular conception of the library from a male to a female?

Several factors aided the change, like World War I, which took men away from the home front and created or expanded professions in the postwar era. The woman suffrage movement was at its height, although women did not need to force their way into this profession. The Depression saw probably the greatest flowering of the female librarian. Salaries were low everywhere, but a man could not expect to raise a family on a librarian's wage. He turned to other professions, leaving the public library, and possibly the schools, to women.

The rise of the graduate school may have contributed to the present male dominance by gradually adapting itself to the needs of the male librarian. The graduate school, the growth of interest in professionalism, and the rise of certification, increased in importance from the Depression years onward. A male-female polarity might be at work here. The male opts for control and seeks to establish guidelines in order to create a profession which would include the qualities which he finds necessary to himself.

Following World War II and the rise in affluence, men began again to enter the profession in significant numbers. Salaries increased, and with the increase came the various new technocratic positions in new cooperative library ventures which, when financed by State and Federal funds, offered salaries at unheard-of rates. These positions were filled mainly by male librarians.

The male librarian today brings something new to the profession, something about which the nineteenth-century male was never concerned. The male librarian wants first, before proving himself as a librarian, to prove himself as a male. He does not want to be considered as belonging to the female stereotype. He wants personally to exclude himself from the sexual characteristics which have in the popular mind characterized the female librarian. His maleness is in question. He must demonstrate those qualities which distinguish himself from females. By emphasizing these qualities, such as aggressiveness, he concludes he can experience a larger association with other males, such as businessmen and Federal career men, rather than with the narrow-minded purveyors of his own profession who, by coincidence, are mostly female.

There are decisive characteristics which are considered male and female. When we consider what constitutes maleness and femaleness, we might compile a list such as this:

Male	*Female*
aggressiveness	retiring disposition
aloof	maternal
commanding	relinquishing authority
bureaucratic	personal
extrovert	introvert
man of action	delays decisions
impersonal	sensitive

In examining these qualities, we find that they are sexual characteristics which have been with mankind throughout history: the male, the maker of decisions, the molder of destiny; the female, the watcher in the wings. Lewis Mumford, in *The City In History,* endows cities with sexual characteristics. The city of the past was maternal, the protector of its inhabitants. The city of today is being destroyed by many forces and becomes like a male in its impersonality.

Along with other influences arising in the twentieth century which have acted upon the library profession has been another social change of vast importance: the rise in power and dominance of the mass media together with advertising. As the librarian watched the hold of the mass media upon the public mind, he gradually began to think that he could use some of their techniques *pro bono* library. After all, the library must continuously convince taxpayers and municipal authorities of its effectiveness, and what better way to do this than to use lessons learned from the mass media and advertising?

A few years ago, a meeting of librarians in New York City was held at one of the largest and oldest advertising agencies in the country. Following the meeting, the librarians toured the agency which occupied several office floors. The keynote of the agency—and this is probably similar with others dealing in "public relations"—was its pretentiousness. Each office was styled in a particular period, while each office "door" was a wood or iron gate, again of a particular period. The executive dining room—hand-hewn tables and a huge fireplace—had been brought intact from an old inn in New England.

The juxtaposition of styles, the use of styles for effect instead of for reasons of taste, the indifference to historicity, the lack of anything solid and real, all are elements of the mass mind, mass media atmosphere about us. Here today, forgotten tomorrow. Nothing is truly permanent as one fact, or style, or creation, will be succeeded by another fact, style, or creation. Nothing is as important as the present.

For libraries to fall into this error of thinking would be disastrous. Unfortunately, the doing over of yesterdays is a male trait. Women tend to preserve and conserve. Housekeeping is for women. The stories of female librarians saving things are legion. Local history collections have been built up by female librarians. Men, tending towards sweeping, panoramic views of life, are not savers. Traditionally they are not concerned about details. They only make decisions.

Again, we are referring only to sexual traits. There are certainly excellent, conscientious local history librarians who are male, as there are, by advertising agency standards, excellent female advertising — or mass media — executives.

The male librarian when dealing with people, be they other librarians or members of the public, does best if he possesses some of the feminine characteristics, for the human contact benefits by the qualities of warmth and personal attention which are inherent in the feminine personality. The female librarian, however, who assumes the personality of the male administrator becomes neither male nor female.

One of the talked-out books of 1966 was *Our Children Are Dying* by Nat Hentoff. The book is a description of the public and private agonies of Elliott Shapiro, principal of P.S. 119, one of the ghetto schools in Harlem. The book is a paean to Dr. Shapiro and his methods in combatting the education establishment and educational apathy. In reading the book, one is struck with astonishment at how ordinary Dr. Shapiro is. No intellectual or outstanding personality, he. What Hentoff considers remarkable is the amount of personal, thoughtful attention Dr. Shapiro gives to everyone, child and adult. This principal is generous, kind, and a decent human being. Are these traits so lacking in school principals today that their appearance is unusual and has to be documented in a book? Will we have to do something for librarians soon and have a book written about a single, compassionate librarian?

I am not saying that male librarians are suspect, or that female librarians are to be prized. I believe that all of us err on the side of the angels from time to time. However, at this difficult period of history when standards do not really exist, when the whole two thousand years of civilizing influences are being thrown out the window, it behooves all librarians to remember the feminine side of the personality and, when we are harassed by the pettiness of some library details, to lean toward those qualities which are judged to be feminine. The hard-hitting masculine man deceives no one. The library profession, like teaching, social work, and medicine — any profession dealing face to face with people — should guard well its feminine qualities.

Are there important considerations which should be taken into account when comparing the librarian of 1876 with the librarian of 1969? The nineteenth-century librarian had a single-mindedness of purpose which would be almost impossible to maintain today. That librarian considered his books the prime object of his concern. Today, the librarian is bombarded on all sides by library materials, social issues, complexity of organization — all of which he must deal with intelligently and forcefully. His range is more far-reaching.

However, until libraries consist of a computer wall which the user plugs into at home, the librarian must continue to deal with people. He should be aware of the more desirable qualities which are best needed in dealing with people, qualities often considered feminine. As long as he recognizes the necessary feminine side to the profession, no harm will be done. In fact, more people should then be turning to their public libraries for the warmth and understanding which they find lacking in their offices, cities, and government.

The Liberated Librarian?
A Look at the "Second Sex"
in the Library Profession

by Janet Freedman

"Let us consider women in the grand light of human creatures who in common with men are placed on earth to unfold their faculties," pleaded Mary Wollstonecraft [Godwin] in her introduction to *A Vindication of the Rights of Women*.[1] Nearly 200 years later a United States Presidential Commission on the Status of Women was established to develop plans for advancing the full partnership of men and women in our national life.[2] The awareness of this discouraging lack of progress has elicited the concern of radical college women and middle-aged mothers. Whether demanding an immediate end to an oppressive "sexual caste system" or advocating moderate schemes for accommodating family and career life, today's women seem determined to reverse the frustrations which have marked the history of feminism. Does the new feminism have implications for the library profession? What is the potential for women librarians today?

It is ironic that the profession which was 90 percent female in 1940 and is still numerically dominated by women may prove especially difficult to women trying to challenge stereotyped limitations on sex roles. The general rule that "it is harder for a woman to be appointed or promoted to a leadership position than it is for a man,"[3] certainly applies to library employment where men occupy the top posts and receive the greatest remuneration. A recent career guide to librarianship stated ". . . it is a fact recognized by both men and women that men will advance further and at a more rapid pace than women. In other words, men attain higher salaries and top posts at a younger age with less experience than do their feminine counterparts. City administrators prefer men to head large public libraries. Men usually head large university libraries, also. The trend toward male administrators is a growing one and is a factor in attracting men to the profession."[4] Data gathered by Richard and Ida Simpson corroborate the sexual discrimination against women in top administrative library positions.[5]

The male ascendency has benefited the profession in many ways. In line with prevalent cultural norms, salaries have risen sharply to satisfy the material needs of the "heads of families" entering the library field after World War

Reprinted from *Library Journal* 95 (May 1, 1970):1709-1711. Published by the R. R. Bowker Co., a Xerox Company. Copyright © 1970 by Xerox Corporation.

II.[6] The male recruits have often offered more dynamic leadership than the females whom they replaced.

It is frequently overlooked, however, that the women entering the library profession in recent years resemble their predecessors in anatomy only. They too have been attracted to the vital and exciting challenge of discovering human solutions to the knowledge explosion. With most of the creative posts dominated by men, women are likely to be utilized for their "housekeeping" talents in serials, acquisitions, and cataloging work, or for their "patience and warmth" in school libraries and children's departments. At a time when women are aspiring to and receiving high positions in many previously "closed" fields, their chances for upward mobility in the library profession appear to be considerably reduced.

Female librarians customarily and with justification blame sexual discrimination on male egotism. This is borne out by the fact that male librarians usually hire other males as their chief administrative associates, leaving only the "middle management" positions for female professionals. In a chapter contributed to Etzioni's *The Semi-Professions and Their Organization,* the Simpsons mention other considerations including women's traditional reduced commitment to work, lower motivation, and discontinuous work histories.[7]

The belief in masculine superiority is shared by most females who offer little support to members of their sex challenging the male dominance of administrative posts. As Simone de Beauvoir points out in her classic work, *The Second Sex,* "neither men nor women like to be under a woman's orders."[8] She suggests that frequently a woman's feeling that she is the victim of discrimination gives rise to "exaggerated affection of authority and lack of ease" in dealing with subordinates—a situation which mars the effectiveness of many female librarians.

Married women with high professional aspirations are occasionally envied and resented by single colleagues.[9] This point may have validity in the library profession where statistics imply that many women may not have become librarians if they had married.[10]

Other difficulties face the female married librarian, including the woman who does not aspire to administration but wishes to continue her career. Despite the protests of some militant women, the husband's job usually dictates where a couple settles. Many locales offer very few professional library positions as compared with opportunities in other fields, notably teaching. Even where potential opportunities exist the familiar problem of the foggy public image of the librarian often prevents the establishment and funding of needed professional positions. Part-time positions, other than in cataloging or subprofessional work, are not plentiful. Library scheduling is rarely flexible and less easily accommodates combining career and family life than does nursing or teaching, for example.

Married women with household responsibilities may not be able to find a challenging—or, often, even a dull—full- or part-time job. Anxious to utilize their education and professional experience, many women volunteer their services to school, public, and religious libraries. While outstanding contributions are made by volunteer librarians, their generous gift of time and talent sometimes delays trustees or school officials in their consideration of more permanent—and more expensive—solutions to library needs. The lack of salary usually weakens the commitment of the volunteering librarians and the agency receiving her services. Little money for necessary supplies and clerical assistance is available outside the library's formal budget. Some women who have embarked on volunteer projects discover they are bogged down with typing and other routine clerical tasks. Often the program discontinues altogether when the particular volunteer is no longer available.

It is often deplored, but nonetheless evident, that librarianship is a low-status occupation. Despite the frequent use of the term, it may never achieve the status of a true "profession."[11] For this reason recruitment of top people of both sexes will continue to be a problem. Sex discrimination within the field, particularly at a time when women are challenging employment barriers and striving to gain new levels of prestige, will make it difficult for librarianship to attract highly motivated females. Of course, many women consider the opportunity for service and personal satisfaction as important as chances for mobility and high status. But among this group of potential candidates there may be many women who are discouraged by the difficulties of combining library work with family responsibilities. Kindred professions certainly allow increased opportunity for significant part-time work and offer easier re-entry for those who interrupt their careers during the years when family concerns are most pressing.

The present employment outlook must change if libraries are to attract qualified women and keep those already prepared for the profession. Possible solutions are plentiful and should be thoughtfully considered by librarians, libraries, graduate schools, and professional associations.

Equality of opportunity should be stressed by all libraries. Although sexual discrimination in hiring is now illegal, evidence cited earlier indicates that it is practiced. Rather than employ the conventional excuses for *not* hiring women, libraries should consider the opportunities, many of which can be mutually beneficial, for accommodating their particular job requirements.

Many women obviously want to combine marriage and career. The present difficulties in locating household help and the current shortage of day care centers usually make full-time employment hard if not impossible. Part-time opportunities must be created. Hiring two women to fill one job opening offers both librarian and library a creative solution. There are very few professional positions which cannot conceivably be shared. Hypothetically, a public library could utilize two childrens' specialists, one an outstanding program planner and public relations expert, the other concentrating on book selection. Division could depend on other considerations than professional duties. It is conceivable that the two women would prefer handling a wide variety of skills, alternating to prevent the tediousness which often accompanies library work. Budgetary considerations often prevent libraries from providing important services and overload the schedules of present staff. A highly qualified professional employed on a part-time basis could certainly alleviate these situations.

Temporary employment opportunities can also be created if librarians are willing to present trustees with the wisdom of a scheme which seems to speak for itself in the potential offered. Housewives who do not want to accept a formal work commitment may welcome the chance to contribute professional skills at a professional rate of remuneration on a temporary basis. Such occasions include special projects or periods of increased work. Libraries should certainly have substitutes for professional staff members who are ill or vacationing. If, indeed, a provided professional service is valuable, it certainly should not be curtailed when the permanent staff member is not available.

Substitutes and temporary workers may become permanent staff if and when they decide to return to full-time work. Their professional skills and knowledge of progress in the field will not be dated and re-entry into an interrupted career will undoubtedly be easier. Both librarians and libraries would have been afforded the opportunity for mutual observation and evaluation. As with school systems, libraries could easily gather lists of professional substitutes and potential temporary employees. Library schools and professional associations are additional sources of temporary specialists.

Professional associations should make an effort to keep in touch with the many women who are not presently employed in libraries but who perhaps look forward to re-entering the field. The dialogue between those temporarily "outside" the work world and active professionals also suggests reciprocal benefits. Nonworking librarians may keep informed of current professional thought, while offering employed librarians a more objective view of certain issues than can be seen by those most closely involved.

Library schools have great potential for improving the position and enlarging the opportunities for women in the profession. Rather than furthering the prevalent myth that women cannot be successful administrators, graduate schools should try to attract female candidates who can fill leadership positions. Instead of discouraging women in the light of their career limitations, library schools should innovate in reducing these restrictions. Recognition of the problem of interrupted employment can be remedied by alumni institutes which can keep temporarily housebound librarians informed in the areas of their specialty and of professional concerns in general. In cooperation with libraries, courses can be established where necessary to renew skills and make re-entry into the job market smoother.

It is hoped that some of these ideas will encourage further discussion and promote other practical suggestions for making the library profession a rewarding field for both men and women. The new decade promises real change in the status of women in all areas of life. The formerly negative image of the "feminine" professions can be transformed if both sexes cooperate in recognizing problems and offering creative solutions. By setting precedents in this and other areas, librarianship may yet receive a positive public image and deserve to consider itself a vital profession which can attract highly competent men and women.

REFERENCES

1. [Godwin], Mary Wollstonecraft. *A Vindication of the Rights of Women* (New York: Norton, 1967), p. 33.

2. *American Women: Report of the President's Commission on the Status of Women, 1963.* (Washington, DC: Government Printing Office, 1963).

3. Ginzberg, Eli, ed. *Life Styles of Educated Women.* (New York: Columbia Univ. Pr., 1966), p. 95.

4. Wallace, Sarah Leslie. *So You Want To Be a Librarian.* (New York: Harper, 1963), p. 86.

5. Simpson, Richard L. and Ida Harper Simpson. "Women and Bureaucracy in the Semi-Professions," *The Semi-Professions and Their Organization.* Amitai Etzioni, ed. (Free Press, 1969), p. 222-23.

6. Bird, Caroline. *Born Female: the High Cost of Keeping Women Down.* (New York: McKay, 1968), p. 98-100.

7. Simpson, *op. cit.*, p. 228-30.

8. de Beauvoir, Simone. *The Second Sex.* H. M. Parshley, trans. and ed. (New York: Knopf, 1968), p. 701.

9. *Ibid.*, p. viii.

10. Simpson, *op. cit.*, p. 214.

11. Goode, William J., "The Theoretical Limits of Professionalization," *The Semi-Professions and Their Organization.* Amitai Etzioni, ed.

Overdue: Taking Issue with the Issues

by John Carey

It is not surprising that we in the library field recognize the need to re-examine every aspect of our profession, surrounded as we are with upheaval in a society sick of pollution, prejudice, and war. We seek the relationship of these social issues to the library—a long overdue self-examination.

I cannot help but feel, however, that the general hysteria of our times has made our self-criticism less meaningful. There is a tendency for us to jump on bandwagons instead of intelligently seeking our real problems and their solutions. The demand for controversial journal articles and library conference programs has created a radical rhetoric of pat answers to fad issues. It is hoped that this article will contribute a more realistic appraisal of some of the issues.

REPRESSION OF FEMALE LIBRARIANS—HUMBUG!

Typical of some of the thinking which is now in vogue is the article "The Disadvantaged Majority" by Anita Schiller.[1] Professor Schiller decries the lack of research in this area, socks it to us with some statistics, and concludes that sexual prejudice in the library profession has defrauded women of their just rewards in terms of salary and status. She even points to a conspiracy, suggesting that the "implicitly desired goal of the present policy of the American Library Association may be that women eventually will cease to enter the field."[2]

Studies support the fact that women, who form 80 percent of our profession, are receiving lower salaries and are less likely than men to be chosen for the highest professional positions. One cannot, however, jump to the conclusion that this is due to a conspiracy or to prejudice. Implicit in the Schiller article is the belief that this difference in salary and status is a problem at all. I wonder if it really is.

There are several factors which account more realistically for the difference in the way the profession rewards men and women. One of the first to come to mind is the good, old-fashioned law of supply and demand. If one can grant that there may be times when it is justifiable to employ a librarian of one particular sex, then it is clear that if the sex is male, the starting salary will

Excerpted from the February 1971 issue (592; 594) of the *Wilson Library Bulletin*. Copyright © 1971 by the H. W. Wilson Company.

often have to be higher than if it were female. The job market for male librarians is simply tighter.

A comparison of the career patterns of men and women librarians also shows many significant factors which affect salary and status.

For example, a good many women librarians are married and a good many have children. This means that they either enter the profession after bearing their children, or that they take time off during their careers to attend to things at home. In either case, it is natural and perfectly justifiable that a person whose career starts late or is interrupted during the developmental years is less likely to get the prestigious jobs or draw the highest salaries. Studies of librarians consistently show the male librarians, as a group, are typically younger than women.[3]

Married women are also less free to plan their moves from job to job than their male counterparts, and this affects their rewards from the profession. Taking the right job at the right time, or conversely leaving a job at the right time is extremely important in the advancement of a librarian's career. Yet a female librarian married to a man established in a certain area may be forced to choose from a very limited number of opportunities during her entire career. On the other hand, she may find that she will have to move with her family to a new area which does not offer any job suited to her experience and talents. She may move back and forth among school, college, and public library jobs as they present themselves. Although none of these situations tends to advance any librarian's career, one certainly cannot blame their results on the profession or on prejudice.

The most puzzling and disturbing aspect of the library feminist's claims is understanding how this great majority of librarians—four out of every five—can be so held down by the small remaining percentage. This claim only strengthens the suspicion that despite what anyone says, women are more passive and less keenly professional than men.

REFERENCES

1. Schiller, Anita R. "The Disadvantaged Majority." *American Libraries* (April, 1970), pp. 345-349.

2. *Ibid.*, p. 346.

3. *Ibid.*, p. 345.

A Healthy Anger

by Helen Lowenthal

As librarians, we pride ourselves on our understanding of freedom—intellectual freedom, personal freedom, political freedom. We point with pride to *Portnoy's Complaint* and *Soul on Ice* on our shelves; with equal pride we point to publications of the Birch Society and the DAR. We are pleased that our liberalism gives readers a choice in the literature they read. We shudder at the thought of a library which expresses a single point of view, for certainly all freedom rests on the freedom of choice.

Women's liberation aspires to exactly that: the freedom of choice and equality of opportunity. As women, we are restricted in choosing careers, life styles, and behavior. We are channeled into the roles that we must play as women, and deviancy from these roles is considered abnormal behavior. Women who choose to step out of their traditional roles are branded "unfeminine" and must suffer the consequences of abnormal behavior. Men, too, suffer from being forced into restrictive roles, but the suffering of men is the suffering of the master who is chained to the slave: both are bound, but the conditions of their bondage are different.

Nowhere is woman's inequality and her lack of choice more plainly evident than in librarianship, the profession which claims such a profound understanding of freedom. Many a woman librarian is smug in the knowledge that her professional colleagues are predominantly women. Her smugness and contentedness have no foundation. Perhaps she ought to address a few questions to herself:

Why did she select librarianship as a career?

What were her options and how free was her choice?

Why are there so many women librarians?

Once she "chose" librarianship, how free was she to choose her position in the hierarchy of the field?

Once she reached her level of competency (women's progress is usually halted before the Peter principle applies), was she rewarded on an equal basis with men in salary, recognition, and attitudes towards her?

When I was ready to graduate from college, my parents asked me what I was going to do. I replied that I did not know, but that I was *not* going to teach. Aghast, they asked, "Well then, what *are* you going to do?" So it goes with daughters. From the time we are born we are channeled into teaching, nursing, social work, and librarianship. For some reason, I was not expected

Reprinted from *Library Journal* 96 (September 1, 1971): 2597-2599. Published by R. R. Bowker Co., a Xerox company. Copyright © 1971 by Xerox Corporation.

to become a doctor, lawyer, or college professor, as were all of the boys I grew up with.

Women are handicapped psychologically in that society's expectations for them are lower than they are for men. In those rare cases when a woman decides that she wants to enter the "male" professions, she is not patted on the back as are her male counterparts. We women confront raised eyebrows: "Won't you feel bad taking up a man's place in medical school?" and "Won't that interfere with marriage?" With no outside encouragement, we develop a "nigger mentality" and decide that we don't really want the prestigious positions anyway. We shuffle along, contented with serving others selflessly and stifling the urge to serve ourselves. I firmly believe that people cannot adequately satisfy others until they are satisfied with themselves. As women, we are the living denial of this statement.

So we choose librarianship, firm in the belief that we were meant to help others. If we are not helping our children and husbands, we are helping the public. If altruism is such an important quality in furthering social progress, why haven't more men entered the service professions? Why are these professions comprised predominantly of women?

Perhaps in librarianship it is because recruitment takes place on two different levels, one for each sex. Women are equal, but they are separate. This acts in the interest of women as well as it did of Blacks before *Brown vs. the Board of Education.* In any hierarchy, by definition, there are fewer individuals at the top and more at the bottom. I maintain that women are recruited for the bottom and men for the top, and that this fact explains the disproportionate number of women in the field.

The appeal in recruiting women to librarianship is not only to our helping, serving-others, maternal "instincts" (instincts we are *taught* from the day we are born), but also to our "housewife" qualities. Those of us in public services play mother to our patrons and those in technical services "keep house" within our institutions. Melvil Dewey admitted it: "The natural qualities most important in a library are accuracy, order (or what we call the housekeeping instinct)" and "executive ability . . ."[1]

Mr. Dewey mentioned executive ability as a librarian's quality. If we are looking for men in the hierarchy of librarianship, we would be advised to look to the top. Considering the percentage of men in librarianship, they overwhelmingly dominate the executive, administrative positions in the field. The higher we look, the more men we see. There are a number of studies which bear out this fact, and casual observation affirms their statistics.

In a 1968 thesis, Ben Bradley studied the characteristics of heads of the 50 largest academic and 50 largest public libraries, based on volume count. Of the public library heads, 86 percent were male, and *all* of the academic library heads were male.[2] Are we to believe that in the academic library field, two-thirds of which is female, there were no qualified women to fill any of those positions?

In *Esquire*, April 1964, an article entitled "Young Man, Be a Librarian" claims, "Most of the top jobs in the profession want male librarians to fill them as the running of library systems in most large urban areas of the nation is truly big business." Adrian Paradis tells us that "Men fill most of the top administrative posts . . ."[3] It's no secret. Men are the patricians and women the plebians in library science. With their Y-chromosomes, men inherit the top seats in the field; they are the aristocracy, the chosen few.

And we shuffle along and say, "But I really don't want to be an administrator. I truly enjoy doing the less prestigious work." This may again be a result of our nigger mentality or it may just be the absolute truth, but in either case we must realize that *we have not had a choice.* We frequently complain about the way things are being run, but we dare not aspire to taking over administrative positions. After all, everyone knows how level-headed and practical men are and how emotional and impractical women are. There are exceptions, of course, but we women know our place—at the bottom of the hierarchy.

Even if the library field placed fewer restrictions on women's ability to rise to the top, the restrictions imposed by society and our culture would have to be confronted.

> Because of the lack of geographic mobility of the professional married woman, she cannot follow the opportunities in her field but must make the most of those that exist wherever she happens to be. Such a situation leads to exploitation . . . She will, for she must, accept conditions that her male counterpart would not . . . though this sort of exploitation often occurs with the knowledge and even with the approval of the woman, it impedes her professional advancement and hence increases the likelihood that she will find herself in a situation where she is superior in ability, training, or seniority to the requirements of her job and to the men classified as her equals or even as her immediate supervisors.

So we find women in their subjunctive role. Now, given "our place," how are we regarded and how are we treated by people within the profession and those outside it?

The librarian image is nothing new to any of us. The outside world stereotypes us as either effeminate males or old-maid, bookish females. In either case we are far from filling the ideal sexual roles that society and Madison Avenue dictate we should strive for. Women are supposed to be married; when little girls are asked what they want to be when they grow up, the answer is inevitably "a mother," and this presupposes marriage. Although we are allowed to be intelligent—or rather, "educated"—we should not be more intelligent than our male counterparts. As any popular woman's magazine will tell us, the main reason we should pursue knowledge and broaden our horizons is so that we will be more interesting or helpful to men. Imagine a wife telling her husband to take a course so she'll find him more interesting!

Far worse than the treatment the outside world gives us is the total lack of recognition and respect from within the profession. When we enter the field, we are aware of the former, but the latter is hard to accept.

Anita Schiller's study of academic librarians' salaries indicated that in that group the median salary for men was $1500 more than that of women, and furthermore, as these librarians grow older, acquire more experience, and move further up the hierarchy, the gap widens.[5] These are examples of attitudes towards women expressed in dollars. There are other reflections of these attitudes.

My experiences in library school abound with instances of male chauvinism, a term that we in the women's liberation movement use when a person—of either sex—builds up the male ego at the expense of the female ego. (Strange, how the words "female ego" seem foreign on the tongue.)

At Simmons, where 84 percent of the students were female, only about one-third of the voting faculty was female, and neither of the two top administrators was female.

At an alumni function I attended, the entire head table was male, except for one woman, who was at least 50 years old. When the man at the microphone introduced her, he referred to her as the only "girl" at the table. His calling her a girl was vaguely reminiscent of a white person calling a 60-year-old black man "boy."

In library school courses where we used the case method, competent library administrators or promising young library students are consistently depicted as men, whereas the women are described as crotchety, conservative, and eccentric. And the worst part of these indignities is our unawareness that they exist. How subtle are the forces that elevate man's dignity above woman's and convince us that this is how things should be! What a brainwashing job has been done!

Who is to blame for the inequality and partiality towards men we see in our profession and in our culture? Men, women, the ruling powers in the profession (whoever they may be), the family unit which forces women to choose between a career and marriage are some possible scapegoats. But no amount of scapegoating will correct the situation. What are the positive steps we can take to correct such a deep-seated problem?

First, we must be aware of what is happening. How can we be free to choose a way of life if we are not aware of all possible choices? Up to now we have believed when we have been told that women must act in a certain way and men in another. We have not questioned; we have, nodding and smiling, accepted what we were told. We have clutched our femininity and masculinity as a child clutches its security blanket. What is femininity if not a set of attitudes and behavior, inculcated by sinister but effective brainwashing techniques, which give us security and limit our freedom to behave in other ways? How many of our feminine trappings are inherent in our biological makeup and how many are conditioned? We must challenge old assumptions at every step of the way and expand our consciousness enough to reject invalid assumptions about the traditional male and female roles.

Second, we must not be afraid of developing a healthy anger at situations and individuals which help perpetuate the inequalities in the sex roles. "Let it all hang out." We must not be afraid of being mocked for daring to believe that we are entitled to more than we are getting. Mockery is the male-dominated society's strongest weapon. By refusing to take us seriously, our mockers totally negate our worth. There is nothing funny about the black man's getting a smaller piece of the pie than the white man; no less funny is this similar discrimination against women.

Finally, and most important, as women we must drastically change our attitudes about ourselves and cast off our nigger mentality. We must reassess our capabilities and try to win back what has been taken from us. We can no longer accept "You're a woman" as a reason for being shortchanged. Our choices in all areas of life have to be at least as free as those of our male counterparts. We must ally with other women rather than compete with them. Women across the country are uniting and discovering common problems and common angers. The most oppressive force we must face in liberating ourselves is not at home, nor at work, but in our minds.

REFERENCES

1. Dewey, Melvil. *Librarianship as a Profession for College-Bred Women.* (Boston, MA: Library Bureau, 1886).

2. Bradley, Ben W. *A Study of the Characteristics, Qualifications and Succession Patterns of Heads of Large U.S. Academic and Public Libraries.* Thesis, University of Texas, M.L.S., 1968.

3. Paradis, Adrian A. *Librarians: Careers in Library Service.* (New York: McKay, 1959).

4. Bailyn, Lotte. "Notes on the Role of Choice in the Psychology of Professional Women." *Daedalus,* Spring 1964, p. 700-10.

5. Schiller, Anita R. "Academic Librarians' Salaries," *College and Research Libraries,* March 1969, p. 101-11.

The Tender Technicians: The Feminization of Public Librarianship, 1876-1905

by Dee Garrison

"The law of nature destines and qualifies the female sex for the bearing and nurture of the children of our race and for the custody of the homes of the world," stated the Wisconsin Supreme Court in 1875 when ruling that women could not be admitted to their bar. The judges conceded that the "cruel chances of life" might leave some women free of the sacred female duties. "These may need employment, and should be welcome to any not derogatory to their sex and its proprieties."[1] Most Americans of the time would have agreed with the Court that only financial need justified a woman's going to work and that only limited jobs should be opened to her. But in the decades before and after 1900 Americans became the unobservant participants in a social revolution, as profound changes took place in the attitudes toward women and their work. The American public libraries played an important role in the revolution, for the feminization of librarianship proceeded rapidly. In 1852 the first woman clerk was hired at the Boston Public Library;[2] by 1878 fully two-thirds of the library workers there were female.[3] In 1910 78½ percent of library workers in the United States were women; only teaching surpassed librarianship as the most feminized "profession."[4]

Educated women, while meeting resistance in other more established professions, flooded into library work during the last quarter of the nineteenth century for a variety of reasons. Librarianship was a new and fast-growing field in need of low-paid but educated recruits. With a plentiful number of library jobs available, male librarians offered no opposition to the proliferation of women library workers, partly because women agreed that library work matched presumed feminine limitations. Librarianship was quickly adjusted to fit the narrowly circumscribed sphere of women's activities, for it appeared similar to the work of the home, functioned as cultural activity, required no great skill or physical strength and brought little contact with the rougher portions of society. For all these reasons, Melvil Dewey could predict, when writing at the turn of the century of the ideal librarian, that "most of the men who achieve this greatness will be women."[5] The feminization of librarianship, however, had unexpected long-range results. The prevalence of women would profoundly affect the process of professionalization and the type of service the library would provide. The nature of library work itself, one of the

Copyright © 1972, by Peter N. Stearns. Reprinted from the *Journal of Social History*, Vol 6 #2 pp. 131-159, by permission of the editor.

few sources of economic opportunity open to educated women in the late nineteenth century, would serve to perpetuate the low status of women in American society. Above all, female dominance of librarianship did much to shape the inferior and precarious status of the public library as an important cultural resource and to cause it to evolve into a marginal kind of public amusement service.[6]

The rapid growth of libraries in size, number and complexity between 1876 and 1905 was an important cause of the feminization of librarianship. The monumental 1876 "Report on Public Libraries" listed 3,682 libraries containing a little over twelve million volumes.[7] Total yearly additions of library books in the nation passed the one million mark in 1876.[8] A conservative estimate raised the total to forty million volumes held in 8,000 libraries in 1900.[9] Because a heavy demand for trained librarians coincided with other national developments, particularly the advance of women's education and the increase of women workers, many women found employment in library service. Very probably, women would have flocked into any new field into which their entry was not opposed. Because male librarians heartily welcomed women into library service, the eventual feminization of the library staff was assured.

The low cost of hiring women was perhaps the most important reason that male library leaders welcomed women assistants. The public library, supported by taxes and voluntary donations, was by necessity obliged to practice thrifty housekeeping. Trustees and taxpayers expected that the major portion of the yearly income would be invested in books. Because women were notoriously low-paid, the annual cost of library administration could be appreciably lowered by the introduction of women workers. Frederick Perkins, in an 1876 article entitled "How to Make Town Libraries Successful," recommended that "women should be employed as librarians and assistants as far as possible." Perkins was no crusader for women's equality; he only pointed out that the hiring of women, along with the use of "mechanical appliances . . . better arrangements of book rooms and other sufficient contrivances of that American ingenuity," would lessen the excessive cost of library administration.[10] Justin Winsor, speaking at the 1877 conference of British and American librarians in London, emphasized the importance of women workers in American libraries.

> In American libraries we set a high value on women's work. They soften our atmosphere, they lighten our labor, they are equal to our work, and for the money they cost—if we must gauge such labor by such rules—they are infinitely better than equivalent salaries will produce of the other sex . . . We can command our pick of the educated young women whom our Colleges for Women are launching forth upon our country—women with a fair knowledge of Latin and Greek, a good knowledge of French and German, a deducible knowledge of Spanish and Italian, and who do not stagger at the acquisition of even Russian, if the requirements of the catalogue service make that demand. It is to these Colleges for Women, like Vassar and Wellesley, that the American library-system looks confidently for the future.[11]

The limited opportunities open to educated women for paid employment served to bring larger numbers of competent women than competent men into low-paid library jobs during this period. Of the eight leading women librarians of the time, four had some college and the rest at least a high school education.[12] In view of the constant references made in library literature to the necessity of finding workers with an educated knowledge of books, a high intelligence and preferably a familiarity with a few languages, it is safe to assume that most women entering library service at this time were either self- or formally-educated to at least the extent expected of an urban school teacher.[13] The same economic factors were at work in librarianship and teaching, for educated women, with few other job opportunities flocked into both fields, with a depressing effect on wages. Library work required similar qualifications to teaching and was little worse in pay. In librarianship women could exercise their presumed special feminine talents and could, besides, remain isolated, in a way teachers could not, from the rough workaday world.[14]

The feminine movement into new occupations like nursing and teaching or clerical and industrial employment began in the middle of the nineteenth century when both the right to individuality and the myth of women's sphere held extremely important places in American popular thought. Two such conflicting ideas could not exist together unless individualism was reserved for man alone. Thus man took the world and all its activities as his "sphere," while confining women to domesticity and the guardianship of culture. Women were just as guilty of inconsistency. The gradual expansion of women's claim to the right of individual choice was on the whole unaccompanied by any feminine calls for radical social change. Instead, as each new job became filled by women, charming theories were developed by both sexes to explain why the feminine mind and nature were innately suited to the new occupation. Thus it was decided that teaching was much like mothering; women, it was said, were uniquely able to guide children into piety, purity and knowledge. Women were cleared to work as writers, musicians and artists because of their inherent sensitivity, elevated moralism and love of beauty. Women doctors and nurses were intuitively kind, sympathetic and delicate of touch. The woman social worker expressed inborn feminine qualities of love, charity and idealism. Factory, business and clerical work fit the feminine nature, for women were naturally industrious, sober and nimble-fingered, as well as better able than men to endure the boredom of detailed or repetitive tasks. These various expansions of the work of women served to modify the concept of woman's proper sphere but the process was gradual and involved no radical threat to traditional social ideals.[15] Yet each expansion led to others, with a snowballing effect, so that within a hundred years the limits of woman's claim to individual freedom of choice had undergone considerable and drastic change.

This redefinition of woman's sphere, always in accord with the characteristics presumed to be innately feminine, also came to encompass librarianship as one of the proper fields open to women. The course to library work had already been cleared for women because libraries held books and books denoted Culture with a capital "C." By the late nineteenth century, women's sphere decidedly included the guardianship and enjoyment of culture. It was believed that through their refining and spiritualizing influence women could exalt all human society. It would be almost impossible to overemphasize the Victorian conviction that men were physically tamed and morally elevated by the sway of the gentle female. Moreover, by the 1870s American popular literature was consciously designed to please feminine readers. Therefore the advent of women to library work required little stretching of the popular ideal regarding the female, for "books . . . should be treated by reverent hands

. . . should be given out as a priest dispenses the sacrament, and the next step to this ideal ministry is to have them issued by women."[16]

> The librarian . . . is becoming . . . the guardian of the thought-life of the people . . . The library, in its influence, is whatever the librarian makes it; it seems destined to become an all-pervading force . . . moulding [sic] public opinion, educating to all of the higher possibilities of human thought and action; to become a means for enriching, beautifying, and making fruitful the barren places in human life . . . Librarians have an important part to play in the history of civilization and in the conservation of the race.[17]

Women in librarianship were merely making more visible the female position as the guardian of cultural ideas.

Just as the concept of "culture" had been generally accorded to the care of women, so the functions of providing education and of overseeing charity to the poor had been deemed suitable fields for female concern. The provision of education and moral uplift to the masses was a prominent mission of the early library; thus, women library workers, with their presumed inborn talents and temperaments, seemed uniquely suited to the new field of librarianship. The popular library brought the librarian "in hourly contact with her constituency of readers, advising, helping and elevating their lives and exerting a far-reaching influence for good not to be exceeded in any profession open to women . . ."[18] The great mass of men in all fields worked to secure prestige or a higher income but the librarian worked "with as distinct a consecration as a minister or missionary . . . The selfish considerations of reputation or personal comfort, or emolument are all secondary."[19] For Melvil Dewey, library work offered more opportunity to the altruistic than did the work of the clergyman or teacher. The library would reach those who never entered a church or who did not go to school.

> Is it not true that the ideal librarian fills a pulpit where there is service every day during all the waking hours, with a large proportion of the community frequently in the congregation? . . . [The library is] a school in which the classes graduate only at death?[20]

Dewey encouraged educated women who might ordinarily have become teachers to consider a library career. Physically the library was less exacting than the school. The librarian avoided the "nervous strain and the wear and tear of the classroom" and escaped the bad air of crowded rooms. Dewey could think of no other profession "that is so free from annoying surroundings or that has so much in the character of the work and of the people which is grateful to a refined and educated woman."[21] The genteel nature of library work would compensate, he believed, for the regretable fact that women librarians normally received half the pay of men librarians and often received even less than urban teachers did.

As women became dominant in library work, library literature began to reflect the concept that the ideal library would offer the warmth and hospitality of the home to its patrons. To nineteenth-century man, of course, woman's sphere was, above all, the home, for which she was originally intended and which she was so exactly fitted to adorn and bless. Not surprisingly, it was anticipated that the feminine influence of the librarian would soften the library atmosphere. Like a visitor to a home, the reader must be welcomed; he must be given kind and individual attention; he must be treated with tact and gentle manners. Not the cold impersonality of the business world should pervade but rather the warmth of the well-ordered home, presided over by a gracious and helpful librarian. Counsel like the following is pervasive in the library literature of the 1870s and 1880s:

> Something may be said of the desirableness of making the library wear a pleasant and inviting look. The reading-room offers perhaps the best opportunity for this. A reading-room lately seen has a bright carpet on the floor, low tables, and a few rocking-chairs scattered about; a cheerful, open fire on dull days, attractive pictures on the walls, and one can imagine a lady librarian filling the windows with plants. Such a room is a welcome in itself, and bids one come again.[22]

It was this ideal of the librarian as the accommodating and heartily receptive hostess which Miss Theresa West had in mind when she said that "the personal equation of the librarian may easily become the exponent of the power of the library."[23] On the surface the likening of the library to the home was but one of several devices which library leaders used to entice the reluctant patron and to make the library into a more "popular" institution. Operating more subtly, underground, were the effects of the prevalence of women in library work. Just as the school had been likened to the home, in order to make more acceptable the dominance of women teachers, so did the library readjust to reflect the widening of woman's sphere. The position of librarian required a certain "gracious hospitality" and here "women as a class far surpass men." Women would not feel humiliated by serving, by playing in the library the part they played in the home: "Here it is said her 'broad sympathies, her quick wits, her intuitions and her delight in self-sacrifice' give her an undoubted advantage."[24]

Women workers were also preferred, it was generally conceded, for the tedious job of cataloging. Again, it was the unique nature of woman which qualified her for this work because of her "greater conscientiousness, patience and accuracy in details."[25] Because women had greater ability than men to bear pain with fortitude, women had stored great reserves of patience and thus could perform the most monotonous tasks without boredom. All the routine, repetitive work of the library was quite generally agreed to fall within the scope of women's special talents.[26]

It is evident that the role of domesticity imposed upon women also worked to create the emphasis which was early given to library service for children.[27] By 1900 the children's library had "passed its first stage—all enthusiasm and effervescence—"[28] and had moved into its current position as a major department of the public library. From the beginning, the supervision of children's reading was given over to the woman librarian.

> The work for children in our libraries, like many other of our best things, is woman's work. To them it owes its inception, its progress and present measure of success, and its future is in their hands.[29]

Here in the children's sections was woman's undisputed domain. And here the librarians waxed eloquent over the attributes and accomplishments of the reigning queen. Work with children is "the most important, and in its results, the most satisfactory of all library work," reported Minerva Sanders. "As our personal influence is exerted, in just such a proportion will our communities be uplifted."[30] Another librarian commented that woman, alone, has "that kind sympathetic second-sight that shall enable her to read what is often obscure in the mind of the child."[31] Edwin M. Fairchild summed up the pre-

vailing attitude toward woman's natural role in library work—not as a
bluestocking, but as a traditionally defined female with intrinsic traits.

> The chief source of enthusiasm for the children's library is the librarian . . .
> [She] needs to be . . . a woman grown, herself the realization of the education-
> al ideal, which by the way is not the smart, but the intelligent, great souled
> woman . . .[32]

Originally conceived and theoretically maintained as an educational institution, the children's department was, in fact, even by the turn of the century, becoming mainly a provider of recreational reading for pre-adoles-
cents.[33] Misgivings over the nature of library service to children were rarely
expressed, however. Most often, sentimentality over-ruled any attempt at a
realistic assessment of the work being accomplished in the children's department. The romantic air of enthusiastic tenderness so prominent in any discussion of children in the library is in sharp contrast to the more normal tendency
of librarians to indulge in searching self-criticism in every other phase of library work. This incongruity becomes more understandable when it is
remembered that the children's section of the library was created and shaped
by women librarians. Here, as in no other area, library women were free to
express, unchallenged, their self-image. Because their activities did not
exceed the Victorian stereotype of the female, their endeavors remained substantially unquestioned and unexamined by male library leaders.

Despite the respect paid them, however, women soon learned that they
were seldom paid the same as men who were doing the same work; and that
even though women easily dominated the library field in numbers, male librarians headed the largest and most prestigious libraries. In the library literature of this period there is hardly a hint that the hundreds of women librarians across the country were seriously disturbed at the inequality which was
freely admitted to be their lot.[34] Rather, one finds feminine pride repeatedly
expressed over the prevalence of women in the library, at the increased participation of women in the national association and of America's flattering contrast with England where women were meeting resistance in library work. A
situation which really amounted to the exploitation of women in the American library was publicly touted as a liberal concession to women in America
and was contrasted with women's supposedly less favorable position in the
Old World to indicate the superiority of American freedoms and the liberal
attitudes of the male leaders of the American library movement.[35]

The twelve women present at the 1876 American Library Association
meeting set the submissive tone which few women librarians were to
challenge. They were "the best of listeners, and occasionally would modestly
take advantage of gallant voices, like Mr. Smith's, to ask a question or offer a
suggestion."[36] The next year Miss Caroline Hewins had the distinction of being the first woman to speak up at the national convention; she asked if the
dog tax were used to support a library outside Massachusetts. Perhaps this
small temerity earned her the reputation of fearless spokesman for it was Miss
Hewins who presented in 1891 the first general discussion of the "woman
question" in the *Library Journal.*

Library work was difficult for women, Miss Hewins said. For a salary
varying from three to nine hundred dollars annually, a library assistant must
write steadily six or seven hours a day, know half a dozen languages, be
absolutely accurate in copying, "understand the relation of all arts and

sciences to each other and must have . . . a minute acquaintance with geography, history, art and literature." A successful woman librarian would work eight to ten hours a day and "those who are paid the highest salaries give up all their evenings." Miss Hewins added that "librarians and library attendants sometimes break down from overwork." With unconscious humor, the intrepid Miss Hewins had a remedy for impending exhaustion—"plenty of sleep and nourishing food, with a walk of two or three miles every day."[37] Presumably this stroll was to be taken in the hours of early dawn or late evening.

The year after Miss Hewin's article appeared there was an abortive attempt to establish a Woman's Section in the national organization. The sole meeting of women in 1892 was a tame affair, with only the barest expression of stifled rage at women's low wages and subordinate position. An official statement secured from 25 of the nation's most prominent libraries revealed that "women rarely receive the same pay for the same work as men."[38] But no matter "The palm of honor and of opportunity waits for her who shall join a genius for organization . . . to the power of a broad, rich, catholic and sympathetic womanhood." In "the long run" the woman librarian "will win appreciation."[39]

The Woman's Section of the American Library Association did not meet again, although the 1892 session appointed a committee to report at the next conference in Chicago. There was no formal explanation of the failure of this committee to report but it may be that a protest movement, sparked by Miss Tessa Kelso of the Los Angeles Public Library, would explain the demise of the Woman's Section. Miss Kelso stoutly disapproved of any deference paid to women as a group.[40]

> In the . . . 14th American Library Association Conference I note that there is a movement toward establishing a woman's section . . . For years woman has worked, talked, and accepted all sorts of compromises to prove her fitness to hold the position of librarian, and to demonstrate that sex should have no weight where ability is equal. In all these years the accomplishment is seen in the table of wages paid women librarians in comparison with those paid men . . . For women to now come forward with the argument that a woman librarian has a point of view and such limitation that they must be discussed apart from the open court of library affairs is a serious mistake . . . The use of the name of the association should not be permitted in such a direction . . .[41]

Such a truculent defense of women's equality, however, was not in accord with the expressed attitude of most women librarians. They accepted with little protest the traditional view of women as inherently limited in the working world. Certainly women library leaders had no utopian plans for woman's sexual and social emancipation. Of course they wanted to do things not customary for women in the past, such as managing a library with pay equal to men's, but this they considered as no more than a slight modification of the traditional ideal, and certainly not as a basic change in the male-structured view of women. As late as 1896 the influential Mary Ahern, editor of *Public Libraries*, warbled that "no woman can hope to reach any standing . . . in the library profession . . . who does not bring to it that love which suffereth long and is kind, is not puffed up, does not behave itself unseemly, vaunteth not itself, thinketh no evil . . ." Every woman owes it to herself to live up to the ideals expected of womanhood; "no woman striving ever so hard to play the part of a man has ever succeeded in doing more than to give just cause for a blush to the rest of her kind." Every woman in library work should seek not "to detract from the reputation so hardly earned of being faithful conscientious workers."[42]

In 1904 one hundred representative libraries were asked by the American Library Association to comment on the limitations of women library workers.[43] Economic reasons were most often cited to explain women's low pay scale; women who did not demand as much salary as men were in abundant supply. Women were generally acknowledged to be hampered by their "delicate physique" and "inability to endure continued mental strain." Mary Cutler (now Mrs. Fairchild), an important woman library leader, commented that she could not see how women's physical disability could ever be eliminated. Whether women would ever hold high positions in the library "may remain perhaps an open question." While having decided advantage wherever "the human element predominates," Mrs. Fairchild went on, women too frequently lacked the will to discharge executive power and most trustees "assume that a woman would not have business capacity." Reviewing all the facts she concluded that "on account of natural sex limitations, and also actual weakness in the work of many women as well as because of conservatism and prejudice, many gates are at present closed to women."[44]

Recognition of women's limited potential was probably justified when applied to women library workers in general. The average woman accepted the current ideal which taught that her success in life would be judged by her marriage and not by her work. With this concept central in her mind, she was being wholly practical if she spent much of her time in conforming to the popular ideal of "femininity" rather than in thinking about business achievement. Women librarians who had given up hope for marriage were also less apt to strain for advancement since they realized that society would discourage them from a display of "male" aggressiveness. Of course, some talented and energetic women librarians did realize their ambitions to a considerable degree, primarily because these ambitions were exceedingly modest and did not threaten the prevailing notion of woman's place.

Perhaps the most striking point to be made about women's adaptation to library work is the extent to which they supported the traditional feminine concern for altruism and high-mindedness. They invoked the Victorian definition of proper female endeavors at the same time as they were widening it. Librarianship, when defined as self-denying and spiritual, offered women the opportunity not to change their status but to affirm it, not to fulfill their self but their self-image. When women's advance became justified in terms of the good they could do, rather than of their human right to equality, it became conditional in nature.

Even if some librarians did not subscribe to the concept of woman's sphere, with all its connotations, they had to appear to do so in order not to offend the many who did. Not to surrender to the Victorian mystique was to run the terrible risk of being judged deviants in their society, of being judged abnormal because of a challenge to well-established norms. Perhaps, too, both men and women librarians wished to avoid any real discussion of the injustice which library women suffered because of the eagerness of all library leaders to establish librarianship as a profession. To publicize the prevalence of women in the library or to increase their influence could only harm the drive toward professionalization. A woman-dominated profession was obviously a contradiction in terms.

Librarians have been absorbed to a marked degree, from 1876 to the present, with the question of professionalization. Melvil Dewey and other early library leaders made repeated claims to professional status.[45] Not until the Williamson report of 1923 was there open and general admission among librarians that significant elements common to professional work were lacking in librarianship.[46] In the effort to win professional standing, librarians have concentrated upon improvements in their system of library schools. The education of librarians, it has been commonly lamented, includes too much detail and attention to method, only producing good craftsmen and technicians. True professional education, on the other hand, should present a systematic body of theory and a scientifically-based abstract knowledge upon which the profession rests.

Throughout the debate among librarians as to how best to receive recognition as professionals, the dominant influence of women on librarianship has been strangely shunted, buried under a multitude of words concerning recruitment, accreditation, curriculums and other factors thought to be inhibiting professionalization. There has been no systematic consideration given to the way in which feminization has shaped, in a most significant way, the development of library education and the entire range of activities associated with the field of library work. Carl White, who has written the best study of library education as it developed before 1923, gives thoughtful and scholarly attention to the social and educational setting in which library education began and relates it brilliantly to the traditions which remain today from that early inheritance.[47] Yet White curiously refrains from considering the effect of the prevalence of women workers upon the shaping of those traditions. Only sociologist Peter Rossi, in a symposium of 1961, has tackled the existence of feminization head-on and applied it to library development. Rossi commented upon the puzzling absence of any real consideration being given to the influence of women upon library history.

> I kept expecting . . . some comment on *the major reasons* [italics mine] why librarians find it difficult to achieve a substantial spot in the array of professions. Any occupation in which there is a high proportion of women suffers a special disability . . . Women depress the status of an occupation because theirs is a depressed status in the society as a whole, and those occupations in which women are found in large numbers are not seen as seriously competing with other professions for personnel and resources. It is for this reason that professions such as education, social work, and librarianship develop within themselves a division of labor and accompanying status along sex lines.[48]

Rossi added that the status of librarianship could be raised by a radical division of labor such as that accomplished in medicine where nursing was done by females and doctoring by males. This sharp differentiation between male and female librarians, however, runs counter to the central development of library history. Once formed, the solutions—both planned and accidental—found workable by nineteenth-century librarians closed the possibility of starting over with a clean slate. For this reason it is important that librarians assess the basic meaning of feminization and give precise attention to their early history, for the dominance of women is surely the prevailing factor in library education, the image of librarianship and the professionalization of the field. Women's role in the library was established in the last 25 years of the nineteenth century. An examination of the principal factors in this period of library history should include an emphasis upon the underrated effect of women students in library schools and its relationship to the constant search of librarians for professional standing.

The process of professionalization has received increasing attention by sociologists and historians in recent years.[49] Although it is generally agreed that professions have certain characteristics differentiating them from other occupations, there is no agreement on the precise nature of those characteristics. The conceptual model for this study will be devised so as to examine the professionalization of librarianship under three headings: service orientation, knowledge base and degree of autonomy. These components of professionalization will be examined, first as they apply to nineteenth-century librarianship in general and then as they relate to the feminization of the field.

The service orientation of librarianship exhibits most of the qualities expected in the ethical code of a profession. The professional, in contrast to the non-professional, is primarily concerned with his client's needs or with the needs of society, rather than with his own material interests. A profession also has direct relevance to basic social values on which there is widespread consensus. In law and medicine, for example, the services provided by the professional are justice and health. In librarianship the basic social value served is education. Early library leaders were firm in their commitment of the library to educational purposes; they definitely relegated the recreational function of the library to a secondary place. William Poole's comment typifies this view.

> Our public libraries and our public schools are supported by the same constituencies, by the same methods of taxation, and for the same purpose; and that purpose is the education of the people . . . If public libraries shall, in my day, cease to be educational institutions, and serve only to amuse the people and help them to while away an idle hour, I shall favor their abolition.[50]

The librarian also showed a professional acceptance of the ideal of sacrificial service to the community. Librarianship was deemed to be second only to the ministry in its aims and standards.[51] Additionally, librarians had the sense of community which is common to professionals. They felt an affinity with other librarians in a way which the plumber, for example, does not feel for all other plumbers. Librarians, like the ministers with whom they liked to compare themselves, sensed an identity as a group, sharing a common destiny, values and norms.

The service and collectivity orientation of librarianship, then, conform to certain important characteristics of a profession. The characteristics used in the definition of the term "profession" are variables, forming a continuum along which an occupation's rise to professionalism can be measured. Although librarianship certainly showed a number of professional traits, significant elements of a truly professional code of service were missing. Specifically lacking in the librarian's professional service code are a sense of commitment, a drive to lead rather than to serve and a clear-cut conception of professional rights and responsibilities. The feminization of library work is a major cause of these deficiencies.

The concentration of women served to lower a professional work-commitment within librarianship. The culture defined woman's responsibility to the home as her primary one and this definition was all-pervasive before 1900. It was perfectly understandable, for example, that Theresa West would in 1896 leave her job as the leading woman librarian heading an important library when she married Henry Elmendorf. Indeed, it would have been shocking if she had chosen otherwise. Nineteenth-century complaints of high employee turnover and of low commitment to excellence among library workers are directly related to the place which women accepted in society. For the library assistant of the nineteenth century to become highly work-committed would require from her an atypical value orientation.[52] The majority of librarians were no doubt eager to marry and to leave library work. Of the eight women leaders selected for this study, five were unmarried and one was a widow. Of the two who married, late in life, both continued to work in the library field, although not as head librarians. All eight of these women were highly educated by the standards of their time. In each case, professional success, high status, extensive training and spinsterhood served to increase their vocational commitment. Despite the positive work commitments demonstrated by these women leaders, it remains generally true that within the field of librarianship, from 1876 to the present, the dominance of women significantly lessened a trend toward professional, life-long commitment to the field of library service.[53]

In established professions the practitioner assumes the responsibility for deciding what is best for his client. Whether or not the client agrees with him is theoretically not a factor in the professional's decision. Thus in the medical field, the doctor does not give the patient whatever treatment he requests, but instead prescribes the treatment which, for professional reasons, the doctor thinks is correct. In contrast to this professional attitude, librarians tended to "serve" the reader, rather than to help him. They felt a strong obligation to meet the needs of the public and were self-consciously sensitive to requests and complaints of the client.[54] This is partly a result of the tax-supported nature of the library and of its early efforts to attract a large public following. But this passive, inoffensive and non-assertive "service" provided by the librarian is also a natural acting-out of the docile behaviorial role which females assumed in the culture.[55]

Theoretically the nineteenth-century library could have developed a less demand-oriented code of service. John Dana, Melvil Dewey, William Fletcher and William Poole often urged the librarian to lead his community, to educate the reader and the public. These men strongly felt that the librarian's role was to teach the standards that the public *should* want, not merely to provide access to what the public *did* want. Dewey argued that it was unwise "to give sharp tools or powerful weapons to the masses without some assurance of how they are to be used."[56] The public library, said William Fletcher,

> . . . has too often been regarded somewhat as a public club, a purely democratic association of the people for mutual mental improvement or recreation . . . The public library is an educational and moral power to be wielded with a full sense of its mighty possibilities and the corresponding danger of their perversion.[57]

The assumption of a definitive intellectual leadership, however, did not come to characterize the public librarian. Modern librarians have laid the blame for their general passivity and inferior status upon various factors: the lack of a scientifically-based abstract body of knowledge; the public's lack of differentiation between the "professional" librarian and the library clerk and the inherently weak position of the librarian as implementor rather than creator of intellectual and cultural advance. Rarely given its due as a determinant is the overwhelming presence of women in librarianship. The negative traits for which librarians indict themselves—excessive cautiousness, avoidance of controversy, timidity, a weak orientation toward autonomy, little business sense, tractability, over compliance, service to the point of self-sacrifice and willingness to submit to subordination by trustees and public—are predominantly "feminine" traits.[58] Dana and others who sought to give librarianship a position of community leadership and intellectual authority were vastly outnumbered by the thousands of women who were shaping library development across the country. There is no evidence to indicate that these women opposed society's views of woman's nature and function. The traditional ideals of feminine behavior held by women librarians and the reading public had a profound impact upon the development of the public librarian's nonassertive, non-professional code of service.

The second component of library professionalization—the body of knowledge—does not contain as many professional attributes as does the service ideal of librarians. Professional knowledge is generally defined as that knowledge which (1) is organized in abstract principles, (2) is continually revised or created by the professionals, (3) places strong emphasis upon the ability to manipulate ideas and symbols rather than physical objects and (4) requires a long enough term of specialized training so that the society views the professional as possessing skills which are beyond the reach of the untrained layman. William Goode has commented,

> Librarians themselves have found it extremely difficult to define their professional role and the knowledge on which it rests. To use a phrase like 'specialization in generalism' is sufficient . . . The repeated calls which librarians have made for a 'philosophy of librarianship' essentially expresses the need to define what *is* the intellectual problem of the occupation.[59]

In short, the librarian does not know who he is. Is he a library mechanic, having to do with such clerical, technical work as cataloguing, shelf arrangement and signing-in-and-out management? Or is he an expert guide, with considerable training in knowledge retrieval and organization?

One point, at least, seems clear. Despite the expressed desire of librarians to become admired professionals whose expertise would make available the world of knowledge, the system of library education which developed in the nineteenth century was a form of schooling, in origin and by design, which merely produced good craftsmen, trained to perform jobs which were chiefly mechanical in nature. This relatively low level of training, which made a small intellectual demand on the student, did not evolve entirely because of the feminine majority in library schools. The rate of expansion in both size and numbers of libraries was the first influence. The demand for a rapid production of library workers encouraged library schools to grind out graduates after only a brief course of instruction in the fundamental skills of library economy. The older system of in-service training could not produce enough self-made librarians to satisfy the manpower needs of the country. Carl White has outlined the second great influence on library education—the nineteenth-century development of technical education to fill the vacuum created by the breakdown of the classical curriculum and the medieval system of apprenticeship.[60] Library leaders were aware that a concentrated practical training has been demonstrated in other fields to produce the same results as learning by doing, but in less time and more systematically. Thus, detailed instruction in technical routines became the solid core of library training. Library education was in no sense designed to cultivate intellectual leadership, to produce trained high-level administrators or to develop an abstract knowledge base for library science.

The predominance of women in library schools, on library-school faculties and in library work functioned as an unmentioned but inflexible framework into which "professional" education would have to be fitted. An emphasis upon the influence of women is not meant to downgrade the other elements which shaped library education or to deemphasize the other inherent weaknesses in the librarian's claim to professional status, nor is it meant to impose chauvinistic attitudes upon male library leaders. Nineteenth-century librarians, however, were men and women of their time, governed by traditional views of woman's role in society. They were faced with an unorthodox problem—how to devise "professional" training for young women. Their answer was caught between the upper and the nether millstones. The upper millstone was their hope that librarians would become indispensable educational leaders, with professional scope and value. The nether millstone was the reality of the library school student—a woman who most likely lacked scholarly ambitions or preparation, had no life-long vocational commitment and whose attitudes toward feminine sex roles led her to accept, and expect, administrative controls, low autonomy and subordination to clerical, routine tasks.[61]

No study of why library training developed as it did would be complete without a consideration of how it was influenced by the thought of Melvil Dewey. Dewey so molded library education that the whole period before 1923 is called the "Dewey period." Librarians, too, have their folk heroes; Dewey's whirlwind passage through library history is the source of much of librarianship's most colorful annals. The narrators who have given accounts of intimate contact with Dewey share a common characteristic—they are breathless, either with admiration or with rage.

Tall, powerfully built, astonishingly handsome, Melvil Dewey was priggishly devoted to the truth as he saw it. He had no use for the trivial frolics of life; wasted time was to him a moral issue. He even developed in his wife the habit of writing precise compilations of how each minute of the day had been spent. He was, above all, pragmatic, looking only for what was workable, then and there, to produce the desired results. Dewey has been called a "man-child," for his idealism, enthusiasm and impatience with any obstacle. Childish too was his simplistic assessment of the world and his mission in it. There is something maddeningly pretentious about a man who can decide, at 17, "to inaugurate a higher education for the masses,"[62] and who can write, at age 76, in the same shallow prose,

> As I look back over the long years, I can recall no one I ever intentionally wronged, or of whom I should, now, ask forgiveness . . . I have tried to do right, and so, if my race is run, I can go down into the last river serene, clear-eyed and unafraid.[63]

Yet burning zeal can carry one very far. Dewey's contributions to library development are unequaled by any one man and his personal courage and unflinching faith in his mission will long be admired. It was Dewey who initiated library school education and aggressively promoted his standards of technical training in library mechanics.

A predominant characteristic of Dewey's, and important for its relationship to library education development, is his inordinate fondness for women.

His men friends were few; his women friends appear to have been numerous. All through his life he preferred the company of women to men. He worked with them, played with them and repeatedly got into trouble over them.

The trouble began as early as 1883 when Dewey hired six young women graduates of Wellesley to assist him in the organization of the Columbia University Library. At that time Columbia College was closed to women. Four years later Dewey again scandalized the campus by his insistence that women students be admitted to the first library school ever established. When the Trustees refused to allow Dewey classroom space because of the presence of women in the school, he furnished an unused storeroom on the campus and opened on schedule in defiance of the Trustees' orders. Shakily supported by President Frederick A. P. Barnard, the library school survived until 1889 when Dewey submitted his resignation to the Trustees shortly before his impending dismissal. During the time at Columbia, Dewey was sharply criticized for his open recruitment of women students and for his startling application form which included in it a request for height, weight, color of eyes, color of hair and a photograph.[64] Little tempered by time, Dewey's congenial intimacy with women set wagging in 1905 the "tongue of slander in sex matters," which even his eulogistic biographer concedes to have sent "stories sweeping like storms among the library leaders of the nation."[65] Dewey apparently had been guilty of some vaguely defined, but unorthodox, familiarities. The scandal prompted his wife to write scorching letters to the tale-bearers.

> Women who have keen intuitions know by instinct that they can trust Mr. Dewey implicitly. He has so many proofs of this and is so sure of his own self-control, that unconsciously his manner has grown more and more unconventional and familiar . . . It is most unwise for any man to pass the bounds of convention, and he has been frequently warned of the danger. Knowing that I was absolutely free from jealousy and understood him perfectly, he has doubtless gone farther than with a wife who felt it necessary to watch her husband . . . A wife who has lived more than a quarter of a century with her husband is surely the best judge as to whether he is pure minded . . .[66]

Dewey's compatibility with women gave him insight which was unusual among men of his time. This remarkable statement was delivered before the Association of Collegiate Alumnae in 1886:

> Would a father say to his son, 'My boy, your mother and I are lonely without you, you must stay at home, go out to afternoon teas with us, and keep us company in the big, empty house. I have enough for us all, so there is no need of your bothering your head about supporting yourself.' Would he expect his son to be happy under such circumstances? Why, then, his daughter?[67]

Dewey had sincere respect for the intellect of women and successfully contended that Mary Salome Cutler should be chairman of the library exhibit committee for the World's Columbian Exposition of 1893 because she was the most highly qualified candidate. He has often been praised because his defense of women's capabilities led him at times to suffer real personal sacrifice, as at Columbia. Any admiration for his support of women's rights, however, must be tempered by a recognition that Dewey had an unusually strong personal desire for feminine company and an equally strong indifference to the presence of men. Indeed, his role as champion of women is a complex and intriguing one, for beneath it lies a grating note of paternalism. He did not call on women to assert themselves but instead set himself up as their valiant spokesman.

Dewey, with a progressive (as well as erotic) affinity for women, was obviously deflected by his sexist attitudes from his progressive design for a strong, highly intellectual new profession. The library school curriculum which Dewey devised at Columbia and later continued at the New York State Library School ruled out any "attempt to give general culture or to make up deficiencies of earlier education." Dewey, in a characteristically pragmatic decision, would reconcile the library needs of the country with the status of women in society by concentrating upon schooling which would teach the technical skills necessary to perform work on the lower rungs of the library ladder. The American Library Association's committee on the proposed library school at Columbia remarked that those who came to the school would probably wish to become administrators. Dewey quickly corrected them; the committee was told that "the plans all contemplate special facilities and inducements for cataloguers and assistants who do not expect or desire the first place."[68]

By 1905 library education had crystallized around Dewey's core of practical instruction of routine detail to a predominantly female force. Yet even though librarians had established library education as a system of non-professional training for library mechanics, they continued to wonder at the "appalling misconception" in the public mind of their "professional" qualifications and to bemoan the fact that the public had made them "the poorest paid professionals in the world."[69] In that year the American Library Association found an answer of sorts to the dilemma—the great librarians, it was agreed, were born, not made.

> Pools and Winsors are not and never will be wholly produced by library schools . . . Such eminent examples are born librarians. The born librarian will not need a school to teach him principles of classification . . . he will evolve systems of classifications and cataloging, and methods of administration without ever going near a school . . . But there will never be many of him, and there will be thousands of library employees.[70]

It was for the low-level employee "that our schools are at present intended."[71] In the discussion that followed a consensus was reached by important library spokesmen like E. C. Richardson, Frederick M. Crunden, S. S. Green, Melvil Dewey and Herbert Putnam.[72] It was agreed that librarians of genius had no need of formal training. Unconsciously the national association had focused upon a central library truth. While females from the library schools became clerks and assistants and heads of small libraries, the most honored and well-paid librarians were men. The "best" librarians of the time were indeed not made, but born—born male.

The prevalence of women librarians also served to strengthen a non-professional bureaucratic system of control and low autonomy base for the library worker. In librarianship, as in teaching and social work, the dominance of women made more likely the development of an authoritative administrative structure with a stress on rules and generally established principles to control the activities of employees. In these feminized fields the highest success was secured through promotion to the administrative levels of the organization. This is in contrast to the pattern within established professions. In university teaching, for example, the productive practitioner is usually more honored within his profession than is the high level administrator of the university. Within librarianship and other feminized occupations, compliance to sex roles caused women to assume low levels of autonomy. Because sexist attitudes still prevail in the society, this basic situation has undergone little change since the nineteenth century.[73]

The changing image of librarianship graphically illustrates the many alterations which feminization brought to library work in the late nineteenth century. To call the public image of librarianship a stereotype does not make it an entirely erroneous concept for the popular image of librarians is a by-product of deeper social realities. In the 1870s the popular concept of the librarian was that of a pre-occupied man in black—a collector and preserver who was never so happy as when all the volumes were safely on the shelf. He was thought to be ineffectual, grim and "bookish." Library literature of this period reflects the attempt of librarians to replace the image of the "old" librarian with a picture of the "new" librarian.

> The mechanical librarian is no more a finality than the acquisitive and conservative librarian. He is succeeded by . . . a type who is not content with removing the obstacles to circulation that his predecessors have built up, but tries actually to foster it; who leans more to the missionary and pastoral side of librarianship; who relies more on personal intercourse; who goes in for reference lists and annotated and interesting bulletins; who does not so much try to make it easy for an interested public to help itself among the books as to create an interested public.[74]

The popular image had shifted by 1905 to portray the librarian as a woman. The public's mental image of the librarian was consistently deprecatory. Meek, mousy and colorless had been added to the original "old" male librarian's traits of eccentricity, frustration, grouchiness and introversion. The public librarian came to be stereotyped as an inhibited, single, middle-aged woman.[75] Librarian Harold Lancour quipped that he had heard so much about this lady that he was "growing rather fond of the old girl."[76] Howard Mumford Jones, musing on the caricature of the librarian, suggested that the image was "partly the product of limited budgets, and in part the product of genteel tradition. . . . This is not to say that all librarians are maiden ladies, but enough of them are to rank librarians with school teachers, Y.W.C.A. secretaries and social workers as persons less likely to go to night clubs than are receptionists or department-store buyers."[77] Unlike the librarians who had shaped public library standards, Jones understood well the chief reason why professionalization continued to elude library workers: the training of librarians should include more about the insides of books and "less technical lore about what to do with the books as an object in space."

The feminization of public librarianship did much to shape and stunt the development of an important American cultural institution. The socially designated sexual roles which women elected to act out had a major influence upon the development of the library's "homey" atmosphere and its staff of "helpful" non-assertive hostesses. Increasingly librarians are seeking to change the traditional role of the public librarian. The hope is to establish librarianship on a scientifically-oriented, abstract-knowledge base and to train the librarian as the indispensable expert in knowledge retrieval. The communication explosion has decidedly created a need for such a person; as the printed material grows to an unmanageable mass certainly someone, if not the public librarian, will move in to perform this vital function. However, until the librarian deals with the implications of feminization—with its varied inhibitory effects on intellectual excellence and leadership—progress toward professionalization will be limited. So long as sexist attitudes essentially govern the society, the basic situation which supported the service ideal and knowledge base of the nineteenth-century librarian seems unlikely to change.

FOOTNOTES

1. Robert W. Smuts, *Women and Work in America* (New York: Columbia University Press, 1959), 110.

2. Charles Evans, ed. *The Athenaeum Centenary* (Boston: The Boston Athenaeum, 1907), 42. William Poole is generally credited with the hiring of the first woman librarian at the Boston Athenaeum in 1857. Poole's predecessor had barred women from the staff on the grounds that part of the library should be closed to impressionable female minds.

3. "The English Conference: Official Report of Proceedings," *Library Journal*, II (January-February, 1878), 280. The *Library Journal*, organ of the American Library Association, is hereafter cited as *LJ*.

4. Joseph Adna Hill, *Women in Gainful Occupations, 1870-1920*, Census Monograph, No. 9 (Washington: Government Printing Office, 1929), 42. Librarianship has been termed a "profession" by the U.S. Census and is used in that sense here. Hill cites 43 women library workers in 1870, 3,122 in 1900 and 8,621 in 1910. See Sharon B. Wells, "The Feminization of the American Library Profession, 1876-1923" (unpublished Master's thesis, Library School, University of Chicago, 1967) for statistics on the number of women employed in all American libraries, including public libraries, and the number of women enrolled in library schools. Miss Wells counts 191 men and 18 women managing collections of over ten thousand volumes in 1875.

5. Melvil Dewey, "The Ideal Librarian," *LJ*, XIX (January, 1899), 14.

6. This analysis of the feminization of public librarianship rests upon a larger study of the socio-economic backgrounds and social and literary ideals of 36 library leaders in the period from 1876 to 1900. The selected librarians represent the profession's most influential spokesmen and are primarily the heads of urban libraries in the east, although important western library leaders are also included in the group.

7. U.S. Bureau of Education, *Public Libraries in the United States of America: Their History, Condition and Management*, Special Report, Part I (Washington: Government Printing Office, 1876), iii. Hereafter cited as "1876 Report."

8. Carl M. White, *The Origins of the American Library School* (New York: The Scarecrow Press, Inc., 1961), 14.

9. R. R. Bowker, "Libraries and the Century in America: Retrospect and Prospect," *LJ*, XXVI (January, 1901), 5.

10. "1876 Report," 430. It is interesting to note that Perkins, who deserted his family to go West and to become the surly librarian at the San Francisco Public Library, left behind his young daughter, Charlotte Perkins Stetson Gilman, who later became a noted spokesman for women's rights.

11. "The English Conference. . . ."

12. The eight women among the selected 36 library leaders are: Mary Bean, Eliza G. Browning, Mary Cutler, Theresa Elmendorf, Caroline Hewins, Hannah James, Mary Plummer and Minerva Sanders.

13. Because librarians, at least until about 1885, were so vocal in their contempt for the low intellectual abilities of teachers in general, I deduce that most women librarians were better educated or of higher social standing than were most women teachers.

14. Mabel Newcomer, *A Century of Higher Education for American Women* (New York: Harper and Brothers, 1959) offers a good overview of the employment opportunities open to educated women in the late nineteenth century. The economic causes which she cites of the predominance of women teachers can also be applied to the feminization of librarianship. In 1870 three-fifths of all teachers were women. Also see, Robert E. Riegel, *American Women: A Story of Social Change* (Cranbury, New Jersey: Associated University Presses, Inc., 1970). 132-200.

15. Aileen S. Kraditor, ed. *Up from the Pedestal* (Chicago: Quadrangle Books, 1968) and William L. O'Neill, *Everyone Was Brave* (Chicago: Quadrangle Books, 1969).

16. Richard le Gallienne, quoted in M. S. R. James, "Women Librarians," *LJ*, XVIII (May, 1893), 148.

17. Linda A. Eastman, "Aims and Personal Attitude in Library Work," *LJ*, XXII (October, 1897), 80.

18. "Library Employment vs. the Library Profession," *Library Notes*, I (June, 1886), 50.

19. *Ibid.*, 51.

20. Melvil Dewey, "Libraries as Related to the Educational Work of the State," *Library Notes*, III (June, 1888), 346.

21. Melvil Dewey, "The Attractions and Opportunities of Librarianship," *Library Notes*, I (June, 1886), 52. See also, Melvil Dewey, Address before the Association of Collegiate Alumnae, March 13, 1886, *Librarianship as a Profession for College-Bred Women* (Boston: Library Bureau, 1886).

22. Lilian Denio, "How to Make the Most of a Small Library," *Library Notes*, III (March, 1889), 470.

23. Theresa H. West, "The Usefulness of Libraries in Small Towns," *LJ*, VIII (September-October, 1883), 229.

24. Mary Salome Cutler Fairchild, "Women in American Libraries," *LJ*, XXIX (December, 1904), 162.

25. *Ibid.*

26. Celia A. Hayward, "Woman as Cataloger," *Public Libraries*, III (April, 1898), 121-23. "Female Library Assistants," *LJ*, XIV (April, 1889), 128-29; John Dana, "Women in Library Work," *Independent*, LXXI (August 3, 1911), 244.

27. Robert Weibe, *The Search for Order: 1877-1920* (New York: Hill and Wang, 1967), 122-23, discusses how sexual roles were expressed in this period by women social workers, lawyers and doctors in their service to children.

28. *LJ*, XXV (August, 1900), 123.

29. *Ibid.*

30. Minerva Sanders, "Report on Reading for the Young," *LJ*, XV (December, 1890), 59.

31. Annie Carroll Moore, "Special Training for Children's Librarians," *LJ*, XXIII (August, 1898), 80.

32. E. M. Fairchild, "Methods of Children's Library Work as Determined by the Needs of the Children," *LJ*, XXII (October, 1897), 26.

33. Sophy H. Powell, *The Children's Library: A Dynamic Factor in Education* (New York: H. W. Wilson Co., 1917), 1-7, 191-96, 255-71, is a careful study of the limited educational function of the children's section of the library. For a history of the development of library service to children see Harriet G. Long, *Public Library Service to Children: Foundation and Development* (Metuchen, New Jersey: The Scarecrow Press, Inc., 1969) and Effie L. Power, *Work With Children in Public Libraries* (Chicago: American Library Association, 1943).

34. For examples of women's mild tone see, Mary S. Cutler, "What a Woman Librarian Earns," *LJ*, XVII (August, 1892), 90; Mary E. Ahern, "The Business Side of a Woman's Career as a Librarian," *LJ*, XXIV (July, 1899), 62; Martha B. Earle, "Women Librarians," *Independent*, XLIX (February 18, 1897), 30.

35. "Woman's Meeting," *LJ*, XVII (August, 1892), 89-94.

36. "Proceedings," *LJ*, I (November 30, 1876), 90.

37. Caroline M. Hewins, "Library Work for Women," *LJ*, XVI (September, 1891), 273-74.

38. Cutler, 90.

39. *Ibid.*, 91.

40. "Library Association of Central California," *LJ*, XXII (June, 1897), 308. Miss Kelso later became a successful businesswoman in the field of publishing and remained an outspoken feminist.

41. Tessa L. Kelso, "Woman's Section of the A.L.A.," *LJ*, XVII (November, 1892), 444.

42. Ahern, 60-62.

43. Fairchild, 153-62.

44. *Ibid.*, 162.

45. Melvil Dewey, "The Profession," *LJ*, I (September, 1876), 5-6; Ernest C. Richardson, "Being a Librarian," *LJ*, XV (July, 1890), 201-02.

46. The first library school opened in 1887 at Columbia College. As a result of Williamson's critical survey of library schools in 1923, the curriculum standards in library education were revised and a national system of accreditation was established. Charles C. Williamson, *Training for Library Service: A Report Prepared for the Carnegie Corporation of New York* (Boston: The Merrymount Press, 1923); Sarah K. Vann, *The Williamson Reports: A Study* (Metuchen, New Jersey: The Scarecrow Press, Inc., 1971); C. Edward Carroll, *The Professionalization of Education for Librarianship* (Metuchen, New Jersey: The Scarecrow Press, Inc., 1970). For discussions of library professionalization see: Phillip H. Ennis (ed.), *Seven Questions About the Profession of Librarianship* (Chicago: University of Chicago Press, 1961); Pierce Butler, "Librarianship as a Profession," *Library Quarterly*, XXI (October, 1951), 235-47; Robert D. Leigh, *The Public Library in the United States* (New York: Columbia University Press, 1969); Robert D. Downs (ed.), *The Status of American College and Univer-*

sity Librarians (ACRL Monograph, No. 22 [Chicago: American Library Association, 1958]); William J. Goode, "The Theoretical Limits of Professionalization," *The Semi-Professions and their Organization: Teachers, Nurses, Social Workers,* ed. Amitai Etzioni (New York: The Free Press, 1969), 266-313.

47. White, *passim.*

48. Ennis, 83.

49. A. M. Carr-Saunders, *The Professions* (Oxford: Clarendon, 1933); T. A. Caplow, *The Sociology of Work* (Minneapolis: University of Minnesota, 1954); Ernest Greenwood, "The Attributes of a Profession," *Social Work,* II (June, 1957), 139-40; Howard M. Vollmer and Donald Mills (eds.), *Professionalization* (Englewood Cliffs, New Jersey: Prentice-Hall, 1966); Ronald M. Pavalko, *Sociology of Occupations and Professions* (Itasca, Illinois: F. E. Peacock Publishers, Inc., 1971); Raymond M. Merritt, *Engineering in American Society* (Lexington, Kentucky: University Press of Kentucky, 1969); Daniel H. Calhoun, *Professional Lives in America* (Cambridge, Massachusetts: Harvard University Press, 1965); Kenneth S. Lynn (ed.), *The Professions in America* (Boston: Houghton Mifflin Company, 1965).

50. William F. Poole, "Buffalo Conference Proceedings," *LJ,* VIII (September-October, 1883), 281. See also, William H. Brett, "The Present Problem," *LJ,* XVIX (December, 1894), 5-9; S. S. Green, *Libraries and Schools* (New York: F. Leypoldt,   3), 56-74; Max Cohen, "The Librarian as an Educator and Not a Cheap-John,   7, XIII (November, 1888), 366-67; Melvil Dewey, "Public Libraries as Public Educators," *LJ,* XI (June, 1886), 165.

51. Charles Knowles Bolton, "The Librarian's Duty as a Citizen," *LJ,* XXI (May, 1896), 219-22; S. S. Green, "Personal Relations Between Librarians and Readers," *LJ,* I (November 30, 1876), 74-81.

52. Smuts, 36.

53. For a thorough documentation of characteristic behavior of women workers see Richard L. and Ida Harper Simpson, "Women and Bureaucracy in the Semi-Professions," in Etzioni, 196-265. The nineteenth-century woman would demonstrate even more strongly the traits which the Simpsons outline.

54. Ennis, 7, 9; Marjorie Fiske, *Book Selection and Censorship* (Los Angeles: University of California Press, 1959), 100-12.

55. Sociologist Talcott Parsons has also noted "the tendency for women to gravitate into 'supportive' types of occupational roles, where functions of 'helpfulness' to the incumbent of more assertive and ultimately, in the social function sense, more responsible roles, is a major keynote." Parsons points to sex composition as "both a symptom and a partial determinant" of the pattern of "the 'quietness', the rather passive character of the attributes of librarians as a group, wishing as it were to be unobtrusively 'helpful' but avoiding assertiveness." Talcott Parsons, "Implications of the Study," *The Climate of Book Selection,* ed. J. Periam Danton (Berkeley: University of California, 1959), 94-95.

56. U.S. Bureau of Education, *Report of Commissioner of Education, 1887-1888* (Washington: Government Printing Office), 1033.

57. William Fletcher, *Public Libraries in America* (Boston: Roberts Brothers, 1894), 32-33.

58. My interviews with a leading university librarian and with several public librarians indicate a recent twentieth-century trend toward male homosexuals

in library work. Their presence may be connected to the role-playing assumed by librarians in general. That is, to the extent that the homosexual male takes on the characteristics of femininity, he proves quite adaptable to playing a female service role. It may be, too, that male homosexuals, having been driven from most of the high status professions by prejudice, find women less hostile to their presence and thus feel more comfortable in a feminized working environment. On this point, note the formation of the Task Force on Gay Liberation during the 1970 American Library Association annual meeting.

59. William E. Goode "The Librarian: From Occupation to Profession?" Ennis, 13.

60. White, 32-33.

61. Normal schools were faced with similar problems during this period. A predominantly bureaucratic control is evident in school-teaching and librarianship. See Simpson and Simpson, 196-221.

62. Fremont Rider, *Melvil Dewey* (Chicago: American Library Association, 1944), 8.

63. Grosvenor Dawe, *Melvil Dewey: Seer, Inspirer, Doer* (Albany, New York: J. B. Lyon Company, 1923), 76.

64. Ray Trautman, *A History of the School of Library Service: Columbia University* (New York Columbia University Press, 1954), 3-23.

65. Dawe, 70.

66. Letter from Annie Godfrey Dewey, June 15, 1906, cited in Dawe, 70.

67. Dawe, 91-92.

68. "Report of the Committee on the Proposed School of Library Economy," *LJ*, X (September-October, 1885), 293.

69. Lutie E. Stearns, "The Question of Library Training," *LJ*, XXX (September, 1905), 68, 70.

70. "Fifth Session," *LJ*, XXX (September, 1905), 167-68.

71. *Ibid.*

72. *Ibid.*, 164-76.

73. Simpson and Simpson, 260-65. For current feminist protest see, Anita R. Schiller, "The Widening Sex Gap," *LJ*, LXXXXIV (March 15, 1969), 1098-100; Janet Freedman, "The Liberated Librarian," *LJ*, LXXXXV (May 1, 1970), 1709-711; Anita R. Schiller, "The Disadvantaged Majority: Women Employed in Libraries," *American Libraries*, IV (April, 1970), 345-49.

74. "Editorial," *LJ*, XVII (September, 1892), 371. For discussions of the old and new librarian see "The New Librarians," *LJ*, XV (November, 1890), 338; R. R. Bowker, "The Work of the Nineteenth Century Librarian for the Librarian of the Twentieth," *LJ*, VIII (September-October, 1883), 247-50.

75. William H. Form, "Popular Images of Librarians," *LJ*, LXXI (June 15, 1946), 851-55; Robert Leigh and Kathryn W. Sewny, "The Popular Image of the Library and of Librarians," *LJ*, LXXXV (June 1, 1960), 2089-091.

76. Ennis, 74.

77. Howard Mumford Jones, "Reflections in a Library," *Saturday Review*, XXXXIII (April 9, 1960), 34.

Women in Librarianship

by Anita R. Schiller

INTRODUCTION

References to women in librarianship can be uncovered in hundreds of reports, surveys, and articles. Yet this subject is rarely the primary focus of investigation. Only a handful of studies pinpoint this subject at the start or begin with the question, "What is the status of women in librarianship?"

One of the very few that did, written almost three-quarters of a century ago, began, curiously enough, with the researcher disclaiming any interest in the topic:

> The inquiry does not particularly interest or attract me, but I am glad to undertake it because of my confidence in the judgment of our (ALA) president who thinks that such a statistical statement, with a slight analysis of the statistics, will be of value.[43]

Fairchild's report itself showed that women's representation in the ALA rose from the role of "the best of listeners" in 1876, to a representation of nearly one-third on the program in 1902. Overall, Fairchild believed, there was "practically no discrimination with regard to sex in the American Library Association."

But women's place in the library field itself was "quite another question." Basing her conclusions on a national survey of one hundred libraries of all types, she stated that, broadly speaking, women librarians "hold a large number of important positions, seldom the most important. They do not hold positions offering the highest salaries and apparently they do not receive equal remuneration for the same work."[43]

Fairchild's "slight analysis" turns out to have been a rather substantial one for the time and is the latest survey I know of that was undertaken solely to determine the status of women in librarianship in the United States. Her initial reluctance to undertake the survey at all tells us as much about discrimination on one level as her own assessment of it does on another.

"Women in librarianship" has not been regarded as a distinct research area. With one possible exception, a master's thesis on the feminization of the profession,[132] no extensive national study, since Fairchild's brief but quite comprehensive inquiry, has been made. The lines laid out by Fairchild seem to have expressed, in a general way, what was to follow for the next seventy years.

At the same time, the predominance of women in librarianship has been called a "touchy" subject,[87] and despite Munthe's own significant contribution (a chapter in his book, *American Librarianship from a European Angle*), a review of the literature bears this out. The disinclination to examine this allegedly sensitive issue has had serious consequences for research. It has meant that data of major importance have not ordinarily been collected. Where they have, usually they have been gathered as part of a larger study, and statistics on women have been submerged in a mass of other data.

Moreover, where these statistics have not reaffirmed the tacit faith that there is equal opportunity for women in librarianship, the findings, until very recently, have been widely disregarded by the profession at large. As late as 1965, the relative status of women in the profession was a moot question. Was women's status equal to men's or wasn't it?

Responding to a charge made elsewhere[62] that there was discrimination against women in librarianship and that there was only "tokenism at the top," with women strongly under-represented in major positions, an editorial in the *Library Journal* supplied some other figures, gathered on its own. (See page 155.) These suggested the opposite. (The implication was quite clear that women controlled the power positions.) The editorial concluded: "We are not brave—or foolish—enough to take sides on *this* issue."[84]

According to the editor, there simply wasn't enough "statistical ammunition" to document the charge of discrimination. In one sense this was true enough. Data on this issue have been fragmentary at best. Much of what we know now has emerged since this editorial was written. Yet now, in retrospect, it seems quite likely that librarians were reluctant to put together the bits and pieces of information they had, to perceive their own condition.

Recent research in other fields[e.g., 63] suggests the possibility that the will to believe in equality, or perhaps in male superiority, may have been a major obstacle to perception. Librarians may well have unconsciously, but understandably, internalized the prevailing social view of the inherent worthiness and capability of the male and the corresponding inadequacy of the female.

If this is even partly correct, the profession's thinking would go something like this: If men are represented in the field, and particularly at the top levels where they would be more visible, librarianship would receive some measure of status in the larger society. Correspondingly, to deny male superiority in librarianship would have been, in a sense, to deny it the same status as other professions—something neither men nor women librarians would have wanted to do.

While this is a speculative point, it is worth considering because overt discrimination against women is but one facet, very important to be sure, of the disadvantaged role of women in librarianship. It relates also to current research on women in fields other than librarianship. Recent findings and analyses give strong support to the view that on-the-job discrimination has its roots in the assignment of sex roles that precedes (though also includes) what occurs at the work site. A British study explains how the scope of that particular research project was enlarged from a narrow focus to a much broader one:

> What it is reputable to state or deny in public about family relationships and women's careers has been changing fast. One index of this change is the evolution which occurred within [this] . . . project itself, over and above the shift just mentioned from concern with top jobs to concern with the whole range of people from whom recruits to top jobs may be drawn. As compared to previous research, the project is distinctive in at least three respects. It focuses on issues affecting men and women together rather than on women's problems as such. It analyzes the interplay between changing family or sex roles and roles at work, rather than

study work and family issues separately. It insists on the complexity of solutions as well as of problems and . . . [emphasizes] the many angles and uncertainties of a far-reaching revolution in a major area of culture and social organization.[49]

In fact, in Sweden, women's liberation is known as the "sex role" issue, a conceptualization that permits a comprehensive approach to a condition that far transcends job discrimination. Sex-typing of occupations, as well as all other social activities, is the definitional means by which inequality is imposed in the home, in education, and on the job. Accordingly, what needs to be considered is not only the question of whether women hold this or that administrative position, but how the profession is regarded and why librarianship has been stamped as a woman's occupation.

In explaining the applicability of the term "sexism," sociologist Jessie Bernard amplifies this issue. She writes:

> The term *sexism* was brilliant. The word racism had begun to appear in the dictionaries only in the late 1960's. Until then the word *prejudice* had seemed adequate for analysis of most racial situations. Only by the late 1960's did it appear that a new concept was needed to refer to a situation in which quite unprejudiced people were, willy-nilly, engaged in discriminatory practices. More than prejudice alone had been responsible for discrimination in the past and its continuance into the present. Adverse discrimination was found to be built into all institutions. . . . Now young women were protesting that in the same way, discrimination against women — *oppression* was the term they frequently used — was also built into all our institutions. The term became essential in the study of sex relations as it had in race relations, because adverse discrimination was surviving legal banning.[14]

In brief, the status of women in librarianship reveals an explicit pattern of discrimination (which we shall document further along). But the origin of the condition of the disadvantaged majority in this one field is not to be found in the arbitrary behavior of prejudiced males (though this often does exist). Rather, there is an extremely complex interaction of the larger society's male/female role prescriptions in every category of existence, both inside and outside the home, and that same society's socioeconomic dynamic and structure that has kept libraries and the library profession far down on its preferred resource allocation scale.

THE STATUS OF WOMEN LIBRARIANS

A review of national surveys of librarians over the past twenty-five years reveals a consistent pattern: a continuing existence of significant salary and position level differentials between men and women. At no time during this period has the status of women librarians been equal to men's. Not unexpectedly, this is in accord with current research findings on women in all fields.[e.g., 8, 41, 46, 127, 128]

The major work, *The Public Librarian,* based on a survey in 1947-1948, continues to stand out as the classic study on the characteristics of librarians, although it is now long out of date.[23] Undertaken as part of the Public Library Inquiry, this study examined the economic and educational status, personal characteristics, and careers of library personnel. It contains more significant analyses and breakdowns of the data by sex than most studies provide.

Bryan's findings pointed to a "dual career structure for librarians differentiated on the basis of sex — an accelerated career for the minority, composed of men, and a basic library career, established within considerably lower limits for the majority, who are women."[23] However alien the "dual career structure" concept may be, it has governed in practice.

During the same period, the U.S. Bureau of Labor Statistics (BLS),[121] with the cooperation of the American Library Association, undertook a comprehensive survey of the economic status of library personnel, covering "professional and nonprofessional library employees working in all states in the country in all types and sizes of libraries."

As in Bryan's survey, women earned less, on the average, than men in both the professional and nonprofessional categories. In professional positions, the median salary for women librarians ($2,975) was about 75 percent of the median salary for men ($3,975). About one out of *ten* men librarians and one out of a *thousand* women librarians earned $7,000 or more (p. 68). Other tables reveal that at any given amount of general or professional education, women's salaries were also lower than men's. No data on position levels were supplied, but children's librarians, among whom the concentration of women has always been particularly high, earned the lowest salaries of all types of positions. Children's librarians also had lower levels of education.

Two ALA surveys followed (American Library Association, 1953, 1956). These surveys, like the BLS survey before them, stand out from all later ones because they covered the entire profession. Still, not one of the tables includes breakdowns by sex, and nowhere in the text of the reports is there any mention of men or women. Since 1956, national surveys of librarians have covered only portions of the librarian population.

National Salary Data, 1960-1972

Salary differentials between men and women have been reported for public librarians;[40] academic librarians;[76] state library consultants;[103] federal librarians;[64] deans of library schools and library science doctorates;[32] directors of large public libraries;[33] members of the American Association of Law Libraries;[17, 66] members of the Special Libraries Association (SLA);[113] and members of the American Library Association.[80]

TABLE I

SALARY DISTRIBUTION (1970) OF ALA MEMBERS BY SEX

	Salaries	
	Men[a]	Women[b]
Average salary (FT)	$14,471	$10,874
5th Percentile	$ 8,250	$ 6,700
25th Percentile	$10,500	$ 8,736
50th Percentile	$13,500	$10,400
75th Percentile	$17,200	$12,600
95th Percentile	$24,500	$16,620

[a] Number of respondents: 2,778.
[b] Number of respondents: 9,030.

Higher salary ranges for men are characteristic. Table I shows the salary distribution of members of the American Library Association who responded to a 1970 questionnaire. Overall, women's salaries were about 75 percent of men's. One out of every four men earned over $17,200, but only one out of every twenty women earned over $16,620. Other data from the same survey disclose that women earned lower salaries than men, regardless of education or job level.[80]

Another survey[103] indicated that salary differentials between men and women widened with experience. Among college and university librarians with less than five years' experience, the median salary for women was 92 percent of that for men, but among those with twenty or more years of experience, women's salary was only 70 percent of the men's (see Table II).

Even where men and women had equal amounts of education and experience, salary differentials persisted. Among men and women whose highest degree was the M.L.S., the salaries of women with ten years or more of professional experience were only 85 percent of the salaries of their male colleagues.[103]

Data on the salaries of men and women with the doctorate in library science reveal even more striking inequities. The median salary for women with this degree was $13,800, while for men it was $18,300.[32] As Table III indicates, salary differences between the sexes were pronounced at all age levels.

This survey also found that among deans of accredited library schools the median salary for women was $15,800; for men, $22,300. Reporting on the salaries of deans and doctorates together, the authors of this survey noted that "nearly one-third of the men are paid more than the highest paid female."[32] The conclusion of this study was unmistakable. Women in librarianship could not, even with the doctoral degree, expect to achieve equal status with men.

In the past few years, other surveys have confirmed for different portions of the profession, what has now become a widely accepted fact. Even in federal employment, women are classified at lower levels than men, and earn

TABLE II

MEDIAN SALARY OF ACADEMIC LIBRARIANS (1966-1967) BY NUMBER OF YEARS EXPERIENCE, BY SEX

Number of years professional experience	Men		Women		Women's salary as % of men's
	Per-cent	Median salary	Per-cent	Median salary	
Under 5	35.5	$ 7,330	31.6	$6,750	92
5-9	23.0	8,950	18.6	7,465	83
10-14	17.2	10,235	12.6	8,080	79
15-19	11.7	10,750	11.6	8,275	77
20 and over	12.6	12,570	25.6	8,745	70
	100.0	$ 8,975	100.0	$7,455	83%

TABLE III

MEDIAN SALARIES OF LIBRARY SCIENCE DOCTORATES[a]
BY SEX AND AGE

Age	Men (N=83)	Women (N=24)	Women's salary as % of men's
21-30	— (0)	(only 1 case)	—
31-40	$16,300 (18)	$13,700 (7)	84
41-50	19,100 (18)	11,200 (4)	59
51-60	19,200 (35)	15,200 (5)	79
over 60	19,800 (12)	14,200 (7)	72
All ages	$18,300	$13,800	75%

[a] Excludes library school deans.

correspondingly lower salaries. In 1967, there was a difference of two grades between men and women librarians, and a salary differential of $1,788.[64]

Recent surveys of the members of various library associations indicate similar patterns. A study of law librarians, for example, reported that 22 percent of the men, compared to 1 percent of the women, earned $20,000 and over. At the opposite end of the scale, 16 percent of the men, compared to 51 percent of the women, earned less than $10,000.[66] Summarizing another survey of law librarians a short time earlier, the *Library of Congress Information Bulletin* reported: "A distressing fact was reconfirmed by this study—the discrimination in women's salaries. . . . Something must be done about the salaries of women, as they represent one-half of the law library community."[17]

Similar conclusions were reached in the survey by the Special Libraries Association, the third salary survey undertaken by this group but the first to include salary distributions by sex. Analyzing certain high income categories by sex, the authors of this report concluded: "In all instances (geographic, job function, subject, and highest academic degree) men's salaries clustered above the overall mean and women's salaries clustered below the mean. In spite of the perhaps independent effects of geographic location, library subject, academic degree, and job title, there is evidence for a real male-oriented sex bias in salaries reported for all categories."[113]

Until 1972, none of the salary surveys of current library school graduates (begun in 1951 and published annually in *Library Journal*) included data by sex, but in response to a request from the ALA Social Responsibilities Round Table Task Force on Women, these figures will now be reported.[50] Although the first such report, on 1972 graduates, was not scheduled for publication until June 1973, one library school, on its own initiative, gathered the figures for 1971.[50]

This report made a particularly telling point about discrimination, because it showed that women whose professional training was identical with men's began their library employment with a salary handicap. Average and median salaries for women were lower than men's in all types of libraries. With or without experience, women earned less than men with the same professional education. The lowest salary for men was $1,900 higher than the lowest salary for women. The average salary for men with no professional experience or additional graduate study was $8,899; for women $8,425.[21]

Also not a national survey but included here because it is unusually comprehensive, an affirmative action report on the status of women in one large university library[29] analyzed promotion patterns for all librarians employed there, from the time of their appointment to their current classifications. Finding that men had been promoted much more rapidly than women, the report emphasized the cumulative effects of salary losses to women over a long-term period.

Position Level

As we have seen, women fare poorly in comparison with men in the salaries they receive. In the matter of job holding, the disadvantaged condition of the woman librarian is, if anything, more striking. Women's underrepresentation in top jobs also accounts to some degree for overall salary differentials.

To grasp fully the degree of discrimination against women in the level of position held, it is essential first to review the woman/man-power situation in librarianship. Although we do not have up-to-date figures on the percentages of women in each of the various components of the profession, and even those figures that are available have certain limitations, they are at least indicative. Various surveys[103] have reported the following: *Although roughly 80 percent of librarians were women*, among school librarians, 94 percent were women; among public librarians 87 percent were women; among special librarians 72 percent were women; and among academic librarians 67 percent were women.

Do women accordingly share equally in the administrative and policy-making jobs in this profession in which they are so heavily represented? Indeed, the question of "sharing equally" in the decision-making machinery is itself an ambiguous conception. For even if the disparity in sex ratios in the separate portions of the profession are accepted as given, a reasonable bench mark for sharing equally would be whether or not women were represented in the job positional ladder according to their proportion in whichever library category was being considered. Thus, in school librarianship, where women constitute 94 percent of the professional workers, equal participation in the administrative machinery would require that the same percentage of the administrative positions in school librarianship be held by women.

Yet, the evidence overwhelmingly indicates that instead of women participating in top library policy-making posts in some manner roughly proportionate to their numbers in the field, they are systematically underrepresented and sometimes almost totally excluded.

What better place to begin this inquiry than in our national library? The Library of Congress is an institution, one would hope, whose practices might be regarded as providing a model for less prestigious and more modest systems and units across the country. In fact, the Library of Congress exemplifies the national pattern of a pyramidal labor force arrangement, where a large number of women are concentrated at the bottom and a smaller number of men are ensconced at the top.[75] Table IV shows the percentage of women employed in the various grades from GS 1 through GS 18 and above. It includes all employees, librarians and others. The GS 9 level is the beginning position for those with the master's degree in library science. At this grade level, 54 percent of the individuals were women. Grades 16-18 are considered "supergrade" positions, and women held 4 percent of them. At the highest level, above GS 18, no women were represented.[75]

TABLE IV

LIBRARY OF CONGRESS PERSONNEL STATISTICS[a]
MAY 1972
GRADE LEVEL BY SEX

GS	Total	Men	Women	% Women
1-8	2,058	835	1,223	59
9	423	196	227	54
10	34	16	18	53
11	435	215	220	51
12	355	180	175	49
13	201	135	66	33
14	129	99	30	23
15	70	60	10	14
16-18	55	53	2	4
Above 18	3	3	0	0
	3,763	1,792	1,971	52%

[a]All grades/all series.

The Library of Congress pattern of discrimination against women in the level of job held is replicated in libraries nationally. Four recent reports, all parts of a large-scale manpower research project initiated at the University of Maryland's School of Library and Information Service, examined the situation of library administrators in each of the four major types of libraries.[24-27] In each case, only the chief administrator and only the larger and more complex organizations were included in the population universe. The concentration of men in the top administrative positions in all types of libraries, except school libraries, is apparent from Table V.

Note that even in the one category where women do retain more top administrative positions, the school libraries, the percentage of men who are top supervisors is higher than their employment overall in that category.

Stratification of the position hierarchy by sex is demonstrated still further by a 1971 survey of large public library systems serving populations of 100,000 or more. The figures show that even within this top level grouping, where men directors outnumber women by nearly two to one, "the larger the library, the more likely that the director will be male. Forty percent of directors are female in libraries serving populations of 100,000 to 399,000. But for populations in the range of 400,000 to 749,000 only 20 percent are female and the figure drops to 10 percent for the largest populations, 750,000 or more."[33]

These studies verify, beyond any further doubt, Bryan's earlier statement that the profession harbors a "dual career structure." These conditions for male/female employment of librarians are not of recent origin. Several studies, using biographies of achievement, confirm the inferior levels of attainment of women librarians while demonstrating at the same time the profession's easy acceptance of this discrimination.

TABLE V

CHIEF ADMINISTRATORS OF LARGE LIBRARIES BY TYPE OF LIBRARY, BY SEX[a, b] (PERCENT DISTRIBUTION)

Type of library	Chief administrator	
	Male (%)	Female (%)
Academic (Libraries in institutions with enrollments of 3,000 or more)	92	8
Special (Special libraries and information centers with staffs of 10 or more)	63	37
Public (Libraries serving populations of 100,000 or more)	61	39
School (Libraries in systems with enrollments of 25,000 or more)	19	81

[a] Source: Bundy and Wasserman, 1970a, pp. 77-79; 1970b, pp. 73-76; 1970c, pp. 79-80; 1970d, pp. 76-77.

[b] Based on a selected sample of 198 out of 458 large academic libraries; and a universe of 427 large special libraries and information centers; 248 large public libraries; and 150 large school systems which have school library supervisors.

In four separate studies covering *Who's Who in America (WWA)* volumes 1940-41, 1944-45, 1948-49, and 1956-57, between two-thirds and four-fifths of all librarians counted were men.[70, 73, 78, 109] Although the large majority of all librarians are women and in 1956 women constituted nearly 90 percent of the profession, of the 431 librarians listed in *WWA* for that year, 74 percent were men.[109] Women librarians are not particularly visible even in *Who's Who of American Women*. Its editors have actually commented on the small number of women librarians included there.[47]

A study of job mobility brought out some interesting data on the proportions of men and women at the top of the academic and public library position hierarchies.[59] Examining the careers of 1,316 chief public and college librarians listed in *Who's Who in Librarianship* (listing in this volume, incidentally, is self-determining), and applying a numerical scale, which was weighted by position level and size of library, Harvey asked: "Were males more likely to be found at the higher levels than were females?" The answer was "yes." Men dominated in college libraries, where they held nine-tenths of the top level positions, and in public libraries where they held two-thirds of all top level positions. (Top level, as used here, is not simply a top administrator, but a top administrator in a large library.)

Harvey also asked: "Did other studies find males so clearly dominant?" His answer was, "Yes, they did." Harvey's review of previous research on this question led him to this conclusion quite emphatically. He found, in fact, that despite the claims of one previous writer, R. S. Alvarez, who stated that women "had as good a chance of reaching the top as their male colleagues,"[1]

Alvarez' findings showed otherwise. Reviewing Alvarez' dissertation on public librarians,[2] Harvey stated that "60 percent of his (Alvarez') public libraries with more than 140,000 volumes were run by men, who made up only 10 percent of his entire study. In fact, the division between the sexes was so great that he [Alvarez] suggested that it was possible to think of the librarians of the smaller cities as women and the librarians of the larger cities as men."[59] Actually this important generalization applies even more forcefully to academic librarians.

A survey of chief college library administrators provided data that showed, for example, that men held the majority (63 percent) of all surveyed positions in colleges with enrollments of 1,500 to 5,000, while women held a majority of these positions (57 percent) in institutions where enrollments were 1,500 or less (Blankenship, 1967). When the largest institutions are also taken into account, the disproportions are much greater. In the late 1960's, not one of the fifty largest academic libraries in the United States were headed by a woman.[103] Moreover, there were "no women among the directors of the 74 libraries in that elite group known as the Association of Research Libraries."[67]

Clearly, the conclusion of the United States Bureau of Labor Statistics' *Occupational Outlook Handbook* that "men are more frequently employed than women in executive and administrative positions in large library systems,"[122] is all too accurate. But the degree of women's exclusion from high positions not only varies with the size of the library, but relates as well to the various components of the profession. The higher the status of a library field, the less likely that women occupy important administrative jobs in it. A study of *The Image and Status of the Library and Information Field* states that "there is a clear status hierarchy *within* the field, with academic librarians and the more technologically oriented special librarians occupying top position, while the public librarian and school librarian being considered lower status."[129] It is not unlikely that the sexual composition of the profession by type of library has something to do with this status hierarchy. Put otherwise, is status low because women dominate the field? Or (and we will return to this further along) are women forced into low status fields?

Some Salary Comparisons

Overall, women in the labor force earn substantially less than men. In 1970, the median salary income for all professional and technical year-round full-time women workers ($7,878) was 67 percent of the median salary for men.[123] ($11,806) Comparable figures for all men and women librarians are not available.

ALA and SLA salary surveys indicate that women's salaries were about three-quarters of the men's, and this may imply that the relative position of women to men in librarianship is slightly better than that of women to men professionals overall. But since the salary figures for librarians apply only to members of these associations, the two sets of figures are not really comparable. A report on federal librarians' salaries[64] indicates that salaries of women librarians are somewhat higher than salaries for all women professionals in the federal civil service, but here too, caution should be applied in generalizing from the data.

A report on manpower trends[19] assembles some preexisting salary surveys and contrasts salaries in librarianship with those in other fields. Statistical coverage of salaries in librarianship has been spotty, and the picture remains incomplete. From what can be pieced together, men with the library science doctorate seem to fare very well.[32] Generally, however, salaries in librarianship make a poor showing in contrast to other fields. Two studies on the compensation of college and university librarians are illustrative, but neither of these reports provides salary breakdowns by sex.[30, 61]

Reports on beginning salaries of current graduates in librarianship and in other fields for 1971, show that bachelor's degrees in the natural sciences and related fields bring higher salaries than the master's degree in librarianship. In 1971, estimated average beginning annual salaries for graduates with a bachelor's degree were $10,620 for men in engineering and $10,608 for women in engineering and technical research (however few they may have been). In chemistry the figures were $9,912 for men and $9,744 for women; in mathematics and statistics, $9,672 for men; $9,312 for women.[115] Current graduates with the master's degree in library science (with and without experience) earned an average salary of $8,846.[50] While we have come to expect higher salaries in the sciences generally, these differentials seem particularly striking, for they indicate that higher levels of education in librarianship offer less compensation than lower levels of education in these male-typed occupations.

A significant analysis of discrimination in librarianship is provided in the Berkeley report.[29] This report states that the economic effects of discrimination against women's occupations hit men, as well as women, librarians. Calling attention to this point, data are reproduced there from a larger study, which documents this conclusion for librarianship, as well as for other women's fields. According to this study "the more educated labor in several 'female' occupations is not rewarded by a proportionately higher income."[92]

Table VI shows that educational levels of men and women in these occupations tend to be higher, but income levels tend to be lower than those for the total male labor force. In these "female" occupations, higher educational levels do not "pay off" for men or women. These occupations (see Table VI, footnote *b*) account for 71 percent of all women in professional and technical work, 98 percent of all women in clerical work, and 42 percent of all female workers.

Other data support the conclusion that men, as well as women, are underpaid in librarianship.

A ranking of earnings for the year 1959 in 321 selected occupations placed male librarians 219th, just below bus drivers.[102] A report on the salaries of federal librarians showed that men librarians earn, on the average, $1,788 annually more than women librarians, but $1,821 *less* than average civil service salaries for male professionals in all fields.[64]

Although an examination of recent trends may reveal that salary differentials between men in librarianship and men in other professional fields may now be narrowing, low salary scales in librarianship have affected men as well as women. But women, claims the Berkeley report, are "victims of a double discrimination—first by being consigned to a women's profession and hence exploited as a source of cheap labor, and second, within the profession itself."[29] In this sense, a "woman's profession" may be described as a field poorly rated by a market society, which has placed profitability ahead of social utility.

Trends

Few studies have examined the status of women in librarianship at any point in time, so comparisons from one time to another are difficult at best. It is not unlikely that women in top library positions reached a peak during the 1920's, although possibly even before. Their situation probably corresponded, at least in some degree, to what was taking place in other fields, particularly in academia.[eg., 13]

Yet it is quite clear that whatever it was at its high point, women's representation in certain key positions has diminished rapidly in recent years.[106] Here too, there is a parallel with other fields and especially with other women's professions. Testimony from the National Education Association on the Equal Rights Amendment reported that in 1970, 78 percent of all elementary school principals in the United States were men, whereas in 1928, 55 percent of the elementary school principals were women.[116] A parallel dramatic reversal has occurred in librarianship as well.

In 1950, 50 percent of the deans and directors of accredited U. S. library schools were men. In 1970, the corresponding figure was 81 percent. A similar trend is apparent among the journal editors of national library periodicals. In 1950, about one-half of the national library periodicals were edited by women. In 1971, the figure dropped to one-third. This shift has resulted in part from the introduction of new journals (e.g., the *Journal of Library Automation* and *Library Technology Reports* are edited by men).

In the mid-sixties, *all* of the fifty largest academic libraries were headed by men, although there had been four women among the immediate predecessors in these fifty positions.[22] The libraries of the elite women's colleges, traditionally directed by women, have been the scene of male takeovers. Men librarians, for the first time in these institutions' histories, stepped into the top positions at Barnard in 1967 and at Smith in 1968.

A few directorships in the top fifty academic libraries have been regained by women in the past few years, but appointments of women to these positions remain exceptional. As we have noted elsewhere, the largest libraries are traditionally headed by men, and this pattern is being consolidated, not broken. Another report, covering a longer span of years, showed that in 1930, three-quarters (73 percent) of the libraries in the nation's seventy-four largest academic institutions accredited by the American Association of Universities were headed by men. A check of these same institutions in 1967 found that 95 percent of these libraries now had men directors.[103]

For public libraries a similar story unfolds. Of the fifty largest public libraries, by number of volumes, forty-three of the directorships were held by men in the mid-sixties. Of the immediate predecessors in these positions, thirty-nine were men.[22] Maloney (1971) has also reported on this trend in twenty-six large public libraries for the years 1969, 1950, and 1930.

State librarians and heads of state library extension agencies are a group of top leadership positions where a particularly dramatic shift has occurred. The trend began to accelerate during the sixties, a few years after the passage of the Library Services Act. Thereafter, federal funds and matching grants from the states began to be disbursed to these agencies to strengthen public library development, and millions of dollars were added to their combined budgets. As these positions acquired greater responsibility and influence, they were increasingly assigned to men.

TABLE VI

RELATIVE INCOME AND EDUCATIONAL STANDING OF SELECTED OCCUPATIONS 1960[a,b]

Occupation	Ratio of median number of school years completed in occupation to median for total male labor force[c]		Ratio of median income in occupation to median for total male labor force[d]	
	Male	Female	Male	Female
Total	1.00	1.09	1.00	0.59
Professional workers				
Dancers and dancing teachers	1.12	1.12	0.83	0.61
Dietitians and nutritionists	1.14	1.19	0.76	0.68
Librarians	1.50	1.46	1.01	0.77
Musicians and music teachers	1.34	1.33	1.03	0.29
Nurses	1.17	1.19	0.84	0.71
Recreation and group workers	1.36	1.32	1.00	0.78
Social and welfare workers	1.49	1.48	1.04	0.87
Religious workers	1.47	1.21	0.77	0.49
Elementary teachers	1.53	1.48	1.03	0.85
Teachers, n.e.c.	1.48	1.45	1.10	0.74
Therapists and healers	1.48	1.45	0.97	0.83
Clerical workers				
Library attendants and assistants	1.23	1.18	0.55	0.54
Physicians' and dentists' office attendants	1.12	1.12	0.68	0.53
Bank tellers	1.14	1.12	0.84	0.63
Bookkeepers	1.14	1.12	0.89	0.64
File clerks	1.12	1.10	0.75	0.59
Office-machine operators	1.13	1.12	0.96	0.68
Payroll and timekeeping clerks	1.13	1.12	1.00	0.73
Receptionists	1.13	1.13	0.77	0.57
Secretaries	1.15	1.14	1.05	0.71
Stenographers	1.14	1.14	1.02	0.70
Typists	1.13	1.13	0.80	0.64
Telephone operators	1.11	1.10	1.07	0.67
Cashiers	1.08	1.08	0.78	0.53
Clerical workers, n.e.c.	1.12	1.12	0.99	0.66
Sales workers				
Demonstrators	1.08	1.09	—[e]	0.50
Hucksters and peddlers	0.92	1.09	0.82	0.16

In 1950, a large majority (80 percent) of the state librarians and state library agency directors were women. In 1959, women still held 76 percent of these positions, but by 1970 they became the minority, when their representation dropped to 48 percent. Although there were a few replacements of men by women in the fifty state offices during the past decade, the overall trend has persistently favored the men; the movement has been rapid and there is no sign of deceleration. While half of the fifty state library associations in 1970 had women presidents, as late as 1960 women held a two-thirds majority of these positions.

The evidence is overwhelming. Women are being systematically eliminated from leadership positions in an occupation in which they constitute four-fifths of the membership. The apparent irony is that the wipe-out rate began to accelerate as support for libraries increased. Whether, or how, women's position will be affected by current reductions in library support is difficult to predict, but it would be most unfortunate if budget cuts, rather than affirmative action turn out to be a decisive factor.

Women Librarians in the Professional Associations

Discrimination against women is deeply embedded in the operating conditions of the library profession. In salaries received and in positions held, women in librarianship fare far worse than men. In contrast to most other professions, however, the level of participation by women librarians in their national and state associations is extraordinarily high. Women's active role in the American Library Association began relatively early in the Association's history, and just past the turn of the century, women constituted 30 percent of those listed on the annual conference program as participants. The first woman president was elected in 1911. Throughout its history, seventeen out of the eighty-nine presidents of the ALA (through 1972) were women: two per decade between 1911 and 1939, and three per decade since 1940. This three-per-decade quota has a good chance of being exceeded in the 1970's. Still, no woman has ever served as ALA executive secretary, except for one joint appointment in 1890-91.

Comparisons with other professions in this respect are startling. As recently as 1968, women comprised only 7.3 percent of the total membership of the American Political Science Association, and only 4.8 percent of the

Footnotes to Table VI:

a Source: U. S. Bureau of the Census, *1960 Census of Population:* Subject Report PC(2)-7A, *Occupational Characteristics,* Tables 9 and 28.

Reprinted with permission from Valerie Kincade Oppenheimer, *The Female Labor Force in the United States.* University of California, Institute of International Studies, Berkeley, California, pp. 100, 101. (Population Monograph Series, No. 5.)

b Includes occupations in which at least 51 percent of the workers were female and where the median school year completed was greater than 11.1—the median for the total male experienced civilian labor force.

c Experienced civilian labor force.

d Wage and salary workers in the experienced civilian labor force who worked 50-52 weeks in 1959.

e Base not large enough to compute a median.

"paper givers" at its annual conference that year.[106] Of the fifty-six presidents elected from the founding of the American Sociological Association through 1968, only one was a woman[41] and only one has been elected since. The American Bar Association has never had a woman president. Of thirteen presidents of the American Federation of Teachers during its first fifty-four years, two were women.[116] The first woman president of the American Association for the Advancement of Science was not elected until 1969. And in 1970, The National Press Club voted to admit women after The Women's Press Club voted to admit men.[91] The British Library Association elected its first woman president in 1966.[138]

Women are also represented in significant proportions on ALA's boards and committees. In 1972-73, half of the members of the Executive Board and seven executive secretaries of the ALA's thirteen divisions were women. Of the members of Council elected in 1972, women accounted for 61 percent. These recent figures may reflect rising affirmative action concerns on the part of the ALA membership. Not all sections of the Association have offered this high degree of participation to women, and their underrepresentation in official positions has been noted in the past. An editorial entitled, "The Weaker Sex?"[131] pointed out that women constituted only 30 percent of the ALA Council in that year. Certain enclaves remain largely male-dominated. Tuttle reports that "in spite of an occasional female President, the Association of College and Research Libraries tends to lean toward male domination. . . . Its journal, *College & Research Libraries,* has never had a female editor."[120] Since that was written, the ACRL has appointed its first woman Executive Secretary.

Contrasted with the backwardness of other professional associations that have barred women from active participation, or even from membership, the ALA has a record of relative achievement. But in proportion to women's representation in the profession-at-large, women are still underrepresented in top level offices. Data showing women's representation in the ALA Council and other leadership positions over a continuing period have not been compiled, although the basic source materials exist. Without a more complete record, it is impossible to describe trends. As the ALA approaches its centenary, the history of women's role in the Association remains unwritten.

LIBRARIANSHIP AS A WOMAN'S OCCUPATION

The Traditional Research Framework

Traditional research on women in the library profession is based on the assumption that there is a kind of Gresham's Law operating in librarianship. According to this law, bad money drives out good. Applied to librarianship, women drive out professional standards. This notion surfaced some years ago in more popular form, in an essay contest entitled: "Should the Preponderance of Women in the American Library Profession Be Considered an Evil?"[98] Most research on women in librarianship tends to assume that it is, implying that women have imposed the "weaknesses" of their sex upon their profession.

This assumption is not limited to librarianship. It is prevalent, too, in the literature of the sociology of occupations. For example, the term "feminization" of an occupation implies not simply that the ratio of women to men who have entered an occupation is large, but that the occupation, defined as men's work to begin with, now takes on allegedly feminine traits.

Librarianship has been called "brittle," because of its single women and professionally uncommitted, because of its married women. It has also been seen as lacking in a scientific outlook because women, in general, are not drawn to the natural sciences.[57] As a woman's occupation, librarianship has been identified as conservative, bureaucratic, and overly strong in its personal, "service" orientation.[97] The most comprehensive overview of characteristics associated with teaching, nursing, social work, and librarianship labels all of them as "semi-professions" whose "main intrinsic appeal . . . is to the heart, not the mind."[111] While these descriptions tell us how women who work in the professions are regarded in a society that defines women's role by their sex, they have also had some influence in determining the popular image of these professions, particularly among practitioners.

More significantly, they have assisted in concealing the origins of librarianship's disadvantaged condition. This is particularly observable in the customary explanation of the historical condition of impoverishment of the profession. For it is in this area of librarianship that Gresham's Law is applied most widely. In the matter of salaries, for example, it is claimed that "the predominance in the profession of women librarians has . . . facilitated retention of salary structures which would be unacceptable to a largely male profession."[61] Put this way, the predominance of women appears as the *cause*, rather than as the *result* of the profession's marginality. A historical perspective may help to illuminate this important distinction.

The Feminization of the Profession

Women came into librarianship relatively early in the development of the profession in the United States. The first women library clerks were employed in the Boston Public Library when that institution was established in 1852, and the first woman librarian was hired by the Boston Athenaeum in 1857. Shortly before, women had not been welcome there even as library users.[132]

Census figures show, however, that by 1870 women constituted 20 percent of the 213 librarians in the United States reported for that year. Other evidence indicates that there were probably more librarians—both men and women—during this period, than these figures suggest.[132] It also seems clear, however, that while men predominated, women, even at that early date, represented a significantly larger proportion of the librarian population than standard practice has allowed in the professions generally. In 1964, nearly a century later, women still constituted only 8 percent of the scientists, 6 percent of the physicians, 3 percent of the lawyers, and 1 percent of the engineers in the United States.[125]

The attendance figures at the founding conference of the American Library Association in 1876 (11 percent of the participants were women) indicate also that women participated in the library profession relatively early.

Although the data are incomplete Table VII indicates that women entered the profession in rather substantial numbers between 1870 and 1900 and accounted for the major portion of its growth. According to Wells,[132] librarianship began with men in the majority but was fully established as a woman's profession by 1910. Examining how teaching became a woman's profession, Oppenheimer[92] has concluded that women did not *displace* men but may have *replaced* them. Simply in terms of numbers alone, the figures in Table VII would seem to support this conclusion in librarianship also.

TABLE VII

DECENNIAL CENSUS DATA ON THE NUMBER OF LIBRARIANS, BY SEX 1870-1970[a]

Year	Total	Men	Women	Percent women
1870	213	170	43	20
—[b]				
1900	4,184[c]	1,059	3,125	75
1910	7,423[d]	1,594	5,829	79
1920	15,297[e]	1,795	13,502	88
1930	29,613	2,557	27,056	91
1940	36,347	3,801	32,546	90
1950	55,597	6,330	49,267	89
1960	83,881	12,045	71,836	86
1970	121,852	22,001	99,851	82

[a] Source: See U.S. Census of Population for the following years:
　　1870—Vol. 1, pp. 676, 686.
　　1900—Vol. 2, pt. 2, p. 505; and Special Reports. *Occupations at the Twelfth Census*, pp. XXXIV, XXXV
　　1920—Vol. 4, *Occupations*, chapter 2, p. 42.
　　1930—Vol. 5, *General Report on Occupations*, p. 20.
　　1940—Vol. 3, *The Labor Force*, pt. 1 p, 75.
　　1960—Vol. 1, *Characteristics of the Population*, pt. 1, p. 528.
　　1970—Subject Report PC(2)-7C, *Occupation by Industry*, p. 241.
[b] In 1880 librarians were classified as "Authors, lecturers and literary persons;" in 1890 as "Authors and literary and scientific persons."
[c] Based on the classification "Librarians and assistants."
[d] Excludes catalogers, who were counted as "Library Assistants" (not shown).
[e] Includes catalogers, who were counted as "Librarians."

Wells' study richly documents the historical record of women's entry into librarianship and is a major contribution to the research literature. Several reasons are advanced to explain why librarianship became a woman's profession: the encouragement of women by the profession's male leadership, not only to become librarians, but to pursue library education, is seen as a major factor. This occurred during a period of rising educational opportunities for women and the simultaneous expansion of library service. Other factors such as women's allegedly natural suitability for library work along with the availability of an educated work force at low pay, are also considered.

The First Professional School

When Melvil Dewey established the first library school at Columbia University in 1887, women comprised the majority (seventeen out of twenty) of the entering class. Although Dewey had expected from the start that more women than men would be enrolled, and he had the support of President Barnard in admitting women to the school, he had been explicitly forbidden by the trustees to do so. Dewey's open admissions policy led to a formal hearing which resulted in his dismissal and the demise of the school. Dewey moved the school to Albany shortly thereafter.

The opening of librarianship's first professional school to women and Dewey's debacle with the Columbia trustees constitute an important chapter in librarianship and in the history of women's rights in the United States.

Did Feminization Bring Low Salaries, or Vice Versa?

The conditions under which the school began suggest why the profession's male leadership encouraged women to join. Recalling his early days at Columbia's first School of Library Economy some years later, Dewey is reported to have said: "I distinctly remember we cald it first the Library School of Economy, thinking of getting the most possible out of the appropriations not available."[36] The spelling is in Dewey's phonetic style.

According to an administrative history of the school, its operation was to involve no expense to the Columbia Corporation; instruction was to be given by library staff members in addition to their other duties; and the school was to be conducted in the library building with whatever accommodations could be found there.[36]

Although slightly less stringent limitations applied when the school moved to the New York State Library at Albany, there, too, it received less than minimal support, and the instructional staff received no compensation beyond what was paid for work in the library itself. Taking the two sets of restrictions together (Columbia's and Albany's), "it ment that the promoters of the original scool effort were compeld to make bricks without straw."[36]

The situation was much the same in libraries, where an educated work force was needed but the necessary financial support was lacking. Dewey's recruitment appeal to "college-bred" women, which warned, at the same time, that "salary hunters" should stay away, is illustrative.[39]

The fact that the first question asked by a woman at a library conference related to the use of the dog tax as a source of library support indicates further how pinched library budgets were and that all possibilities were being exploited. This question, incidentally, was raised at the ALA's second annual meeting in 1877.[43]

In the same year, Justin Winsor succinctly summarized the reasons for encouraging women to become librarians when he addressed the Conference of Librarians in London:

> In American libraries we set a high value on women's work. They soften our atmosphere, they lighten our labour, they are equal to our work, and for the money they cost . . . they are infinitely better than equivalent salaries will produce by the other sex. For from £ 100 to £ 160 a year we can command our pick of the educated young women whom our colleges for women are launching forth upon our country. . . . It is to these colleges for women like Vassar and Wellesley that the American library system looks confidently for the future.[35]

The appeal to women to join this labor force was also made socially acceptable by emphasizing that it was women's "spiritual qualities," their "innate" willingness to serve, and their "housekeeping instinct" which so well suited them for librarianship.

Since women with college training had few other professional outlets and were virtually barred from the men's professions, they responded to the call. According to Wells,[132] a survey of the occupations of women college graduates in 1918 listed librarianship third, after teaching and social work, as the most common occupation. Considering how women "took over" these fields, it can also be suggested that the sex-typing of these professions for women depended upon the sex-typing of other professions for men. In this sense, librarianship was able to capitalize on the sexual segregation which excluded women from most other professions.

Oppenheimer's research on women's occupations in the United States led her to conclude that the demand for female labor in several female occupations is typically associated, not only with cheapness and availability, but also with educational requirements. "Women's education is not a gratuitous accompaniment of the job but *characteristic of the demand itself.*"[93] [Italics for emphasis added.]

Another characteristic of demand in such professions as school teaching, nursing, social work, and librarianship is that it is heavily concentrated in the nonprofit sectors of the economy.[124] Low salaries, which are typically attributed to the predominance of women in these professions, may be regarded alternatively as a reflection of the low priority the market economy has placed on the public sector.

This brings us back to the beginning of this section where we said that low salaries in librarianship are the result, rather than the cause, of the profession's marginality. This suggests that the reason for low salaries in librarianship is not the predominance of women. On the contrary, *women predominate in librarianship because salaries are low.* This distinction could get us out of the vicious circle Munthe described: "Women took over the library positions because the low salaries did not attract men, and the salaries were low because the positions were held by women."[87] Yet if salaries were low to begin with, this has been a continuing condition.

If salary levels in librarianship do not depend upon the sexual composition of the profession, but serve instead to determine it, the implication is that more men will enter the field if salary levels are raised. This is the reverse of the traditional solution, which has recommended that men be recruited to librarianship in order to raise salaries. Obviously, this question is a complex one, and cultural factors, too, play an important role. Research on women's occupations by Oppenheimer,[93] Gross,[58] and others has opened up approaches and lines of analysis and suggests that this is a fertile field for further exploration.

Bureaucracy, Hierarchy, and Lack of Autonomy

Simpson and Simpson[111] have reviewed a substantial body of research on the women's professions. As was noted earlier, librarianship, along with social work, school teaching, and nursing, has been labeled a "semi-profession." This description downgrades most women professionals in the United States. School teaching and nursing alone, accounted, in 1960, for roughly two-thirds of all women professionals.

In contrast to such male-typed professions as law, which are characterized by autonomous collegial control, the "semi-professions" are identified with bureaucracy, hierarchy, and lack of autonomy. Simpson and Simpson argue "that one reason for this pattern is the prevalence of women in the semi-professions."[111]

An alternative view could just as well be posited—that women have been recruited to librarianship precisely to accommodate a hierarchical structure, which relies on large numbers of subordinates. In any event, the association of women's professions with bureaucratic and hierarchical patterns of control seems well established.

Comparing the differences in personnel structures between academic libraries (where women predominate) and academic faculties (where men predominate), a recent survey described their respective career ranks. While 20 percent of the faculty were at the lowest rank of instructor and 50 percent held the two highest ranks, among librarians 50 percent held the lowest basic rank and only a few librarians held high career positions. As the profession of librarianship is now structured, advanced position can be achieved only by becoming an administrator in a large library, which means joining a caste that is apart from the rest of the professional ranks. This survey concluded further that "an imbalance between the compensations of faculty and librarians may well be symptomatic of two equally serious problems: minimization of the role and organizational requirements of (libraries) . . . and the possibility of exploitation."[61]

A second survey, a year later, reexamined the finding of a "relatively small number of librarians at the top and a wide base of very low-paid positions at the bottom." The conclusion this time: "The statistics again confirm the pyramidal structure of the profession. . . . Contrast this situation with university faculties where a rectangular structure, albeit an imperfect one, prevails."[30]

How little autonomy the academic librarian has enjoyed is well illustrated by a recent article describing the participation of academic librarians in one institution in the search for a library director as *a new experience,* but one which was written up to encourage others to press similarly for a voice in their own affairs.[52] Yet, it may well be that academic librarians, as the higher status portion of the profession, have more autonomy in their work environment than do those in other subfields of librarianship.

At any rate, strict and petty rules governing personal behavior on the job, as well as regulations covering minute details of professional practice have been commonplace. Library staff manuals would provide a good source for examining this matter further. Reporting on his visit here from Norway, Munthe remarked on the contents of one such manual with incredulity. He wondered, in fact, how such a detailed code could be kept up to date.

Materials on library careers and recruitment are other useful sources of information, both on the actual nature of library work and on the character of the appeals that are made to others to join it. (For the earlier period, see, for example, New York State Library School, 1911.) One recent article suggests that women have been encouraged to enter librarianship for one set of reasons—to become subordinates and routine workers—men, for another. For men, the appeals emphasize that they will quickly become administrators.[77]

It has been noted that cheapness, availability, and education were the constituents of demand for women workers. It is possible, too, that dependency and submissiveness were additional qualifications. Although these characteristics have been encouraged in women generally and are widely regarded as feminine traits, they may also have been stressed for women workers as specific requirements for the jobs they were hired to do. On salary matters, at least, these "feminine" qualities were not simply tolerated, but clearly expected.

Again, as with the issue considered in the previous section, there is an important matter of emphasis. While women are seen to have affected the structure of librarianship,[111] this assumes a one-way relationship where women impose hierarchical patterns on the profession from the bottom up. The present analysis, on the other hand, suggests that the profession has not simply been acted upon by women, but has itself been instrumental in utilizing this marginal work force to advantage by keeping it in its place. While this is most likely a two-way process, spurred and reinforced by broader socioeconomic and cultural forces, traditional conceptualizations have emphasized only one factor, while minimizing or ignoring the other.

Women Librarians and Unions

Although the link between librarians and unions has never been strong,[9] librarians' unions have considered the status of women in libraries as an important issue. A resolution, introduced at the ALA Conference in 1919 by Library Employees Union 15590 of Greater New York, read as follows:

> WHEREAS, The present low and inadequate salaries paid to librarians in the public libraries is due solely to the fact that all of the rank and file are women, and
>
> WHEREAS, All the highest salaried positions are given to men by the board of trustees, and
>
> WHEREAS, The present policy of library boards is to remove women from all positions of responsibility and largest financial returns, and replace them with men only, and
>
> WHEREAS, This discrimination is based on sex, and not on any superiority of intelligence, ability, or knowledge on the part of the men appointed; therefore be it
>
> RESOLVED, That we are against this system of removing women without reason, and are in favor of throwing open all positions in library work, from Librarian of Congress down to that of page, to men and women equally, and for equal pay.[3]

A fascinating description of how this resolution made its way to the floor of the conference, and was then voted down by a count of 121 to 1, included this comment; "It was notable that four fifths or more of the audience were women."[3] The ALA's third woman President also spoke against the resolution.

More recently, at the University of California, Berkeley, union activity again centered around the woman issue. Pressure from the American Federation of Teachers and the Association of State, County and Municipal Employees was evidently instrumental in the creation of a library-appointed Affirmative Action Program Committee for Women. The resulting report reflected considerable union input.[29]

CHARACTERISTICS AND CAREERS

Most of the surveys cited in Section II, A on salaries contain some data on the personal and other characteristics of men and women librarians. After the work by Bryan in 1952, Morrison's study[86] is probably the most comprehensive. A revised version of a doctoral dissertation completed in 1961, it includes an added bibliographic review of developments from 1960 to 1967. Particularly useful for its description of the librarian's personality (summarized briefly in Morrison, 1963), this basic work also covers social backgrounds, education, and other career factors. Over a third of the tables provide data by sex. Farley's dissertation[44] devotes some attention to women library administrators. Stone[117] and Kortendick and Stone[71] examine factors relating to professional development and educational needs, and report some findings by sex.

With few exceptions, masters' theses, biographical studies, and surveys of local or regional populations have been excluded from this review. Although Massman's survey of faculty status (1972) is not national in coverage, it warrants inclusion, however, because of its wide bibliographic range, and because it focuses in some detail on women in librarianship. Surveys by Clayton (1970) and DeWeese (1972) are limited to single institutions, but are also worth noting, because they are relatively recent and bring out some new data on men and women librarians.

Students and faculty in the accredited library schools are described in White and Macklin's (1970) report on education, careers, and professionalization. Part of the University of Maryland's manpower research project,[see also 19, 24-27, 97, 129] this study includes an examination of the similarities and differences in career expectations of men and women.

Few studies describe minority women librarians, although they are mentioned by Pollard[96] and Bock.[18] Figures on minority employment by sex have been reported for central libraries in the federal government.[48] Josey's, "The Black Librarian in America," includes some biographical accounts by individual women librarians.[68]

Personal Characteristics

The typical woman worker at the turn of the century was single. So was the typical woman librarian. Wells[132] examined census data for 1920 and found that 7.4 percent of the women librarians at that time were married — a percentage that was similar to, but somewhat lower than, the 9.7 percent for women teachers. The 1960 census reports this figure for women librarians at 43 percent. Comparable percentages for women have also been reported for social workers (48 percent); secondary school teachers (53 percent); nurses (57 percent); and elementary school teachers (59 percent).[7] Simpson and Simpson[111] found that women librarians and social workers in every age category were less likely to be married than women in these other professions. No single factor can account for this, but one possible explanation for the differences might be that the more flexible work schedules in nursing, and the shorter work day and longer vacations in teaching, were more compatible with family schedules than were the more standardized working hours in librarianship and social work.

Also, image reinforces reality. In the popular stereotype, these two professions — librarianship and social work — are more closely identified with single women than are nursing and teaching, and it is not unlikely that this has had some impact, too. As Jesse Shera once said, "Little girls don't play librarian." The fact that little boys don't either is not without significance. Yet it seems likely that for girls this may relate to marital status.

In librarianship, men are much more likely to be married than women are. This is the case in other occupations, too, for married men overall are more likely to be employed than are married women. Still, married women are coming into librarianship in growing numbers. The most striking change in the growth of the national female labor force is the increasing participation of married women. In 1970, nearly 60 percent of all working women were married, compared to 30 percent in 1940. This trend has been reflected to some degree in librarianship, although it has not been examined in detail. In addition, the sharply increased overall labor force participation of married women in the upper age groupings is probably a factor in what appears to be the increasing age levels of women librarians.

Dropout Rates

The rising representation of married women in librarianship has encouraged some to focus on the dropout rate, but data on this question remain fragmentary.

A postcensal survey found that about 20 percent of those who stated in 1962 that they had been public librarians in 1960 had changed occupations by the reporting date. Among those who had changed occupations during the two-year period, women constituted 88.3 percent. Among those who remained as librarians, it was 87 percent. The data do not supply any indication of marital status, reasons for leaving, or the nature of the new occupation. While the apparently large number of persons who left librarianship during the two-year interval was, as Drennan suggested, "startling," he pointed out also that the results remain inconclusive.[40]

While that survey reported on those who had left the profession, two others[71, 103] reported on those who had returned. In the first of these surveys, on college and university librarians, 15 percent of the women stated that they had left library work at some earlier point for marriage or family reasons and had later returned to library work. Six percent of the men had left for military service. Altogether, marriage and family were the major reasons women had left, and further education was the chief factor in men's departure. In both surveys, a rather substantial number of librarians (more than two out of every five) indicated that they had left library work at some point and later returned to it. Since this figure tells us only about those who had returned, it underestimates the loss of professional labor power which results when those with professional training leave. How many women withdraw from the field permanently for marriage or family remains an unanswered question. Two reports from abroad have made some effort to provide some information on this question. In Great Britain[130] and in New Zealand,[89] this matter has been examined in order to overcome "social wastage of women, particularly those who are graduates and those who hold a professional qualification."[130]

Wells (1967) supplies some interesting retrospective figures, drawn from the Williamson (1923) report on library education. Of the nearly five thousand graduates of the library schools Williamson surveyed through 1921, 66 percent of the men, and 62 percent of the women were still in library work as of that date. While women who married generally left, there weren't many who married. As attention focused on single women librarians, their lack of marital "status," and on personality characteristics, we may have lost sight of the relative stability of women's library careers compared to men's during that period. While this tells us only about the past, it might well be kept in mind when thinking about the present.

Turnover

While women who leave library work for marriage or family reasons are seen to disrupt the stability of library operations in individual institutions, there is no evidence that women are any more likely than men to quit their jobs. Bryan's[23] survey of public librarians found that there was more turnover in small libraries than in larger ones and substantially greater turnover among subprofessionals than among professionals. Examining the turnover rates of men and women librarians, she concluded: "The generally prevalent idea that turnover is greater among professional women than among men is not borne out by these statistics."[23]

Simpson and Simpson[111] reported that as in libraries, turnover rates for men and women did not differ greatly in teaching, or in social work either. A major problem here, however, is that regardless of what the facts are, employers *think* women bring higher turnover rates, and act accordingly.[92]

Studies of men and women in other occupations have shown that turnover is more closely associated with the kind of job and its salary than it is with sex.[e.g., 126]

Mobility

Harvey's study[59] of chief public and academic librarians examined mobility patterns and concluded that "males were more mobile than females." Morrison[86] has noted quite legitimately, however, that despite the implications of Harvey's data, they did not bear directly on the willingness or unwillingness of women to move from one job to another. Morrison's data also led him to some different conclusions from those that Harvey had drawn earlier. Although two other studies[100, 112] report greater mobility for men than for women, data on this question remain scanty. Even so, we would expect to find that married women librarians are less mobile than men, for traditional patterns are that the wife's geographical mobility depends on the husband's. A counterforce could begin to operate here, however, as job opportunities for women receive more attention and as careers become regarded as significant for wives, as well as for husbands.

Education

Differences in educational levels between men and women librarians have been reported in most of the national surveys of the various librarian populations, although the extent of the differences varies somewhat between one survey and another. These surveys are cited in Section II, A on salaries. Apart from census data, which do not distinguish between professional and academic degrees and which have certain other limitations for this purpose as well, figures on the educational characteristics of the current labor force are not available for the profession overall. The ALA Salary Survey[80] reports type and level of degree by sex, but this applies to ALA members only.

During the past decade, about four out of every five master's degrees conferred in library science went to women. At the doctoral level, the majority of all degrees have gone to men. From 1928 through August 1965, 220 doctoral degrees in library science were conferred in the United States. Of this total, 159 (72 percent) went to men; 61 (28 percent) to women.[81] Table VIII indicates that women's representation has improved recently, although they remained in the minority. (Since the total number of degrees awarded in any given year is small, it would seem unwise to take the figure for any single year as representative.)

TABLE VIII

LIBRARY SCIENCE DOCTORATES BY SEX, 1928-1969/70[a]

Year	Total No.	Total Percent	Men No.	Men Percent	Women No.	Women Percent
1928-(Aug.) 1965	220	(100)	159	(72)	61	(28)
1965/66-1969/70	114	(100)	75	(66)	39	(34)
1965/66	19	(100)	14	(74)	5	(26)
1966/67	16	(100)	10	(62)	6	(38)
1967/68	22	(100)	15	(68)	7	(32)
1968/69	17	(100)	12	(71)	5	(29)
1969/70	40	(100)	24	(60)	16	(40)
TOTAL	334	(100%)	234	(70%)	100	(30%)

a Source: Marco (1967) and U.S. Office of Education, *Earned Degrees Conferred.*

Whether or not women's somewhat improved representation during the most recent period can be attributed in any way to the Higher Education Act Fellowships for doctoral study is difficult to say. One survey reported before they were introduced that very few public librarians had held research or teaching assistantships to support their education at any level, but that men were more likely to have held assistantships than women.[40]

Figures on doctoral dissertations in progress, as of September 1971, suggest that the slight relative improvement for women is continuing at least if present ratios hold through the granting of degrees. The breakdown of the total (212) is 129 men (61 percent), and 83 women (39 percent).[55]

THE CURRENT SCENE

Stirrings of interest in the status of women in librarianship began to become noticeable around 1969. Since then, articles and discussion in the library press have appeared with increasing frequency. Accelerating interest within the profession can probably be attributed to three major factors: the sweeping national impact of the women's movement; the legal support for affirmative action programs provided by federal laws and regulations; and the growing recognition, supported by national survey findings in librarianship, that position and salary differentials between men and women in this profession, as in all occupations, were substantial.

One woman librarian, appointed in 1971 to the directorship of one of the nation's fifty largest academic libraries, commented: "My appointment was, I believe, influenced by the changing role of women. I doubt that this could have occurred five or even three years ago. Three years ago when I was appointed Associate Librarian, that was an innovation."[90]

As late as 1970, and possibly even after that, classified advertisements that specified sex as a qualification for certain library positions (e.g., "desires innovative young man") had continued to appear in library periodicals. While it is difficult to date the first official action for equal opportunity for women in librarianship, an editorial announcement in *American Libraries* of a policy requiring that all listed positions be open to all applicants, probably counts among the first.[110] The editorial stated that "overt or covert references to the sex of a job applicant or the sex desired for any position in a given library" would be edited out. Claiming, too, that such terms as "salary negotiable" had been used, not only "to hide embarrassingly low salary offers," but also "to make higher initial offers to male applicants," the editorial also asked that all future position listings specify salary ranges.

Interest in affirmative action for women was spurred by the ALA's Activities Committee on New Directions for ALA (ACONDA) and particularly by the late Shirley Olofson, who was one of its members. (Some of the accomplishments of ACONDA are described by Curley in another chapter of this volume.) At Olofson's request, a paper on what the ALA should do to improve the status of women librarians was submitted to the Committee. Included originally as a section of the ACONDA report, this paper, published in a slightly revised version some months later, urged the ALA to take a stand for affirmative action and offered some recommendations.[104]

Wood[138] discusses some of the issues raised there and elsewhere in a succinct review of the grounds on which discrimination against women has been opposed or justified. Covering most of the periodical literature from 1969 through mid-1971, this review also highlights some earlier research. The journal in which this article appeared was the second library periodical to devote an entire issue to women in librarianship.[99] The first was published a few months earlier.[74] One of the early appeals for heightened awareness came from Barber.[10] Articles by Detlefsen and Schuman[37] and Hathaway[60] discuss some women's liberation movement issues and how they relate to librarianship.

The images of women's role transmitted by children's books;[45, 119] library subject headings;[12] and textbooks used in library schools,[83] have also begun to be noted and examined. The messages carried by these materials indicate that sex-typing has been reinforced by libraries themselves as they reflect and reproduce the distortions of a wider reality.

A positive sign of interest in change is reported in an exchange of letters between a library school student and the publisher of *American Men of Science*.[83] Although women scientists had been included before, the title of this reference work now reads *American Men and Women of Science*. The exclusion of women from other reference books has also begun to receive attention. While past omissions and distortions were not willful or intended, they become recognizably apparent along with the increasing participation of women in today's world. A brief item from Jessie Bernard to the Sociologists for Women in Society *Newsletter*, states: "I have just noted in the *International Encyclopedia of the Social Sciences* that although the article on "Affection" is signed by Margaret K. Harlow, her first name is not indexed. Her husband's is, though. See for yourself, Volumes 1 and 17, pp. 124 and 237 respectively. Maybe we need a continuing column of odds and ends like this, mostly odd."[15]

One particularly provocative article on book selection and pornography suggested that women's role in society has caused them to be more restrictive than men in library book selection.[69] The author was quite legitimately called to task for his prejudiced attitude,[118] but this is a question that may warrant further examination.[28, 94]

A few items in the library press have pinpointed the need for flexible scheduling and part-time work opportunities for married women.[51, 56] This subject has received attention, also, in Canada[e.g., 20] and in Great Britain.

Several other subjects of developing interest have also been brought out in the affirmative action reports prepared in individual colleges and universities. While most such reports do not single out libraries for special consideration, those that do, have made a contribution to the literature of women in librarianship, because of their intensive and detailed focus. Examining conditions in one large university library, one such report showed how the discriminatory sex-typing of librarianship has affected not only librarians, but also library technicians and assistants — men, as well as women.[29]

Library technicians and assistants were included in the earlier surveys cited in this review, but in the later surveys, after 1956, they have been considered separately from professional workers. Current concern with the position of women in librarianship may create new identifications of interest in all classes of library workers. At the same time, the drive toward faculty status for librarians in college and university libraries may create a pull in the opposite direction. The fact that each of these two sets of identifications is, in part, a response to a broader pattern of discrimination against women may serve in some measure to unify these apparently opposite forces.

Another activity we have not yet described is the participation of women librarians in the bibliography of the field.[95] Other bibliographies on women, which do not single out librarianship, have also appeared in the library press.[e.g., 11, 53, 54, 108] Two more ambitious undertakings, begun and issued on a continuing basis, are Hughes' bibliography[66] on the legal and economic aspects of women's employment and Whaley's *Women Studies Abstracts (1972)*. Spiegel, librarian at the Business and Professional Women's Foundation (Washington, D.C.), has also compiled several widely used bibliographies on sex roles, discrimination, etc. Two books on women were also produced by librarians in 1972.[72, 134]

Outside librarianship, bibliographies of women's studies are being generated widely. Because libraries themselves have not taken as active a part in collecting and organizing current materials as the needs dictate, the Women's History Research Center (Berkeley, California) has attempted to fill part of the gap by developing an archive of the women's liberation movement. A particularly useful source for keeping up to date on current information on women is the *Spokeswoman*.

Task Force on Woman

Plans for a Task Force on the Status of Women in Librarianship started at the ALA's midwinter meeting in January, 1970. Formed within the Social Responsibilities Round Table (SRRT), the Task Force held its first meeting in June, 1970.[107] A resolution on equal opportunity for women in librarianship, adopted at that meeting, was passed by the ALA membership in January, 1971, and was later approved by the Council. In contrast to the majority opposing a similar resolution some fifty years before (see Section III, F), this time there were few objections. The 1971 resolution on women and another, adopted at the same time, on equal opportunities for minorities, appears in *American Libraries.*[42]

Beginning in August 1970, the Task Force issued an occasional newsletter.[6] An article on women's caucuses, committees, and commissions in the professions lists this as one of five newsletters published by the more than twenty comparable caucuses that had been formed in the major academic and professional associations.[91] When the Professional Women's Caucus, a nonlibrary organization formed to improve communication across disciplines, held its first conference, the papers presented there included one on women in librarianship.[133]

The SRRT Task Force was established primarily in response to the inequalities in library employment, and this has remained a major interest. Two of the ongoing projects, as of the end of 1972, were developing a roster of women seeking career opportunities, and a survey of nepotism practices in libraries. It has also been concerned with a range of other issues that go beyond the question of status alone. Now renamed the Task Force on Women, its activities have been described by Rudy.[101]

In January, 1972, an ad hoc ALA Committee on Equal Opportunity in Libraries was established by the ALA Council. This committee has been charged to develop major policy statements on discriminatory practices in library recruitment, employment, training, and promotion.

A report on the status of women in Canada illuminates an important perspective. Recognizing that the female professions traditionally have been underpaid and have continued to be rewarded inequitably at a time of increasing demand for these service professions, the report recommends that pay in federal employment *"be set by comparing these professions with other professions in terms of the value of the work and the skill and training involved".*[31] In this context, current interest in affirmative action for women can be seen to relate as well to affirmative action for librarianship.

REFERENCES

1. Alvarez, R. S. (1938). Women's place in librarianship. *Wilson Bulletin for Librarians* 13, 175-178.

2. Alvarez, R. S. (1939). "Qualifications of Public Librarians in the Middle West." Unpublished dissertation, University of Chicago.

3. American Library Association, Asbury Park Conference (1919). *Library Journal* 44, 516-539.

4. American Library Association. Board on Personnel Administration (1953). "Salaries of Library Personnel, 1952." Prepared by H. Timmerman. American Library Association, Chicago, Illinois. (Mimeograph copy.)

5. American Library Association. Board on Personnel Administration (1956). "Salaries of Library Personnel, 1955." Prepared by H. Timmerman. American Library Association, Chicago, Illinois. (Mimeograph copy.)

6. American Library Association. Social Responsibility Round Table. Task Force on the Status of Women (1970-   ). *Newsletter* No. 1 (August).

7. Archibald, K. A. (1971). "The Supply of Professional Nurses and Their Recruitment and Retention by Hospitals." The New York City Rand Institute, New York. (R-836-NYC.)

8. Astin, H. S., Suniewick, N., and Dweck, S. (1971). "Women: a Bibliography on Their Education and Careers." Human Service Press, Washington, D.C.

9. Baker, E. F. (1964). "Technology and Woman's Work." Columbia University Press, New York.

10. Barber, P. (1969). Ladies in waiting. *Synergy* No. 24 (December), pp. 22-25.

11. Bayefsky, E. (1972). Women and work. *Ontario Library Review* 56, 79-90.

12. Berman, S. (1971). "Prejudices and Antipathies: A Tract on the LC Subject Heads Concerning People." Scarecrow Press, Metuchen, New Jersey.

13. Bernard, J. (1964). "Academic Women." Pennsylvania State University Press, University Park, Pennsylvania.

14. Bernard, J. (1971). "Women and the Public Interest." Aldine-Atherton, Chicago, Illinois.

15. Bernard, J. (1972). (Letter.) *Sociologists for Women in Society Newsletter* 2 (September), 6.

16. Blankenship, W. C. (1967). Head librarians: How many men? How many women? *College & Research Libraries* 28, 41-48.

17. Blondell, H. M., and Nabors, E. (1970). Reports of the 63rd Annual Meeting of the American Association of Law Librarians. *Library of Congress Information Bulletin* 29 (July 23), A54-A60.

18. Bock, E. W. (1969). Farmer's daughter effect: the case of the Negro female professionals, *Phylon* 30, 17-26.

19. Bolino, A. C. (1969). "Supply and Demand Analysis of Manpower Trends in the Library and Information Field." Catholic University of America, Department of Economics, Washington, D.C. (ED 038 986.)

20. Bow, E. (1972). Interrupted careers; the married woman as librarian. *Ontario Library Review* 56, 76-78.

21. Bower, B. (1972). "Placement of 1970/71 SLS Graduates: Is Sex Discrimination a Reality?" University of California, Los Angeles, School of Library Service, Los Angeles, California. (Departmental Announcements and Memoranda, April 20, 1972.) (Mimeograph copy.)

22. Bradley, B. W. (1968). "A Study of the Characteristics, Qualifications, and Succession Patterns of Heads of Large United States Academic Libraries." Unpublished master's report, University of Texas.

23. Bryan, A. I. (1952). "The Public Librarian." Columbia University Press, New York.

24. Bundy, M. L., and Wasserman, P. (1970a). "The Academic Library Administrator and His Situation." University of Maryland, School of Library and Information Services, College Park, Maryland. (ED 054 796.)

25. Bundy, M. L., and Wasserman, P. (1970b). "The Administrator of a Special Library or Information Center and His Situation." University of

Maryland, School of Library and Information Services, College Park, Maryland. (ED 054 799.)

26. Bundy, M.L., and Wasserman, P. (1970c). "The Public Library Administrator and His Situation." University of Maryland, School of Library and Information Services, College Park, Maryland. (ED 054 797.)

27. Bundy, M. L. and Wasserman, P. (1970d). "The School Library Supervisor and Her Situation." University of Maryland, School of Library and Information Services, College Park, Maryland. (ED 054 798.)

28. Busha, C. H. (1970). Student attitudes toward censorship and authoritarianism. *Journal of Education for Librarianship* 11, 118-136.

29. California, University of, Berkeley. Library Affirmative Action Program for Women Committee (1971). "A Report on the Status of Women Employed in the Library of the University of California, Berkeley, with Recommendations for Affirmative Action." (Processed.) (ED 066 163.)

30. Cameron, D. F., and Heim, P. (1972). "How Well Are They Paid? Compensation Structures of Professional Librarians in College & University Libraries, 1970-71." Council on Library Resources, Washington, D.C. (The Second Survey.)

31. Canada. Royal Commission on the Status of Women in Canada (1970). "Report." Saannes Publications, Toronto, Ontario.

32. Carpenter, R. L., and Carpenter, P. A. (1970). The doctorate in librarianship and an assessment of graduate library education. *Journal of Education for Librarianship* 11, 3-45.

33. Carpenter, R. L., and Shearer, K. D. (1972). Sex and salary survey: selected statistics of large public libraries in the United States and Canada. *Library Journal* 97, 3682-3685.

34. Clayton, H. (1970). Femininity and job satisfaction among male library students at one midwestern university. *College & Research Libraries* 31, 388-398.

35. Conference of Librarians (1878). "Transactions and Proceedings of the Conference of Librarians held in London. October 1877." Trübner, London.

36. Dawe, G. G. (1932). "Melvil Dewey: Seer: Inspirer: Doer, 1851-1931: Biografic Compilation." Lake Placid Club, Essex Co., New York.

37. Detlefsen, E. G., and Schuman, P. (1970). Women's liberation movement-I. *Wilson Library Bulletin* 44, 962 ff.

38. DeWeese, L. C. (1972). Status concerns and library professionalism. *College & Research Libraries* 33, 31-38.

39. Dewey, M. (1886). "Librarianship as a Profession for College-Bred Women." Library Bureau, Boston, Massachusetts.

40. Drennan, H. T. and Darling, R. L. (1966). "Library Manpower: Occupational Characteristics of Public and School Librarians." U. S. Government Printing Office, Washington, D.C. (OE-15061.)

41. Epstein, C. F. (1971). "Woman's Place: Options and Limits in Professional Careers." University of California Press, Berkeley, California.

42. Equal employment opportunity: affirmative action plans for libraries (1971). *American Libraries* 2, 977-983.

43. Fairchild, S. C. (1904). Women in American libraries. *Library Journal* 29, 157-162.

44. Farley, R. A. (1967). "The American Library Executive: An Inquiry into His Concepts of the Function of His Office." Unpublished dissertation, University of Illinois.

45. Feminists on Children's Literature (1971). A feminist look at children's books. *Library Journal* 96, 235-240.

46. Ferriss, A. L. (1971). "Indicators of Trends in the Status of American Women." Russell Sage Foundation, New York.

47. Fie, if thy name be woman! (1959). *Library Journal* 84, 556.

48. FLC personnel statistics (1972). *FLC Newsletter, Federal Library Committee* No. 67 (September), p. 16.

49. Fogarty, M. P., Rapoport, R., and Rapoport, R. (1972). "Women and Top Jobs: The Next Move." Political and Economic Planning, London. (Vol. 38, Broadsheet 535.)

50. Frarey, C. J., and Learmont, C. L. (1972). Placements and salaries, 1971: a modest employment slowdown. *Library Journal* 97, 2154-2159.

51. Freedman, J. (1970). The liberated librarian? *Library Journal* 95, 1709-1711.

52. Galloway, L. (1972). Academic librarians participate in the selection of a director of libraries. *College & Research Libraries* 33, 220-227.

53. Galloway, S. (1972a). A starting point. *Wilson Library Bulletin* 46, 696-697.

54. Galloway, S. (1972b). The new feminism: its periodicals. *Wilson Library Bulletin* 47, 150-151.

55. Garrison, G. (1972). Research record. *Journal of Education of Librarianship* 12, 211-213.

56. Gilliam, B. H. (1970). Housewife-librarian (Letter). *Library Journal* 95, 3704.

57. Ginsburg, E., and Brown, C. A. (1967). "Manpower For Library Service." Columbia University, Conservation of Human Resources Project, New York. (ED 023 408).

58. Gross, E. (1968). Plus ça change . . .? The sexual structure of occupations over time. *Social Problems* 16, 198-208.

59. Harvey, J. F. (1957). "The Librarians Career: a Study of Mobility." University of Rochester Press, Rochester, New York. (ACRL Microcard Series, No. 85.)

60. Hathaway, G. W. (1970) Women's liberation movement II. *Wilson Library Bulletin* 44, 963 ff.

61. Heim, P., and Cameron, D. F. (1970). "The Economics of Librarianship in College and University Libraries, 1969-70: a Sample Survey of Compensations." Council on Library Resources, Washington, D.C.

62. Holden, M. Y. (1965). The status of women librarians. *Antiquarian Bookman* 36, 647-648. (Originally published as "Discriminatory Practices in the Recruiting of Women for Leading Positions in the Profession of Librarian.")

Address before Convention of National Women's Party, Washington, D.C., May 24, 1965).

63. Horner, M. S. (1969). Fail: bright women. *Psychology Today* 3 (November), 36-41.

64. Howard, P. (1970). The state of federal libraries. *In* "Bowker Annual of Library and Book Trade Information, 1970," pp. 257-264. R. R. Bowker, New York.

65. Hughes, M. M. (1970). "The Sexual Barrier: Legal and Economic Aspects of Employment." (Supplement Number One, 1971; Supplement Number Two, 1972.) M. M. Hughes, 2422 Fox Plaza, San Francisco, California.

66. Hughes, M.M. (1971). Sex-based discrimination in law libraries. *Law Library Journal* 64, 13-21.

67. Jordan, R. T. (1965). In defense of women (Letter). *Library Journal* 90, 5126.

68. Josey, E. J., ed. (1970). "The Black Librarian in America." Scarecrow Press, Metuchen, New Jersey.

69. Katz, B. (1971). The pornography collection. *Library Journal* 96, 4060-4066.

70. Korb, G. M. (1946). Successful librarians as revealed in *Who's Who in America. Wilson Library Bulletin* 20, 603-604.

71. Kortendick, J. J., and Stone, E. W. (1971). "Job Dimensions and Educational Needs in Librarianship." American Library Association, Chicago, Illinois.

72. Kritchmar A. (1972). "The Women's Rights Movement in the United States: A Bibliography and Sourcebook." Scarecrow Press, Metuchen, New Jersey.

73. Labb, J. (1950). Librarians in *Who's Who in America. Wilson Library Bulletin* 25, 54-56.

74. *Library Journal* (1971). (Issue on women) 96, 2567-2603.

75. Library of Congress personnel statistics (x972). *FLC Newsletter, Federal Library Committee* No. 67 (September), p. 17.

76. Long, M. A. (1965). "The State Library Consultant at Work." Illinois State Library, Springfield, Illinois. (Research Series, No. 6.)

77. Lowenthal, H. (1971). A healthy anger. *Library Journal* 96, 2597-2599.

78. Lyle, G. R. (1940). They have made their mark. *Library Journal* 65, 947-950.

79. Maloney, R. K. (1971). The "average" director of a large public library. *Library Journal* 96, 443-445.

80. Manchak, B. (1971). ALA salary survey: personal members. *American Libraries* 2, 409-417.

81. Marco, G. (1967). Doctoral programs in American library schools. *Journal of Education for Librarianship* 8, 6-13.

82. Massman, V. F. (1972). "Faculty Status for Librarians." Scarecrow Press, Metuchen, New Jersey.

83. Meadows-Hills, G. H. (1971). Women's liberation and the reference book. *RQ* 11, 63-65.

84. Moon, E. (1965). Tokenism at the top? *Library Journal* 90, 4019.

85. Morrison, P. D. (1963). The personality of the academic librarian. *College & Research Libraries* 24, 365-368.

86. Morrison, P. D. (1969). "The Career of the Academic Librarian: A Study in the Social Origins, Educational Attainments, Vocational Experience, and Personality Characteristics of a Group of Academic Librarians." American Library Association, Chicago, Illinois. (ACRL Monograph No. 29.)

87. Munthe, W. (1939). "American Librarianship from a European Angle." American Library Association, Chicago, Illinois.

88. New York State Library School (1911). "Librarianship: an Uncrowded Calling." New York State Education Department, Albany, New York.

89. New Zealand Library Association. Professional Section (1969). Women in professional library work· survey of women library graduates, 1946-65. *New Zealand Libraries* 32, (Fヒ ·ㅡㅗ ry), 4-31.

90. Of sex and administration (ᵢϑ71) *Protean* 1 (December), 20-31.

91. Oltman, R. M. (1971). Women iu the professional caucuses. *American Behavioral Scientist* 15, 281-302.

92. Oppenheimer, V. K. (1970). "The Female Labor Force in the United States: Demographic and Economic Factors Governing its Growth and Changing Composition." University of California, Institute of International Studies, Berkeley, California. (Population Monograph Series, No. 5.)

93. Oppenheimer, V. K. (1972). The sex labeling of jobs. *In* "Readings in Population" (W. Peterson, ed.), pp. 136-145. Macmillan, New York.

94. Parsons, T. (1959). Implications of the study. *In* "The Climate of Book Selection: Social Influences on School and Public Libraries" (J. P. Danton, ed.), pp. 77-96. University of California, School of Librarianship, Berkeley, California.

95. Philadelphia SRRT. Women's Liberation Task Force (1970). "Women in Libraries." (Mimeograph copy.)

96. Pollard, F. M. (1964). Characteristics of Negro college chief librarians. *College & Research Libraries* 24, 281-284.

97. Presthus, R. (1970). "Technological Change and Occupational Responses: A Study of Librarians." U. S. Office of Education, Bureau of Research, Washington, D.C. (ED 045 129.)

98. Problems: a monthly department of discussion (1933). *Wilson Bulletin for Librarians* 8, 230-231.

99. Robson, L., ed. (1971). The professional woman. *Protean* 1 (December), 1-56.

100. Rothenberg, L., Rees, A. M., and Kronick, D. A. (1971). An investigation of the educational needs of health sciences library manpower. IV. Characteristics of manpower in health sciences libraries. *Medical Library Association Bulletin* 59, 31-40.

101. Rudy, M. (1972). Women. *Library Journal* 97, 731-732.

102. Rutzick, M. A. (1965). A ranking of U. S. occupations by earnings. *Monthly Labor Review* 88, 249-255.

103. Schiller, A. R. (1968). "Characteristics of Professional Personnel in College and University Libraries." University of Illinois, Library Research Center, Urbana, Illinois. (ED 020 766.) [Also published by Illinois State Library, Springfield, Illinois, 1969. (Research series, No. 16.)]

104. Schiller, A. R. (1970). The disadvantaged majority: women employed in libraries. *American Libraries* 1, 345-349.

105. Schiller, A. R. (1971). Report on women in librarianship. *American Libraries* 2, 1215.

106. Schuck, V. (1971). Femina students rei publicae: notes on her professional achievement. *In* "Women in Political Science: Studies and Reports of the APSA Committee on the Status of Women, 1969-1971." American Political cal Science Association, Washington, D.C.

107. Schuman, P. (1970). Status of women in libraries: task force meets in Detroit. *Library Journal* 95, 2635.

108. Schuman, P., and Detlefsen, G. (1971). Sisterhood is serious: an annotated bibliography. *Library Journal* 96, 2587-2594.

109. Seeliger, R. A. (1961). "Librarians in *Who's Who in America*, 1956-1957." Unpublished master's thesis, University of Texas.

110. Shields, G. R. (1970). Discomfort to the enemy. *American Libraries* 1, 115.

111. Simpson, R. L., and Simpson, I. H. (1969). Women and bureaucracy in the semi-professions. *In* "The Semi-Professions and Their Organization" (A. Etizioni, ed.), pp. 196-265. The Free Press, New York.

112. Special Libraries Association. Personnel Committee (1967). A study of 1967 annual salaries of members of the Special Libraries Association. *Special Libraries* 58, 217-254.

113. Special Libraries Association. Personnel Committee (1970). SLA salary survey. *Special Libraries* 61, 333-348.

114. *Spokeswoman* (1970-   ) Susan Davis, 5464 South Shore Drive, Chicago, Illinois.

115. Stieber, G. (1971). Beginning salaries for college graduates, June 1971. *NEA Research Memo* 1971-5 (January).

116. Stimpson, C., ed. (1972). "Women and the 'Equal Rights' Amendment: Senate Subcommittee Hearings on the Constitutional Amendment, 91st Congress." (Edited in conjunction with Congressional Information Service.) R. R. Bowker, New York.

117. Stone, E. W. (1969). "Factors Related to the Professional Development of Librarians." Scarecrow Press, Metuchen, New Jersey.

118. Teander, J. (1972). (Letter.) *Library Journal* 97, 801.

119. Trumpeter, M., and Crowe, L. D. (1971). Sexism in picture books. *Illinois Libraries* 53, 499-503.

120. Tuttle, H. W. (1971). Women in academic libraries. *Library Journal* 96, 2594-2596.

121. U. S. Bureau of Labor Statistics. Division of Wage Statistics (1950).

"Economic Status of Library Personnel, 1949." Prepared by L. M. David. American Library Association, Chicago, Illinois. (Mimeograph copy.)

122. U. S. Bureau of Labor Statistics (1966). "Occupational Outlook Handbook, 1966-67." U. S. Government Printing Office, Washington, D.C. (Bulletin No. 1450.)

123. U. S. Bureau of the Census (1971). "Current Population Reports." U. S. Government Printing Office, Washington, D.C. (P-60, No. 80.)

124. U. S. Department of Labor (1970). "Manpower Report of the President." U. S. Government Printing Office, Washington, D.C.

125. U. S. Women's Bureau (1966). "Fact Sheet on Women in Professional and Technical Positions." U. S. Women's Bureau, Washington, D.C. (WB67-164.)

126. U. S. Women's Bureau (1969a). Facts About Women's Absenteeism and Labor Turnover." U. S. Government Printing Office, Washington, D.C.

127. U. S. Women's Bureau (1969b). "1969 Handbook on Women's Workers." U. S. Government Printing Office, Washington, D.C. (Women's Bureau Bulletin 294.)

128. U. S. Women's Bureau (1971). "Fact Sheet on the Earnings Gap." U. S. Government Printing Office, Washington, D.C.

129. Walters, J. H. (1970). "Image and Status of the Library and Information Services Field." U. S. Office of Education. Bureau of Research, Washington. D.C. (ED 045 130.)

130. Ward, P. L. (1966). "Women and Librarianship." The Library Association, London. (Library Association Pamphlet No. 25.)

131. The weaker sex? (1938). *Library Journal* 63, 232.

132. Wells, S. B. (1967). "The Feminization of the American Library Profession." Unpublished master's thesis, University of Chicago.

133. Wetherby, P. (1970). Librarianship: opportunity for women? *In* "Sixteen Reports on the Status of Women in the Professions." (The Professional Women's Conference, April 11, 1970, New York.) KNOW, Pittsburgh, Pennsylvania.

134. Wheeler, H. R. (1972). "Womanhood Media: Resources for Knowing About Women." Scarecrow Press, Metuchen, New Jersey.

135. White, R. F., and Macklin, D. B. (1970). "Education, Careers and Professionalization in Librarianship and Information Science." U. S. Office of Education. Bureau of Research, Washington, D.C. (ED 054 800.)

136. Williamson, C. C. (1923). "Training for Library Service. A Report Prepared for the Carnegie Corporation of New York." Merrymount Press, New York.

137. *Women Studies Abstracts* (1972-   ). S. S. Whaley, ed., v.1-.

138. Wood, M. S. (1971). Sex discrimination: the question of valid grounds. *Protean* 1, (December), 32-40.

An Investigation of Female Leadership in Regional, State, and Local Library Associations, 1876-1923

by Margaret Ann Corwin

This study was undertaken to extend the thesis of Sharon B. Wells on "The Feminization of the American Library Profession, 1876-1923," which concluded that women never dominated the top positions in the profession nationally. This study tested the hypothesis that female librarians did provide leadership in state organizations, local associations, and state positions during the years 1876-1923. The method employed was simply to list all persons who held the executive positions in particular national associations, and to compare the sex distribution with that of the persons who held executive positions in state library associations, library commissions, and local library associations. The data are derived from a sample of such listings for every third year during the period. The data indicate that women made up 31 percent of the officers in national library associations for the years 1890-1923; they also show that women tended to be better represented when the office was not a governmental position; only 20 percent of the state librarians were women. However, during the same period, 56 percent of the officers in library commissions, 60 percent of those in state associations, and 68 percent in local associations were women. Thus, the hypothesis—that women were more active in leadership roles on the local and state scene than at the national level—is supported by the data. While the proportion of women in such leadership roles never equaled their proportion in the profession overall, they were probably more active than might have been predicted considering the cultural climate of the period covered by the study.

The question of the status of women in the American library profession is an early and enduring one. From the beginning, the phenomenon of women librarians has been given separate consideration in the literature. *The Bibliography of Library Economy* by H. G. T. Cannons [1], which covers the periodical literature of librarianship from 1876 to 1920, contains almost two pages on the subject of women librarians. Every volume of *Library Literature,* which has covered the periodical indexing since Cannons, lists at least one citation under the headings "Women as Librarians," or "Women Librarians," with the 1936-39 volume containing twenty citations. Most of the articles deal with librarianship as a vocation for women or with discrimination in the library field. Until very recently, there have been few attempts to evaluate the contributions of women to librarianship or to assess the significance and influence of women in the profession.

One study centered on this important and largely uncharted aspect of American library history is the master's thesis by Sharon B. Wells entitled "The Feminization of the American Library Profession, 1876-1923" [2]. Wells's conclusion was that although women were becoming increasingly prominent in the profession during this period, they never completely dominated the top positions, they never administered the largest libraries, and they never received the highest salaries.

Building upon the Wells thesis, the present study investigates the extent to which women were playing leadership roles in the profession during the 1876-1923 period, concentrating on the state and local levels rather than on the national scene. Its hypothesis is that despite the fact that women held the lower prestige positions nationally in the profession during this early period, they were actively providing leadership in state organizations and local associations.

A NOTE ON METHODOLOGY

The data for this research are based upon a determination of the sex of each person in positions of leadership in national, state, and local associations during the 1876-1923 period. Since almost all of the state and local associations began after 1890, and there would thus be little comparable data for the early period, early data on the American Library Association and on state librarians are treated only briefly. The data were gathered from published lists of officers of the national associations;[1] U.S. Bureau of Education reports; the *American Library Index* (later *American Library Annual*); state publications such as bluebooks; press reports of elections of officers as found through Cannons and *Library Literature;* and, in some cases, for verification, through correspondence with state librarians. The names of the president and secretary of a particular group in a specific year who served for more than six months of the year in question were used to represent the "positions of leadership." If both sets of officers served exactly six months (the election being on July 1), the officers for the latter six months were chosen. While all the officers of the national associations from 1890 were used to provide a large enough sample, a selection of officers for the state associations, clubs, and commissions was made by using the officers for every third year beginning with 1890 up to 1923. For the years 1911, 1914, and 1917 data were taken from the *American Library Index* and the *American Library Annual.* For the period of 1890-1908 and for 1920 and 1923, records of elections were used.

Executive officers of national associations of a general character — American Library Association, Special Libraries Association, and Catholic Library

---

[1] The sources used were the ALA Handbook, 1929 [3], the CLA Handbook, 1946 [4], and Shove [5, vol. 2, pp. 14-16].

Association—and those of broad influence—National Association of State Librarians and Association of American Library Schools—were compared with state librarians, and officers of state library associations and local library clubs, including library school and college library associations, to determine the degree to which women were represented at the various levels.

For the purpose of this study, it is assumed that public recognition, as evidenced in election or appointment to executive offices and to positions of responsibility, is one useful indicator of "leadership." A second assumption is that the sex of a person can be deduced from a given name. Dictionaries of given names were used for reference, but if there were any doubts as to which sex was designated by a name, an attempt was made to find a reference to the person for which a pronoun was used. For names such as "Jessie" and "Jesse," or "Marion" and "Marian," the spelling was assumed to indicate the sex of the person involved. A few unusual first names were presumed to be female, as in the case of the traditional feminine endings (in "Lura," for example). For names in which there was an initial and a second name given, the second name was used to determine the sex (for example, G. Seymour Thompson, who was assumed to be male). While there may be occasional exceptions to the reliability of these factors as indicators of the sex of the individual, the exceptions are believed to be too infrequent to influence the results significantly.

With a small percentage of the names, no clues as to the sex referred to could be deduced. Many of these were last names with which only initials were given, and clarification was not available elsewhere. Because an overwhelming number of such names which could be verified turned out to be male, these names for which clarification was unavailable were arbitrarily determined to be male as well. Out of 660 names for the state library associations, 262 were determined to be male; 393 were female, and only five were uncertain and therefore counted as male. For local library associations, 106 of the names were established as male, 252 as female, and eleven were uncertain. For library commissions, 119 names were determined to be male, 154 female, and three uncertain and taken as male. On the lists of state librarians, 266 names were established to be male, 112 as female, and fourteen were uncertain and assigned to the male category. The error factor of the data is considered too small to be significant; in any case, the assignment of all such names to the male category suggests that the data here presented, if in any way distorted, tend to underestimate only slightly the number of women in positions of leadership.

The historical period 1876-1923 has been chosen for several reasons. In the first place, this is the time span of the earlier thesis, and the present study attempts to gather data to parallel and compare with the previous findings. But, more important, the years from 1876-1923 were a period of significance for both the library profession generally and specifically for the economic activity of women. As Wells has already suggested, there was a growing number of women entering the profession and the labor force during this period. In addition, the years between the founding of the ALA in 1876 and the publication of the Williamson Report in 1923 mark both the initial step in the formation of the profession and the establishment of professional standards for the library schools. Trends in any aspect of librarianship during this period have a special historical significance in the development of American librarianship.

NATIONAL ASSOCIATIONS

During the fourteen-year period 1876-89, there is little statistical material available on which to base a discussion of the involvement and activity of women in the profession on the local scene. The ALA was the only association considered in this study which was formed and active in this period. As table 1 illustrates, one woman was elected in 1889, the last year of this period, to the position of recorder.

The 1876 study of public libraries [6] was used as a basis for determining who held positions as state librarians during the year covered by the document. Five out of thirty-seven persons taken to be state librarians during this year were women. Again, these data suggest that women were more active on state than on national levels (see table 10).

While table 2 suggests that men made up less than one-third of the profession in 1900, less than one-fourth in 1910, and less than one-eighth in 1920, men filled over twice as many positions of leadership in national associations as women between 1890 and 1923 (see table 3). Further, men filled 81 percent of the presidential positions and 63 percent of the secretarial positions (see table 4).

As would be expected from the role women played in the development of the library schools, women were very active in the Association of American Library Schools, filling over three times as many elective offices as men (see table 3). However, the office of president, even here, was held about as frequently by men as by women. In each of the other national associations, men were elected to executive offices more than twice as frequently as women (see table 3).

TABLE 1

TOTAL NUMBER OF OFFICES IN THE ALA HELD BY MEN AND WOMEN BEFORE 1890, WITH BREAKDOWN BY YEAR

Year	Men		Women	
1876	2		0	
1877	3		0	
1878	2		0	
1879	3		0	
1880	2		0	
1881	3		0	
1882	3		0	
1883	3		0	
1884	3		0	
1885	3		0	
1886	3		0	
1887	4		0	
1888	4		0	
1889	4		1	
Total: 43	42	(98%)	1	(2%)

TABLE 2

EMPLOYMENT STATISTICS ON LIBRARIANS, 1900-1920

Year	Total	Men		Women	
		Number	Percent	Number	Percent
1900	2,915	803	28	2,112	72
1910	7,423	1,594	21	5,829	79
1920*	15,297	1,795	12	13,502	88

SOURCE—U.S. Bureau of the Census, "Occupational Trends in the United States, 1900-1950," by David L. Kaplan and M. Clarie Casey, Working Paper no. 5 (Washington, D.C: Government Printing Office, 1943), pp. 10, 16, 22.

*The classification of cataloguers in libraries with librarians' assistants and attendants in 1910, and with librarians in 1920, accounts partially for the large increase in the number of librarians in 1920.

TABLE 3

TOTAL NUMBER OF TIMES MEN AND WOMEN HELD OFFICES IN NATIONAL LIBRARY ASSOCIATIONS, 1890-1923

Association and Office		Number of Men		Number of Women	
American Library Association:					
President		31		3	
Secretary		37		1	
Treasurer		34		0	
Other		8		32	
Total	146	110	(75%)	36	(25%)
Association of American Library Schools:					
President		4		5	
Secretary/Treasurer		0		9	
Total	18	4	(22%)	14	(78%)
Catholic Library Association:					
President		3		0	
Total	3	3	(100%)	0	(0%)
Special Libraries Association:					
President		13		2	
Vice-president		12		7	
Secretary		9		8	
Total	51	34	(67%)	17	(33%)
National Association of State Librarians:					
President		25		1	
Vice-president		34		15	
Secretary		11		15	
Total	101	70	(69%)	31	(31%)
Total	319	221	(69%)	98	(31%)

The officers of the American Library Association, probably the most prestigious of the library associations during this period, further illustrate the tendency for women in all organizations to cluster in lower-prestige positions. Men were elected approximately three times as frequently as women to American Library Association offices. Further, while women were elected four times to the positions of president or secretary, men were elected sixty-eight times during this period. No woman was elected treasurer, while men were elected thirty-four times. Women filled other positions, such as recorder and registrar, approximately four times as frequently as men (see table 3, "Other" under American Library Association).

Table 5, a triennial breakdown of national data to compare with state and local data sampled in similar fashion, suggests no clear pattern for the activity of women at the national level. Never does the number of women exceed the number of men, despite the fact that men were never more than one-third of the profession. Women in leadership positions were, nevertheless, beginning to appear in larger numbers after the turn of the century.

TABLE 4

TOTAL NUMBER OF TIMES MEN AND WOMEN HELD OFFICES IN NATIONAL LIBRARY ASSOCIATIONS BY OFFICE HELD, 1890-1923

Office	Total Number	Men Number	Percent of Total	Women Number	Percent of Total
President	87	76	87	11	13
Secretary	90	57	63	33	37
Other	112	88	62	54	38

TABLE 5

TOTAL NUMBER OF OFFICES HELD BY MEN AND WOMEN IN NATIONAL ASSOCIATIONS, 1890-1923, BY THREE-YEAR PERIODS

Year	Men	Women
1890-92	12	4
1893-95	12	3
1896-98	15	5
1899-1901	17	8
1902-4	16	11
1905-7	20	10
1908-10	24	6
1911-13	27	3
1914-16	23	10
1917-19	22	14
1920-22	24	18
1923	9	6

REGIONAL AND COLLEGE LIBRARY ASSOCIATIONS

The figures suggest that although women were twice as active as men on a regional level, in regional college associations, women were outnumbered four to one in positions of leadership (see table 6). The sample is small because these associations began rather late in the period covered. Because of the sample size, the trend can only tentatively be postulated.

STATE ASSOCIATIONS AND STATE LIBRARY COMMISSIONS

In state library associations and state library commissions, women filled 59 percent of the executive positions of secretary or president during 1890-1923 (see table 6). In the breakdown by year (table 7), men outnumbered women in state associations before 1908; from that year on there were consis-

TABLE 6

TOTAL NUMBER OF TIMES MEN AND WOMEN HELD OFFICES OF PRESIDENT AND SECRETARY IN SAMPLE OF REGIONAL, STATE, AND LOCAL ASSOCIATIONS, 1890-1923

	Men		Women	
Level	Number	Percent of Total	Number	Percent of Total
State	388	41	547	59
Regional-general	4	29	10	71
Regional-college	9	82	2	18
Local	117	32	252	68

TABLE 7

NUMBER OF ELECTIVE OFFICES HELD, BY SEX, 1890-1923

Year	Total		State Associations		Local Associations		Library Commissions	
	Men	Women	Men	Women	Men	Women	Men	Women
(1887)	2	0	. . .	. . .	2	0	. . .	. . .
1890	4	4	3	2	1	1	0	1
1893	22	12	15	9	4	2	3	1
1896	29	22	21	15	5	3	3	4
1899	36	33	21	14	7	13	8	6
1902	45	43	23	23	11	9	11	11
1905	56	51	33	27	13	13	10	11
1908	60	72	32	37	14	21	14	14
1911	63	88	29	44	18	27	16	17
1914	62	106	30	47	17	39	15	20
1917	43	120	20	57	8	43	15	20
1920	42	120	20	58	9	38	13	24
1923	41	128	20	60	8	43	13	25
Total	505	799	267	393	117	252	121	154

Note.—Number based on the sample of state and local associations and agencies.

tently more women than men in each type of organization. It should be remembered that in 1910, men were 21 percent of the profession, and, in the figures for 1908 and 1911, they were clearly far better represented than their numbers in the profession would suggest. By 1920, men represented 12 percent of the profession, yet they held one-third of the leadership positions in state associations during that year. Nevertheless, women were far better represented in executive offices around 1920 on a state level (approximately 74 percent, fifty-eight women to twenty men in 1920) than on a national level (43 percent, twenty-four men to eighteen women in the years 1920-22).

In state library commissions, women filled 56 percent of the positions (see table 8). In the breakdown by year, women began consistently to outnumber men by 1911. Men and women were more equally represented on the commissions than in the state library associations in the breakdown by date; in 1923, men represented only slightly more than one-third of the persons in major offices in state library commissions.

TABLE 8

PERCENTAGES OF TOTAL ELECTIVE OFFICES, BY SEX AND LEVEL

Level	Total Number of Persons	Percent Male	Percent Female
State associations	660	40	60
Local associations	369	32	68
Library commissions	275	44	56
Total	1,304	39	61

Source.—Table 7.

LIBRARY CLUBS

In library clubs, the most local of the organizations, women represented 68 percent of the executive officers (see table 8). Until 1908, women were outnumbered by men in such positions. However, after 1917, women outnumbered men by four and sometimes five to one. Not even at this level, however, were women represented in leadership positions in the same proportion to which they were present in the total population of librarians in 1920, where they made up 88 percent of the profession.

CUMULATIONS

When the sample of state associations, local associations, and state library commissions are cumulated by year, men consistently outnumber women until 1908 (see table 7). In 1899, women represented 48 percent of the persons holding executive positions, by 1900 they made up 72 percent of the total population of librarians. In 1911, they made up 58 percent of the persons holding such positions and 79 percent of the population. In 1920, they held 74 percent of the executive positions and represented 88 percent of the population. Thus, the data strongly suggest that while women were present in leadership positions in increasing numbers throughout the period 1890-1923, they were never active in proportion to their representation in the total population of librarians during this period.

The breakdown of the data on state associations, state library commissions, and local associations by region provides insight into the activity of women in executive positions in various parts of the country (see table 9). In the East, the difference was small, men holding 47 percent of the positions, while women held 53 percent. In the South and Southwest regions, women held 63 percent, while men held 37 percent of the executive positions. In the West, women made up 64 percent of the persons holding such positions. In the Midwest, women were most active, filling 69 percent of the offices.

STATE LIBRARIANS

Twice as many men as women held the position of state librarian throughout the period 1890-1923; the percentage of women in that office consistently hovers around 30 percent (table 10). This representation of men is larger than the percentage of men represented in executive positions in all the national associations (69 percent), but not higher than the percentage of men represented in the most prestigious library association, the American Library Association (75 percent).

A QUALIFICATION

The Spanish-American War of 1898 and World War I must be considered in interpreting the data for the years 1899 and 1917. While it is difficult to determine the degree to which male librarians during these periods were absent from professional activities on war duties, women were represented in a somewhat higher proportion in these offices during the war years. Although the wars may account for a temporary increase in leadership roles, the long-term trend was certainly toward increasing female leadership in the profession at both state and local levels. There was a rather dramatic drop in male librarians from 1914 to 1917 (see cumulations in table 7) which surprisingly continued well beyond the years of the First World War. It is possible that a significant number of men preferred not to return to librarianship after the war, while young men starting their careers chose to enter higher-paying professions. The disruption of social traditions by the war probably helped to create a postwar climate in which women could be increasingly active in occupations such as librarianship, especially after they had the opportunity to prove themselves in positions vacated by men in war service.

CONCLUSIONS

During the three decades between 1890 and 1923, women were becoming increasingly involved in librarianship; these women appear to have assumed leadership roles on a regional, state, and local level rather than the national level, particularly when the position was not related to politics. Perhaps in some measure this reflects the inferior legal status of women during almost all of the period. It is also probably due to the fact that women were fixed in a smaller geographical area by home and family. Despite these and other handicaps, women were nevertheless active in state and local library organizations.

TABLE 9
TOTAL NUMBER OF ELECTIVE OFFICES HELD, BY SEX AND REGION, 1890-1923

		Men		Women	
East:					
	Connecticut		10	23	
	Delaware		8	0	
	Maine		30	8	
	Maryland/District of Columbia		22	6	
	Massachusetts		42	65	
	New Hampshire		16	17	
	New Jersey		13	17	
	New York		59	66	
	Pennsylvania		31	25	
	Rhode Island		8	6	
	Vermont		3	27	
	West Virginia		0	8	
	Total	510	242 (47%)	268 (53%)	
Midwest:					
	Illinois		15	42	
	Indiana		18	21	
	Iowa		12	43	
	Kansas		7	18	
	Michigan		11	43	
	Minnesota		10	37	
	Missouri		13	29	
	Nebraska		3	23	
	North Dakota		5	12	
	Ohio		20	14	
	South Dakota		3	11	
	Wisconsin		24	25	
	Total	459	141 (31%)	318 (69%)	
South and Southwest:					
	Alabama		13	7	
	Arkansas		5	6	
	Florida		3	5	
	Georgia		8	18	
	Kentucky		2	15	
	Louisiana		2	4	
	Mississippi		3	7	
	North Carolina		3	16	
	Oklahoma		1	13	
	South Carolina		3	3	
	Tennessee		6	16	
	Texas		12	14	
	Virginia		11	0	
	Total	196	72 (37%)	124 (63%)	
West:					
	Arizona				
	California		17	14	
	Colorado		15	17	
	Idaho		0	14	
	Montana		1	11	
	Nevada				
	New Mexico				
	Oregon		1	9	
	Utah		4	9	
	Washington		10	5	
	Wyoming		2	8	
	Total	137	50 (36%)	87 (64%)	

Note—Number based on the sample of state library associations, local library associations, and library commissions.

TABLE 10

STATE LIBRARIANS BY SEX AND YEAR FOR SELECTED YEARS

Year	Men	Women
1876	32	5
1891	29	8
1896	26	11
1903	31	10
1908	33	12
1911	33	13
1914	33	14
1917	33	14
1920	31	14
1923	31	16
Total for 1890-1923: 392	71%	29%

The results of the comparison of national with state and local associations is in agreement with trends that have been suggested in the literature. In the first decade and a half after the formation of the profession, it has been recognized that female librarians did not attain positions of prominence, despite their numbers. Observers of women in the American library field have also recognized that later, women were far better represented in libraries holding less than 10,000 volumes than in libraries with over 100,000 volumes, whether academic or public. Some writers have given preliminary substantiation to the idea that men held major administrative positions out of proportion to their numbers in the profession. This study confirms that men were indeed greatly overrepresented in national associations. As suggested in the analysis of officers in national associations, the results of this study are also in agreement with the idea that in prestigious organizations, women were more likely to be in subordinate than in superordinate positions.

While the findings of this study indicate that women were very active in associations at the local, state, and regional levels, it is apparent that even so, their participation is never in proportion to their numbers in the profession. When the offices were governmental positions, women were even less likely to be involved. In regional as in state associations, women seem to have been relatively active. There are indications, however, that in regional college associations the scholarly male tradition was dominant. Women are best represented in leadership positions in local associations. When the inferior legal status of women and the traditional social role of the woman are taken into account, female librarians were probably more active in leadership positions in the library field than might initially have been expected.

REFERENCES

1. Cannons, Harry George Turner. *Bibliography of Library Economy: A Classified Index to the Professional Periodical Literature in the English Language Relating to Library Economy, Printing, Methods in Publishing, Copyright, Bib-*

liography, Etc., from 1876-1920. (Chicago, IL: American Library Association, 1926).

2. Wells, Sharon B. "The Feminization of the American Library Profession, 1876-1923." M.A. thesis, University of Chicago, 1967.

3. ALA Handbook, 1929. "Past Officers." Compiled by Mrs. Henry J. Carr. *American Library Association Bulletin* 23 (November, 1929):732-34.

4. CLA Handbook, 1946. "A List of Its Officers, Committees, Units, Publications, Constitution, and Members." *Catholic Library World* 17, no. 8, pt. 1 (May, 1946):236.

5. Shove, Raymond P. "Association of American Library Schools." *Encyclopedia of Library and Information Science.* (New York: Marcel Dekker, 1969).

6. U.S. Bureau of Education. *Public Libraries in the United States of America; Their History, Condition, and Management.* Special Report, pt. 1. (Washington, DC: Government Printing Office, 1876).

Women and Librarianship in 1975

by Patricia Layzell Ward

1975 has been designated as International Women's Year and this has created interest in occupations where traditionally there has been a high proportion of women. It would therefore seem to be a reasonable time to reexamine the balance of the sexes in librarianship and to see whether there are any apparent changes taking place. An earlier report examined this question in 1963.[1] At this time major changes were about to take place in professional education with the introduction of the two-year course and the trend towards direct entry to the profession. There was a shortage of staff in libraries, and a possible way to overcome this might have been to encourage qualified married women not working in libraries to return to their careers. It was suggested that a possible career pattern for women was that of being married at 26 and retiring at 28, having worked 3 or 4 years before qualifying and for 4 or 5 years after attending library school.

However, this picture has changed dramatically during the past 12 years.

The proportion of women to men in the UK library schools has stayed constant during the past five years, for since 1970 nearly three-quarters of the students have been women.

TABLE 1

ENROLLMENT OF WOMEN AND MEN IN UK LIBRARY SCHOOLS, 1965-74

Year	Men		Women		Total
1965	439	27%	996	73%	1,595
1967	604	28%	1,536	72%	2,140
1969	742	28%	1,886	72%	2,638
1971	678	26%	1,885	74%	2,563
1973	685	26%	1,927	74%	2,613
1974	661	26%	1,882	74%	2,543

Source: Annual census of students. *Libr. Assoc. Rec., 1965-74.*

A more dramatic picture of change emerges if the number seeking election to the Register of chartered librarians is shown as men, and the percentage of women shown as married and unmarried at the time of election. In 1947 45 percent seeking election were men and 4 percent were married women; by 1972 the percentage of men had fallen to 28 percent and the percentage of married women has risen to 28 percent of the total.

The men still outnumber the women in seeking election as Fellows, although the percentage fell between 1950 and 1970. Of a total of 77 Fellows elected in 1950, 60 or 78 percent, and in 1970 14 of a total of 20, or 70 percent, were men.

The notion that marriage put an end to a career for women has now died. Women now have the freedom of choice as to whether they intend to continue in their careers without break. In 1953 the percentage of the total number of chartered librarians who were married women not gainfully employed was 5 percent; by 1965 this had risen to 12 percent. In 1972 it was only 14 percent, despite the increase in the percentage of married women among chartered librarians.

TABLE 2
PERSONS SEEKING ELECTION TO THE REGISTER OF CHARTERED LIBRARIANS, 1947-72

Year	Total	Men		Women			
				Unmarried		Married	
1947	230	103	45%	117	51%	10	4%
1952	262	112	43%	149	57%	1	21%
1957	307	114	47%	156	51%	37	12%
1962	419	147	35%	214	51%	58	14%
1967	695	237	34%	307	44%	151	22%
1972	1,319	374	28%	581	44%	364	28%

Source: Libr. Assoc. Rec., 1947-73.

TABLE 3
THE PERCENTAGE OF MARRIED WOMEN NOT GAINFULLY EMPLOYED SHOWN IN RELATION TO THE TOTAL NUMBER OF CHARTERED LIBRARIANS, 1953-72

Year	Total number of chartered librarians	Total number of women not gainfully employed	Percentage of women not gainfully employed
1953	3,582	176	5
1958	4,602	332	7
1968	8,056	1,029	13
1970	9,766	1,282	13
1972	11,808	1,612	14

Source: LA Yearbook, 1953-72.

Of the women who were chartered librarians working in libraries in 1973, 43 percent were married women as compared with 13 percent in 1953.

In examining the career patterns of a sample of chartered librarians,[2] it was found that among the married women who have a break in their careers that this could last from one year to thirty years. It was also found that it was not only women who had breaks in careers or who left librarianship before the normal age of retirement; a certain number of men were not maintaining their membership of the Library Association and had possibly left the profession. Of 98 listed in the *Record* in 1953 as having been elected as Associates, only 76 were now listed in the *1973 Yearbook*. One hundred and thirty-six were elected in 1958 and 110 were still on the Register; 186 were elected in 1963— 137 were still on the Register. Of 228 elected in 1968, only 183 were still on the Register in 1973.

TABLE 4

WOMEN CHARTERED LIBRARIANS WORKING IN LIBRARIES SHOWN BY MARITAL STATUS, 1953-73

Year	Total women chartered librarians working in libraries	Married women chartered librarians working in libraries	
1953	1,382	182	13%
1958	1,872	309	17%
1963	2,306	491	21%
1968	2,950	901	31%
1973	5,322	2,292	43%

So the proportion of qualified women working in the profession continues to maintain a high level, and we have had the benefits of equal pay for a number of years. However, the proportion of women in the most senior posts does not appear to be high. Preparing a detailed analysis of the exact percentages is near impossible due to the differences in labels given to similar posts in different types of libraries, but just looking through the names of chief librarians of academic, public or special libraries, few women are seen, and since the reorganization of local government the number of women chiefs of public library systems has fallen. It is believed that only one university, two polytechnic chiefs and three public library chiefs are women. One reason for this probably lies in the number of women who retired in the post-war period to raise a family and who have not returned to their careers for a number of reasons. It is likely that there are fewer women committed to advancement in their careers who are in the appropriate age group for the most senior posts.

From a recent investigation it does appear that there is a tendency for the younger age groups to continue their careers without a break and although progress is slow, the establishment of crèches in universities and in industry will help women to be able to continue a career and have a family.

As yet women have not organized themselves within the profession in the UK as have women librarians in the US, where the Social Responsibility Round Table held a highly successful conference for women librarians at

TABLE 5

LATEST MEMBERSHIP STATISTICS PROVIDED BY LA MEMBERSHIP DEPARTMENT

Categories	November 1974 Total personal membership November 1974 = 21,166		February 1975 Total personal membership 28 February 1975 = 21,770		
	Total personal membership November 1974	Categories as percentage of total personal membership November 1974	Women members February 1975	Categories as percentage of women members 1975	Women members as a percentage of total personal membership February 1975
Graduate Fellows	624	2.95%	239	1.63%	1.10%
Non-Graduate Fellows	1,284	6.07%	406	2.77%	1.86%
Graduate Associates	3,436	16.23%	2,228	15.20%	10.23%
Non-Graduate Associates	9,183	43.39%	6,835	46.64%	31.40%
Graduate Members	2,260	10.68%	1,577	10.76%	7.24%
Non-Graduate Members	4,379	20.69%	3,371	23.00%	15.48%
Total	21,166		14,656		67.31%
Chartered Members	14,527	68.63%	9,708	66.24%	44.59%
Non-Chartered Members	6,639	31.37%	4,948	33.76%	22.72%
Total	21,166		14,656		67.31%

Rutgers University in 1974 and plans another to precede the ALA annual conference in San Francisco in 1975. They also issue regularly *Women in libraries.*

REFERENCES

1. Layzell Ward, P. *Women in Librarianship.* Library Association, 1966.

2. Layzell Ward, P. *A Study of the Geographic and Occupational Mobility of Professional Librarians Related to Their Education.* Unpublished PhD thesis. University College London, 1974.

3. Schiller, Anita. Women in Librarianship. In: *Advances in Librarianship,* vol. 4, (New York: Academic Press, 1974):103-147.

> Anita Schiller has recently published an interesting overview of women in librarianship in which she discusses the status of women librarians, librarianship as a women's occupation, characteristics of careers and the current scene. She draws from the published literature of North America, Europe and Australia, and also gives an account of the work of SRRT's Task Force on the status of women in librarianship.

American Librarianship

by Anne E. Brugh
and Benjamin R. Beede

In the United States we find [in librarianship] . . . the elysium of women.
[M. S. R. James, 1902][1]

Librarianship is . . . a dead end for women.
[Phyllis Wetherby, 1970][2]

Relatively little has been written about women in American librarianship,[3] considering the numerical predominance of women in the field and the number of journals in which librarians may express themselves. The problem has not been to assist women to enter the field, since it has been long considered a women's preserve, but to ensure that women librarians receive equitable treatment. Salary discrimination is both a source of controversy and closely related to exclusion of women from major administrative posts. Another controversial issue is the degree to which women's predominance in the field has kept librarianship a "semiprofession."

The object of this paper is to review publications of the past five years which offer a new perspective on women in librarianship. Emphasis is given to work on salary discrimination, the socioeconomic and historical bases for discrimination in the structuring and development of the library profession, and the actions women are taking to change the patterns of inequality that have been uncovered.

Several federal reports document the basic problems facing women in the field. A general survey prepared in 1974 showed that 97,000 women made up 84 percent of all librarians in 1970.[4] The largest proportion of these women worked in school libraries, where prestige is lowest; and the smallest proportion worked in academic libraries, where prestige is highest. An important factor affecting the prospects of women is the increasing number of men entering the field. There were 18,000 men librarians in 1970, compared with 10,000 in 1960.[5] Another study showed that men librarians earn more than women librarians, but that they earn less in that profession than do men in

Reprinted with permission from *Signs: a Journal of Women in Culture and Society* 1 (Summer, 1976):943-955. Reproduced by permission of the authors and publisher.

other professions. Women librarians, on the other hand, have salaries comparable to those of other professional women. Because the feminine image of librarianship is said to exert a negative influence on the profession, many administrators are actively encouraging men to become librarians; consequently, men advance farther and faster than women.[6] Bureau of the Census statistics indicate that, from the beginning, women in library work received lower salaries than men for comparable work. Men almost invariably held the highest-paid administrative positions in large libraries.[7]

As early as 1886, Melvil Dewey, one of the leading American librarians of the nineteenth century, asserted that men receive higher salaries than women because women have poorer health than men, lack business and executive training, and do not plan to work permanently. Even if an individual woman did not have these disabilities, she would have to accept lower pay "because of the consideration which she exacts and deserves on account of her sex."[8] He observed, however, that women's salaries should improve as they obtained more education and experience. Dewey has been assailed often by feminists for these sexist assumptions, although he did much to open the profession to women. Much less well known than this address is his speech at the Second International Library Conference in 1897. Dewey described what he regarded as the ideal qualifications for "a great librarian." He then added, "When I look into the future, I am inclined to think that most of the men who will achieve this greatness will be women."[9] Rather than attacking Dewey for his sexist beliefs in the 1880s, it might be more fruitful to ascertain why his prediction of 1897 was not fully realized during the next seventy years.

An explanation lies in the ascription of roles in the library profession on the basis of sex. Not only are occupations sex typed,[10] but categories of jobs within a field can be and are assigned by sex. One way to describe this situation is through the application of the theory of caste: "The concept of *caste* conveys how social roles are determined by birth rather than by achievement. In a society not conditioned by *caste*, work roles would be assigned or chosen according to individual aptitudes."[11] Perhaps the fact that men and women came to have different career paths within the field resulted in librarianship becoming a "semiprofession" in which women made up the vast majority of practitioners. One report speaks of the "four classic female professions — education, library science, social work, and public health."[12] An excellent analysis of diverging career patterns of women and men in librarianship is Wanda Auerbach's survey of the status of women in academic libraries.[13] Auerbach, a librarian and social worker, tried to determine what progress women had made in fighting for their rights. She found discrimination in academic libraries to be more serious than in public libraries. This was not a new finding.[14] Nevertheless, Auerbach had much to contribute to the discussion of women in library service. She described a "harem" model to explain library staffing patterns. A division of labor exists in which men hold leadership roles and women fill subordinate posts. The same model is applicable to other fields where women predominate numerically, such as nursing, teaching, and social work.[15] In these "semiprofessions," little autonomy devolves on the individual practitioners; advancement, moreover, comes through the assumption of administrative duties, rather than through professional achievement.

Auerbach cited the common reasons offered for differentiating between men and women librarians in appointment, promotion, and salary determination:

1. Women are more tractable than men.
2. Women are less intellectually and educationally ambitious than men.
3. Women are less committed to their professional careers than men.
4. Women do not like to work for other women and accept the cultural prescription that they should defer to men.

She argued that discrimination cannot be justified on such grounds. Role expectations imposed by society have such a powerful impact that "a mutually reenforcing relationship then persists between the organization that discriminates against women and the cultural norms which seem to give such discrimination a valid foundation."[16]

An intensive study by two sociologists confirmed the accusations made by practitioners such as Auerbach.[17] Pointing to the fact that studies of advancement by women in the professions have usually dealt with occupations in which women are very much in the minority, Carol Kronus and James Grimm believed it would be valuable to study a field in which there was a significant representation of both sexes but in which women made up the majority. They found men coming to dominate librarianship to an increasing degree. Using several criteria such as the sex of deans of library schools, of editors of major library periodicals, and of presidents of state library associations, the researchers determined that the percentage of women in each category was falling. Only among school librarians were women represented in leadership roles roughly proportionate to their numbers. "One could almost posit a 'vacuum' concept of female power, in which women get promoted to top positions only in the complete, rather than relative, absence of male alternatives."[18]

The authors discussed the reasons often given for women not moving into leadership roles in librarianship. They did not assess their accuracy, but they did evidence surprise at the results. "Is it possible that one finds less administrative talent and ambition among 75,000 women than among 13,000 men?" The authors applied the concepts of "employment queues" and "promotion queues" to the position of women librarians. This approach led to a conclusion that, "although they are not bypassed when it comes to filling routine library positions, they are clearly rejected in favor of men as promotion candidates. In broader terms, we find no necessary connection between a group's position on the employment and promotion queues. This suggests that the two queues are independent, possibly resulting from a different mix of objective and subjective criteria used to array groups on the two continuums."[19] Changes can only occur when there are shortages of individuals in the preferred groups or when employers take a more favorable view of groups that have been given second preference. The authors asserted, "Neither of these conditions is present in librarianship today, so in this field where women predominate, men dominate."[20]

One of the catalysts in prompting more intensive studies of women librarians has been the findings of various salary surveys within recent years. The first major survey of the current decade was sponsored by the Special Libraries Association, an organization consisting primarily of librarians employed by private firms. When a special committee reported the data for 1970, it was not reticent about stating, "There is evidence for a real male-oriented bias in salaries for all categories" of librarians. Education, status as a director, and other factors had little effect; there was an overall differential of 25 percent between men and women, in favor of male librarians.[21]

The American Library Association made a survey in 1970-71 which also showed salary gaps between the sexes. The association's Library Administration Division reported the data without comment. "The principal salary determinants are academic degree, type of employer, and sex."[22] No matter what their background, women on the average ran $2,000-$3,000 behind their male counterparts. The average salary for full-time librarians was $14,471 for men and $10,874 for women.[23] This was an important survey, for the association was making a distinction between the salaries of men and women for the first time.

Carlyle Frarey and Carol Learmont of Columbia University made an inquiry into sex distinctions in salaries and job opportunities in library science as part of a general survey in 1971.[24] This was the first year in this series of studies that the impact of sex was considered. The compilers sent questionnaires to thirty-nine graduate schools of library science to learn whether deans believed discrimination against women existed. The vast majority denied there was any discrimination or stated they had insufficient data to make a judgment. The authors inferred, "Our simple question elicited a response and some suggestive statistics that imply real inequities, at least in some places. Obviously the time is here when we need to keep better statistical information upon which to base our judgments and to rely less upon what we suppose or feel to be true."[25] This brave beginning was negated by the very conservative approach they took in succeeding years. Their next survey seemed to "imply discrimination," but they were unwilling to analyze possible trends because of the lack of comparable data from earlier years. Frarey and Learmont suggested educational and experience differences might explain some of the patterns in salary distribution. They concluded that "time, space, and the lack of comparable data preclude a full discussion of this issue in our 1972 report."[26] The 1973 survey continued comparisons between sexes but did not exhibit much enthusiasm for the subject. Although asserting that "women generally fare somewhat less well in salaries than do men," the compilers were unwilling to make generalizations. "Whether the salary differentials reflect real discrimination is not clear since we have insufficient data concerning such relevant variables as education, experience, and mobility to make any assessment." As a result, they threw up their hands. "It seems unlikely that we will ever be able to make an in-depth analysis of the differences and the reasons for them."[27] They did not recognize that there could be discriminatory forces in library education and in the availability of employment opportunities which helped to determine the salary level of women librarians. Their latest report says even less about sex differences than the previous three. Figures are reported, but there is little analysis. The current data "reinforce what we have long known: that whether or not there is any real discrimination intended or practiced, men, in general, fare better in their beginning salaries than do women."[28]

Fortunately, there have been library educators willing to come to grips with the problem. Two library school professors, Raymond L. Carpenter and Kenneth D. Shearer, initiated a series of surveys in 1971 which dealt forthrightly with sex discrimination. Although their data was limited to major American and Canadian public libraries, it is of general interest. Public libraries are a pure type which facilitates comparisons between men and women. In academic and special libraries, differences in education may exist which can be used to explain away discriminatory patterns in salary and promotion. This distinction cannot be maintained in public libraries, where both men and women rarely have more than a master's degree in library science.

The first Carpenter-Shearer survey showed there was a gap of approximately 30 percent between the median salaries of men and women library directors. A disproportionate number of men were directors, and the larger the library, the more likely the director was to be a man. Libraries headed by men tended to receive more support from their communities. Salaries for new librarians, whether male or female, were usually higher in libraries headed by men. The average per capita budget (the amount of money allocated to a library by a local government unit divided by the population of the unit) manifested the same pattern. The authors asserted sex differences in salary and library support should be eliminated: "We have a long way to go in attaining a reasonable approximation of 'equal pay for equal work.' But through our professional organizations and unions we can insist that differences in pay for equal work at least be independent with respect to the director's gender."[29]

According to their next survey, published about a year later, sex patterns had not changed much. The gap in per capita support between libraries headed by men and women had narrowed but was still substantial. The 30 percent salary advantage of men persisted.[30] Because of "the continuation of differences in salary and per capita statistics by sex [the authors decided to make] an exploration of what may be a result of sexism in a 'female' occupation."[31] Carpenter and Shearer asked rhetorically whether such differences were the consequence of the superior fitness of men for administration or the result of discrimination. They concluded that discriminatory patterns in American society were the root cause. They discussed the reasons commonly given for appointing men to directorships in preference to women—for example, that women are oriented toward their families and not toward their jobs.

The authors did not endorse these arguments, but they believed opponents of sexism should examine and understand sexist assumptions in order to combat them more effectively. They stressed the need for continuing education opportunities and encouraging women who might want to become administrators. Other recommendations included discussion groups in libraries to consider sex attitudes and related topics, efforts by library directors and other librarians to improve salaries, and attempts by directors to raise per capita support.

The professional association, as Carpenter and Shearer pointed out, is one major means of effecting change in the library field. Nevertheless, the historical record suggests that problems exist in exploiting this means. A recent study of women's participation in state and local library associations between 1890 and 1923 concluded that women were more active in these associations than at the national level.[32] At neither level were women represented in proportion to their numbers in the profession. Despite this, the record of women seemed quite good, considering the sexist societal patterns prevalent in the years studied. Gradually, women began to outnumber men in holding leadership posts in the associations; they went over the 50 percent mark in 1908. The trend was accelerated by World War I, when the numbers of men both in the profession and active in library associations declined.

More evidence on the role of women in the professional associations appeared in a report by Phyllis Wetherby at a conference of professional women in 1970. Noting the greater number of men now being attracted to library work and their continued gravitation to administrative positions, Wetherby scored the major library associations for having failed to do anything about discrimination against women. As late as 1969, although the American Library Association and the Special Libraries Association "regularly gather[ed] statistics on salaries . . . neither has yet seen fit to analyze the differences in salaries for men and women."[33] Other areas of discrimination included membership on the faculties of library schools and the holding of offices in professional organizations. With respect to the associations, Wetherby made the telling point that women help to select men in preference to women "when they have the opportunity to elect officers. . . . In the American Library Association's 100-year history, only 14 of the 52 Presidents have been women."[34]

Another attack on sexism in the professional associations, especially the American Library Association, came from Anita R. Schiller, probably the leading proponent of sex equality in the library profession.[35] She contrasted librarianship with occupations in which there were efforts to make up for past exclusion of women by a strong recruitment program. The library profession, particularly as embodied in the American Library Association, seemed content with the status quo. Schiller believed that this inaction might be attributed to the fear of many librarians that making an issue of discrimination would emphasize the predominance of women in the field and thereby degrade the profession in the eyes of outsiders. Schiller asserted that, instead of a badge of shame to be concealed, the large number of women in the occupation offers librarianship the opportunity to become the first profession to establish equality for both sexes.

Within the American Library Association, women's role in librarianship has become a matter of concern primarily to a task force of the Social Responsibilities Round Table (SRRT).[36] While the Task Force on Women is keeping the issue alive, the status of women would probably be improving more rapidly if there were more commitment at higher levels of the association. Many librarians are skeptical about achieving change through the American Library Association. As a result, Women Library Workers, an organization outside the framework of the association, has been formed. This group will cooperate with the SRRT Task Force on Women but will remain independent. Its first newsletter was issued in September 1975. Presumably, this publication will become an important medium for the discussion of issues confronting women librarians.[37]

Trade unionism is another path for women who wish to increase their vocational opportunities and protect their economic and social interests. As the Twentieth Century Fund recently observed, *"Unions can and should play a key role in the struggle to bring equal opportunity to women."*[38] This principle has been applied to librarianship by Joan Dillon.[39] She warned that the gap between the earnings of men and women is widening and cited statistics that demonstrated the need for women to look to unions in order to gain their share of economic resources. While approximately 10 percent of women workers belong to unions, their median income is 70 percent higher than that of nonunion women. She described changes in union organization and in union attitudes which allow women more voice in the movement. Dillon reminded readers that, while the majority of librarians are women, men hold most of the significant positions in the field. Her advice to women was, " 'If you haven't got a union, fight to get one! If you have a union, fight to make it fight.' "[40]

Another important form of activity is an affirmative-action program. Wendy De Fichy described the role an affirmative-action committee may play in enabling women to overcome discrimination and advance to managerial posts. The committee should first determine the existing status of women employees and study current employment practices. To do this, De Fichy stressed, the committee must have the full support of top management. The committee should then map out plans to increase "the percentage of women in management, effect anti-discrimination policies and improve the attitude of workers toward women managers."[41] To overcome past discrimination, libraries should fill managerial vacancies with women whenever possible, until the percentage of women in library management equals the percentage of women employed as librarians. Library schools can assist affirmative action with courses encouraging women to become administrators and programs which allow women to return to work after rearing their children.

Before attempting to change social conditions, one needs to know precisely how they have arisen. Within the past few years, several efforts have been made to examine the early years of the American library profession to determine how sexist preconceptions took root. The development of children's librarianship in the late nineteenth and early twentieth centuries reflects some of the problems faced by women. It was a women's field from the beginning. As Margo Sasse pointed out, "American women . . . originated what has been called America's most valuable contribution to the library world—library service to children."[42] Yet the status of children's librarians was and is low in relation to other groups of librarians. Sasse showed that children's librarians, who should be regarded as pioneers, have been excluded in the main from major biographical sources such as *Notable American Women, 1607-1950.* Sasse concluded that "a necessary reordering of priorities should both provide tribute to the women founders of children's service and a realignment of the status of those currently providing children's services."[43]

One of the best studies directed to women in the early history of the profession was prepared by Dee Garrison, a historian at Rutgers University. Using her library experience and her training as a historian, Garrison traced the process by which librarianship became a "woman's job" in public libraries between 1876 and 1905. The moral halo that surrounded women in the nineteenth century combined with the cultural atmosphere of the public-library movement to make the field a natural one for women. The assumed ability of women to perform jobs requiring great attention to detail suggested the availability of women for cataloging books, a subspecialty which was and has remained among the lowest paid and least prestigious types of library work. There were several negative effects of the feminization of public libraries. Municipalities did not seem to support libraries so vigorously as women came to predominate on their staffs. The influx of women also lowered salaries. "The same economic factors were at work in librarianship and teaching, for educated women, with few other job opportunities flocked into both fields, with a depressing effect on wages."[44]

The second half of Garrison's article deals with the professionalization of librarianship. The predominance of women hampered this process because of the nature of nineteenth-century society and the role of women therein. Married women were discouraged by law and social custom from working. This shortened the careers of women who married. Those who did not marry were regarded with little respect, since the goal of every woman was conceived to be to find a husband. When she failed, she was regarded as an ineffective human being with little to contribute. According to Garrison, "The negative traits for which librarians indict themselves—excessive cautiousness, avoidance of controversy, timidity, a weak orientation toward autonomy, little business sense, tractability, overcompliance, service to the point of self-sacrifice, and willingness to submit to subordination by trustee and public—are predominantly 'feminine' traits."[45]

Some recent articles explore in depth the validity of the stereotypes of the female librarian and attempt to assess their job satisfaction. David Lee and Janet Hall investigated the stereotypes by comparing female college students and female library school students.[46] Using Cattell and Eber's *Sixteen Personality Factors Questionnaire,* which scores subjects on a scale for self-assurance versus apprehensiveness, reserved versus outgoing personality, humbleness versus assertiveness, and other traits, the authors found the occupational stereotype disproved. "[In] contrast to the occupational stereotype, this group of library science students was *not* found to be more rigid, conscientious, conventional, conservative, tense, or less intelligent or less stable than the college female norm group."[47] Three scores on the scale which revealed significant differences between the two groups (more intelligent, experimenting, self-sufficient) reflected favorably on the prospective librarians.

Susanne Wahba compared the sources of job satisfaction for women and men librarians in order to measure the effects of the differential treatment women receive in libraries.[48] Porter's *Need Satisfaction Questionnaire* was used to measure the individual's rating of his or her job. Such a rating was based on the subject's perception of the fulfillment or nonfulfillment of the following needs: security, social esteem, autonomy, and self-actualization. The study showed that women receive less satisfaction from their work than do men. This conclusion points to the need for studying the conditions under which women work to determine more specifically where improvements should be made. By exposing the differential treatment given to men and women, the investigators helped to disprove the assertions of sexists that women are satisfied with their present role in the profession.

Besides action through professional organizations, trade unions, and other structures such as affirmative-action committees, the literature promotes consciousness raising for the individual librarian as a remedy for some of the problems women face in the profession. Many articles state clearly that change will not occur until more women librarians rethink their attitudes. In "A Healthy Anger," Helen Lowenthal suggested that women librarians have developed a "nigger mentality," that is, a degree of conditioning to male prejudices that teaches them not to strive above their "natural" station. Lowenthal was one of the few writers to criticize librarianship as a career for women. She argued that a lack of options forced many women into the field. Once within it, they overadapted: "[We] shuffle along and say, 'But I really don't want to be an administrator. I truly enjoy doing the less prestigious work.' This may . . . be the result of our nigger mentality or it may just be the absolute truth, but in either case we must realize that *we have not had a choice.*"[49]

Perhaps Lowenthal's most significant contribution to the discussion of women in librarianship was her consideration of the dual stereotype. Among nonlibrarians, members of the profession are often regarded as pedantic old maids. Within the field, women are viewed as conservative and unbusiness-like. Courses in library school which employ the case method of teaching administration frequently reflect this stereotyping. Lowenthal's remedies were more in the direction of consciousness raising than political and legal action. She wanted women to recognize the narrow parameters which govern their options. Like many others in the women's movement, Lowenthal stressed the need for women to be angry when faced with discrimination. "The most oppressive force we face in liberating ourselves is not at home, nor at work, but in our minds."[50]

Another plea for women to look honestly at their status in the library world came from Helen Tuttle. Like Lowenthal, Tuttle firmly asserted, "Women must change their own attitudes and activities before they can change the attitudes of others."[51] It seemed to her that married women who are librarians should pursue their careers as seriously as do their husbands. Relocation decisions should take into consideration the careers of both husband and wife, and they should avoid any undue restrictions on the professional advancement of either.

The fight for equality of the sexes in librarianship is far from over, as can be seen from the publications discussed in this survey. To conclude, something should be said about the importance of further research and writing to the struggle. To at least one librarian writing in 1972, many of the recent articles seemed sexist, whether or not the authors professed sympathy with women's liberation. Mary Wood also found the literature deficient. "The labor of attacks and counter-attacks has been redundant, weakened by a lack of definitions, largely undocumented, sporadic in data collection, and impaired by a reluctance to draw from the bodies of anthropological, sociological or biological theory. Whether from the male or female viewpoint, a continuing polemic seems fruitless."[52] Over the past three years, there seems to have been a definite improvement in the quality of articles on women in librarianship. Scholarly historical and sociological treatments have been made of several facets of the problem. Moreover, there seems to have been some movement away from rhetoric about women's degradation in libraries and toward substantial proposals for remedying existing problems.

Research on women in the "semi-professions," including librarianship, can take several forms: "First, research could focus . . . on the degree to which women in the semi-professions are interested in responsibility and advancement. Second, research might focus on the degree to which the semi-professions are bureaucratically oriented and structured, making them particularly vulnerable and sensitive to female career interruption. . . . Third, research could . . . study the relationship between (changing) occupational structures and sex-typed employment in the semi-professions."[53] Research of this kind can help to define goals and to collect the data needed, if women in librarianship are to make the profession something more than a dead end for the majority of practitioners.

FOOTNOTES

1. "Women Librarians and Their Future Prospects," *Public Libraries* 7 (January 1902):5.

2. Phyllis Wetherby, "Librarianship: Opportunity for Women?" in *Sixteen Reports on the Status of Women in the Professions* (New York: Professional Women's Caucus, 1970), p. 2.

3. The most useful bibliography consulted was "Women in Librarianship, 1920-1973," in *Women in Librarianship: Melvil's Rib Symposium.* Margaret Myers and Mayra Scarborough, eds. (New Brunswick, NJ: Rutgers University Graduate School of Library Service, 1975). Additional citations were supplied by Lillian A. Hamrick, librarian. U.S. Department of Labor Library: Lelia Alexander, Women's Action Program. Office of the Secretary, U.S. Department of Health, Education, and Welfare; and Jenrose Felmley, librarian, Business and Professional Women's Foundation, Washington, D.C.

4. U.S. Department of Labor Bureau of Labor Statistics, *Library Manpower: A Study of Supply and Demand,* Bulletin no. 1852 (Washington, DC: Government Printing Office, 1975), p. 12.

5. Ann Kahl, "What's Happening to Jobs in the Library Field?" *Occupational Outlook Quarterly* 18 (Winter, 1974):21.

6. U.S. Department of Labor, p. 26.

7. Rudolph C. Blitz, "Women in the Professions, 1870-1970." *Monthly Labor Review* 9 (May, 1974):36.

8. Melvil Dewey, "Librarianship as a Profession for College-bred Women" (address delivered before the Association of Collegiate Alumnae, March 13, 1886), p. 20.

9. Melvil Dewey, "Relation of the State to the Public Library," in *Transactions and Proceedings of the Second International Library Conference, Held in London, July 13-16, 1897* (London, 1898), p. 22.

10. See Cynthia Fuchs Epstein, *Women's Place: Options and Limits in Professional Careers* (Berkeley: University of California Press, 1970), pp. 151-66.

11. Carol Andreas, *Sex and Caste in America* (Englewood Cliffs, NJ: Prentice-Hall, Inc., 1971), p. 48.

12. Eli Ginzberg et al., *Life Styles of Educated Women* (New York: Columbia University Press, 1966), p. 76.

13. Wanda Auerbach, "Discrimination against Women in the Academic Library," *University of Wisconsin Library News* 17 (February, 1972):1-11.

14. Anita R. Schiller, *Characteristics of Professional Personnel in College and University Libraries.* Research Series no. 16 (Springfield: Illinois State Library, 1969), p. 76.

15. Auerbach, pp. 1-2.

16. Ibid., pp. 5-6.

17. Carol L. Kronus and James W. Grimm, "Women in Librarianship: The Majority Rules?" *Protean* 1 (December, 1971):4-9.

18. Ibid., p. 7.

19. Ibid., p. 8.

20. Ibid., p. 9.

21. "SLA Salary Survey, 1970," *Special Libraries* 61 (July-August, 1970):348. There was no decrease in this differential through 1973. See "Equal Pay for

Equal Work: Women in Special Libraries" (New York: Special Libraries Association, 1976), pp. 3, 7.

22. "ALA Salary Survey: Personal Members," *American Libraries* 2 (April, 1971):410.

23. Ibid., p. 411.

24. Carlyle J. Frarey and Carol L. Learmont, "Placement and Salaries, 1971: A Modest Employment Slowdown," *Library Journal* 97 (June 15, 1972): 2154-59.

25. Ibid., p. 2159.

26. Carlyle J. Frarey and Carol L. Learmont, "Placements and Salaries, 1972: We Hold Our Own," *Library Journal* 98 (June 15, 1973):1886.

27. Carlyle J. Frarey and Carol L. Learmont, "Placements and Salaries, 1973: Not Much Change," *Library Journal* 99 (July, 1974):1774.

28. Carlyle J. Frarey and Carol L. Learmont, "Placements and Salaries, 1974: Promise or Illusion?" *Library Journal* 100 (October 1, 1975):1767.

29. Raymond L. Carpenter and Kenneth D. Shearer, "Sex and Salary Survey," *Library Journal* 97 (November 15, 1972):3685.

30. Raymond L. Carpenter and Kenneth D. Shearer, "Sex and Salary Update," *Library Journal* 99 (January 15, 1974):103.

31. Ibid., p. 101.

32. Margaret Ann Corwin, "An Investigation of Female Leadership in Regional, State, and Local Library Associations, 1876-1923," *Library Quarterly* 44 (April, 1974):133-41.

33. Wetherby, p. 1.

34. Ibid., p. 2.

35. Anita R. Schiller, "The Disadvantaged Majority: Women Employed in Libraries," *American Libraries* 1 (April, 1970):345-49.

36. This organization grew out of the National Women's Liberation Front for Librarians, which was formed in 1969.

37. The next issue was planned for January 1976.

38. *Exploitation from 9 to 5: Report of the Twentieth Century Fund Task Force on Women and Employment* (Lexington, MA: Lexington Books, 1975), p. 17.

39. "Union Women," *Booklegger* 1 (March-May, 1974):21-24.

40. Ibid., p. 23.

41. Wendy De Fichy, "Affirmative Action: Equal Opportunity for Women in Library Management," *College and Research Libraries* 34 (May, 1973):198.

42. "Invisible Women: The Children's Librarian in America," *Library Journal* 98 (January 15, 1973):213.

43. Ibid., p. 217.

44. Dee Garrison. "The Tender Technicians: The Feminization of Public Librarianship, 1876-1905," *Journal of Social History* 6 (Winter, 1972-73):133.

45. Ibid., p. 146.

46. David L. Lee and Janet E. Hall, "Female Library Science Students and the Occupational Stereotype: Fact or Fiction?" *College and Research Libraries* 34 (September, 1973):245-67.

47. Ibid., p. 267.

48. Susanne Patterson Wahba, "Job Satisfaction of Librarians: A Comparison between Men and Women," *College and Research Libraries* 36 (January, 1975):45-51.

49. *Library Journal* 96 (September 1, 1971):2597.

50. Ibid., p. 2599.

51. Helen W. Tuttle, "Women in Academic Libraries," *Library Journal* 96 (September 1, 1971):2595.

52. Mary S. Wood, "Sex Discrimination: The Question of Valid Grounds," *Protean* 1 (December, 1971):38.

53. James W. Grimm and Robert N. Stern, "Sex Roles and Internal Labor Market Structures: The 'Female' Semi-Professions," *Social Problems* 21 (June, 1974):704.

Towards a Feminist Profession

by Kathleen Weibel

Redefinition of the role and position of women in society has again become a major social movement. Parallelling the first wave of feminism which culminated in the right to vote, the "women's movement" has made its way from the organization of a small number of middle-class women to a broad based movement of women working in homes, industry and offices, gay women, single parents, and others. Their rejection of traditional social, sexual, and economic dependencies has already made an impact on individuals, both male and female, and on the institutions of society. The future of this movement ranges from potentially revolutionary to mildly reformist, with the ever-present danger that a male dominated power structure may become female controlled but equally oppressive. The direction of the women's movement will not evolve in a vacuum; a host of factors will help shape it, including the condition of the economy, racism, and scientific discoveries. With this in mind, then, what is the impact of the women's movement on librarianship?

One might expect it to be considerable. Librarianship as a profession is 84 percent female (unless otherwise noted all figures are taken from the U.S. Bureau of Labor Statistics' *Library Manpower*).[1] If statistics were available on all those employed by libraries, the percentage of females would most probably be higher. To varying degrees, issues of the women's movement such as child care, role definition, equal pay and opportunity have become concerns of the institutions which define libraries: schools, colleges and universities, business, government, etc., as well as concerns of the constituencies served by these libraries. Executive orders and legislation on equal pay and opportunity have also had a direct impact on a number of libraries, including the Library of Congress.

On the other hand, libraries have not been noted for their quick institutional response to social movements. Within the profession itself, organized activity on the part of women came a bit later than in other professional or academic groups, including those such as nursing also dominated in number by women. Organized participation in the overall women's movement has not yet developed as a vigorous concern of the profession. No library defined group, for example, is listed among the 75 diverse organizations (American Nurses Association, National Gay Task Force, Hadassah, etc.) contributing to the creation of the U.S. National Women's Agenda.[2]

While discussion of women in librarianship and action on the issues raised by women have increased greatly in the last five years, knowledge of the status of women librarians and their impact on library service is still limited to scattered data and research, and opinion pieces such as this. Anita Schiller has culled a description of female librarians from the literature which most librarians can corroborate from individual experience: women do not predominate, in top administrative positions, in large libraries, or in the "status" branches of the profession. The salaries of women are generally lower than those of men, and the average salaries of the profession are generally lower than those of similar male dominated professions.[3] The role of women in the initial development of the field is currently being explored by Garrison, among others. Schiller points out that the profession has not considered women an appropriate concern for a directed research effort since 1904.

It is the purpose of this article to explore the future impact of the women's movement on librarianship with the year 2000 the upward boundary. Anyone reading the projections of futurists written as recently as five years ago knows the pitfalls of this type of forecast (since cliches about our rapidly changing society are all too true). Our limited knowledge of the position of women in librarianship and the factors determining it, coupled with the fluctuation and conflict within the women's movement, and the potential for backlash against women's liberation, complicate the precariousness of such predictions. But, since problems, trends, and questions can be identified and discussion generated from futuristic musings, I'm willing to take on the role of seer.

The women's movement has effected librarianship primarily in matters relating to employment. The affect on services and the nature of the profession is more subtle, if it yet exists. Certainly this effect is more difficult to observe and measure than the more visible discrimination suits, for example, although the impact of such actions is also difficult to determine. Assuming that the women's movement continues at least at its current strength, its impact could be felt by librarianship in three general modes: 1) as *a women's profession* in which females make up the majority of the work force; 2) as *a feminized profession* with the "negative" connotations of characteristics labeled female, such as passivity, emotionalism, and intuitiveness; 3) and as *a feminist profession* operating on a feminist value system wherein traditional roles based on sex and power are no longer extant and life choices and ability determine functions. Of the three areas, the last is the most speculative, but the most far-reaching in its implications.

Librarianship as a woman's profession has received more attention in the literature and limited data gathering than the other two. The problems of a feminized profession have also been discussed directly and in the many considerations of the profession's *image*. Little research has been done in this area. Librarianship as a feminist profession has received the least consideration although the newly formed Woman Library Workers seems to be attempting to grapple with it, as a "growing sisterhood of non-submissive, life affirming women who are committed to action programs in democratically run libraries."[4]

A WOMEN'S PROFESSION

Once fields become established as men's or women's professions they are very hard to change.

[Anita Schiller][5]

Librarianship will continue to include enough women to remain a women's profession during the next 25 years. Whether the percentage of women will equal or continue to surpass the percentage of men depends on a number of factors. Although men have been attracted to librarianship in growing numbers in recent years, a proportionate increase in the number of women entering the field has caused the percentage of females to drop only a few points. The ratio of men to women in the under 45 age group is higher, however, than in the total profession. As of this writing, 44 percent of all employed librarians are age 45 and over. Almost half the women in the profession are in this age group and are likely to retire during the next 25 years. The ratio of male to female librarians replacing this 44 percent of the profession, and in the under 45 age group now practicing, will determine the sex characteristic of the profession in the year 2000.

What the influence of the contracting job market on the entrance of men and women into the profession will be, is difficult to say. Fields such as engineering and law, which had previously not been overly receptive to women, are now actively recruiting and may very well draw women away from the traditional women's fields. Consideration of desexualization of role may also make men feel freer to enter the women's professions.

At the same time that librarianship is placing a growing emphasis on the hard sciences as undergraduate preparation, fields traditionally dominated by men, business, industry, and academe, actively seek women with these qualifications to meet affirmative action quotas. Librarianship may not be able to compete for these women as a career option, meaning that entrants into the profession with scientific preparation are even more likely to be men.

The question of people with advanced academic qualifications in other professions, the humanities, and social sciences, moving into librarianship due to job shortages in their own fields will probably have an influence, but it is difficult to suggest a direction in terms of sex in these fields. Interest in part-time work and job sharing currently voiced by both men and women, but usually associated with women, will influence the availability of positions and qualified women to fill them. The effect of re-entrants into the profession, who will probably be women, and drop-outs who may be either male or female, must also be considered. A safe projection, then, is that librarianship will continue to be a women's profession although the percentage of women will drop below the present 84 percent mark.

Librarianship as a whole may remain a women's profession in 2000, but men may very well predominate in certain types of libraries, particularly academic where they now account for 44 percent of the professionals. Special and public libraries will also reflect a change in the male:female ratio, with special libraries possibly swinging toward balanced employment of men and women. Even in school libraries, where women dominate in numbers greater than their percentage of the total profession, men may make considerable inroads. Projection by type of library must take into account growth possibilities in each type. Enrollments in elementary and high schools, for example, are expected to pick up during the 1980s and to drop in higher academic institutions during this period. Whether more men or women will move into the school library field where jobs should be more plentiful is an open question.

Staffing of the various library functions will also reflect the change in the numbers of men in the profession. In the case of administration, the push towards equal opportunity may counterbalance the projected increase in the number of males. Certainly it has already been an acknowledged factor in restructuring of procedures used to fill positions and in the actual filling of some jobs. It is safe to say that we will probably see more women administrators in the traditionally male dominated top positions in the larger, more prestigious libraries. Whether women will retain their rapidly diminishing predominance as administrators of the smaller institutions, particularly public libraries, is more questionable. These institutions are not as visible, the pressures in them less, and possibilities for reaction against the historical dominance of women greater.

At the same time that women have been pushing for admittance to higher positions, they have also sought the development of lateral career structures. Women who do not want to be administrators are actively seeking personal and financial recognition of their contribution to the profession. Revised career structures would also benefit those men who do not wish to take the administrative route which they are sometimes unwillingly nudged into. The plight of the excellent reference librarian, for example, forced into administration to advance his or her career has been a concern of the profession long before the women's movement. This additional impetus should speed the process. It may have a positive effect on services, as well as influence the balance of male:female administrators.

A gender breakdown of aspects of librarianship other than administration is not readily available (a telling fact in itself). Since the profession is 84 percent female and more males than females hold the bulk of administrative positions, one might conclude that the technical support and reader services are composed of women. There is a general impression that men may be more populous in the automation and information science areas of the field than in reader services. We just don't know. In public and school library youth services, an area most would agree is truly dominated by women, and where other factors, such as the long proposed merger of the two institutions' services and the growing acceptance of men working with children are known, questions can be raised. What will be the scope of opportunity for men and women in this service? Will men be more sought after than women? Otherwise, projection beyond a statement that change will occur because of the adjustments in the sexual makeup of the profession as a whole is not possible.

A FEMINIZED PROFESSION

I hope you won't repeat that quote from Justin Winsor again!
[A Feminist Librarian Friend]

"That quote" refers to Winsor's 1878 summary of the value of women in librarianship as cheap well-educated labor with the additional service, softening, and housekeeping instincts needed in the profession[6] and characterizes much of the sentimental comment on women in library literature. Sentimentality is not the only response to women. An anti-feminine bias on the part of both men and women also exists and manifests itself in characterizations of niggling spinsters, uncommitted mothers, and the sheer number of women in the profession as a weakness. In fact much of the literature of women in librarianship treats feminine dominance as a problem: the problem of a feminized profession.

An acceptance and even affinity for bureaucratic and hierarchical structures, humanitarian service rooted in the emotions, task rather than intellectual orientation, and compliance are the hallmarks of the feminized professions and are the subject of innumerable articles in the literature of librarianship. Whether one attributes these characteristics to the dominance of women alone, not at all, or in combination with other factors such as association with the educational, cultural, and nonprofit segments of society, these do seem to be the acknowledged generalizations about the profession and are voiced both within and outside of librarianship. Simpson and Simpson cataloged these and related tendencies and characteristics of feminized or semi-professions and concluded in the late sixties that "so long as our family system and the prevailing attitudes of men and women about feminine roles remain essentially as they are now, this basic situation seems unlikely to change."[7]

The women's movement, however, is challenging prevailing attitudes toward female and male roles. In addition, the literature concerning sex differentiation indicates socialized and not innate origins for the roles and characteristics identified by Simpson and Simpson and seen in library literature.[8]

Librarians concerned with the sexism of children's materials acknowledged the importance of socialization to the challenges of the women's movement. But what of the adults who inhabit Libraryland? Library literature offers no response. To project a defeminized profession it is necessary to move outside librarianship—toward those who are attempting to define feminist, not feminized, values and structures.

Women are seeking to define themselves through control of their bodies, equality in their relationships, and freedom of choice in their careers. Participatory rather than hierarchical structures, the development of the individual as well as of the collective movement, and, responsibility rather than dependence are goals of the women's movement. Rather than replacing passive with aggressive behavior, new models such as assertiveness are being explored. As women pursue these and other changes it seems reasonable to expect that their work styles will reflect them.

Activity on the part of women librarians for their own liberation as women and as librarians has been growing. There is a proliferation of their literature, for example, *Women Library Workers* and *Emergency Librarian,* as well as an increase in the number of articles elsewhere. They are organizing new professional associations or groups within existing organizations such as the SRRT Women's Task Force. There is regional and local organizing of library women in Massachusetts, Chicago, California, New York and Connecticut. For those librarians active in or supportive of the women's movement, and this includes men as well as women, the characteristics of a feminized profession are in opposition to their commitments. These commitments require an assertive response to client information needs, practiced in an open flexible institution.

At the same time library literature indicates an increasing interest in nonhierarchical or collegial management styles, more autonomous practice of the profession, and flexible approaches to career ladders. If the increase in library science doctorates is any indication of an attempt to build a more knowledgeable base from which to design services, the profession is also moving away from its emotionalistic roots. Convergence of these with the similar interests of the library women's movement should strengthen librarianship so that the image can be overcome and the profession is no longer "feminized" in the pejorative sense.

The impact of women's challenge to traditional male and female roles in the next quarter century will also help shape the character and values of the men and women who choose to enter the profession. The direction and degree of their role redefinition will mirror the changing agenda and influence of the women's movement. Librarianship's own redirection will influence the values and characteristics of those who choose to enter the field. If the profession does not keep pace with the challenges of the women's movement and its own innovators, it may remain a feminized profession in the worst sense of the term, no matter whether males or females dominate in the year 2000.

A FEMINIST PROFESSION

> *I hate not men but what it is men do in this culture, or how the system of sexism, power dominance and competition is the enemy—not people, but how men, still created that system and preserve it and reap concrete benefits from it.*
> [Robin Morgan, *Monster,* p. 83.]

Discussion of librarianship as a feminist profession is highly speculative. Consideration of the potentials of feminist values is essential to making the women's movement more than just a numbers game. The purpose of the women's movement is not more women administrators, male children's librarians, or clerk typists. These are manifestations of the central issue: the development of role-free human beings, they are not ends in themselves.

A feminism built on humanitarian values and advocacy of women's full participation in political, social, and economic spheres shares a call for the redistribution of power with other social movements. Feminism further calls for a transformation of our concepts of power: compassion and support rather than aggression and dominance. As a value system as well as a social movement, feminism demands a change in basic assumptions as well as an alteration in life style. While feminism is associated with the women's movement, belief in and actualization of its value system are not confined to women. Men may have a limited role in the women's movement, but they have a full role in the struggle for human freedom which is here labeled feminism. How they choose to develop that role is up to them as individuals and as a social grouping.

The potential for feminist librarianship lies in the men and women of the profession who hold feminist values. Their ability to implement the changes in the assumptions of the profession and to build new approaches is unknown. Brief examination of library employment and services through the focus of feminism is the only projection possible.

If librarianship accepted the feminist values of eliminating the dominant or single breadwinner per living unit and encouraged more people to work while balancing time for personal and community activities, the profession would be characterized by job sharing, serial, and part-time work arrangements. Individuals choosing these work styles would have the same benefits and career options as those who choose full-time work. Continuing education not confined to job related subjects will be available for all levels of employees with adequate counseling time and general encouragement provided. Acceptance of the potential for individual contribution should result in creative job design possibly crossing current professional/nonprofessional lines as well as participatory decision-making. Equal pay for equal work is, of course, a given, as are just payment for ability and effort accompanied by adjustment based on need.

Implementation of feminist rooted library services would be based on a concept of equal services for all users: SDI for children as well as scientists. Free access to information will continue as a central tenet of librarianship in the year 2000. However, demystification of information and advocacy will be given equal billing. Rather than attempting to build institutional empires, libraries will act as catalysts in the larger communication environment. Service plans will be flexible and designed with user input and evaluation. Because feminist values imply a reworking of national priorities, more financial support will be available for institutions such as libraries, if they respond to needs in a feminist and humanist mode.

These employment and service scenarios drawn for feminist librarianship are but one possibility on a wide spectrum of potential. The year 2000 could just as readily see us only inches ahead of our present view of the profession or even behind it. Women and the women's movement are *not* meant to be portrayed as saviors of humankind nor of librarianship. A process of defining and working towards a realization of feminist values, however, is relevant and possible.

That spectre of a truncated women's movement, bereft of feminism, must also be raised. Freedom of choice for women, at the expense of the caring, warmth, and sensitivity to others so often associated with them, may be empty. In the thrust to redefine male and female roles, women must not become men; nor can men be permitted the continued dehumanization of their role.

For librarianship, triumph of the women's movement without feminist values may result in meaningless proliferation of networks, self-perpetuating institutions, service built on expediency, and a lowering of capacity to meet the user needs to a level below that of its worst days as a "feminized" profession.

REFERENCES

1. U.S. Department of Labor, Bureau of Labor Statistics. *Library Manpower: a Study of Demand and Supply.* Washington, D.C.: U.S. Government Printing Office, 1975.

2. Meyerson, Bess. "A Call to Action: The National Women's Agenda," *Redbook,* (November, 1975), p. 71-75.

3. Schiller, Anita R. "Women in Librarianship." In Voigt, Melvin, ed., *Advances in Librarianship,* v. 4. (New York: Academic Pr., 1974).

4. *Women Library Workers.* Special issue. September 1975, p. 6.

5. Schiller, Anita R. "The Status of Women." In Sellen, Betty-Carol and Joan Marshall, eds., *Women in a Women's Profession: Strategies.* Proceedings of the Preconference on the Status of Women in Librarianship sponsored by the American Library Association, Social Responsibilities Round Table, Task Force on the Status of Women: Douglass College, Rutgers Univ., July 1974.

6. Conference of Librarians (1878). "Transactions and Proceedings of the Conference of Librarians held in London. October 1877." Trübner, London.

7. Simpson, Richard L. and Ida Harper Simpson. "Women and Bureaucracy in the Semi-Professions." In Etzioni, Amitai, ed., *The Semi-Professions and Their Organization.* The Free Pr., 1969.

8. Maccoby, Eleanor E. and Carol N. Jacklin. *The Psychology of Sex Differences.* (Stanford, CA: Stanford Univ. Pr., 1974).

9. Morgan, Robin. *Monster.* (New York: Random House, 1972).

PART

VI

BIBLIOGRAPHY

Introduction

This annotated bibliography includes print and nonprint materials on the role of women in librarianship from 1876-1976. Coverage focuses on women in the library profession in English-speaking countries, although the scope of the bibliography is international.

Materials are included if they contribute to an understanding of the role of women in librarianship. Biographical items are not included unless they are collective biographies discussing women in a context larger than their own careers. Materials on such issues as the image of librarians, or on groups of library workers, such as library assistants who are primarily women, are included only if they specifically address their topic as a woman-related issue.

The bibliography was compiled by searching the "Women Librarians" section in *Cannons Bibliography of Library Economy,* which covers the literature of librarianship from 1876-1920; the sections on "Librarians," "Librarianship," "Librarianship as a Career," "Men Librarians," and "Women Librarians" in *Library Literature* which covers the literature written from 1920 to the present. Bibliographies on women in librarianship, including: 1) the American Library Association Social Responsibilities Round Table Task Force on Women bibliography, "Women in Librarianship, 1892-1976"; 2) bibliographies appended to major works on women in librarianship such as Dee Garrison's "The Tender Technicians" (1972-73); and 3) indexes to major library journals of Great Britain and the United States such as the *Library Association Record* and *Library Journal* were also searched. Seminal works in librarianship such as the Williamson Report (1923-01) were also perused for comments and discussions pertinent to the topic.

ORGANIZATION BY DATE

Arrangement of the bibliography is chronological by publication date of the material cited. Citations with the same date of publication are arranged alphabetically by author. Within each year, those publications with the year as the only date precede those which are dated by month. Materials with seasonal publication dates fall in this order: Spring before March; Summer before June; Fall before September; and Winter before December. Materials with a publication date of more than one month (e.g., March/April) are found after the first month of that date, for example:

1940-07 Lyle, G.R. "They Have Made Their Mark." *Library Journal* 65 (November 15, 1940):947-950.

An examination of the 187 librarians listed in the 1940-41 edition of *Who's Who in America* who are still active in the profession. Of the total 235 librarians listed forty-four were women. The analysis of the 187 is not broken down by sex although it is noted that seventeen of the women included hid their age by omitting birthdays and college graduations.

1941-01   Freer, P. "The Profession in South Africa." *Ontario Library Review* 25 (February 1941):62-64.

Reprint of [1940-05].

1941-02   Liddle, H. "Resigned on Marriage." *Library Assistant* 34 (April 1941):67-68.

Women do not become unfit for work when married, so they should not be forced to resign.

1941-03   Matthews, Mrs. R.E.S. "Married Women Librarians." *Library Journal* 66 (August 1941):650-651.

Discusses how married women suffer much more discrimination than single women in all fields.

1943-01   "Letter to the Editor." *Library World* 46 (December 1943):84.

An opinion that women are being held in lower positions by male supervisors.

IDENTIFICATION NUMBERS AND LETTERS

An identification number composed of the year of publication and sequence within that year has been assigned to each item with the exceptions of letters in response to articles, reviews, and editorial replies. These are indented and entered below the item to which they pertain first by date and then alphabetically by author. Where letters generate other letters additional sequences are identified by further indentation and entered below the letters to which they refer, for example:

†1949-03   Munn, R. "It's a Mistake to Recruit Men." *Library Journal* 74 (November 1, 1949):1639-1640.

Opposes recruiting more "average run-of-the-mine [men] simply to get men . . . It will operate against the profession, both by filling it with men of mediocre caliber and by discouraging the entrance of superior women." Because of the low salaries, librarianship will remain a woman's profession and should be kept attractive to capable women.

> **Letters:**   McCann, E. "Let Them Come In." *Library Journal* 74 (December 1, 1949):1802.
>
> Suggests concentrating on making the librarian's work clear to the public so that more capable men and women will be drawn to the profession. More men may be needed in the profession because "any group where a man is out-numbered 250 to 1 is not going to permit him to make a proper adjustment to the task at hand."
>
> Brown, T. A. "Recruiting Men." *Library Journal* 74 (December 15, 1949):1842.
>
> Verse parody of Munn's argument.
>
> Obler, [Sic] E.M. "Men Librarians." *Library Journal* 75 (January 15, 1950):66; 98.
>
> Argues that Munn's view that the present economic status and position of librarians will not improve is a counsel of despair. Claims that men make better administrators than women because of various physiological and psychological reasons.

Letter: Heathcote, L.M. "Men Librarians." *Library Journal* 75 (April 1, 1950):518; 520.

Claims that women resent inferior type of man entering profession, not men as such. Questions Obler's statements on men and women as administrators.

McDonough, E. "Men Librarians." *Library Journal* 75 (March 15, 1950):422; 478.

Argues that delimitation of field into "women's work" and "men's work" is unfortunate, causing suspicion and mistrust.

ENTIRE ISSUES DEVOTED TO WOMEN

Newsletters on women in librarianship are included, but individual issues were not analyzed, as indexes to these newsletters have been or will be prepared. [See 1923-01 for example.]

Entire issues of journals, books, or proceedings of conferences devoted to women in librarianship have an identification number which is shared by all articles or papers. Articles or papers are further distinguished by a letter notation which also shows this relationship, as in:

1974-12 "Women's Issue." *Librarians for Social Change* 5 (n.d.).

Entire issue of journal edited by Librarians for Social Change Feminist Group. Includes articles and bibliographies on sexism in children's literature, library service to women, women's libraries in the U.S. and Britain, sexism in classification and in language, and guides to sources of information on women's rights in Britain.

1974-12A "Editorial." *Librarians for Social Change* 5 (n.d.):3.

Explains rationale for a Feminist Group in the British organization, Librarians for Social Change. Women "usually do get equal pay, but . . . usually *don't* get the jobs!" This may be because of women's social conditioning and multiple roles as well as discrimination. The Feminist Group and this issue of *Librarians for Social Change* hope to change the "conditioning that turns us into sterile, narrow-minded bosses and slaves instead of the free and loving humans we could be."

1974-12B Alexander, R. "De-Manning in Cuba." *Librarians for Social Change* 5 (n.d.):8.

Comments on the decision of the Cuban government to declare over thirty occupations, including librarianship, "women's work" because of the need for more men for hard physical labor in the sugar cane fields. Author feels this is counter to statements by Fidel Castro and a form of counter-revolutionary oppression.

1974-12C "Female Library Staffs — An Opinion From the Opposite Sex." *Librarians for Social Change* 5 (n.d.):9-12.

Review of and commentary on an article which appeared in *Toshokan Zasshi* on the male librarian's opinion of the increasing number of women librarians in Japanese libraries [1973-25D]. Summary indicates that the author is of two minds: wishing women to develop their capacities so that they may have equal opportunity to gain administrative posts (at present only one woman out of 15 is promoted to a responsible position), but also somewhat sad to see male domination decline. Includes results from a January 1973 survey of women members of the Japanese Library Association which indicated most women are in reader's or children's services.

SPECIAL SYMBOLS

Asterisk (*) citations refer to items which were identified but which could not be obtained for examination. No annotations accompany these citations. Dagger (†) designates articles which may be found in the anthology portion of this book. Whenever possible reprints have been listed as individual citations for ease in procuring the materials, but the annotations have not been repeated. Within annotations previous citations are referred to by identification number where knowledge of these materials will clarify the user's understanding of the material at hand. Author and subject indexes keyed to identification numbers are provided.

1876-1879

†**1876-01**   Bixby, Mrs. A.F. and Howell, Mrs. A. *Historical Sketches of the Ladies' Library Associations of the State of Michigan.* Adrian, Michigan: Times and Expositer Steam Print, 1876.

At the regular monthly meeting of the Adrian Ladies' Library Association held in April, 1875, the Association decided that "the work accomplished by the women of Michigan in the accumulation of libraries is a noble one, well worthy of honorable mention this centennial year" and that communication should be sent to the several Ladies' Associations of Michigan asking "unity of action in the preparation of a volume containing the history of library work, to be presented to the Women's Department at the International Centennial Exhibition." Twenty-six associations responded with histories of their efforts.

1876-02   U.S. Bureau of Education. *Public Libraries in the United States. Part I: Special Report.* Washington, DC: Government Printing Office, 1876.

Women are mentioned briefly throughout the report, the basic source on libraries for this period. For example, F.B. Perkins comments that women are suited to the duties of a library assistant but frequently do not get along together as well as men (p. 430).

1876-03   "Editorial." *Library Journal* 1 (November 30, 1876):90.

In commenting on the first meeting of the ALA, the presence of women is noted: "The minority of ladies was a welcome and suggestive feature, for the library field offers one of the most promising solutions of the difficult question of woman's opportunities for worldly work: they were the best of listeners, and occasionally would modestly take advantage of gallant voices, like Mr. Smith's, to ask a question or offer a suggestion."

***1877-01**   Hanaford, P.A. *Women of the Century.* Boston: B.B. Russell, 1877.

1877-02   "Librarians in Congress." *London Times* (October 6, 1877):10.

Report of the Librarians' Conference [1878-01] includes Lloyd P. Smith's and Justin Winsor's remarks on the employment of women in American libraries.

†**1878-01**   *Transactions and Proceedings of the Conference of Librarians Held in London.* October, 1877. London: Chiswick Press, 1878:177.

Comments by Lloyd P. Smith, Justin Winsor, and William Frederick Poole on the role, status and pay of women employed in American libraries.

1878-02   "Proceedings of the Conference of Librarians, London, October 2-5, 1877: Sixth Setting: The Executives of a Library—Their Qualifications, Functions, Vacation and Salaries." *Library Journal* 2 (January-February 1878):280-282.

Comments by Lloyd P. Smith, Justin Winsor, and William Frederick Poole on the role, status and pay of women employees in American libraries are included in the discussion (p. 280-281). Also in [1878-01].

1878-03   Poole, W.F. "Lady Librarians and Poole's Index." *Library Journal* 3 (May 1878):127.

Comments on excellent work done on the index by women.

1878-04   "Ladies as Librarians." *The Young Ladies Journal* 15 (October 1878):685.

Number 95 in a series on "Women's Domestic, Useful and Lucrative Employments," the article proposes librarianship as a suitable field for British women because they can live on low salaries; also the experience in America indicates that women make capable library assistants.

1879-01   "The Success of the Conference." *Library Journal* 4 (July-August 1879):278

Overview of the 1879 American Library Association conference which includes the comment, "much would remain unsaid without reference to the ladies whose presence at this Conference, in force, sets an example that will not be lost at future gatherings" (p. 278).

1879-02   Poole, W.F. "Proceedings of the American Library Association, Boston - 1879: Committee on Poole's Index." *Library Journal* 4 (July-August 1879):299.

"While all have done their work well, it is due to the ladies, who have taken their share of indexing, that we should state that theirs is among the best of the work that has been sent in, the neatest in penmanship, the most accurate in details and in comformity to the Committee rules and requiring the least revision."

1879-03   "Employment of Young Women in Free Public Libraries." *Library Journal* 4 (November 1879):410.

Report of Thomas Baker's address [1880-01] to the Library Association's second annual meeting held in Manchester, the city whose public library was the first in Great Britain to hire women.

1880-1889

†**1880-01**   Baker, T. "The Employment of Young Women as Assistants in Free Public Libraries." In *Transactions and Proceedings of the Second Annual Meeting of the Library Association of the United Kingdom Held at Manchester, September 23, 24, and 25, 1879.* London: Chiswick Press, 1880:32-3; 95; 122.

Recounts the experiences of the Manchester Public Library, the first British public library to hire women library assistants. In discussion (p. 95) Rev. J.M. Guilding cites a successful woman librarian and "thoroughly endorses" Thomas Baker's paper. Prof. Leopold Seligmann notes that the question is closely connected with the rights of women and that the Americans had brought women librarians to the conference. "The true criterion was how far a lady librarian could promote the true objects of a library and not the fact that they could be got for smaller salaries than men." Hiring of women is also noted in a report of a visit to Manchester libraries (p. 122).

1880-02   "Statistical Report on the Public Free Libraries of the United Kingdom." (Appendix II - I) In *Transactions and Proceedings of the Second Annual Meeting of the Library Association of the United Kingdom Held at Manchester, September 23, 24, and 25, 1879.* London: Chiswick Press, 1880: Appendix following p. 138.

Statistical data include responses to question 16: "Are female assistants employed? If so, how many, and at what wages?" Provides an overview of the employment of women in 1878.

1880-03   "A Lady Has Been Appointed to the Post." *Library Journal* 5 (January 1880):26.

News item on the appointment of a woman to the Free Library of Blackpool, Lancashire.

1880-04   "Report of the Library Association's December Monthly Meeting" *Library Journal* 5 (January 1880):13-14.

Summarizes Mr. C. Walford's "Talk About American Libraries and Librarians" in which Walford comments on the skill of women working in Boston libraries and the state of their health (p. 14).

1882-01   Tedder, H.R. "Librarianship as a Profession: Women as Librarians." In *Transactions and Proceedings of the Library Association of the United Kingdom Fifth Annual Meeting Cambridge 1882.* London: The Library Association, 1882:171-172.

In the context of a larger article on the duties of the librarian the author includes a section supporting the employment of women. Though he includes a reiteration of Justin Winsor's comments [1878-01] on women as cheap labor he notes, "I hope it may not be understood that the sole reason for advocating librarianship as a field for the employment of women is that they fill subordinate positions for less money than men."

1883-01   "The New York Free Circulating Library." *Library Journal* 8 (March-April 1883):47-8; 53.

Report of a plan to raise funds to employ women in the library.

1886-01   Dewey, M. *Librarianship as a Profession for College Bred Women.* Boston: Library Bureau, 1886.

Address delivered before the Association of Collegiate Alumnae. Notes that college bred women are preferred at the Library School of Columbia College because they are the best material in the country, have a wide culture and broad views, have proven themselves in advanced work, and do better in library skills than those without college.

1886-02   Dewey, M. "Library Work vs. the Library Profession." *Library Notes* 1 (June 1886):50-51.

Differentiates between two types of library work (routine and moral) and notes that there will always be women fond of books to do the routine work as the supply of help at low prices will always exceed the demand.

1886-03   "Ladies in Libraries" *Library Journal* 11 (October 1886):420.

Comments, reprinted from the *London Saturday Review,* on the problems for serious scholars using the British Museum reading room, chief of which is the presence of women. Author concludes that some women are also serious scholars and that separate facilities for men could not solve the problem of distractions in the reading room.

†1886-04   Dewey, M. "Women in Libraries: How They Are Handicapped." *Library Notes* 1 (October 1886):89-92.

Justifies lower pay for women (even though they do the same work as men) on grounds of poor health, weakness, lack of business and executive training, lack of permanence in plans and considerations given to women because they are physically less able to help out in emergencies. Final line: "There are many uses for which a stout corduroy is really worth more than the finest silk." Originally read at the Association of Collegiate Alumnae [1886-01].

1887-01   "Women as State Librarians." *Library Journal* 12 (May 1887): 195-196.

A list of women state librarians in ten states and territories.

1887-02   Schwartz, J. "Three Little Maids from the Library School." *Library Journal* 12 (November 1887):511.

A parody of Gilbert and Sullivan, written by the "Poet-Laureate of the *Library Journal,*" dedicated, by permission, to Melvil Dewey.

1889-01   Black C.E. "New Career for Women: Librarians." (London) *The Queen* (February 23, 1889):235.

Notes that there are one or two libraries in which women are employed and since it seems likely that they will be employed in free libraries in the future a description of a librarian's work might be interesting for women.

*1889-02   "Female Library Assistants." *New Orleans Times-Democrat* (March 24, 1889).

1889-03   "Female Library Assistants." *Library Journal* 14 (April 1889):128.

Reprint of an article [1889-02] praising the work of several clerical assistants in the Howard Memorial Library.

1890-1899

1890-01   James, M.S.R. "People's Palace Library." *The Library* 2: (1890): 341-351.

A report of the People's Palace exhibition library to which women were appointed as librarians. James comments that women do not wish to oust men from their positions (p. 342).

1890-02   "Proceedings of the American Library Association, Fabyans, White Mountains, NH - 1890: Trustees Section." *Library Journal* 15 (December 1890):135-136.

P.T. Sexton, chairman of the section, congratulates the "one noble woman" trustee in attendance and goes on to note, "If I could single out any one ground of encouragement for the hope which this association gives humanity, it is based upon the fact that so large a number of the librarians of the country are women." He also acknowledges women as influential in the lives of successful men and notes that when men take on the superior characteristics of women "the millenium will have dawned."

1891-01   "Proceedings of the American Library Association, San Francisco - 1891: Speeches at the Banquet at the Palace Hotel." *Library Journal* 16 (December 1891):140-148.

Comments on the role of women in the Midwest as opposed to California and on the fact that women were not usually present at similar California gatherings. In a toast to the ladies their role as culture keepers and nurturers is appreciated.

1891-02   Hewins, C.M. "Library Work for Women: Some Practical Suggestions on the Subject." *Library Journal* 16 (September 1891):273-274.

The requirements for library work and alternative preparations for a library career are described in this article reprinted from the *Hartford Courant.* "Those who read only novels or seek easy work for a few hours a day need not apply."

1891-03   Clifford, L.M. "Women As Librarians." *Monthly Packet* (1 or 2?) (1891 or 1892?):42-46.

Sees Walter Besant (who suggested ladies as librarians at the People's Palace as "opening out a wide field for women,") describes the duties of a librarian as something a woman can manage quietly and comfortably.

1892-01   James, M.S.R. "Women Librarians." *The Library* 4 (1892): 217-224.

James reiterates the role of women in British Libraries up to 1892 and cites the lack of business training as a major reason women have not advanced. Comments on the fact that at the ALA conferences more women than men may attend, while at the Library Association women are in a "hopeless minority."

†1892-02   "Proceedings of the 14th American Library Association Conference, Lakewood-1892: The Woman's Meeting." *Library Journal* 17 (August 1892):89-94.

Report of the first meeting of a proposed women's section.

Letter: Kelso, T. "Woman's Section of the ALA." *Library Journal* 17 (November 1892):444.

Protests the establishment of a separate women's section because standards should not be based on sex. "There is but one standard of management for a live business and sex has nothing to do with that standard."

†1892-02A   Cutler, M.S. "What a Woman Librarian Earns." *Library Journal* 17 (August 1892):89-91.

Comments on what a female librarian does vs. what she is paid, listing some reasons for the low pay. Ends with remarks on what she is to do to maintain and improve her position.

†1892-02B   Sargent, M.E. "Woman's Position in Library Service." *Library Journal* 17 (August 1892):92-94.

Attacks the theory that men make better head librarians than women.

*1892-03   James, M.S.R. "Women as Librarians." *Philadelphia Press* (November 27, 1892).

1892-04   James, M.S.R. "Women Librarians." *Review of Reviews* 6 (December 1892.):579.

A portrait of the author and excerpts of her paper published in *The Library* [1892-01].

1893-01   Cowell, P. *Public Library Staffs.* Library Association Series, No. 3. London: Library Association, 1893:13-14.

Questions why women in Britain have not done as well as librarians in America. Author notes, "If a young woman on her appointment to a library could bring herself to put all thoughts of marriage in the background," she might gain an honorable reputation in librarianship.

1893-02   James, M.S.R. "American Women as Librarians." *The Library* 5 (1893):270-274.

A report on the status, education and pay of American women librarians gleaned from observation and conversation. Charges of women's ill health are refuted.

1893-03   James, M.S.R. "Women Librarians" *Library Journal* 18 (May, 1893):146-148.

Slightly condensed version of an article published in *The Library* [1892-01].

*1893-04   "Interview with M.S.R. James." *Young Woman* (September 1893).

1894-01   Fletcher, W.T. *Public Libraries in America.* Boston: Roberts Brothers, 1894.

Librarianship is cited as a fine field for women's work as women are showing marked abilities especially in the "missionary" features of public library work (p. 84-85). Statistics which list the 100 largest libraries show 50% are run by women, but a close examination of library size show that men run the larger libraries (50,000+ volumes), while women directors are concentrated in libraries with 10-20,000 volumes (p. 148-151).

†**1894-02**   Richardson, Miss. "Librarianship as a Profession for Women."
The Library 6 (1894):137-142.

Argues that women are suited to library work. Hindrances to their entrance and advancement in British librarianship may stem from their socialization and the lack of a library school which could put them on an equal educational footing with men.

***1894-03**   "Library Work for Women." (Rhode Island) *Providence Journal*
(January 10, 1894).

1894-04   Underhill, A. "A Plea for a Neglected Profession" *Vassar Miscellaney* (2 or 3?) (February 1894):184-188.

"Librarianship as a profession has attracted college men, but it has had few recruits from college women" because college women are not familiar with librarianship and the need for women in the profession. Library work and requirements to enter the profession are explained.

1894-05   Bateson, M. "Librarianship." Part of the series, "Professional Women on Their Professions." (London) *The Queen* (March 31, 1894):503.

Interview with the People's Palace Librarian, M.S.R. James, includes her comments on the different status of women in the U.S. and Britain.

1895-01   Bailey, N. "Indexing," *Professional Women Upon Their Professions.*
Edited by M. Bateson. London: Horace Cox, 1895:114-120.

Discusses the suitability of indexing as a profession, but notes most women lack the general knowledge required of a good indexer.

1895-02   James, M.S.R. "Librarianship." In *Professional Women Upon Their Professions.* Edited by M. Bateson. London: Horace Cox, 1895:110-115.

Reprint of an interview in *The Queen* [1894-05] in a collection of interviews on women in the professions.

1895-03   Petherbridge, Miss. "The American Library School." *The Library*
8 (1895):65-74.

Within the context of an article which gives an overview of the American Library School, several comments are made on women: 1) women, especially from Wellesley, dominate in numbers (p. 65); 2) Dewey's 1886 address [1886-01] on "Librarianship as a Profession for College Bred Women" is summarized (p. 68); 3) libraries are increasingly willing to pay men and women the same salary (p. 69); 4) exceptional women graduates such as Mary Wright Plummer and Katherine Sharp are mentioned (p. 70). Petherbridge concludes that the "new woman" claims a right to share in work and not be isolated.

1896-01   Kroeger, A.B. "Report on the Congress of Women Librarians at Atlanta." *Library Journal* 21 (December 1896):57-58.

Report of the Congress of Women Librarians held as part of the 1895 Cotton States and International Exposition. The Congress was arranged by Anne Wallace to create interest in the public library movement.

1897-01   Greenwood, T. "Salaries and Women Librarians." In *Greenwood's Library Year Book 1897: A Record of General Library Progress and Work.* London: Cassell and Co., 1897:93-94.

Greenwood comments on the low salaries of librarians and few positions available for women "against whom a dead set is made by many librarians on various ridiculous grounds . . . Altogether the outlook is not very promising for women who desire to become public librarians earning a living wage, and until a radical change occurs, it is not worth an intelligent girl's trouble to train herself for work which can hardly be said to exist."

1897-02 Omega. "Female Assistants." *The Library* 9 (1897):78-79.

Letter reviewing reasons women are not employed equally with men in British libraries. Concludes that women's lack of "business facility" and "inventive imagination" are the chief reasons they have not risen beyond the assistant level.

Letters: Iconoclast. "Female Assistants." *The Library* 9 (1897):357.

Excerpts from a letter from an anti-female librarian who notes women are so utterly devoid of business habits that they cannot stick a postage stamp of the correct value on a letter. His proof is that letters from U.S. library schools, where there are many women, are stamped incorrectly half the time.

P. "Female Assistants." *The Library* 9 (1897): 208.

Castigates Omega's assertions about women's mental inferiority and asks where do women have a chance? States that given the opportunity women will invent methods of work which do not rely solely upon mere mechanical aids for their success.

1897-03 Earle, M.B. "Women Librarians." *Independent* 49 (February 18, 1897):30.

A recruitment article which details the activities of librarians, necessary training, and the fact that women may find a place in the library profession. Remarks on salaries note: "Women do not in this as in most vocations receive the same pay as men . . . working among books is considered an attractive and 'genteel' employment; because many library trustees will take advantage of a woman's willingness to work for less than she earns when she knows her work is useful." Notes that one prominent male librarian asks women applicants if they keep their bureau drawers in order.

1897-04 Jellison, A.M. "Library Association of Central California." *Library Journal* 12 (June 1897):308.

Report of the Association's May meeting which was designated as "Ladies Night," the topic being "Women in the Service of the Public Library." Papers are listed and briefly summarized: "Woman as Trustee," "Woman at the Delivery Desk," "Woman as Benefactor," and "Women in Library Work."

1897-05 Fairchild, E.M. "Proceedings of the American Library Association, Philadelphia - 1897: Methods of Children's Library Work as Determined by the Needs of Children." *Library Journal* 22 (October 1897):23.

Notes that a children's librarian must be a woman "grown," who must take the children of the community to her heart.

1897-06 "The International Library Conference." *Public Libraries* 2 (October 1897):410-420.

Overview of the conference which includes a summary of Mathews's paper on library assistants and competitive examinations [1898-01] giving considerable attention to women in libraries (p. 414).

1898-01 Mathews, E.R.N. "Female Library Assistants and Competitive Examination." In *Transactions and Proceedings of the Second International Library Conference Held in London July 13-16, 1897.* Edinburgh: Morrison and Gibb Limited, 1898:40-43.

Provides background on the history of the employment of women in British libraries; gives a detailed account of the personnel policy developed by the Bristol Public Library for women library assistants. Discussion follows; Alderman J.W. Southern of the Manchester Public Library Committee comments favorably on the employment of women in that library and in libraries generally (p. 231).

1898-02   Rawson, H. "The Duties of Library Committees." In *Transactions and Proceedings of the Second International Library Conference Held in London July 13-16, 1897.* Edinburgh: Morrison and Gibb Limited, 1898:27.

Comments that "on our staff is the considerable number of 84 women" and that they are perfectly suitable. More women are employed in the libraries of Manchester than are engaged in all other libraries in Great Britain.

1898-03   Tedder, H.R. "The Evolution of the Public Library." In *Transactions and Proceedings of the Second International Library Conference Held in London July 13-16, 1897.* Edinburgh: Morrison and Gibb Limited, 1898:13-18.

Notes "it is a subject for congratulations that women find an increasing place among us" (p. 18).

1898-04   Sharp, K.L. "Librarianship as a Profession." *Public Libraries* 3 (January 1898):5-7.

Focuses on the qualifications of a librarian and the technical competencies needed. A rebuttal to those who see library work as not needing formal training. Need for college bred men and women is emphasized.

1898-05   Hayward, C.A. "Woman as a Cataloguer." *Public Libraries* 3 (April 1898):121-123.

Asked to speak on women as cataloguers, Hayward prefers to speak to the qualifications needed by both men and women cataloguers. She comments that the world has too long been arranged "after the fashion of a Quaker meeting - men on this side, women on that, with a dead line between added."

*1898-06   "Women's Employment - To Correspondents." (London) *The Queen.* (April 9, 1898).

1898-07   D, B.L. "Notes and Comments." *The Library Assistant* 5 (May 1898):47-48.

Details sources of tension between men and women in librarianship which can be solved only when there is equal pay for equal work and women make a full commitment to their career, as women "very largely have themselves to blame." Reprints item [1898-06] describing opportunities for women in librarianship and who to contact for further information on entry into the field.

1898-08   D, B.L. "Notes and Comments." *Library Assistant* 1 (June 1898): 60-61.

Two letters are commented upon but not printed in their entirety. One agrees with [1898-07], noting women should earn the same as men, while the other sees as positive the employment of women in libraries which are short of funds. Includes a quote from [1893-01] on the employment of women in libraries who are steadier and more thoughtful than men for half the pay.

1898-09   Crunden, F.M. "Proceedings of the American Library Association, Lakewood-on-Chautaqua - 1898: Special Training for Children's Librarians." *Library Journal* 23 (August 1898):82.

Writer notes that the children's librarian should be a woman who not only possesses the qualities of intelligence, tact, enthusiasm, and self-devotion which all librarians have, but a sympathetic nature and love of children.

*1898-10 "Educated Women as Librarians." *Hearth and Home* (October 6, 1898).

1898-11 "Educated Women as Librarians." *Library Assistant* 1 (November 1898):103.

Reprint of [1898-10] from *Hearth and Home* which advocates educated women entering the profession who will prove far superior to uncultivated men, who now dominate. Suggests that educated women begin applying for all library posts even if advertisements indicate men only so that authorities will grow accustomed to the idea of women librarians. The introduction to the reprint expresses displeasure with the idea of single women replacing men who support families.

1898-12 "Hearth and Home." *Library Assistant* 1 (December 1898):115.

Reprints an advertisement from *The New Zealand Observer* for a "Lady Assistant" for the library. Jokes about "Lady Assistants" who marry.

*1898-13 Interviews in "Occupations for Women and Their Compensation." (New York) *Tribune Monthly* 9 (December 1898).

1898-14 James, H.P. "Women in American and British Libraries." *The Library World* 1 (December 1898):89-90.

A discussion of the reasons more U.S. libraries than British libraries are in the hands of women. Reasons given: 1) British libraries have an older tradition and were built up by men; 2) American women have more economic independence; 3) the public library in America is mandated to serve the people; 4) American women have better chances for education; 5) American women have a better opportunity to learn business; 6) American women do not have as much tradition to overcome.

1899-01 Petherbridge, Miss. "Indexers," and "Librarians." *English Woman's Yearbook, 1899:*57-58.

Two short articles on indexing and librarianship as careers for women included with similiar articles on other fields. Indexing "is peculiarly suited for well-educated women" who are inclined to the sedentary rather than active life. It is "so peculiarly suitable for women because it requires the infinite capacity for taking pains, the thorough conscientiousness, good common sense, and at the same time the quickness and versatility of mind which are supposed to be essentially womanly qualities." Indexing is highly paid and training is absolutely essential. In the section on librarianship the steps necessary to become a librarian are described: work in a library, take the Library Association classes and examination. Women are not prominent in British libraries, as they are in American libraries, for two reasons: "(a) the difficulty in getting trained; (b) the very poor remuneration and the very limited outlook that await the librarian at the end of her training." Since M.S.R. James resigned from her post in 1894 there has been no prominent woman manager of a British library.

1899-02 Vernyey, E. "Village Libraries." *The Library* 10 (1899):24-28.

Although this article does not focus on women *per se* it does speak of village librarians as women and by its tone communicates that the community spirit needed in a small library is feminine.

1899-03 Dewey, M. "The Ideal Librarian." *Library Journal* 24 (January 1899):14.

Dewey comments that a "great librarian must have a clear head, a strong hand and . . . a great heart . . . and, when I look into the future, I am inclined to think that most of the men who achieve this greatness will be women."

*1899-04 "Women as Librarians." *Home Life* (April 15, 1899).

1899-05   "Women as Librarians." *Library Assistant* 1 (May 1899):209.

Reference to an article in *Home Life* [1899-04] which contains a well informed statement on women in libraries.

1899-06   Ahern, M.E. "Women as Librarians in the Business World." *Public Libraries* 4 (June 1899):257-261.

Partial printing of Ahern's speech at the 1899 Atlanta ALA Conference. Complete text available in Conference proceedings [1899-13].

1899-07   Brown, J.D. "Women as Librarians at Clerkenwell." *Library Assistant* 1 (June 1899):219.

A brief notice indicating the salary and work-week of women and the examinations required.

1899-08   Dyer, B.L. and Lloyd, J. "Women Librarians in England." *Library Assistant* 1 (June 1899):219-222.

Three tables: 1) rate supported libraries with women librarians; 2) a comparative table contrasting women and men assistants; 3) private and other libraries with women assistants.

1899-09   "May Meeting: Women in Libraries." *Library Assistant* 1 (June 1899):212-213.

Report of Wire's paper [1899-11] and discussion of the suitability of women for library work. Discussion included comments that women should be employed because the low salaries would not be acceptable to men; girls were best at mechanical work where there was no hope of promotion; and it would be unsuitable to hire women in the event that they might marry co-workers.

1899-10   Selby, W.L. "Women as Librarians in Bristol." *Library Assistant* 1 (June 1899):217-219.

Discusses Bristol libraries run by women as the "survival of the fittest." Since men were replaced by women there has been less friction with the public and an increase in use. Although the initial reason for hiring women is their willingness to come for less money, the public turns out to prefer them. Argues that the fact that women marry creates a higher turnover and therefore a younger, more energetic staff.

1899-11   Wire, G.E. "Library Assistants in the United States." *Library Assistant* 1 (June 1899):214-217.

Compares the status of American and British library assistants: America has more women and they can begin only after having graduated from high school, whereas in Britain ladies begin after grammar school. He concludes by saying that women are employed in the U.S. because they stay longer than men, are more loyal, trustworthy, faithful, don't complain about the salary, and have endeared the library to the populace due to faithfulness, conscientiousness, genius, and patience. If instead, half-paid, half-hearted men had been employed, libraries would not be so well off.

1899-12   "Women Librarians." *Library Assistant* 1 (July 1899):226.

Reports on the Librarians Section at the 1899 International Congress of Women [1900-01] and lists speakers.

†**1899-13**   Ahern, M.E. "The Business Side of a Woman's Career as a Librarian." *Library Journal* 24 (July 1899):60-62.

Speech, given at the 1899 American Library Association conference, stating what is expected of a woman librarian, such as dignity, executive ability and no concessions because she is a woman.

1899-14 "Women in Librarianship." *Library Assistant* 1 (August 1899):237-238.

Comments that at the 1899 International Congress of Women [1900-01] unrepresentative women spoke on women librarians and incorrect remarks were made on the percentage passing the Library Association examination.

1899-15 "Women in Librarianship." *Library Assistant* 1 (August 1899):246.

Refers to editorial [1899-14] which condemned the International Congress of Women and quotes F.H. Low's article from *The Nineteenth Century* 48 (August 1899):192 which criticizes the Congress for only featuring successful women. Also criticizes one of the speakers, Miss Petherbridge, for making statements that make entry seem easier than it is.

1899-16 Smith, L.T. "On Openings for Women in Library Work." *Library Association Record* 1 (November 1899):719-724.

Paper read to the International Congress of Women, 1899 [1900-01]. Discusses the evolution of libraries and librarianship and the place of women. Compares the British and American opportunities and cites examples.

1899-17 James, M.S.R. "Women in Librarianship at the Late Congress." *Library Assistant* 2 (December 1899):44-45.

Reply to criticisms [1899-15] of the sub-section accorded to women librarians at the Women's Congress [1900-01]. It was appended to the program at the eleventh hour and therefore had little time to secure a representative selection of speakers.

1899-18 Petherbridge, Miss. "Miss Petherbridge and the Congress." *Library Assistant* 2 (December 1899):45.

Response to [1899-15] which criticizes writer's remarks. She notes that her remarks were extempore and not reported at all. Therefore she was quoted in a confused manner. She clarifies comments made at the Congress.

*1899-19 "Questions and Answers Column: Librarian." *Girls Own Paper* (December 2, 1899).

1900-1909

†1900-01 "Women Librarians." In *The International Congress of Women of 1899: Women in the Professions.* Volumes I & II. Edited by The Countess I. Aberdeen. London: T. Fisher Unwin, 1900: Vol. I: 8; Vol. II: 211-232.

The International Congress of Women of 1899 was intended to bring together persons of experience from all parts of the world who could provide facts regarding the position, work and opportunities of women at the end of the nineteenth century and who could trace the history of various phases of women's progress in various lands. Conference transactions are reprinted in seven volumes. Sections devoted to women in libraries are annotated below.

1900-01A Garnett, Dr. "Women Librarians - Opening Remarks." In *The International Congress of Women in 1899: Women in the Professions.* Volume II. Edited by The Countess I. Aberdeen. London: T. Fisher Unwin, 1900:211.

Urges women not to accept low salaries and praises the general fitness of women for employment in libraries.

†1900-01B Plummer, M.W. "The Training of Women as Librarians." In *The International Congress of Women of 1899: Women in the Professions.* Volume

II. Edited by The Countess I. Aberdeen. London: T. Fisher Unwin, 1900: 211-218.

Summarizes the state of U.S. library education and the history of the four extant schools (Albany, Pratt, Drexel and Armour) which train women as well as men. Discussion by M.H. Jones, Miss Petherbridge, Francis Hardin Hess, and Dr. Garnett focuses on women as indexers.

†1900-01C   James, M.S.R. "Women and Their Future in Library Work." In *The International Congress of Women of 1899: Women in the Professions.* Volume II. Edited by The Countess I. Aberdeen. London: T. Fisher Unwin, 1900:219-224.

"It is a source of great wonderment to everyone who has considered the subject that so few women have been employed in British libraries in really responsible positions." James considers the situation in all library types focusing on Britain, but mentioning Italy, Norway, Sweden, Austria, Germany, Switzerland, France, Hawaii, Canada, Australia and the U.S. The U.S., she notes, is "the elysium of women . . . It is almost the exception not to find women in libraries, where they have proved themselves indispensable as organizers, administrators, catalogers and indexers." The discrepancy between the employment of women in Britain and America is due to the fact that British men distrust women in a business capacity and that there is no precedent. James maintains that women can do the work and more women on boards would help women's positions and promotions, as well as women librarians pursuing business training, attending meetings, taking the Library Association exams and being careerists.

1900-02   "School for Women Librarians." *Library Assistant* 2 (March 1900):88.

News item mentioning that a training school for women librarians has been opened in Berlin offering two courses: one for six months to prepare for public library work and one for three years to prepare for work in scientific libraries.

1900-03   James, M.S.R. "Women Librarians and Their Future Prospects." *Library Association Record* 2 (June 1900):291-301.

Paper read before the International Congress of Women of 1899, published in the Congress Transactions [1900-01C]. Paper is only slightly changed from the original.

1901-01   Norrenberg, Dr. C. "Woman as Librarian." *Public Libraries* 6 (March 1901):156-158.

Work in libraries is within the German concept of womanliness. There are fewer women in German libraries than in U.S. libraries because women are suited to public library work rather than scholarly librarianship and the public library movement is not as strong in Germany as in the U.S. The qualifications for work in German public libraries are described.

*1901-02   Anderson, H.C.L. "Women as Library Assistants." *Library Record of Australasia* 2 (October 1901 or 1902?):99.

1902-01   Henry, W.E. *Librarianship: What It Implies.* Indianapolis: William B. Burfurd, 1902.

A selection of quotations on librarianship including letters on the qualifications "requisite in a librarian for a small town." Herbert Putnam, Librarian of Congress, comments that "For the salary usually paid in such a position an efficient woman is more likely to be secured than a man of equivalent efficiency who would be content to remain in the position" (p. 18). Johnson Brigham, State Librarian of Iowa, says, "He (and when I say 'he' I mean 'she'; for I believe that more women are better adapted to library work than men) should be thorough; aggressively neat; uniformly, not aggressively, polite; sympathetically helpful and tactful" (p. 20-21).

1902-02 James, M.S.R. "Women Librarians and Their Future Prospects." *Public Libraries* 7 (January 1902):3-7.

This article, excerpted from [1900-01C], a paper James read before the International Congress of Women of 1899, does not include the bibliographical references which appeared in [1900-03], the *Library Association Record's* reprint of the same paper.

†1902-03 Chennell, F.E. "Lady Assistants in Public Libraries." *Library World* 4 (March 1902):245-248.

Argument against women because they deter men from filling lower ranks and therefore reduce pool of potential directors. Since women marry they break the continuity of training.

1902-04 "Libraries and Librarians." *Library World* 4 (April 1902):276.

News item from a Cardiff paper is reprinted which states that over one hundred young women applied for positions as library assistants causing the editors to wonder if Chennell's comments [1902-03] have gone unheeded. Editors also wonder why no woman champion has appeared to refute Chennell.

1902-05 "The Desk Assistant: An Imaginary Conversation." *Library Journal* 27 (May 1902):251-254.

Dialogue between female desk assistant and male librarian covering ideal characteristics for such work: the librarian's expectations, the desk assistant's request for a living wage and finally her realization that her work is more than mechanical.

†1902-06 Pierce, K.E. "Women in Public Libraries: A Reply to Mr. Chennell." *Library World* 4 (May 1902):286-288.

A reply to Chennell's [1902-03] argument against women in the library which refutes his indictments. Pierce notes that Chennell has given no reason for men to have a freehold as exclusive managers of libraries. Seven points are made: 1) there is no proof that women are inferior to men; 2) libraries haven't been able to hire men or couldn't afford to, so women have been hired; 3) libraries queried have found women more steady and reliable than boys and not as liable to matrimony as was thought; 4) women have *not* been responsible for a general lowering of salaries; 5) the last census shows more women than men, therefore they need a livelihood; 6) American women have distinguished themselves more than English men; and 7) Chennell only utters fears, not facts.

1902-07 Chennell, F.E. "The Lady Assistant - A Rejoinder." *Library World* 4 (June 1902):319-322.

Author responds to Pierce's reply [1902-06] and says she has perverted the truth. He responds to the seven points she makes. His tone throughout is cavalier and contemptuous of women.

1902-08 Pierce, K.E. "Women in Public Libraries." *Library World* 5 (July 1902):14-15.

Another sally in the Chennell controversy [1902-03; 06; 07] Pierce cites women who have become doctors and lawyers, castigates Chennell's slur on library boards who have chosen women and affirms her belief that women are just as "well-suited, mentally and physically."

1902-09 "Women Librarians and Assistants. (A Report form Various Libraries)." *Library World* 5 (July 1902):7-14.

314   *The Role of Women in Librarianship*

Prompted by the Chennell-Pierce controversy [1902-03; 06; 07; 08] the editors have undertaken a survey on women in libraries, the results of which are reported. Quotes from respondents and a library-by-library response to questions on salaries, difficulties encountered, policies, and experience with women workers are included. "It is impossible to resist the conclusion that women have completely vindicated their right to rank as first-class librarians."

1902-10   Chennell, F.E. "The Woman Assistant Again." *Library World* (August 1902):40-43.

Chennell, originator of controversy criticizing women [1902-03; 06; 07; 08], "subsides gracefully" though not without a few more sarcasms, and a poem. He admits his views have been modified.

1902-11   Herself. "The Case of the Desk Assistant." *Library Journal* 27 (October 1902):876-878.

Describes schedules and salaries of desk assistants as a supplement to [1902-05]. Schedules are regarded "simply as problems in arithmetic, unrelated to the human constitution," (p. 876) and often result in physical damage to the woman assistant.

1903-01   Brown, J.D. "Women Librarians and Assistants." In *Manual of Library Economy*. London: Scott, Greenwood and Co., 1903:87-89.

Compares employment of women in British and U.S. libraries. Prejudice against women is a problem in both countries. In Great Britain, however, there are not as many opportunities, and salaries are not high as in the U.S., so British women have more obstacles to overcome. Equal pay for equal work is strongly advocated. Bibliography included.

1903-02   McMillan, M. "Some Causes of Ill Health Among Library Workers." *Public Libraries* 8 (November 1903):412-414.

Dicusses psychological reasons for women's ill health. These include lack of participation in policy making, lack of freedom to complain, "nerves," worrying about families and financial burdens.

1904-01   Hawley, F.B. "Some Non-technical Qualifications for Library Work." *Library Journal* 29 (July 1904):360-362.

Excerpts from a lecture to Pratt Institute Library School discussing qualities such as sympathy, desire to please and cheerfulness; non-technical qualities owed to the fact that most librarians are women. Women may become as business-like as men ("and thereby lose half our claim as women") but cannot produce the same results as men of equal ability.

1904-02   "Library Assistants: Shortcomings and Desirable Qualifications." *Library Journal* 29 (July 1904):349-359.

Lengthy discussion of the characteristics of desk assistants who are assumed to be women. Supervision is also touched on: "probably a man can keep a set of women assistants at a higher level than could a woman of the same rank" (p. 349-350). Among the shortcomings are lack of executive ability, lack of interest in the work at hand, wastefulness and ill-health. Desirable qualities include tact, punctuality, adaptability, precision and accuracy.

1904-03   "The City of Berlin Has Recently and for the First Time Appointed Two Women." *Public Libraries* 9 (December 1904):518.

Brief note on the appointment of women to People's libraries in Germany.

†1904-04   Fairchild, S.C. "Address Delivered at Library Section of International Congress of Arts and Science. St. Louis, MO, September 22, 1904: Women in American Libraries." *Library Journal* 29 (December 1904):157-162.

Report of a survey of one-hundred libraries on the place of women in the library field undertaken at the request of the ALA President, Herbert Putnam. Women greatly outnumber men and hold "a creditable proportion of administrative positions but seldom one involving large administrative responsibility," particularly in the larger or more scholarly libraries. "They do not hold the positions offering the highest salaries, and broadly speaking, apparently they do not receive equal remuneration for the same grade of work." Women's willingness to work for lower salaries, "delicate physique," unbusiness-like character, conservatism, lack of originality and a sense of proportion, lack of contact with "the world of affairs" and lack of temperament suitable to supervision, as well as shunning of responsibility are cited as factors leading to the condition of women in librarianship. There are exceptions and these women do hold responsible positions. Women excel in positions requiring the "human element" and may prefer to work in those and other lines where they can, if they will, equal men. Women in American librarianship, Fairchild concludes, have accomplished much although "many gates are at present closed to women."

1905-01 "Women in Public Libraries." *Library Assistant* 4 (January 1905):212.

Comments that Carnegie Libraries have opened up many positions for women bookishly inclined.

1905-02 "Women and Libraries." *Public Libraries* 10 (June 1905):318.

Report on Fairchild's survey [1904-04] on women in the profession reprinted from the Bangor, Maine *Commercial.*

1905-03 Stearns, L.E. "Proceedings of the American Library Association Conference, Portland - 1905: The Question of Library Training." *Library Journal* 30 (September 1905):68-71.

Stearns notes that women hurt themselves by accepting lower salaries than men for equal service and by their willingness to work for "the love of it."

1907-01 Boston Athenaeum Staff. *The Athenaeum Centenary.* Boston: The Boston Athenaeum, 1907:41-42.

History of the Athenaeum notes that the Athenaeum was a man's institution until the opening of the Beacon Street building when Mrs. Harnden was admitted to the staff in 1857 followed by Mary A. Beon and Sarah E. Gill.

1907-02 Brown, J.D. "Women Librarians and Assistants." In *Manual of Library Economy.* Revised edition. London: The Library Supply Co. 1907:73-74; 78.

Comments similar to those in first edition [1903-01] but the number of women employed has increased from twelve to fifteen percent. Bibliography included.

1907-03 "Men in Library Work." In the *Annual Report of New York State Library School: Albany.* (1907):216-217.

Dispels the "popular apprehension library work is women's work" and demonstrates that men have always been preferred for the chief positions and that there is a preference for men as chief librarians. Compares salaries to professions such as academic teaching.

1907-04 Hartham, D. "Lovely Woman in the Library." *Library World* 9 (1907):360-393.

A diatribe against women in libraries by "a mere male" indicting them as lovely but lacking initiative. Style is witty but insidious.

1907-05 Pierce, K.E. "Women in Libraries." *Library World* 9 (1907):440-441.

Pierce, who established herself as a champion of women in the Chennell controversy [1902-03; 06; 07; 08; 10] again responds to a man's attack on women [1907-04]. She has found the work of female library assistants to be more than adequate and does not find Hartham's "general tone of contemptuous superiority" amusing.

1907-06   Brunner, M.A.R. "The Library as a Place for Women." *Library World* 10 (1907):137-139.

The role of women in German libraries is discussed. Opinion is that the majority of librarians queried were favorably inclined towards employment of female assistants.

1907-07   "The Librarian." *Boston Evening Transcript* (September 4, 1907):16.

Observations on the dominance of women in library positions: men are outnumbered at the American Library Association; all but one of the important library schools are managed by women; both library magazines are edited by women; small libraries are headed by women; and eighty to ninety percent of the staffs are women. Questions whether the dominance of women has been a "helpful or injurious" influence. Notes that foreign librarians make merry over the American female dominated situation.

1907-08   "The Librarian." *Boston Evening Transcript* (September 11, 1907):19.

Continues discussion begun in [1907-07]. Uses data from the 1900 Census to demonstrate that women are dominant in number. Compares the U.S. situation to Germany where women are considered more suited to public and popular libraries rather than scholarly or scientific libraries.

1907-09   "Scarcity of Men in Library Work." *New York Evening Post* (November 1907).

Expresses concern at the declining number of men in the library profession. The decline indicates a "serious weakness both in the general library movement and in the standing and management of the library schools." It is expected that women should be in preponderance but positions of responsibility are multiplying and though women can fulfill some of these, in many cases a man is needed.

1907-10   Hitchler, T. "The Successful Loan-Desk Assistant." *Library Journal* 32 (December 1907):554-559.

The qualifications of the desk assistant are described, among them maturity, good health, a sense of responsibility and humor and a "neat, clean and pleasing personal appearance." The assistant is assumed to be a woman. The fact that there are more women in the profession is postulated to account for the willingness of many to work for less salary out of love of the work. However, "the woman worker of today has a family to take care of or someone dependent on her for support almost as frequently as has the man who works" so money is a requirement and a fit salary must be offered to keep qualified workers.

1907-11   "Library Notes from Germany — Women in German Libraries." *Public Libraries* 12 (December 1907):394-395.

Overview of position of women in German libraries. Women are employed more frequently now, but in the lower ranks where they are not content to stay. Education is an issue and training for women is described.

1908-01   Gilbert, M. "The Education of the Library Assistant - (2)." *Library Assistant* 6 (January 1908):52-55.

One of three papers on the education of the library assistant read at the Library Assistant Association meeting, December 11, 1907. Gilbert was asked to treat the subject from the standpoint of women, but feels there is no difference in the work done by men and women, nor in the education required of either. She urges women to qualify for the Library Association examination. In the discussion reported Miss Clark agrees with Gilbert, "that the question of sex should not count" (p. 60).

1908-02 "A hopeful view of this subject—." *Boston Evening Transcript* (March 18, 1908):19.

Reports that while the numerical proportion of women in library work is far greater than men, "the actual weight of influence is not against men." The positions open for men far exceed the supply (according to the New York State Library School).

*1909-01 May, G.E. "Librarians." *Public and Social Work.* Boston: Central Bureau for the Employment of Women, 1909:20-25.

*1909-02 Richardson, A.S. "Work in Libraries." *Girl Who Earns Her Own Living.* Dodge, NY, 1909:74-76.

1909-03 "Women Librarians." *Public Libraries* 14 (June 1909):233.

Note inviting women librarians to correspond with editor, Mary Eileen Ahern, who has been asked to speak on "Women librarians" at the Quinquennial Congress and International Council of Women in Toronto June 17-30.

1909-04 "The Librarian." *Boston Evening Transcript* (June 2, 1909):23.

Suggests as one reason for the small number of men in library work the stringent moral requirements of being a librarian. Sees library schools as inflicting the same rules against smoking and drinking as schools for the ministry. Suggests the more manly fields of medicine and law be used to measure the moral habits of male librarians.

1909-05 "Librarianship for College Men." *Reserve Weekly* December 21, 1909.

Article urging college men to consider librarianship because men are wanted in higher paying library jobs and the work may be pleasing to men of scholarly tastes.

1910-1919

1910-01 Rathbone, J. "Library Work for Women." In *Vocations for the Trained Woman. Part I.* New York: Longmans for the Woman's Educational and Industrial Union, 1910:215-220.

Discusses career potential, salary range, and work in all types of libraries. The more important positions in library work are held by men but all are open to women.

*1910-02 Rebbins, M.E. "Library Training." In *Vocations for the Trained Woman. Part I.* New York: Longmans for the Woman's Educational and Industrial Union, 1910:221-226.

*1910-03 "Women Assistants." *Libraries, Museums and Art Galleries' Year-Book 1910.* (November 1910):277.

1910-04 Bostwick, A.E. "Labor and Rewards in the Library." *Public Libraries* 15 (January 1910):15.

Speech delivered to the graduating class of the Library School, Atlanta, Georgia, June 1, 1909, which asks and answers why librarians' wages - particularly those of women - are so low: the physical weakness of the average woman, the lack of value placed on women's work, the attitude of women themselves, the law of supply and demand and lack of public understanding of library work.

1910-05 Bascom, L. "Library Work for College Women." *Kappa Alpha Theta* 24 (May 1910):321-328.

Discusses the attractions and compensations of library work for college women on the basis that there is no profession that satisfies so thoroughly many of the womanly qualities that most naturally find expression in the care and culture of a home. Also compares the variety of librarianship with the narrowness of teaching. Requisites are given: efficiency, enthusiasm, and an all-around education. Salaries are quoted with no disparity between men's and women's salary. Schools are described.

1910-06 Feagan, S. "Women Librarians." *Library Association Record* 12 (May 16, 1910):224-226.

Reflections on the role of women in libraries as it has changed since 1900. Feagan notes there is no great demand for women librarians sufficient to justify women undergoing expensive library training. She advises girls to "have another string in their bow."

1910-07 "Bargains in Library Assistants." *Public Libraries* 15 (July 1910):284-285.

Editorial criticizing libraries which hire women college graduates at less than living wages when they would have preferred men but were unable to secure them. Finds the policy of writing joyful reports about such practices particularly disturbing. Emphasizes that as part of the public, librarians should receive a decent salary - "their right to a just consideration is not annulled by the fact that they administer the public's institution."

1910-08 Coatsworth, M.L. "The Female Assistant From Her Own Standpoint." *Library Assistant* 7 (August-September 1910):217-218.

Summary and discussion of a meeting of the North Eastern Branch where Coatsworth read her paper, "A Small Protest on Behalf of the Female Assistant."

*1911-01 Bird, M.M. "Library Work." In *Women at Work*. London: Chapman, 1911:233-234.

*1911-02 Brewer, F.M. "Library Work." In *Choosing an Occupation*. New York: Board of Education, 1911:77-79.

1911-03 New York State Library School. *Librarianship as a Profession.* Albany, NY: Education Department, 1911.

A pamphlet of reprints, including general discussion of librarianship as a profession, to interest men and women in library work. The introduction notes that librarianship offers men the best chances for success.

1911-03A "Men in Library Work." In *Librarianship as a Profession.* Albany, NY: Education Department, 1911:11-13.

Reprint of [1907-03].

1911-03B "Scarcity of Men in Library Work." In *Librarianship as a Profession.* Albany, NY: Education Department, 1911:14-15.

Reprint of [1907-09].

1911-03C Bascom, E.L. "Library Work for College Women." In *Librarianship as a Profession.* Albany, NY: Education Department, 1911:22-26.

Reprint of [1910-05].

1911-03D Rathbone, J. "Library Work for Women." In *Librarianship as a Profession.* Albany, NY: Education Department, 1911:27-32.

Reprint of [1910-01].

1911-04   Clarke, O.E. "Librarianship for Women." *The Library Assistant* 8 (February 1911):24-25.

Criticizes a *Queen* article (January 14) for giving inaccurate information about library training and for implying that women make better librarians than men.

1911-05   "Editorial." *Library Journal* 36 (July, 1911):321-322.

In commenting on the ALA 1911 Pasadena Conference, the election of Theresa West Elmendorf, first woman president of ALA, is noted as, "a fitting recognition of the growing importance of women in the library profession" (p. 322). Mention is also made of the fact that in earlier days women "pulled the coat sleeves of Dr. Poole or Mr. Lloyd Smith with modest requests that one of these kindly gentlemen would speak up in a meeting on their behalf" (p. 322).

1911-06   Reed, M. "Women's Work in Libraries." *The Librarian and Book World* 2 (August 1911):32-33.

The first in a series of columns on "anything of interest to women librarians and assistants." Women earn less and are studying for positions they have little hope of attaining. The issue of whether women do the same work as men is raised but unresolved. The author flatly states women do not flirt more with borrowers than men, an issue of concern to the profession.

1911-07   Dana, J.C. "Women in Library Work." *Independent* 71 (August 3, 1911):244-250.

Cites librarianship as the most attractive of all occupations now open to women because of the agreeable surroundings, pleasant work, and contact with intellectual people. Skills needed are discussed at length.

1911-08   Reed, M. "Women's Work in Libraries." *The Librarians and Book World* 2 (September 1911):76-77.

Raises the question of whether women willing to work for "pocket money" are lowering the salaries of librarians. Cites examples of this in other occupations.

1911-09   Reed, M. "Women's Work in Libraries." *The Librarian and Book World* 2 (October 1911):115-116.

Comments on a position advertised for a woman librarian at a very low salary. The Library Assistants Association has called attention to the "injustice" and the author encourages them.

1911-10   Reed, M. "Women's Work in Libraries." *The Librarian and Book World* 2 (November 1911):149-150.

Because of their career patterns women may not favor compulsory retirement and pension fund contributions.

1911-11   Reed, M. "Women's Work in Libraries." *The Librarian and Book World* 2 (December 1911):185-186.

Reed reprints response by Mary Eileen Ahern to a remark in a previous column [1911-09]. Ahern considered the remark typical of women's "propensity to be personal in their dealings" which hinders their public career. Reed apologizes.

1912-01   "Wandsworth Borough Council and Female Assistants." *The Librarian and Book World* 3 (1912):33.

Announcement that Wandsworth Public library will employ female assistants as vacancies in the male staff occur. This change is thought necessary since libraries cannot pay enough to employ men at senior levels.

1912-02   "Wandsworth Borough Council and Female Assistants." *The Librarian and Book World* 3 (1912):144.

Announcement that the Wandsworth Public Library will not employ women since "male labor should not be displaced by female when hundreds of men were walking about the streets unemployed."

1912-03   "Wandsworth Borough Council and Female Assistants." *The Librarian and Book World* 3 (1912):230.

Final announcement that women will not be employed at Wandsworth Public Library.

1912-04   Reed, M. "Women's Work in Libraries." *The Librarian and Book World* 2 (January 1912):228-229.

Musings on why women librarians hire female staffs while male librarians have both all female and mixed staffs.

1912-05   Reed, M. "Women's Work in Libraries." *The Librarian and Book World* 2 (February 1912):269-270.

Criticizes the library section of the 1912 *Englishwoman's Yearbook*. Comments on the better wages and working conditions of women working for commercial as opposed to art bookbinders.

1912-06   Reed, M. "Women's Work in Libraries." *The Librarian and Book World* 2 (March 1912):307-308.

Excerpts from the *National Negro School News* describing library service to Blacks in the United States.

1912-07   Reed, M. "Women's Work in Libraries." *The Librarian and Book World* 2 (April 1912):348-349.

Comments on "voluntary girl assistants" on the library staff. Reed feels this practice does little good for the women in libraries.

1912-08   Reed, M. "Women's Work in Libraries." *The Librarian and Book World* 2 (May 1912):388-389.

Strong arguments for equal pay for equal work in librarianship and for an end to "blind alley employments" of women as circulation assistants only.

1912-09   Reed, M. "Women's Work in Libraries." *The Librarian and Book World* 2 (June 1912):426-427.

Decries dress codes for women but not for men in libraries. If, however, libraries insist, "the least such a library should do would be to buy the girls' dresses."

>   **Letter:**   Griffiths, M.E. "Correspondence." *The Librarian and Book World* 3 (August 1912):18.
>
>   Disagrees with Reed on the "question of overalls (*not* uniforms) for female assistants," because there are very few libraries where women work and even fewer where they wear other than their own clothes. In any case the idea is a good one and Reed's comments show "a very peculiar idea of the mental capacity of the women engaged in Public Libraries."

1912-10   Reed, M. "Women's Work in Libraries." *The Librarian and Book World* 2 (July 1912):466-467.

Comments on a recruitment article published in *The Lady*. Reed is not sure it is wise to actively encourage women to enter librarianship where there may not be enough positions for them.

1912-11   Reed, M. "Women's Work in Libraries." *The Librarian and Book World* 3 (August 1912):19-20.

Comments on reactions in the regular press and by Maude Griffiths [1912-09-letter] to her column [1912-09] on dress codes in libraries. Griffiths' letter is responded to line by line and the resentment of "many girls . . . obliged to wear certain styles of dress" and hair styles is restressed.

1912-12   Gerard, E. "Librarianship from a Woman Assistant's Point of View." *Assistant Librarian* 9 (August-September 1912):164-171.

Reiterates the history of women in British libraries (beginning in 1871 at Manchester) to the present when seven hundred women are employed — mainly in humble positions. Criticizes women for lack of initiative and professional activity. Outlines skills needed for women to advance.

1912-13   Reed, M. "Women's Work in Libraries." *The Librarian and Book World* 3 (September 1912):64-65.

Poor working conditions and long hours for library assistants are discussed. Reed urges women library assistants to exercise, go outdoors and take advantage of the games and amusements available to them.

†1912-14   Putnam, H. "The Prospect: An Address Before a Graduating Class of Women." *Library Journal* 37 (December 1912):651-658.

Lengthy comments by the Librarian of Congress on women moving into the service work force (which he approves of) and on the limitations faced by women which are caused by superior traits of men such as manliness, a sense of proportion, insight and power. Women, however, have offsetting qualities: devotion, loyalty, absorption. The distinction between male and female natures: the one dynamic, the other static, are discussed and career and life advice given.

1913-01   Countryman, G.A. "Librarianship." In *Vocations Open to Women Bulletin.* University of Minnesota, 1913:18-19.

Article does not discuss women in libraries as such but the duties, opportunities and requirements for librarianship are described for a female audience.

*1913-02   Laselle, M.A. and Wiley, K.E. "Library Work." In *Vocations for Girls.* Boston: Houghton, 1913:66-72.

1913-03   Reed, M. "Women's Work in Libraries." *The Librarian and Book World* 3 (January 1913):235-236.

After a lapse of three months Reed begins her column again and reports on the status of women working in libraries. There has been much discussion of whether girls and women assistants are taking work from male assistants. Reed objects to the low salaries of women which hurts the profession as well as women themselves.

1913-04   Barnum, M.F. "Opportunities for College Women in the Library Profession." *Bostonia* 14 (April 1913):1-7.

Librarianship, its opportunities and requirements, is discussed in general as a profession for women. Librarian's salaries are compared favorably with teaching (librarianship: $500-$600; teaching: $500).

1913-05   Gerard, E. "The Women's Standpoint." *The Library Assistant* 10 (June 1913):108-109.

Criticizes the profession for limiting the opportunities of women assistants for advancement.

1913-06   "A Few Brickbats From a Layman." *Public Libraries* 18 (July 1913):277-279.

Critique of women librarians, many of whom know little about taxation, their base of public support. Suggests that women librarians, who have failed in another line of work, wish a soft job or are most concerned with salary, be removed from the profession. Describes three types of librarians: the show librarian, business librarian, and middle-of-the-road librarian.

1913-07   Reed, M. "Women's Work in Libraries." *The Librarian and Book World* 4 (August 1913):9-10.

A letter appearing in a number of "ladies papers advertising a course in librarianship for girls" causes the author to ask what the Library Association can do to maintain its control of the educational standards of the profession.

1913-08   "Women Assistants and L.A.A." *Library Assistant* 10 (December 1913):228.

Editorial comments that as women become more prevalent in assistant positions, they have weakened the Library Assistants Association by not joining. Commends women who are trying to remedy the situation.

1914-01   Reed, M. "The Status of the Lady Librarian." *The Librarian and Book World* 4 (March 1914):278-279.

In response to a letter circulated by women librarians and assistants questioning the position of women in British libraries, the author suggests that it would be counter to the professionalization of librarianship to raise women to chief positions. She states that women have brought about "one good thing" — in libraries they have reduced the "ridiculously long hours that used to be worked all over the country."

1914-02   "The Women's Committee." *The Library Assistant* 11 (April 1914):61-62.

News item announcing a meeting of the Committee of Women Librarians and Assistants to discuss "methods by which women may be induced to take more active interest in their profession and to cooperate with their male colleagues in their efforts to raise the status of librarianship."

1914-03   "Women as Employees." *Public Libraries* 19 (May 1914):196.

Extract from address of Louise Connolly at a meeting of Long Island Library Club. Deplores women librarians' lack of ambition and compares their attitude to that of eager young men. Calls for a rewards system for women in pay, recognition and free time to assure greater achievement. Especially emphatic about the need for "*free time* for free development."

1914-04   Reed, M. "The Attack on Women." *The Librarian and Book World* 5 (August 1914):10; 13.

Response to criticism of women in libraries, which Reed feels has increased since women librarians and assistants formed their own society. Women have worked for low salaries of which Reed disapproves but these low wages did enable libraries to purchase more books. Salaries remain low, not because of the number of women, but because library work is not seen as worth a reasonable salary.

1914-05   "Library Work for College Girls." *American Educational Review* 36 (October 1914):33.

Young women are encouraged to consider library work as the profession of teaching is becoming over-crowded. "In the small city the girl librarian is, even more than the school teacher, the dispenser of culture." Library work, salaries, hours, and library training are briefly described.

1914-06   Reed, M. "Women, Libraries, and the War." *The Librarian and Book World* 5 (October 1914):75-76.

Questions bringing untrained women library assistants into the profession to temporarily replace those who have joined the war effort.

*1915-01   Weaver, E.W. "Librarianship." In *Profitable Vocations for Girls.* New York: Barnes. 1915:138-148.

†1915-02   Feagan, M. "Women Assistants and the War." *Library World* 17 (January 1915):197-200.

Sees the war, though regrettable, as an opportunity for women to show they are as competent as men.

> **Comment:**   Eratosthenes. "They Also Serve Who Only Stand and Wait." *The Library World* 17 (February 1915):239.
>
> Comment by regular writer for *Library World.* Sees Feagan's argument as "Now is your chance, girls; the men are going to the war, very soon many more will be forced to go; let us grab their places." Characterizes her as heartless.

> **Letters:**   Clarke, G.E. "Women Assistants and the War." *The Library World* 17 (February 1915):240-241.
>
> States that it is inconceivable that Feagan should suggest that women should strain every nerve to oust and supplant their male competitors. Exhorts women to sacrifice and volunteer and stop all diatribes against men.

> A Woman Librarian. "Women Assistants and the War." *The Library World* 17 (February 1915):240.
>
> Agrees with Feagan but says we must not lose sight of the services rendered by men and perhaps the situation will lead to better mutual understanding.

> Feagan, M. "Women Assistants and the War." *The Library World* 17 (March 1915):271.
>
> A response to correspondence about her original article and a restatement of her main thesis: "men have seen to it that women have not had the opportunity of knowing their ability . . . and I was urging women to be sufficiently man-like in their methods to take it."

1915-03   Reed, M. "The Great War: Part IV; Women's Work." *The Librarian and Book World.* 5 (January 1915):170-171.

Encourages women to volunteer in the war effort and asks the names "of any girl or women assistants from our libraries, who had become war nurses or members of the V.A.D. or who had 'enlisted' for any other work."

1915-04   R., F.B. "Misnamed Educational." *Public Libraries* 20 (February 1915): 62.

Reprint of article from *American Education Review* [1914-05] which F.B.R. calls "inane, so colorless and at the same time so full of error that as one librarian in writing of it expresses it, 'it arouses one's wrath.' " Sections on salaries, assistants' hours and library training which F.B.R. finds offensive or incorrect are italicized and briefly commented upon.

1915-05   "An Important Movement." *Public Libraries* 20 (March 1915):119-120.

At the "4th vocational conference on opportunities for women in occupations other than teaching" in Madison, Wisconsin, interest was so great in librarianship as a vocation and profession that the lecture and discussion period was more than doubled. The idea of giving career advice and information to young women should be considered by other colleges and universities.

1915-06   F., S.A. "The Library Assistants' Association: Liverpool and District Associations of Assistant Librarians." *Library Association Record* 17 (March 1915):131-132.

Summary of Gilbert's Address on "The Position of Women in Library Work To-Day," [1915-11] which outlines the history of women in Brttish libraries, points out notable women in America and then exhorts British women librarians to move forward in the profession.

1915-07 Zenodotus. "Women and the L.A. Council." *The Library World* 17 (March 1915):269-270.

Hopes that the Association of Women Librarians which is planning to run a woman candidate for the Library Association Council will not succeed since qualifications, not sex, should determine election.

Letter: Fearnside, K. and Pierce, K.E. "Woman Candidate for Library Association Council Election, 1915." *The Library World* 17 (April 1915):299-300.

Refutes Zenodotus' uninformed statement about a movement to forward a woman candidate for the Library Association Council. States that there is no "Association of Women Librarians" nor has there ever been any suggestion that one be formed. There are two committees: one to explain to girl assistants the need for training; the other in connection with a woman candidate for the Library Association Council. Because women are a numerically small body in the Library Association it was felt that a group effort might be the best way to elect a woman to the Council. A copy of the letter sent to women librarians to raise support is included. The writers ask that when the election takes place that the candidate be considered on her own merits.

1915-08 Reed, M. "Women Assistants." *The Librarian and Book World* 5 (April 1915):254-255.

Discusses the increase in the employment of women as library assistants due to the war. Raises questions as to their future. If after the war there are plenty of other jobs for men, the women may continue in library work. Also raises the issue of a growing prejudice against women because of the vocal interest of some in becoming chief librarians.

1915-09 Smith, F.E. "Interesting College Women in Library Work." *Library Journal* 40 (April 1915):263.

Report on the University of Wisconsin's fourth vocational conference February 10-12, 1915. Purpose was to introduce young women students to occupations other than teaching. Mary Eileen Ahern spoke on librarianship and Mary Emogene Hazeltine, preceptor of the Wisconsin Library School, provided statistics on the school's graduates.

*1915-10 Intercollegiate Bureau of Occupations. "Library Work," *Opportunities in Occupations Other Than Teaching.* New York, July 1915:4.

1915-11 Bonnefoy, A. "Women as Librarians - a French Viewpoint." *Library Journal* 40 (September 1915):657-658.

Excerpt from A. Bonnefoy's *Place aux Femmes! Les Carriers feminines, administratives et liberales,* in which he quotes an article from *Revue Internationale de l'Enseignement* which explains why women are more suited to work in libraries than men: it is indoor work, a subordinate role and requires affability. Bonnefoy is reported to agree and suggest that women assistants gradually replace men.

†1915-12 Gilbert, M. "The Position of Women in Public Libraries," *The Library World* 18 (October 1915):100-105.

Summarizes the position of women in British, U.S. and European libraries. Emphasizes the necessity of obtaining the proper qualifications for library work if women are to advance. Describes the efforts of the Library Assistants' Association Committee of Women Librarians and Assistants founded in 1913.

1915-13 Johnson, E.M. "The Special Library and Some of Its Problems." *Special Libraries* 6 (December 1915):157-161.

Along with a description of the duties in a special library is the information that women are preferred over men as special librarians because they will accept lower salaries. Despite this statement Johnson is inclined to think that service is considered over sex when actual hiring is done.

*1916-01 Shoemaker, H.R. *Library Work.* Philadelphia Bureau of Occupations for Trained Women, 1916.

*1916-02 Hazeltine, M.E. "Opportunities for College Women in Library Work." (One of series: "The New World and the College Woman") *The Bookman* February, 1916.

1916-03 Newberry, M.A. "Women and Library Work." *Michigan Women* (May 6, 1916).

1916-04 Newberry, M.A. "Women and Library Work." *Michigan Library Bulletin* 7 (May-June 1916):93-94.

Women have contributed to the library movement as founders and users of libraries. Women now hold prominent positions in the library work force and statistics are offered to support this. Various aspects of library work are described, the rewards of which are subjective, not objective. Reprint of [1916-03].

*1916-05 Hazeltine, M.E. "Opportunities for College Women in Library Work." *Wellesley College News* June 1916.

Reprint of [1916-02].

1916-06 "College Women in Library Work." *Wisconsin Library Bulletin* 12 (July 1916):277.

Summarizes [1916-07] and its publication history. Praises Mary Emogene Hazeltine's career as one that has opened up opportunities in library work to women "and men as well."

1916-07 Hazeltine, M.E. "Opportunities for College Women in Library Work." *Wisconsin Library Bulletin* 12 (July 1916):289-292.

Reprint of [1916-02], describes various types of library work in answer to the question: "What is this field that offers so much to the new woman?"

*1916-08 Heron-Maxwell, B. "Women Librarians: a Profession that Wants Recruits." *Daily Mail* August 16, 1916.

1916-09 "Editorial." *Library World* 19 (September 1916):57-59.

Editor feels Heron-Maxwell's article recruiting women to librarianship [1916-08] misleads women as opportunity is not as great as portrayed. Several of the women quoted by Heron-Maxwell are members of the Committee of Women Librarians and Assistants, one of whose purposes was to present accurate information on women in library work. The editor appeals "to these ladies to keep hereafter to their own excellent rule."

1916-10 "Inadequate Salaries of School Librarians." *Library Journal* 41 (October 1916):752-754.

A Cleveland educational survey reported that librarians have more educational training than teachers, but get less pay and no pension, thus providing less incentive for women to become librarians.

1916-11 "Editorial." *Library Journal* 41 (December 1916):863.

Introduction to memorial addresses honoring Mary Wright Plummer notes that Herbert Putnam chose to emphasize in his speech [1916-12] "the value of the work in libraries of women who constitute in America the large majority of the profession and so differentiate it from the library calling of other countries." The achievements of several women other than Plummer are outlined.

1916-12   Putnam, H. "The Woman in the Library." *Library Journal* 41 (December 1916):879-881.

Address given at symposium in honor of the memory of Mary Wright Plummer. Details the virtues of women. "The lack in women of the abilities which have been characteristic of men may be made good by the ampler social and business experience which the times assure; but the lack in men of the qualities characteristic of women, can never be made good except through the auxiliary cooperation of women themselves" (p. 879). The library schools provided the route for women to enter the profession in America and thus bring complimentary feminine qualities to librarianship.

*1917-01   Bennett, H. *Women and Work.* New York: Appleton, 1917:215.

*1917-02   Hirth, E.P. "Library Work." In her *Classified List of Vocations for Women.* New York: Intercollegiate Bureau of Occupations, March 1917:22-23.

1917-03   "Editorial." *Library Journal* 42 (July 1917):506.

Editorial comment on the retirement of Eliza Gordon Browning from the Indianapolis Public Library. Her successor, a man, will receive double her salary. A protest is entered on "behalf of a large majority of the profession that the salaries of women should be more nearly on a par with those of masculine incumbents or successors."

1917-04   Gardner, M.C. "The Training of Library Apprentices." *Library Journal* 42 (July 1917):524-528.

Stresses the various attributes a woman should possess if she is to be an efficient library worker.

1917-05   "Man or Woman." *Public Libraries* 22 (July 1917):278.

Comments on Miss Browning of Indianapolis who, in announcing her resignation, stated that the position has "grown to a man's job." Editorial notes that women do themselves a disservice by showing such little regard for their own abilities and that Eliza Gordon Browning, an equal rights advocate, seems inconsistent in her statement.

1917-06   Hasse, A.R. "Women in Libraries." *Journal of the Association of Collegiate Alumnae* 11 (October 1917):73-80.

Discusses deficiencies in librarians and quality of those trained. Asks the Association of Collegiate Alumnae to look at librarianship as an area in which government support (as compared to support for weather or geological surveys) is insufficient. Closes with the observation that college women can change librarianship.

1917-07   Power, R.L. "Business Education for Business Librarians." *Special Libraries* 8 (November 1917):135-139.

Recognizes a need for business courses to be included along with library science courses to produce a more qualified business librarian. Brief statement that women business librarians seem little more than file clerks, showing lack of initiative.

†1918-01   Ahern, M.E. "Up in Arms." *Public Libraries* 23 (January 1918):24.

Thinks points raised about women in war work earlier in issue by "two women prominent in library service" . . . are "well taken." [1918-02; 03] "If one were justified at any time in saying that library work is a 'man's job,' it would occur in regard to a library that was in a community of 33,000 men, but there is room even then for women to assist."

†1918-02   One of the Women. "Why Not a Woman's Auxiliary?" *Public Libraries* 23 (January 1918):22.

Letter calling for an auxiliary committee of women librarians to provide back up service to the war camp libraries since women are anxious to serve but are not permitted to work in the camps. Recounts the work of women librarians in raising funds to support the ALA war service effort.

†1918-03   A Woman. "Women in Library War Service." *Public Libraries* 23 (January 1918):19.

Letter relating that the War Department refuses to allow women to work in the camp libraries, which limits the services offered because most librarians are women. Suggests that "women themselves organize to carry on where they see things to be done and that are not being done by men."

1918-04   Hasse, A.R. "Women in Libraries." *Library Journal* 43 (February 1918):141-142.

Excerpts from [1917-06]. Library schools are criticized for emphasizing the technical as opposed to professional side of librarianship. The failure to appreciate the possibilities of professional work has without doubt been one of the prime causes in keeping library salaries for the rank and file as low as they are. College educated women have a role to play in the reworking of library resources to meet public requirements for an information service which Hasse says the public libraries, as presently organized, are unable to provide.

1918-05   Johnson, E.M. "Library Work as a Vocation for Women: a Bibliography." *Special Libraries* 9 (April 1918):99; 106-107.

Forty-eight annotated entries, mostly from contemporary authors and journals, prepared by the librarian of the Women's Educational and Industrial Union, Boston.

1918-06   Van Kleeck, M. "A Census of College Women." *Journal of the Association of Collegiate Alumnae* 11 (May 1918):557-591.

Report of 1915 survey analyzing the present status of women graduates of Barnard, Bryn Mawr, Mount Holyoke, Radcliffe, Smith, Vassar, Wellesley, Wells and Cornell. Of the 16,739 women included, 293 were in library work. Salary and graduate education data are provided for librarians and other occupation groups. A profile of the group as a whole is also given.

1918-07   Jennings, Mrs. J.T. "Statistics of Women in Library Work." *Library Journal* 43 (October 1918):737.

Analysis of statistics from the *Journal of the Association of Collegiate Alumnae*]1918-06]. Briefly compares earnings of teachers, social workers, librarians and business women and the post-graduation education of teachers to librarians. Librarianship has the' lowest median earnings of the four professions. The larger percent of teachers having graduate work is suggested as a reason for salary differences between teaching and librarianship.

*1919-01   Reed, M. "Women and Libraries in the New Age." *The Librarian* 9 (May 1919):133.

Comments on the fact that there may be more support for public libraries which, since the war, have been more and more staffed by women. Reed warns these women not to anticipate achieving the higher posts although they can expect to make more than pocket money in the new age.

1919-02   Bowker, R.R. "Address: Catalogue Section-Trustees Section." *American Library Association Forty-first Annual Meeting Papers and Proceedings, Asbury Park, New Jersey, June 23-27, 1919.* In *ALA Bulletin* 13 (July 1919):382-385.

Responding to Maude Malone's points on unions [1919-03], Bowker notes that there is no profession in which women were more honored or had more control of a professional organization.

1919-03   Malone, M. "Address: Catalogue Section-Trustee Section." *American Library Association Forty-first Annual Meeting Papers and Proceedings, Asbury Park, New Jersey, June 23-27, 1919.* In *ALA Bulletin* 13 (July 1919):379-382.

In the context of a speech on unions Maude Malone notes, "We all know that the large proportion of library workers are women. We all know that the women make up 90 per cent of the working force; that all the large, more important positions in the library world have been cornered by men." She also notes the women always enter library service through lower grades while directors are always men. Selection of upper officials is not made on the basis of superiority of intelligence or ability but simply on the basis of sex.

1919-04   "American Library Association: Asbury Park Conference: Sixth Session. Resolutions. Presented by the Library Employees' Union, 15590, Greater New York." *Library Journal* 44 (August 1919):521-522.

Text of resolution for equal pay and opportunity for women in librarianship. Discussion, in which Alice Tyler and R.R. Bowker address the achievements of women in librarianship, is summarized. The resolution was defeated by members attending the conference 121 to 1. Maude Malone is reported not to have voted.

1919-05   "An Open Letter to Women Library Assistants." *Library Assistant* 14 (October 1919):292.

Letter notes there is still a deep-rooted prejudice against the employment of women. Hope is expressed that the new Library School will provide training for women and that the LAA will appoint a new women's committee on the status of women in the profession.

1920-1929

*1920-01   Hand, T.W. *A Brief Account of the Public Libraries of the City of Leeds, 1870-1920.* Leeds: Leeds Public Library (?), 1920:25-26.

1920-02   Sayers, W.C.B. "Women Librarians and Assistants." In J.D. Brown's *Manual of Library Economy* (revised and rewritten by W.C. Berwick Sayers.) London: Grafton and Co. 1920:96.

Comments are similar to those in earlier editions, [1903-01; 1907-02] but somewhat shorter. Percentage of women employed in Britain has not changed from second edition [1907-02].

†1920-03   Peacock, M. "Sex Disqualification." *The Library World* 22 (February 1920):344-347.

A strong denunciation of sex discrimination in British libraries following World War I which notes, "in the history of library labours, we have reached the critical and dangerous point for women when, openly, sex is no disqualification, yet in secret reality it is a most powerful hardship."

1920-04   Bowker, R.R. "Women in the Library Profession: First Article." *Library Journal:* 45 (June 15, 1920):545-549.

While women have become prominent in American librarianship they are not yet treated with absolute equity. The activities of women in the ALA are described and biographical sketches of Minerva Sanders, Caroline Hewins, Theresa Elmendorf, Mary Wright Plummer and Alice Tyler are described.

Letter: Squires, T. "Masculine versus Feminine Librarians." *Public Libraries* 25 (October 1920): 435-436.

Letter from Library Employees' Union 15590, 463 Central Park West, N.Y.C. castigating Bowker for stating that no woman could replace Herbert Putnam as head of the Library of Congress. Questions the qualifications of highly placed men as opposed to the library education of women who advance "to even modest position in the service."

1920-05 Doad, M. "The Inarticulate Library Assistant." *Library Journal* 45 (June 15, 1920):540-543.

Before the war opened opportunities for "cultural women with trained minds" outside librarianship and teaching, there was always a waiting list for library assistant positions and not much opportunity for creative expression or advancement in the work. There was also little chance for an enriching life outside of work because of poor salaries. Since the Armistice, women have continued to resign from libraries and seek other positions. Opportunities for assistants to take on more responsibility and to develop their own ideas, and the creation of an organization through which they can voice their concerns, are urged.

1920-06 Hadley, C. "The ALA and the Library Worker." *Library Journal* 45 (June 15, 1920):534-540.

In a paper on the condition of American library workers the fact is noted that the National League of Women Workers called attention to the bad example set by libraries "for not only were library workers underpaid, but this by comparison was preventing workers in other educational and social fields from obtaining what otherwise would be granted them" (p. 538).

1920-07 Bowker, R.R. "Women in the Library: Second Article." *Library Journal* 45 (July 1, 1920):578-589.

Though public libraries of America have been chiefly run by women, not many leading municipalities have as yet made women their chief librarians. Biographical sketches of prominent women include: Electra Doren, Ellen E. Coe, Jessie Hume, Ann Wallace, Gratia Countryman, Mary Hannah Johnson and Mary F. Isom. Comments also include the contributions of women to library architecture.

1920-08 Bowker, R.R. "Women in the Library Profession: Third Article." *Library Journal* 45 (August 1920):635-640.

The last article in the series [1920-04; 07] chronicles the achievements of women state librarians, library educators and other outstanding women, Mary Eileen Ahern, Elizabeth Claypool Earl, Sarah Askew, Salome Cutler Fairchild, Adelaide Hasse, Mrs. H.J. Carr, and Mary L. Titcomb are included.

Letter: Dewey, M. "A Correction." *Library Journal* 45 (August 1920):658.

Letter written in simplified spelling correcting errors in Bowker's series. Recounts Theresa Elmendorf's refusal of the chief librarian position in Buffalo, preferring instead the more "difficult" bibliographic work.

1920-09 "Editorial." *Library Journal* 45 (August 1920):646.

Call for librarians to encourage young people to enter librarianship, a difficult task because of low salaries. "The library schools need more women - not to speak of a few more men."

1920-10   "Editorial." *Library Journal* 45 (August 1920):647.

Commentary on the "Women in the Library" series [1920-04; 07; 08] requesting information and reminiscences of other early leaders. Reference is made to Dewey's letter in the same issue which corrects several points [1920-08-letter].

1920-11   Power, R.L. "Women in Special Libraries." *Library Journal* 45 (September 1920):691-695.

Contends that the success of women in special library work is greater than in public librarianship. Supports contention with brief sketches of Mary L. Erwin, Beatrice Carr, Florence Spencer, Alice Rose, Marion Glenn, Ethel M. Johnson, Marie Fay Lindholm, Claribel R. Barnett, Maud A. Carabin, Sarah E. Ball and Ethel Cleland.

1921-01   "Women in Libraries." *Library Assistant* 15 (April 1921):131-132.

Notes that the Library Assistant's Association is represented in the London Society for Women's Service. Includes a letter from the Society commending the LAA for its stand on equal pay and requesting that the Association help the society by 1) taking action where women make less than men for the same work; 2) protesting when women are arbitrarily dismissed in favor of men; and 3) protesting against ads for library jobs which specify male or female. The LAA council approved the first and second points but not the third since they recognized that there were some positions for which only men or women were suitable.

1921-02   Reed, M. "The Loyalty of Women in the Library Profession." *The Librarian and Book World* 10 (May 1921):168-170.

"There is no excuse for these long hours, low pay and wearing work" now that the rate of library support has been increased.

1921-03   "We Have Been Looking Over the Results." *The Library World* 21 (October 1921):52.

News item noting the increase of women passing the School of Librarianship examinations, belonging to the Library Assistant Association, and to the Library Association. The high exam scores of women are taken as indication that "the best men are not entering the library profession."

†1921-04   "Men versus Women Librarians." *Library Assistant* 15 (November 1921):206-207.

Takes issue with the Winchester Library which offers less per year to a woman than a man; describes the low esteem of librarianship for a man.

1921-05   Best, M.S. "Women and Librarianship." *Library Association Record* 23 (December 15, 1921):399-409.

Author feels that women can bring virtues of sympathy, courtesy and reliability to library work, but their outlook is limited.

1922-01   Frost, M. "Women as Librarians and Library Assistants." *Library Assistant* 16 (April 1922):52-54.

Equal remuneration for women is discussed and recommended since discrimination has thus far prevailed.

1923-01   Williamson, C.C. *Training for Library Service: A Report Prepared for the Carnegie Corporation of New York.* New York: Carnegie Corporation, 1923; reprint ed., Ann Arbor, Michigan: University Microfilms, 1969.

Benchmark report on the status of library education includes discussion of the problems caused by the lack of distinction between professional work, for which college educated men and women are required, and the work of assistants which "can be performed just as well (perhaps better) by a young woman with a high school education and a little appropriate instruction and experience" (p. 4). Also discusses the problems of recruiting men into a profession which is known as woman's work "largely because it is generally looked upon as clerical" (p. 107). General statistics on graduates of library schools as of 1921 are broken down by sex for graduates still in library work and women graduates who have married (p. 78).

†**1925-01** Thorne, W.M. "Librarianship as a Career for Women." *Library Assistant* 18 (January 1925):21-22. Continued (February 1925):33-35.

Discusses the domination of the professions by men and the slow entrance of women to librarianship in Great Britain. Discusses the opportunities and qualifications for a librarian.

1925-02 Simmons, E.B. "The Women Behind the Books." *The Woman Citizen* 10 (June 27, 1925):7-8; 28.

Article is part of a series on vocations for women. Simmons notes that only "first-class" salaries prevent library work from being the ideal profession for women. Advises women who want to make money to go into business. Reasons that librarianship is peculiarly suited to women include "house-keeping ability, a gift for teaching, social instinct, patience and tact" — all qualities traditionally woman's. Notes that most librarians are women though men hold the top administrative posts. Highlights successful women such as Linda Eastman, Anna Mulheron, Gratia Countryman, Mary Eileen Ahern, and Sarah Askew. Women in department head positions are cited. The role of the Reader's Advisor is seen as ideal for women. Qualifications are given.

1926-01 Leuck, M.S. "The Genteel Professions." In her *Fields of Work for Women.* New York: D. Appleton and Company, 1926:116-125.

Librarianship, with teaching, is discussed as a ladylike profession "to which the girl who has failed to achieve matrimony can retire without losing her womanly qualities." Capable, ambitious girls' salaries and working conditions are lowered because of those who enter for this reason. Training, salaries and possible openings are discussed at length. "Except for the highest positions . . . there is little discrimination in favor of men."

1926-02 "Women Librarians Fifty Years Ago," *Libraries* 31 (June 1926):270-271.

Excerpt from P. Hanaford's book, *Women of the Century* [1877-01], relating to women librarians. The quote, in regard to newspaper accounts of the 1876 Librarians Conference, notes that although women attended the conference, no mention was made of the special capability of women for library work. Significant women librarians are noted. The excerpt was sent to *Libraries* by T. Hanison Cummings whose letter accompanies it. Cummings thought the excerpt relevant to the approaching fiftieth anniversary of the ALA.

1926-03 Bowker, R.R. "Seed Time and Harvest-The Story of the ALA." *Library Journal* 51 (October 15, 1926):880-886.

Speech made before the semi-centenary conference of the ALA, October 6, 1926, acknowledges the contribution of three women: Caroline Hewins, Minerva Saunders and Mary Wright Plummer (p. 882). The negative reaction of the trustees of Columbia College to women attending the library school founded by Dewey is noted (p. 884).

1927-01 Hatcher, O.L. "Library Work." In author's *Occupations for Women.* Richmond, Virginia: Southern Woman's Educational Alliance, 1927:345-363.

An overview of the various types of library jobs, training schools, and entrance qualifications needed for library work. Special section focuses on "Women in Library Work in Atlanta," since the only school in the South for the professional training of librarians is located there. Details of library positions in the Atlanta area are noted.

*1927-02   "The Woman Librarian: an Interesting Career." (Liverpool, England) *Liverpool Courier* (January 6, 1927).

*1927-03   A Woman Librarian. "Why I Like My Work." (Manchester, England) *Manchester Guardian* (February 21, 1927).

1928-01   Tillie, H.A. "Women in Librarianship." *Library World* 31 (December 1928):144-145.

Speaks against the hypocrisy of a society which at the same time praises women as qualified librarians and offers the administrative positions to men.

*1929-01   Hill, J.A. *Women in Gainful Occupations, 1870-1920.* Census Monograph, No. 9 Washington, DC: Government Printing Office, 1929:42.

1929-02   McNiece, T.S. "Women as Library Workers." In her *The Library and Its Workers.* New York: H.W. Wilson Company, 1929:17-18.

Introduction to the section on women in McNiece's anthology summarizes and comments on the role of women in the nineteenth century public libraries.

1929-02A   "Women as Library Workers." In *The Library and Its Workers.* Edited by T.S. McNiece. New York: H.W. Wilson Company, 1929:19-20.

Reprints comments of Justin Winsor and William Frederick Poole [1878-01] on the role of college women in librarianship.

1929-02B   Fairchild, S.C. "Women in American Libraries." In *The Library and Its Workers.* Edited by T.S. McNiece. New York: H.W. Wilson Company, 1929:21-29.

Reprint of [1904-04].

†1929-03   Wyer, J.I. "Women in College Libraries." *School and Society* 29 (February 16, 1929):227-228.

Letter to appointing officers of colleges and universities drawing their attention to "a neglected yet thoroughly competent and reasonably plentiful source of library personnel" - women.

1929-04   "Women in College Libraries." *Library Journal* 54 (April 1929):319.

Summary of Wyer's *School and Society* letter [1929-03]. "A review of the most important college libraries now run by women shows that while women are holding their own in the women's colleges, in colleges for men or co-educational institutes, they are represented, with very few exceptions, only in small relatively unimportant institutions."

1929-05   Woodhouse, C.G. and Yeomans, R.F. "Library Work." In their *Occupations for College Women; A Bibliography.* Greensboro, NC: Institute of Women's Professional Relations, October, 1929:143-146.

Bibliography of readily available materials devoted to occupations suitable for college women. The section on librarianship includes recruitment literature and articles describing qualifications and training of librarians.

1929-06   "A Composite Picture of the Rank and File in the Library Profession." *Library Journal* 54 (October 1, 1929):810-812.

Summary of the report of the ALA Committee on Salaries, Insurance and Annuities giving detailed breakdown of library assistants' education, salaries and budgets, including personal expenses. While the data is not broken down by sex, references in the article indicate that the library assistants responding to the survey were women.

1930-1939

*1930-01   Countryman, G.A. *Library Work as a Profession.* Minneapolis: Woman's Occupational Bureau, 1930.

1930-02   Spaulding, Mrs. H.W. "The Public Library and the Woman's Club." *Iowa Library Quarterly* 11 (July 1930):105-106.

Shows parallels between the development of the Iowa Federation of Women's Clubs and that of the public library and the continued involvement of club women in library work.

1931-01   Buck, Mrs. J.L.B. "Libraries and Women's Clubs." *Virginia Libraries* 4 (1931):63-64.

Reports the work of volunteer women in organizing establishment of public libraries. Notes that the Virginia Federation of Women's Clubs adopted as its slogan, "A Library in Every County in the State."

1931-02   Shera, J.H. "Handmaidens of the Learned World." *Library Journal* 56 (January, 1931):21-22.

Notes that the low status of librarianship is not due to the predominance of women (though the masculine minded might think so) but rather to inadequate intellectual stimulus.

1932-01   Dawe, G. "Fighting for Progress." In his *Melvil Dewey: Seer: Inspirer: Doer.* Essex County, NY: Lake Placid Club, 1932:184-205.

Chapter on founding of the first library school includes discussion of resistance to women students.

1932-02   Randall, W.M. "The College Library Staff." In his *The College Library: A Descriptive Study of the Libraries in Four-Year Liberal Arts College in the United States.* Chicago: American Library Association and the University of Chicago Press, 1932:51-66.

In his chapter on the college library staff Randall comments that large libraries are under the control of men although women have more professional training. Men are chosen for their academic training (p. 63-64).

*1933-01   Hanson, J.C.M. "Amerikansk og Europeisk bibliotekyesen." In *Festschrift: Overbibliotekar W. Munthe pa 50 arsolagen.* Oslo, 1933.

†1933-02   Sanders, S.H. "Problems; A Monthly Department of Discussion: Should the Preponderance of Women in the American Library Profession be Considered an Evil?" *Wilson Bulletin for Librarians* 8 (December 1933): 230-231.

Letter submitted to the *WLB* monthly "Problems" column. Writer is disturbed that so many American libraries are run by the female sex. In England the number of women holding senior posts would be negligible and rightly so since patrons would "certainly have much less confidence in a woman." Men read more widely than women. Women should have routine jobs but men, as in England, should hold responsible positions. Responses are asked from readers and prizes offered.

> **Responses:**   †Borden, A.K. "First Prize." *Wilson Bulletin for Librarians* 8 (March 1934):403-404.
>
> Defends the role of women in the profession by a litany of details women perform so well. "There is no denying the great strides forward that have been made under feminine organizing direction in such matters as the proper arrangement of pamphlet collections . . ." Sees the "most serious problem con-

fronting the library profession today - the annual loss through matrimony of so much feminine talent."

†Shera, J.H. "Second Prize." *Wilson Bulletin for Librarians* 8 (March 1934):404-405.

Responds, "Yes!" to Sanders but goes on to explain that the library and the classroom have been the only places for women to go. Exhorts society to accept women in all professions. Affirms the need for more equal representation by men in the field.

†Reuben from Ohio. "Third Prize - Tie." *Wilson Bulletin for Librarians* 8 (March 1934):405-406.

Writer calls American public libraries "Over-Rachelized" and explains that while women make good executives their distinctly feminine traits are handicaps. Specifically: lack of objectivity, inability to take criticism, squabbles with other women, inclination to accept fads, etc. Women also prefer the concrete to the general, already formulated ideas rather than creatively thinking for themselves. They can't deal with blueprints or mechanics, can't understand the needs of male readers, and don't read widely but indulge in light fiction.

†Hyatt, R. "Third Prize - Tie." *Wilson Bulletin for Librarians* 8 (March 1934):406-407.

Asks if Englishmen's attitudes toward women don't account for Sanders' ideas. In America women have longer been accepted as equal to men whereas in England women have been kept suppressed. Cites accomplishments of capable women.

Bowman, H.B. "Other Replies." *Wilson Bulletin for Librarians* 8 (March 1934):407.

Cites growth of American libraries, high circulation and many male borrowers as refutation of Sanders' viewpoint.

Litchfield, D.H. "Other Replies." *Wilson Bulletin for Librarians* 8 (March 1934):407.

Responds that Sanders is wrong. Senior posts in almost all large libraries in America are held by men while women do most of the minor clerical work.

Praeger, J.W. "Other Replies." *Wilson Bulletin for Librarians* 8 (March 1934):407; 409

School librarian writes he is the only male of 150 school librarians in his district and that he feels a need for more men librarians. He also feels that the effect of male librarians would be helpful in changing the "sissy" image of librarians held by the general public.

1934-01   Wellard, J.H. "Old Problems and Young Men in English Librarianship." *Wilson Bulletin for Librarians* 8 (February 1934):346-347; 371.

In the context of a discussion of the old and new guard in British librarianship the author notes that in Great Britain the profession has not yet succumbed to the preponderance of women as in the United States. This is essential for librarianship if it is not to lose its vigor and vitality.

1934-02   Scoggin, M.C. "The Retort American." *Wilson Bulletin for Librarians* 8 (March 1934):391-392.

Responds to [1934-01], and defends women by noting that intelligent individuals of both sexes have something of value to contribute. Summed up: "in the American profession, women predominate *although there is no discrimination against men;* in the English profession men predominate *because there is discrimination* against women."

1934-03 Bollert, E. "Bedarf und Nachwuchs im Wissenschaftlichen Bibliothekarsberuf." (trans: Demand and the Rising Generation in the Research Librarian's Profession.) *Zentralblatt fur Bibliotekswesen* 51 (May 1934): 263-268.

Survey of librarians in German university and research libraries and their educational backgrounds. Notes that fewer librarians are trained than needed to replace the loss through retirement, etc. Includes statistics showing that only 6.6 percent (53 of 802) of university level librarians are women (who were not admitted to the profession until after World War I). Of those only five have full-time civil service positions. The rest are employed in temporary positions or being trained.

1935-01 Headicar, B.M. *A Manual of Library Organization.* London: G. Allen and Unwin Ltd. and the Library Association, 1935:42; 59.

Several sections pertain to women. Headicar notes salaries (p. 42) should be equal and women should not be hired to save money though there are "perfectly valid reasons used against women to justify lower salaries": 1) greater percentage of absences; 2) inability to do a year's work without breaking down; 3) liability of women to err in moments of emergency; and 4) inability to maintain discipline (p. 59). But he also notes, "however, that women have some compensating qualifications," which tend "to level matters up," such as better concentration and more patience. Their best work comes when they are under the control of a man.

1935-02 Joeckel, C.B. *The Government of the American Public Library.* Chicago: The University of Chicago, Press, 1935.

Description, analysis, and evaluation of the position of the public library in the structure of government in the United States. Women's role on library boards is included. In cities of over 30,000 surveyed "library control" is reported as still largely a masculine affair (p. 236). "The right of women to serve on library boards seems no longer to require special protection" (p. 189).

*1935-03 "Women Passed Over in Public Service. Striking Examples of How Promotions Are Withheld By the Authorities! By Our Special Commissioner." *Australian Women's Weekly* (February 23, 1935).

†1936-01 Smith, S.W. "Librarianship-Stop-Gap or Profession?" *Wilson Bulletin for Librarians* 10 (March 1936):454-455; 458.

Librarians' salaries are low because women use the profession as a stop-gap until marriage and so are not willing to work to improve salaries. Recruitment of men is suggested as a solution.

Letter: Stokes, K.M. "In Defense of Women." *Wilson Bulletin for Librarians* 10 (April 1936):544-545.

Response to Smith from a woman who states: "those who have made library work their profession cannot fail to be incensed." Some women are more suited to professional work than housework. Spirited young ladies will not want to go to library school if "dry talk of equal pay for men and women doing the same work is ridiculous." Refutes arguments that in our social system men are providers and women homemakers by asking what of women without fathers, husbands or brothers who may be the sole support of aged parents. Smith's suggestion that salaries be on the basis of their relative needs sounds like "a Mussolini."

1937-01 Wilson, L.R. "The American Library School Today." *Library Quarterly* 7 (April 1937):211-245.

Under subtopic, "Students," the 1,184 students enrolled in library school during the 1936-37 year are analyzed by sex. Table 16 shows that first year students include 953 women and 112 men; advanced students (those pursuing the Masters and PhD degrees) include 71 women and 48 men.

1937-02   Bixler, P.H. "Thoughts While Becoming. a Librarian." *Wilson Bulletin for Librarians* 11 (June 1937):684-687.

One section of the article, "The Woman Question," notes that until women become politically astute their status will not equal men's.

1937-03   Lemaitre, H. "Hongrie. Association des Bibliothecaires et des Archivistes de la Hongrie." *Archives and Bibliotheques* 3 (1937-38):311-312.

Brief survey of the Hungarian Association of Archivists and Librarians, its history and conferences. Notes that forty-four of eighty-two students are women (in the spring 1937 courses). Students' qualifications are advanced university studies and language skills.

1938-01   Leuck, M.S. "The Genteel Professions." In her *Fields of Work for Women.* New York: D. Appleton and Company, 3rd Ed. 1938:136-149.

Extensively revised from [1926-01]. Emphasizes shift in library training to a formalized school situation and higher salaries. Includes lengthy description of the reader advisor position, which "comes nearer to the dreams of the girl who becomes a librarian because she loved books than does any other division of her profession."

> **Review:**   Winning, M. *Library Journal* 63 (November 1, 1938):838.
>
> Reviewer wonders if, as men enter the field, Leuck might not change the headings under which librarianship appears: "The Genteel Professions." Overall, a positive review.

*1938-02   Speight, P.M. and Hartmann, E. "Survey of Conditions Relating to the Employment of Women in Libraries." In *Survey of Professional and Semi-Professional Careers for Women in the Union.* Edited by the South African Association of University Women. Johannesburg Branch. Johannesburg, South Africa: South Africa Association of University Women, 1938:57-60.

1938-03   Goldstein, F. "Library Work for Jewish Girls." *B'nai B'rith Magazine* 52 (February 1938):202/203.

Description of public library work, the qualities and preparation needed to become a librarian with specific counseling for Jews who must face the anti-Semitism which exists "in this field as in others."

1938-04   Harnack, A. von. "Die Italienischen Bibliotheken." (trans: The Italian Librarians) *Zentralblatt für Bibliothekswesen* 55 (March 1938):156-164.

Outlines high positions held by women in Italian academic libraries — positions which men will not take because of low salaries.

1938-05   "Tribute to Cleveland and Its Feminine Staff." *ALA Bulletin* 32 (March 1938):203.

Praise for high degree of "conscientiousness, special training and professional competence" of staff.

†1938-06   "Weaker Sex?" *Library Journal* 63 (March 15, 1938):232.

Editorial regarding scarcity of qualified candidates for administrative posts laments the fact that young women are overlooked for top jobs while young men, often of unproved ability, are recommended and pushed. Points out that a disproportionate number of library administrators are male and opens a forum to discuss the problem.

> **Letters:**   †Barker, T.D. "In Reply to the Weaker Sex." *Library Journal* 63 (April 15, 1938):294-295.
>
> Notes a number of supporting facts on discrimination against women including the fact that the ALA nominating committee would not nominate a dis-

tinguished woman because not enough time had elapsed for a women to be considered for president. An analysis of ALA officers showing discrimination in practice is included.

†Curtis, F.R. "In Reply to the Weaker Sex." *Library Journal* 63 (April 15, 1938):294.

Feels that though women are equal, the fact that men can go to men's organizations and places where policies are made before formal action is taken may tip things in their favor.

†Daniels, M. "In Reply to the Weaker Sex." *Library Journal* 63 (April 15, 1938):296.

Sees the problem as three-fold: trustees, boards, the profession itself. Trustees and committees search the country over for a man, excellent or mediocre, old or young, while women with better qualifications must take the back seat. Writer calls for a "Lady Pankhurst who will champion the cause of women in the library profession."

Mann, M. "In Reply to the Weaker Sex." *Library Journal* 63 (April 15, 1938):295-296.

A reasoned statement calling for mutual respect while writer notes that women have introduced new and inventive patterns.

Reese, R. "In Reply to the Weaker Sex." *Library Journal* 63 (April 15, 1938):295.

Applauds editorial and notes "one needs only go to a few meetings . . . to realize how much better chance even second rate young men have than the best women."

Tyler, A.S. "In Reply to the Weaker Sex." *Library Journal* 63 (April 15, 1938):294.

Places blame on library boards who assume institutions are more highly recognized and influential if a man is at the head; on Library Schools who feel "men must have the jobs" when asked for recommendations; and on an influential group of male librarians within the ALA.

Hunt, M.L. "Men vs. Women." *Library Journal* 63 (May 1, 1938):342.

Author feels women should work for their own advancement; that utmost concern of both men and women should be for the betterment of the profession.

†Savord, R. "Men vs. Women." *Library Journal* 63 (May 1, 1938):342-343.

Blames both men and women for sex discrimination in jobs. Notes she is not a "detestable" feminist but laments the fact that a generation of young women are being over-looked for young men who have not yet served their normal period of apprenticeship. Proposes that the new ALA trustees section take up the issue.

Taber, F.T. "Men vs. Women." *Library Journal* 63 (May 1, 1938):343.

Glad to finally see in print revelation of the policy that men are given desirable positions over better qualified women. She notes that even in library school men are given preferential treatment for fellowships.

†Lightfoot, R.M. "Further Discussion." *Library Journal* 63 (June 1, 1938):438.

Points out that men are more represented in administration in all professions; claims prejudice exists towards male librarian's image.

Banning, M.C. "Women as Administrators." *Library Journal* 63 (August 1938):569.

Regrets that sex should influence administrative choice but thinks militant feminist attitude toward condition equally bad.

1938-07   Shilling, M.W. "Women in Librarianship." *South Africa Libraries* 5 (April 1938):186-190.

A refutation of arguments against women in librarianship inspired by B.M. Headicar [1935-01]. Speaks for better salaries for women and gives employment statistics as well as qualifications of women in South Africa.

1938-08   Goldstein, F. "Library Work for College Women." *Library Service News* 7 (April 1938):26-27.

A reprint of Goldstein's "Library Work for Jewish Girls" [1938-03] with all references to Jews and anti-Semitism removed.

1938-09   Committee to Study the Status of Married Women in the Library Profession. "Status of Married Women." *ALA Bulletin* 32 (June 1938):402.

Report of survey of seventy libraries to determine attitude toward hiring and promoting married women. Majority reported placements were according to ability and educational qualifications.

1938-10   Beust, N.E. "Do You Want to Be a Librarian?" *American Girl* 21 (September 1938):8-10.

Tells of educational requirements for librarianship and the types of positions in various departments of the library with special emphasis on the joys of service to children.

†1938-11   Alvarez, R.S. "Women's Place in Librarianship." *Wilson Bulletin for Librarians* 13 (November 1938):175-178.

Argues that women hold the majority of administrative positions in librarianship and leading positions in library associations. Provides figures from his dissertation [1939-01] showing that women predominate.

> **Letter:**   Kaiser, W.H. "War Between the Sexes." *Wilson Bulletin for Librarians* 13 (January 1939):336.
>
> Objects to Alvarez's conclusion that women hold the majority of power positions in librarianship. Places data in columns for easy comparison to demonstrate that none of the figures presented in article show women to have a share of the administrative positions proportionate to their number in the profession.

1939-01   Alvarez, R.S. "Qualifications of Heads of Libraries in Cities of Over 10,000 Population in the Seven North-Central States." Ph.D. thesis. The University of Chicago, 1939.

Heads of 241 public libraries in Mid-western cities of over 10,000 population were studied. Information on professional qualifications, salaries, advancement, and activities are presented in detail and sometimes broken down by sex. The larger the library the more likely the head is a man. Men who head libraries in cities above 35,000 are more frequently appointed from outside the local community, more often college graduates, and received larger salaries than did women in similar positions. Women tend more often to be library school graduates and report more previous experience in library work. Alvarez concludes that "library work is unusual in the extent to which its administrative positions are open to women." Among his recommendations is that recruitment of men be given more attention.

1939-02   Koch, E. "Die Bibliothek der Technischen Hochschule und die Industrie." (trans.: The Library in the Technical Institute and in Industry.) *Zentralblatt für Bibliothekswesen* 56 (1939):470-484.

Surveys the library in German technical institutes and services to industry. Includes a sharp critique of women in the middle levels of librarianship who lack knowledge of scientific literature, are slow in processing technical books, and to whom logical, systematic accounting is unknown or abhorrent. Koch proudly announces that for the past year his was one of the few libraries functioning without women workers and he has received only the most favorable reactions.

†**1939-03**   Munthe, W. "Librarianship — a Feminine Vocation?" In his *American Librarianship from a European Angle:* Chicago: American Library Association, 1939:155-160.

Observations on the impact of the numbers of women in American librarianship. The over-feminization of the profession is both a cause and a result of low salaries. Men must be attracted to the profession to increase salaries and counter the sentimentality, lack of inclination towards advanced study, gossipy tone and missionary spirit of women. Women have made outstanding contributions to librarianship in the areas of service to children and use of fiction but skills are needed to serve professional men as well.

†**1939-04**   Stokes, K.M. "Warning — Soft Shoulders." *Wilson Bulletin for Librarians* 13 (March 1939):470-471.

Criticizes women librarians for their failure to respond to Stewart Smith's article [1936-01]. Hers was the only letter to the editor. Argues for the right and ability of married women to pursue their careers if they choose. Warns women not to expect soft treatment because they are women; they must be librarians first in order to get equality.

Letter: Graham, C.S. "A Vulnerable Minority." *Wilson Bulletin for Librarians* 13 (May 1939):625.

Agrees with Stokes and adds that attitudes and legislation on working married women affect all women.

1939-05   Stephens, E. "Gunpowder Women of the ALA." *California Library Association Bulletin* 1 (September 1939):9-13.

A letter summarizing the 1939 ALA convention. Reports the conversations of several women on the role of women in the profession. A return to the "Plummer-Isom" tradition is sought.

1940-1949

1940-01   Carnell, E.J. "Library Policy: Great Britain, United States, New Zealand." In *Proceedings and Papers of the Twelfth Conference of Representatives. and Members.* Wellington, New Zealand. February 21-23, 1940. Wellington, New Zealand: New Zealand Library Association, 1940:43-54.

In comparing U.S. and British libraries Carnell notes that British libraries employ a large percentage of young girls who will leave the field for marriage thereby solving the problem of full salaries. Tells her listeners that they will be "astounded" to hear that in the U.S. there are not only married women employed but women with children. Criticizes regulations that say women must resign when they marry.

1940-02   Quigley, M. "Books, Books, Books." *Mademoiselle* (January 1940):82; 113-114; 116.

Belies the spinster image of the librarian by explaining the librarian's exciting day — a day which "teems with men" wherein a pretty girl can take a man's mind off business. Qualifications and salaries for library work are cited.

1940-03   Glauning, O. "Der Weibliche Mittlere Dienst." (trans.: The Female in Middle-Level Library Service.) *Zentralblatt fur Bibliothekswesen* 57 (April 1940):164-167.

Response to Koch [1939-02]. Gives samples of excellent female librarians and library workers in Munich and Leipzig. Blames any shortcomings women may have compared to male workers on their poorer education — a fact which libraries exploit, making it impossible for women to rise in the hierarchy. In a footnote another male librarian, Bollert, concurs with Glauning.

†1940-04   Cowper, R.S. "Not in Our Stars." *Library Association Record* 42 (June 1940):166-167.

Urges women in librarianship to "set [their] house in order." Stabilization of women in librarianship is essential not only to gain the immediate goals of equal pay for equal work, but as a safeguard against totalitarian forces which some day may threaten democracy even in England.

1940-05   Freer, P. "Address by the President." *South African Libraries* 8 (July 1940):3-6.

An examination of factors contributing to the poor esteem in which libraries are held by the general public: libraries bring no revenue; places called "libraries" might be as insignificant as a village hall; the employment of women aggravates the situation since their enfranchisement is too recent for the recognition of equal pay for equal work. Women also marry and resign, which is detrimental to the development of the profession.

1940-06   Wolf, I. "Noch Einmal: die Frau im Mittleren Bibliotheksdienst." (trans.: Once More: The Woman in Middle Level Library Service.) *Zentralblatt für Bibliotekswesen* 57 (August-September 1940):406-408.

Response by a woman librarian to specific points in Koch's accusations [1939-02]. Argues that German women's lack of ability is because of the education of female library workers, not their sex. Points out that due to the war between 50% and 100% of the middle level library workers in research libraries are women. Were Koch's experiences a true indication of women's abilities, the entire library system would be in a disasterous condition which it clearly is not.

1940-07   Lyle, G.R. "They Have Made Their Mark." *Library Journal* 65 (November 15, 1940):947-950.

An examination of the 187 librarians listed in the 1940-41 edition of *Who's Who in America* who are still active in the profession. Of the total 235 librarians listed forty-four were women. The analysis of the 187 is not broken down by sex although it is noted that seventeen of the women included hid their age by omitting birthdays and college graduations.

1941-01   Freer, P. "The Profession in South Africa." *Ontario Library Review* 25 (February 1941):62-64.

Reprint of [1940-05].

1941-02   Liddle, H. "Resigned on Marriage." *Library Assistant* 34 (April 1941):67-68.

Women do not become unfit for work when married, so they should not be forced to resign.

1941-03   Matthews, Mrs. R.E.S. "Married Women Librarians." *Library Journal* 66 (August 1941):650-651.

Discusses how married women suffer much more discrimination than single women in all fields.

1943-01   "Letter to the Editor." *Library World* 46 (December 1943):84.

An opinion that women are being held in lower positions by male supervisors.

1945-01   "Dis nie Meisie-werk Nie." (trans.: It's Not Just Girl's Work.). *Cape Libraries* 3 (April 1945):2.

A metamorphosis is occurring in the concept of librarianship as a profession. Rising interest in the library has led to a reevaluation of a librarian's job from that of a leisure-time occupation for refined ladies to that of a profession in which men might be interested in South Africa. Outlines the two kinds of education offered, the correspondence course or the course at Cape Town University.

1946-01   Library Association. "Royal Commission on Equal Pay." *Library Association Record* 48 (March 1946):56-57.

Statement submitted by the Library Association to the Royal Commission in favor of maintaining an equal balance between men and women in the profession for four reasons: 1) "there are many tasks for which women are most suitable (e.g., work with young people)"; 2) "there is in most library services more work suitable for the relatively junior assistant than for the senior" hence a high turnover is needed in the field and this can be gained by employing women, a high percentage of whom leave for marriage; 3) there are considerable administrative responsibilities involved in senior positions and men have more capabilities in these areas; and 4) successful librarianship requires long years of experience; therefore, the men needed to fill "senior administrative and specialized posts must start their careers at an early age." Thus both men and women are needed in the field. Equal pay for men and women should avoid over-feminization while not reversing the turnover rate essential to the profession.

1946-02   Korb, G.M. "Successful Librarians as Revealed in *Who's Who in America.*" *Wilson Library Bulletin* 20 (April 1946):603-604; 607.

Analysis of librarians listed in *Who's Who 1944-45* which includes breakdown by sex. "The Who's Who library is a man's world by three to one. This is in contrast to the proportions in the profession where women outnumber men by nine to one." Only two of the 55 women listed have married; "the women who rose to success placed a career above marriage." Twenty of the women and two of the men did not reveal their ages. The typical leader of the profession is a 58 year old male.

1946-03   "Liegeligt antal af mandlige og Kvindelige bibliotekarer br tilstraebes." (trans.: Equal Number of Men and Women Librarians Should Be Sought.) *Bogens Verden* 28 (June-July 1946):46.

Quotes a statement by the Library Association to a Commission on Equal Pay for Men and Women [1946-01] expressing the desirability of recruiting and training more men for administrative library positions (since "experience has shown that more men than women are able to take up administrative responsibility — the outstanding female administrators notwithstanding"). The Danish writer urges the Danish library world to follow the English recommendation and make a concerted effort to attract more men to library work in order to have an equal representation of both sexes.

†**1948-01**   Enser, A.G.S. "Shall the Misses Be Masters?" *Library Association Record* 50 (May 1948):124-125.

Membership registers in the 1937 and 1947 Library Association *Year Books* are examined to determine whether librarianship is becoming over-feminized. The answer is yes, more women than men entered the field during the decade studied. Men, however, hold the highest professional posts, "and herein lies the only crumb of comfort to male members (but for how long?)" The post war years may see the balance of male and female more equalized but the "real answer to the problem lies in equality of pay between the sexes, since this would obviate that so prevalent practice of obtaining quantity without quality in public library staffing by the employment of cheap rate female labour."

Letter: Cook F.E. "Shall the Misses Be Masters?" *Library Association Record* 50 (July 1948):195.

Scathing response to Enser. Asks whether we should be concerned with over masculinization if we are called upon to be concerned with the increased feminine membership of the Library Association. Asks for a rank and salary study of women in the largest public libraries.

Letters in response to F.E. Cook:

Broome, E.H. "Shall the Misses Be Masters?" *Library Association Record* 50 (September 1948):249.

A lengthy defense of the hard-working male compared to the frivolous female employee meant as a refutation to Cook. Women who rise to the position of chief librarian should be the exception rather than the rule.

Enser, A.G.S. "Shall the Misses Be Masters?" *Library Association Record* 50 (September 1948):250.

Protests that his article was not meant to be an attack against women nor a questioning of their efficiency, but a proof of the over-feminization of public librarianship. Cook's letter is termed a "naughty, petulant outburst" and is responded to point by point.

Gardner, F.M. "Shall the Misses Be Masters?" *Library Association Record* 50 (September 1948):249.

Refutes the letter from Cook, one of whose assertions was that men develop more slowly than women, with data from intelligence tests that show girls are only three tenths of a year ahead of boys in development.

Firby, N.K. "Shall the Misses Be Masters?" *Library Association Record* 50 (August 1948):226.

Submits a quote from a speech by Baker [1880-01] read before the Library Association in 1879 in which employment of women is recommended.

Greenslade, C. "Shall the Misses Be Masters?" *Library Association Record* 50 (August 1948):225.

Notes that Enser, "while admitting that war-time conditions have affected the proportion of men to women qualifying in recent years, has underestimated the allowance to be made on this account."

Haywood, J.C. "Shall the Misses Be Masters?" *Library Association Record* 50 (August 1948):225-226.

Considers that preference for women is preventing the entrance of men into the profession since a) women in the general and clerical division under the National Service Acts receive lower salaries and b) are not liable for service. The remedy for a) is equalization of salaries, though no simple remedy will overcome b). While it may be more difficult for men to enter librarianship, once in they advance more rapidly than women. Librarians should be concerned that the fittest persons, irrespective of sex, become librarians.

Moore, M.S. "Shall the Misses Be Masters?" *Library Association Record* 50 (August 1948):226.

Further analysis of Enser's tables shows that there is little reason for women to obtain the more prestigious Fellow of the Library Association (F.L.A.) since the best positions are earmarked for men.

Murison, W.J. "Shall the Misses Be Masters?" *Library Association Record* 50 (August 1948):226.

More statistics demonstrate that while the number of women entering the profession is increasing the number of women in chief librarianships is not increasing proportionate to their percentage of the profession and, in fact, is proportionate to their number ten years ago.

Whitehouse, R.D.E. "Shall the Misses Be Masters?" *Library Association Record* 50 (August 1948):225.

Refutes Enser with later statistics and offers as counter the U.S. experience where the preponderance of female staff has not resulted in the decay of libraries.

1948-02   Unger, N.A. "Why Women Work." *ALA Bulletin* 32 (June 1948):403.

A letter recommending *Why Women Work*, a pamphlet reporting economic reasons for women working, which "will go far toward disabusing administrators of the fairly malevolent idea that women work for 'pin money'."

1948-03   Metcalfe, J. "Librarianship: Qualification and Recruitment at Home and Abroad." *New Zealand Libraries* 11 (December 1948):278-281.

General comments reprinted from the *Australian Commonwealth Office News,* June 1948, which include references to women in librarianship. Author notes that women in Great Britain receive more equal pay than in Australia but that the proportion of women is less: there women could be encouraged to enter the profession so that a fifty-fifty balance could be obtained at all levels. More cultured men look to library work in Great Britain while in Australia books are considered "sissy." More "certainly good girls" come forward as entrants than "certainly good boys."

1949-01   Garceau, O. *The Public Library in the Political Process.* New York: Columbia University Press, 1949.

Report on the government and politics of the public library undertaken as part of the Public Library Inquiry. Notes that while there were "some women in the sample who were astute in city or county government far beyond most of the men librarians, it remains true that the majority of women we met retained a deep distrust of politics, a feeling of acute helplessness . . ." (p. 89). While women librarians do not participate in the councils of political power such as the Rotary Club, which tend to be male, this handicap is not seriously crippling (p. 114-115). Reference is also made to complaints that Carl Milam, Executive Secretary of The American Library Association, favored men librarians over more deserving women librarians for important vacancies in the profession (p. 171).

1949-02   U.S. Department of Labor Statistics. "Librarians." *Occupational Outlook Handbook, 1949.* Washington, DC: U.S. Government Printing Office, 1949:109-110.

Notes that there are "about 30,000 trained librarians, of whom 90 per cent are women," and that there is considerable turn-over in this field because many young women marry and leave their jobs. Also both men and women find positions in other fields where librarianship is an asset (p. 109).

†**1949-03**   Munn, R. "It's a Mistake to Recruit Men." *Library Journal* 74 (November 1, 1949):1639-1640.

Opposes recruiting more "average run-of-the-mine [men] simply to get men . . . It will operate against the profession, both by filling it with men of mediocre caliber and by discouraging the entrance of superior women." Because of the low salaries, librarianship will remain a woman's profession and should be kept attractive to capable women.

Letters: McCann, E. "Let Them Come In." *Library Journal* 74 (December 1, 1949):1802.

Suggests concentrating on making the librarian's work clear to the public so that more capable men and women will be drawn to the profession. More men may be needed in the profession because "any group where a man is out-numbered 250 to 1 is not going to permit him to make a proper adjustment to the task at hand."

Brown, T. A. "Recruiting Men." *Library Journal* 74 (December 15, 1949):1842.

Verse parody of Munn's argument.

Obler, [Sic] E.M. "Men Librarians." *Library Journal* 75 (January 15, 1950):66; 98.

Argues that Munn's view that the present economic status and position of librarians will not improve is a counsel of despair. Claims that men make better administrators than women because of various physiological and psychological reasons.

Letter: Heathcote, L.M. "Men Librarians." *Library Journal* 75 (April 1, 1950):518; 520.

Claims that women resent inferior type of men entering profession, not men as such. Questions Obler's statements on men and women as administrators.

McDonough, E. "Men Librarians." *Library Journal* 75 (March 15, 1950):422; 478.

Argues that delimitation of field into "women's work" and "men's work" is unfortunate, causing suspicion and mistrust.

1950-1959

1950-01   David, L.M. *Economic Status of Library Personnel, 1949.* Chicago: American Library Association, 1950.

Report of survey undertaken by the U.S. Department of Labor, Bureau of Labor Statistics. Earnings of women were lower than men in both the professional and non-professional library positions. Most of the women library workers surveyed were single and had no dependents. Tables break down data on sex by education, race, marital status, dependents, salary and region, and salary and education.

1950-02   Leigh, R.D. *The Public Library in the United States.* New York: Columbia University Press, 1950.

General report of the studies making up the Public Library Inquiry, including Garceau [1949-01] and Bryan [1952-01]. Includes judgment "that actually there is a dual career structure in the public library field, one for men and one for women" (p. 196).

1950-03   Banister, J.R. "Just How Right Is Mr. Munn?" *Library Journal* 75 (February 1, 1950):141-142; 155.

Refutes Munn's arguments [1949-03] that it is a mistake to recruit men with the following: 1) recruiting has no effect on quality, only on quantity; 2) Munn's measurements of mediocrity are questionable; 3) a librarian's salary is enough on which to support dependents; 4) women as well as men have dependents and so need adequate salaries.

Letter: Sass, S. "Men Librarians." *Library Journal* 75 (April 1, 1950):520.

Has no wish to enter controversy between Munn [1949-03] and Banister but disputes Banister's claim that librarians are paid as well as other professions and offers salary statistics on chemists and engineers as evidence.

1950-04 Labb, J. "Librarians in *Who's Who in America.*" *Wilson Library Bulletin* 25 (September 1950):54-56.

Study of the background, education and characteristics of librarians (all administrators) listed in *Who's Who in America* notes: "In the profession as a whole, according to the 1940 census, there are 36,347 individuals, of which 3,801 are men and 32,546 women . . . However, of the persons worthy of listing in *Who's Who in America, 1948-1949* there are 256 men librarians, while 124 are women." Also notes only thirteen of the 124 women were married as opposed to 242 of the 256 men. None of the individuals listed were school librarians.

1951-01 U.S. Department of Labor, Bureau of Labor Statistics, "Librarians." *Occupational Outlook Handbook,* 1951 Edition. Washington, DC: U.S. Government Printing Office, 1951:118-119.

Notes that about "30,000 trained librarians were employed in late 1949, of whom 90 per cent were women" and that turnover is considerable in the field because young women marry and leave their jobs or both men and women move into other fields (p. 118).

1951-02 Enser, A.G.S. "Figures and Facts." *Library Association Record* 53 (January 1951):14-15.

A comparison of the register of members in the 1947 and 1950 editions of the *Library Association Yearbook* similar to that undertaken by the author for an earlier period [1948-01] to generalize the feminization of the profession. Over the past two years the intake ratio is one male to every three females; prior to that it was one male to six females. More men than women are seeking to qualify as Fellows of the Library Association, a more prestigious credential than Associate of the Library Association, the credential more women hold. More married women are continuing to work than before the war. The author leaves interpretation of the figures gathered to the reader.

1951-03 Hintz, C.W. "Personnel Administration - Discrimination, Despotism, Democracy." *PNLA Quarterly* 16 (October 1951):15-22.

Out of 129 woman respondents to a Pacific Northwest Library Association's survey, 65.1% feel discrimination exists against females.

†1952-01 Bryan, A.I. *The Public Librarian: A Report of the Public Library Inquiry of the Social Science Research Council.* New York: Columbia University Press, 1952.

Report of a study of public library personnel undertaken as part of the Public Library Inquiry. Data are analyzed by sex. Conclusions drawn about male and female librarians and the position of women in the public library include: 1) women predominate but not in high administrative positions except in smaller libraries; 2) male librarians hold consistently higher academic qualifications than women, whose qualifications tend to be from experience or library training programs; 3) tensions between men and women, particularly expressed by middle management women, were found and attributed to the "gradual shift from a women's occupation to a 'co-educational' profession."

*1952-02   Stjernqvist, H. "Bibliotekar - Statistik 1950." (trans.: Statistics on Librarians in 1950.) *Bibliotekaren* 14 (1952):21-30.

*1952-03   Whittock, J.M. "Study of the Interests of the Female Students Enrolled in the School of Library Science, Drexel Institute of Technology, as Measured by the Strong Vocational Interest Blank and the Kuder Preference Record." Master's thesis. Drexel Institute of Technology, 1952.

1952-04   Vivian, M.E. "Discrimination Against Women in the Professions; A Survey of Recent Literature." *PNLA Quarterly* 16 (January 1952):83-89.

Mentions research done on discrimination towards women, followed by bibliography on status of women in professions.

1954-01   Hamner, P.N. "The Ladies' Library Associations of Michigan: A Curious Byway in Library History." Master's thesis. Western Reserve University, 1954.

Historical survey of the Ladies' Library Associations of Michigan, which were responsible for the development of public libraries in Michigan communities during the last half of the nineteenth century.

1954-02   Trautman, R. *A History of the School of Library Service, Columbia University.* New York: Columbia University Press, 1954.

The history of, and resistance to, women students at Columbia in 1886-1888 is outlined (pp. 12-13; 18-19). It is also noted that when Carl M. White accepted a position as Dean of the School in 1943, one of his conditions was a gradual reduction of women on the faculty (p. 51).

*1954-03   "Britisk Bibliotekar Besoker Norske Biblioteker." (trans.: British Librarian Visits Norwegian Libraries.) *Bok og Bibliotek* 21 (November 1954):274-275.

1956-01   Wilson, L.R. and Tauber, M.F. *The University Library.* New York: Columbia University Press, 1956.

In a discussion of academic rank for librarians the authors note that one of higher education administration's major objections to faculty status for librarians is the fact that library staffs are predominantly women (p. 322).

†1956-02   Wilden-Hart, M. "Women in Librarianship." *Assistant Librarian* 49: (May 1956):78-80.

Feels women's inherent faults cause them to be passed over for many awards and opportunities.

1957-01   Douglass, R.R. "Personality of the Librarian." Ph.D. thesis. University of Chicago, 1957.

General purpose was to ascertain the extent to which the library profession "selects" members with a characteristic personality configuration. Hypotheses confirmed included: the male librarian is more feminine in his interests than men in general and is characterized as more sensitive and passive than men in general. Men are more theoretical and aesthetic than women librarians. Women are found to be strong in social and religious values and weak in the economic and political.

1957-02   Harvey, J.F. *The Librarian's Career: A Study of Mobility.* Rochester, NY: University of Rochester Press for the Association of College and Reference Librarians, 1957 (ARCL Microcard Series. No. 85).

Report of a study undertaken to analyze aspects of job behavior as revealed in the job histories of academic and public library chiefs listed in *Who's Who in Library Service*

1943. Factors correlating with vertical and horizontal mobility were sought. Among the summary conclusions: those who reached higher advancement levels tended to be older married males; low achievement levels were more likely held by younger single females. Sex, itself, was an important discriminator between the vertically mobile and the immobile. "Chief librarianship, as found in this study, was a man's world, even though 70 percent of the practitioners were female, since men held the better positions and were always more mobile than females" (p. 145).

*1957-03   Holt, L.C. "Study of Western Reserve University Library School Graduates 1934-1953." Master's thesis. Western Reserve University, 1957.

1957-04   U.S. Department of Labor, Bureau of Labor Statistics. "Libraries." *Occupational Outlook Handbook,* 1957 Edition. Washington, DC: U.S. Government Printing Office, 1957:183-185.

Notes that in 1950 more than 55,000 librarians were employed of whom almost ninety percent are women. About two-thirds of these women were employed in public libraries or public school libraries. "In recent years, more men have been entering the library field partly because of the increased salaries being offered, the growing emphasis on library service in scientific and technical fields, and improved opportunities for advancement to administrative positions" (p. 183). In discussing the employment outlook, many additional openings are anticipated because of the "turnover among young women in the field who leave their jobs for marriage and family reasons" (p. 184).

1957-05   Lightfoot, R.M. Jr. "In Defense of Nepotism." *Library Journal* 82 (June 15, 1957):1610-1616.

Urges that each applicant be considered solely on basis of merit and not denied positions if related to another employee of an organization. This is particularly crucial to librarianship where "there is a strong tendency for male librarians to marry female librarians." Responses from fourteen library administrators to his proposal ranging from approval to opposition are quoted.

1957-06   Hamilton, W.J. "American Librarianship: Some Women." *Library Review* 16 (Winter 1957):238-247.

Personal reminiscences women who were outstanding librarians. Mentions many names in this cursory survey; gives particular attention to Linda Eastman, Sarah Bogle and the women who worked for H.W. Wilson.

1958-01   Sammons, W. "Preface." *Who's Who of American Women Volume I* (1958-1959). Chicago: The A.N. Marquis Company, 1958:7-9.

While describing the procedures used to collect data for the biographical entries the fact that comparatively few librarians are included is questioned. The author concludes that while librarianship is dominated by women, they do not make contributions proportionate to their number. Harvey's [1958-02] analysis is quoted to support this judgment.

1958-02   Harvey, J.F. "Variety in the Experience of Chief Librarians." *College and Research Libraries* 19 (March 1958):107-110.

Sex differential is viewed as the most important personal characteristic influencing achievement of administrative positions, since men were likely to have wider varieties of job experience, and greater mobility than females. A summary of [1957-02].

1958-03   Shores, L. *A Profession of Faith: The First Annual Mary C. Richardson Lecture.* Geneseo, New York: State University Teachers College, March 27, 1958.

Recruitment lecture extolling the merits of librarianship. In a section rebutting Alice Bryan's [1952-01] composite picture of librarians as "inhibited old maids," Shores notes that it is not universally true that most librarians are women and that in the U.S., where women are in the majority, most administrative posts are held by men. Regarding Bryan's insinuation that librarianship is effeminate, Shores cites Bryan's own reports of masculinity and femininity tests which show male librarians to be masculine and women normal, not at all all old maids: 64% of those women who were unmarried desired marriage, and 37% were willing to give up librarianship for home-making.

1959-01   Paradis, A.A. *Librarians Wanted.* New York: David McKay Company, Inc. 1959.

Notes that "for many years women dominated the library field because it was considered women's work and did not pay enough to enable a man to support a family," but that has changed and men, who fill most of the top administrative posts, will advance and earn high salaries (p. 229).

1959-02   Parsons, T. "Implications of the Study." In *The Climate of Book Selection: Social Influences on School and Public Libraries.* Edited by J.P. Danton. Berkeley: University of California, School of Librarianship, 1959.

In a discussion of Marjorie Fiske's *Book Selection and Censorship: A Study of School and Public Libraries in California* the sex composition of librarianship is briefly examined. The tendency of women to gravitate into supportive types of occupations is noted but the question of whether this is due to preference or barriers in other professions is not examined. The predominance of women "should be considered both a symptom and a partial determinant of the pattern with which we are concerned" — the presence of anomie in librarianship (p. 94-95).

1959-03   U.S. Department of Labor, Bureau of Labor Statistics. "Librarians." *Occupational Outlook Handbook,* 1959 Edition. Washington, DC: U.S Government Printing Office, 1959:200-203.

Discussion of where librarians are employed notes that "by far the majority of librarians are women, and most of them are employed in public libraries or in the libraries of public schools." The influx of men into the field is commented on and attributed to higher salaries, emphasis on library service by many fields, and improved opportunity for advancement to administrative positions (p. 201). High turnover in the field because of young women "who leave their jobs for marriage and other reasons" is also noted.

1959-04   Angoff, A. "The Male Librarian - An Anomaly?" *Library Journal* 84 (February 15, 1959):553-556.

The public tends to look on the male librarian with pity, surprise and disrespect. If the excitement of library work can be communicated "a new and more vigorous type of male librarian will become more prevalent."

Letters: McGaw, H.F. "Answer to Angoff." *Library Journal* 84 (May 1, 1959):1348; 1350.

Comments that Angoff overdoes the hyperbole and that what librarianship needs is independent-minded people — strong women being better than weak men. "If a man is hesitant about choosing a profession in which there is a preponderance of women, let him choose a career where his timidity will not matter."

Stone, L.H. "Visit to Another World." *Library Journal* 84 (May 1, 1959):1350.

Compares England, where there are many more male librarians, with the U.S. in a reversal of Angoff's plight.

1959-05   "Fie, If Thy Name Be Woman!" *Library Journal* 84 (February 15, 1959):556.

Extract from the preface to *Who's Who of American Women* [1958-01] reprinted in the "hopes that aroused females and their protective male colleagues will have something to say."

Letters: Paulus, M. "Why Lady Librarians Don't Get Into Who's Who!" *Library Journal* 84 (April 15, 1959):1166.

The writer, "a very average librarian of a very average library system in a very average town," is in *Who's Who in American Women,* but wonders why others more qualified failed to make it. Contends most librarians were probably too busy to bother to fill in the questionnaire about who they are and how good they are.

Colton, G.A. "Women Administrators." *Library Journal* 84 (June 1, 1959):1712.

"The argument over who make better administrators, men or women, is fruitless because this is an individual difference and few administrators are equally good in all areas." The Harvey article [1958-02] quoted in the excerpt is criticized because it equates the position of chief librarian with administrator and uses indefinite terms to describe statistics.

Harvey, J.F. "Apply, If Thy Name Be Woman!" *Library Journal* 84 (June 1, 1959):1712; 1714.

Urges people to read the original paper [1957-02] on which the article [1958-02] quoted in the preface excerpted from *Who's Who in American Women* [1958-01] was based. Claims he is not prejudiced against women but was reporting the results of an objective study which showed career patterns for women which did not lead to administrative posts.

1959-06   Haslam, D.D. "Why More Men Librarians in Britain?" *Library Journal* 84 (October 15, 1959):3084-3085.

Feminization of librarianship in Great Britain and the United States is compared. Feminization is an evolutionary process stemming from sociological development due to the emancipation of women, particularly the practice of married women continuing their work; equal pay; the increasing admission of women to the profession and to high administrative posts coupled with creeping inflation. In the U.S. this process has reached a more advanced stage and hence librarianship is more feminized than in Great Britain although the percentage of British male librarians is also decreasing.

1959-07   Baxter, S.G. "Analysis of Membership in the American Library Association Held by Individuals and Institutions in Texas in 1957." *Texas Library Journal* 35 (December 1959):118-121.

Among the factors analyzed is sex: 15% of the ALA members were male; 85% female. Eighty percent of the eighty-two male members were from public libraries. Women were more evenly divided amongst type of library but 40% were school librarians. About 35% of male ALA members did not belong to the Texas Library Association; slightly more than 25% of the women did not. About 44% of the men were listed in *Who's Who in Library Service* as opposed to about 30% of the women.

1960-1969

1960-01   Angoff, A. "The Male Librarian - An Anomaly?" In *Of, By and For Librarians.* Edited by J.O. Marshall. Hamden, Connecticut: The Shoe String Press, Inc. 1960:321-326.

Reprint of [1959-04].

1960-02   Elliott, L.R. "Salute to the Vanguard." *Texas Library Journal* 36 (March 1960):7-10.

Brief sketches of seven Texas women librarians active from 1900-1950's: Dorothy Amann, Cleora Clarton, Julia Ellen Grothaus, Julie Bedford Idesan, Jennie Scott Scheuber, Maude Durlin Sullivan and Elizabeth Howard West. Their career patterns and accomplishments are analyzed. The author comments that when he came to Texas "they welcomed the brash trespasser so graciously that one wonders if the petticoat predominance were not becoming a wee bit monotonous." He closes the article with "And who are the present successors of this valiant vanguard in voile? Nearly all males. It's a dreary bookscape!"

1961-01   Morrison, P.D. "The Career of the Academic Librarian: A Study of the Social Origins, Educational Attainments, Vocational Experience, and Personality Characteristics of a Group of American Academic Librarians." Ph.D. thesis. University of California, Berkeley. 1961.

Results of survey to: 1) discover how college and university librarians compare with members of other professions; 2) identify the characteristics which differentiate those holding one kind or level of position from others; 3) explore the ways in which background and career factors are interrelated; and 4) gather and evaluate the reactions of librarians to their experience. Data were gathered in 1958 from 707 academic librarians. Findings include the fact that male librarians derive greater satisfaction from collegial relations than do female who tend to be isolated from the rest of the academic community. Tabular data are analyzed by sex throughout. Findings on *education* note that the phasing out of the second-year master's program closes one feminine pathway to success since women tend not to go into doctoral programs (p. 161); and on *career decision* findings note that men enter the field later than women (p. 188) and women who go into academic librarianship are discouraged if they have strong ambitions for advancement.

*1961-02   Seeliger, R.A. "Librarians in *Who's Who in America, 1956-1957.*" Master's thesis. University of Texas, 1961.

1961-03   U.S. Department of Labor, Bureau of Labor Statistics. "Librarians." *Occupational Outlook Handbook,* 1961 Edition. Washington, DC: U.S. Government Printing Office, 1961:250-255.

Entry prepared by the Women's Bureau, notes that, "approximately 85% of all librarians are women" and most of them are employed in public and school libraries. "Nearly 25% of the graduates who earned a bachelor's, masters or Ph.D. degree in library science in 1959 were men." The rationale behind the male influx into librarianship is commented upon briefly (p. 252). The turnover rate, due to the number of young women "who leave their jobs for marriage and other reasons" is also noted (p. 245).

1961-04   Schultz, S. "Panel on Professional Library Personnel: Remarks on Women in Librarianship." In *American Theological Library Association Fifteenth Annual Conference.* Summary of Proceedings. Washington, DC, June 13-15, 1961:100-101.

Among other barriers, equity between male and female theological librarians is hampered because women are barred from ordination which is frequently required for faculty status.

1961-05   Glass, M. "The Syllabus." *Assistant Librarian* 54 (May 1961):101-102.

Letter on the two year syllabus which recounts author's experience: a year in library school and library work after marriage. She has now been informed that "a woman's career finishes on marriage" and the only job available to her is shelving books. Questions whether women will be willing to undergo two years of preparation for such treatment.

†**1961-06**   Simsova, Mrs. S. "Married Women in Libraries." *Assistant Librarian* 54 (July 1961):130-132.

Article written in response to Glass's letter [1961-05]. Women now continue with their careers after marriage. Problems do occur with the birth of the first child, after which, if she takes leave from the profession to rear the child, a woman will have a difficult time re-entering the profession. Some solutions are discussed and women are encouraged to pursue their qualifications as librarians, despite concern that their effort will be wasted.

Letters: Dzielski, B.M. "Married Women in Libraries." *Assistant Librarian* 54 (September 1961):181.

Considers Simsova's article reasonable but questions devoting two pages to the topic. The author has never encountered discrimination; "frankly, if we expect to have our cake and eat it too, we can hardly complain of a little indigestion!"

Chambers, N. "Married Women in Librarianship." *Assistant Librarian* 54 (October 1961):201.

Part-time professional positions and the return of people to the profession after a number of years' absence is detrimental to the growth of librarianship. Suggests non-professional positions "for ladies of experience, with good judgment, fully rounded personalities and integrated home lives to control the flocks of young ladies who will seek jobs as 'librarians,' as indeed they do now, with no intention of qualifying and no interest in the future of librarianship beyond the next day."

Letters in response to above letters:

Divers, M. "Married Women in Librarianship." *Assistant Librarian* 55 (February 1962):33-34.

Disagrees with Chambers' letter. Bringing up a family does not cause women "to become incapable of anything other than mothering." The absence from library work may provide a fresh perspective. Questions whether Chambers considers "readers" who could benefit from the skills of married women librarians.

Stirling, S. "Married Women in Librarianship." *Assistant Librarian* 55 (February 1962):33.

Chambers' letter "was enough to provoke every qualified librarian mother in the country." With the shortage of librarians, the library profession "cannot afford to ignore married women who desire to return to librarianship."

Serwadda, G.W. "Married Women in Librarianship." *Assistant Librarian* 54 (October 1961):201-202.

Opposes married women with children working because the care of a family is a full time vocation. Questions whether home life can be happy if the wife and mother works.

Glass, S.T. "Married Women in Librarianship." *Assistant Librarian* 54 (December 1961):236.

Says much of the point of her earlier letter [1961-06] was missed because her address was left off. She lives in Northern Ireland; in England she had been unable to find employment after marriage. Agrees with Serwadda that a woman should stay at home when her children are young.

Stallybrass, O.G.W. "Married Women in Librarianship. *Assistant Librarian* 54 (December 1961):236-238.

Argues that women can have children and carry on their professional life if child care is adequate. Feels part-time librarians are professionals too. If other professions employed part-time practitioners, why not librarianship?

Turnbull, K.R.M. "Married Women in Librarianship." *Assistant Librarian* 54 (December 1961):238-239.

Calls Chambers' and Serwadda's thinking "muddled and obsolete." Opposes "total dedication" to librarianship as neurotic. Argues for the re-entry of women into the profession but at this point, after her own experience, advises young women to seek careers more sympathetic to their needs.

Shields, L.G. "Married Women in Librarianship." *Assistant Librarian* 55 (February 1962):32-33.

Feels not enough attention has been given to refuting the reasons given by previous letter writers who oppose the employment of married women. A married woman with a cooperative partner may have less domestic responsibility than a single woman. Men leave positions for promotions or pay increases just as much as women leave for pregnancy. Experiences in her work situation during the past 14 years are recounted. "To-day an intelligent woman in a necessary and satisfying profession is not, as in the 1930s, driven to illicit unions or sublimation of natural instincts; surely the community as a whole is so much the better for it."

Cloke, D.R. "Married Women in Librarianship." *Assistant Librarian* 55 (February 1962):33-34.

Recounts personal experiences in support of proposition that women can combine career and family although now no longer working in a library. When she married she was told she had "forfeited any possibility of promotion." When she chose to return to the library after the birth of her first child she was downgraded and given a lower salary. In spite of this she worked and neither home nor job suffered. At the birth of her second child she "felt it more graceful to retire."

1961-07   Goode, W.J. "The Librarian: From Occupation to Profession." *Library Quarterly* 31 (October 1961):306-320.

At the conclusion of a lengthy essay on why librarians will never reach full professional status, Goode notes that librarians will increase their prestige partly by recruiting more men "who are usually more concerned with building a career, and who therefore invest more heavily in it" (p. 319).

1961-08   Harvey, J.F. "Advancement in the Library Profession." *Wilson Library Bulletin* 36 (October 1961):144-147.

Summarizes his 1957 study [1957-02] and 1958 *CRL* article [1958-02] in a more popular style.

1961-09   Joyce, C. "The Suppliant Maidens." *Library Journal* 86 (December 15, 1961):4246-4249.

Presents an extract from a letter of the Trustees of the Wellesley (Mass.) Free Library to the town personnel board in which higher salaries for librarians are requested in order to attract a better class of librarians. Asserts "there is nothing accidental about either the lowness of professional salaries or the drive to raise them. Library work, like the other women's professions . . . rates . . . as woman herself rates . . . not very high." He discusses the letter, which did result in higher salaries, as no model since it hinges its arguments on benefit to the community rather than the need for librarians to be treated as professionals.

*1962-01   Parrott, S. "Analysis of the Biographies of Librarians Listed in *Who's Who of American Women, 1958-1959.*" Master's thesis. Atlanta University, 1962.

1962-02   Rossi, P.H. "Discussion." In *Seven Questions About the Profession of Librarianship.* Edited by P.H. Ennis and H.W. Winger. Chicago: University of Chicago Press, 1962:82-83.

Responding to a paper on the status of the profession Rossi asks why the high proportion of women in librarianship are not alluded to. He argues that any profession with as many women as librarianship "suffers a special disability." The division of labor in medicine with nursing a female occupation and doctoring masculine is suggested for librarianship.

1962-03   "Survey to Be Made of Part-time Jobs for Women." *Library Journal* 87 (December 1, 1962):4406-4407.

Announces survey by the Alumnae Advisory Center of part-time job opportunities in the New York City area to be undertaken with the aid of a $17,000 grant from the Carnegie Corporation. Librarianship is one of the fields to be examined. "The first time that any organization has set out to study the ways in which this resource (married women librarians who do not wish to work full time) might best be tapped."

1962-04   Shera, J. "Little Girls Don't Play Librarian." *Library Journal* 87 (December 15, 1962):4483-4487.

"In the late 19th century, librarianship came to be regarded as a kind of consolation prize for matrimonial disappointment." A recruitment article that explores the image of the librarians (rife with comments on the old maid stereotype) in order to define librarianship as a meaningful profession in spite of such images.

1963-01   Logsdon, R.H. and Logsdon, I.K. *Library Careers.* New York: Henry Z. Walck, Inc., 1963.

Includes brief comment on librarianship as a gratifying career for men (p. 17) though women librarians feel men have had a distinct advantage when choices are made for administrative posts. Aimed at high school students.

1963-02   U.S. Department of Labor, Bureau of Labor Statistics. "Librarians." *Occupational Outlook Handbook,* 1963-1964 Edition. Washington, DC: U.S. Government Printing Office, 1963:241-245.

Caption under photo (p. 242) of a male librarian states, "A growing number of librarians are men." Text notes several thousand positions will be vacated each year by young women who leave their jobs to take care of their families (p. 244).

1963-03   Wallace, S.L. "Men vs. Women." In her *So You Want to Be a Librarian.* New York: Harper and Row, 1963:85-86.

"Librarianship is a good field for women and they will feel no discrimination because of their sex at the beginning levels . . . However, it is a fact recognized by both men and women that men will advance further and at a more rapid pace than women."

1963-04   "Cheesecake and Charter." *Liaison: The News Sheet of the Library Association* (June 1963):38.

Reports the selection of a library assistant as Borough Road College Rag Queen. Comments that the "physical attributes of women librarians seem to be increasingly noticed and publicized." Quotes from a feature on the Newcastle City libraries in the local paper which devotes considerable attention to describing the women assistants.

1963-05   Morrison, P.D. "The Personality of the Academic Librarian." *College and Research Libraries* 24 (September 1963):365-368.

Group profile based on Ghiselli "Self Description Inventory," administered in 1958 to 676 academic librarians in all parts of the United States. The section on sex (p. 367-368) reports that women scored higher on the personality inventory than men but are concentrated in the lower ranks. Among major executives, scores for men and women are alike.

1963-06   Meyer, E.P. *Meet the Future: People and Ideas in Libraries Today and Tomorrow.* Boston: Little, Brown and Co., 1964.

Notes that since World War II men have been flocking into librarianship which makes the field more inviting and stimulating to women in the field (p. 177-178).

1963-07   G., A. "Young Man, Be a Librarian." *Esquire* 69 (April 1964):8.

Exhorts men to look to library science as a wide open field with reasonably high pay in a pleasant environment. Most top jobs want males, since running library systems in large urban areas is big business. Also there is increasing demand for men in the scientific and industrial libraries. Notes that librarianship, which requires a short time of study, makes an ideal second career.

*1963-08   Waligora-Rittinghaus, J. "Frau und Bibliothek; zum Frauen-Kongress der Deutschen Demokratischen Republik." (trans.: Woman and Library; on the Occasion of the Women's Congress of the German Democratic Republic.) *Bibliothekar* 18 (June 1964):561-568.

1965-01   Long, M.L. *The State Library Consultant at Work.* Springfield, Illinois: Illinois State Library, 1965.

Salary differentiation between men and women is cited (p. 14). Notes difference in male/female responses on job satisfaction, e.g., men like to travel more (p. 35-36). Men tend to hold higher degrees (p. 43-44) partly because of their younger age. Women have more work experience (p. 45).

1965-02   Sullivan, P. "School Library Service." In *The Library Reaches Out: Reports On Library Service and Community Relations by Some Leading American Librarians.* Edited by K. Coplan and E. Castagna. New York: Oceans, 1965: 241-256.

Notes that men have been attracted to the field because of opportunities for administrative advancement and increasing emphasis on non-print instructional materials.

1965-03   U.S. Department of Labor, Bureau of Labor Statistics. "Librarians." *Occupational Outlook Handbook,* 1966-67 Edition. Washington, DC: U.S. Government Printing Office, 1965:250-255.

Notes several thousand people will be needed to replace young women librarians who leave their jobs to care for families (p. 254).

1965-04   Mannix, Mrs. I.G. "Then as Now." *Assistant Librarian* 58 (March 1965):50.

Reprint of 1899 letter requesting information "respecting the employment of girls in Free Libraries" and reprint of reply: librarians are not well paid; girls are "received in one or two of the large provincial libraries for a period of four years"; training is advised.

1965-05   Roberson, B.E. "Library Trustees and Library School Directors: What Are You Looking For?" *PNLA Quarterly* 29: (April 1965):195-197.

Library school graduate at age fifty offers her success story to prove older women are good potential source of help.

1965-06   Shera, J.H. "A Better Class of Mouse." *Wilson Library Bulletin* 39 (April 1965):677.

Various reasons for the departure of librarianship from the scholarly tradition are discussed: standardization, rise of the popular library movement, change of patron type and the feminization of the profession. "Even though we hold no brief for the view that women are necessarily intellectually inferior to men . . . in the popular mind the hierarchy of the professions is still sex-linked."

1965-07   "Librarians Rank 219th in Earnings Out of 321 Selected U.S. Occupations." *Library Journal* 90 (May 15, 1965):2231.

News item summarizing findings on librarians' median annual earnings compiled from 1960 U.S. Census data and reprinted with data on 321 occupations by M.A. Rutzick in the *Monthly Labor Review*, March, 1965. Librarians rank 219 when compared to male workers; but third when compared to female workers.

†1965-08   Holden, M.Y. "The Status of Women Librarians." *Antiquarian Bookman* 36 (August 23, 1965):647-648.

Address at 1965 convention of National Women's Party (NWP). Where and how women are employed in librarianship is the key to discrimination against women. Tokenism exists in top positions. The failure of women to advance rests on women's difficulties in acquiring advanced degrees and male policy makers' selection of male librarians. Support of young professional women by the NWP is urged.

†1965-09   Moon, E.E. "Tokenism at the Top? Women in Minority." *Library Journal* 90 (October 1, 1965):4019.

Editorial reacting to Holden's address [1965-08] to the National Women's Party. Cites current statistics on women in the profession such as: 60% of heads of state library agencies are women, seven of the national library periodicals' editors are women and both the American and British Library Association president-elects are women. Chastises Holden for not having up-to-date information and presenting a "selectively simple case."

>**Letter:**   Jordan, R.T. "In Defense of Women." *Library Journal* 90 (December 1, 1965):5126.
>
>Despite the figures quoted by Moon, the writer concurs with Holden [1965-08]. Points out that the 74 Association of Research Libraries members have male directors, that the number of women state library agency heads has been steadily declining and that men are over-represented in the ALA. Urges the profession to devote time to the problem of discrimination against women as well as "against Negroes in connection with libraries."

1965-10   Shera, J.H. "Kinder, Küche, und Bibliotheken." *Wilson Library Bulletin* 40 (December 1965):365.

Discussion of the Carnegie Corporation grant to the Graduate School for Library and Information Science of the University of Pittsburgh for the professional education of mature women whose family responsibilities are no longer as demanding as they once were. The grant is seen as an opportunity for serious research into the labor problem of professions such as librarianship, social work, and nursing, which attract a high. proportion of women. "Inherent dangers" in part-time programs such as lack of contact with other students, lack of identification with the educational community, and, upon graduation, no part-time positions are discussed. Possible conflict between family and job are seen as a hindrance to the growth of the library profession since the family, in Shera's opinion, should properly come first.

1966-01   Drennan, H.T. and Darling, R.L. "The Public Librarian." In their *Library Manpower: Occupational Characteristics of Public and School Librarians*, Washington, DC: U.S. Government Printing Office, 1966:1-14.

Analysis of results of public librarians' response to the Postcensal Study of Professional and Technical Manpower, which aimed at identifying significant characteristics of many different kinds of workers. Data are broken down by sex. Male public librarians reported higher salary rates and earnings although women have generally served longer. Estimated to represent 13% of total public librarians, men are over-represented by 6% in the upper echelon positions and occupy nearly 50% of the directorships of larger libraries and 27.2% of the directorships of medium sized agencies.

†1966-02   Ward, P.L. *Woman and Librarianship.* London: The Library Association, 1966.

Report of an investigation undertaken to determine if there is a shortage of trained librarians and whether there is a pool of qualified married librarians willing to re-enter the field. This is found to be true, and conditions necessary to ensure the fullest possible use of women in libraries are examined. Active steps are recommended to change the situation.

> **Reviews:**   Jordan, M.R. "Libraries and Marriage." *Assistant Librarian* 59 (April 1966):86.
>
> Agrees with the Ward recommendations but says they are self-evident.
>
> Heathcote, L.M. "Wives in British Libraries." *Library Journal* 91 (May 15, 1966):2462-2463.
>
> Reports methods and results of Ward's study. Comments on prejudice against women in British libraries.
>
> Ditmas, E.M.R. *Journal of Documentation* 22: (June 1966):154.
>
> Summarizes Ward's findings. Gives background on decision to undertake study.

1966-03   "Library Education and the Talent Shortage." *Library Journal* 91 (April 1, 1966):1761-1773.

An *LJ* poll of library administrators' response to the *ALA National Inventory of Library Needs,* which predicts 100,000 vacancies in libraries. The respondents are all male. Ervin J. Gaines comments that "the talent reservoir is kept low by the high proportion of women, who necessarily withdraw from the profession for marriage and motherhood, thus creating a higher job mortality than is good for stable operations." He notes that higher salaries would attract more men, and that women who do remain and attain supervisory positions are usually unmarried (p. 1770-1771). Herbert F. Mutshler comments that "we have lost a great potential talent area in women over thirty-five because of the profession's reluctance to make training easily available (p. 1772-1773)."

1966-04   "Hiring of Married Librarians Recommended in British Study." *Library Journal* 91 (April 15, 1966):20-23.

News item summarizing Ward study [1966-02].

1966-05   "Married Women Who Are Also Chartered Librarians." *Library World* 67 (May 1966):334.

Ward report [1966-02] welcomed because married women librarians have deplored lack of opportunity to obtain employment. Recommendations summarized. Questions feasibility of part-time work in small or specialized libraries because of limited labor market.

1966-06   Davies, G.R. "First Lady." *Library Journal* 91 (September 15, 1966):4052-4053.

Account of the Library Association's meeting and speech of its first woman president, Lorna Paulin. Paulin is reported to have stressed the role of women in county libraries.

1966-07   Cronin, A. "The Second Career." *Drexel Library Quarterly* 2 (October 1966):339-344.

Urges the library profession to recognize the potential of women over forty who are considering returning to school for retraining. Suggests re-examining library school admission standards and creating part-time jobs.

1966-08   "Equal Pay in the Public Library of South Australia." *Australian Library Journal* 15 (October 1966):191.

News item noting that the South Australian government has "implemented the first stage of a five year scheme to equate salaries for female librarians in the Libraries Department with those for males."

1966-09   "Refresher Course for Married Women." *Assistant Librarian* 59 (October 1966):196.

News item advertising a weekly course for women who have been away from the profession for at least six years. Patricia Ward, who directed study of married women librarians [1966-02], is listed as contact person.

1966-10   Sass, S. "Ranking Librarianship as a Career." *Special Libraries* 57 (November 1966):667.

Letter to editor quoting figures on salaries of librarians compared to other male occupations from March 1965 *Monthly Labor Review.* Comments that "recruiting men into the library profession in any appreciable numbers is not likely in view of the fact that education requirements are so far out-of-line with expected earnings."

1967-01   Farley, R.A. "The American Library Executive: An Inquiry into His Concepts of the Function of His Office." Ph.D. dissertation. University of Illinois, 1967. (DAI Number: 67-11851).

Descriptive study of male and female executives in American libraries with budgets of over $300,000. Data are broken down by sex and responses of women analyzed in a separate chapter (p. 62-72). Among the conclusions: "There is no evidence in this data to indicate that female library executives were less scientific as administrators than male library executives. The only difference observed was that women tended to be more personal in their approach to administrative problems" (p. 84).

1967-02   Ginsburg, E. and Brown, C. *Manpower for Library Services.* Bethesda, MD: ERIC Document Reproduction Service, ED 023 408, 1967.

Analysis of the "state of library manpower and the outlook for the future." Librarianship is approached as a field which makes use of a large number of women, a fact which is seen to cause a "certain brittleness," low salary structures, lack of scientific knowledge, and the gap between a service expectation and the realities of librarianship as management. Recommendations include the easing of entrance and re-entrance for mature married women on a part- or full-time basis and recruitment efforts aimed at men during their career decision-making points, because librarianship tends to be a second career choice for them.

1967-03   Wells, S.B. "Feminization of the American Library Profession, 1876 to 1923." Master's thesis. University of Chicago, 1967.

Discusses the introduction of women to American librarianship, Dewey's role, the position of formal library training in aiding the feminization process, and the status of women in a feminized profession.

1967-04   Blankenship, W.C. "Head Librarians: How Many Men? How Many Women?" *College and Research Libraries* 28 (January 1967):41-48.

Notes men may hesitate to enter college library work because it is over feminized and most administrative posts are held by women. Provides data to demonstrate that this is not necessarily so. A questionnaire sent to 660 heads of U.S. college libraries resulted in 414 responses. Results indicate a nearly equal number of men and women librarians; however, men tended to head larger publicly supported institutions whereas women headed smaller private institutions.

1967-05   McMahon, A. *The Personality of the Librarian: Prevalent Social Values and Attitudes towards the Profession.* Adelaide: Libraries Board of South Australia, 1967.

Study of thirty Tasmanian librarians working in public, university and special libraries. Results are broken down by sex. The findings agree with Douglass [1957-01] and Morrison [1961-01] that librarians lack the traits most closely associated with forceful leadership. Male librarians are described as sensitive, prone to worry, somewhat overcontrolled and insecure. Female librarians are also sensitive and idealistic, withdrawn socially and somewhat depressed and insecure.

1967-06   Gambee, B. "The Great Junket: American Participation in the Conference of Librarians, London, 1877." *Journal of Library History* 2 (January 1967):9-44.

In a lengthy article on the 1877 conference there are several references to women notably the Smith-Wilson-Poole exchange on the shortage of women librarians in England [1878-01] (p. 37) and a tribute to Annie Godfrey Dewey who made the trip to the 1877 conference.

1967-07   Shores, L. "Students." *Drexel Library Quarterly* 3 (January 1967):59-64.

Notes that as regards the typical library school student the use of the masculine pronoun is tending to become a fact of life rather than a convenience of English usage. Under the sub-heading, "Sex," the reasons for the increasing recruitment of men are given as the increase in library salaries, the opening of the audio-visual field with its emphasis on mechanical and electronic equipment, and the growth of information science. Male students are seen to be more masculine "due to increasing vigilance of admission officers for evidence of homosexuality" and due to the influx of men attracted to library opportunities as well as men recruited from the armed forces. Female students are seen to be more feminine. Library schools have included beauty contest winners, models, stage and dance performers. The marriage index for librarians is becoming more favorable. There is an increasing number of women divorcees in library schools.

1967-08   "Brighter Librarianship as She is Practised: The Miss Library World Finals - March 11th, 1967." *Assistant Librarian* 60 (April 1967):58-59.

Report of the first Miss Library World beauty contest held to celebrate National Library Week.

1967-09   "A Study of 1967 Annual Salaries of Members of the Special Library Association." *Special Libraries* 58 (April 1967):217-254.

Most analyses not divided by sex, but mobility profile shows men more able to move for better positions than women.

1967-10   Marco, G. "Doctoral Programs in American Library Schools." *Journal of Education for Librarianship* 8 (Summer 1967):6-13.

Study of doctoral programs gives an overview of extant programs: admission and GRE requirements, credit required and type of courses. Placement of doctoral recipients is reported with a breakdown by sex. Total degrees granted are also broken down by sex: as of August, 1965 — 159 men and sixty-one women.

1967-11   Pritchard, D. "Recruiting Men to Librarianship." *Florida Libraries* 18 (June 1967):15-17.

Reviews literature on role of men in librarianship. Gives ten suggestions for recruiting men including recruiting in men's colleges, and recruitment articles in journals such as *Playboy.*

1967-12 White, R.F. and Macklin, D.B. *Education, Careers and Professionalization in Librarianship and Information Science.* Bethesda, MD: ERIC Document Reproduction Service, ED 054 800, October, 1967.

Analysis of the procedure by which individuals enter librarianship and are prepared for the positions in the field, undertaken as part of the University of Maryland Manpower in the Library and Information Science Profession Research Program. Data from a mail survey of students and faculty in all accredited library schools and from visits to a majority of the schools are analyzed by sex. Among the findings: over 60% of the women students indicated a wish to combine career and family in some way, most preferring part-time to full-time work; library education may attract career oriented women and family oriented men; a higher proportion of male students prefer an academic setting for their work and a relatively larger proportion of women to men in all age groups favor the school setting.

1967-13 Whyte, J. "The Library Profession and Library Education in Australia: A Man's World." *Library Journal* 92 (November 15, 1967):4120-4122.

Brief history of the library movement in Australia and the role of the Library Association of Australia. "While most positions in libraries, except the top ones, are still filled by women, an increasing number of men are entering the profession . . . Equal pay is a fact in the professional grades of university librarianship and in the state of New South Wales, and the first steps have been taken to implement equal pay scales in South Australia."

1968-01 Bradley, B.W. "A Study of Characteristics, Qualifications and Succession Patterns of Heads of Large U.S. Academic and Public Libraries." Master's thesis, University of Texas, 1968.

Survey of the fifty largest public libraries showed 86% had male directors. Of the fifty largest academic libraries 100% were directed by males.

*1968-02 Chamberlain, E.R. *The Librarian and His World.* London: Victor Gollancz, 1968.

1968-03 Ingraham, M.H. "The Director of Libraries." In his *The Mirror of Brass: Compensation and Working Conditions of College and University Administrators.* Madison: University of Wisconsin Press, 1968:199-210.

A questionnaire sent to administrators of colleges listed in the *1965-66 Education Directory* was the impetus for the book. The survey determined, regarding libraries, that 93% of the university and 64% of the public college directors of libraries are men. In the private colleges 52% of the directors are women. The median age of male directors is forty-nine (fifty-five in universities, forty-seven in colleges), while the median age of women is fifty-five (p. 199).

1968-04 Library Advisory Council (England). *Report on the Supply and Training of Librarians.* London: Her Majesty's Stationery Office, 1968.

Study of the numbers of qualified librarians likely to be required in the foreseeable future, and of the arrangements for their education and training. The life of a working librarian is affected most seriously by the proportions of men and women in the profession. The percentages of women among librarians newly admitted to the Library Association's professional register have increased steadily since 1930: 1930 - 50%; 1940 - 55%; 1950 - 60%; 1960 - 65%. By 1967 women constituted 72% of the students and will probably constitute 70% of new librarians in the 1970s. Male librarians seldom leave the profession before normal retirement and have a working life of thirty-five years. Only about 10% of women librarians make a life-long career of librarianship. The average initial working life of the other women librarians is less than five years. About 10% of women who return after marriage do so for about fifteen years (pp. 9-10). Report does not envisage married women entering librarianship in sufficient numbers to justify the provision of special courses (p. 26). Concern is expressed about the low proportion of male recruits to librarianship which leads to a high rate of staff turnover because of the shorter professional life which can be expected of a female librarian. Because of their longer professional lives, men fill most senior positions so it is important to attract sufficient numbers of men (p. 27). The need for higher salaries in order to attract male entrants is noted (pp. 26-27). Attractiveness of short training for women who intend to marry is emphasized (p. 45).

1968-05   U.S. Department of Labor, Bureau of Labor Statistics. "Librarians." *Occupational Outlook Handbook, 1968-69 Edition.* Washington, DC: U.S. Government Printing Office, 1968:213-217.

Notes several thousand librarians will be needed each year to "fill positions vacated by young women who leave their jobs to care for their families." Re-entry opportunities for women are seen as favorable (p. 216).

1968-06   Bundy, M.L. and Wasserman, P. "Professionalism Reconsidered." *College and Research Libraries* 29 (January 1968):5-26.

While focusing on professionalism, article makes several comments about librarianship as a feminine profession with a service orientation (p. 8).

1968-07   Hooper, J. "Half a Librarian Is Better Than None . . ." *Canadian Librarian* 24 (January 1968):338-340.

Advocates part-time employment, particularly for women with families who want to stay in profession.

1968-08   Ladenson, A. "Fair Labor Standards Act as Applied to Libraries." *ALA Bulletin* 62 (April 1968):399-401.

Amendments to the Fair Labor Standards Act (P.L. 89-601) will affect libraries. The history of the legislation, which was first adopted in 1937, and the legal implications of the new amendments for libraries' employment and payroll policies are given. The law prohibits employers from discriminating on the basis of sex in payment of wages for equal work.

1968-09   Ormsby, A. "For Want of a Year." *Assistant Librarian* 61 (April 1968):91.

A letter from a married librarian who questions the regulations of the Library Association as they apply to the life of the young married librarian who may have to take time off from her career for personal reasons. She seeks comments from librarians in similar circumstances.

Letters: Haslam, D.D. "For Want of a Year." *Assistant Librarian* 61 (July 1968):148-149.

Response from the Deputy Secretary of the Library Association sympathizing with Ormsby. Since her letter, Library Association regulations have been loosened in "hardship" cases. Also clears up references to people who qualified under previous charter regulations.

Seymour, G. "For Want of a Year." *Assistant Librarian* 61 (July 1968):148.

Recounts similar experience and financial loss caused by lack of a charter. Calls for a Library Association section entitled "Disillusioned Married Women."

Underhill, A. "For Want of a Year." *Assistant Librarian* 61 (July 1968):148.

Has experienced similar problems with the Library Association, which will not accept part-time work for charter requirements; writer also has problems finding care for her children because teachers and nurses are given priority in local nursery schools. Wonders if the Library Assistant's Association can help.

1968-10   Blackburn, R.T. "College Libraries — Indicted Failures: Some Reasons - and a Possible Remedy." *College and Research Libraries* 29 (May 1968):171-177.

Article identifies sources of conflict between the academic library and the teaching faculty. A major factor is the number of women librarians versus the predominantly male faculty which creates a doctor-nurse type relationship (p. 173). One solution is that, although female librarians can't grow beards they can "have long, straight hair, leotards, and miniskirts" (p. 176).

1968-11   Seymour, G. "Part-time Posts for Married Women." *Library Association Record* 70 (May 1968):134.

Same letter sent to the *Assistant Librarian* [1968-12] pointing out difficulty in obtaining part-time work in libraries.

Letters: Bradley, G. "Part-time Posts for Married Women." *Library Association Record* 70 (July 1968):186-187.

Argues against part-time employment; claims it is not efficient library practice.

Jones, D.E. "Part-time Posts for Married Women." *Library Association Record* 70 (August 1968):213.

Writer suggests routes other than public libraries to Seymour.

Phillips, J.P. "Part-time Posts for Married Women." *Library Association Record* 70 (August 1968):213.

A letter in support of Seymour from another qualified woman who cannot get a part-time position.

1968-12   Seymour, G.M. "The Path of the Part-timer." *Assistant Librarian* 61 (May 1968):108.

Points out the difficulty in obtaining part-time work in libraries. Warns prospective librarians to consider other careers. Same letter sent to the *Library Association Record* [1968-10].

Letters: Bassett, J.M. and others. "The Path of a Part-timer." *Assistant Librarian* 61 (July 1968):149.

Letter from ten librarians in Westcliff-on-Sea, Essex, affirming the difficulty in getting part-time work. Retirement problems are also pointed out. "We are becoming convinced that this is all part of a conspiracy by the male members of the profession to keep women out of the top jobs."

Lowe, P.A. "The Path of a Part-timer." *Assistant Librarian* 61 (August 1968):183.

Reports that writer finally found a part-time job but at a poor pay rate. "Let Mrs. Seymour and other qualified potential part-timers be prepared not only to be determined but also devalued."

Letter: Paulin, L.V. "The Path of a Part-timer." *Assistant Librarian* 61 (October 1968):230.

Comment on Lowe's letter. Part-time positions are sometimes hard to fill because married women aren't mobile and can't go where a part-time post is.

1968-13   Blinston, J. "All Those Lovely Girls." *Assistant Librarian* 61 (July 1968):150.

Letter in response to Leonard C. Guy's article in the *Assistant Librarian* 61 (May, 1968) wherein Guy refers to "all those lovely girls (and the few tired looking boys) who pass annually through library school." Writer suggests if fewer lovely girls are hired in the first place then fewer will disappear to get married.

> **Letter:**   Guy, L.C. "All Those Lovely Girls." *Assistant Librarian* 61 (September 1968):204-205.
>
> Serious response to Blinston notes that there are some harsh facts regarding librarianship that he has overlooked. Since two-thirds of the applicants to library schools are women, and since the profession needs men, the admission standards are higher for women than men.

1968-14   Clayton, H. *An Investigation Into Personality Characteristics Among Library School Students at One Midwestern University.* Bethesda, MD: ERIC Document Reproduction Service, ED 024 422, July 1968.

Study to investigate whether distinctive personality characteristics could be determined among students wishing to enter academic library work. Data are broken down by sex and a chapter devoted to analysis of men and women. Males scored higher on femininity scales than females; females presented personality profiles similar to nurses. Overall finding is that librarians are less outstanding as a group than students in other areas.

1968-15   Holbrook, F. "The Faculty Image of the Academic Librarian." *The Southeastern Librarian* 18 (Fall 1968):174-193.

In a lengthy article on faculty-librarian relations, author notes that the many women in librarianship may hinder relationships with faculty, who are mostly male (p. 182).

1968-16   Porter, D.M. "Married Women and Librarianship." *Assistant Librarian* 61 (October 1968):226-227.

Excerpts recent letters in *Assistant Librarian* [1968-12-Letters: Bassett, Haslam, Seymour, Underhill] to show Ward's [1966-02] recommendations have not been implemented.

*1969-01   Magrill, R.M. "Occupational Image and the Choice of Librarianship as a Career." Ph.D. thesis, University of Illinois, 1969 (DAI Order N. 70-13,404.)

1969-02   Morrison, P.D. *The Career of the Academic Librarian: a Study of the Social Origins, Educational Attainments, Vocational Experience, and Personality Characteristics of a Group of American Academic Librarians.* ACRL Monograph no. 29 Chicago: ALA, 1969.

Revision of author's thesis [1961-01]. Includes an update in the final chapter, "Developments Since 1960," which summarizes research from 1958-1968.

1969-03   Reeling, P.A. "Undergraduate Female Students as Potential Recruits to the Library Profession." DLS thesis, Columbia University, 1969.

Study to evaluate the relative effectiveness of selected library recruitment activities in stimulating undergraduate female students to consider or reject a career in librarianship; to determine to what extent it is possible to isolate and define measurable characteristics which typify undergraduate female students who are potential recruits to librarianship; and, to identify those factors that have influenced them to consider and reject librarianship. A comparison of the group rejecting library science and the students favoring a library career is made.

1969-04 Schiller, A.R. *Characteristics of Professional Personnel in College and University Libraries.* Research series no. 16. Springfield Illinois State Library, 1969. (Also published as ED 020 766).

The objectives of this study were to describe the characteristics of librarians employed on the staffs of U.S. higher educational institutions and to identify and examine relevant manpower issues. Two-thirds of academic librarians are women; data are analyzed by sex. The large proportion of women is shown to have many ramifications and the profession is urged to devote special attention to improving the utilization and status of women.

1969-05 Schwarz, C. *Dokumente zur Geschichte des bibliothekarischen Frauenberufs im wissenschaftlichen Bibliothekswesen Deutschlands: 1907 bis 1921).* (trans.: Documents Relating to the History of Women Professional Librarians in German Research Librarianship: 1907 to 1921.) Schriftenreihe der Universitats-Bibliothek zu Berlin, Nr. 5. Berlin: Universitäts-Bibliothek zu Berlin, 1969.

First milestones on the tortuous path leading to acceptance of women as professional librarians in Prussian university and state libraries. The initial historical overview is followed by three documents addressed to the Prussian Ministry of Culture, dated 1908, 1910, and 1919 respectively, each strongly favoring the entrance of women. The first, from the Director of the Berlin University Library, and the second, from the Head Librarian of the Prussian Royal Library, are of an advisory nature. Both these men had employed women from around 1900 on, mainly in temporary positions which men did not want because of lack of job security. The results were so positive that the authors felt permanent civil service positions for women should be created, and provided practical guidelines to that end, including exam requirements, duties and salary scales (always less than their male counterparts'). The third document is a demand from the Alliance of German Women's Groups (*Bund deutscher Frauenvereine*) for equal consideration for professional positions and equal pay.

1969-06 Simpson, R.L. and Simpson, I.H. "Women and Bureaucracy in the Semi-Professions." In *The Semi-Professions and Their Organization.* Edited by A. Etzioni. New York: Free Press, 1969:196-265.

Asserts that semi-professional organizations, which include libraries, are more bureaucratic than professional ones because of the prevalence of women. Semi-professionals lack autonomy and there is a great emphasis on hierarchical rank with duties differentiated by level. As one goes up the ladder, administrative tasks replace the semi-professional ones; therefore the primary task loses prestige while supervision and administrative activities are most rewarded. Lack of mandate, necessity for bureaucratic control, and weak orientation toward autonomy are forces instrumental in this trend. Characteristics of women in the semi-professions include upward mobility, late occupational choice, a feeling of inadequacy to succeed in other fields, and the appeal of the fields to the heart, not the mind. In a section on discrimination, against women the authors state that low motivation and discontinuous work histories of women raise questions about discrimination. The societal belief in male superiority also makes it difficult for women to move up the hierarchy. Includes justification for sex differentials because women have less education and discontinuous work careers. Sees no change as long as society holds values about feminine sex roles.

1969-07 Stone, E.W. *Factors Related to the Professional Development of Librarians.* Metuchen, NJ: Scarecrow Press, 1969.

Study includes 1956 and 1961 MLS graduates, with some background information on women in terms of education, experience, salary and need for continuing education.

1969-08   Reynolds, A.L. and King, C. "Why Not Partnership Librarians?" *Bay State Librarian* 58 (February 1969):3-4.

Proposal for administrators to consider two part-time employees to fill one full-time position, particularly for women who wish to remain in field but have small children.

1969-09   "Women in Professional Library Work." *New Zealand Libraries* 32 (February 1969).

Issue devoted to a report of the Professional Section of the New Zealand Library Association (NZLA), which undertook a survey of the professional careers of women library school graduates from 1946 to 1965, similar to that of Patricia Ward's in Great Britain [1966-02]. Includes the response to the survey given at the 1968 NZLA Conference. Survey instruments are printed as appendices (p. 28-31).

1969-09A   Professional Section of the New Zealand Library Association. "A Survey of Women Library School Graduates 1946-1965 by the Professional Section of the N.Z.L.A." *New Zealand Libraries* 32 (February 1969):4-14.

Summary report of survey. Women comprise 75% of the total 1946-1965 graduates of the Library School. If about two-thirds will marry and have children the later group will represent about 50% of total graduates. If at any given time 60% of the professionally qualified married women are working, 50-55% in libraries, they will comprise 30% of professional librarians; if for one third of their married working lives they want and obtain part-time work, then one-third professionally qualified married women will be part-time, and will amount to 10% of the profession.

1969-09B   "Comments by Library School Women Graduates, Now Married, on the Question of Returning to Professional Library Work." *New Zealand Libraries* 32 (February 1969):15-18.

A variety of comments from the survey [1969-09A]. Women want to work for additional income because of too much time on their hands, interest in librarianship, and desire to continue their careers. Husband's attitudes varied. Volunteer work, indecision about returning to work, and the problems of part-time work were also reported.

1969-09C   McEldowney, W.J. "Women in Professional Library Work: Some Comments." *New Zealand Libraries* 32 (February 1969):19-23.

Comments by a prominent university librarian: part-time workers cause problems in scheduling but these can be coped with, as long as there are not too many cases; questions estimates of number of women willing to return to work.

1969-09D   "A Summary of the Discussion Following Mr. McEldowney's Comments on the Report." *New Zealand Libraries* 32 (February 1969):25-31.

Report of comments on the survey focusing on part-time work and passage of two resolutions: 1) that the study be extended; 2) that the survey be published and sent to women library school graduates.

1969-10   Reamer, P. "Consider the Wife as Librarian." *ALA Bulletin* 63 (March 1969):309.

Letter discussing difficulties recruiting women for the profession and problem of lack of mobility of married women.

1969-11   Schiller, A.R. "Academic Librarians' Salaries." *College and Research Libraries* 30 (March 1969):101-111.

One out of every five librarians in American academic libraries were polled as to current salary. Mean salary was $8,425. Men's salaries were higher than women's. Women tended to be most heavily concentrated at lower ranges of the salary distribution. While one-fifth of all respondents earned $10,000 or more, only 12% of the women did so compared to 37.3% of the men. The median salary for men, $8,990, was higher than the median salary for women, $7,455. Mean salary was $8,425. The difference between the mean salaries of men and women was even larger. Women made $7,746; men made $9,598.

1969-12 "The Educated Housewife." *Library Journal* 94 (March 15, 1969):1100.

Excerpts from [1966-07].

1969-13 Schiller, A.R. "The Widening Sex Gap." *Library Journal* 94 (March 15, 1969):1098-1100.

Statistics supporting the contention that women librarians are likely to become increasingly disadvantaged in relation to men.

> **Letter:** Ford, O. "Ask Any Woman." *Library Journal* 94 (May 1, 1969):1819.
>
> Contends women are poor administrators and that women don't like to work for other women. Men are in administrative positions because women want them there.

†**1969-14** Sable, A.P. "The Sexuality of the Library Profession: the Male and Female Librarian." *Wilson Library Bulletin* 43 (April 1969):748-751.

Deals with history of male dominance of the profession and stereotyped characteristics of male and female.

1969-15 Strain, P.M. *"LJ's* Sex Gap." *Library Journal* 94 (May 1, 1969):1819-1820.

Letter reporting that in the last six months, *LJ's* "People" column carried 128 announcements of appointments or change of status affecting male librarians to seventy-two of females. More pictures of men are also included.

> **Response to Letter:** "Ed. Note." *Library Journal* 94 (May 1, 1969):1820.
>
> "*LJ's* 'People' page reports important personnel changes . . . we don't make the appointments."

1969-16 Marchant, M.P. "Faculty - Librarian Conflict." *Library Journal* 94 (September 1, 1969):2886-2889.

A proposal for mediation between librarian and faculty value systems includes the comment that the low status of librarians is part of the male-female syndrome. Since librarians are largely women the male faculty tend to attribute inferior status to librarians. Marchant notes, "Female librarians may accept this professionally as they do in society at large. Male librarians, who are increasing their penetration into the profession, resent it strongly and vocally. As a consequence, the upper reaches of the library staff, which are heavily populated by men, tend to have faculty status even when the lower positions don't" (p. 2887).

> **Letter:** Anderson, P.S. "Marchant's Misogyny." *Library Journal* 95 (May 1, 1970):1680.
>
> Protests Marchant's call to recruit more male librarians to improve faculty-librarian communication.

> **Letter:** Hopkins, J. "No Misogynist at All." *Library Journal* 95 (August 1970):2588-2589.
>
> Argues that Dewey was not a misogynist as Anderson had stated.

1969-17   Brown, W.L. "The Public Library Scene." *Australian Library Journal* 18 (October 1969):321-323.

Reports on a meeting of the Victorian Branch of the Library Association of Australia on the subject of equal pay. Speakers showed how advertisements offered two different salaries (the female $856 less per year) for precisely the same job (p. 321).

1969-18   Coffin, J.E. "Library Work for Housewives." *Library Association Record* 71 (November 1969):337.

Letter seeking ideas from "lady librarians [who] have managed to put their hard-won qualifications to use, while successfully running a home and coping with a family."

Letters: Kilvington, B. "Library Work for Housewives." *Library Association Record* 72 (January 1970):34.

Shares Coffin's interest in hearing the solutions of others: "I finally gave up in desperation, and returned to work full-time as a school librarian and employed the services of an *au pair*."

Parker, M.B. "Library Work for Housewives." *Library Association Record* 72 (January 1970):33-34.

Response detailing sources of assistance and describing author's solution to same problem: volunteer work and lobbying for a branch library in which she hopes to get a job.

Saunders-White, P. "Library Work for Housewives." *Library Association Record* 72 (January 1970):34.

Relates own difficulties integrating marriage and career which were solved by taking a teaching position which ultimately led to the founding of a school library. Urges others to become "tutor-librarians."

Florey, C.C. "Library Work for Housewives." *Library Association Record* 72 (February 1970):74.

Urges married women librarians who cannot find a use for their library training to immigrate to Australia where "we cannot afford to waste married women by letting them vegetate at home."

Letters generated from above letters:

Horton, A. "Library Work for Housewives." *Library Association Record* 72 (June 1970):245.

The conditions of work for women with family responsibilities in Australia is difficult to generalize. Part-time employment exists but child care facilities "will need considerable improvement before married women are able to have the freedom they deserve."

Lidgett, D.H. "Library Work for Housewives." *Library Association Record* 72 (June 1970):245.

The Australian opportunities for women which Florey describes exist only in Western Australia. In South Australia "it's the employers' market." After four years the author is totally unemployable unless she will work full time.

Metcalfe, J. "Library Work for Housewives." *Library Association Record* 72 (September 1970):320.

Florey's "glowing account" of the opportunity for women librarians in Australia requires some balance. Australian housewives "complain of a lack of adjustment to their needs, as both workers and students." Women [in New South Wales] "at least in the professional grades have equal pay with men. For whatever reasons, however, chief librarianships are mainly held by men as in Great Britain." Librarians considering immigration should get proper information before making a decision.

Addis, F.E. "Library Work for Housewives." *Library Association Record* 72 (April 1970):171.

Letter seeking comments from "anyone who has been able to use their library qualifications working in their own home." Writer is pleased to see that others share her concerns.

1969-19   Ramsden, M. "Hanging Together." *Assistant Librarian* 62 (November 1969):158-164.

In his presidential address Ramsden discusses the preponderance of women in the profession noting that many females leave the field at an early age for marriage — only 10% of women entrants making librarianship a lifelong career and 82% leaving within five years of their entrance to the profession. "If we are considering long term continuous recruitment, it is to the men that we must look, since, notwithstanding the overall preponderance of women, men make up 81% of long term recruits; and consequently the more senior posts in the profession are filled by men." The results of the exam given at Aberystwyth showed that of 136 taking the test, the top ten scorers were women, and of the ten lowest, seven were men. The need to recruit better men and retain these outstanding women, or at least attract the women back when their families are grown, is obvious. Much of Ramsden's talk is derived from the *Report on the Supply and Training of Librarians* [1968-04].

Letter: Nicholson, D. "Local Government Difficulties." *Library Assistant* 63 (February 1970):28.

Agrees with Ramsden on the need to attract women with grown families, but wonders if he knows legislation must be passed to do so due to the Superannuation Acts, which make re-entry difficult.

1969-20   Barber, P. "Ladies in Waiting." *Synergy No. 24* (December 1969):22-25.

Asks women to become aware, active, and questions why women are perpetuating inferiority complexes by saying they would rather work under a man.

1969-21   "Librarians Moving More, Mobility Study Shows." *Library Journal* 94 (December 1, 1969):4332.

News item reporting findings of study of sample of librarians listed in 1966 edition of *Who's Who in Library Service* done by Betty Duston. Men moved farther, went abroad more frequently, and were more likely to come to librarianship from some other profession than women.

1970-

*1970-01   Bullard, C.G. "Professionalization: A Study of Librarianship." B.A. Honors thesis. University of New South Wales, 1970.

1970-02   Bundy, M.L. and Wasserman, P. *The Administrator of a Special Library or Information Center and His Situation.* Bethesda, MD: ERIC Document Reproduction Service, ED 054 799, 1970.

A total of 150 special libraries or information centers having staffs of ten or more were selected for the sample in this survey conducted for the Maryland Manpower Project. Ninety-five respondents completed this mailed questionnaire of whom 40% were women. "Occupation of Wife" and "Wife Working at Present" were reported for respondents (p. 70-71). The average male population for this type of facility is 38%. In

30% of the institutions men occupy more than 50% of the professional positions. It is noted that 21% have no men on their staffs as opposed to 49% of the academic libraries surveyed for the manpower project (p. 47). [1970-13]

1970-03   Carroll, C.E. *The Professionalization of Education for Librarianship.* Metuchen, NJ: Scarecrow Press, 1970.

Study analyzing social process of professionalization through history of library education particularly during the period 1940-1960. Influx of men into librarianship from 1949 on, when the Master's degree became the basic professional degree (p. 61-68), is examined. The predominance of men in the doctoral programs is discussed; also considered is women's preference for the sixth-year Master's as a form of advanced study before it was abolished (p. 132; 200; 207).

*1970-04   Cass, F.M.B. "Librarianship in New South Wales: Social History of a 'Professional' Occupation." B.A. Honors thesis. University of New South Wales, 1970.

1970-05   Howard, P. "The State of Federal Libraries." In *Bowker Annual of Library and Book Trade Information; 1970.* New York: R.R. Bowker, 1970:257-264.

Under the subheading "Personnel," the trends developing in federal libraries are outlined. Statistics for men and women are given. Notes that male librarians are generally two GS grades above women — a salary differential of $1,788. While women are paid slightly higher ($500) than other women in professional federal positions, men are paid quite a bit less than men ($1,921) in other professional federal positions.

1970-06   Presthus, R. *Technological Change and Occupational Response.* Bethesda, MD: ERIC Document Reproduction Service, ED 045 129, 1970.

Part of study entitled "A Program of Research into the Identification of Manpower Requirements, the Educational Preparation and the Utilization of Manpower in the Library and Information Profession." Study is intended to contribute to the understanding of the library occupation and its capacity to accommodate to several pervasive changes now confronting the field, including moves toward professionalization and unionization, reorientation toward working-class clients, and automation. Career commitment by librarians is seen as low due to the fact that a high proportion are women. This enhances the negative control aspects of bureaucratic norms while threatening some of their positive efficiency values. "Girls" are taught to defer to authority, to mediate interpersonal relations by submission, to achieve their ends by indirection, to employ psychological sanctions in dealing with each other, and to avoid direct conflict. Such factors account for the tendency of women to accept bureaucratic control. The low career commitment of women is reinforced by their choice of a service profession (p. 25). Responses to questions asked on the "organizational and authority structures" of libraries are broken down by "professional-clerical" and "male-female." Discussion of occupational commitment finds women have a tenuous commitment to change and innovation. Responses to "occupational values" questions are broken down by "librarian-clerical" and "male-female." Conclusion is that "conflict avoidance, order, and dependency are apparently common needs among librarians, some 80% of whom are women. These bureaucratic values which do not typically inspire strong demands for professional control of one's work milieu, including any new techniques, seem to be aggravated by the uncertain career commitment and the personal 'service' orientation often characteristic of 'female' occupations" (p. 108).

1970-07   U.S. Department of Labor, Bureau of Labor Statistics. "Librarians." *Occupational Outlook Handbook,* 1970-71 Edition. Washington, DC: U.S. Government Printing Office, 1970:233-237.

Notes 85% of all librarians are women, but men are more often executives and administrators or in libraries concerned with science and technology (p. 235).

1970-08   Shields, G.R. "Editor's Choice: Discomfort to the Enemy." *American Libraries* 1 (February 1970):115.

Editorial announcing *American Libraries'* new policy of editing "any overt or covert references to the sex desired for a position in a given library" out of classified advertisements. Such phrases as "salary negotiable," which "were too often used to make higher initial offers to the male applicant," will also be deleted.

1970-09   Darter, P. "One Point of View — Born a Woman." *Assistant Librarian* 63 (March 1970):42; 44.

Opinion piece describing the status of women librarians in Great Britain. Although only 28% of the professional entrants are men they will get preference over their female colleagues. Strategies to change women's role are discussed, which include a change in regulations concerning superannuation.

1970-10   Murphy, E.D. "Women and Blacks: Sexual Discrimination in the Library Profession." *Library Journal* 95 (March 15, 1970):959.

Letter pointing out parallel between Blacks' and women's struggle for equal opportunity.

1970-11   Schiller, A.R. "The Disadvantaged Majority: Women Employed in Libraries." *American Libraries* 1 (April 1970):345-349.

Proposes actions by ALA to ameliorate situation of women who, though in majority, are discriminated against. These are: 1) openly state the willingness of the association to deal with the issue; 2) institute and support a comprehensive research program on the status of women in librarianship; 3) open channels of communication for discussion of equality of opportunity in the profession; 4) establish a special committee on the status of women; 5) announce a stated minimum salary for all librarians which is consistent with going minimum salary rates for comparable educational qualifications in other professions where women do not necessarily predominate; 6) support measures designed to promote the rights of all women; and 7) develop a long-range action program designed to effect significant change and improvement for women.

Letters: Denis, L. "Discrimination Discussed." *American Libraries* 1 (July 1970):644.

Disputes Schiller's analysis of discrimination against women in librarianship. Offers evidence from a survey of 1960-1967 graduates of Canadian library schools which indicates that salary differences "are due to a number of factors completely unrelated to willful discrimination."

Plate, K. "Discrimination Discussed." *American Libraries* 1 (July 1970):644.

Criticizes Schiller for superficial treatment of problem. Cites studies showing men are more mobile, have more advanced degrees and tend to do more research than women, thus accounting for so-called discrimination against women.

Response to Letters: Schiller A. "Schiller Responds." *American Libraries* 1 (July 1970):644-645.

Schiller refutes Denis and Plate: 1) they ask different questions from the ones she addressed; 2) the research they cite is scattered and not conclusive; and 3) she asks what can be done; they, on the other hand, say "this we know," and stop there.

1970-12   Wetherby, P. "Librarianship: Opportunity for Women?" Series: *Sixteen Reports on the Status of Women in the Profession.* New York: Professional Women's Caucus, April, 1970.

Report to the Conference of Professional and Academic Women, April 11, 1970, asserts that "Librarianship is an open sesame for men, a dead end for women." Supports this with review of recent literature and examination of status of women librarians and library educators in Pittsburgh, Pennsylvania.

1970-13   Bundy, M.L. and Wasserman, P. *The Academic Library Administrator and His Situation. Final Report.* Bethesda, MD: ERIC Document Reproduction Service, ED 054 796, May, 1970.

Analysis of the characteristics of administrators and of the organizations and environments in which they function; one part of the University of Maryland Library Manpower Study. Data were gathered from a mail survey of academic library administrators in institutions having 3,000 students or more. Of the total of 161 replies, 7% were women and 93% men. Men make up 37% of the total professionals in academic libraries. Proportion of male professionals in institutions is reported: only 17% have staffs composed of men in 50% or more of the total professional positions (p. 46). The section on background and career of academic library administrators includes table on "Occupation of Wife" and "Wife Working at Present Time" (p. 75).

1970-14   Detlefsen, E.G., and Schuman, P. "Overdue: Women's Liberation Movement - I." *Wilson Library Bulletin* 44 (May 1970):962; 964-982.

Discusses re-emergence of an organized women's movement, women's sex role socialization, and the position of women in librarianship. Librarianship has been considered an acceptable profession for women in all but its administrative aspects. The profession must adapt to the changing role of women to remain valid and must also provide information on women-related issues to the society as a whole.

1970-15   Hathaway, G.W. "Overdue: Women's Liberation Movement - II." *Wilson Library Bulletin* 44 (May 1970):963; 965.

All people play double roles of oppressor and oppressed. One of the results of women's oppression is the female role socializations women bring to the workplace which lead to inappropriate behavior such as passivity, rigidity, ambiguity. Libraries are urged to respond to the information needs produced by the women's movement and to provide freedom for women's "options for the future within and without the institution."

> **Letter:**   Deur, B. "Don't Call Us . . ." *Wilson Library Bulletin* 45 (September 1970):34.
>
> "Spare us from such 'sympathetic' male chauvinists as Mr. Hathaway!" Hathaway deals in myths, which solidarity among women will overcome.

†1970-16   Freedman, J. "The Liberated Librarian? A Look at "The Second Sex" in the Library Profession." *Library Journal* 95 (May 1, 1970):1709-1711.

Surveys aspects of, and suggests possible solution to, male ascendancy in librarianship.

> **Letters:**   Brass, L.J. "Team Employment." *Library Journal* 95 (September 1970):2853.
>
> Report of librarians who submitted a team application, which was turned down because an experienced librarian was available. Gives arguments in favor of part-time work and supports Freedman's call for a substitute system in libraries.
>
> Lilley, S. "The Woman Question." *Library Journal* 95 (September 15, 1970):2853.
>
> Congratulates *LJ* on finally getting to the woman question. Librarianship, which is so concerned with intellectual freedom and professionalism, should also consider the place of women in the profession.

Smith, R.K. "The Woman Question." *Library Journal* (September 15, 1970):2853.

Questions "just which sex is the second sex?" Reports that in New York Chapter of SLA all officers are women.

Swarm, E. "Professionalism Over Emphasized." *Library Journal* 95 (September 15, 1970):2853-2854.

Takes issue with Freedman's statements on lack of salary weakening the commitment of volunteers. Cites the work of church librarians.

Gilliam, B.H. "Housewife-librarian." *Library Journal* 95 (November 1, 1970):3704-3705.

Reports her experiences as a part-time librarian; refutes typical arguments against part-time professionals; and laments lack of financial aid to part-time library students.

1970-17   Carpenter, R.L. and Carpenter, P.A. "The Doctorate in Librarianship and an Assessment of Graduate Library Education." *Journal of Education for Librarianship* 11 (Summer 1970):3-45.

Among many items surveyed is one showing that salaries for men with doctorates are far better at each age level for each type of position than for women.

1970-18   Nyren, K. "Spiro and the Rotten Kids." *Library Journal* 95 (July 1970):2403.

A tongue-in-cheek editorial on women's liberation with an obscure message.

Letter: Deur, B. "Non-support of Women." *Library Journal* 95 (October 15, 1970):3416.

Nyren's attempt to be supportive reveals his lack of understanding of women's liberation.

1970-19   Herring, M.G. "Reports of the 63rd Annual Meeting of the American Association of Law Libraries Held in Washington, DC, June 28 - July 2, 1970: A Panel Discussion." *Library of Congress Bulletin* 29 (July 23, 1970): A-56-A-57.

Report of a panel presentation, "Law Library Salaries," includes review of salaries by Carlyle J. Frarey based on a survey of Law Library Association members. Fifty-three percent of those responding were women. The median salary for women law librarians was $8,500, while for men it was $13,000. One of Frarey's general conclusions: "something must be done about the salaries of women."

1970-20   Detlefsen, E.G. "Women's Liberation Meeting at the ALA Conference." *AB Bookman's Weekly* 46 (July 20-27, 1970):90.

Describes beginning of SRRT Task Force on Women.

1970-21   "Detroit 1970: Another Opening, Another Show." *American Libraries* 1 (July-August 1970):660-684.

Included in this lengthy conference review is the report of the presentation of a motion, defeated by ALA membership, to condemn practices of discriminatory sexism, and not plan future ALA meetings in places which practice such discrimination (p. 676-677).

1970-22   Forsman, C. "Up Against the Stacks: Task Force on Status of Women in Libraries." *Synergy* No. 25 (July-August 1970):9.

Discusses issues of salary and promotion discrimination, underrepresentation of women in library education and administration of libraries, and the need for improved working conditions.

1970-23 "SLA Salary Survey: 1970." *Special Libraries* 61 (July-August 1970):333-348.

Shows that in all categories of survey (job function, subject, highest academic degree) men's salaries clustered above overall mean and women's clustered below mean.

1970-24 [ALA Social Responsibilities Round Table. Task Force on Women.] *SRRT Task Force on the Status of Women in Librarianship.* (August 1970) No. 1.

Newsletter reporting projects of the Task Force and giving general news of women's materials and activities. Continued by [1970-30].

1970-25 Bundy, M.L. and others. *The School Library Supervisor and Her Situation. Final Report.* Bethesda, MD: ERIC Document Reproduction Service, ED 054 797, August 1970.

Report of survey of school library supervisors in U.S. school system with enrollments of 25,000 or more to which ninety-nine of 150 replied. The study is part of the Maryland Manpower Series. Eighty percent of the respondents are women "Occupation of Husband" and "Husband Working at Present Time" are reported (p. 71). The report as a whole is a group profile of women, half of whom are over fifty years of age, who choose librarianship as a second career, most likely after teaching.

1970-26 Schuman, P. "Status of Women in Libraries: Task Force Meets in Detroit." *Library Journal* 95 (August 1970):2635.

Identifies areas of action needed: administrative guidelines; investigation of materials portraying women; discrimination clearinghouse; and information services for women. Describes origins of SRRT Task Force on Women.

1970-27 "ALA 1970: Notes and Comments: Further Goodies." *Wilson Library Bulletin* 45 (September 1970):17.

Report of "group [SRRT] espousing many special causes traditionally apart from library business" including founding meeting of the SRRT Task Force on Women.

1970-28 Geller, E. "Up Against the Wall: Highlights of The Detroit Conference, American Library Association, June 27 - July 3." *School Library Journal* 17 (September 1970):21-24.

Included in conference report is mention that "Women's Lib made its first official appearance with a meeting that pulled over 200 people" and a brief account of women's actions (p. 22).

*1970-29 Angoff, A. "All Male Library Staff." *Teaneck Points of Reference* 3 (October 1970).

1970-30 [ALA Social Responsibilities Round Table. Task Force on Women.] *ALA/SRRT Task Force of Women in Librarianship Newsletter.* (November 1970) No. 2.

Continues [1970-24]. Continued by [1971-16].

1970-31 Regnier, F.D. "Librarianship - A Woman's Profession?" *University of Wisconsin Library News* 15 (November 1970):11-13.

A review of Schiller [1969-13] with Schiller's figures compared to salary data at the University of Wisconsin—Madison Memorial Library. Regnier finds that Memorial follows the national pattern and notes that it is obvious librarianship is not a woman's profession and "equal opportunities" is a meaningless cliché.

1970-32   Oltman, R.M. *Campus 1970: Where Do Women Stand? Research Report of a Survey on Women in Academe.* Washington, DC: American Association of University of Women. December 1970.

Among many other topics in study, this survey shows women less likely to be head librarians in higher education institutions with enrollment over 10,000 and in public institutions; more likely in private schools or with enrollment under 1,000 (p. 14).

*1971-01   Corbett, E.V. *Librarianship.* London: Sunday Times Career Books, 1971.

1971-02   Horrocks, N. "The Carnegie Corporation of New York and Its Impact on Library Development in Australia: A Case-study of Foundation Influence." Ph.D. thesis. University of Pittsburgh, 1971.

In discussing the plans for the Australian Institute of Librarians, the opposition of women librarians in New South Wales to an organization of a profession in which they felt discriminated against is mentioned. References are also made to the hiring of women by the Public Library of New South Wales, a pioneer in the employment of women, and to allegations of sex discrimination in the awarding of Carnegie grants for overseas study (pp. 257-258).

1971-03   Kortendick, J.J. and Stone, E.W. *Job Dimensions and Educational Needs in Librarianship.* Chicago: American Library Association, 1971.

A total of 365 federal librarians completed a mailed questionnaire and twenty top-level administrators were interviewed in this study. The study's basic purpose was curriculum development at the post-Master's degree level that would equip the middle and upper-level personnel in libraries for the changes confronting them. Women made up 73.4% of the respondents; however "generally the higher the grade, the higher percentage of men holding these federal library posts — a similar pattern is noted among the non-administrators" (p. 65). Data are not generally analyzed by sex.

1971-04   McCauley, E.B. "The New England Mills Girls: Feminine Influence in the Development of Public Libraries in New England 1820-1860." D.L.S. thesis, Columbia University. 1971.

Historical study dealing with the relationship of the industrial revolution in cotton, which used large numbers of young women, and the development of public libraries to which all members of the community, including women, had access. In an era which denied women fundamental rights the pre-Civil War mill villages offered certain liberating advantages which women had never experienced before. In the villages, studied progress toward the development of public library collections was precipitated by the existence of literate female populations, who were experiencing a condition approaching equality with men in the labor market and were reaching out for equal opportunities in other fields of human aspiration.

1971-05   Shaffer, K.R. *Decision Making: A Seminar in Public Library Management.* Hamden, Connecticut: Linnet Books, 1971.

A collection of seventy-five situations portraying "administrative problems characteristic of public libraries," many of which contain stereotypes of male and female roles: directors are male, troublesome staff members and trustees female. "Gray-skinned Ladies in Gray Dresses" concerns the dowdy dress of women librarians; "Companionate Marriage" deals with the problems incurred in hiring married women; and "Author! Author!" considers the failure of a male reference librarian to put "his real vocational steam into his profession and his job."

1971-06   Rothenberg, L., Rees, A.M., and Kronick, D.A. "An Investigation of the Educational Needs of Health Sciences Library Manpower: IV. Characteristics of Manpower in Health Science Libraries." *Bulletin of the Medical Library Association* 59 (January 1971):31-40.

Shows male professionals in survey had highest rates of job and geographic mobility and salaries.

1971-07   The University of Michigan School of Library Science Alumnus in Residence 1971. *Women in the Library Profession: Leadership Roles and Contributions.* Ann Arbor: University of Michigan School of Library Science, (n.d.)

A collection of papers prepared by five distinguished women alumnae of the Michigan Library School to honor the centennial of the admission of the first woman to the University of Michigan. Brief biographies and portraits of the alumnae are included: Martha Boaz, F. Bernice Field, Clara Jones, Mary Jo Lynch, Faith Murdoch.

1971-07A   Boaz, M. "And There Were Giantesses in Library Education." In *Women in the Library Profession: Leadership Roles and Contributions.* Ann Arbor: University of Michigan School of Library Science, (n.d.):1-10.

Boaz begins her paper by commenting that she would prefer to talk about men but accepts her topic. A brief history of women in library education is given followed by biographical sketches of forty women library educators.

1971-07B   Field, F. "Technical Services and Women." In *Women in the Library Profession: Leadership Roles and Contributions.* Ann Arbor: University of Michigan School of Library Science, (n.d.):11-15.

Reviews developments in acquisitions, cataloging and technical services. Brief biographical sketches of women contributing to these specialties are given. Opportunities for women in technical services are reviewed.

1971-07C   Jones, C. "Women in the Inspiration of Librarianship." In *Women in the Library Profession: Leadership Roles and Contributions.* Ann Arbor: University of Michigan School of Library Science, (n.d.):16-19.

Jones comments on the role of librarians as inspirers of future librarians. She recounts her initiation into librarianship and women who inspired her. Jones believes that men have also made significant contributions to librarianship and are the reason for the rise in salaries in recent years.

1971-07D   Lynch, M.J. "Women in Reference Service." In *Women in the Library Profession: Leadership Roles and Contributions.* Ann Arbor: University of Michigan School of Library Science, (n.d.):20-23.

Argues that many women choose librarianship for the wrong reasons, such as the availability of part time work. Women, however, have made significant contributions to librarianship and should become more assertive. The work of Alice Kroeger, Isadore Mudge and Constance Winchell is reviewed.

1971-07E   Murdoch, F. "Standard Bearers for School Libraries." In *Women in the Library Profession: Leadership Roles and Contributions.* Ann Arbor: University of Michigan School of Library Science, (n.d.):24-27.

Reviews the emergence of school libraries as an educational force. Biographical sketches of Frances Lander Spain, Mary Peacock Douglas, Mary Garver and Frances Henne are included.

1971-08   Weber, D.C. and Rogers, R.D. *University Library Administration* (New York, H.W. Wilson, 1971).

Under the topic, "Staff Selection and Appointment," problems in hiring faculty wives are discussed. Throughout, the director is referred to as male (p. 31).

1971-09 Schuman, P.G. "Sugar and Spice." *School Library Journal* 17 (January 1971):5.

Editorial discusses idealized aspects of women's liberation and then goes on to note that even in "traditional" female professions such as librarianship, men dominate in administrative positions. Calls for librarians to realize the crippling effects of sexism in children's literature.

1971-10 "Behind the Library Counter, the Image Is Starting to Change." *New York Times* (January 15, 1971):24.

Discusses the image of the librarian but turns aside the old image with comments like, "Dunbar, a well-curved 29-year-old, wearing a quantity of blue eyeshadow." In an attempt to show it's not really a female profession article notes thirty-nine of the nation's largest libraries are run by men. One woman notes that her consciousness has been raised as she recognizes women are the heads of only two major libraries — Dallas and Detroit.

†**1971-11** Carey, J.T. "Overdue: Taking Issue With the Issues." *Wilson Library Bulletin* 45 (February 1971):592-594.

Refutation of Schiller [1970-11] noting that careers for women are interrupted by children or interrupted by husbands' moves. He implies that women must be passive and less professional than men since, while in the majority, they are still dominated by men.

Letters: DeBoard, J.A. "Taking Issue with 'Taking Issue With the Issues' of Female Librarians." *Wilson Library Bulletin* 45 (April 1971):780.

Point by point refutation of Carey's argument: with "many librarians in administration holding such views, it would be amazing to see women advance to any degree in the field."

Osborne, J. "Law Library." *Wilson Library Bulletin* 45 (April 1971):781.

Asks how Carey would justify discrimination on the basis of sex in light of Title VII of the 1964 Civil Rights Act.

Price, S. "Mediocrity." *Wilson Library Bulletin* 45 (April 1971):781.

"Why should talented women be held down on the basis that most women are mediocre? Talented men don't have to answer for mediocre men, do they?"

Shaw, B. "Passive - Humbug." *Wilson Library Bulletin* 45 (April 1971):780-781.

For the most part feels Carey's remarks are fair but disagrees that women are more passive than men. "Someday it will be as unthinkable to label all members of one sex as passive as it is today to label all members of any race stupid."

Starr, C. "Obvious." *Wilson Library Bulletin* 45 (April 1971):781.

The prejudice which exists against women in librarianship is "that of the whole male-supremacy society that we live in today." Questions whether violence, which she deplores, would not more immediately effect change.

1971-12 Hughes, M. "Sex-based Discrimination in Law Libraries." *Law Library Journal* 64 (February 1971):13-22.

Survey shows that male head librarians have higher salaries than women, that there is a concentration of males in large law school libraries and they tend to achieve administrative positions at a younger age than women.

1971-13   "Of Note." *American Libraries* 2 (February 1971):137-146.

Included in series of brief news items is summary of Angoff's "gem on an all-male staff for a library [1970-29] (p. 138-139)." Who would make coffee or cookies; carry on the children's room; put in extra hours "commiserate with the female public at the circulation desk," etc. if there were no women working in libraries?

> **Letter:**   Cassell, K.A.   "Sex-role   Kidding."   *American   Libraries*   2 (March 1971):235-236.
>
> Was both amused and disturbed by Angoff and hopes he was only joking. "Sex role conditioning is a problem which needs serious consideration by all of us."

1971-14   Maloney, R.A. "The 'Average' Director of a Large Public Library." *Library Journal* 96 (February 1, 1971):443-445.

Study of directors in twenty-six libraries in 1969, 1950, and 1930, with analyses of age, sex, training, etc. showing fewer women in top positions.

1971-15   T., P.A. "Salaries in Three States: Victoria." *The Australian Library Journal* 20 (March 1971):33.

In a review of recent actions on library staff salaries in Victoria, an equal pay case for a library assistant which could not be substantiated is mentioned. Movement toward parity, however, is noted.

1971-16   "Headin' For the Last Roundup: Equal Opportunity for Women." *American Libraries* 2 (March 1971):265-266.

Part of 1971 Midwinter conference review. Report of unanimous ALA Council passage of resolution on "Equal Opportunity for Women in Librarianship" presented by the ALA SRRT Task Force on Women. Resolution is printed in full.

1971-17   [ALA Social Responsibilities Round Table. Task Force on Women.] *ALA/SRRT Task Force on the Status of Women in Librarianship Newsletter.* (April 1971) No. 3.

Continues objectives of [1970-24; 1970-30]. Continued by [1972-11].

1971-18   Maguire, C. "Survey of Library Employment in N.S.W." *The Australian Library Journal* 20 (April 1971):26.

News item on the Encel survey [1972-03]. Reports, "the most important theme will be the implications of the fact that the great majority of librarians are women. . . . The preponderance of women imposes on librarianship special problems in gaining recognition as a profession."

1971-19   Malcolm, S.F. "Women's Lib." *The Australian Library Journal* 20 (April 1971):32.

Letter inquiring why do "ladies providing biographical details for the *Journal's* Notes on Contributors supply birth dates while men do not." Author suggests she may join "women's lib" because of this practice. Editor replies it is because women supply birthdates and "coy men" do not.

1971-20   Manchak, B. "ALA Salary Survey: Personal Members." *American Libraries* 2 (April 1971):409-417.

Discloses salary figures which indicate inequities between men and women.

1971-21   "Association News: Standing Committee: A Report: Discrimination in Advertisements." *The Australian Library Journal* 20 (May 1971):43.

Item noting that the editor of the *Journal* sought authority to refuse advertisements seeking librarians which discriminated on the basis of sex. The request was denied on the grounds that "library authorities may legitimately seek to employ 'male only' or 'female only' librarians."

1971-22   Colley, A.W. "More Women's Lib." *The Australian Library Journal* 20 (May 1971):47.

Letter pointing out "the prominence given to the birthdates of the two female contributors" in the March issue of the *Journal.* Writer asks whether this is intended as discrimination against women.

1971-23   Shaffer, K.R. "Decision Making." *Library Journal* 96 (May 15, 1971):1677-1680.

Excerpts from author's *Decision Making: A Seminar in Public Library Management* [1971-04] describing situations confronting library administrators and recommending solutions. Included are situations on women interviewing men for library positions and a mother whose family responsibilities conflict with working.

Letters: Bryant, J. "Sexism or Sensibility." *Library Journal* 96 (August 1971):2410.

Compliments Shaffer. "How rare it is today to read something sound and at the same time entertaining."

Cowan, L. "Sexism or Sensibility." *Library Journal* 96 (August 1971):2410.

Short letter complimenting Shaffer.

Forth, S. "Sexism or Sensibility." *Library Journal* 96 (August 1971):2409.

Brief letter in support of Shaffer's article.

Klein, H. "Sexism or Sensibility." *Library Journal* 96 (August 1971):2409.

"Shaffer's attitude exemplifies the typical male prejudice on which many discriminating administrative decisions in all occupational fields are based."

Martin, P.T. "Sexism or Sensibility." *Library Journal* 96 (August 1971):2410.

Criticizes Shaffer's "companionate" marriage situation. "Surely it is time for the profession to dispense with such obtuse generalizations masquerading as conventional wisdom."

Powell, J.W. "Sexism or Sensibility." *Library Journal* 96 (August 1971):2410.

Letter criticizing Shaffer's approach as "cutesy Dear Abby."

Robbins, R.W. "Sexism or Sensibility." *Library Journal* 96 (August 1971):2409-2410.

Letter in support of Shaffer's "cheerful decisiveness."

Russell, N. "Sexism or Sensibility." *Library Journal* 96 (August 1971):2409.

Comments on Shaffer as a teacher. Urges that librarians "truly concerned with administrative problems skip purchasing the book."

Vernon, C. "Sexism or Sensibility." *Library Journal* 96 (August 1971):2410.

Describes female staff of library where author works and criticizes Shaffer for "damning female parents as a class."

Hanssen, N. "More on Shaffer." *Library Journal* 96 (September 15, 1971):2710.

Letter objecting to the tone and substance of the excerpts printed from Shaffer's book, particularly the anti-homosexual, anti-female bias.

Dziura, W.T. "More on Shaffer: Pro . . ." *Library Journal* 96 (October 15, 1971):3256.

Letter on responses to Shaffer which are characterized as "the hysterical wails in response to an emotional misreading. . . . All unwittingly provided exquisite proof of the very problems presented in the Shaffer article."

Taborksky, T. ". . . And Con." *Library Journal* 96 (October 15, 1971):3256.

If women received equal pay for equal work they too could afford services to substitute for their personal services in the home.

Aldrich, R.D. "Shaffer Defense." *Library Journal* 96 (November 15, 1971):3701.

Letter in support of Shaffer, interpreting his statement on married women as employees as meaning that in our present society "if you hire married women you have to realize that their first responsibility is to their home and family."

Yaranella, M. "Judging Virility." *Library Journal* 96 (November 15, 1971):3701.

Comments on Shaffer's chauvinism; wonders what special skill has been developed to judge virility within the confines of the ordinary job interview.

1971-24 Maguire, C. "A Mirror for Librarians." *The Australian Library Journal* 20 (August 1971):27.

Report of Professor Sol Encel's address to the New South Wales Branch of the Library Association of Australia in which Encel outlined the methodology and findings of his study [1972-03]. Eighty-six and one-half percent of the survey respondents were women as contrasted to the figure of 30 percent for women in the Australian work force generally. Encel also found that women encountered special difficulties in realizing their professional aspirations.

1971-25 "Shadows of the Future: Confrontation." *Library Journal* 96 (August 1971):2442-2443.

Included in the review on SRRT action at the 1971 ALA conference is a report of the SRRT Women's Task Force demonstration picket line at the Newbery-Caldecott Awards Dinner protesting sexism in children's literature. Also reports the male chauvinism awards to Kenneth Shaffer for *Decision Making* [1971-05] and John Carey for his article in *Wilson Library Bulletin* [1971-11].

1971-26 "ALA 1971: Notes and Comments: Women." *Wilson Library Bulletin* 46 (September 1971):26; 28.

Report of SRRT Task Force on Women activities at 1971 ALA Convention: alternative Newbery-Caldecott Awards Dinner and a visual presentation on sexism and children's literature.

1971-27 "Issue on Women." *Library Journal* 96 (September 1, 1971).

Entire issue devoted to articles and bibliographies on women, includes an annotated bibliography by Pat Schuman and Gay Detlefsen and "The Legal Status of Women" by Kay Ann Cassell.

Letters: Crutwell, A. "Women's Lib Reactions." *Library Journal* 96 (October 15, 1971):3255.

Enumerates major and minor tasks of a female library assistant. Response to "Women's Lib issue of September" by a non-professional who describes the many responsibilities she has as a library assistant. "For [her] share of the "assistance" [she] receives the magnificent yearly sum of $3,400 and must be duly thankful for having a job at all" — a situation typical of women's work.

Josey, E.J. "Orchids!" *Library Journal* 96 (November 15, 1971):3701.

"Bravo for the Sept. 1 issue . . . since I am a member of the largest oppressed minority group in this country, I support all oppressed groups—."

Zimmerman, K. "Quest for Equality." *Library Journal* 96 (November 15, 1971):3700.

Notes that the Sept. 1 issue encourages her own quest for equality. Relates two incidents of sexual discrimination which also affected her husband. "Let's help both sexes by getting equal rights and benefits."

1971-27A Gerhardt, L.N. "Melvil! Thou Shouldst Be Living." *Library Journal* 96 (September 1, 1971):2567.

Angry editorial introducing issue on women.

1971-27B Tuttle, H.W. "Women in Academic Libraries." *Library Journal* 96 (September 1, 1971):2594-2596.

Discusses discrimination against women in academic librarianship, the roles both men and women take on, and sexism in language. Urges women to believe in their own potential and ability and then develop their own careers.

Letters: Lainer, D.L. "Women's Lib Reactions." *Library Journal* 96 (October 15, 1971):3255.

Expresses appreciation for Tuttle's article.

Ruef, J. "Women's Lib Reactions." *Library Journal* 96 (October 15, 1971):3255.

Acknowledges unfair treatment of women in librarianship and society in general which two groups prolong: female Uncle Toms, and radicals like Tuttle who promote the concept that women are superior to men.

McElney, B. "Men Are Human Too." *Library Journal* 96 (November 15, 1971):20.

Criticizes Tuttle's classification of men as killers. Suggests that part of the equal pay for equal work issue should be a definition of "work."

Piternick, G. "Wo-Manly Word Play." *Library Journal* 96 (December 15, 1971):22.

Caustic response to Tuttle's article belittling her discussion of expunging male dominance from our language.

1971-27C Jacobson, B. "Woman's Work . . . A Job Description." *Library Journal* 96 (September 1, 1971):2596.

Brief description of the many responsiblities of a woman with family attending library school.

†1971-27D   Lowenthal, H. "A Healthy Anger." *Library Journal* 96 (September 1, 1971):2597-2599.

Call to direct anger at situations which perpetuate inequalities between the sexes in the profession.

Letter: Moore, I.P. "A Healthy Anger." *Library Journal* 96 (November 15, 1971):3700-3701.

"Therefore, all you Liberationists: *Stop trying to make me unhappy!. . .* I'd rather be a competent, happy unliberated woman."

1971-28   "Cary Is New Copyright Head; Ringer Sues, Charging Bias." *Publisher's Weekly* 200 (September 6, 1971):29.

Announcement of George D. Cary's appointment as Register of Copyrights to succeed Abraham L. Kaminstein. Includes a brief interview with Barbara A. Ringer who is filing suit in the U.S. District Court for the District of Columbia, requesting a restraining order to halt the implementation of Cary's appointment on the ground that the Civil Service failed to observe its own regulations. Sex discrimination is one of her charges.

1971-29   "Assistant Copyrights Register Charges Bias." *Wilson Library Bulletin* 46 (October 1971):126.

Background of Barbara A. Ringer's battle to gain position as Register of Copyrights, a case which involves sex discrimination.

1971-30   "Equal Employment Opportunity: Affirmative Action Plans for Libraries: Woman Power." *American Libraries* 2 (October 1971):983.

Reprints text of ALA resolution on Equal Opportunity for Women in Librarianship and briefly discusses affirmative action and women.

1971-31   "Copyright Appointment Nixed by D.C. Court Order." *Library Journal* 96 (October 15, 1971):3261.

Report that District Court, Judge William Jones, has ordered the appointment of George D. Cary as Register of Copyrights of the Library of Congress cancelled as a result of a discrimination suit brought by Barbara A. Ringer.

1971-32   "Race and Sex Bias Are Issues as Ringer Takes LC to Court." *Library Journal* 96 (October 15, 1971):3262-3263.

Analysis of Barbara A. Ringer's tactics in taking her discrimination case to court and through the administrative procedures of the Library of Congress. Summary of a telephone interview with Ringer, who was denied an interview for the position of Register of Copyright.

1971-33   "Affirmative Action Committee for Women Appointed at UC." *Library Journal* 96 (November 1, 1971):3552-3553.

University of California at Berkeley library staff charged with developing program to ensure women optimum employment and promotion.

1971-34   "Circuit Court Nullifies LC's Appointment of Cary." *Library Journal* 96 (November 1, 1971):3543.

Report of Circuit Court decision in case of Barbara A. Ringer. The interview stage of the appointment has been re-opened because of the decision that L. Quincy Mumford,

Librarian of Congress, had not followed LC employment regulations. LC's newly established Fair Employment Office is in the process of examining Ringer's charges of sex and racial discrimination.

1971-35   Wagner, S. "Cary Renamed Register of Copyrights." *Publisher's Weekly* 200 (November 8, 1971):29.

Notes that although George D. Cary was renamed Register of Copyrights by the Librarian of Congress, L. Quincy Mumford, the issue is not entirely closed, for a discrimination complaint by Barbara A. Ringer is pending. Background on the case is given.

1971-36   Library Affirmative Action Program for Women Committee. University of California, Berkeley. *A Report on the Status of Women Employed in the Library of the University of California, Berkeley, with Recommendations for Affirmative Action.* December 1971. Also available as an ERIC document: ED 066 163.

Documents that women are concentrated at lowest levels with diminishing opportunities for advancement: presents recommendations for changes in hiring, recruitment, training. Model for subsequent policies of other libraries.

1971-37   "The Professional Woman." *Protean* 1 (December 1971).

Entire issue devoted to articles on sexism in librarianship, includes a general paper by Sheila Tobias on psychological and social harms to women on the job.

1971-37A   Kronus, C.L. and Grimm, C.W. "Women in Librarianship: The Majority Rules?" *Protean* 1 (December 1971):4-9.

Analyzes the nature of and connection between the employment and promotion queues for men and women in librarianship. No necessary connection is found. There may be more women in librarianship, but they are not dominant in power positions.

1971-37B   Ackerman, P.; Ellis, E.G.; Nyren, D.; Tucker, M.; Tuttle, H.; Whitney, V. "Of Sex and Administration." *Protean* 1 (December 1971):20-31.

Six women library administrators respond to questions on sex discrimination, support staff, affirmative action, implications for librarianship of changes in women's roles and Ken Shaffer's *Decision Making: A Seminar in Public Library Management* [1971-05].

1971-37C   Wood, M.S. "Sex Discrimination: The Question of 'Valid Grounds.' " *Protean* 1 (December 1971):32-40.

Review of the literature of women in librarianship pointing out discrimination patterns and rationales given for discrimination. Notes the rhetorical nature of the bulk of the literature, calls for more research and the suggestion of solutions.

1971-37D   Robson, L. "Making an Issue of It." *Protean* 1 (December 1971):54-56.

Closure to *Protean* issue examining the pervasiveness of sexism in librarianship. Summarizes action taken within the ALA to equalize the position of women; suggests areas for ongoing concern including reporting of salary data by sex, nepotism and research needed. Cautions that paraprofessional development and the definition of ourselves must not be forgotten.

1971-38   Schiller, A.R. "Aware: Report on Women in Librarianship." *American Libraries* 2 (December 1971):1215-1216.

Review of women's representation in top positions shows rapid decline; also reports on affirmative action plans in academe.

1971-39   Schuman, P.G. "SLJ News Roundup: Racism, Sexism, Chauvinism." *School Library Journal* 18 (December 1971):23-24.

Actions by women and minorities in cases of discrimination and on behalf of non-stereotyped literature are noted. The work of the SRRT Task Force on Women is mentioned and concern is expressed over competition between predominantly female school librarians and predominantly male audiovisual directors for the head-of-media-center jobs.

1971-40   Shephard, S. "Sic 'em II." *American Libraries* 2 (December 1971):1140-1141.

Letter calling for women to unite and reclaim their rightful place as leaders in libraries. Prominent women of the past such as Mary Wright Plummer, Margaret Mann and Minnie Earl Sears are cited as models. Fact that inferior men are promoted over admirable women is expanded in protest against the gay rights movement in libraries.

> **Letter:**   Bowman, L.J. "Getting the Great Ladies Together." *American Libraries* 3 (February 1972):117.
>
> Ironic response to Shepherd which gently pokes fun at the reverse sexism of her letter.

1971-41   Katz, B. "The Pornography Collection." *Library Journal* 96 (December 15, 1971):4060-4066.

In a discussion of pornography Katz asks if "the great hassle in libraries over censorship result[s] primarily from the too-shrill and puritanical dominant voice of the woman librarian?" (p. 4062). He quotes Richard Schickel's opinion that women don't know why men are so turned on by sexy films. Perhaps, says Katz, this explains why so few women are involved with library censorship. He concludes with these observations: "The obvious fallacy of this hypothesis is that sex may be important in shaping sensibility, yet in terms of evaluating magazines or books the determinant should be intelligence. And neither sex has a corner on that" (p. 4062).

> **Letters:**   McShean, G. "Censorship and Chauvinism." *Library Journal* 97 (March 1, 1972):801-802.
>
> Writer defends Katz, who has been denounced by female members of the Bay Area SRRT at their January meeting. He states that the article as a whole is solid and that women in general haven't really defended intellectual freedom.
>
> Tenander, J. "Censorship and Chauvinism." *Library Journal* 97 (March 1, 1971):801.
>
> Writer is offended and amazed at Katz' presentation of women librarians as repressed and uninvolved in censorship problems. His remarks are "obnoxious" and "unnecessary."

1972-01   Bundy, M.L. and Wasserman, P. *The Public Library Administrator and His Situation,* Urban Information Series Publication No. 6. College Park, MD: Urban Information Interpreters Inc., 1972.

One part of the executive study portion of the Program of Research into the Identification of Manpower Requirements, the Educational Preparation and the Utilization of Manpower in the Library and Information Profession. Data reported and analyzed were gathered from a mail survey sent to administrations of public libraries serving populations of 100,000 or more; 102 (71%) responded. Women make up 38% of the group but data are not broken down by sex. "Occupation of Wife," and "Wife Working at Present Time," are reported (p. 75). The average male population of library staffs is 15% and the contrast with academic libraries (37%) noted. "In only 22%

of the responding institutions, do men occupy more than 20% of the professional staff positions and the upper limit is 40%" (p. 49).

1972-02   Cass, F.M.B. *Librarianship in New South Wales, A Study.* Occasional Papers in Librarianship No. 12 Adelaide: Libraries Board of South Australia, 1972.

A study of the emergence and development of librarianship in New South Wales origi- nally done as an honors thesis in sociology [1970-04]. Particular attention is paid to the roles of H.C.L. Anderson and W.H. Ifould in the feminization of the profession. The influx of women into librarianship is seen as a direct result of the policies of these librarians, particularly relating to pay levels, entrance requirements and views of the role of women. The current situation is also examined from the point of view of sex. Males as a proportion of the professional membership of the Library Association of Australia are on the decrease while married women are on the increase. The academic achievement level of both sexes is dropping. Professional employment is examined by sex, marital status for women, and educational level for the major classes of librarians. Married women re-entering the work force tend to be unqualified or have received their library qualifications many years ago; these women tend to be employed in local government libraries. Women who re-enter the work force who have their degrees tend to be employed in institutions of higher education. In Appendix I data from the 1970 Library Association of Australia sponsored study of librarianship in New South Wales directed by S. Encel [1972-03] are presented in tabular form "to supplement and intensify the information from documentary sources upon which [the] thesis is based."

1972-03   Encel, S., Bullard, C. and Cass, M. *Librarians: A Survey.* Sidney, Australia: New South Wales University Press Pty. Ltd., 1972.

Report of a 1969 survey of libraries in New South Wales, Australia and excerpts from Cass's and Bullard's theses [1970-04; 1970-01]. Two chapters are devoted specifically to women in librarianship. A history of the role of sex in the development of the li- brary profession in New South Wales is given through brief analysis of the work and influence of H.C.L. Anderson and W.H. Ifould, male librarians who brought women into library work and promoted policies directed towards a subordinate role for them (p. 15-31). The current situation of women is analyzed by type of library, work loca- tion, marital status, age, and salary range as compared with men. Women's easy sub- mission to male bureaucratic control is posed as running counter to the profes- sionalization of librarianship.

*1972-04   Kuhn, A. and Poole, A. *The Background and Career of the Graduate Librarian.* Sheffield, England: Sheffield University, Higher Education Re- search Unit, Department of Sociological Studies, 1972.

1972-05   Massman, V.F. *Faculty Status for Librarians.* Metuchen, NJ: Scarecrow, 1972.

Study reviews the history of the struggle for faculty status by academic librarians and some of the arguments advanced in support of that objective. Reports on the similarities and differences between librarians and faculty members in the broad areas of preparation, contributions, and rewards. All data are broken down by sex. Notes that the problems of academic librarianship have sometimes been attributed to the fact that it is a feminine profession (p. 66). Table 6 shows the percentage of male and female librarians from 1870 to 1960 (p. 67). Conflict between faculty (mostly male) and librarians (mostly female) is seen to arise because of sex (p. 18). Massman views the high proportion of women in librarianship as having serious implications for the profession since fewer women earn the doctorate; women are less interested in re- search and publishing; less mobile (and therefore less competitive for administrative positions); and the victims of unwarranted and self-imposed discrimination (pp. 66- 73).

1972-06   Shores, L. "Library School Students." In *Library Education*. Littleton, Colorado: Libraries Unlimited Inc., 1972:64-71.

Reprint of [1967-07].

1972-07   U.S. Department of Health, Education, and Welfare. *Library Statistics of Colleges and Universities: Institutional Data, Part B, Fall 1971: Basic Information on Collections, Staff, and Expenditures.* Washington, DC: U.S. Government Printing Office, 1972.

One of three reports of the fall 1971 survey of U.S. college and university libraries which had an 86% response rate. Table 2, "Regular Library Staff (FTE). By Term of Employment, Type of Position, and Sex, College and University Libraries, By Institution: Aggregate United States, Fall 1971" (p. 53-96), breaks down employees by category and sex for each of the 2519 libraries responding to the survey. Categories include librarians, other professional staff, clerical, and other staff. Data are not analyzed until [1973-14].

1972-08   U.S. Department of Labor, Bureau of Labor Statistics. "Librarians." *Occupational Outlook Handbook,* 1972-73 Edition. Washington, DC: U.S. Government Printing Office, 1972:248-252.

Notes more than 85% of all librarians are women, but men are more frequently employed in executive and administrative posts and in libraries concerned with science and technology (p. 251).

1972-09   DeWeese, L.C. "Status Concerns and Library Professionalism." *College and Research Libraries* 33 (January 1972):31-38.

Among factors examined, marital status rather than sex was a predictor of concern.

1972-10   "George D. Cary Made Register of Copyrights." *Wilson Library Bulletin* 46 (January 1972):468.

Brief notice that Cary has been reappointed Register of Copyrights in spite of Barbara A. Ringer's protests.

1972-11   [ALA Social Responsibilities Round Table. Task Force on Women.] *ALA Social Responsibilities Round Table Task Force on Women Newsletter.* (February 1972) No. 4.

Continues objectives of [1970-24; 1970-30; 1971-17]. Continued by [1972-42].

1972-12   Auerbach, W. "Discrimination Against Women in the Academic Library." *University of Wisconsin Library News* 17 (February 1972):1-11.

Includes data on ratio of men to women directors of public vs. academic libraries; also statistics of sex imbalance in University of Wisconsin-Madison Memorial Library.

1972-13   Dunbar, G. "Discrimination in Library Schools." *American Libraries* 3 (February 1972):113-114.

Argues that older women are not given entrance to library schools.

1972-14   Rudy, M. "Women." In "Reports on Programs, Plans and Projects of SRRT Task Forces." *School Library Journal* 18 (February 1972):30-31.

Detailed history of the SRRT Task Force on Women. Future projects include day care at ALA conventions, production of a packet of materials on developing and filing discrimination charges, a survey of library policies on maternity leave, and support of the passage of the ERA in the Senate.

1972-15   Washington Library Association, SRRT Task Force on the Status of Women in Librarianship, and Associated Students of University of Washington Women's Commission. "University of Washington Libraries Discrimination Against Women: Preliminary Report." Seattle, February 1972. (Mimeographed).

Data gathered from the staff of the University of Washington libraries include graphic representations of the inequities between male and female librarians. One-third of the men receive salaries of $15,000 or more compared with one one-seventy-fourth of the women. Two-thirds of the men receive salaries over $10,000, while four-fifths of the women receive salaries under $10,000. Only one-eighth of the men earn less than $8,500, while one-third of the women do so. Only one man earns less than $8,000 while one-sixth of the women do so. The situation with respect to rank is similar. While women outnumber men three to one, only one of the top six administrative ranks is held by a woman. Recommendations are made to bring the University of Washington libraries into conformity with the University Policy of Equal Opportunity Employment: Salary adjustments should be made and women be given equal treatment.

1972-16 Rubinstein, H.L. "Chauvinism in Academe." *Library Journal* 97 (February 1, 1972):437-438.

Letter calling attention to a book "equally misogynist and distasteful" as Shaffer's *Decision Making* [1971-05]: *University Library Administration* by R.D. Rogers and D.C. Weber [1971-08]. Particularly objects to passage on faculty wives as a labor source and to the assumption that library directors will be male.

1972-17 Erlich, M. "He-Libes vs. Women's Lib." *Unabashed Librarian* No. 3 (Spring 1972):17-18.

A parody on the women's movement in librarianship.

1972-18 "Calm, Cool, and Sort-of-Collected: Resolution on Statistical Study of Librarianship." *American Libraries* 3 (March 1972):255.

Text of resolution from the SRRT Task Force on Women calling for the ALA to request that the U.S. Bureau of Labor Statistics undertake a nation-wide statistical study of librarianship.

1972-19 "Equal Pay in Queensland." *The Australian Library Journal* 21 (March 1972):68.

News item announcing the Queensland government's recent approval of equal pay for both sexes in a range of State Public Service employee catagories, including most library staff. Women librarians and library assistants had their salaries raised to what were formerly male rates. Also, notes a claim on behalf of Brisbane Municipal Library staff which includes the concept of equal pay.

1972-20 Lundie, M. "Discrimination in *Aust. Lib. J.*" *The Australian Library Journal* 21 (March 1972):75.

Letter criticizing the printing of advertisements for librarians which quote differing job salaries for males and females.

1972-21 Plotnik, A. "ALA Midwinter: Hot Winds, Cold Winds, Ups and Downs: SRRT's Ups and Downs." *Wilson Library Bulletin* 46 (March 1972):647.

Included in the report of SRRT action at ALA midwinter are comments on the lessening of women's militancy.

1972-22 University of Washington Libraries. Office of the Director. "Response to Preliminary Report on University of Washington Libraries' 'Alleged Discrimination Against Women.'" Seattle, March 1972. (Mimeographed).

Responds to report issued by the Task Force on the Status of Women of the Washington Chapter of SRRT and the Women's Commission of the Associated Students of the University of Washington [1972-15]. Notes that no females with the necessary qualifications could be found for administrative posts in most cases. Tries to show that it is inevitable that men have better positions due to lack of female applicants.

1972-23   "UC Affirmative Action Report Scores Sex and Job Bias." *Library Journal* 97 (March 15, 1972):958.

News item summarizing the Berkeley Affirmative Action Report [1971-35].

1972-24   Schiller, A.R. "The Origin of Sexism in Librarianship." *American Libraries* 3 (April 1972):427-428.

Notion that libraries are peripheral institutions is not due to women, but to distorted social condition and outlook; article includes summary of Berkeley Library report on status of women [1971-36].

*1972-25   Bower, B. "Placement of 1970/71 SLS Graduates: Is Sex Discrimination a Reality?" University of California, Los Angeles School of Library Service. Departmental Announcements and Memoranda, April 20, 1972. (Mimeographed).

1972-26   Fielding, F.D.O. "A Valediction on a Non-profession." *The Australian Library Journal* 21 (May 1972):162-164.

An assessment of the validity and relevance of the Encel report on libraries in New South Wales [1972-03]. Reviews the chapters analyzing the movement of women into librarianship because the pay wasn't high enough to attract men. Discusses recommendations point by point. The Library Association of Australia does not need to ensure equality of representation for women as recommended because women are in the majority. The author agrees that the LAA should "unequivocally assert the equality of the sexes in all spheres of library activity," and while agreeing that the LAA should support equal pay for equal work notes that "nothing the LAA could do would stop the tide towards equal pay in government employment."

1972-27   Pottinger, J.S. "The Drive for Employment Equality." *Protean* 2 (Summer 1972):6-11.

Explains how HEW insures nondiscriminatory hiring practices and why affirmative action programs are necessary in some cases.

1972-28   Andrews, C.R. "Proof Positive." *American Libraries* 3 (June 1972):585-586.

A letter about women in administrative and vital positions. Lists eight such positions at Case Western Reserve University Library held by women.

1972-29   Bayefsky, E. "Women and Work: a Selection of Books and Articles." *Ontario Library Review* 56 (June 1972):79-90.

Bibliography of general works on subject as well as short section on women in librarianship and new approaches to work patterns.

1972-30   Bow, R. "Interrupted Careers: the Married Woman as Librarian." *Ontario Library Review* 56 (June 1972):76-78.

Argues that women are discriminated against in librarianship but that the shortage of women in top administration is also due to the career constraints of married women. Part time and shared work and more nine-to-five jobs are needed for mothers so they can continue to climb career ladders and keep in touch with the field during childbearing years.

1972-31 Brown, W.L. "Association News: Discrimination in Australian Library Journal." *The Australian Library Journal* 21 (June 1972):214.

Notes that the standing committee considered Lundie's complaint [1972-20] on sex based salaries in advertising but "as it was a late item on the agenda, consideration of it was deferred to the next meeting."

1972-32 "The University of Washington Library and Femlib." *Wilson Library Bulletin* 46 (June 1972):948.

Report of women's group charges contained in [1972-15] that the library discriminates against women in personnel practices; and the director's response [1972-22] maintaining that there is no policy of conscious discrimination.

1972-33 Frarey, C.J. and Learmont, C.L. "Placements and Salaries, 1971: a Modest Employment Slowdown: Salaries and Employment Opportunities for Women." *Library Journal* 97 (June 15, 1972):2154-2159.

Annual survey of ALA accredited library school graduates' placements and salaries which indicates that in the future data will be broken down by sex and that in response to the question: "In your opinion are women discriminated against?" Nineteen stated no; four yes; and sixteen that they could not tell. One school did provide data which clearly showed discrimination against women.

1972-34 "SRRT Groups Take Action on Women's Rights Issue." *Library Journal* 97 (June 15, 1972):2136-2137.

Briefly explains SRRT Task Force on Women roster of women qualified to fill administrative and specialist positions in libraries. The activities of Task Force on Women's Issues in Librarianship formed in Massachusetts are also explained. Notes that not all librarians support such action: "*LJ* has received more than one letter from female librarians condemning preferential hiring practices as both unfair and unethical."

1972-35 "Affirmative Action Program Implemented at Berkeley." *Library Journal* 97 (July 1972):2326.

News item on changes and corrective policies [1971-36] begun at University of California.

1972-36 Annan, G.L. "Women's Lib - Librarians' Lib." *Bulletin of the Medical Library Association* 60 (July 1972):492.

Letter to the editor pointing out that in medical libraries "once a woman's world . . . top positions are solely for men." Urges the MLA to respond to this inequity.

1972-37 "At Its Last Meeting—." *The Australian Library Journal* 21 (August 1972):294.

Note from the editor indicating that at the July 1 meeting of the Standing Committee Lundie's letter [1972-20] was considered and the editor authorized to refuse advertisements in which salary was differentiated by sex.

1972-38 Berry, J. "The Changing of the Guard: SRRT Week." *Library Journal* 97 (August 1972):2528-2529.

Included in report of SRRT activities during the 1972 ALA conference is mention that "1,000 jammed the meeting of the SRRT Women's Task Force to hear practical advice on how women can gain equal rights where they work."

1972-39 Hazell, J. "Standards and Status." *The Australian Library Journal* 21 (August 1972):293-294.

Letter by convener of the Library Association of Australia's Committee on Standards and Status calling for information from those directly affected by unequal pay for equal work. While eliminating advertising which offers sex based pay from the Australian *Library Journal* may be useful, the "nature and extent of problems within the profession" must be identified so that concrete proposals may be made for the future.

1972-40   Wagner, S. "Miss Ringer Wins Examiner's Support for Copyrights Post at Library of Congress." *Publishers Weekly* 202 (August 21, 1972):58.

Background on Barbara A. Ringer's fight to gain the post of Register of Copyrights includes in-depth coverage on the Hearing Examiner's report which supported Ringer's case. Sex discrimination was one element in her complaint against the Library of Congress.

1972-41   Little, C. "Librarianship: a Female Profession?" *Michigan Librarian* 38: (Autumn 1972):10-11.

Indicates how Michigan library situation reflects national scene with statistics on top administrative positions demonstrating that most directors of academic libraries are male (40 of 62); half of the directors of the largest public libraries are male (seventeen of thirty-four). Two of the three library school deans are male; the state librarian and the president of the Michigan Library Association are male - even though four out of five librarians are female. Sees the problem as partly cultural because of women's reluctance to assert themselves; partly the fault of the profession for its failure to encourage women to strive for administrative positions; and partly the fault of the power structure which controls libraries (universities, trustees, city councils) which is mostly male and adheres to the accepted cultural pattern of placing men in administrative posts.

1972-42   ALA Social Responsibilities Round Table. Task Force on Women. *ALA-SRRT Task Force on Women Newsletter.* September 1972 Vol. 2 No. 1. - June 1974 Vol. 3 No. 6.

Continues [1970-24; 1970-30; 1972-16; 1972-11]. Continued by [1974-51]. Note: Vol. 2 No. 3 January 1973 is entitled *ALA-SRRT Task Force on Women Newsletter - Pre-Midwinter.*

1972-43   Brown, W.L. "Association News: Standing Committee: A Report: Discrimination in Advertising." *The Australian Library Bulletin* 21 (September 1972):346.

Report of action based on Lundie's letter [1972-20]. It "was resolved that the editor of *The Australian Library Journal* be authorized to refuse advertisements that specify different rates of pay for male and female librarians."

1972-44   Brown, W.L. "Association News: Standing Committee: A Report: Encel Report." *The Australian Library Journal* 21 (September 1972):345.

Report of the Library Association of Australia sub-committee criticizing the Encel report [1972-03] as not comprehensive enough and failing to define adequately the term, "librarian." The report's emphasis on the preponderance of women in librarianship as a major factor is also criticized.

1972-45   "Equal Pay Claim." *The Australian Library Journal* 21 (September 1972):343.

News item on the equal pay claims of female student librarians at the state library of Tasmania. Women students are paid $476 per year less than men even though equal pay is operative for qualified librarians.

1972-46   "F.L.C. Personnel Statistics." *FLC Newsletter, Federal Library Committee* Number 67. (September 1972):16.

Statistics broken down by race and sex on central federal libraries staff demonstrate that men are disproportionately represented at the highest levels.

1972-47 "Library of Congress Personnel Statistics." *FLC Newsletter, Federal Library Committee* Number 67 (September 1972):17.

LC personnel statistics broken down by sex exemplify the national pattern of a pyramidal labor force arrangement, where a large number of women are concentrated at the bottom and men are ensconced at the top.

1972-48 "LC Asks Examiner to Reconsider Findings in Barbara Ringer Case." *Library of Congress Information Bulletin* 31 (September 1, 1972):393-394.

Report of L. Quincy Mumford's request to reconsider the Hearing Examiner's report that Barbara A. Ringer be appointed Register of Copyrights.

1972-49 Wagner, S. "Mumford Asks Examiner to Review Ringer Case." *Publishers Weekly* 202 (September 4, 1972):24.

News item reporting Librarian of Congress L. Quincy Mumford's request for a reconsideration of a Hearing Examiner's finding that Barbara A. Ringer was wrongfully denied the post of Register of Copyrights because of patterns of discrimination in employment at the library. Background of the case is given.

1972-50 "Statistics Show More Women in Higher Grades at Library." *Library of Congress Information Bulletin* 31 (September 8, 1972):402-403.

Report comparing the percentage of women at the Library of Congress in Federal Civil Service Grades with the Federal Government as a whole. LC fares better at all levels above grade 6. However, the higher the grade, the fewer the women.

1972-51 "Hearing Officer Tells LC to Appoint Ringer to Copyright Post." *Library Journal* 97 (September 15, 1972):2791-2792.

Report of Ernest Waller's (Hearing Examiner) findings at the Library of Congress which indicate a consistent pattern of discrimination. Waller recommends that Ringer be hired with retroactive wages.

1972-52 Savage, N. "Barbara Ringer and LC." *Library Journal* 97 (September 15, 1972):2789.

Editorial on the duel between the Library of Congress and Barbara A. Ringer notes that bias against women also extends to candidates who are against racial discrimination. George D. Cary, who was awarded the post, was motivated to apply by his concern for the effects on morale of someone like Ringer, who had asserted she would promote Blacks to rectify discrimination patterns at LC. Evidence that discrimination at LC is rampant is mounting.

1972-53 "LC Weighs Court Battle vs. Ringer Appointment." *Wilson Library Bulletin* 47 (October 1972):124.

Tallies major points in the LC-Ringer battle: 1) Barbara A. Ringer's support by a Federal Hearing Examiner in her claim that she was denied the post of Register of Copyrights as a result of sex discrimination; 2) examiner declined the Library of Congress' request for reconsideration; 3) the question is now in the hands of the Librarian of Congress.

1972-54 "Opinion on Barbara Ringer." *American Libraries* 3 (October 1972):940.

Federal Examiner's Report found that Barbara A. Ringer was denied promotion because of sex bias. Also notes that there is a consistent pattern of discrimination against women at the Library of Congress. Recommends an Affirmative Action Program. Gives some detail on the case.

1972-55   "Report on Ringer Case Challenged by Mumford." *Library Journal* 97 (October 1, 1972):3103.

Report of L. Quincy Mumford's request that the Hearing Examiner in the appeal of Barbara A. Ringer reconsider his findings: that Ringer had been denied the Register of Copyrights post because of her sex and because she had advocated appointment of Blacks to high positions at the Library of Congress. Background on Ringer and case given.

1972-56   "Librarian Upholds Decision on Cary Appointment." *Library of Congress Information Bulletin* 31 (October 13, 1972):446.

Notice detailing L. Quincy Mumford's decision to stand by his appointment of George D. Cary to the position of Register of Copyrights even though Cary's appointment was based on error according to the Hearing Examiner's report.

1972-57   Cass, F.M. "Librarians: A Survey; A Reply to the L.A.A." *The Australian Library Journal* 21 (November 1972):425-433.

Response to criticisms reported in [1972-44]. Cass does not refer to general comments but makes a point-by-point, page-by-page response to a series of specific criticisms including those on Chapters 2 and 3 of the report [1972-03], which focus on women. Criticisms and the passage criticized are printed next to Cass's response. Further evidence is offered to support the contentions that women were employed in libraries because the pay was not high enough to attract men and that women are discriminated against in the profession.

1972-58   Encel, S. "Encel Replies." *The Australian Library Journal* 21 (November 1972):444-445.

Letter in reply to criticisms of his study [1972-03] as reported in [1972-44] and refuted by Cass [1972-57]. Encel responds to five points including suggestion that the researchers misinterpreted the attitude of the Library Association of Australia toward women librarians. Discrimination against women "is part of the Australian scene," including librarianship, and has been documented fully in the report.

1972-59   "People and Events: Item." *New Library World* 73 (November 1972):441.

Report of an 1889 clipping on the suggestion of Constance Black, librarian of the People's Palace library, that librarianship would be a suitable career for women.

1972-60   "R.I. Title II Consultant Quits: Protests; Too Few Women." *School Library Journal* 19 (November 1972):14.

News item reporting that Ruth Wade Cerjavec has resigned her position as Title II and Library Consultant for the Rhode Island Department of Education. Quotes from letter and interview indicate that her resignation was caused by failure of the Department to provide women with leadership roles.

1972-61   Wylie, E. ". . . As Others See Us." *The Australian Library Journal* 21 (November 1972):445.

Letter from American on advertisements for Australian librarian openings in the *New York Times* which imply that men are wanted. Careful wording is suggested "for a profession which does not have a good record of appointing women to senior positions."

1972-62   "Hearing Officer Rebuffs LC: Refuses Ringer Case Review." *Library Journal* 97 (November 1, 1972):3525.

Ernest Waller, appointed by the U.S. Civil Service Commission to serve as arbitrator in the Barbara A. Ringer case for the Library of Congress' Equal Opportunity Office, refuses to alter his report. L. Quincy Mumford, the Librarian of Congress, refuses to accept his recommendation. The case will go to court.

1972-63 "LC Claims Substantial Gains on Affirmative Action Front." *Library Journal* 97 (November 1, 1972):3525-3526.

News item reporting the Library of Congress claims "that it has put all other federal agencies in the shade by employing more women in GS grades six through 18." Notes that this claim is contradicted by opinions handed down by Hearing Officer in discrimination cases brought against LC.

1972-64 Carpenter, R.L. and Shearer, K.D. "Sex and Salary Survey; Selected Statistics of Large Public Libraries in U.S. and Canada." *Library Journal* 97 (November 15, 1972):3682-3685.

Analysis of 1971 data show median salary for male directors 30% higher than women; library expenditures 30% higher under male directors; beginning professional salaries under male directors 6.5% higher.

1972-65 Berry, J. "Death of a Movement." *Library Journal* 97 (November 15, 1972):3663.

Editorial discussing the effects of sexism on municipal budgets. Quotes from Carpenter and Shearer's study [1972-64]. Feels "if being a woman adversely effects the ability of a library director to get support for her library, it is not because of *her* sex. The problem is with the other gender." Suggests a consciousness raising campaign to show the effects of sexism. Such a campaign should be directed at trustees and city halls. Closes with a suggestion that the Melvil Dui Marching and Chowder Society once again attempt to open its doors to women because "the bright young man movement is dead."

Letter: See [1972-66 Letters: Lowenthal].

1972-66 "I Was the Mainstay of the Public Library until I Discovered Smirnoff." *Library Journal* 97 (November 15, 1972):3671.

Reproduction of an advertisement for Smirnoff's Vodka showing a sensual young woman who has given up the library for vodka.

Letters: Lowenthal, H. "Sexist Stereotype." *Library Journal* 98 (March 1, 1973):667.

Letter in response to editorial [1972-65] and the Smirnoff Vodka ad in the same issue. The editorial tells us nothing new. The fact that the stereotyped Smirnoff ad is printed only a few pages after the editorial shows how much the editor has to learn.

Willar, A. "Sexist Stereotype." *Library Journal* 98 (March 1, 1973):667.

Letter criticizing *LJ* for apparent favorable reaction to Smirnoff Vodka ad.

Finn, F.R. "Of Hoydens and Dullards." *Library Journal* 98 (May 1, 1973):9.

Unlike Lowenthal and Willar, writer finds nothing offensive in the Smirnoff ad. "The only sexist thing that the poster even hints at is the misconception that libraries are chiefly used by women, and this I would call sexual discrimination against the male population."

1972-67 Garrison, G. "Research Record." *Journal of Education for Librarianship* 12 (Winter 1972):211-213.

Report on dissertations in progress breaks down data by sex. Women account for eighty-three, men for 129.

1972-68   "Boston Women Librarians Tackle Sexist Attitudes and Employment Practices." *Bay State Librarian* 61 (December 1972):7.

Describes concerns, activities and future plans of the Boston Area Task Force on Women's Issues in Librarianship, a chapter of ALA's Social Responsibilities Roundtable. The objectives of the group are to make librarians aware of women's issues in librarianship, particularly the exposition of discriminatory practices in employment, and to make librarians aware of the ways in which media present an unfair portrayal of women in society.

1972-69   Brown, W.L. "Editorial." *The Australian Library Journal* 21 (December 1972):459.

Comments on issue include note that the data on salary and sex reported by Garlick [1972-70] "seem to indicate that women, no matter what their experience and qualifications, do not generally reach the top."

1972-70   Garlick, M. "LAA Salary Survey, 1971-72: Interim Report." *Australian Library Journal* 21 (December 1972):498-502.

Results of salary survey sent to 5,919 private members of the Library Association of Australia to which response was approximately 50%. Results are displayed in tables and no analysis is provided. Tables include "Salary by Qualifications by Sex," "Salary by Experience by Sex," and "Salary by Sex." More women than men are in the lower salary ranks and while the number diminishes with qualifications and experience, the ratio of females to males is still higher in the lower ranks.

1972-71   Metcalfe, J.W. "Librarianship: A Survey Report and Two Theses." *The Australian Library Journal* 21 (December 1972):486-493.

Critique of *Librarians; a Survey* [1972-03], Cass's thesis [1970-04], also published as an occasional paper by the Libraries Board of South Australia [1972-02] and Bullard's thesis [1970-01]. *Librarians; a Survey* contained excerpts from both Cass's and Bullard's earlier work. Metcalf questions the "credibility generally and in detail" of the report. Does not agree that the feminization of the profession had any relationship to the rate of pay as postulated by Cass.

1972-72   "Personnel Statistics Listed for Federal Libraries." *Library Journal* 97 (December 1, 1972):3837.

Summarizes comparative employment figures for men and women from the Federal Library Committee newsletter [1972-47]: of 3,763 employees, 52.3% are women. Women are in the majority in GS-2 to GS-11 positions, dropping as the positions go higher, except for GS-18 where they comprise 25% of those employed.

†1972-73   Garrison, D. "The Tender Technicians: The Feminization of Public Librarianship, 1876-1905." *Journal of Social History* 6 (Winter 1972-73):131-159.

Argues that librarianship was one of the few fields open to women in the late nineteenth century especially since it appeared similar to the home in its provision of a comfortable atmosphere. The feminization of librarianship is seen as having long-range results on the status of the public library causing it to evolve into a marginal kind of public amusement service.

1973-01   Carpenter, R.L. and Shearer, K.D. "Sex and Salary Survey." In *Bowker Annual* 18th ed. New York: R.R. Bowker, 1973:406-414.

Reprint of [1972-64].

1973-02   Catalyst. *Library Service: Career Opportunities Series: C17.* New York: Catalyst, 1973.

A recruitment pamphlet developed by the American Library Association and Catalyst, the national non-profit organization dedicated to expanding employment opportunities for college-educated women who wish to combine career and family responsibilities. Includes a section on the status of women in librarianship and several reports of the careers of successful women librarians as well as general descriptions of the field.

1973-03   Cheda, S. "That Special Little Mechanism." In *Canadian Library Association Twenty-eighth Annual Conference Proceedings.* Sackville, New Brunswick. June 16-22, 1973. Ottawa, Ontario: Canadian Library Association, 1973:106-115.

Outlines myths and barriers women face in the profession as well as suggestions for actions to overcome masculine mystique, which is a device that prevents women from full participation in the library world.

1973-04   Corwin, M.A. "An Investigation of Female Leadership in State Library Organizations and Local Library Associations, 1876-1923." Master's thesis, University of Chicago Graduate Library School, 1973.

See [1974-30] for summary annotation.

1973-05   "Editorial." *Emergency Librarian* 1; Number 1 (n.d.):1.

Reports "explosion" set off by Sherrill Cheda's speech at Canadian Library Association June 20, 1973 [1973-03]. It resulted in the resolution to commission and fund studies on the status of women in the profession and the first Canadian Librarians' underground newsletter (*Emergency Librarian*).

1973-06   Frarey, C.J. and Learmont, C.L. "Placements and Salaries, 1971: a Modest Employment Slowdown." In Bowker Annual. 18th Edition. New York: R.R. Bowker, 1973:393-405.

Reprint of [1972-33].

1973-07   Jensen, R. "Family, Career, and Reform: Women Leaders of the Progressive Era." In *American Family in Social-Historical Perspective.* Edited by M. Gordon. New York: St. Martin's Press, 1973:267-279.

Report of study of sample of 879 autobiographical questionnaires filled out by 9,000 prominent women in the early part of the twentieth century. Responses were coded into forty variables and analyzed. "With the striking exception of the apathetic librarians, it appears that women who held responsible positions in competition with men were more pro-suffrage, while those with basically private lives were less supportive." Only 6% of the librarians supported the suffrage amendment as opposed to 43% of the physicians and 40% of the social workers, for example (p. 273). Most working women had designated female roles - sopranos, deans of women, specialized health services to women, etc. "Perhaps only those thoroughly cowed librarians had to out-qualify men for their jobs" (p. 274).

1973-08   Kelly, T. *A History of Public Libraries in Great Britain: 1845-1965.* London: The Library Association, 1973.

In this lengthy history, women are mentioned several times *in passim:* the first women were employed in 1871 at Manchester though resistance continued in other places (p. 103); Liverpool began to employ women in 1898 due to a shortage of funds - a move so successful that by 1904 they occupied all but senior level posts (p. 141-142); prejudice against women died hard, and up to 1897 only Manchester, Bradford, Bristol and Aberdeen, of the large towns, employed them, although small towns with short funds more often included women. World War I is given as the chief factor for the eventual predominance of women (p. 204); this growth of the predominance of women was one of the biggest changes between 1911-1931. Of the professional staff employed in municipal libraries, 58.3% were women by 1932 although women never rose above branch level.

1973-09   "News Flash!" *Emergency Librarian* 1; Number 2 (n.d.):2-3.

Report on the development of the Canadian Library Association Task Force on the Status of Women in Canadian Libraries. Committee Chairperson, Dr. Sheila Bertram, chose Shirley Wright, Annemarie Mayer, Sherrill Cheda and Phyllis Yaffe to serve on the Committee. The first meeting resulted in the decision to cover five areas: 1) a directory of Canadian libraries from which to conduct 2) a national inquiry on salary; 3) a day of women's programming at CLA; 4) smaller studies; 5) oral histories and bibliographies.

1973-10   "Precis of Discussion Groups Following 'Theme Day' Speech, CLA June 20, 1973. Sackville, New Brunswick." *Emergency Librarian* 1; Number 1 (n.d.):2-3.

Reports the overwhelming response to a discussion group on "women in the library profession" and issues raised: 1) need for day care; 2) need for men and women to have a choice to fulfill themselves within the profession; 3) need for females to seek administrative positions. A Fair Policy Committee was proposed on pregnancy leave as an unalienable right. Other suggestions for action included a permanent column in the *Canadian Library Journal* referring to the status of women in the profession; a task force investigating the status of women in libraries; documentation of cases of discrimination in libraries.

1973-11   Ramsden, M.J. *The Association of Assistant Librarians: 1895-1945.* Edinburgh: Association of Assistant Librarians, 1973.

History of the Association of Assistant Librarians makes several mentions of women in the organization. An attempt to bar their membership by the steering committee was not carried through at the founding of the Association and by 1899 there were seven women included in the 129 member Association. These included M.S.R. James, Alice E. Smith, and Miss Petherbridge — the latter, whose remarks at the International Congress of Women in 1899 on the subject of women in librarianship obliged her to resign (p. 4). Early issues of the Association's journal, the *Library Assistant,* focused on controversial topics of the time such as women in the profession (p. 36). The first woman to be elected President of the Association was Ethel Gerard in 1918. World War I saw increasing numbers of the "fair sex" join the Association (p. 86).

1973-12   Taylor, M.R. "External Mobility and Professional Involvement in Librarianship: A Study of the Careers of Librarians Graduating from Accredited Library Schools in 1955." Ph.D. thesis, Rutgers University, 1973. (DAI Order no.: 73-27, 986).

Shows that the librarian who seeks advancement becomes involved in professional activities to further career; that immobile women are apt to earn less and are older; males earn higher salaries, have more formal education and move more readily from one state to another.

1973-13   Tucker, S.A. *Salary Survey of Colorado Librarians.* Denver: Colorado Library Association, 1973.

Shows men have more experience, education, and mobility than women; however, women who are equal in these aspects do not earn salaries equal to those of men.

1973-14   U.S. Department of Health, Education and Welfare. *Library Statistics of Colleges and Universities Fall 1971: Analytic Report (Part C).* Washington, DC: U.S. Government Printing Office, 1973.

Report analyzing data collected in the fall of 1971, including [1972-07]. Women constituted 77% of academic librarians. When data are sub-divided by level of staff, 86%

of clerical staff, 65% of the professional librarians, and 75% of the other professionals are women. The highest single group of women in academic libraries are in privately controlled four-year institutions where 94% of the clerical workers are women (p. 11). Table D is titled "Number and Percent, by Sex, of Full-time-equivalent (FTE) Staff in College and University Libraries by Level of Staff and Control and Type of Institution: Aggregate United States, Fall 1971 (p. 12)." Data are broken down by public; private; public and private total; four-year institutions with and without graduate students; and two-year institutions; and by sex of total staff, librarians, other professional and clerical, and other staff.

1973-15   Wheeler, H.R. *Placement Services in Accredited Library Schools.* Bethesda, MD: ERIC Document Reproduction Service, ED 078 847, 1973.

Surveys practices in posting job notices, handling dossiers, word-of-mouth advertising, and discriminatory actions. Emphasis on women.

1973-16   Yaffe, P. "IPLO Workshop on Women." *Emergency Librarian* 1; Number 2 (n.d.):8-9.

Report of IPLO (Institute of Professional Librarians of Ontario) workshop held October 26, 1973, on "The Female Librarian: How Far Does She Have To Go and How Will She Get There?" After Maryon Kantaroff spoke on the dehumanizing restraints of sex roles, small groups discussed women in administration, children's literature, political action, and strategy for change.

1973-17   "Issue on Women." *School Library Journal* 19 (January 1973).

Entire issue devoted to women and sexism. Includes articles on the treatment of women in children's encyclopedias, high school women, the Women's History Research Center, feminist resources for schools, and a study of sexism in children's literature.

> **Letter:**   Hiebing, D. "More . . ." *School Library Journal* 19 (May 1973):5.
>
> Brief letter calling for more issues or articles devoted to subjects covered in the feminist issue.

1973-17A   Schuman, P. "Editorial." *School Library Journal* 19 (January 1973):199.

Editorial introducing issue on women. Includes Isaac Asimov's comment to the New York Library Association, "L-I-B — Let's Ignite Bras," and the audience reaction.

> **Letter:**   Asimov, I. "Chopped Libber." *School Library Journal* 19 (March 1973):57.
>
> Asimov responds to Schuman's editorial questioning whether her comments constitute a racial slur. He states he is not a male chauvinist but "in point of fact, a woman's libber."

1973-17B   Sasse, M. "Invisible Women: the Children's Librarian in America." *School Library Journal* 19 (January 1973):213-17.

Lauds notable women leaders and founders of children's services; notes that *The Dictionary of American Biography* excludes women who are children's librarians so that their accomplishments are undervalued and unrecognized.

1973-18   Day, A.E. "Those Library Ladies." *New Library World* 74 (January 1973):5-6.

Discussion of letter written in the 1880s by Dr. Ernest A. Baker on the woman librarian. Baker's analysis of women's role in British and U.S. librarianship is reviewed, and a plea made for an end to factors limited by sex shaping and influencing recruitment to the profession.

1973-19   "LAA Salary Survey, 1971-72: School Librarians." *The Australian Library Journal* 22 (February 1973):27-28.

Results for school librarians of salary survey conducted among members of the Library Association [1972-70]. Results are given in tables, including "Salary by Sex" (p. 27), but not analyzed. Male librarians tend to cluster in the higher salary ranges.

1973-20   Krevitt, B.I. "SRRT Status on Women Task Force." *LC Information Bulletin* 32 (February 16, 1973):A-34-A-35.

Report of January 30, 1973 meeting of SRRT Task Force on Women. Child care for the 1973 ALA annual conference, a survey of library school placement, plans for a preconference in 1974, and discussion groups were considered.

1973-21   Alvarez, R.S. "Profile of Public Library Chiefs; a Serious Survey with Some Comic Relief." *Wilson Library Bulletin* 47 (March 1973):578-583.

Reports results from a survey of directors of largest U.S. public libraries (largest not defined) which indicate a movement toward the appointment of men as public library directors. Most of the results are not broken down by sex with the exception of attitudes towards unionization. Library directors were asked, "Are your clericals as sharp and attractive as those in business offices?" Yes, replied most; one commented, "We've got some lookers."

1973-22   Cass, F.M.B. "W(h)ither a Female Profession?" *Australian Library Journal* 22 (March 1973):49-55.

Urges changes in education to help women get training in mathematics for increased use of data processing in libraries. Tables depicting salary of men and women are presented. Recruitment of women with math and computer backgrounds is seen as critical to the survival of the profession.

> **Letters:**   Jacob, M.E. "Librarians and Numeration." *Australian Library Journal* 22 (May 1973):164.
>
> Reports results of a test given to librarians at the University of Sidney Library which shows little difference between men and women on an IBM math test.

> **Letter:**   Howard, P. "Cass and Women." *Australian Library Journal* 22 (July 1973):237-238.
>
> Response questioning Jacob and pointing out that the socialization of women was the main point of Cass's article.

> Campbell, D.V.A. "Librarians and Computers." *Australian Library Journal* 22 (June 1973):145-196.
>
> Response from a data processing instructor who criticizes Cass's ignorance of what librarians need to know about computers — how to use services, an appreciation of what computers can produce and how enquiry terminals are operated — no mathematical competence at all.

1973-23   Marks, R.J. "Why Not Men in Children's Librarianship?" *Pennsylvania Library Association* Bulletin 28 (March 1973):67-70.

Parallels predominance of women in children's librarianship but not library administration to the predominance of women in elementary school teaching. Argues that "more males should be recruited to children's librarianship at the same time that more women are recruited as directors of those very same libraries."

1973-24   Ramsay, M. "W(h)ither (C)ass." *Australian Library Journal* 22 (March 1973):55-59.

Reply to [1973-22] in the form of a "daydream." Sarcastic references to homosexuals as Ramsay asks whether Cass ascertained if homosexuals display the mathematical characteristics of their own or the opposite sex (right down his alley "as a member of Camp. Inc.")

Letter: Bielski, J. "Librarians and Computers." *Australian Library Journal* 22 (June 1973):196.

Writer takes issue with Ramsay's references to Cass's homosexuality and the former's frivolous tone on an important topic. As a teacher of girls, Bielski notes she would like to be able to steer them out of the profession if it is becoming obsolete in its present form.

*1973-25 "Special Series - Female Librarians." *Toshokan Zasshi* 67 (March 1973):76-90.

Special issue on women in Japanese libraries.

*1973-25A Ikenaga, S. "Female Librarians in the U.S. and Canada." (Title translated by Japanese Translation Centre.) *Toshokan Zasshi* 67 (March 1973).

*1973-25B Kimura, T.; Ueno, C.; Sasaki, S.; Okazaki, S. and Ito, A. "A Week of Female Librarians' Work." (Title translated by Japanese Translation Centre.) *Toshokan Zasshi* 67 (March 1973).

*1973-25C Tanaka, T. "Work and Life of Female Librarians - a Report on the Results of a Questionnaire." (Title translated by Japanese Translation Centre.) *Toshokan Zasshi* 67 (March 1973).

*1973-25D Tazawa, K. "Female Librarians from the Standpoint of Male Librarians." (Title translated by Japanese Translation Centre.) *Toshokan Zasshi* 67 (March 1973).

*1973-26 Llewellin, D. "Discrimination in the Library System Said Rooted in Library Schools." *The St. Catherines Standard* Ontario, Canada (Thursday, March 1, 1973).

1973-27 "Judge Rules in Ringer Case." *Library of Congress Information Bulletin* 32 (March 9, 1973):78.

Brief note of U.S. District Court Judge's decision in favor of Barbara A. Ringer against the Librarian of Congress ordering that the plaintiff's motion for summary judgment be granted in her sex discrimination case.

1973-28 Berry, J. "A New Management Mood: SRRT Midwinter." *Library Journal* 98 (March 15, 1973):832.

Brief mention of planned 1974 SRRT Preconference on Women and Librarianship included in report of SRRT actions at ALA 1973 Midwinter meeting.

1973-29 Rosenberg, K.C. and Savak, P. "ALA Committee Membership: a Statistical Survey." *Library Journal* 98 (March 15, 1973):842-845.

Survey of constituency of ALA Committees 1968-1971 using data drawn from a variety of sources. Sex is one variable analyzed. The ratio of male committee members to female appears to be increasing.

1973-30 Clubb, B., and Yaffe, P. "Try It, You'll Like It." *Canadian Library Journal* 30 (March - April 1973):96-100.

Urges women to realize family and career can coexist.

1973-31   Beckman, M. "Woman: Her Place in the Profession." *IPLO Quarterly* 14 (April 1973):129-134.

Women don't rise to the top of librarianship in comparison to their number in the profession because of society itself, the history of the profession, and social conditioning which makes men more career oriented. Many of these problems originate in the library schools. Women must make it to the top as individuals, not through a women's liberation movement in librarianship. "Women have to be prepared to work twice as hard as any man doing the same job."

1973-32   "Judge Rules Against LC on Copyright Register Appointment; Register George D. Cary Resigns." *Wilson Library Bulletin* 47 (April 1973):635.

Report of the U.S. District Court order to vacate the appointment of George D. Cary as Register of Copyrights. Seen as insuring the appointment of Barbara A. Ringer.

1973-33   "Women in Archives." *The American Archivist* 36 (April 1973).

Special issue devoted to women in archives, women in the academic professions, the failure of historians to include women's history, difficulties in documenting women's history, and a program of action for women in archives.

1973-33A   Deutrich, M.E. "Women in Archives: Ms. versus Mr. Archivist." *The American Archivist* 36 (April 1973):171-181.

Notes the lack of attention paid to women archivists in the profession. (Only twenty-three women have held officer posts in the professional association as opposed to 121 men; only thirty-seven women have been elected to Council as opposed to 173 men.) Women have also not held top positions in government or state archives, have failed to publish, and have failed to receive any of the awards of the Society of American Archivists.

1973-33B   Freivogel, E.F. "Women in Archives: The Status of Women in the Academic Professions." *The American Archivist* 36 (April 1973):183-201.

Looks at the general pattern of discrimination against women in the academic professions. Mentions women's caucuses in the Society of American Archivists, American Historical Association, and ALA. Executive order 11246 prohibiting sex discrimination in universities is examined. Asks why, if one-third of the SAA are women, do they make up such a low percentage of administrative and officer posts?

1973-33C   Crawford, M.I. "Women in Archives: A Program for Action." *The American Archivist* 36 (April 1973):223-232.

Notes that women need to publish more and obtain advanced degrees in order to achieve parity with men in the professions. Suggests long range goals for women in the SAA, which include creation of a job roster, child care at conferences, and development of equal opportunity guidelines.

1973-34   "SRRT Task Force on Women Serves as Job Clearinghouse." *Library Journal* 98 (April 1, 1973):1673.

Announces roster for women interested in administrative and specialist positions in libraries.

1973-35   "Three Union Suits Filed Against UC Regents." *Library Journal* 98 (April 1, 1973):1078.

News item describing three suits filed against the Board of Regents of the University of California. All three involve librarians and their position as members of a "women's profession."

1973-36   "Court Rules Against LC in Ringer Case." *Library Journal* 98 (April 15, 1973):1228; 1230.

Report of District Court Ruling that the Library of Congress did not comply with its own procedural regulations regarding discrimination when it appointed George D. Cary to the post of Register of Copyrights and thus had "prejudiced the rights of the plaintiff, Barbara Ringer, in seeking the appointment." Details of the case, which involves sex discrimination, are given.

1973-37   "Union Librarians at UC Win Court Round in Calif." *Library Journal* 98 (April 15, 1973):1237.

News item reporting that the University of California has been ordered to submit a dispute over librarians 1972-1973 salaries to arbitration. "The AFT has made sex discrimination its main issue, arguing that librarianship, because it is classed as a 'woman's occupation', is the lowest paid of all UC academic occupations." A complaint on similar grounds filed with the Equal Opportunity Commission in San Francisco is also described.

1973-38   DeFichy, W. "Affirmative Action: Equal Opportunity for Women in Library Management." *College and Research Libraries* 34 (May 1973):195-201.

Outlines steps for determining status, assessing policies affecting hiring, parental leave and promotion, and strategies to attain managerial positions.

1973-39   Turner, D. "Overproduction of Librarians?" *Library Association Record* 75 (June 1973):119.

Letter written in response to D.G. News's "Overproduction of Librarians?" *Library Association Record* 75 (April 1973) which discussed the employment picture for new librarians. Turner asks: what about the "great army of unemployed female librarians who cannot return to a professional post?"

Letters: Ward, P.L. "Overproduction of Librarians?" *Library Association Record* 75 (June 1973):119.

Supports Turner's question. Asks whether stabilized percentage of women librarians reported in Library Association home membership (12% to 13% from 1966 to 1973) is the result of ease in returning to librarianship or the fact that women are staying in their posts and meeting family obligations. Asks women to write to her about their career patterns.

Love, G.M. "Overproduction of Librarians." *Library Association Record* 75 (August 1973):164.

Remains a member of the Library Association even though she is in the home because she plans to return to librarianship. Other professions welcome returning women - why not librarianship?

Ray, S.G. "Overproduction of Librarians." *Library Association Record* 75 (August 1973):163-164.

Thinks women are both finding it easier to return to the profession (although not always as professionals) and to meet family obligations while working, although this is not an easy task. Expresses concern for women who take on family obligations, never find a suitable post, and are lost to librarianship.

Ward, P.L. "Overproduction of Librarians." *Library Association Record* 75 (September 1973):184.

Reports on response to her letter requesting information on career patterns. It appears that 1) women are now making more conscious decisions about having children, and 2) part-time posts, outside the populous areas, which use the special skills trained for are difficult to obtain.

1973-40   U.S. Bureau of the Census. *Census of the Population: 1970.* (Subject Reports - Final Report PC (2) - 7A Occupational Characteristics). U.S. Government Printing Office, June 1973.

Gives median earnings, weeks worked, school years completed, age for men and women librarians from 1970 census (Table 1).

1973-41   Wagner, S. "Barbara Ringer Continues to Fight for LC Position." *Publishers Weekly* 203 (June 11, 1973):132-133.

News item on Barbara A. Ringer's continuing battle to win appointment as Register of Copyrights. Details her taking a sex discrimination case to the U.S. Court of Appeals.

1973-42   Frarey, C. and Learmont, C.L. "Placements and Salaries, 1972: We Held Our Own." *Library Journal* 98 (June 15, 1973):1880-1886.

First time that annual review includes data on salary differentials between men and women graduates for all categories. The median starting salary for women graduates of ALA accredited library education programs is less than that for men.

1973-43   "Action on Women's Lib Front: Two Suits in Motion." *Library Journal* 78 (July 1973):2037.

Outlines charges of discrimination on basis of sex filed by Helen Wheeler; mentions NOW efforts to suspend tax-free status of universities and foundations until discrimination is ended.

1973-44   Jouly, H. "Die dressierte Bibliothekarin; Gedanken über die Frauen in einem nahezu weiblichen Beruf." (trans.: The Well-trained Librarian; Thoughts on Women in an Almost Exclusively Female Occupation.) *Buch und Bibliothek* 25 (July 1973):622-623.

Discusses the unfortunate situation that, although women comprise 80% of West German librarians, only around 20% are in well-paid administrative positions, since the few men in the field are given preference. Various reasons for this are cited and possible remedies offered.

> **Letters:**   See [1973-45 Letters: Weber, Buchholz, Hut, Endell, Rosher].

1973-45   Krauss, G. "Überlegungen zur beruflichen Emanzipation der Bibliothekarinnen (trans.: Reflections on the Professional Emancipation of Women Librarians)" *Buch und Bibliothek* 25 (July 1973):623-624.

Enumerates the ways in which women themselves help perpetuate the myth that they are unfit for leading positions in the library; recommends they demonstrate self-confidence in seeking greater responsibility.

> **Letters:**   Weber, B. "Nicht unterprivilegiert, sondern temperamentlos?/Noch einmal: die Bibliothekarin im Beruf. (trans.: Not Underprivileged, but Without Spirit?/Once again: the Female Librarian at Work.) *Buch und Bibliothek* 25 (August 1973):734.
>
> Responds to previous discussions by Jouly [1973-44] and Krauss [1973-45] concerning professional emancipation of female librarians by calling for a sociological investigation of the problem. Provides a list of questions which should be posed such as: Why do people seek leadership positions?
>
> Buchholz, R. "Die Bibliothekarin im Beruf - das Gesprach geht weiter." (trans.: The Female Librarian at Work - the Discussion Continues.) *Buch und Bibliothek* 25 (October 1973):830.

Sees professional isolation as the greatest obstacle to emancipation of the female librarian. Suggested remedies are cultivation of library work which extends beyond the local level and workshops dealing with the problems of women administrators. Also responds to Jouly [1973-44].

Hut, U.; Niebuhr, B.; Prober, M.; and Wiese, E. "Gleichberechtig-ung — endlich offentlich diskutiert." (trans.: Equal Rights — Openly Discussed at Last.) *Buch und Bibliothek* 25 (October 1973):830-831.

Sees it as a positive sign that the question of equal rights for female librarians is being brought out in the open and finds that solidarity is necessary. However, real "emancipation" must include both men and women and should ideally involve less enslavement to a job for both sexes. Also responds to Jouly [1973-44].

Endell, F. "Wenn man Mich fragt/Zum Problem der Bibliothekarin im Beruf." (trans.: If You Ask Me: the Problem of the Female Librarian in the Profession.) *Buch und Bibliothek* 25 (October 1973):831-832.

A veteran librarian supports the traditional role of women in the profession as mediators "between books, readers, co-workers and - the boss" (p. 831). She feels they are especially suited for small libraries, or for hospital or children's collections. Also responds to Jouly [1973-44].

Letters in response to above letters:

Bastian, L. "Chefin werden oder Mensch bleiben/Thema: Emanzipation." (trans.: Boss or Human Being - Theme: Emancipation.) *Buch und Bibliothek* 25 (October 1973):1019-1020.

Challenges Endell's contention that women librarians should be "mediators" rather than "bosses." Stresses that women should have the same chances for advancement as men; also that administrators of both sexes would do well to exhibit the humane qualities traditionally reserved for women. Courses on management psychology are needed, and qualified women must be encouraged to participate.

Rosher, "Die Bibliothekarin - gesehen von einem Altbibliothekar." (trans.: The Female Librarian, from the Viewpoint of a Veteran Male Colleague.) *Buch und Bibliothek* 25 (October 1973):1020-1022.

A retired librarian first gives token support to equal opportunities for women, then finds them decidedly inferior in too many instances. Feels they are not scholarly or versatile enough in their interests, that they should try to emancipate themselves through "stronger involvement" in public — especially political — matters. Also responds to Jouly [1973-44].

1973-46 Ridgeway, T. "The Latest Image?" *Library Journal* 98 (July 1973):2026.

Letter commenting on unflattering female librarian image in *Occupational Outlook Handbook*. [1972-08, p. 249].

1973-47 Berry, J. "Localism in Las Vegas." *Library Journal* 98 (August 1973):2231-2242.

Report of the 1973 ALA conference includes two sections on women: "SRRT Women," a brief report of SRRT Task Force on Women activities at the conference (p. 2238) and "Women," a report of the SRRT Task Force on Women LAD/PAS Economic Status, Welfare and Fringe Benefits Committee program which featured Wilma Scott Heide, President of the National Organization of Women (p. 2241).

1973-48 Horrocks, N. "Serenity at Sackville: A Report on the Canadian Library Association Conference." *Library Journal* 98 (August 1973):2245-2247.

Included in overview of CLA conference is report of Sherril Cheda's speech, "That Special Little Mechanism," [1973-03] and a successful resolution at the Annual General Meeting calling on Council to consider funding a study of the status of women in the profession (p. 2245-2246).

1973-49   "Salary Statistics: University and Library Reports." *Library Journal* 78 (August 1973):2226.

Shows women concentrated in lower salary ranks; widest gap between men and women at university level; narrowest gap in two-year colleges.

1973-50   Tarr, S.A. "The Status of Women in Academic Libraries." *North Carolina Libraries* 31 (Fall 1973):22-32.

Surveys factual and statistical information in library literature as well as general studies of academic community on women and myths regarding women workers.

1973-51   "ALA News: Documentation: Membership." *American Libraries* 4 (September 1973):506.

Included in 1973 annual conference report is text of resolution passed by membership urging California legislators to appropriate funds to equalize academic librarians' salaries with those of other non-teaching academic staff not in a "women's" profession.

1973-52   Eshelman, W.R. "The Wiltings, Winnings, Losings, Loathings, Fears and Fortunes of 8,500 American Library Association Conferees Who Went to Las Vegas." *Wilson Library Bulletin* 48 (September 1973):58-69.

Two reports of women's activities are included in overview of 1973 ALA Conference. "Further Winners" reports on Wilma Scott Heide's speech and panel reaction by Clara Jones, Virginia Whitney and "Lillian G-r-r-rhardt" (p. 62). "Women and Unions" includes mention of resolution passed supporting increase in pay for librarians as a women's profession and male reaction to it (p. 67).

1973-53   Gerhardt, L.N. and Cheatham, B.M. "Breaking Even in Las Vegas: a Report of the 92nd Annual American Library Association Conference: The Youth Divisions." *School Library Journal* 20 (September 1973):28-33.

Included in 1973 ALA Conference overview is brief report of Wilma Scott Heide's speech and comment on the few "librarians present who hold positions in public or school library service for children and young adults (p. 31)."

1973-54   Lee, D.L. and Hall, J.E. "Female Library Science Students and the Occupational Stereotype: Fact or Fiction?" *College and Research Libraries* 34 (September 1973):265-267.

Compares group of library school women with general college student norms; they are similar in personality.

1973-55   "Barbara Ringer Appointed Register of Copyrights." *Library of Congress Information Bulletin* 32 (September 14, 1973):319; 325.

Official Library of Congress notice of Barbara A. Ringer's appointment. Her outstanding career as an internationally famous expert on copyright and law is outlined. No mention is made of her legal battle with LC to win the position.

1973-56   "SRRT Task Force Reports on Women's Job Roster." *Library Journal* 98 (September 15, 1973):2502.

Summary of an evaluation of the job roster, which contains names of women librarians seeking new positions and pertinent data on them. Although there were 102 requests for the roster from employers, only one hiring has been reported.

1973-57 Wagner, S. "Ringer Appointed Register; Long Legal Fight Ends." *Publishers Weekly* 204 (September 17, 1973):31.

Notice that Barbara A. Ringer has won the position of Register of Copyrights after a two-year battle which included charges of sex discrimination against the Library of Congress.

1973-58 "Barbara Ringer Named Register of Copyrights." *Wilson Library Bulletin* 48 (October 1973):120.

Notice that Barbara A. Ringer has finally won her legal battle to be appointed Register of Copyrights.

1973-59 "Draft - ALA Equal Opportunity Policy." *American Libraries* 4 (October 1973):560-561.

Statement which ALA Council later approved in January 1974 (with minor changes) involving Association in promoting employment equity.

1973-60 "Women's Issue." *New Library World* 74 (October 1973).

Includes articles from women making a contribution to the profession on how to do research, junior librarians, and international librarianship. Several articles also deal with women's issues.

> **Letters:** Jones, N. "Your Slip Is Showing." *New Library World* 74 (December 1973):269-270.
>
> Lengthy letter criticizing women's issue for the cover, style, and missing of the central issues: motivation; commitment; the question of inherent difference between men and women; the hierarchical structures of libraries; staff development; and the need for role models for women.
>
> Scrivens, G. "Your Slip Is Showing." *New Library World* 74 (December 1973):270.
>
> Letter protesting the sex exploitation of the women's issue cover.

1973-60A Plaister, J.M. "Why a Women's Issue?" *New Library World* 74 (October 1973):251-261.

The editor of the issue on women isn't sure why women are to be the subject of an issue, but concludes, why not? She herself feels women are not discriminated against; rather they do not apply for the top jobs. The intent of the issue was not "women's lib", although it has crept in.

1973-60B McNeill, E. "Women and Their Associations." *New Library World* 74 (October 1973):220-221.

Fewer women than men are active in professional associations because of individual women's choice and the societal conditioning of all women. Solutions are proposed.

1973-60C Ward, P. "Women and Librarianship - Ten Years On." *New Library World* 74 (October 1973):221-223.

A review of the events in the ten years since Ward's study of women in librarianship [1966-02]. Refresher courses for women have not been successful. Part-time positions seen to be increasing. Women are now entering the profession fully trained because of the elimination of part-time studies. Data suggest women may be moving in and out of the labor market more easily.

1973-60D Fransella, M. "Marriage and the Profession." *New Library World* 74 (October 1973):223-224.

Report of the author's "completely undistinguished and unambitious approach (to the profession) for the married women in librarianship."

1973-60E   Burt, D. "Twenty-five Years On." *New Library World* 74 (October 1973):224-225.

Autobiographical account of a librarian who left work, raised a family and returned to school.

1973-60F   Beals, S. "From the Cradle." *New Library World* 74 (October 1973):225-226.

View of the library profession by a "comparative newcomer." Questions the scarcity of women at the top of the profession. Recounts the anti-women comments of one of her tutors in library school.

1973-61   "Barbara Ringer Wins LC Register of Copyrights Post." *Library Journal* 98 (October 15, 1973):2951.

News item noting that Barbara A. Ringer has won the position of Register of Copyrights at the Library of Congress after a long series of court battles and a discrimination investigation. Details of the case are given.

1973-62   "Barbara Ringer Named Register of Copyrights." *American Libraries* 4 (November 1973):590.

Barbara A. Ringer's victory over sex discrimination is touted as "dramatic." Concludes her appointment as Register of Copyrights finally came to her because she was the best qualified. Background on the legal battle is included.

1973-63   Walker, G.M., "Editor Castigated." *The Australian Library Journal* 22 (November 1973):427.

Letter questioning inclusion of advertisements offering different rates of pay to male and female librarians in light of the journal's policy against accepting such advertisements.

1973-64   Young, S.E. "Editor Castigated." *The Australian Library Journal* 22 (November 1973):427.

Letter asking why an advertisement offering higher pay for male than for female librarians appeared in the September 1973 issue of the *Australian Library Journal* despite a statement in the advertisement section that "Advertisements which specify different rates of pay for male and female librarians will not be accepted."

Response to Letters: "The Editor Is Humbled." *The Australian Library Journal* 22 (November 1973):427.

Editor responds that one advertisement in question [1973-63; 64] just slipped by; the other is for library assistants, not librarians, and "was not seen to be in conflict with the Standing Committee's resolution on 'librarians.' "

1973-65   Gaver, M.V. "Women in Publishing and Librarianship." *AB Bookman's Weekly* 52 (November 26, 1973):1819-1824.

Summarizes recent studies of women in publishing and discusses briefly the careers of prominent women in the field. Reviews the status of women in librarianship, "really a mirror profession to publishing." In both fields women must prepare themselves for top jobs, assist other women and undertake action to equalize treatment of both sexes.

Letter: Tuttle, C.E. *AB Bookman's Weekly* 53 (March 18, 1974):1084.

Letter praising Mary V. Gaver's article and noting prominent women in the Tuttle Company. Adds that women figure "very strongly" in the area of rights and permissions, especially foreign rights: "They seem to do a better job than men in this area. Perhaps because there is a great deal of detail and follow-up work included in it." No comment is made on Gaver's discussion of women in libraries.

1973-66 Swanick, M.L.S. "Women and the Profession." *APLA Bulletin* (Atlantic Provinces) 37 (Winter 1973):118-119.

Summarizes Sherrill Cheda's speech at the Canadian Library Association [1973-03].

1973-67 Whitten, J.N. "The Melvil Dui Chowder and Marching Association." *The Library Scene* 2 (Winter 1973):19-20.

History of the nineteen year old, all male, Melvil Dui Association. Women have asked to be invited, but there are no procedures for making a decision to admit them in the informal organization. Eric Moon made an issue of the male exclusivity in 1970, "but no action was or could be taken in respect to the non-constitutional situation."

1973-68 Cheatham, B.M. "SLJ News Roundup: Discrimination/Sexism." *School Library Journal* 19 (December 1973):14-15.

Report of activities of women and minorities during 1973. Included is mention of Barbara A. Ringer's victory in her case against the Library of Congress.

1973-69 Rochester, M. "Librarianship Students in Australia." *Australian Academic and Research Libraries* 4 (December 1973):154-160.

Summarizes two surveys on library school enrollment in Australia: 1) notes that only 20% of the students in March of 1973 were males as compared to 26% in the U.K.; 2) an analysis of professional characteristics and employment of 1972 graduates breaking down data by sex.

1973-70 "SLA Salary Survey 1973." *Special Libraries* 64 (December 1973): 594-628.

Sex bias found in 1970 survey persists [1970-23]; $12,900 mean annual salary for women is only 75% of the $17,200 mean for men. Correlations also reported between age and sex; race and sex.

1973-71 Foster, A. "Female Librarian: How Far Does She Have to Go and How Will She Get There?" *Feliciter* 19 (December 1, 1973):16.

Brief report of October 26, 1973 IPLO workshop. Among topics discussed were the problems of women in administration, women's passive acceptance of junior positions, the use of language to maintain the status quo, the necessity for balanced sex roles in children's literature, and methods of social and political action.

1974-01 Blake, F. "CLA Women's Programme: Feature Speaker." In *Canadian Library Association Twenty-Ninth Annual Conference Proceedings*. Winnipeg, Manitoba. June 21-28, 1974. Ottawa, Ontario: Canadian Library Association, 1974:146-152.

Calls for documenting instances of discrimination, publicizing action taken and organizing.

1974-02 Bryum, M. "Women in Management." In *Every Librarian a Manager: Proceedings of a Conference Sponsored by Indiana Chapter, Special Libraries Association and Purdue University Libraries and Audio-Visual Center*. West Lafayette, Indiana: Purdue University. September 27-28, 1974: 42-57 (n.d.)

A discussion of where women are today in management: salary comparisons, position percentages, myths of women in management, with a section on librarianship.

1974-03 Carpenter, R.L. and Shearer, K.D. "Sex and Salary Update." In *Bowker Annual* 19th ed. New York, 1974:310-322.

Reprint of [1974-15].

1974-04 "CLA Women's Programme: CLA Workshop: Women's Day." In *Canadian Library Association Conference. Twenty-Ninth Annual Conference Pro-*

ceedings. Winnipeg, Manitoba June 21-28, 1974. Ottawa, Ontario: Canadian Library Association, 1974:146.

Summary of CLA Women's Day organized by Phyllis Yaffe. The program included book displays, guerilla theater, panels on personal experiences and workshops on career development, Women's Resource Centers, and women in unions.

1974-05   Feldman, S.D. *Escape from the Doll's House: Women in Graduate and Professional School Education.* New York: McGraw-Hill, 1974.

Examination of the training and experiences of women in graduate and professional schools, particularly how they are regarded by faculty and fellow graduate students and on their self-images and career expectations. Extensive use is made of the data collected in the Carnegie Commission's National Survey of Faculty and Student Opinion conducted in 1969. Library science is included. Among the findings: the higher the library science degree, the fewer women receive it (p. 7). Women are the majority of bachelor and graduate library science degree recipients and faculty, which is the case in only two other disciplines: nursing and home economics; although women represent only 60% of faculty in library science as opposed to 96% and 89% in the others (p. 44-45). Library science is viewed as a feminine academic discipline (p. 41). Male library science students have a slightly higher view of the discipline's prestige (p. 49) than females. More male than female library science faculty members engage in paid consulting; no female faculty members report an institutional income over $20,000 (p. 55). Slightly more women faculty than men have a strong orientation to teaching, but more male graduate library science students than female have this orientation (p. 60). Forty-three percent of male library science faculty score zero in a research activity index; 74.9% of the women score zero (p. 63). Female library science graduate students rate the humanities more important than males do and mathematics as less important than males (p. 66). As with other fields men in library science are more likely to view female students as less dedicated than men, although this prejudice is not as great as in more male-dominated fields (p. 71).

1974-06   Frarey, C.J. and Learmont, C.L. "Placements and Salaries, 1972." In *Bowker Annual* 19th ed. New York: R.R. Bowker, 1974:295-310.

Reprint of [1973-42].

1974-07   Garrison, D. "The Tender Technicians: The Feminization of Public Librarianship, 1876-1905." In *Clio's Consciousness Raised* Edited by M. Hartman and L.W. Banner. New York: Harper and Row, 1974:158-178.

Slightly revised version of [1972-73].

1974-08   Rochester, M.K. "Manpower Analysis." In *Outpost: Australian Librarianship '73.* Proceedings of the 17th Biennial Conference held in Perth, August 1973. Perth: Westbooks Pty. Ltd, 1974:586-592.

Data on status of women in Australia and Great Britain is analyzed and implications drawn for Australian librarianship manpower planning: librarians will come from chiefly middle-class backgrounds, be more literate than numerate, and be mostly married women. Part-time work must be provided.

†1974-09   Schiller, A.R. "Women in Librarianship." In *Advances in Librarianship* v. 4. Edited by M.J. Voight. New York: Academic Press, 1974:103-147.

A major literature review and analysis of the status of women in librarianship. National surveys of librarians are seen to reveal a consistent pattern of significant salary and position level differentials between men and women (pp. 107-123). The traditional research framework, "women drive out professional standards," is explored as a basic assumption of the sociology of occupations. The feminization of the profession is examined historically, economically, and sociologically. Women librarians and unions are briefly touched upon. Characteristics and careers of women librarians are analyzed with focus on personal characteristics, dropout rates, turnover, mobility, and education. The final section, "The Current Scene," details efforts of women librarians to rectify the unequal position of men and women in libraries. Activities of the SRRT Task Force on the Status of Women in Librarianship are summarized (pp. 137-141). A lengthy bibliography is included.

*1974-10   Tierney, C.M. "Women in American Librarianship: An Annotated Bibliography of Articles in Library Periodicals, 1920-1973." Research paper, Kent State University, 1974.

1974-11   U.S. Department of Labor, Bureau of Labor Statistics. "Library Occupations: Librarians." *Occupational Outlook Handbook 1974-75 Edition.* Washington, DC: U.S. Government Printing Office, 1974:212-215.

Notes that 85% of librarians are women. Men make up 35% of university staffs and are numerous in law, science and technology libraries (p. 213).

1974-12   "Women's Issue." *Librarians for Social Change* 5 (n.d.).

Entire issue of journal edited by Librarians for Social Change Feminist Group. Includes articles and bibliographies on sexism in children's literature, library service to women, women's libraries in the U.S. and Britain, sexism in classification and in language, and guides to sources of information on women's rights in Britain.

1974-12A   "Editorial." *Librarians for Social Change* 5 (n.d.):3.

Explains rationale for a Feminist Group in the British organization, Librarians for Social Change. Women "usually do get equal pay, but . . . usually *don't* get the jobs!" This may be because of women's social conditioning and multiple roles as well as discrimination. The Feminist Group and this issue of *Librarians for Social Change* hope to change the "conditioning that turns us into sterile, narrow-minded bosses and slaves instead of the free and loving humans we could be."

1974-12B   Alexander, R. "De-Manning in Cuba." *Librarians for Social Change* 5 (n.d.):8.

Comments on the decision of the Cuban government to declare over thirty occupations, including librarianship, "women's work" because of the need for more men for hard physical labor in the sugar cane fields. Author feels this is counter to statements by Fidel Castro and a form of counter-revolutionary oppression.

1974-12C   "Female Library Staffs — An Opinion From the Opposite Sex." *Librarians for Social Change* 5 (n.d.):9-12.

Review of and commentary on an article which appeared in *Toshokan Zasshi* on the male librarian's opinion of the increasing number of women librarians in Japanese libraries [1973-25D]. Summary indicates that the author is of two minds: wishing women to develop their capacities so that they may have equal opportunity to gain administrative posts (at present only one woman out of 15 is promoted to a responsible position), but also somewhat sad to see male domination decline. Includes results from a January 1973 survey of women members of the Japanese Library Association which indicated most women are in reader's or children's services.

1974-12D   "From the *Guardian*, 24. II. 73." *Librarians for Social Change* 5 (n.d.):12.

Report of the Royal Borough of Kensington and Chelsea's search for a new librarian. When a woman was found to be among the applicants one of the committee growled, "We don't want a bloody woman as chief officer."

1974-12E   "How They See Us." *Librarians for Social Change* 5 (n.d.):13.

Discussion of British recruitment monographs by Chamberlain [1968-02] and Corbett [1971-01] which denigrate the role of women in libraries indicating that they work best at routine tasks and do not enter the field as a long term career since marriage is their main objective. Also notes that most important offices are held by men.

1974-12F   Ronan, C. "Letter!" *Librarians for Social Change* 5 (n.d.):20.

Describes failure of the Library Association to assist women who are trying to qualify as librarians part-time and also run a home; and difficulties of married women, once they are chartered, in getting promotions and obtaining child care. Calls on women to "make your voices heard and bring this disgraceful wastage to an end."

> **Response:**   "The Editor Replies." *Librarians for Social Change* 5 (n.d.):20.
>
> In support of Ronan's points, the case is cited of a married woman under twenty-one whose grant to pursue a librarianship degree course had been cut by more than half because she was married.

1974-13   "Issue on Women." *School Library Journal* 20 (January 1974).

"The need for constant vigilance about the status of all women in the nation's work force" is the focus of this issue. Articles on library service to women, feminist criticism, and librarians are included.

1974-13A   Gerhardt, L.N. "Of Times, Changes, and Votes." *School Library Journal* 20 (January 1974):5.

Editorial comments on changes in women's library-leadership positions between 1920s and 1970s; "career opportunities for women have shrunk." The return of men from the war and the attempt to change the image of librarianship to attract them is raised as a causal factor.

1974-13B   Heide, W.S. "On Women, Men, Children, and Librarians." *School Library Journal* 20 (January 1974):17-21.

Compilation of Heide's comments on women, similar to those made in her speech to the 1973 ALA annual conference. Outlines career concerns of women and social pressures affecting library service.

*1974-14   "Rhode Island Women in Libraries Form Chapter of ALA SRRT." *RILA Bulletin* 46 (January 1974):2.

1974-15   Savage, N. "News Report - 1973: Women." *Library Journal* 99 (January 1, 1974):31.

Report of 1973 library service to women and actions of women in librarianship including charges of discrimination against pregnant women at the San Francisco Public Library and comments on the ALA insurance plan which costs women under thirty almost twice as much as men.

1974-16   Carpenter, R.L. and Shearer, K.D. "Sex and Salary Update." *Library Journal* 99 (January 15, 1974):101-107.

Shows continuation of differences in salary by sex in public libraries serving populations over 100,000; that male directors earn 30% more than female; that per capita support and beginning professionals' salaries are better under male directors. Updates earlier study [1972-64].

1974-17   "Ontario College Librarians Seek Faculty Benefits." *Library Journal* 99 (January 15, 1974):95-96.

Charges teaching faculty receive larger salaries and higher benefits because predominately male; reports that librarians (predominately female) at Ontario's College of Applied Arts and Technology file class-action complaint.

1974-18   "CLA Women's Day." *Emergency Librarian* 1 (February 1974):9.

Announcement of June 24, 1974 as Women's Day at the Canadian Librarian Association meeting in Winnipeg.

1974-19 "College Librarians Fight Discriminatory Conditions." *Emergency Librarian* 1 (February 1974):13.

Report of librarians' fight at Ontario's College of Applied Arts and Technology to achieve equal status with predominately male groups at the institution.

1974-20 Eshelman, W.R. "Calif. L.A. 1973: The Sea Closes on Moses: The Women, God Bless 'em." *Wilson Library Bulletin* 48 (February 1974):452-453.

Included in overview of the 1973 California Library Association Conference is a report on "The Effective Woman Executive" preconference, a practical training program run by three men. On the second day an impromptu panel of women challenged the program, but the bulk of the participants chose to let the program go on.

Letters: Armstrong, C.J. "Bravo, Stefan Moses." *Wilson Library Bulletin* 48 (April 1974):636-637.

Praises preconference and objects to "intrusion of dissident librarians" who objected to business orientation and all male speakers.

Wick, S.L. "Giving *WLB* the Business." *Wilson Library Bulletin* 48 (April 1974):634.

Takes issue with Eshelman's reporting of the preconference. Granted the preconference was mistitled in view of the fact that it was not specifically directed at women, but questions what special points could have been made concerning women only. Approves of the business orientation of the preconference speakers.

1974-21 "Toward Liberated Librarianship." *Emergency Librarian* 1 (February 1974):10-11.

Report of an IPLO (Institute of Professional Librarians of Ontario) workshop held at the University of Toronto, October 26, 1973, on the "Female Librarian." Recommendations included abolition of sexist references and stereotyping in library literature, administration courses taught by women who can act as role models, and more emphasis on women-related sources in basic courses. The IPLO workshop also recommended Canadian Library Association support of the ALA Task Force on the Status of Women in Librarianship.

1974-22 "UC Union Seeks Back Pay in Discrimination Grievance." *Library Journal* 96 (February 15, 1974):440.

News item reporting suit filed by local 1695 of the American Federation of State, County and Municipal Employees at the University of California seeking retroactive pay increases for librarians and others on charges of sex discrimination in the 1972-1973 cost-of-living salary adjustments.

1974-23 Phelps, L. "Is There Equal Opportunity for Women in Public Library Management?" *West Virginia Libraries* 27 (Spring 1974):10-12.

Presents factual evidence to prove the thesis that there are a disproportionate number of men in top administrative positions in libraries. Administrative personnel figures for 1972 in West Virginia are given. Lillian Bradshaw is quoted: "Only if women are aggressive enough to seek out the positions and apply for them is there equal opportunity for women." Allie Beth Martin is quoted as indicting women for their failure to obtain special training and managerial skills.

1974-24 "By, For, About Women." *New York Library Association Bulletin* 22 (March 1974):3.

Description of the planned ALA-SRRT Women's Task Force preconference on women prior to the 1974 ALA annual conference.

1974-25   Berry, J. "Money Comes First: SRRT Is Back." *Library Journal* 96 (March 15, 1974):732-733.

Reports that during 1974 Midwinter meeting the SRRT Task Force on Women devoted most of its six meetings to planning the 1974 Preconference, "Women in a Women's Profession: Strategies."

1974-26   "Connecticut SRRT Task Force: Women's Information Explosion." *Library Journal* 99 (March 15, 1974):724.

Rundown of activities of Connecticut Women in Libraries, a recent affiliate of ALA's Social Responsibilities Roundtable. These include a program featuring Shelia Tobias speaking on women's studies, children's books, a two-day state-wide conference: "The Humanism Explosion-Implications for Public Libraries," and a survey of the self-image of Connecticut librarians. Print, video, or audio material from these activities is available.

1974-27   Dillon, J. "Union Women." *Booklegger* 1 (March - June 1974):20-24.

Overview of union women. Notes that librarians are changing and that in San Francisco's city employees' strike librarians won a reputation for being the most organized, dependable and militant.

1974-28   Huish, L. "The Convention of Sexism." *Booklegger* 1 (March - June 1974):49-53.

Summary of actions taken by California Library Association members on the thirty-dollar 1973 CLA Preconference, "The Effective Woman Executive — Meeting the Management Challenge," which was scheduled with all-male speakers. A four-page discussion of the Preconference by five members of the Bay Area SRRT, covering the program, "counter program," and their reactions, is included.

1974-29   Broderick, D.M. "How I Became Radicalized." *Emergency Librarian* 1 (April 1974):15.

Dorothy Broderick tells the story of serving on the Appointments, Promotions and Tenure Committee of the Dalhousie School of Library Service. When voting on the appointment for a woman, one male faculty member noted, "she will bring to our faculty a level of femininity not now present." Broderick notes that in the future she will apply the same standard to male applicants.

1974-30   "CLA Women's Day." *Emergency Librarian* 1 (April 1974):32.

Notice of Women's Day at the Canadian Library Association meeting. Fay Blake will speak.

†1974-31   Corwin, M.A. "Investigation of Female Leadership in Regional, State and Local Library Associations, 1879-1923." *Library Quarterly* (April 1974):133-144.

Data indicate women made up 31% of national library association officers 1890-1923. Shows women more active in leadership roles on state and local levels.

1974-32   Geirsson, F. "Stranglehold Broken: U. of T. Library Staff Revolts." *Emergency Librarian* 1 (April 1974):6-10.

Details of Anne Woodsworth's challenge to the University of Toronto Library when she protested the inequity in salary between herself and a male in a comparable post. Notes that this spark has made Toronto's library hasten its emergence into the twentieth century. Includes a letter from Woodsworth to the Chairman on the Task Force on the Conditions of Employment for Non-Academic Female Staff detailing her attempts to alleviate the salary discrepancy, her subsequent resignation, her decision to appeal and call into question the University's inadequate or non-existent policies on grievances, librarian promotion criteria, and lack of females in library administration.

1974-33   Inskip, R. "College Librarians Fight Discriminatory Conditions." *Emergency Librarian* 1 (April 1974):20-21.

Details the quest of College of Applied Arts and Technology librarians in Ontario to achieve parity with teachers and counselors, who are mostly male.

1974-34   Blitz, R.C. "Women in the Professions, 1870-1970." *Monthly Labor Reviews* 97 (May 1974):34-39.

Historical review of women in the professions, including librarianship. Women's culture-oriented college education suited the liberal arts background required in librarianship. Suggests that overall women have not achieved as much progress in the professions as initial examination of statistics might indicate.

1974-35   Hiebing, D. "Women in a Women's Profession: a Unique Pre-Conference." *Mountain/Plains Library Association Quarterly* 19 (Summer 1974):22-23.

Gives viewpoint of one attendee at the ALA-SRRT Task Force on Women's 1974 Preconference. She lists her positive experiences at the event.

1974-36   Grimm, J.W. and Stern, R.N. "Sex Roles and Internal Labor Market Structures: the 'Female' Semi-professions." *Social Problems* 21 (June 1974):690-705.

Report of research on men employed in "female" semi-professions (nurses/librarians/social workers/teachers) concludes that men are disproportionately represented in the administrative components. In academic librarianship men are twice as likely to hold chief librarian positions while women predominate in the lowest status categories.

1974-37   "San Diego Librarians Protest 'Sex' Inequities." *Library Journal* 99 (June 1, 1974):1507.

News item reporting plans of staff at San Diego Public Library to bring into its Civil Service negotiations statistics documenting the charge that both male and female library professionals are paid less by the city than are professionals in traditionally "male occupations" — despite wide disparities in job qualifications.

1974-38   Cheda, S. "Women in the Library Profession." *Emergency Librarian* 1 (June - August 1974):27-32.

Bibliography.

1974-39   Crocker, A. "Women in Librarianship Conference." *Emergency Librarian* 1 (June - August 1974):26-27.

Report of a Canadian Conference organized by Dorothy Broderick at the Atlantic Provinces Library Association Conference held on May 24-26, 1974, in Halifax.

1974-40   Kannins, M. "Women's Day at the CLA." *Emergency Librarian* 1 (June - August 1974):5-6.

Report of Women's Day at the Canadian Library Association which included Fay Blake's keynote speech [1974-01]. Seen by Kannins as the "high point of an otherwise plodding conference."

1974-41   Frarey, C.J. and Learmont, C.I. "Placement and Salaries, 1973: Not Much Change." *Library Journal* 99 (July 1974):1767-1774.

Reviews 1973 ALA accredited library school graduate placements and salaries, including comparison of men and women graduates. "The evidence from last year and this is pretty unequivocal: women generally fare somewhat less well in salaries than do men."

1974-42 "The Library as a Feminist Resource." *Bay State Librarian* 63 (July 1974):13.

Summarizes a program sponsored by the Boston Area Task Force of SRRT/Women in Libraries. Speakers were feminists whose topics included women as health care consumers; the share series, programs at Salem State College on women's issues; women and literature; and "The Woman Alone." Feminist periodicals and reference sources were on display.

1974-43 "Rutgers to Pay Some $375,000 in Bias Compensation." *Library Journal* 99 (July 1974):1752-1753.

News item reporting that after conducting a comprehensive review of male and female faculty members (including librarians) New Jersey's Rutgers University has decided to pay more than $375,000 in compensation to women and ethnic minority group faculty members.

1974-44 "ALA's 93rd Annual Conference — Strategy, Structure and Specialization." *Library Journal* 99 (August 1974):1901-1911.

Report on 1974 ALA Conference includes sections, "Strategies for Women" (p. 1902), which summarizes the SRRT Task Force on Women Preconference, and "Women's Box Score" (p. 1902-1903), reporting the results of resolutions brought to ALA from the Preconference. Conclusion: "women did not achieve total victory but they did score well at ALA, bringing both raised consciousness of the problem and considerable tactical skill to the Council and Membership meeting floor."

1974-45 "EEOC Finds Sex Bias at LSU; Rules in Wheeler's Favor." *Library Journal* 99 (August 1974):1892.

Reviews case of Helen Wheeler who charged LSU with disparate treatment of sexes and wage differentials.

1974-46 " 'Sex Inequities' in San Diego: Battling for Higher Wages." *Library Journal* 99 (August 1974):1892-1893.

Report of San Diego city management's inattention to efforts to bring the salaries of librarians up to the levels of traditionally male occupations. The librarians now plan to ask for a complete reclassification of library positions "to make us equal to other professionals within the city of San Diego."

1974-47 "SRRT Women's Job Roster Replaced by Bulletin." *Library Journal* 99 (August 1974):1892.

Resume screening service replaced by job listings.

1974-48 "Wage Disparity; Sex Bias is the Primary Cause." *Feliciter* 20 (August 1974):1.

Cites case of Ontario community college librarians who earn as much as $5,000 less a year than equally qualified teachers and counselors. College of Applied Arts and Technology academic librarians are demanding wage parity and citing sex bias as a major cause of the inequity. They are backed by the Ontario Status of Women Council.

1974-49 Ad Hoc Committee on the Status of Women in the Archival Profession. *Report on the Status of Women in the Archival Profession.* Philadelphia, PA: Society of American Archivists, August 29, 1974.

Analysis of Society of American Archivists members' questionnaire responses, which profile the "average" woman archivist as white with an M.A. earning about $12,000 with a 1:1 chance of not having published an article. The "average" male would earn about $15,000 with a 3:2 chance of having published. Conclusion to the report notes that men predominate in the higher administrative positions and archivists must take corrective action to end discrimination.

1974-50 Schlachter, G. and Thomison, D. "The Library Science Doctorate: A Quantitative Analysis of Dissertations and Recipients." *Journal of Education for Librarianship* 15 (Fall 1974):95-111.

Among other conclusions: production of female doctorates accelerated in 1970's; however, their proportion of total doctoral degrees granted remained constant. No significant relationship existed between sex and type of degree received or research method employed.

1974-51 ALA Social Responsibilities Round Table. Task Force on Women. *Women in Libraries: Newsletter of ALA/SRRT Task Force on Women.* (September 1974) Vol, 4 - no. 1 - . Available from Kay Cassell, 44 Nathaniel Blvd. Demar, New York 12054.

Continues [1970-24; 1970-30; 1971-17; 1972-11; 1972-42]. Newsletter regularly features reviews of women's materials, national women's concerns, and activities of the Task Force.

1974-52 Eshelman, W.R. "A Wary-eye View of ALA/NY." *Wilson Library Bulletin* 49 (September 1974):58-61.

Report of 1974 ALA conference includes brief mention of SRRT Task Force on Women Preconference and defeat of resolution on sexist terminology. The resolution drew a tie vote broken by President Jean Lowrie who "laughingly referred to herself as, 'your chairman.' "

1974-53 Gerhardt, L.N. "ALA's 93rd Annual Conference." *School Library Journal* 21 (September 1974):29-35.

Conference report begins with summary of SRRT Task Force on Women Preconference, "Women in a Women's Profession: Strategies," and a report of resolutions brought to ALA (p. 29-30). Passed: affirmative action policies should be considered in the accreditation of library schools. Defeated: call for revolving top library management positions every three years; call for elimination of inequities between administrative and service positions; and a directive that all ALA publications cease employing sexist terms.

1974-54 Horn, Z. "California Library Association Conference Revisited: Myths about Women Managers and Libraries as Businesses." *Wilson Library Bulletin* 49 (September 1974):40-42.

Critique of CLA preconference on "The Effective Woman Executive." "The basic fault in the preconference was its insensitive disregard of the very people it aimed to help." Questions the assumption that libraries are businesses and management asexual. Responds to Wick and Armstrong [1974-20 Letters] in text and boxed section: "Facts on the Women's Panel." Women had protested the packaged preconference when the brochure first appeared; speakers were contacted and arrangements made with them for the panel of women to participate. The audience was impatient with the active participation called for by the panel.

1974-55 *Libraries in the Southeast: Preliminary Findings of the Southeastern States Cooperative Library Survey.* Atlanta, Georgia Institute of Technology, September 1974.

Data given for number and percent of professional personnel by type of position and sex as well as by sex and salary range. Fewer than 3% of women earned over $16,000 while 20% of men exceeded this.

1974-56 "SRRT Publications for Women." *American Libraries* 5 (September 1974):434-435.

Announces change in job roster for women. Roster will now list positions above starting level rather than list women seeking such positions.

1974-57 "Women Have Their Day at Canadian LA." *Wilson Library Bulletin* 48 (September 1974):77-78.

Summarizes Women's Day program at 1974 conference.

1974-58 Struble, L. "NOW and the Dollar." *Library Journal* 99 (September 15, 1974):2108.

Letter protesting NOW's stand on volunteers as quoted in *LJ/SLJ Hotline* (June 17,1974). Women should not be motivated by money. Volunteer work is personally satisfying and many librarians have benefited from it.

1974-59 Swaim, C. "Disgusted NOW." *Library Journal* 99 (September 15, 1974):2108.

Clarifies NOW's position on women volunteers, which author feels was misinterpreted in *LJ/SLJ Hotline* June 17, 1974. Voluntary activities which serve to maintain women's dependency are distinguished from change-directed activities which lead to more active participation in decision-making. Women volunteers are exploited by libraries in which they are used to pick up the slack in government negligence or in the organization's fund raising.

Letters: Deale, H. "Chauvinism NOW?" *Library Journal* 99 (November 15, 1974):2918.

States that Swaim's attitude is chauvinistic. Women are not being denied work because of volunteers. Some women do not need remuneration for their work and shouldn't be denied the opportunity to work.

Marshall, N. "NOW vs. Volunteers." *Library Journal* 99 (November 15, 1974):30.

Serving on boards of libraries, etc. denotes the prerogatives of decision-making "which is not volunteer work but volunteer management" — a task men gladly take on. "Volunteer work by women cannot be construed to mean the same as volunteer work by men; the former is vassal labor, the latter feudal management." Also responds to Struble [1974-58].

1974-60 Cheda S. "That Special Little Mechanism." *Canadian Library Journal* 31 (September-October 1974):422-427; 430-432.

Reprint of [1973-03] with illustrations depicting bosomy women in clinging dresses.

Letters: Cheda, S. "Cheda Illustrations Raise Storm." *Canadian Library Journal* 32 (February 1975):4.

Author disclaims the sexist cartoons which accompanied her article. An editor's note pleads the lack of money for a quality artist caused the poor pictures; but the editor also defends the pictures by noting they are taken from cues in the text.

McDonough, I. "Cheda Illustrations Raise Storm." *Canadian Library Journal* 32 (February 1975):4.

Applauds article but deplores illustrations which perpetuate sexism and pander to the male sense of humor.

Smart, A. "Cheda Illustrations Raise Storm." *Canadian Library Journal* 32 (February 1975):5.

Comments that the cartoons are degrading and ugly stereotypes of women.

Windreich, L. "Cheda Illustrations Raise Storm." *Canadian Library Journal* 32 (February 1975):4.

Notes that the illustrations are excessively vulgar, grotesque and are a travesty in terms of the author's message.

1974-61 "Annual Conference: Business as Usual in New York." *American Libraries* 5 (October 1974):473-475.

Report of 1974 ALA annual meeting including membership resolutions on affirmative action as a criteria for accreditation of library education programs (p. 473) and on the right to protest discrimination without fear of retribution (p. 473-474). Also reports council action on resolutions brought from the SRRT Preconference on Women (p. 474).

1974-62 Broderick, D. "Getting It Together." *Emergency Librarian* 2 (October 1974):25-27.

Summary of the two day SRRT Task Force on Women 1974 Preconference. Urges the Canadian Library Association to consider a similar all-women event.

1974-63 "National Feminist Network Formed By Librarians." *Emergency Librarian* 2 (October 1974):31.

Description of SHARE (Sisters Have Resources Everywhere), a network of feminist librarians, and other actions taken at the ALA-SRRT Task Force on Women Preconference.

1974-64 "Women's Program Committee Sponsors Management Seminars." *Library of Congress Information Bulletin* 33 (October 25, 1974):347; 349-350.

Report of two seminars for principal library managers and supervisors sponsored by the Federal Women's Program Committee in the Library of Congress. The purpose of the seminars is to increase understanding and awareness of problems shared by women in society in general and in Federal Service in particular.

1974-65 " 'Impact '74' Conference - OALT/ABO: Women in Library Service." *Feliciter* 20 (November 1974):28.

Summary of Phyllis Yaffe's address to the Ontario Association of Library Technicians/Association des Bibliotechniciens de l' Ontario (OALT/ABO). Yaffe reviews the place of women in librarianship, myths women are forced to battle, patriarchal hierarchical management style, the need for role models, and actions being taken by women working in Canadian libraries to change their position.

1974-66 Holmstrom, E.I. and Holmstrom, R.W. "The Plight of the Woman Doctoral Student." *American Education Research Journal* 11 (Winter 1974):1-18.

Data from 1969 study show women received discriminatory treatment in doctoral programs, although women in education and library science found more favorable climates than other academic areas.

1974-67 Cheatham, B. "Recapping a Restive Year." *School Library Journal* 21 (December 1974):11-14.

Section on women (p. 14) summarizes 1974 activities: SRRT Task Force on Women Preconference; women's activities at ALA and NOW actions on textbooks.

Letter: Cassell, K. "For the Record." *School Library Journal* 21 (February 1975):4.

Corrects Cheatham's statement that none of the SRRT Task Force on Women's Preconference resolutions had passed at the 1974 ALA annual conference.

1974-68 Klement, S. "Feminism and Professionalism in Librarianship: an Interview with Sherril Cheda." *Canadian Library Journal* 31 (December 1974):520-524.

Topics covered include unions, community involvement, librarianship as a "passive" profession, and women in the Canadian Library Association.

1975-01 American Library Association SRRT Task Force on the Status of Women. *Women in a Woman's Profession: Strategies. Proceedings of the Preconference on the Status of Women in Librarianship.* Douglass College, Rutgers University, July 4-6, 1974. (n.d.)

Includes abstracts of keynote address on the status of women by Anita Schiller and of presentations on self-image, education, affirmative action, career development, unions, regional and local organizing and tactics; reports of workshops on the above, and on feminist values are also included. Preconference resolutions presented to ALA; some participant response to the experience of the Preconference; Women in Librarianship: A Bibliography; and a list of participants are appended.

Review: See [1975-09 - Reviews. Bergman].

1975-02 American Library Association. SRRT Task Force on the Status of Women. *Women in a Woman's Profession: Strategies.* Videotape. Edited by Carol Ansheim. New York: Brooklyn College Library, 1975.

Overview of the SRRT Task Force on Women's July 1974 Preconference [1975-01]. Includes excerpts from the following: Anita Schiller's address and the question period which followed; presentations on workshops; the self-image and feminist values workshops, including the decision to produce a *SHARE Directory* [1975-18]; and discussion of whether to support Helen Wheeler's discrimination case. Concludes with "gut reactions" of a group of participants.

1975-03 Braunagel, J. "Job Mobility as Related to Career Progression of Female Academic Librarians in the South." Ph.D. thesis. Florida State University, 1975. (DAI 76-16, 515).

Mobility and career progression of both male and female academic librarians were investigated to determine the influence of job mobility on the women's careers, as related to similar data for men. Nine major hypotheses were tested. Results indicate that overall mobility patterns cannot be held accountable for salary or position differences between men and women.

1975-04 Frarey, C.J. and Learmont, C.I. "Placements and Salaries 1973." In *Bowker Annual* 20th ed. New York: R.R. Bowker, (1975):263-278.

Reprint of [1973-42].

1975-05 Grotzinger, L. "Katherine Sharp and Margaret Mann." In *Women in the Past as Leaders in the Library Profession.* American Library Association. Library History Round Table 1974 Program. Audio Cassette Library for Professional Librarians. L-427. Los Angeles: Development Digest 1975: tape 2.

Reviews lives and accomplishments of Margaret Mann and Katherine Sharp. Discusses them in the context of the accepted roles for women in the latter part of the nineteenth - early twentieth century. Refers briefly to the role of women in librarianship as a whole and the type of women drawn to the profession.

1975-06 McCarthy, C. *Developing Libraries in Brazil, with a Chapter on Paraguay.* Metuchen, NJ: Scarecrow Press, 1975.

Differentiates between the commonly used title, *bibliotecarios,* (male librarian), and the seldom used *bibliotecaria,* (female librarian), as indicative of the domination of the patriarchal society. Ninety-five percent of all librarians are women (p. 45). Notes that marriage is no obstacle: generous maternity leaves are given and since working class women work as maids, professional women can pursue their careers (p. 55). Explains low salaries are a function of the fact that most librarians are women and most women are "kept" by a husband or a father; because wages are low, librarianship remains a female occupation (p. 181).

1975-07 Maidment, W.R. *Librarianship.* London: David and Charles, 1975.

Guide to library careers. When discussing administrators' comments that, "the masculine pronoun is appropriate because a high proportion of the chief officers' posts go to men, the preponderance of women recruits to librarianship being more than balanced by their earlier loss to the profession at marriage or motherhood (p. 70)."

1975-08 Morrison, P.D. and Gilbert, N. "Characteristics of Students," In *The Administrative Aspects of Education for Librarianship: A Symposium.* Edited by M.B. Cassata and H.L. Totten. Metuchen, NJ: Scarecrow Press, 1975:200-229.

Statistics on men and women library school students. Possible effects of the feminist movement on librarianship discussed. Long-term trends, however, are dangerous to predict. Psychological traits of students are analyzed. Authors' studies show that "traits such as initiative, spuriously labeled as 'masculine,' are as prevalent among women as among men who choose librarianship as a career."

1975-09 Myers, M. and Scarborough, M. *Women in Librarianship: Melvil's Rib Symposium.* New Brunswick, NJ: Rutgers Graduate School of Library Service, 1975.

Four papers on background and status of women in librarianship including one on sociological and psychological aspects by Caroline Sherif, and one on sex discrimination against women in libraries by Herman Greenberg. Discussion (p. 63-81) includes questions from the audience such as, "How many female deans of library schools are there?"; "How come we've never heard all this before?" and insightful, lengthy answers from the panelists. "Federal Laws and Regulations Concerning Sex Discrimination in Educational Institutions," (p. 83-90) and a bibliography, "Women in Librarianship, 1920-1973," (p. 91-112) are included.

Reviews: Blake, F.M. *Library Journal* 100 (July 1975):1296.

A positive review which points out that the "higher-ups" in librarianship stayed away from the conference in droves demonstrating that they regard the status of women in librarianship as a non-subject.

Morris, S. *Booklegger* 2 (July/August 75):31.

Review praises symposium as far better than the usual fare for such get-togethers.

Cheda, S. *Emergency Librarian* 3 (September/October 1975):29.

The symposium is seen as a valuable contribution to the literature of feminist librarianship.

Grosch, A.N. *Journal of the American Society for Information Science* 26 (November-December 1975):353.

After noting this review is somewhat out of place in *JASIS*, reviewer comments that this volume may help both sexes work together to give women professionals a fairer role.

Bergman, S.B. *College and Research Libraries* 37 (January 1976):74-76.

Reviewed with the *Proceedings of the Preconference on the Status of Women in Librarianship* [1975-01], volume is seen as indicative of the urgent need to end sex discrimination in librarianship.

Schuman, P.G. *School Library Journal* 22 (March 1976):84.

Thorough summary of the symposium with insightful comments on the merits of various contributions.

1975-09A   Schiller, A.R. "Sex and Library Careers." In *Women in Librarianship: Melvil's Rib Symposium,* Edited by M. Myers and M. Scarborough. New Brunswick, NJ: Rutgers Graduate School of Library Service, 1975: 11-20.

Notes that although Dewey was dedicated to equal opportunity for women, his reasons for championing their place in libraries was also due to the savings libraries could experience by employing them rather than men. Examines the current status of women in various occupations noting they earn lower salaries than men, are concentrated in lower level jobs and are segregated in female roles. Finds the same is true of librarianship.

1975-09B   Greenberg, H. "Sex Discrimination Against Women in Libraries." In *Women in Librarianship: Melvil's Rib Symposium.* Edited by M. Myers and M. Scarborough. New Brunswick, NJ: Rutgers Graduate School of Library Service, 1975:49-62.

Sees discrimination against women in libraries as indicative of the condition of women as employees in other occupations and professions. Discusses attitudinal changes women must make in order to succeed in reversing discrimination.

1975-10   "Our Cultural Institutions: Libraries." In *The Creative Woman: A Report of the Committee on the Arts and Humanities.* National Commission on the Observance of International Women's Year. Washington, DC: U.S. Government Printing Office, 1975:17-20.

Overview of the status of women in librarianship and archives drawing heavily on Schiller [1974-09], the 1975 Bureau of Labor Statistics report [1975-13], the ad hoc Committee on the Status of Women of the Society of American Archivists Report [1974-49], and communications from the ALA SRRT Task Force on Women. Points out that although librarianship has been called a "women's profession," "The men are taking over — taking over, that is, more and more of the top jobs."

1975-11   Pond, P.B. "Mary Evelyn Hall." In *Women in the Past as Leaders in the Library Profession.* American Library Association, Library History Round Table; 1974 Program. Audio Cassette Library for Professional Librarians, L-427. Los Angeles: Development Digest, 1975: Tape 1.

Reviews studies on women in librarianship by Wells [1967-03], Corwin [1973-04] and Sasse [1973-17B]. Gives brief biographical information on five women who were pioneers in school librarianship. Focuses on Mary Evelyn Hall.

1975-12   Rhodes, L.G. "A Critical Analysis of the Career Backgrounds of Selected Black Female Librarians." Ph.D. thesis, Florida State University. 1975 (DAI Order No. 75-26, 810).

Oral history techniques were used to capture first-hand the reflections of Black female librarians who witnessed and participated in more than five decades of the traumas of segregation, but rose to positions of dignity.

1975-13 U.S. Department of Labor, Bureau of Labor Statistics. *Library Manpower - A Study of Demand and Supply.* (Bulletin 1852) Washington, DC: U.S. Government Printing Office, 1975.

The results of a study of library personnel resources undertaken to identify and analyze factors influencing manpower needs and to develop projections of demand for library personnel. Analysis of demographic characteristics of library workers includes sex, which is compared with type of employing library for librarians and library assistants, and age for librarians (p. 12-15). Analysis of earnings includes comparison with the male and female work forces (p. 21-24). The role of women in librarianship is also considered in projecting demands (p. 60).

*1975-14 Wahba, S. "Difference Between Career Pay of Women and Men: a Longitudinal Study of Librarians and Teachers Pay." (contact author at Baruch Graduate Center, 257 Park Ave., So. New York, New York 10010).

*1975-15 Cartier, C.R. "La Femme Noyée." (trans.: The Drowned Woman) *Argus* 4 (January 1975):4-9.

1975-16 Deutrich, M.E. "Women in Archives: A Summary Report of the Committee on the Status of Women in the Archival Profession." *The American Archivist* 38 (January 1975):43-46.

Summary [1974-49] which finds men do far better in salaries and positions than women, even if education and experience are control factors.

1975-17 Schuman, P.G. "Make Your Point: Cutting the Marshmallow." *School Library Journal* 21 (January 1975):31.

Reiterates attempts to organize women librarians and notes lack of establishment (i.e. ALA) support for the SRRT Women's Task Force. Proposes a women's caucus unencumbered by bureaucracy and functioning on both local and national levels.

1975-18 *Sisters Have Resources Everywhere: A Directory of Feminist Librarians.* Compiled by C. Leita and R. Feinberg. San Francisco: ALA/SRRT Task Force on Women, 1975.

Directory of feminist women librarians, the majority of whom attended the 1974 SRRT Task Force on Women Preconference. Talents, concerns, and resources are listed for each woman and indexed. The Directory is arranged by state.

1975-19 Wahba, S. "Job Satisfaction of Librarians: A Comparison Between Men and Women." *College and Research Libraries* 36 (January 1975): 45-51.

Shows men and women attach same importance to security, social, and self-esteem needs; women regarded self-actualization and autonomy needs as having lower importance.

1975-20 Savage, N. "News Report 1974: Women and Discrimination." *Library Journal* 100 (January 1, 1975):27.

Report of 1974 "progress in focusing attention on discriminating practices" against women and minorities. Mentions suits at Louisiana State University and correction of salary inequities at Rutgers among others.

1975-21 Holcomb, M. "Semiannual Report on the LC Federal Women's Program." *Library of Congress Information Bulletin* 34 (January 17, 1975): A25-A30.

Analyzes statistics on status of women in the Library of Congress and outlines Federal Women's Program Coordinator program activities in 1974.

1975-22   Freedwoman, J. "Staying Alive." *Booklegger* 2 (January - February 1975):509.

Describes Boston Area Women in Libraries group, as well as personal account of creating change in work environment.

1975-23   "Women in Library Administration." *Wisconsin Library Bulletin* 71 (January - February 1975):46.

Report of November 25-26, 1974, Women in Library Administration Conference held in Madison, Wisconsin, which drew ninety-five participants. Speakers are listed and their comments summarized.

1975-24   Cassell, K. "The Concerns of Women." *New York Library Association Bulletin* 23 (February 1975):6.

Announces an ad hoc NYLA committee on the concerns of women in the library profession.

1975-25   Smart, A. "Women - the 4/5 Majority." *Canadian Library Journal* 32 (February 1975):14-17.

An overview of the concerns of women in librarianship by Chairperson of the CLA Standing Joint Committee on the Status of Women. Focuses on education, status, work situations, and administration.

1975-26   "Women: Women's SRRT Maps Strategy; New Job Bulletin Ready." *Library Journal* 100 (February 1, 1975):255.

News item announcing plans for a women's conference at the 1975 San Francisco ALA conference, and that it is subscription renewal time for the *TFW Bulletin Board*, a job listing service.

1975-27   Arksey, L. "The Part-time Librarian: A Summary of Support." *PNLA Quarterly* 39 (Spring 1975):4-9.

Arguments supporting part-time work for professional librarians which at present is of interest to more women than men. Suggests male dominance of library administration may perpetuate difficulty in obtaining part-time professional work.

1975-28   Gerhardt, L.N. and Cheatham, B.N. "ALA Midwinter Meeting: SLJ's Report of Council and Youth Divisions." *School Library Journal* 21 (March 1975):72-75.

In section titled, "He/She/Persons - et al," passage of an ALA resolution against the use of sexist terminology in ALA documents is noted (p. 74). Section on American Association of School Librarians includes praise for revision of the Division's by-laws to eliminate sexist terminology (p. 25).

1975-29   "On the Back Burner: No Time for Women." *Wilson Library Bulletin* 49 (March 1975):489-490.

Report of cut-off of debate in mid-discussion on resolution to establish a standing Council Committee on the Status of Women because of a technical ruling on time.

1975-30   "Speaking Softly, Carrying a Big Agenda; Highlights of the ALA Midwinter Meeting 1975: SRRT Women in Their Year." *American Libraries* 6 (March 1975):156.

Report on the action and activities of the SRRT Task Force on Women: discussion of the formation of a separate women's caucus; plans for a mini-conference at the 1975 annual conference; follow-up on the submission of a list of women candidates for the

American Libraries editorship; and a proposal for a Standing Committee on the Status of Women in Librarianship.

1975-31 "ALA Midwinter in Chicago: Women." *Library Journal* 100 (March 1, 1975):428.

Report of actions at conference: sexist terminology in publications banned; the ALA Washington Office's disinterest in more "muscle to pursue women's rights," and the failure of a resolution on the Status of Women in Librarianship to get before Council because of time.

1975-32 Miller, M. "Women Doctorates and School Media Development." *Media Spectrum* 2 (Second Quarter 1975):5-6.

Calls for more women doctorates in the media field and offers advice to women seeking a Ph.D. as a way of contributing to the field.

1975-33 "Celebrating the Year of the Woman: Melvil's Rib Symposium." *American Libraries* 6 (April 1975):249.

Announces the publication of articles from a symposium at Rutgers University on the hiring and status of women in librarianship [1975-09].

> **Letter:** Buffum, C.W. "Why Dewey Really Left Columbia." *American Libraries* 6 (June 1975):335.
>
> Criticizes lack of research shown by quote from *Melvil's Rib Symposium* in announcement. Dewey's school at Columbia moved to Albany with him; it did not close. "As for the bit that 'women students were in the majority,' Melvil Dewey was reported to be very much a lady's man."

1975-34 Fain, E. "Manners and Morals in the Public Library: A Glance at Some New History." *Journal of Library History* 10 (April 1975):111-116.

A review of Garrison's "The Tender Technicians: The Feminization of Public Librarianship 1876-1905," [1972-73], which Fain sees as a counter-balance to Michael H. Harris' "The Purpose of the American Public Library: A Revisionist Interpretation of History," *Library Journal* 98 (September 15, 1973).

1975-35 Garrison, D. "Rejoinder." *Journal of Library History* 10 (April 1975):111-116.

Rejoinder to Fain [1975-34]. In defense of her article [1972-73] Garrison points out that unlike schools, the public library did not have the power to force the masses to make use of its offerings and librarians found it necessary to attract a clientele if the library were to survive as an institution. Garrison sees the elitist nature of early public library leadership and the predominance of women in librarianship as culminating in the library hostess of the late 1880's - "a middle class lady who does indeed demonstrate some of the stereotypical traits of that grim, prim librarian, who has become a commonplace figure in American popular thought." She suggests the hypothesis that the social objective of most women library leaders can best be compared to the conservative reform efforts of women workers.

1975-36 Manson, R.A. "Let's Name Names." *Canadian Library Journal* 32 (April 1975):97-99.

Advocates stating specific individual names when describing discrimination examples in the literature; also discusses sexist subject headings.

1975-37 "MLA Midwinter Conference." *Bay State Librarian* 64 (April 1975):89.

Summarizes featured speech at Massachusetts Library Association where Dr. Gail Parker of Bennington College analyzed some of the causes and impact of feminization on the profession.

1975-38   Newiss, J. "Whatever Happened to Women's Lib?" *Library Association Record* 77 (April 1975):97.

A letter noting that in 1900 there were twenty-five women chief librarians in Great Britain while in 1975, though about 67% of library staff are now female, only 5% of 122 chief librarians are women in public libraries in England, Wales and Northern Ireland.

Letters in response to and generated by J. Newiss: Bainbridge, J. "Women in Librarianship." *Library Association Record* 77 (June 1975):145-146.

Cites two reasons for the decline in the number of senior women: 1) because of the loss of men in World War I women had more opportunities in librarianship; these women have now retired, 2) with the emphasis on formal education for librarianship, men have felt the profession more suitable. Urges librarians "to consider the wider aspects of the needs of working women."

Duckett, P.N. "Women in Librarianship." *Library Association Record* 77 (June 1975):146.

Encourages consideration that motherhood need not end library careers; part-time work is suggested.

Letter: Southan, B.M. "Women in Librarianship." *Library Association Record* 77 (September 1975):223.

Concurs with Duckett. Qualified librarians with children who wish to work are sometimes forced to "accept nonprofessional part-time posts."

Letter: Palmer, D.M. "Women in Librarianship." *Library Association Record* 77 (November 1975):271.

Urges women like Southan to seek work in industrial libraries and chastises those who won't do non-professional work. "In industry there just isn't room for distinction between grades of posts except in the very large libraries."

McNeil, E. "Women in Librarianship." *Library Association Record* 77 (June 1975):145.

The discrimination Newiss points out exists in university libraries and library education, too. Suggests that even if women are directors they have been paid less than their male counterparts.

Moores, E.F. "Women in Librarianship." *Library Association Record* 77 (June 1975):146.

Agrees with Newiss and decries assumption that the female is thought more suitable for certain posts, i.e., children's librarian.

Ralph, A.C. "Women in Librarianship." *Library Association Record* 77 (October 1975):253.

Recounts experiences attempting to find part-time work. Urges the Library Association to "give real consideration to [this] inconsistency in their approach to women in librarianship," and develop more imaginative approaches to the use of available labor, particularly female.

Letters: Holt, E. "Women in Librarianship." *Library Association Record* 77 (December 1975):289.

Questions Ralph's blaming of the library system for wasting the public money spent to train her because part-time work is not available. If Ralph feels so strongly about her obligation to the public, she should make other arrangements.

Tennant, P.M. "Women in Librarianship." *Library Association Record* 77 (December 1975):289.

Sympathizes with Ralph from the point of view of one facing the choice of career or marriage and family. Comments on the incongruity of articles in the same issue as Ralph's letter urging graduate training. Shall women spend more time in training only to not find work if they choose to raise a family?

†1975-39   Ward, P.L. "Women and Librarianship in 1975." *Library Association Record* 77 (April 1975):82-83.

Updates some of the data given in [1966-02]. "The proportion of qualified women working in the profession continues to maintain a high level, and we have had the benefits of equal pay for a number of years. However, the proportion of women in the most senior positions does not appear to be high" (p. 82). It appears there is a tendency for the younger age group of women to continue their careers without a break. While the establishment of day care centers in industry and at universities helps women to continue a career and have a family, progress is slow. British women librarians have not organized as they have in the United States.

1975-40   "Women in Administration: Wisconsin Meeting." *Library Journal* 100 (April 15, 1975):718.

Report of a conference held in Madison, Wisconsin on women in administration which included speakers from Bulgaria, Norway, and Nigeria, as well as U.S. speakers including Allie Beth Martin.

1975-41   "Women: Sex Discrimination." *Library Journal* 100 (April 15, 1975):718.

Brief news item reporting that a McGill University spokesman has acknowledged that there are salary differences in different departments because some are more established than others. These tend to be predominately male as opposed to the "new" library school — established in 1927, where the faculty is predominately female.

1975-42   "Association." *Emergency Librarian* 2 (April-June 1975):37.

Notice that ALA's SRRT Task Force on Women is holding a day of programs devoted to women at the 1975 San Francisco Conference.

1975-43   "CLA Status of Women." *Emergency Librarian* 2 (April-June 1975):31-32.

Outlines plan for the Canadian Library Association's Status of Women Standing Committee open meeting.

1975-44   "Colorado Librarians Eliminate Sexist Language." *School Library Journal* 21 (May 1975):14.

News item reporting the passage of a resolution requiring that "all future publications and documents of the Colorado Association of School Librarians be revised to avoid sexist terminology."

1975-45   "Every Woman's Day." *American Libraries* 6 (May 1975):299.

Announces SRRT Task Force on Women all-day program for women at San Francisco conference.

1975-46   Feinberg, R. and Cassell, K. "No More Li'l - Ole - Me Librarians." *New York Library Association Bulletin* 23 (May 1975):1; 6.

Presents the previous options for women in librarianship; nature of changes needed; and plans for International Women's Year.

1975-47   Oakley, M.C. "Ms. V. or Mrs. P." *School Library Journal* 21 (May 1975):5.

Letter noting the incongruity of an article which first discusses the abolition of sexist terminology and then refers to Lu Ouida Vinson as "Mrs. Ira Phillips."

1975-48   Potter, C. "Women and Libraries: a Conversation with Jo Thorpe." *Cornell University Libraries Bulletin* (May 1975):12-13.

Summary of an interview with the retiring head of the Cornell University Reference Department. Early in her career she recognized that men held the prestigious and financially rewarding positions, but decided "to accept the inequality between men and women in library work," rather than take on the role of an activist. Women, not men, have changed the "old maid" image of librarianship. Changes in the status of women librarians are probably due to changes in their status in society.

1975-49   West, C. "Librarians in San Francisco: We Became New." *Booklegger* 2 (May/June 1975):1-2.

Detailed participant's report of the SRRT Women's Conference, Sunday, June 29; SRRT's "Women in Unions Program"; and the founding of Women Library Workers, Tuesday July 1, during the 1975 ALA conference.

1975-50   Millar, R. "Library School: Only Singles Need Apply." *Canadian Library Journal* 32 (June 1975):221-223.

Deplores physical inaccessibility of library schools which sets obstacles for wives and mothers wishing to enter profession.

1975-51   "Women in Unions." *American Libraries* 6 (June 1975):349.

Announcement of SRRT program on the role of women in the labor movement, especially in public and academic libraries, scheduled for 1975 ALA conference.

1975-52   Grotzinger, L. "The Proto-feminist Librarian at the Turn of the Century: Two Studies." *Journal of Library History* 10 (July 1975):195-213.

Slightly different form of the speech given before the American Library History Round Table July 9, 1974 [1975-05].

1975-53   Stephens, E. "Gunpowder Women of the ALA — Memories of a Library Conference as Seen from a San Francisco Penthouse." *California Librarian* 36 (July 1975):56-61.

A reprint of a letter written about the 1939 American Library Association Conference [1939-05].

1975-54   "Anita Schiller's Librarianship." *Emergency Librarian* 2 (July-August 1975):10-11.

An interview with Anita Schiller, where she expresses her views on women in librarianship and her philosophy on library management which features a restructuring of relationships between librarians.

1975-55   Broderick, D. "Women — 4/5 Ignored." *Emergency Librarian* 2 (July-August 1975):5-6.

A critical examination of the 1975 Canadian Library Association convention session devoted to "Women in the Profession."

1975-56   Cheda, S. and Yaffe, P. "A Declaration of Independence." *Emergency Librarian* 2 (July-August 1975):7-8.

Account of women's activities at the ALA 1975 conference held in San Francisco and the birth of Women Library Workers, a feminist organization separate from ALA.

1975-57 "Ladies Day at CLA." *Emergency Librarian* 2 (July-August 1975):3-4.

Report on the Canadian Library Association Status of Women Standing Committee program at the 1975 CLA convention in Toronto. Resolutions were sponsored by the Committee on issues such as equal salary scales for all part-time library employees, equal maternity and paternity leave, universal childcare, and elimination of sexist terminology from CLA publications.

1975-58 Powell, J. "Excuse Me, My Dear Division — But What Did You Say Was Your Reason for Being?" *American Libraries* 6 (July - August 1975):414-415.

Opinion piece on school librarians, the merging of the library and audiovisual segments of media service in schools, and the related associations, particularly the American Association of School Librarians (AASL). Author suggests that the emerging power struggle between the Association for Educational Communications and Technology (AECT) and the AASL may be "an interesting and not insignificant example of a power struggle between the two sexes, since it is evident that the majority of school librarians are women and the majority of AV people have historically been men."

1975-59 Gillett, M. ". . . Faintly the Inimitable Rose." *Canadian Library Journal* 32 (August 1975):277-279.

Reviews contemporary struggle against discrimination in both the teaching and library professions.

1975-60 Nyren, K. and others. "The Transitional Conference." *Library Journal* 100 (August 1975):1377-1386.

Included in 1975 ALA Annual Conference overview are brief reports of the SRRT Task Force on Women resolution requiring editorial guidelines on sexism for ALA publications (p. 1380) and the founding of Women Library Workers (p. 1386).

1975-61 Farley, J.R. "SRRT Program." *LC Information Bulletin* 34 (August 1, 1975): A152-A153.

Report of SRRT program on "Women in Unions," which took place during the 1975 ALA annual conference. The remarks of the four speakers are summarized, and a common theme noted, as best expressed by Bonnie Krawczyk: "The time for organizing is now, while the women's movement is so strong."

1975-62 Wahba, S.P. "A Longitudinal Study of Career Pay of Men and Women Librarians." *LACUNY Journal* 4 (Fall 1975):13-18.

Brief summary of longitudinal study of men and women librarians from three large non-unionized private universities. Each subject was followed throughout the years of employment, during the period 1960 to 1970, to determine the nature and degree of differentiation between the career pay of men and women. The study shows: 1) that the average pay of women is lower than that of men; 2) that pay levels and increments are not contingent upon job performance; 3) that pay levels and pay variability are different for men and women, a difference which appears to be constant from year to year; and 4) this difference seems to be determined outside the employing organization by means of the entry pay.

*1975-63 "WIT [Women in Instructional Technology] in Dallas [1975 AECT Convention]." *Florida Media Quarterly* 1 (Fall 1975):4.

1975-64 Comstock, E. "Down with Feminists." *Rhode Island Library Association Bulletin* 48 (September 1975):18-19.

Article written by a male librarian originally appearing in the *Phoenix-Times Newspapers* (July 23-24, 1975) categorizing feminists as an "aberrant breed of career-oriented women," destroyers of the home and traditional values.

1975-65   Gerhardt, L.N. et. al. "ALA 99 and One to Go: Status of Women." *School Library Journal* 22 (September 1975):26-27.

Report on the Women's Fair at the ALA's 94th conference in San Francisco and founding of Women Library Workers later in the conference week.

1975-66   Harper, P. "Turning Point: Uppity Women, Unite!" *Wilson Library Bulletin* 50 (September 1975):50.

Report of the founding of Women Library Workers, the Women's Fair, and SRRT presentation on "Women in Unions" at the 1975 ALA conference.

1975-67   Kelly, M. "Women in Library Land: a Dilemma for Women." *New Mexico Libraries Newsletter* 3 (September 1975):2.

Questioning the "sexual sorting pattern characteristic of society and of librarianship" is essential. Women need to understand their psychological handicaps; at the same time institutions must remove prejudice against women.

1975-68   McKinven, M.J. "Library Women Forge New National Caucus: SRRT Task Force on Women Continues Feminist Drive within ALA." *American Libraries* 6 (September 1975):483-484.

Report on the founding of Women Library Workers, the Women's Fair, SRRT's "Women in Unions" program and other women's activities during the 1975 ALA conference. Women Library Workers resulted from the need for "a vehicle more exclusively devoted to the women's movement than ALA" but "was not created in a spirit of rivalry."

1975-69   Sharma, R.N. "Do We Need Cooperation or Liberation in the Libraries?" *Library Scene* 4 (September 1975):11-15.

Feels the women's liberation movement has not aided the profession; advocates working cooperatively to achieve increased status for both men and women. Criticizes Anita Schiller's writings on the grounds that she has misused statistics, then goes on to quote raw statistics in an effort to prove women are fairly treated.

1975-70   "Women's Issue." *Northern Libraries* (October 1975).

Issue of mimeographed Rhode Island Librarians' Newsletter devoted to women.

1975-70A   Comstock, E. "Down with Feminists." *Northern Libraries* (October 1975):7-8.

Reprint of [1975-64].

1975-70B   Comstock, E. "It Wasn't Me . . . But." *Northern Libraries* (October 1975):8-10.

Article written by male librarian originally appearing in the *Warwick Beacon* (August 20-21, 1975) commenting on response to his earlier piece [1975-64] which was "a report on someone else's thinking." Criticizes the intolerance of feminists who responded to his attack and describes the value of the traditional role of women.

1975-70C   Boucher, S. and Zetzer, H. "Reflections on Sexism." *Northern Libraries* (October 1975):10-12.

Response to Comstock [1975-70A, -70B] by two women librarians defining feminism as a movement advocating equality for women and men, not destruction of the family; and emphasizing choice of role, not a sexually determined role.

1975-71   Goldstein, R.K. "The Status of Women in the Administration of Health Science Libraries." *Bulletin of the Medical Library Association* 63 (October 1975):386-395.

Results of a survey of large health science libraries in the U.S. demonstrate that the relative position of men and women is comparable to that prevalent in other libraries. Medical schools and the largest libraries are most likely to be administered by men. The percentage of women who are directors of large bio-medical libraries has declined radically since 1950.

1975-72   Kumar, P.S.G. "Women and Librarianship: Significance of 1975." *Herald of Library Science* 14 (October 1975):221-224.

Women are suitable for librarianship because of their patience, sympathy and perseverence. In India, as elsewhere, they outnumber men in the profession, but drop out because of marriage and household duties; hence, their contribution to the profession is negligible. "It is difficult for an Indian woman to play the dual role of housewife and professional life." Concludes with "firsts" for Indian women in librarianship.

1975-73   "Special Report: Women Show Their Strength at CLA." *Wilson Library Bulletin* 50 (October 1975):101.

With its theme, "the four-fifths minority," the Canadian Library Association recognized International Women's Year. Although the meeting tended to be low-keyed, an equality resolution was passed.

1975-74   Trehan, G.L. "Women Librarians of India." *Herald of Library Science* 14 (October 1975):247.

Poem acknowledging work of women, ending with line, "The profession welcomes thy tribe today, and may thee get equal status and pay."

1975-75   Wallace, S.L. "Editor's Note." *The Quarterly Journal of the Library of Congress* 32 (October 1975):257-259; 412.

A review of the issue of women's role in libraries from the founding of the Columbia Library School to roughly 1911. Wallace profusely quotes Dewey [1886-01]; Cowell [1893-01]; an 1896 inquiry into the "condition of the Library of Congress" which includes testimony by Melvil Dewey, Herbert Putnam, and William I. Fletcher; Mary Wright Plummer; and a New York State Library School recruitment booklet [1911-03]. The article serves as the introduction for an issue on "some of the resources available in the nation's library for the study of women."

1975-76   Thwaites, J. "Women in Librarianship — A Statement." *New Zealand Libraries* 38 (October 1975):241-243.

The situation of women in librarianship in the United States and Canada is briefly described. In New Zealand, "there are approximately five times as many women with library qualifications as men, but there is something like an inverse proportion of men in the 'top posts' " (p. 241). The issue in New Zealand "is not that of equal pay but of equal opportunity" (p. 242). A group of women librarians in Auckland has met several times to consider issues. They have formulated a statement which calls for New Zealand librarians to consider part-time positions, maternity leave without loss of either position or prestige, democratic decision-making, and encouragement of women's career aspirations, among other issues.

1975-77   Frarey, C.J. and Learmont, C.L. "Placement and Salaries 1974: Promise or Illusion?" *Library Journal* 100 (October 1, 1975):1767-1774.

Results of annual survey of ALA accredited library school placement of graduates. Data are analyzed by sex. Men, in general, continue to fare better in their beginning salaries than do women.

1975-78   "Wheeler Sues LSU; Sex Bias Is Charged." *Library Journal* 100 (October 15, 1975):1878.

News item reporting that Helen Wheeler, former library science faculty member, has filed a class action suit against Louisiana State University charging that LSU discriminates against women. Background on Wheeler's personal discrimination case is also given.

1975-79   American Library Association. Office for Library Personnel Resources. *Survey of Graduates and Faculty of U.S. Library Education Programs Awarding Degrees and Certificates, 1973-1974.* Chicago: ALA, November, 1975. (Mimeographed).

Results of survey to collect data about the ethnic and sexual composition of the graduates and faculty of library education programs in the U.S. Results show that graduates and faculty are predominantly Whites. Blacks and Asian-Americans are being recruited in proportion to their representation in the pool of college graduates; Spanish surnamed and American Indians are not. Three-quarters of all Master's degrees, three-fourths of all sixth year certificates, and one-third of all Ph.D.'s are awarded to women. On faculties, White males are the largest group holding the majority of positions at all levels except instructor.

1975-80   Gell, M. "Five Women." *Library Journal* 100 (November 1, 1975): 1977-1983.

Interviews five women at the top of the library field and discusses the personal characteristics that led to their becoming successful women administrators: Clara Jones, Barbara A. Ringer, Lillian Bradshaw, Sherrie Bergman, and Margaret Chisholm.

1975-81   Marley, S. "A Comparative Analysis of Library Directorships in Four Midwestern States." *Focus on Indiana Libraries* 29 (Fall/Winter 1975):4-7.

Surveys twenty-five of the largest cities in each of the following states: Indiana, Kentucky, Michigan and Ohio to determine gender of person in public library leadership; shows women directors decreased by 27% between 1951 and 1974.

1975-82   "Women and Librarianship." *Focus on Indiana Libraries* 29 (Fall/Winter 1975):7-8.

A series of short items which includes a comparison of male and female library salaries; a sexist poem; a letter to, and reply from Peggy Barber of ALA on sexism in National Library Week materials; a copy of the California Library Association Resolution on sexism; and a short resource list of materials both on women in libraries and on sex discrimination in general.

1975-83   Boisard, G. "Do Women Hold the Reins of Power in French Libraries?" *Unesco Bulletin for Libraries* 29 (November - December 1975):303-314.

Tables, which break down library workers by sex and marital status, are presented to describe the status of women in French libraries. Though they dominate in numbers, the French women have not been the driving force that American women have, especially in the National Association (there have only been three women presidents of the French Library Association; the first in 1945).

1975-84   Jobozruz, M. "Women Librarians and Documentalists in Hungary." *Unesco Bulletin of Libraries* 29 (November - December 1975):315-318.

Seventy percent of librarians are women, many of whom occupy top positions. Notes there is some problem with women who leave to raise families, though the law gives them this right. Also covers the difficulties women have in raising families, pursuing careers, and attaining advanced degrees.

1975-85   "Women in Libraries." *Michigan Librarian* 41 (Winter 1975):36.
Announces possible topics for a spring workshop titled "Women in Libraries."

1975-86   Boucher, S. and Zetzer, H. "Reflections on Sexism." *Bay State Librarian* 65 (December 1975):8-10.
Reprint of [1975-70C].

1975-87   Cheatham, B.M. " '75 News Roundup: The National Scene: Women." *School Library Journal* 22 (December 1975):26.
Reports of the 1975 Canadian Library Association conference which devoted a major portion of its program to discussion of the role and status of women in librarianship and of the activities of ALA divisions and round tables.

1975-88   Comstock, E. "Down with Feminists." *Bay State Librarian* 65 (December 1975):6-7.
Third reprint of [1975-64] with accompanying pieces contained in [1975-70].

1975-89   Comstock, E. "It Wasn't Me . . . But." *Bay State Librarian* 65 (December 1975):7-8.
Second reprinting of [1975-70B] in library literature.

1975-90   "Librarians Debate the Women's Issue." *Bay State Librarian* 65 (December 1975):6.
Editorial introducing reprints of two articles by Edward Comstock [1975-64; 1975-70B] and response by Susan Boucher and Hannah Zetzer [1975-70C]. The debate does not concern women in librarianship, but is carried on by librarians—"a male director and two female reference librarians"—and provides for "comment and reaction" from Massachusetts librarians.

1975-91   Farnsworth, H.A. "The Position of Women in Libraries: Prone?" *Librarians for Social Change* No. 10 (Winter 1975-1976):5-8.
Outlines the position of women in British libraries since 1900 noting that the number of women in responsible positions has declined. Focuses on the current situation and exhorts British women to be vocal about discrimination against women. Notes the need for more research on women in libraries.

1976-01   Arksey, L. "The Part-time Librarian: A Summary of Support." In *Library Lit. 6 — The Best of 1975*. Edited by B. Katz. Metuchen, NJ: Scarecrow Press, 1976:3-10.
Reprint of [1975-27].

1976-02   Cummings, C.S. *A Biographical-Bibliographical Directory of Women Librarians*. Madison, WI: University of Wisconsin-Madison Library School Women's Group, 1976.
Biographical sketches of 81 historically significant women leaders. Each includes bibliographical citations to biographical sources.

1976-03   "$$$ for Culture and Research." In . . . *To Form a More Perfect Union. . . .: Justice for American Women*. Report of the National Commission on the Observance of International Women's Year. Washington, DC: U.S. Government Printing Office, 1976:37-39.
The U.S. Government and private foundations distribute billions each year in grant programs, but women, including librarians, are not treated equally in the disbursement. The Library Services and Construction Act is cited as an example of grants-in-aid which have had an adverse effect on women. The Arts and Humanities Committee

of International Women's Year [1975-10] found that a few years after the passage of the Act which strengthened library budgets and salaries, "male takeover of top library jobs became apparent."

1976-04   *Equal Pay for Equal Work: Women in Special Libraries.* New York: Special Library Association, 1976.

This brochure presents step-by-step guidelines and procedures for defining, determining, and eliminating gender-based discrimination within special librarianship.

1978-05   Frarey, C.J. and Learmont, C. "Placements and Salaries: 1974" In *The Bowker Annual.* 21st ed. New York: R.R. Bowker, 1976:281-297.

Reprint of [1975-77].

1976-06   Garrison, D. "Women in Librarianship." In *A Century of Service: Librarianship in the United States and Canada.* Edited by S.L. Jackson, E.B. Herling and E.J. Josey. Chicago: American Library Association, 1976:146-168.

Contends that the prevalence of women in librarianship stunted the process of professionalization, served to maintain the low status accorded to women in matters of the intellect, and helped to perpetuate the public library's marginal position as a cultural institution. Presents an historical sketch of the past century and foresees a new era with the advent of activist women's groups within the ALA structure.

1976-07   "Miscellaneous: Women in Libraries." *IFLA Journal* 2 (Number 1, 1976):71-77.

Excerpts from [1975-83].

1976-08   Schiller, A.R. "The Disadvantaged Majority." In *Landmarks of Library Literature: 1876-1976.* Edited by D. Ellsworth and N.D. Stevens. Metuchen, NJ: Scarecrow Press, 1976:219-225.

Reprint of [1970-11].

1976-09   Schiller, A.R. "Women in Librarianship, Status of." *The ALA Yearbook 1976 Centennial Edition.* Chicago: ALA 1976:349-350.

Reviews recent studies but finds the current data lacking and therefore cannot ascertain whether or not the status of women librarians has improved in terms of rank and salary for the profession-at-large.

1976-10   Shearer, K.D. and Carpenter, R.L. "Public Library Support and Salaries in the Seventies." In *The Bowker Annual* 21st ed. New York: R.R. Bowker, 1976:360-370.

Reprint of [1976-43].

1976-11   U.S. Department of Health, Education, and Welfare. *Library Statistics of Colleges and Universities Fall 1973: Summary Data (Part A).* Washington, DC: U.S. Government Printing Office, 1976.

Report based on a survey of college and university libraries conducted in the fall of 1973 covering basic statistics on the library collections, staffing, hours of assistance, salaries etc. Table 1, "Library Staff and Operating Expenditures, College and University Libraries, by Institutional Control and Type: Aggregate United States, 1972-73," breaks down library employees by education and sex for salary ranges and full- and part-time positions. Data are not analyzed.

1976-12   U.S. Department of Labor, Bureau of Labor Statistics. "Library Occupations: Librarians," *Occupational Outlook Handbook,* 1976-77 Edition. Washington, DC: U.S. Government Printing Office, 1976:213-216.

Notes that 85% of librarians are women, but in university libraries 35% of the librarians are male (p. 214).

1976-13 University of Wisconsin - Extension. Department of Communications. *Women in Library Administration.* Madison, Wisconsin: University of Wisconsin, 1976.

Papers and discussions at an Institute held November 24-26, 1974, which included women library administrators from Norway, Nigeria, Bulgaria, and the U.S., as well as women in administration in general, and in fields such as nursing and law.

1976-13A Molholt, P. "Women in Library Administration: An Institute." In *Women in Library Administration.* Madison, Wisconsin, University of Wisconsin, 1976: iv-vi.

An overview of the conference highlighting salient points made by individual speakers and in discussions.

1976-13B Granheim, E. "Libraries, Librarians and Library Administration: In Norway." In *Women in Library Administration.* Madison, Wisconsin: University of Wisconsin, 1976:11-19.

Discusses library structure in Norway. Notes that, though more women than men administer large public libraries, county libraries are more often administered by men because men are more mobile and experienced. Men tend to administer academic and scientific libraries. Exhorts women to take responsibility and top posts.

1976-13C Ogunsheye, F.A. "Libraries, Librarians and Library Administration: In Nigeria." In *Women in Library Administration.* Madison, Wisconsin. University of Wisconsin, 1976:20-27.

After an overview of Nigerian library development, Ogunsheye notes that one-third of this nation's five-hundred librarians are women. The role of polygamy in fostering independence is noted. Outlines her own career.

1976-13D Savova, E.V. "The Role of Women in the Field of Librarianship in the People's Republic of Bulgaria." In *Women in Library Administration.* Madison, Wisconsin: University of Wisconsin, 1976:28-33.

Gives an overview of Bulgarian library development and highlights women who administer libraries. In Bulgaria 95% of all librarians are women.

1976-13E Rossell, G. "Women in Library Administration in the U.S." In *Women in Library Administration.* Madison, Wisconsin: University of Wisconsin, 1976:46-47.

Urges women to apply for top level positions and to encourage and support other women.

1976-13F Martin, A.B. "Women in Library Administration in the U.S." In *Women in Library Administration.* Madison, Wisconsin: University of Wisconsin, 1976:49-52.

Expresses concern at the few women in top library positions and notes that there is a shortage of well qualified women. Participatory management is encouraged as a way to insure that all will have an opportunity to demonstrate competence. New career ladders that recognize those who don't wish to enter administration are discussed as an alternative to vertical promotion.

1976-13G Goggin, M.K. "Women in Library Administration in the U.S." In *Women in Library Administration.* Madison, Wisconsin: University of Wisconsin, 1976:53-56.

Cites statistics and salaries to demonstrate that women are discriminated against and outlines steps for women wishing to enter administration. Comments that women are not publishing enough and cites data from major journals showing women are publishing less than 30% of the items. Encourages higher degrees for women. Sees the role of library education as providing career counseling and problem solving to get women used to the idea of administration.

1976-13H   Arnold, B. "Women in Library Administration: Summary of Discussion." In *Women in Library Administration*. Madison, Wisconsin: University of Wisconsin, 1976:70-71.

Major concerns which surfaced include: 1) not everyone is prepared to accept the responsibilities of top level management - alternate status should be built into jobs; 2) low salaries; 3) need for library education to prepare women to be administrators; and 4) formal continuing education.

1976-13I   "Resolution and Conclusion." In *Women in Library Administration*. Madison, Wisconsin: University of Wisconsin, 1976:99.

Resolutions passed at the end of the general session of the Institute: participants would: 1) work with administration to set goals for management training and participation; 2) give priority to affirmative action goals; and 3) achieve staff development programs for women and minorities.

1976-14   Wisconsin Women Library Workers. *Wisconsin Women Library Workers Newsletter.* (1976 -) (Available from Wisconsin Women Library Workers, P.O. Box 182, West Bend, Wisconsin 53095).

State WLW organization newsletter begun in fall of 1976. Covers chapter's activities, general women's issues, and women's issues in librarianship.

1976-15   "Women in Information Science." *American Society for Information Science Proceedings 39th Annual Meeting.* San Francisco, October 4-9, 1976. Washington, DC: American Society for Information Science, 1976:15.

Announcement of a session designed as an open discussion of the position of women in information science. The session is primarily for those who feel that women are not fully represented at the highest echelons of information science both academically and professionally. Urges those who feel there is no discrimination *not* to attend.

1976-16   Lemke, A.B. "ABC's of Women in Libraries: Access, Barriers, Change." *School Library Journal* 22 (January 1976):17-19.

Speech given November 20, 1975, at the New York Library Association conference covering women's professional concerns: equal pay for equal work; occupational and positional segregation; and women's own attitudes. The use of affirmative action regulations, identification of role models, and developing career strategies are suggested as solutions.

1976-17   Michigan Women in Libraries. *News of Women in Michigan Libraries.* (January 1976-) (Available from B. Rising, 3780 Watuga, Wald Lake, Michigan 48088).

Newsletter contains information and reports on Michigan women's issues and issues of women in librarianship as well as reports of the group's activities.

1976-18   Gerhardt, L.N. "Needed: A Monumental Checkup." *School Library Journal* 22 (January 1976):5.

Editorial on the work of Minerva Sanders, Caroline Hewins and Mary Wright Plummer quoting R.R. Bowker [1926-03]. Also assesses the status of their concerns: service to children, easy access to materials, and library education.

1976-19   Newmyer, J. "The Image Problem of the Librarian: Femininity and Social Control." *Journal of Library History* 11 (January 1976):44-67.

Study examines the historical origins of the assumption that the typical librarian is a kindly old maiden lady and that librarianship itself is a "female occupation: weak, dependent, conservative, and non-intellectual (p. 44). Librarianship is revealed to exhibit a curious pattern of occupational demography as well as a dual set of theories of the profession: one humanitarian; one commercial. Until the 1870's, the popular image of the librarian was of a male. From 1876-1905, unmarried women "began to flood the profession," laying the basis for the image of the librarian as an inhibited, single, middle-aged woman (p. 45). Gradual assumption that humanitarianism could be merged with efficiency encouraged the continuing entrance of women to the field because women could be managed more easily than men (p. 51). Personality tests administered during the 1950s gave a "scientific basis" to the stereotypical image of the womanish librarian, since librarians, both male and female, rated high in femininity (p. 53). As men and women depart from stereotypical roles, factors which once discriminated between male and female have become more similar, thus doing "irreparable damage to the whole idea of discriminating between the sexes in the traditional ways which are reflected in the items of the M-F [masculine-feminine] scales" (p. 60). Concludes that until personality inventories are viewed as scientifically unsound and until the manipulative, social control assumptions behind scientific management and the human relations school of administration are recognized as unworthy of librarianship, the image will persist (p. 62).

1976-20   Sherif, S.; Sharlin, S.; Wise, M.; Weibel, K.; Yao, H. "Ms. Caucus Goes to Library School." Combined Issue. *Booklegger* 3 (January 1976) and *Emergency Librarian* 3 (January/February 1976):10-13.

Details the activities of the Women's Group at the University of Wisconsin-Madison Library School. These include videotapes of job interviews to enable women to learn to handle sexist and illegal questions, videotapes of interviews with activist women librarians and a SHARE directory.

1976-21   Turner, B. "Liberating Library School." Combined *Issue Booklegger* 3 (January 1976) and *Emergency Librarian* 3 (January/February 1976):7-9.

Report of development of women-oriented courses in library school and suggestions for further women-oriented projects for feminist librarians.

†1976-22   Weibel, K. "Towards a Feminist Profession." *Library Journal* 101 (January 1, 1976):263-267.

Analyzes sex segregation within various positions and types of libraries. Projects future for profession in terms of numbers of men and women, so-called female characteristics, and feminism.

1976-23   Women Library Workers. *Women Library Workers.* (January 1976) (Available from Women Library Workers, 555 29th Street, San Francisco, California 94131).

Newsletter of independent national organization whose members are committed to action for democratically run libraries and a feminist society. Contains news of chapter actions, women-related issues, notices of publications on women, information on counter-actions, and the national organization.

1976-24   "LC Minority Employment, December, 1975." *LC Information Bulletin* 35 (January 23, 1976):51.

One of the four tables presented is titled "Breakdown by Sex" and provides GS levels for men and women. Women have increased in GS 5-8, 9-11 and 14-15. Men have increased in GS 1-4, 12-13 and 16-18. Women continue to outnumber men in the lower grades. Men predominate in the higher grades.

1976-25 Bampton, B. "Justice for Teachers - Why Not for Us? *Library Association Record* 78 (February 1976):70;72.

Discusses need for part-time jobs for married professional women librarians. "Is our profession mature enough to respond to this challenge?"

Letters: Burton, D. "Dispel This Prejudice." *Library Association Record* 78 (May 1976):225.

Argues for permanent part-time work and a flexible attitude towards qualified married women.

Charlton, S. "Immaturity of Those Who Choose Motherhood." *Library Association Record* 75 (May 1976):225.

Argues that married women with children who work part-time are an inconvenience to full-time workers and contribute to the oppression of all women. Suggests everyone work part-time so that husbands as well as wives have responsibility for childcare and single persons have more time for their individual pursuits.

Letters in response to S. Charlton: Crossland, J. "Letter." *Library Association Record* 78 (August 1976):375.

Chastises Charlton for considering women without children to be superior to women with children and the antagonism such attitudes cause. Is distressed that Charlton sent her letter from an address shared by the Women's Liberation Workshop, a radical organization. "Radical feminist she may be, but her letter lacks all the feelings of sisterhood that might be expected from anyone calling herself a feminist."

Milton, L.E. "Letter." *Library Association Record* 78 (August 1976):375.

Calls on Charlton to document her statement that "In the vast majority of cases, it is the husband who wants the babies - not the wife."

Ralph, A.C. "Letter." *Library Association Record* 78 (August 1976):375.

Suggests that if Charlton will take on the letter writer's household duties, her husband will pay Charlton the married man's tax relief she criticized: £100 per year.

Walker, F. "Only Single Mothers Have Right to Part-time Work." *Library Association Record* 78 (May 1976):225.

Argues that married women who have children have chosen to do so and cannot "expect their profession to bend its requirements to suit their limited working time." Professional work requires consistency and commitment.

1976-26 "Cable Cars or Cable TV? California LA's Annual Conference." *Wilson Library Bulletin* 50 (February 1976):442-446.

Included in the coverage of the conference is a report of a resolution that urged Oakland Public Library to institute a nationwide search, observe affirmative action guidelines, seek earnestly for a "librarian of standing . . . with substantial experience . . . and with a proven record of creative library achievement." The worry behind this resolution is that a non-librarian staff member of the Oakland Public Library will be appointed director upon receiving his M.L.S.

1976-27 Ina Coolbrith Brigade/San Francisco Bay Area Chapter Women Library Workers. *Women Library Workers - Ina Coolbrith Brigade.* (February

1976-). (Available from Ina Coolbrith Brigade/San Francisco Bay Area Chapter, 37 Sanchez Street, San Francisco, California 94114).

Newsletter of San Francisco area Women Library Workers chapter. Contains chapter news and information.

1976-28 Spencer, P.G. "Aghast-ly Letter." *School Library Journal* 22 (February 1976):4.

Letter reporting that a motion empowering the Virginia Library Association to "commit itself to use of non-sexist terminology in its publications and communications" was defeated at the December 4-6, 1975 VLA Conference.

1976-29 "Title Tattle." *Library Association Record* 78 (February 1976):5-7.

Brief item commenting on the National Union of Journalists suggestion that all women be entitled Ms. "Why can't people be allowed their own chosen style? Some women are not in the least ashamed of being Miss or Mrs., even if others think they should be."

Letter: Brentford, D. "For Any Pam, Vick or Sally . . ." *Library Association Record* 78 (May 1976):227.

Letter addressed "Dear Mr (u) Walter." The notation " 'u' signifies unmarried." Criticizes editor's stance on using forms of address for women indicating marital status.

Response to Letter: "The Editor received . . ." *Library Association Record* 78 (May 1976):227.

Editor replies he doesn't criticize women who withhold marital status but upholds the right of choice to reveal or not reveal. Adds that he is married.

Willies, I. "Letter." *Library Association Record* 78 (August 1976):375.

Questions the use of Ms. He has found Mrs. and Miss useful titles. "I am sure that what Diane [Brentford] wants is for mere males to be equally clearly marked as to marital status."

Response to Letters: "The Ms, Mrs, . . ." *Library Association Record* 78 (August 1976):375.

The editor notes that "The Ms, Mrs., Miss, Mr., Dr. correspondence is now closed."

1976-30 "ALA Library Education Survey Charts Discrimination Progress." *Library Journal* 101 (February 1, 1976):470-471.

News item summarizing ALA's Office of Library Personnel Resources Survey, [1975-79]. Findings include that 80.5% of recipients of degrees and certificates from programs of library education in 1973-74 were women, but men got 63.8% of the doctorates.

1976-31 "Losses in Directorships for Women Pegged." *Library Journal* 101 (February 15, 1976):573.

News item reporting on a survey of four midwestern states reported by *Focus on Indiana Libraries* [1975-81] which finds that male directors of public libraries are in the majority in the largest cities in Indiana, Kentucky, Michigan, and Ohio, while the number of women in leadership positions is decreasing. Decline of female directors between 1950 and 1975: Ohio - 47%; Indiana - 32%; Michigan - 19%; Kentucky - 12% - an overall loss of 27%.

1976-32 Savage, N. "News Report 1975: Women." *Library Journal* 101 (February 15, 1976):588-589.

Report of activities of women in librarianship, such as suits and actions on sexist terminology, included in overview of library events and issues in 1975.

1976-33   "Women Library Workers Plot Strategies." *Library Journal* 101 (February 15, 1976):572.

News item detailing plans by Women Library Workers to expand organization to combat discrimination and deal with issues.

1976-34   Bidlack, R.E. "Faculty Salaries of 62 Library Schools, 1975-76." *Journal of Education for Librarianship* 16 (Spring 1976):258-270.

Results of third survey of ALA accredited library schools broken down by sex for the first time. Deans and directors of twelve schools are women; forty-nine schools are headed by men. The median salary of the ten women deans and directors with fiscal year appointments is $29,707. The median for men with similar appointments is $31,250. Of the 697 full-time faculty members, 408 are men and 289 are women. Women hold 39.8% of the full professorships, 84.3% of the associate professorships and 85.1% of the assistant professorships.

1976-35   Assisi, Sr. C., S.C.(H). "Daughters of St. Elizabeth Ann Seton: Catholic Contribution to Librarianship No. 6." *Catholic Library World* 47 (March 1976):353.

Brief review of contribution of Sisters of Charity to librarianship in past, particularly in library education and report on present activities of nuns in librarianship.

1976-36   Cohn, W.L. "An Overview of ARL Directors, 1933-1973." *College and Research Libraries* 37 (March 1976):137-144.

Compares current Association of Research Libraries (ARL) directors with past directors in order to assess the nature of the new directors. Academic preparation, age, sex and "Destination Upon Leaving Position," are studied. In 1933 there were fifteen women serving as directors. Between 1934 and 1969 only two women were appointed out of the 147 appointments made. During the period of 1970-1973 four women were appointed. All were working at the library which appointed them. It appears that women only reach the top range by staying put and "proving" their abilities to those making the appointments (p. 143).

1976-37   Gerhardt, L.N. and others. "ALA at 99½: SLJ Reports the '76 Midwinter Conference: Women." *School Library Journal* 22 (March 1976):77-78.

Coverage of women's issues at ALA Midwinter. Report of the SRRT Task Force on Women strategy session held to explore means to facilitate the passage of resolutions (daycare, support of ERA, elimination of sexist terminology in ALA publications) through Council. Of most pressing concern: the assurance of a favorable Council vote on the creation of a Status of Women in Librarianship Commitee. ALA President, Allie Beth Martin, appointed an Ad Hoc Committee to define the need for a Standing Committee on Women. The Committee met to draft general guidelines and identify priorities.

1976-38   Harper, P. "Fragments From a Reporter's Notebook: Committee on Women Gets Moving." *Wilson Library Bulletin* 50 (March 1976):526.

Report of the work of the Ad Hoc Committee on the Status of Women in Librarianship and plans to make the Committee permanent.

1976-39   "Libraryland in the Wake of International Women's Year." *American Libraries* 7 (March 1976):138-139.

Discusses the plan to create a Standing Committee on the Status of Women in Librarianship at the ALA's annual conference as well as comparing the status of women librarians in Hungary and France to those in the U.S.

1976-40 "Ten Timely Tales Mother Never Told Us: 'Sexist Terminology' From ALA to be Further Policed." *American Libraries* 7 (March 1976):132.

One of ten capsule summaries of ALA Midwinter 1976. The SRRT Task Force on Women resolution calling for guidelines to tighten controls over use of sexist terminology in ALA publications was passed by Council.

1976-41 "Women in Labor Force Report Released." *Feliciter* 22 (March 1976):4.

Chart covers years 1964-74 in Canada, and shows that although percentage of women in the labor force increased, women's salaries are still lower than men's in all areas, including librarianship.

1976-42 Berry, J. "The Participation Problem: Issues: Women." *Library Journal* 101 (March 15, 1976):788.

Report of 1976 ALA Midwinter Conference activities of Task Force on Women: acceptance of resolution on sexist terminology and advertising and a strategy session on how to get women's resolutions through Council. Meetings of the Ad Hoc Committee charged with determining the need for a Committee on the Status of Women are also covered.

1976-43 Shearer, K.D. and Carpenter, R.L. "Public Library Support and Salaries in the Seventies." *Library Journal* 101 (March 15, 1976):777-783.

Updates their earlier analyses of public libraries serving populations of over 100,000 [1972-64, 1974-16]. Women are still less likely to become public library administrators and are paid less than their male counterparts, but the gaps between public support for libraries directed by women and those directed by men or between salaries paid to entry level librarians in libraries directed by men and those directed by women is narrowing.

1976-44 Medsger, B. "Media Stereotypes of Women and One Modest Attempt at Erasing Some of Them." *California Librarian* 37 (April 1976): 11-15.

Reviews status of women in librarianship as an example of the status of working women. Gives suggestions for changing the media image of all working women.

1976-45 "Oakland Hires Female Director After Bias Charge." *Library Journal* 101 (April 1976):954.

Combined pressure of Women Library Workers and California Library Association on Oakland City Council results in appointment of a woman to directorship of Oakland Public Library.

1976-46 Wallace, Sr. C. "The Four-fifths Minority: Continuing Education for Library Personnel." *Canadian Library Journal* 33 (April 1976):75-79.

Theme address to 1975 Canadian Library Association annual conference gives overview of women in the Canadian work force. Notes that while librarianship is generally viewed as a female profession, the average earnings of men librarians exceed those of women by 18.6%. Suggests consciousness raising for women, role models for women in professional education, a new women's network, and repeated questioning of basic assumptions as steps toward a solution to inequalities.

1976-47 Huff, M. "Vermont Library Association Preconference on Women." *Vermont Libraries* 5 (May 1976):50-52.

Report of Preconference which covered range of subjects, including assertiveness training, volunteerism, and relationship between women and language.

1976-48   Mitchell, L. "Librarian Among Technologists; Perceptions of Subliminal at Splashy AECT Conference." *American Libraries* 7 (May 1976):247-248.

Discusses the formation of WIT (Women in Instructional Technology), women's group of the Association for Educational Communications and Technology (AECT). WIT, formed in the predominantly male AECT to bring women together to share in individual professional growth, to keep sexism out of education, and to encourage women to fight sex discrimination in employment, marked its third birthday.

1976-49   Newman, O.S. " 'Sir' Olga Advises Caution." *Library Association Record* 78 (May 1976):226.

In a letter dealing with hiring practices, the author comments on the fact that many people, "mostly students," address their letters to her, "Dear Sir." When she is freed from answering these letters inquiring about jobs, she may find time to complain about being addressed as "sir."

Letter: Posser, E.M. "Letter." *Library Association Record* 78 (August 1976):375.

Unlike Newman, she is unperturbed when addressed as "Dear Sir," but is annoyed at not being addressed as Dr. having obtained the Ph.D. In a p.s., comments that she is even more annoyed by the German form of addressing a woman Ph.D., married or unmarried, as "Frau Doktor."

1976-50   Wahba, S.P. "Women in Libraries: Part I - Job Satisfaction of Librarians: A Comparison Between Men and Women; Part II - A Longitudinal Study of Career Pay of Men and Women Librarians." *Law Library Journal* 69 (May 1976):223-231.

Part I is a reprint of [1975-19]. Part II is a reprint of [1975-62].

1976-51   "Few Minorities in Minn.: Low Pay for Women." *Library Journal* 101 (May 1, 1976):1077.

Report of the Minnesota Library Association's survey of its Public Library Division. Of 217 respondents, only three were minority group members; women outnumbered men 185 to thirty, but men earned an annual average of $17,911 to the women's $11,784.

†**1976-52**   Brugh, A.E. and Beede, B.R. "American Librarianship." *Signs: Journal of Women in Culture and Society* 1 (Summer 1976):943-955.

Review of publications from 1970-75 which offer new perspectives on women in librarianship. Emphasis is on salary discrimination, the socioeconomic and historical bases for discrimination in the structuring and development of the library profession, and the actions that women are taking to change the patterns of inequality.

1976-53   McLeod, A.J. "Conference on Women and Education: Report to Council." *New Zealand Libraries* 39 (June 1976):126-127.

Report from the New Zealand Library Association's representative to the Conference on Women and Education sponsored by the International Women's Year Committee on Women and the New Zealand Department of Education. It was recommended that the Association hold refresher courses for those men or women temporarily out of the work force because of their child care responsibilities.

1976-54   "Oakland PL Gets Woman Director." *Wilson Library Bulletin* 50 (June 1976):767.

Report of Lelia White's appointment as Director of the Oakland Public Library after a determined campaign by the Bay Area Chapter of Women Library Workers roused the city council to observe affirmative action principles.

1976-55 Holley, E. "Librarians, 1876-1976." *Library Trends* 25 (July 1976):177-207.

In a summary history of librarians over the last century, Holley makes numerous comments on women — their entrance into the profession, participation in ALA, Fairchild's 1904 paper on women [1904-05], and fight for equal recognition and pay.

1976-56 Learmont, C.L. and Darling, R. "Placement and Salaries 1975: A Difficult Year." *Library Journal* 101 (July 1976):1487-1493.

Reviews 1975 ALA accredited library school graduate placements and salaries, including salary differentials between men and women librarians. Women continue to show progress in the higher salary ranges but continue to fall below men in the lower ranges. The median salary for all 1975 women graduates ($9,980) was 96.4% of the men's.

1976-57 Schuman, P.G. "Women Marking Out Their Destiny." *Library Association Record* 78 (July 1976):305; 307.

Traces the development of women librarians organizing and dealing with the question of women in American librarianship in this decade.

1976-58 *SHARE: A Directory of Feminist Library Workers* 2nd Edition. Compiled by C. Leita, M. McKenney, and S. Critchfield. San Francisco: Women Library Workers, July 1976.

SHARE (Sisters Have Resources Everywhere) is a directory of Women Library Workers arranged according to states, with indexing by subject and name. Updates SHARE 1975 [1975-18].

1976-59 Talbot, R.J. *Salary Structures of Librarians in Higher Education for the Academic Year 1975-76.* Chicago: American Library Association, August 1976.

Analysis includes data on the salaries of women and minorities in the professional work force of academic libraries. The wages of academic librarians and faculty members are also compared. Women constitute the majority of academic librarians in all but the top positions and earn less than men in every category.

1976-60 Twin City Women Library Workers. *Women Library Workers Twin Cities Chapter Newsletter.* (August 1976-) (Available from Marti Lyback, 1815 Pierce Street N.E., Minneapolis, Minnesota 55418).

Minneapolis-St. Paul WLW Chapter Newsletter containing information on chapter activities and issues.

1976-61 Grotzinger, L. "Librarian! How Fair the Pages Are." *Michigan Librarian* 42 (Fall 1976):13-21.

Michigan's present library structure is discussed in relationship to the hundreds of women who helped create it. The most obvious feminist contribution lies in the Ladies Library Associations — there were more of them in Michigan in the year of the *U.S, Special Report of 1876* [1876-02] than in all of New England. Part of the reason for their creation was to enable women to have opportunities for education and culture since formal training was often closed to them. Grotzinger goes on to discuss the role of women in school, college and state libraries and focuses on specific women whose contributions were outstanding.

1976-62 Bampton, B. "Lost Talent." *Library Association Record* 78 (September 1976):453.

Letter asking other women librarians seeking part-time employment "interested in joining forces to formulate a scheme which would effectively show what [they] have to offer," to contact her.

1976-63   Gerhardt, L.N. and Others. "Celebrating a Century: ALA '76." *School Library Journal* 23 (September 1976):20-33.

Two reports on women's activities are included in the overview of the ALA 1976 conference. The SRRT Task Force on Women all-day meeting on information and strategies is described in the "SRRT" section (p. 28), under the heading, "Women." The formation of an ALA Council Committee on the Status of Women is detailed; the meeting of two informal discussion groups - women library educators and women library administrators is noted; and Women Library Workers activities are reported (p. 28).

1976-64   Harper, P. "The Dramatic ALA: Women's Place." *Wilson Library Bulletin* 51 (September 1976):32-33.

Report of SRRT Task Force on Women all-day workshop designed to increase the political skills of its participants, and Women Library Workers meeting where chapters reported on goals and projects.

1976-65   "Preliminary Figures Show Academic Salary Patterns." *American Libraries* 7 (September 1976):494.

News item on preliminary results of survey of academic librarians showing that, on the average, women are paid less than men at every level of employment. For full report see [1976-59].

1976-66   "Women Library Workers: The Organizing Drive." *Library Journal* 101 (September 1976):1703.

Discusses continuing drive to increase number of WLW chapters, and the activities of the chapters.

1976-67   Berry, J. et. al. " 'Centering Down': ALA's Centennial Conference: The Status of Women." *Library Journal* 101 (September 1, 1976):1704.

Report of the establishment of the permanent Committee on the Status of Women in Librarianship at the 1976 ALA conference.

1976-68   "Women Library Workers." *Emergency Librarian* 4 (September - October 1976):22-23.

Prints text of Women Library Workers brochure giving statement on purpose, goals and chapter action as an organizing strategy.

1976-69   Yaffe, P. "ALA '76." *Emergency Librarian* 4 (September - October):15.

Report on ALA's establishment of a Standing Committee on Women in Librarianship.

1976-70   "ACRL Survey Shows 35.6% of Academic Library Directors are Women." *Information Hotline* 8 (October 1976):1.

Report of [1976-59].

1976-71   "Salaries of Academic Librarians 1975-76." *College and Research Libraries News* 37 (October 1976):231-234.

Summary of *Salary Structures of Librarians in Higher Education for the Academic Year 1975-76* [1976-59]. Reprints tables.

1976-72   "A Cause for Concern - TV Stereotypes" *School Library Journal* 23 (November 1976):39.

Excerpts from letters sent by the Children's Librarians Association of Suffolk County, Inc., New York to Toyota Motors, the Dr. Pepper Company, and Ex-Lax Inc. protesting the image of librarians, all women, in their TV commercials. Answers from the companies are included.

1976-73 "San Francisco Urged to Hire a Woman as City Librarian." *Library Journal* 101 (November 1, 1976):2214-2215.

News item relates that WLW's San Francisco Bay Area Chapter urged the San Francisco Public Library Commission to appoint a "well-qualified" woman as city librarian.

1976-74 Rinehart, C. and Magrill, R.M. "Characteristics of Applicants For Library Science Teaching Positions." *Journal of Education for Librarianship* 16 (Winter 1976):173-182.

Analysis of library faculty applicants in 1973 and 1975 broken down by sex reveals an increase in women holding the doctorate.

1976-75 "SLA Salary Survey 1976." *Special Libraries* 67 (December 1976): 597-624.

Seventy-nine percent of the respondents to the 1976 Special Libraries Association salary survey are women. Data, cross-correlated by age and sex, reveal a salary gap in favor of men which widens with age. Median salaries of women librarians increased by 18% since 1973, the date of the last SLA survey [1973-70]; men's salaries have risen by 10%. The actual dollar increase in women's median salaries is also higher than men's by $600. While the 1976 data show a narrowing gap, the median salary of women special librarians is still $3,400 (18.8%) less than that of men.

1976-76 "Salary Data for Librarians." *Academe* 10 (December 1976):3-4.

Report of *Salary Structures of Librarians in Higher Education for the Academic Year 1975-76* [1976-59]. Emphasis on AAUP involvement in survey.

1976-77 "Women Librarians Protest Job Bias - with Results." *Christian Science Monitor* (Midwestern Edition) December 3, 1976: Section 1: 38.

Report of $50,000 in back pay and benefits awarded to 18 women librarians at Stanford University, California.

Subject Index to Bibliography

Compiled by Julie Ann Chase

INTRODUCTION

The subject index to the bibliography of *The Role of Women In Librarianship 1876-1976* was prepared from the annotations and is limited to the information contained therein. It is based on the philosophies and indexing guidelines expressed by Joan Marshall in *On Equal Terms* (Neal-Schuman Publishers, 1977).

Subject Headings: Because the entire index deals with women in librarianship, most materials will be located under the subject itself. For example, the employment of women librarians will be found under "Employment Status," not under "Women" or under "Libraries". Exceptions to this are confined to those materials relating to women in a broader sense (for example, "Women—Civil Rights") or to libraries from a user's point of view.

In addition, the heading, "Men Librarians" is used for all material dealing specifically with men librarians.

Access Points: Related subject headings are connected with the use of the terms BT (Broader Term); NT (Narrower Term); and RT (Related Term). Additional access points are provided by the inclusion of cross references from types of libraries, types of services, and geographical areas to the relevant subject headings. Geographical cross references are made from all countries except the United States, and from states in the U.S. where applicable. Cross references are made from all acronyms to the full names of the organizations. Also included are references from divisions or chapters of organizations to the parent name used in the index.

A.A.L.
USE Association of Assistant Librarians
A.A.L.L.
USE American Association of Law Libraries
A.A.L.S.
USE Association of American Library Schools
A.A.S.L.
USE American Association of School Librarians
A.C.A.
USE Association of Collegiate Alumnae

A.E.C.T.
USE Association for Education Communication and Technology
A.H.A.
USE American Historical Association
A.L.A.
USE American Library Association
A.P.L.A.
USE Atlantic Provinces Library Association
A.S.I.S.
USE American Society for Information Science
Academic Librarian—Faculty Relations, 1968-10, 1968-15, 1969-16,
    1972-05
Academic Libraries
USE Administrators, Women—Academic Libraries
    Characteristics of Women Librarians—Academic Libraries
    Discrimination in Employment—Academic Libraries
    Education and Training—Academic Libraries
    Employment Opportunities—Academic Libraries
    Employment Status—Academic Libraries
    Faculty Status
    Men Librarians—Administration—Academic Libraries
    Men Librarians—Characteristics of—Academic Libraries
    Sex Discrimination in Employment—Academic Libraries
    Sex Discrimination in Wages—Academic Libraries
    Wages—Academic Libraries
Administration
USE Administrators, Women
    Men Librarians—Administration
Administrators, Women, 1892-02B, 1902-06, 1902-08, 1912-04, 1938-11,
    1959-06, 1965-08, 1971-14, 1971-37B, 1973-60F, 1975-23, 1975-54
RT   Men Librarians—Administration
Academic Libraries (U.S.), 1958-02, 1963-05, 1967-04, 1968-01, 1968-03,
    1970-13, 1970-32, 1972-28, 1973-38, 1976-36, 1976-70
Federal Libraries (U.S.), 1974-64
Geographic areas by country,
    Australia, 1969-18
    Bulgaria, 1976-13D
    Canada, 1972-30, 1973-16, 1973-71
    Germany, 1973-44, 1973-45
    Great Britain, 1914-01, 1948-01, 1974-12C
    Italy, 1938-04
    Nigeria, 1976-13D
    Norway, 1976-13B
    United States, 1904-04, 1905-02, 1907-09, 1911-03B, 1929-02B, 1933-02,
        1938-06, 1946-02, 1950-04, 1957-02, 1959-05, 1961-08, 1967-01,
        1969-13, 1970-22, 1971-38, 1971-40, 1972-34, 1974-02, 1974-13A,
        1975-80, 1976-13E, 1976-13G
Public Libraries (U.S.), 1894-01, 1952-01, 1971-10, 1972-01, 1973-23, 1974-
    23, 1975-81, 1976-31, 1976-73
School Libraries (U.S.), 1971-39
Special Libraries (U.S.), 1970-02

Advertising, Sexism in
 USE Sexism in Advertising
Affirmative Action, 1973-59
 RT Discrimination in Employment
 NT Affirmative Action for Women
Affirmative Action for Women, 1971-30, 1971-33, 1971-36, 1971-38, 1972-
  23, 1972-27, 1972-35, 1972-54, 1972-63, 1973-38
 BT Affirmative Action
  Women—Civil Rights
 RT Sex Discrimination in Employment
African-American Women Librarians, 1975-12
African-Americans
 USE Library Service to African-Americans
Afro-American Women Librarians
 USE African-American Women Librarians
Age Discrimination in Education (U.S.), 1972-13
 RT Sex Discrimination in Education
Ahern, Mary Eileen, 1909-03, 1911-11, 1915-09, 1920-08, 1925-02, 1976-02
Akers, Susan Grey, 1976-02
Alternate Career Ladders
 USE Horizontal Career Ladders
Amann, Dorothy, 1960-02
American Association of Law Librarians (1970 Conference), 1970-19
American Association of School Librarians, 1975-28, 1975-58
American Historical Association (Women's Caucus), 1973-33B
American Library Association, 1938-06, 1949-01, 1959-07, 1970-11, 1970-
  21, 1973-29, 1975-31, 1976-08
 Committee on Salaries, Insurance and Annuities, 1929-06
 Committee on the Status of Women, 1970-11, 1975-30, 1975-31, 1976-08,
   1976-37, 1976-38, 1976-39, 1976-42, 1976-63, 1976-67, 1976-69
 1876 Conference, 1876-03, 1926-02
 1879 Conference, 1879-01
 1891 Conference, 1891-01
 1898 Conference, 1898-09
 1899 Conference, 1899-06, 1899-13
 Library Administration Division
   Women in Library Administration Discussion Group, 1976-63
 1911 Conference, 1911-05
 1926 Conference, 1926-03
 1939 Conference, 1939-05, 1975-53
 1970 Conference, 1970-21, 1970-26, 1970-27, 1970-28
 1971 Conference, 1971-25, 1971-26
 1973 Annual Conference, 1973-52, 1973-53
 1974 Annual Conference, 1974-44, 1974-52, 1974-61
 1975 Annual Conference, 1975-56, 1975-60
 1976 Midwinter Conference, 1976-37
 Resolution of Equal Opportunity Policy, 1973-59
 Resolution on Equal Opportunity for Women in Librarianship (1971),
   1970-16, 1971-30
 Social Responsibilities Round Table
   1972 Midwinter Conference Meeting, 1972-21

Education and Training—Reentering Women—Australia
Employment—Role Conflict—Australia
Employment Status—Geographic areas—Australia
Equal Pay for Equal Work—Geographic areas—Australia
Married Women—Employment Status—Geographic areas—Australia
Part-time Employment—Geographic areas—'Australia
Sex Composition of Librarianship—Geographic areas—Australia
Sex Discrimination in Employment—Geographic areas—Australia
Sex Discrimination in Wages—Geographic areas—Australia
Sex Role Socialization—Geographic areas—Australia
Wages—Geographic areas—Australia

Baker, Ernest A., 1973-18
Baker, Thomas, 1879-03
Ball, Sarah E., 1920-11
Barber, Peggy, 1975-82
Barker, Tommie, 1976-02
Barnett, Claribel Ruth, 1920-11, 1976-02
Beauty Contests
USE Miss Library World Contest, 1967 (Great Britain)
Beon, Mary A., 1907-01
Bergman, Sherrie, 1975-80
Bertram, Sheila, 1973-09
Besant, Walter, 1891-03
Bibliographies, 1918-05, 1929-05, 1952-04, 1971-27, 1972-29, 1974-09, 1974-10, 1974-12, 1974-38, 1975-01, 1975-09
Black, Constance, 1972-59
Black American Women Librarians
USE African-American Women Librarians
Blake, Fay, 1974-30, 1974-40
Boaz, Martha, 1971-07
Bogle, Sarah, 1957-06, 1976-02
Bookbinders, Women, 1912-05
Boston Athenaeum
USE Athenaeum Library
Bowker, R. R., 1919-04
Bradshaw, Lillian, 1974-23, 1975-80
Brazil
USE Sex Composition of Librarianship—Geographic areas—Brazil
Wages (Brazil)
Brigham, Johnson, 1902-01
Broderick, Dorothy, 1974-39
Browning, Eliza Gordon, 1917-05, 1976-02
Bulgaria
USE Administrators, Women—Geographic areas—Bulgaria
Employment Status—Geographic areas—Bulgaria
Bulletin Board
USE American Library Association—Social Responsibilities Round Table—Task Force on Women—*Bulletin Board*
C.A.S.L.
USE Colorado Association of School Librarians

C.L.A.
USE California Library Association
Canadian Library Association
California
USE Oakland Public Library
San Diego Public Library
San Francisco Public Library
Stanford University Library
Women Library Workers—San Francisco Bay Area Chapter (Newsletter)
California Library Association, 1976-45
1973 Preconference on "The Effective Woman Executive," 1974-20, 1974-28, 1974-54
1976 Conference, 1976-26
Resolution on Sexism, 1975-82
Canada
USE Administrators, Women—Geographic areas—Canada
College of Applied Arts and Technology (Canada)
Education and Training—Geographic areas—Canada
Employment—Role Conflict—Geographic areas—Canada
Employment Status—Support Staff—Geographic areas—Canada
Faculty Status (Canada)
McGill University (Canada)
Married Women—Employment Status—Geographic areas—Canada
Part-time employment—Geographic areas—Canada
Sex Discrimination in Education—Geographic areas—Canada
Sex Discrimination in Employment—Geographic areas—Canada
Sex Discrimination in Wages—Geographic areas—Canada
Sex Discrimination in Wages—Library Schools—Geographic areas—Canada
Sex Role Socialization—Geographic areas—Canada
Sex Typing of Librarianship—Geographic areas—Canada
University of Toronto (Canada)
Wages—Geographic areas—Canada
Canadian Library Association, 1975-43
1973 Conference, 1973-48
1974 Conference (Women's Day), 1974-04, 1974-18, 1974-30, 1974-40, 1974-57
1975 Conference, "Women in the Profession" Session, 1975-55, 1975-73, 1975-87, 1976-46
Standing Joint Committee on the Status of Women, 1975-25, 1975-57
Task Force on the Status of Women in Canadian Libraries, 1973-09, 1973-10, 1974-21
Carabin, Maud A., 1920-11
Career, Family Conflict
USE Employment—Role Conflict
Career Ladders, Horizontal
USE Horizontal Career Ladders
Carey, Miriam Eliza, 1976-02
Carey, John, 1971-25
Carr, Beatrice, 1920-11
Carr, Mrs. H. J., 1920-08

Cary, George D., 1971-28, 1971-31, 1971-35, 1972-10, 1972-52, 1972-56, 1973-32, 1973-36
Case Western Reserve University Library, 1972-28
Cassell, Kay Ann, 1971-27
Censorship
USE Intellectual Freedom
Cerjavec, Ruth Wage, 1972-60
Characteristics of Women Librarians, 1899-03, 1904-01, 1911-11, 1917-04, 1921-05, 1925-02, 1935-01, 1956-02, 1957-01, 1958-03, 1969-06, 1969-14
RT Characteristics of Women Support Staff
Men Librarians—Characteristics Of
Academic Libraries, 1963-05, 1969-04
Geographic areas by country,
Great Britain, 1907-04, 1907-05, 1912-12, 1963-04
India, 1975-72
Tasmania, 1967-05
United States, 1912-14, 1916-12, 1939-03, 1969-03, 1970-06, 1974-09, 1975-08, 1976-19, 1976-22
Public Libraries, 1912-09, 1913-06, 1914-03, 1933-02, 1949-01
Children's Services, 1897-05, 1898-09
Special Libraries, 1917-07
Germany, 1939-02
Characteristics of Women Support Staff, (U.S.), 1904-02, 1907-10
RT Characteristics of Women Librarians
Cheda, Sherril, 1973-09, 1973-48, 1973-66, 1974-68
Cheney, Frances Neel, 1976-02
Children's Librarians Association, Suffolk County, New York, 1976-72
Children's Literature, Sexism in
USE Sexism in Children's Literature
Children's Services
USE Characteristics of Women Librarians—Public Libraries—Children's Services
Employment Opportunities—Public Libraries—Children's Services
Employment Status—Public Libraries—Children's Services
Men Librarians—Children's Services
Chisholm, Margaret, 1975-80
Civil Rights—Women
USE Women—Civil Rights
Clarton, Cleora, 1969-02
Cleland, Ethel, 1920-11
Cleveland Public Library, 1938-05
Coe, Ellen E., 1920-07
College of Applied Arts and Technology (Canada), 1974-33, 1974-48
Colorado
USE Sex Discrimination in Wages (U.S.—Colorado)
Colorado Association of School Librarians
Resolution on Non-sexist terminology, 1975-45
Columbia University, School of Library Service, 1954-02
Colvin, Laura Catherine, 1976-02
Compensation
USE Wages

Conference of Librarians, London (October, 1877), 1877-02, 1878-01, 1878-02, 1967-06
Conference of Professional and Academic Women, 1970, 1970,12
Congress of Women Librarians
    USE Cotton States and International Exposition, Congress of Women Librarians
Connecticut
    USE American Library Association, Social Responsibilities Round Table, Task Force on Women, Connecticut Chapter
Continuing Education, 1969-07, 1973-60C, 1976-13H, 1976-53
Contributions of Women Librarians, (U.S.), 1916-11, 1967-07, 1968-14
Cotton States and International Exposition, Congress of Women Librarians (1895), 1896-01
Coulter, Edith Margaret, 1976-02
Countryman, Gratia Alta, 1920-07, 1925-02, 1976-02
Courses of Study
    USE Education and Training
Cowell, P., 1975-75
Cuba
    USE Employment Status—Geographic areas—Cuba
Culver, Essae Martha, 1976-02
Cummings, T. Harrison, 1926-02
Cutter, Charles Ammi, 1882-01
Denmark
    USE Employment Status—Geographic areas—Denmark
         Men Librarians—Recruiting—Geographic areas—Denmark
Detlefson, Gay, 1971-27
Dewey, Annie Godfrey, 1967-06
Dewey, Melvil, 1895-03, 1920-10, 1932-01, 1967-03, 1969-16, 1975-33, 1975-75
Discrimination against Gays
    USE Homophobia
Discrimination against Homosexuals
    USE Homophobia
Discrimination in Employment, 1938-03, 1970-10, 1971-34, 1971-39, 1972-52, 1975-59
    NT   Equal Pay for Equal Work
         Sex Discrimination in Employment
         Sex Typing of Librarianship
    Academic Libraries (U.S.), 1974-43
    School Libraries (U.S.), 1973-68
Dr. Pepper Company, 1976-72
Donnelly, June Richardson, 1976-02
Doren, Electra Collins, 1920-07, 1976-02
Douglas, Mary Theresa Peacock, 1971-07E, 1976-02
Duties of a Librarian
    USE Job Description
Earl, Elizabeth Claypool, 1920-08
Eastman, Linda Anne, 1925-02, 1957-06, 1976-02
Education, Sex Discrimination in
    USE Sex Discrimination in Education

Education and Training, 1897-03, 1898-14, 1899-11, 1910-05, 1911-03C,
    1917-06, 1926-01
NT   Sex Discrimination in Education
Academic Librarians, 1961-01
   Germany, 1934-03
   United States, 1932-02, 1968-02
Geographic Areas by Country
   Australia, 1973-22, 1973-24, 1973-69
   Canada, 1976-21
   Germany, 1900-02, 1907-11
   Great Britain, 1892-01, 1893-03, 1894-02, 1898-10, 1898-11, 1899-01,
      1899-07, 1908-01, 1911-04, 1912-12, 1913-07, 1914-06, 1915-06,
      1915-12, 1921-03, 1961-05
   Hungary, 1937-03
   South Africa, 1945-01
   United States, 1886-01, 1887-02, 1891-02, 1893-02, 1894-04, 1895-03,
      1910-02, 1914-05, 1916-10, 1916-12, 1918-04, 1918-06, 1920-04,
      1923-01, 1927-01, 1929-02A, 1929-05, 1932-01, 1937-01, 1938-01,
      1938-10, 1940-02, 1950-01, 1970-03, 1971-07A, 1974-05, 1974-34,
      1975-08, 1975-79, 1976-21, 1976-30
PhD Programs (U.S.), 1967-10, 1970-03, 1970-17, 1972-67, 1974-50, 1974-
      66, 1975-32, 1976-30, 1976-74
Post Master's Degree Programs (U.S.), 1971-03
Public Librarians, 1898-04, 1902-03
Public Librarians (U.S), 1952-01
Reentering Women
   Australia, 1972-02
   Great Britain, 1966-09, 1973-60E
   United States, 1965-10, 1966-07, 1969-12
Special Librarians, 1917-07
Technical Services, 1898-05
Educators in Librarianship
USE Library Educators, Women, also specific women
Edwards, Margaret Alexander, 1976-02
Elmendorf, Theresa Hubbel West, 1911-05, 1920-04, 1920-08, 1976-02
Emancipation of Women
USE Women—Civil Rights
Emergency Librarian, 1973-05
Employment—Role Conflict, 1973-10, 1975-84
Geographic Areas by Country
   Australia, 1969-18
   Canada, 1973-30
   Great Britain, 1893-01, 1973-39, 1974-12F
   New Zealand, 1898-12, 1969-09B, 1976-53
   South Africa, 1940-05, 1941-01
   United States, 1933-02, 1965-10, 1966-03, 1969-10, 1971-23, 1971-27C
Employment Benefits, 1911-10, 1914-03, 1916-10
Employment Opportunities, 1897-03, 1911-07, 1912-08, 1915-02, 1915-07,
      1916-02, 1916-07, 1916-08, 1916-09, 1920-05, 1926-01, 1929-05,
      1958-03, 1972-73, 1974-07, 1975-34, 1975-35
Academic Libraries, 1929-03

Geographic Areas by Country
   Great Britain, 1878-04, 1891-03, 1897-01, 1898-06, 1898-07, 1898-10, 1898-11, 1899-05, 1902-04, 1910-06, 1912-01, 1912-02, 1912-03, 1912-10, 1913-05, 1925-01
   New Zealand, 1898-12
   United States, 1894-04, 1898-13, 1899-16, 1910-01, 1911-03, 1911-03D, 1913-01, 1913-04, 1916-06, 1920-09, 1927-01, '1963-06, 1969-03, 1970-12, 1973-15
Public Libraries, 1898-03, 1905-01, 1910-04, 1938-03, 1938-08
   Children's Services, 1938-10
   Public Services, 1938-01
Reentering Women
   Great Britain, 1973-39
   United States, 1965-05, 1967-02, 1973-02
Technical Services (U.S.), 1971-07B
Employment, Part-time
USE Part-time Employment
Employment Reentry
USE Education and Training — Reentering Women
      Employment Opportunities — Reentering Women
Employment, Sex Role Conflict
USE Employment — Role Conflict
Employment Statistics, 1949-02, 1951-01, 1957-04, 1961-03, 1963-02, 1965-03, 1968-05, 1970-07, 1972-08, 1973-46, 1974-11, 1976-12
Employment Status, 1899-01, 1919-01, 1931-02, 1937-02, 1962-04, 1965-09, 1973-18, 1973-65, 1975-09
NT Mothers — Employment Status
Academic Libraries, 1929-04, 1970-32, 1972-07, 1973-14, 1973-50
Archives (U.S.), 1975-16
Federal Libraries (U.S.), 1970-05, 1971-03, 1972-72, 1975-21
Geographic Areas by Country
   Australia, 1948-03, 1971-02, 1971-18, 1971-24, 1972-02, 1972-03, 1972-26, 1972-44, 1972-71, 1974-08
   Bulgaria, 1976-13D
   Canada, 1973-48, 1975-25, 1976-06, 1976-46
   Cuba, 1974-12B
   Denmark, 1946-03
   France, 1915-11, 1975-83, 1976-07, 1976-39
   Germany, 1901-01, 1904-03, 1907-06, 1907-08, 1907-11, 1969-05 (1907-1921)
   Great Britain, 1890-01, 1894-02, 1897-02, 1898-01, 1898-02, 1898-14, 1899-08, 1899-09, 1899-10, 1899-11, 1900-01C, 1900-03, 1902-02, 1902-07, 1902-09, 1903-01, 1907-02, 1910-06, 1914-01, 1920-02, 1948-01, 1951-02, 1965-04, 1970-09, 1974-08, 1974-12E, 1975-91
   Hungary, 1975-84, 1976-39
   India, 1975-72, 1975-74
   Japan, 1973-25, 1974-12C
   New Zealand, 1969-09A, 1975-76
   Nigeria, 1976-13C
   Norway, 1976-13B
   South Africa, 1940-05, 1941-01

Sex Discrimination in Employment — Federal Libraries
Sex Discrimination in Wages — Federal Libraries
Fellows, Jennie Darkas, 1976-02
Feminism and Volunteerism, 1974-58, 1974-59
Feminization of Librarianship
USE Sex Composition of Librarianship
Sex Typing of Librarianship
Field, Francis Bernice, 1971-07, 1976-02
Fletcher, William I., 1975-75
Flexner, Jennie Maas, 1976-02
Forms of Address, 1976-29, 1976-49
Fourth Vocational Conference on Opportunities for Women in Occupations Other Than Teaching (1915), 1915-05, 1915-09
Foy, Mary Emily, 1976-02
France
USE Employment Status — Geographic areas — France
Sex Typing of Librarianship — Geographic areas — France
French Library Association, 1975-83, 1976-07
Frick, Bertha Margaret, 1976-02
Garver, Mary, 1971-07E, 1976-02
Gerard, Ethel, 1973-11
Gerhardt, Lillian, 1973-52
Germany
USE Administrators, Women — Geographic areas — Germany
Characteristics of Women Librarians — Special Librarians — Geographic areas — Germany
Education and Training — Academic Librarians — Geographic areas — Germany
Education and Training — Geographic areas — Germany
Employment Status — Geographic areas — Germany
Equal Pay for Equal Work — Geographic areas — Germany
Sex Discrimination in Education — Geographic areas — Germany
Sex Discrimination in Employment — Geographic areas — Germany
Sex Role Socialization — Geographic areas — Germany
Gill, Sarah E., 1907-01
Glenn, Marion, 1920-11
Granniss, Ruth Shepard, 1976-02
Great Britain
USE Administrators, Women — Geographic areas — Great Britain
Characteristics of Women Librarians — Geographic areas — Great Britain
Education and Training — Geographic areas — Great Britain
Education and Training — Reentering Women — Great Britain
Employment Opportunities — Geographic areas — Great Britain
Employment — Role Conflict — Geographic areas — Great Britain
Employment Status — Geographic areas — Great Britain
Employment Status — Public Libraries — Great Britain
Equal Pay for Equal Work — Geographic areas — Great Britain
Job Description — Geographic areas — Great Britain
Married Women — Employment Status — Geographic areas — Great Britain

Men Librarians—Administration—Geographic areas—Great Britain
Men Librarians—Geographic areas—Great Britain
Men Librarians—Recruiting—Geographic areas—Great Britain
Mothers—Employment Status—Geographic areas—Great Britain
National Library Week, 1967—Great Britain
Part-time Employment—Geographic areas—Great Britain
Sex Discrimination, in Education—Geograpĥical areas—Great Britain
Sex Discrimination, in Employment—Geographical areas—Great Britain
Sex Discrimination, in Employment—Marital Status—Great Britain
Sex Discrimination, in Wages—Geographical areas—Great Britain
Sex Role Socialization—Geographical areas—Great Britain
Sex Typing of Librarianship—Geographical areas—Great Britain
Support Staff—Great Britain
Wages—Geographical areas—Great Britain

Greene, Bella da Costa, 1976-02
Grothaus, Julia Ellen, 1960-02
Guerrier, Edith, 1976-02
Guilding, J. M. Rev., 1880-01
Haines, Helen Elizabeth, 1976-02
Hall, Mary Evelyn, 1975-11
Harnden, Mrs., 1907-01
Hasse, Adelaide, 1920-08
Hazeltine, Mary Emogene, 1915-09, 1916-06, 1976-02
Health problems of women in libraries, 1880-04, 1886-04, 1893-02, 1903-02, 1904-02, 1910-04
Health Science Libraries
USE Administrators, Women—Health Science Libraries
Employment Status—Health Science Libraries
Sex Discrimination in Employment—Health Science Libraries
Sex Discrimination in Wages—Health Science Libraries
Heide, Wilma Scott, 1973-47, 1973-52, 1973-53
Henne, Francis, 1971-07E, 1976-02
Hewins, Carolyn, 1920-04, 1926-03, 1976-02, 1976-18
Hitchler, Theresa, 1976-02
Homophobia, 1971-23; 1971-40; 1973-24
Homosexuals, Discrimination of
USE Homophobia
Horizontal Career Ladders, 1976-13F, 1976-13H
Howe, Harriet Emma, 1976-02
Howland, Anne Wallace, 1896-01, 1920-07, 1976-02
Hume, Jessie, 1920-07
Hungarian Association of Archivists and Librarians, 1937-03
Hungary
USE Education and Training—Geographic areas—Hungary
Employment Status—Geographic areas—Hungary
Hutchins, Margaret, 1976-02
I.W.Y.
USE International Women's Year
Idesan, Julia Bedford, 1960-02

Ifould, W. H., 1972-02, 1972-03
Ina Coolbrith Brigade
    USE Women Library Workers—San Francisco Bay Area Chapter
Indexers, Women, 1878-03, 1879-02, 1895-01, 1899-01, 1900-01B
India
    USE Characteristics of Women Librarians—Geographic areas—India
        Employment Status—Geographic areas—India
Intellectual Freedom, 1971-41
**International Congress of Arts and Sciences, Library Section. 1904
        Conference,** 1904-04, 1929-02B
International Congress of Women, 1900-01
**International Congress of Women, Librarians' Section. 1899 Con-
        ference,** 1899-12, 1899-14, 1899-15, 1899-16, 1899-17, 1899-18,
        1900-01
International Women's Year, 1975-46, 1975-73, 1976-39
Iowa Federation of Women's Clubs, 1930-02
Isbell, Mary Duncan Carter, 1976-02
Isom, Mary Francis, 1920-07, 1939-05, 1975-53, 1976-02
Italy
    USE Administrators, Women—Geographic areas—Italy
James, M. S. R., 1892-04; 1893-04, 1894-05, 1895-02, 1899-01, 1973-11
Japan
    USE Employment Status—Geographic areas—Japan
Job Description, 1899-13, 1910-05, 1911-03C, 1911-06, 1916-03, 1916-04
    Geographic Areas by Country
        Great Britain, 1891-03, 1912-09, 1912-11, 1921-02
        United States, 1892-02A, 1894-04, 1910-01, 1911-03D, 1913-01, 1914-05,
            1915-04, 1931-02
    Public Librarians (U.S.), 1894-01, 1897-04
    Special Librarians, 1915-13
    Support Staff, 1886-02, 1899-09, 1902-05, 1902-11, 1907-10, 1908-01, 1911-
        06, 1912-13, 1916-03, 1916-04, 1921-02
Job Discrimination
    USE Discrimination in Employment
Job Opportunities
    USE Employment Opportunities
Job Roster
    USE American Library Association—Social Responsibilities Roundta-
        ble—Task Force on Women—*Job Roster*
Job Satisfaction, 1965-01, 1975-19, 1976-50
    RT Men Librarians—Job Satisfaction
Job Sharing (U.S.), 1969-08
    RT Part-time employment
Johnson, Ethel M., 1920-11
Johnson, Mary Hannah, 1920-07
Jones, Clara, 1971-07, 1973-52, 1975-80
Jones, William (Judge), 1971-31
Kaminstein, Abraham L., 1971-28
Kantaroff, Maryon, 1973-16
Kelso, Tessa L., 1976-02
Krawczyk, Bonnie, 1975-61
Kroeger, Alice Bertha, 1971-07D, 1976-02

L.A.
USE Library Association
L.A.A.
USE Library Assistants' Association
Library Association of Australia
L.A.D.
USE American Library Association—Library Administration Division
L.A.U.K.
USE Library Association (U.K.)
L.S.U.
USE Louisiana State University
Ladies Library Associations of Michigan, 1876-01, 1954-01, 1976-61
Language, Sexism in
USE Sexism in Language
Law Libraries
USE Sex Discrimination in Employment—Law Libraries
Sex Discrimination in Wages—Law Libraries
LeFevre, Alice Louise, 1976-02
Legal Status of Women
USE Women—Legal Status, Laws, etc.
Librarian's Job Descriptions
USE Job Description
Librarians: A Survey, 1971-18, 1972-03, 1972-26, 1972-44, 1972-57, 1972-58
Librarians—Health
USE Health problems of women in libraries
Library Architecture
USE Architecture
Library Assistants
USE Support Staff
Library Assistants' Association, 1913-08, 1921-01, 1921-03
Committee of Women Librarians and Assistants, 1914-02, 1915-12, 1916-
09, 1919-05
Library Association (U.K.), 1879-03, 1880-01, 1882-01, 1915-07, 1921-03,
1951-02, 1966-06
Library Association of Australia, 1967-13, 1972-26, 1972-58
Library Association of Central California. 1897 Conference, 1897-04
Library Association of the United Kingdom
USE Library Association (U.K.)
Library Associations, Female Leadership, 1973-04, 1973-60B, 1974-31
Library Educators, Women, 1920-08, 1971-07A
Library Employee Unions, 1919-02, 1919-03, 1919-04, 1920-04, 1970-06,
1973-21, 1973-52, 1974-27, 1974-68, 1975-51
Library Journal
Annual Placement and Salary Survey, 1972-33, 1973-06, 1973-42, 1974-06,
1974-41, 1975-76, 1976-05, 1976-56
"People" Column, 1969-15
Library of Congress, 1971-28, 1971-29, 1971-31, 1971-34, 1971-35, 1972-54,
1972-55, 1972-56, 1972-62, 1972-63, 1973-27, 1973-32, 1973-36,
1973-41, 1973-57, 1973-58, 1973-61, 1973-62
Library Schools
USE Education and Training

Sex Discrimination in Employment—Library Schools
Sex Discrimination in Wages—Library Schools
Library Service to African-Americans, 1912-06
Library Service to Women, 1886-03, 1916-03, 1916-04, 1970-26, 1971-04,
    1974-12, 1974-13, 1974-15, 1974-42, 1975-75
Lindholm, Marie Fay, 1920-11
London Conference of Librarians
    USE Conference of Librarians
London Society for Women's Service, 1921-01
Louisiana State University, 1975-20, 1975-78
Ludington, Flora Belle, 1976-02
Lynch, Mary Jo, 1971-07
M.L.A.
    USE Massachusetts Library Association
          Michigan Library Association
McCrum, Blanche Prichard, 1976-02
McGill University, 1975-41
MacPherson, Harriet Dorothea, 1976-02
Male Chauvinism Awards, 1971
    USE American Library Association—Social Responsibilities
          Round Table—Task Force on Women—Male Chauvinism Awards,
          1971
Malone, Maude, 1919-04
Management, Participatory
    USE Participatory Management
Mann, Margaret, 1971-40, 1975-05, 1976-02
Marriage—Career Conflict
    USE Employment—Role Conflict
Married Women—Employment Status
    Geographic Areas by Country
       Australia, 1974-08
       Canada, 1972-30
       Great Britain, 1899-10, 1902-03, 1902-06, 1902-07, 1902-08, 1902-10,
          1946-01, 1951-02, 1961-05, 1961-06, 1966-02, 1966-04, 1968-16,
          1973-60D
       United States, 1923-01, 1938-09, 1940-01, 1946-02, 1950-01, 1962-03,
          1966-03, 1967-02, 1967-07, 1972-06, 1972-09
Martin, Allie Beth, 1974-23, 1975-40, 1976-37
Maryland Manpower Study
    USE University of Maryland Manpower in the Library and Information
          Profession Research Program
Mass Media, Sexism in
    USE Sexism in Mass Media
Massachusetts
    USE American Library Association—Social Responsibilities Round-
          table—Task Force on Women—Boston Chapter
          Athenaeum Library
Massachusetts Library Association (1975 Conference), 1975-37
Master's Degree Programs
    USE Education and Training
Mayer, Annemarie, 1973-10

Medical Libraries
USE Administrators, Women—Health Science Libraries
Employment Status—Health Science Libraries
Sex Discrimination in Employment—Health Science Libraries
Sex Discrimination in Wages—Health Science Libraries
Melvil Dui Marching and Chowder Society, 1972-65, 1973-67
Melvil's Rib Symposium, 1975-09, 1975-33
Men Librarians
Academic Libraries
Great Britain, 1946-01, 1976-07
United States, 1932-02
Administration, 1933-02
Public Libraries, 1917-05, 1973-21, 1974-23
United States, 1907-03, 1907-09, 1911-03B, 1912-01, 1912-02, 1912-03,
1959-01, 1961-09, 1976-03
Childrens' Services (U.S.), 1973-23
Geographic Areas by Country
Great Britain, 1921-04, 1925-01, 1934-02, 1948-01, 1968-04
Tasmania, 1967-05
United States, 1959-04, 1960-01, 1970-03, 1970-16, 1974-36, 1975-48
Job Satisfaction, 1975-19, 1976-50
Recruiting, 1961-07
Denmark, 1946-03
Great Britain, 1969-19
United States, 1908-02, 1909-05, 1911-03, 1911-03A, 1923-01, 1949-03,
1950-03, 1959-01, 1963-01, 1966-10, 1967-02, 1967-07, 1967-11,
1969-16, 1970-08, 1972-06
School Libraries, 1965-02
Men Librarians, Characteristics of, 1899-03
RT Characteristics of Women Librarians
Academic Libraries (U.S.), 1963-05
Geographic Areas by Country
Great Britain, 1921-03, 1934-01
United States, 1909-04, 1912-14, 1957-01, 1968-14, 1969-14, 1975-08,
1976-19
Mentors, 1971-07C
Michigan
USE Administrators, Women—United States, Michigan
Employment Status—United States, Michigan
Ladies Library Associations of Michigan
Sex Composition of Librarianship—United States, Michigan
Michigan Library Association ("Women in Libraries" Workshop),
1975-85
Michigan Women in Libraries (Newsletter), 1976-17
Milam, Carl, 1949-01
Minnesota
USE Sex Discrimination in Wages—Public Libraries—United States,
Minnesota
Women Library Workers—Twin Cities Chapter—Newsletter
Miss Library World Contest, 1967 (Great Britain), 1967-08

Mobility as a factor in advancement, 1957-02, 1967-09, 1969-10, 1969-21,
    1970-11, 1971-06, 1973-12, 1973-13, 1975-03
Moore, Anne Carroll, 1976-02
Morsch, Lucile M., 1976-02
Morton, Florrinell Francis, 1976-02
Mothers, Employment Status of
    BT   Employment Status
    Great Britain, 1961-06, 1975-38, 1975-39
    United States, 1940-01
Ms. as a Form of Address
    USE Forms of Address
Mudge, Isadore Gilbert, 1971-07D, 1976-02
Mulheron, Anna, 1925-02
Mumford, L. Quincy, 1971-34, 1971-35, 1972-48, 1972-49, 1972-53, 1972-56,
    1972-62
Murdock, Faith, 1971-07
N.L.W.W.
    USE National League of Women Workers
N.O.W.
    USE National Organization for Women
N.Y.L.A.
    USE New York Library Association
N.Z.L.A.
    USE New Zealand Library Association
National League of Women Workers, 1920-06
National Library Week, 1967 (Great Britain), 1967-08
National Library Week (U.S.), 1975-82
National Organization for Women, 1974-58, 1974-59
National Union of Journalists, 1976-29
National Women's Party 1965 Convention (1), 1965-08
Nepotism, 1957-05, 1971-37D
New Jersey
    USE Rutgers University
New York Library Association
    Committee on the Concerns of Women in the Library Profession, 1975-24
New Zealand
    USE Employment Opportunities—Geographic areas—New Zealand
        Employment—Role Conflict—Geographic areas—New Zealand
        Employment Status—Geographic areas—New Zealand
        Part-time Employment—Geographic areas—New Zealand
        Sex Discrimination in Employment—Geographic areas—New Zea-
        land
New Zealand Library Association, 1976-53
Newbery-Caldecott Awards Dinner, 1971, 1971-26
Newsletters
    USE American Library Association—Social Responsibilities Roundta-
        ble—Task Force on Women
        Michigan Women in Libraries
        Women Library Workers
        Women Library Workers—San Fr鬼cisco Bay Area Chapter
        Women Library Workers—Twin Cities Chapter
        Women Library Workers—Wisconsin Chapter

Nigeria
  USE Administrators, Women—Geographic areas—Nigeria
       Employment Status—Geographic areas—Nigeria
Norway
  USE Administrators, Women—Geographica areas—Norway
       Employment Status—Geographic areas—Norway
Nun Librarians, 1976-35
O.A.L.T.
  USE Ontario Association of Library Technicians
Oakland Public Library, 1976-26, 1976-45, 1976-54
Oberly, Eunice Rockwood, 1976-02
Ontario Association of Library Technicians, 1974-65
Paraprofessional Employees
  USE Support Staff
Parker, Gail, 1975-37
Participatory Management, 1976-13F
Part-time Employment, 1973-60C, 1975-27, 1976-01
  RT   Job-sharing
  Geographic Areas by Country
    Australia, 1969-18, 1974-08
    Canada, 1968-07, 1972-30
    Great Britain, 1966-05, 1968-11, 1968-12, 1973-39, 1974-12F, 1975-38,
      1976-25, 1976-62
    New Zealand, 1969-09A, 1969-09B, 1969-09C, 1969-09D, 1975-76
    United States, 1962-03, 1965-10, 1966-07, 1967-12, 1969-12, 1970-16,
      1971-07D
Paulin, Lorna, 1966-06
"People" Column
  USE *Library Journal*—"People" Column
People's Palace Library, 1890-01, 1891-03, 1894-05, 1972-59
Perkins, F. B., 1876-02
Petherbridge, Miss, 1973-11
Pettee, Julia Ensign, 1976-02
PhD Programs
  USE Education and Training—PhD Programs
Pierce, Cornelia Marvin, 1976-02
Piercy, Esther June, 1976-02
Plummer, Mary Wright, 1895-03, 1916-11, 1916-12, 1920-04, 1926-03,
      1939-05, 1971-40, 1975-53, 1975-75, 1976-02, 1976-18
Poole, William Frederick, 1878-01, 1878-02, 1911-05, 1929-02A, 1967-06
Pornography
  USE Intellectual Freedom
Post Master's Degree Programs
  USE Education and Training—Post Master's Degree Programs
Professional Associations
  USE Library Associations or names of individual associations
Public Libraries
  USE Administrators, Women—Public Libraries
       Characteristics of Women Librarians—Public Libraries
       Education and Training—Public Librarians
       Employment Opportunities—Public Libraries
       Employment Status—Public Libraries

Employment Status—School Libraries
Men Librarians—School Libraries
Sex Composition of Librarianship—School Libraries
Schuman, Patricia, 1971-27
Scoggin, Margaret Clara, 1976-02
Sears, Minnie Earl, 1971-40, 1976-02
Second International Library Conference (1897), 1897-06, 1898-01,
1898-02, 1898-03
Seligman, Leopold, 1880-01
Sex Composition of Librarianship, 1959-06, 1972-73, 1974-07, 1975-34,
1975-35
BT   Sex Discrimination in Employment
RT   Sex Typing of Librarianship
Geographic Areas by Country
Australia, 1972-02
Brazil, 1975-06
Great Britain, 1968-04, 1975-07
United States, 1907-07, 1907-08, 1957-04, 1959-02, 1959-03, 1962-02,
1965-06, 1970-03, 1970-07, 1970-13, 1974-09, 1975-13, 1975-79,
1976-22
Michigan, 1972-41
School Libraries (U.S.), 1970-25
Special Libraries (U.S.), 1970-02
Sex Discrimination in Education, 1938-06
BT   Education and Training
Geographic Areas by Country
Canada, 1973-31
Germany, 1940-03, 1940-06
Great Britain, 1968-13
United States, 1932-01, 1954-02, 1972-13, 1974-66
Sex Discrimination in Employment, 1928-01, 1934-02, 1971-37A, 1971-
37C, 1971-37D, 1973-33B, 1973-60A, 1975-09A, 1975-09B, 1975-
67, 1976-32
BT   Discrimination in Employment
Employment Status
RT   Mobility as a factor in advancement
NT   Equal Pay for Equal Work
Nepotism
Sex Discrimination in Employment Benefits
Sex Discrimination in Wages
Academic Libraries (U.S.), 1971-27B, 1972-15, 1972-22, 1972-32, 1973-35,
1973-43, 1974-45
Archives (U.S.), 1973-33C, 1974-49
Federal Libraries (U.S.), 1971-28, 1971-29, 1971-31, 1971-34, 1971-35,
1972-46, 1972-47, 1972-50, 1972-54, 1972-55, 1972-56, 1972-62,
1972-63, 1973-27, 1973-32, 1973-36, 1973-41, 1973-57, 1973-58,
1973-61, 1973-62
Geographic Areas by Country
Australia, 1971-02, 1971-21, 1972-03, 1972-26, 1972-44, 1972-57, 1972-
58, 1972-69, 1972-71
Canada, 1973-02, 1973-05, 1973-10, 1973-31, 1973-66, 1974-01, 1974-33,
1974-60, 1975-36
Germany, 1939-02, 1940-03, 1940-06, 1973-44

Sex Role Socialization, 1970-15, 1973-16, 1973-60B, 1975-67
   NT   Sexism in Children's Literature
       Sexism in Mass Media
   Geographic Areas by Country
     Australia, 1973-22, 1973-24
     Canada, 1973-31
     Germany, 1973-45
     Great Britain, 1974-12A
     United States, 1971-11, 1971-13
Sex Typing of Librarianship, 1900-01A, 1902-01, 1910-05, 1911-03C,
     1925-02, 1949-03, 1957-01, 1958-03, 1972-73, 1973-18, 1975-34,
     1975-35
   BT   Sex Discrimination in Employment
   RT   Sex Composition of Librarianship
   Geographic Areas by Country
     Canada, 1974-21
     France, 1915-11
     Great Britain, 1946-01, 1972-59
     United States, 1971-05, 1971-08, 1971-10, 1972-16, 1972-24, 1973-46,
       1973-54, 1974-05, 1974-13A
Sexism
   Advertising, 1972-66, 1976-72
   BT   Sexism in Mass Media
   Children's Literature, 1971-09, 1973-16, 1973-17, 1973-71, 1974-12
   Geographic Areas by Country
     United States, 1971-25, 1971-26, 1971-39
   Language, 1971-27B, 1973-71, 1974-12, 1974-52, 1975-28, 1975-31, 1975-
     45, 1975-47, 1975-82, 1976-28, 1976-32, 1976-40, 1976-42
   Mass Media, 1972-68
   Subject Headings, 1975-36
Shaeffer, Kenneth, 1971-25, 1972-16
Sharp, Katharine Lucinda, 1895-03, 1975-05, 1976-02
Sherif, Carolyn, 1975-09
Sisters Have Resources Everywhere Directory
   USE Women Library Workers—*Sisters Have Resources Everywhere Directory*
Smith, Alice R., 1973-11
Smith, Elva Sophronia, 1976-02
Smith, Lloyd P., 1877-02, 1878-01, 1878-02, 1911-05, 1917-06
Social Responsibilities Round Table
   USE American Library Association—Social Responsibilities Round Table
Society of American Archivists, 1973-33A, 1973-33B
   Women's Caucus, 1973-33B
Sohier, Elizabeth Putnam, 1976-02
South Africa
   USE Education and Training—Geographic areas—South Africa
       Employment—Role Conflict—Geographic areas—South Africa
       Employment Status—Geographic areas—South Africa
       Equal Pay for Equal Work—Geographic areas—South Africa
       Wages—Geographical areas—South Africa
Southern, J. W., 1898-01
Spain, Francis Lander, 1971-07E, 1976-02

466 *The Role of Women in Librarianship*

Special Librarians, Women, 1920-11
Special Libraries
  USE Administrators, Women—Special Libraries
       Characteristics of Women Librarians—Special Libraries
       Education and Training—Special Librarians
       Employment Status—Special Libraries
       Equal Pay for Equal Work—Special Libraries
       Job Description—Special Librarians
       Sex Composition of Librarianship—Special Libraries
       Sex Discrimination in Wages—Special Libraries
       Wages—Special Libraries
Spencer, Florence, 1920-11
Stallman, Esther LaVerne, 1976-02
Stanford University, 1976-77
State Librarians, Women, 1887-01, 1920-08, 1965-09
Stearns, Lutie Eugenia, 1976-02
Stereotyping of Librarianship
  USE Sex Typing of Librarianship
Subject Headings, Sexism in
  USE Sexism in subject headings
Suffrage—Women
  USE Women—Suffrage
Sullivan, Maud Durlin, 1960-02
Support Staff
  NT   Characteristics of Women Support Staff
       Employment Status—Support Staff
       Job Description—Support Staff
  Geographic Areas by Country
    Great Britain, 1910-08, 1912-01, 1912-02, 1913-03, 1913-05, 1913-08, 1914-06
    United States, 1889-02, 1889-03
  Volunteer
    Great Britain, 1912-07
    United States, 1930-02, 1931-01, 1974-58, 1974-59
T.F.W.
  USE American Library Association—Social Responsibilities Round Table—Task Force on Women
Task Force on Women's Issues in Librarianship
  USE American Library Association—Social Responsibilities Round Table—Task Force on Women
Tasmania
  USE Characteristics of Women Librarians—Geographic areas—Tasmania
       Equal Pay for Equal Work—Geographic areas—Tasmania
       Men Librarians—Geographic areas—Tasmania
Technical Services
  USE Education and Training—Technical Services
       Employment Opportunities—Technical Services
Theological Libraries
  USE Employment Status—Theological Libraries

Thorpe, Jo, 1975-48
Titcomb, Mary Lemist, 1920-08, 1976-02
Tobias, Sheila, 1971-37, 1974-26
Tobitt, Edith, 1976-02
Tompkins, Miriam Downing, 1976-02
Toyota Motors, 1976-72
Training
    USE Education and Training
Trustees, Women (U.S.), 1890-02, 1897-04, 1935-02, 1971-05
Tyler, Alice Sarah, 1919-04, 1920-04, 1976-02
Unions
    USE Library Employee Unions
University Library Administration, 1972-16
University of California, 1971-33, 1971-36, 1972-23, 1972-35, 1973-35,
        1973-37, 1973-51, 1974-22
**University of Maryland Manpower in the Library and Information
        Profession Research Program,** 1967-12, 1970-02, 1970-13,
        1970-25, 1972-01
University of Toronto, 1974-32
University of Washington Libraries, 1972-15, 1972-22, 1972-32
University of Wisconsin Memorial Library, 1970-31, 1972-12
Upward Mobility
    USE Mobility as a factor in advancement
V.L.A.
    USE Vermont Library Association
           Virginia Library Association
Vermont Library Association (1976 Preconference on Women), 1976-47
Village Librarians, 1899-02
Vinson, Lu Ovida, 1975-47
Virginia Federation of Women's Clubs, 1931-01
Virginia Library Association
    1975 Conference, 1976-28
    Resolution on Sexist Terminology, 1976-28
Volunteer Workers
    USE Support Staff—Volunteer
           Feminism and Volunteerism
W.L.W.
    USE Women Library Workers
Wages, 1900-01A
    NT Equal Pay for Equal Work
         Sex Discrimination in Wages
    Academic Libraries, 1975-62, 1976-11, 1976-50, 1976-59, 1976-71, 1976-76،
    Geographic Areas by Country
        Australia, 1973-22
        Brazil, 1975-06
        Canada, 1970-11
        Great Britain, 1880-02, 1898-07, 1899-01, 1902-09, 1907-02, 1920-02,
           1965-04
        South Africa, 1938-07

Women, Health of
USE Health problems of women in libraries
Women in Instructional Technology
USE Association for Educational Communications and Technology, Women in Instructional Technology
Women in Library Administration Institute, 1974, 1975-23, 1975-40, 1976-13, 1976-13A, 1976-13B, 1976-13C, 1976-13D, 1976-13E, 1976-13F, 1976-13G, 1976-13H, 1976-13I
Women Indexers
USE Indexers, Women
Women, Legal Status, Laws, Etc., 1971-27
Women Library Educators
USE Library Educators, Women
(Also names of individual women)
Women Library Users
USE Library Service to Women
Women Library Workers, 1975-17, 1975-56, 1975-60, 1975-65, 1975-66, 1975-68, 1976-33, 1976-45, 1976-54, 1976-63, 1976-64, 1976-66, 1976-68, 1976-73
Newsletter, 1976-23
San Francisco Bay Area Chapter (Newsletter), 1976-27
Sisters Have Resources Everywhere Directory, 1974-63, 1975-02, 1975-18, 1976-58
Twin Cities Chapter (Newsletter), 1976-60
Wisconsin Chapter (Newsletter), 1976-14
Women Special Librarians
USE Special Librarians, Women
(Also names of individual women)
Women State Librarians
USE State Librarians
(Also names of individual women)
Women, Suffrage, 1973-07
BT Women—Civil Rights
Women's Group, University of Wisconsin Library School, 1976-20
Women's History Research Center, 1973-17
Women's Movement (1960-), 1970-14, 1970-15, 1970-18, 1970-28, 1971-09, 1972-17, 1975-64, 1975-69, 1975-70A, 1975-70B, 1975-70C, 1975-86, 1975-88, 1975-89, 1975-90
Women's Rights
USE Women—Civil Rights
Woodsworth, Anne, 1974-32
Working Conditions of Librarians
USE Job Description
World War I, 1914-06, 1915-02, 1915-03, 1915-08, 1918-01, 1918-02, 1918-03, 1920-05, 1973-08, 1973-11
Wright, Shirley, 1973-09
Yaffe, Phyllis, 1973-09, 1974-04, 1974-65

Author Index
to Bibliography

Bollert, E., 1934-03
Bonnefoy, A., 1915-11
Borden, A. K., 1933-02 (response)
Boston Athenaeum
  USE Athenaeum Library
Bostwick, A. E., 1910-04
Boucher, S., 1975-70C, 1975-86
Bow, R., 1972-30
Bower, B., 1972-25
Bowman, H. B., 1933-02 (response)
Bowman, L. J., 1971-40 (letter)
Bowker, R. R., 1919-02, 1920-04,
  1920-07, 1920-08, 1926-03
Bradley, B. W., 1968-01
Bradley, G., 1968-11 (letter)
Brass, L. J., 1970-16 (letter)
Braunagel, J., 1975-03
Brentford, F., 1976-29 (letter)
Brewer, F. M., 1911-02
Broderick, D., 1974-29, 1974-62,
  1975-55
Broome, E. M., 1948-01 (letter)
Brown, C., 1967-02
Brown, J. D., 1899-07, 1903-01,
  1907-02
Brown, T. A., 1949-03 (letter)
Brown, W. L., 1969-17, 1972-31,
  1972-43, 1972-44, 1972-69
Brugh, A. E., 1976-52
Brunner, M. A. R., 1907-06
Bryan, A. I., 1952-01
Bryant, J., 1971-23 (letter)
Bryum, M., 1974-02
Buchholz, R., 1973-45 (letter)
Buck, J. L. B., 1931-01
Buffum, C. W., 1975-33 (letter)
Bullard, C., 1972-03
Bullard, C. G., 1970-01
Bundy, M. L., 1968-06, 1970-02,
  1970-13, 1970-25, 1972-01
Burt, D., 1973-60E
Burton, D., 1976-25 (letter)

C.L.A.
  USE Canadian Library Associa-
  tion
Campbell, D. V. A., 1973-22 (letter)
Canadian Library Association,
  1974-04
Carey, J., 1971-11
Carnell, E. J., 1940-01
Carpenter, P. A., 1970-17

Carpenter, R. L., 1970-17, 1972-64,
  1973-01, 1974-03, 1974-16,
  1976-10, 1976-43
Carroll, C. E., 1970-03
Cartier, C. R., 1975-15
Cass, F. M. B., 1970-04, 1972-02,
  1972-57, 1973-22
Cass, M., 1972-03
Cassell, K., 1971-13 (letter), 1974-
  67 (letter), 1975-24, 1975-46
Chamberlain, E. R., 1968-02
Chambers, N., 1961-06 (letter)
Charlton, S., 1976-25 (letter)
Cheatham, B. M., 1973-53, 1973-68,
  1974-67, 1975-28, 1975-87
Cheda, S., 1973-03, 1974-38, 1974-
  60, (and letter), 1975-09
  (review)
Chennell, F. E., 1902-03, 1902-07,
  1902-10
Clarke, G. E., 1915-02 (letter)
Clarke, O. E., 1911-04
Clayton, H., 1968-14
Clifford, L. M., 1891-03
Cloke, D. R., 1961-06 (letter)
Clubb, B., 1973-30
Coatsworth, M. L., 1910-08
Coffin, J. E., 1969-18
Cohn, W. L., 1976-36
Colley, A. W., 1971-22
Colton, G. A., 1959-05 (letter)
Committee to Study the Status of
  Married Women in the Library
  Profession, 1938-09
Comstock, E., 1975-64, 1975-70A,
  1975-70B, 1975-88
Connecticut SRRT Task Force,
  1974-26
Cook, F. E., 1948-01 (letter)
Corbett, E. V., 1971-01
Corwin, M. A., 1973-04, 1974-31
Countryman, G. A., 1913-01, 1930-
  01
Cowan, L., 1971-23 (letter)
Cowell, P., 1893-01
Cowper, R. S., 1940-04
Crawford, M. I., 1973-33C
Crocker, A., 1974-39
Cronin, A., 1966-07
Crossland, J., 1976-25 (letter)
Crunden, F. M., 1898-09
Crutwell, A., 1971-27 (letter)
Cummings, C. S., 1976-02

Shields, L. G., 1961-06 (letter)
Shoemaker, H. R., 1916-01
Shores, L., 1958-03, 1967-07, 1972-06
Simmons, E. B., 1925-02
Simpson, I. H., 1969-06
Simpson, R. L., 1969-06
Simsova, S., 1961-06
Smart, A., 1974-60 (letter), 1975-25
Smith, F. E., 1915-09
Smith, L. J., 1899-16
Smith, L. P., 1878-01, 1878-02
Smith, R. K., 1970-16 (letter)
Smith, S. W., 1936-01
Smith, Toulmin, 1900-01C
Social Responsibilities Round Table
  USE American Library Association Social Responsibilities Round Table
Society of American Archivists, 1974-49
Southan, B. M., 1975-38 (letter)
Spaulding, H. W., 1930-02
Special Libraries Association, 1970-23, 1976-04
Speight, P. M., 1938-02
Spencer, P. G., 1976-28
Squires, T., 1920-04 (letter)
Stallybrass, O. G. W., 1961-06 (letter)
Starr, C., 1971-11 (letter)
Stearns, L., 1905-03
Stephens, E., 1939-05, 1975-53
Stern, R. N., 1974-36
Stirling, S., 1961-06 (letter)
Stjernquist, H., 1952-02
Stokes, K. M., 1936-01 (letter), 1939-04
Stone, E. W., 1969-07, 1971-03
Stone, L. H., 1959-04 (letter)
Strain, P. M., 1969-15
Struble, L., 1974-58
Sullivan, P., 1965-02
Swaim, C., 1974-59
Swannick, M. L. S., 1973-66
Swarm, E., 1970-16 (letter)

"T., P. A.", 1971-15
Taber, F. T., 1938-06 (letter)
Taborsky, T., 1971-23 (letter)
Talbot, R. J., 1976-59

Tanaka, T., 1973-25C
Tarr, S. A., 1973-50
Task Force on Women
  USE American Library Association. Social Responsibilities Round Table Task Force on Women
Tauber, M. F., 1956-01
Taylor, M. R., 1973-12
Tazawa, K., 1973-25D
Tedder, H. R., 1882-01, 1898-03
Tenander, J., 1971-41 (letter)
Tennant, P. M., 1975-38 (letter)
Thomison, D., 1974-50
Thorne, W. M., 1925-01
Thwaites, J., 1975-76
Tierney, C. M., 1974-10
Tillie, H. A., 1928-01
Trautman, R., 1954-02
Trehan, G. L., 1975-74
Tucker, M., 1971-37B
Tucker, S. A., 1973-13
Turnbull, K. R. M., 1961-06 (letter)
Turner, B., 1976-21
Turner, D., 1973-39
Tuttle, C. E., 1973-65 (letter)
Tuttle, H. W., 1971-27B, 1971-37B
Tyler, A. S., 1938-06 (letter)

Underhill, A., 1894-04
Underhill, A., 1968-09 (letter)
Unger, N. A., 1948-02
U.S. Bureau of Education, 1876-02
U.S. Bureau of the Census, 1973-40
U.S. Department of Health and Welfare, 1972-07, 1973-14, 1976-11
U.S. Department of Labor.
  Bureau of Labor Statistics, 1949-02, 1951-01, 1957-04, 1959-03, 1961-03, 1963-02, 1965-03, 1968-05, 1970-07, 1972-08, 1974-11, 1975-13, 1976-12
U.S. National Commission on the Observance of International Women's Year, 1975-10, 1976-03
University of California, Berkeley, Library Affirmative Action Program for Women Committee, 1971-36

Title Index
to Bibliography

Advancement in the Library Profession, 1961-08
Affirmative Action Committee for Women Appointed at CU, 1971-33
Affirmative Action: Equal Opportunity for Women in Library Management, 1973-38
Affirmative Action Program Implemented at Berkeley, 1972-35
Aghast-ly Letter, 1976-28
All Male Library Staff, 1970-29
All Those Lovely Girls, 1968-13
American Librarianship, 1976-52
American Librarianship: Some Women, 1957-06
American Library Association: Asbury Park Conference: Sixth Session. Resolutions. 1919-04
The American Library Executive: An Inquiry into His Concepts of the Function of His Office, 1967-01
The American Library School, 1895-03
The American Library School Today, 1937-01
American Women as Librarians, 1893-02
Amerikansk og Europeisk bibliotekyesen, 1933-01
Analysis of Membership in the American Library Association Held by Individuals and Institutions in Texas in 1957, 1959-07
Analysis of the Biographies of Librarians Listed in *Who's Who of American Women,* 1958-1959, 1962-01
Anita Schiller's Librarianship, 1975-54
Annual Conference: Business as Usual in New York, 1974-61
. . . As Others See Us, 1972-61
Assistant Copyrights Register Charges Bias, 1971-29
Association, 1975-42
The Association of Assistant Librarians: 1895-1945, 1973-11
Association News: Discrimination in Australian Library Journal, 1972-31
Association News: Standing Committee: A Report: Discrimination in Advertisements, 1971-21
Association News: Standing Committee: A Report: Discrimination in Advertising, 1972-43
Assocation News: Standing Committee: A Report: Encel Report, 1972-44
At Its Last Meeting—, 1972-37
The Athenaeum Centenary, 1907-01
The Attack on Women, 1914-04
The 'Average' Director of a Large Public Library, 1971-14
Aware: Report on Women in Librarianship, 1971-38

The Background and Career of the Graduate Librarian, 1972-04
Barbara Ringer and LC, 1972-52
Barbara Ringer Appointed Register of Copyrights, 1973-55
Barbara Ringer Continues to Fight for LC Position, 1973-41
Barbara Ringer Named Register of Copyrights, 1973-58
Barbara Ringer Named Register of Copyrights, 1973-62
Barbara Ringer Wins LC Register of Copyrights Post, 1973-61
Bargains in Library Assistants, 1910-07
Bedarf und Nachwuchs im Wissenschaftlichen Bibliothekarsberuf (trans: Demand and the Rising Generation in the Research Librarian's Profession), 1934-03

Behind the Library Counter, the Image is Starting to Change, 1971-10
A Better Class of Mouse, 1965-06
Bibliotekar—Statistik 1950 (trans.: Statistics on Librarians in 1950), 1952-02
Die Bibliothek der Technischen Hochschule und die Industrie (trans.: The Library in the Technical Institute and in Industry), 1939-02
A Biographical-Bibliographical Directory of Women Librarians, 1976-02
Books, Books, Books, 1940-02
Boston Women Librarians Tackle Sexist Attitudes and Employment Practices, 1972-68
Breaking Even in Las Vegas: a Report of the 92nd Annual American Library Association Conference: The Youth Divisions, 1973-53
A Brief Account of the Public Libraries of the City of Leeds, 1870-1920, 1920-01
Brighter Librarianship as She is Practised: The Miss Library World Finals— March 11th, 1967, 1967-08
Britisk Bibliotekar Besoker Norske Biblioteker (trans.: British Librarian Visits Norwegian Libraries), 1954-03
Business Education for Business Librarians, 1917-07
The Business Side of a Woman's Career as a Librarian, 1899-13
By, For, About Women, 1974-24

CLA Status of Women, 1975-43
CLA Women's Day, 1974-18
CLA Women's Day, 1974-30
CLA Women's Programme: CLA Workshop: Women's Day, 1974-04
CLA Women's Programme: Feature Speaker, 1974-01
Cable Cars or Cable TV? California LA's Annual Conference, 1976-26
Calif. L.A. 1973: The Sea Closes on Moses: The Women, God Bless 'em, 1974-20
California Library Association Conference Revisited: Myths about Women Managers and Libraries as Businesses, 1974-54
Calm, Cool, and Sort-of-Collected: Resolution on Statistical Study of Librarianship, 1972-18
Campus 1970: Where do Women Stand? Research Report of a Survey on Women in Academe, 1970-32
The Career of the Academic Librarian: A Study of the Social Origins, Educational Attainments, Vocational Experience, and Personality Characteristics of a Group of American Academic Librarians, 1961-01
The Career of the Academic Librarian: a Study of the Social Origins, Educational Attainments, Vocational Experience, and Personality Characteristics of a Group of American Academic Librarians, 1969-02
The Carnegie Corporation of New York and Its Impact on Library Development in Australia: A Case-study of Foundation Influence, 1971-02
Cary Is New Copyright Head; Ringer Sues, Charging Bias, 1971-28
Cary Renamed Register of Copyrights, 1971-35
The Case of the Desk Assistant, 1902-11
A Cause for Concern—TV Stereotypes, 1976-72
Celebrating a Century: ALA '76, 1976-63
Celebrating the Year of the Woman: Melvil's Rib Symposium, 1975-33
A Census of College Women, 1918-06
Census of the Population: 1970, 1973-40

Education, Careers and Professionalization in Librarianship and Information Science, 1967-12

The Education of the Library Assistant - (2), 1908-01

The Employment of Young Women as Assistants in Free Public Libraries, 1880-01

Employment of Young Women in Free Public Libraries, 1879-03

Encel Replies, 1972-58

Equal Employment Opportunity: Affirmative Action Plans for Libraries: Woman Power, 1971-30

Equal Pay Claim, 1972-45

Equal Pay for Equal Work: Women in Special Libraries, 1976-04

Equal Pay in the Public Library of South Australia, 1966-08

Equal Pay in Queensland, 1972-19

Escape from the Doll's House: Women in Graduate and Professional School Education, 1974-05

Every Women's Day, 1975-45

The Evolution of the Public Library, 1898-03

Excuse Me, My Dear Division—But What Did You Say Was Your Reason for Being?, 1975-58

External Mobility and Professional Involvement in Librarianship: A Study of the Careers of Librarians Graduating from Accredited Library Schools in 1955, 1973-12

F.L.C. Personnel Statistics, 1972-46

Factors Related to the Professional Development of Librarians, 1969-07

The Faculty Image of the Academic Librarian, 1968-15

Faculty-Librarian Conflict, 1969-16

Faculty Salaries of 62 Library Schools—1975-76, 1976-34

Faculty Status for Librarians, 1972-05

. . . Faintly the Inimitable Rose, 1975-59

Fair Labor Standards Act as Applied to Libraries, 1968-08

Family, Career, and Reform: Women Leaders of the Progressive Era, 1973-07

The Female Assistant From Her Own Standpoint, 1910-08

Female Assistants, 1897-02

Female Librarian: How Far Does She Have to Go and How Will She Get There?, 1973-71

Female Librarians from the Standpoint of Male Librarians, 1973-25D

Female Librarians in the U.S. and Canada, 1973-25A

Female Library Assistants, 1889-02

Female Library Assistants, 1889-03

Female Library Assistants and Competitive Examination, 1898-01

Female Library Science Students and the Occupational Stereotype: Fact or Fiction?, 1973-54

Female Library Staffs—An Opinion From the Opposite Sex, 1974-12C

Feminism and Professionalism in Librarianship: an Interview with Sherril Cheda, 1974-68

Feminization of the American Library Profession, 1876 to 1923, 1967-03

La Femme Noyeze (trans.: The Drowned Woman), 1975-15

A Few Brickbats From a Layman, 1913-06

Few Minorities in Minn. : Low Pay for Women, 1976-51

Students, 1967-07

A Study of Characteristics, Qualifications and Succession Patterns of Heads of Large U.S. Academic and Public Libraries, 1968-01

A Study of 1967 Annual Salaries of Members of the Special Library Association, 1967-09

Study of the Interests of the Female Students Enrolled in the School of Library Science, Drexel Institute of Technology, as Measured by the Strong Vocational Interest Blank and the Kuder Preference Record, 1952-03

Study of Western Reserve University Library School Graduates 1934-1953, 1957-03

The Success of the Conference, 1879-01

Successful Librarians as Revealed in *Who's Who in America,* 1946-02

The Successful Loan-Desk Assistant, 1907-10

Sugar and Spice, 1971-09

A Summary of the Discussion Following Mr. McEldowney's Comments on the Report, 1969-09D

The Suppliant Maidens, 1961-09

Survey of Conditions Relating to the Employment of Women in Libraries, 1938-02

Survey of Graduates and Faculty of U.S. Library Education Programs Awarding Degrees and Certificates, 1973-1974, 1975-79

Survey of Library Employment in N.S.W., 1971-18

A Survey of Women Library School Graduates 1946-1965 by the Professional Section of the N.Z.L.A., 1969-09A

Survey to Be Made of Part-time Jobs for Women, 1962-03

The Syllabus, 1961-05

Technical Services and Women, 1971-07B

Technological Change and Occupational Response, 1970-06

Ten Timely Tales Mother Never Told Us: 'Sexist Terminology' From ALA to be Further Policed, 1976-40

The Tender Technicians: The Feminization of Public Librarianship, 1876-1905, 1972-73

The Tender Technicians: The Feminization of Public Librarianship, 1876-1905, 1974-07

That Special Little Mechanism, 1973-03

That Special Little Mechanism, 1974-60

Then as Now, 1965-04

And There Were Giantesses in Library Education, 1971-07A

They Have Made Their Mark, 1940-07

Those Library Ladies, 1973-18

Thoughts While Becoming a Librarian, 1937-02

Three Little Maids from the Library School, 1887-02

Three Union Suits Filed Against UC Regents, 1973-35

Title Tattle, 1976-29

Tokenism at the Top? Women in Minority, 1965-09

Toward Liberated Librarianship, 1974-21

Towards a Feminist Profession, 1976-22

Training for Library Service: A Report Prepared for the Carnegie Corporation of New York, 1923-01

Index

Employment Opportunities, xxi, 98, 131, 144-5, 214, 241
  Re-entering women, 174-84, 288
  Temporary work, 191-2
  Great Britain, 34
Employment Status. USE Married Women—Employment Status; Mothers—Employment Status
Enser, A. G. S., xxx-xxxi, 123-5
Equal Pay for Equal Work. USE Wage differential between men and women
Equal Rights Amendment, xxii, 233

Fairchild, Mary Salome Cutler, xxxi, 48-55, 208, 214, 222
Fairchild, Edwin M., 205-6
Farley, R. A., 243
Feminism. USE Women's Movement
Fletcher, William I., 211
Frarey, Carlyle, 277
Freedman, Janet, xxxi, 189-93

Garnet, Dr. Richard, xxxi
Garrison, Dee, xxxi-xxxii, 201-21, 280-1
Germany. USE Education and training—Germany
Gilbert, Mizpah, xxxii, 67-71
Goode, William, 212
Government publications, 398-9
Great Britain. USE
  Administrators—Great Britain
  Characteristics of Women Librarians—Public Libraries—Great Britain
  Education and training—Great Britain
  Employment Opportunities—Great Britain
  Married Women—Employment Status—Great Britain
  Support Staff—Great Britain
Green, S. S., 215
Grimm, James, 276

Hall, Janet, 281
Harlow, Margaret K., 247

Harvey, J. F., 230, 245
Hathaway, G. W., 247
Health problems of women in libraries, 53, 55, 65, 148-9, 173. USE also Pregnancy
Hentoff, Nat, 188
Hewins, Carolina, xxxii, 206-7
Historians, xv
Holden, Miriam Y., xxxii, 150-3
Holley, Edward, xv
Howell, A., xxxii, 3-4
Hughes, M. M., 248
Hyatt, Ruth, xxxii, 93-4

I.W.Y. USE International Women's Year
International Congress of Women, 1899, xvii-xviii, 26-37
International Women's Year, 269

James, M. S. R., xxxiii, 29-33
Job description, 13-14, 24, 137-8, 228-9
Job satisfaction, 281
Jones, Mumford, 216
Josey, E. J., 243

Kelso, Tessa L., 207
Kortendick, J. J., 243
Kronus, Carol, 276

Labor, Division of, 209
Ladies Library Association of Michigan, xvi, 3-4
Lancour, Harold, 216
Law librarians, 227
Learmont, Carol, 277
Lee, David, 281
Librarians—Health. USE Health problems of women in libraries
Librarianship as a profession, xiii, xiv, xxii, 191, 197, 209-13, 231-2, 234, 237, 282
Libraries, Women's role in founding them, 3-4
Library assistants. USE Support staff
Library Assistants' Association, xix, 165